O9-AHS-037

TERMINOLOGY FOR MUSEUMS

TERMINOLOGY FOR MUSEUMS

Proceedings of
an International Conference
held in Cambridge, England,
21–24 September 1988

The Second Conference of
The Museum Documentation Association

Edited by
D. Andrew Roberts

PUBLISHED BY
THE MUSEUM DOCUMENTATION ASSOCIATION
WITH THE ASSISTANCE OF THE GETTY GRANT PROGRAM
1990

Proceedings of an International Conference held in Cambridge, England, 21–24 September 1988. The Second Conference of The Museum Documentation Association.

The Conference was jointly organised by The Museum Documentation Association and the Getty Art History Information Program.

The publication of these proceedings has been supported by a grant from the Getty Grant Program.

Published by
The Museum Documentation Association
Building O
347 Cherry Hinton Road
Cambridge CB1 4DH
United Kingdom
(0223) 242848
+44 223 242848

ISBN 0 905963 62 8

Printed in the United Kingdom
by W. S. Maney and Son Limited
Leeds LS9 7DL

CONTENTS

IV INSTITUTION-WIDE INITIATIVES

V CONTROLLING PERSONAL AND CORPORATE BODY NAMES

VI CONTROLLING GEOGRAPHIC DESCRIPTIONS

VII DISCIPLINE DEVELOPMENTS: ARCHAEOLOGY, ANTHROPOLOGY AND ETHNOGRAPHY

IX DISCIPLINE DEVELOPMENTS: SOCIAL HISTORY, DECORATIVE ART, MATERIAL CULTURE, SCIENCE AND TECHNOLOGY

X DISCIPLINE DEVELOPMENTS: NATURAL HISTORY AND GEOLOGY

PREFACE

Based on papers given at the second Conference of the Museum Documentation Association (MDA), *Terminology for Museums* presents a wide diversity of reports about terminology initiatives and plans.

Centred at St Catharine's College and the Babbidge Lecture Theatre in Cambridge from 21–24 September 1988, the conference drew together over 170 colleagues from 18 countries. Eighty-five speakers gave 90 papers in a mixture of plenary and concurrent sessions. The verbal presentations were supported by simultaneous interpretation into English, French and Italian, to produce an international dialogue of unusual diversity for the museum world.

These proceedings have been closely modelled on the structure of the meeting itself. Revised papers from the original speakers have been complemented by additional introductions to each section prepared by the Chair of the corresponding session at the conference. The conference itself ended with a general discussion of the major themes that had emerged during the sessions, points from which have been incorporated into an opening paper (Chapter 2) in the proceedings. In addition, some of the main reference *sources* about museum terminology have been drawn together into a source list, included immediately before an extensive *bibliography*.

Section I includes this review paper and a second scene-setting contribution about museum standards.

Sections II to IV move from an international to a national and institutional perspective, illustrating different ways in which terminology initiatives are being nurtured and promoted. Other specific aspects of institutional developments are also covered in later papers.

Sections V and VI review important developments with controlling personal and corporate body names and geographic names, concepts which recurr in all museum records and which present serious practical problems to documentation staff.

The wealth of initiatives within separate subject areas were covered in the conference by two intensive series of concurrent sessions, when the participants divided into five groups. These discipline developments are presented in *Sections VII to XI* which together form the substantial central core of the book. The divisions were inevitably fairly arbitrary but form a useful framework for examining progress with systems and their application. Each section includes an opening summary by the session Chair; a personal review of discipline developments by a leading specialist in that field; descriptions of terminology control systems; and case studies of work in individual museums.

Section XII examines the experience of a number of users in working with museum terminology, with contributions from a system developer, external researchers and museum professionals.

Finally, some of the technological and policy developments that will be needed if museums are to have improved terminology facilities in the future are assessed in *Section XII.*

ACKNOWLEDGEMENTS

The MDA gratefully acknowledges the advice and financial support provided by the Getty Art History Information Program and the Getty Grant Program. The Art History Information Program (AHIP) jointly organised the conference itself, under the direction of Michael Ester. The Grant Program subsequently agreed to make an essential grant to help fund these proceedings.

Andrew Roberts adds his thanks to Eleanor Fink and John Logan of AHIP, who provided strong support during all stages of preparing for the conference. Eleanor Fink in particular assisted in developing the programme structure and identifying a significant number of important speakers. Without her input, the conference and these proceedings would have been immeasurably weaker.

The MDA and AHIP are very grateful to the speakers for their verbal presentations and subsequent papers. Particular recognition should be made of the Chairs of each session at the conference who have contributed introductions to the papers from their session. The five colleagues who coordinated the lengthy concurrent sessions on discipline developments (Jennifer Stewart, Jennifer Hirsh, Stuart Holm, Mike Budd and Michael Corfield) have played an important role at all stages.

A number of individual contributors have asked to acknowledge help they have received while preparing their papers.

John Perkins (Chapter 9) would like to thank all members of the Conservation Information Network Content Review Boards who work so tenaciously to develop and maintain the data dictionary, along with Janet Bridgland and Kathleen McDonnell for their helpful comments and review.

Susanne Peters (Chapter 10) thanks Leonard Will and David Bearman for comments and valuable suggestions.

John Burnett (Chapter 20) developed the ideas in his paper in discussions with Jane Sunderland of Willoughby Associates. He is also grateful to colleagues, including Helen McCorry, Hugh Cheape and David Clarke, who gave advice on specific points.

Amanda Chadburn (Chapter 37) is grateful to Ben Booth, Helen McMurray, Rebecca Payne, Russell Man and Nigel Clubb, who have discussed her subject or commented on aspects of the paper, and Martin Moss of the English Heritage Records Office mapping section who produced the source for Figure 37.2.

Peter Welsh (Chapter 38) acknowledges his indebtedness to Steven Le Blanc of Questor Systems for his invaluable contributions to the ideas in the paper.

For the discussions on which Chapter 57 is based, John Burnett is indebted to his colleagues on the STOT working party (Dr S. V. Butler, A. King, Dr L. D. Will) and on the Scientific Instrument Commission's sub-committee on terminology (Dr J. A. Bennett, Dr J. Darius and Dr L. D. Will); and to H. McCorry of the National Museums of Scotland.

Eiji Mizushima (Chapter 68) would like to express his gratitude to his superior, Hidenori Yamada, vice-director of the Science Museum and Dr Masahiro Chatani, professor of the Tokyo Institute of Technology, Department of Architecture and Building Engineering. The basic idea of the classification of dwellings comes from his great works.

John Cooper (Chapter 72) thanks Andrew Roberts and Geoffrey Stansfield for advice on earlier versions of his paper, and Gerald Legg and Bill Ely for useful discussions and suggestions.

Charles Pettitt (Chapter 78) thanks David Heppell for bringing some relevant papers to his attention.

Velson Horie (Chapter 82) is grateful for comments, discussions and documents from representatives of major standards organisations, I. Shreeve (British Standards Institute), W. P. Ellis (American Society for Testing and Materials) and A. Ermert (Deutsches Institut für Normung, International Organization for Standardization). Extracts from British Standards can be obtained from them at Linford Wood, Milton Keynes, Bucks MK14 6LE, UK. Extracts from ASTM standards reproduced by permission of the American Society for Testing and Materials.

Gwyn Miles (Chapter 85) would like to thank Vicki Oakley for her assistance in compiling condition reports.

Elizabeth Orna (Chapter 91) thanks the MDA, who gave her her first opportunity of discussing indexing with museum curators many years ago, and who have continued to support her interest in the things museums do with information; Frank Atkinson, who let her try out a museum thesaurus on Beamish material, and all the curators and registrars in the UK and Australia who have talked with her about terminology control since then.

Individual photograph credits accompany the photographs themselves.

Finally, our thanks to staff at W. S. Maney and Son for their advice and skill and to Liz Parker who so ably proofread the galleys.

I
TERMINOLOGY IN CONTEXT

1 TERMINOLOGY IN CONTEXT

D. Andrew Roberts

Museum Documentation Association
Cambridge

Two introductory papers set the scene for the discussion of terminology for museums. The first, by Eleanor Fink and myself, is based on ideas generated during the conference, particularly in a final session which evolved into an open forum. We concentrate on ideas that were raised about future terminology priorities.

David Bearman kindly agreed to provide the keynote contribution at the conference and his paper expands on issues he raised during that presentation. He illustrates the position of terminology standards within the overall corpus of museum information standards. He examines why museums have resisted terminology standards in the past and how more appropriate implementations of these standards will improve their acceptance. He expresses high expectations of the way terminology will help the museum to communicate with its users and how museums will become a key focus for information seekers.

2 TERMINOLOGY FOR USER-FRIENDLY CURATORS

D. Andrew Roberts

Secretary
Museum Documentation Association
Cambridge

Eleanor E. Fink

Getty Art History Information Program
Santa Monica, CA

Introduction

When introducing an interview with the two conference organisers on a Cambridge radio station, the reporter described the theme of the conference as 'terminology for user-friendly curators'. The conference was very much about curators and other users of museum information: how we can extract the best value from the words we use to describe museum collections, whether 'we' are documentation specialists, general curators/cataloguers, outside researchers or members of the public.

The conference and these proceedings concentrate on the terminology or vocabulary applied when recording and retrieving information about objects in collections and related details about people, places, events, etc. Terminology is a fundamental building block on which all museum information systems depend.

In planning the structure of the conference, we were keen to draw together as many practitioners as possible — people with in-depth experience of designing, applying or using terminology facilities — with the hope that this would result in a constructive dialogue and produce a more informed and questioning community.

We felt that many museums would be receptive to reports on terminology products which were relevant to their local needs. During the 1970s and 1980s, there had been a great wave of record production with millions of new manual and, increasingly, automated collection records being drafted. These often conformed to new standards such as those of the MDA and the Canadian Heritage Information Network (CHIN). Our impression was that the developers of these databases were now concerned about the need to improve the standardisation of information, which had often been recorded with limited control and subsequent lack of consistency.

In the same period, there had been a number of important projects to develop original term lists in disciplines such as art, social history and science and technology. We hoped that the designers of these systems would give fresh thought to issues such as how systems should be promoted, supported and developed; how they should be adopted by a museum; how they will be used; and how they will intermesh within a typical, complex multi-disciplinary institution.

1988 was an appropriate time to look at these issues. Many museums were ready to move from an initial database-building phase into a new period of database use. To make really effective use of their records, they needed to pay far more attention to consistent terminology than had been the case in the past. After long development phases, a series of terminology facilities were reaching maturity or undergoing concerted growth and were available for use by museums. In addition, software designers were at last producing packages that offered terminology support capabilities, including the possibility of exploiting automated versions of the new terminology facilities.

We wanted to bring together museum documentation specialists, curators, system developers and internal and external users, and use the opportunity to establish a new dialogue and corpus of information. The success of that mixing is demonstrated in the following chapters. The paragraphs below summarise some of the main points to emerge.

General perception

There was a widespread recognition during the conference that the management or control of terminology will be a key issue for museums in the 1990s. The availability of and efficient use of terminology products will be a major concern, particularly in museums that have established an automated collections database which they need to exploit for collections management and information access purposes.

As a result of the conference, there was a far greater awareness among participants of the range of products that are now available or under active development. This is shown particularly stongly in Sections V–XI in these proceedings. The main results are summarised in the *Sources* digest.

There was also a greater receptivity to evaluating these products for potential internal use. As more products became available and better known, it was recognised that there is less need to design new facilities for adoption by an individual museum. In a number of the following Chapters, reference is made to a decision to develop a local product, because a more general system was still in its infancy or the museum was unaware of any suitable options. Bodies like the MDA and the Getty Trust have a responsibility to provide better information to help reduce duplication of effort of this type.

There was a widespread feeling that internal needs were the first priority for many museums. Terminology systems are more likely to be adopted if they help the museum manage and use its own collections, rather than because of a more altruistic concern to cooperate with other institutions. Conversely, it was appreciated that if museums are increasingly using common systems, information sharing will be more effective.

It was noted that the use of common systems did not necessarily mean that museums will lose the flexibility to deal with local needs. It was presumed that systems will be adapted by individual institutions. Equally importantly, any one institution will be likely to use a wide range of different systems, for example to serve the needs of separate disciplines or different types of enquirer or at different stages in developing a database. The net impact was a far greater awareness of the complexity of the terminology issue, and the need to look critically at the relevance and use of different products by each institution.

During the conference, it was recognised that there was an important balance between the need for terminology *control* and *flexibility*. A number of the contributors stressed the need to retain the richness of terminology while introducing as much consistency as appropriate. As Bearman notes (Chapter 3), we need to aim for systems which allow the use of alternative terms, yet identify their relationships when they are used for retrieval purposes.

Retrieval needs implies users, whether they are museum staff or outside members of the public and researchers with very general or highly specific expertise and familiarity with museum collections. It was stressed that it is important that these users are taken into account before the museum commits itself to a terminology control strategy. The production of collection records is one of the most labour intensive aspects of museum functions: the relevance of the results needs to match up to the investment.

There is, for example, little sense in adopting a complex classification system if its application will place undue demands on staff time and skills or the results are inappropriate to the majority of users. It is essential to assess the level of resources that can and need to be directed to data standardisation and to choose products and strategies commensurate with these resources.

Product development

In considering terminology products, there was concern about the need to develop general guidelines for management areas, such as acquisition method, which are examined independently by many institutions. Similarly, it was felt that there is a need to establish mechanisms whereby museums can benefit from work being undertaken in other communities. For example, developments and research into personal names and place-names being carried out by libraries and geographic organisations are likely to be of direct benefit to museums.

Although there are important initiatives in many areas, there was a particular concern about disciplines like social and industrial history and archaeology, where terminology work seems to be underfunded and disparate. Participants felt there is a need to draw together and support interested specialists in these areas.

Equally, it was felt that there is a need to encourage the acceleration of developments within major current projects, such as the *Art and Architecture Thesaurus*, *Nomenclature* and the *Social History and Industrial Classification*, and to urge a closer dialogue between the teams developing these types of project.

There was a particular need to press for the availability of products in machine-readable form and to pursue their incorporation within a wide range of different software packages.

Pressure needed to be placed on developers to ensure that widely-available products are adequately supported and maintained and that there is an effective liaison with users.

Information and training

It was clear that potential users needed more information about the products that are available or under development; how they will be relevant to a museum; and how they can be used.

There is an onus on developers to be more active in disseminating information about their work. Advising organisations such as the MDA, CHIN and the Museum Computer Network can also be much more effective in acting as a clearinghouse for news. These organisations and the Documentation Committee of ICOM (CIDOC) need to work together to produce and maintain directories of products, etc.

During the Conference, copies of titles distributed by the Book Service maintained by the MDA were available for examination by participants. It was felt to be important that this type of service is maintained and that terminology control facilities should be regarded as a core aspect. With products coming from a wide range of different sources, it is essential that they are actively promoted and readily available.

Product developers and support organisations also needed to be far more effective in providing advice and training to users. Although organisations like the Conservation Information Network have been able to establish a help desk and training services, this is rare within the museum field. It is essential that staff applying widely-adopted products are fully supported in their application.

Research

There is a general need for a greater level of museum-based and academic research into many aspects of the use of museum documentation systems.

With terminology products, the conference participants felt there was a need for far more product evaluation, including assessing the effectiveness of products in a variety of working applications.

More broadly, it would be useful to have recording strategy assessments to identify the effectiveness of different approaches to recording, such as depth of analysis of information, extent of terminology control, etc.

Finally, there should be more research into user needs to clarify the requirements of both documentation staff, curators and end users, and assess the extent to which products fulfil these requirements.

3 FRAMEWORK FOR TERMINOLOGY STANDARDS IN MUSEUMS

David Bearman

Archives & Museum Informatics
Pittsburgh, PA

Common threads in diverse fabrics

The universe of museums is as disparate as any. Museums may range in size from those caring for collections of millions of objects to those having no collections of their own. They may be staffed by thousands of specialised professionals or by one part-time non-specialist volunteer. They may be devoted almost exclusively to research or equally exclusively to public programming. And their focus may be on natural or man-made objects, on the unusual or the typical, on items microscopically small or as large as the landscape.

Institutionally museums may be privately or publicly funded. They may be independent organisations or branches of corporate entities, of non-profit organisations or of government departments. They may be directed by boards, administrators, or their curatorial staffs. They may charge or be free, and may seek support from specific patrons or agencies, from their visiting publics, or from the sale of services, goods, or, even their holdings.

Museums may be hundreds of years old or formed yesterday. They may be bound by wills and legislation to pursue a particular course or may be free to change purposes, and even cease being museums, tomorrow. They may be enabled or burdened by records from their pasts.

Museums may be open or closed to the general public. They may support specialised research or not. They may attract all ages, or focus on the young, adults or the aged. They may have collections on exhibit, or not, and they may vary widely in the percentages of their holdings on display, the percentages of displays from their exhibits, and the frequency with which displays change.

Given these dramatic differences between musuems, what possible areas of standardisation are there, especially if such standards are intended to reach across national boundaries as well? Obviously standards for preservation and conservation of materials will not differ from nation to nation or museum to museum, but what of the more complex issues? What of terminology standards?

Terminology standards are the finest sieves in the hierarchy of information standards. Terminology standards, called *data value standards* by the data processing community, incorporate agreements about information categories, called *data content standards*, since the terms themselves belong to such categories. When implemented to enable communication between systems (rather than simply to establish consistency within a system) they also presume agreements about *data formats or structure* standards and about standard information exchange mechanisms.

These various levels of standardisation can be addressed concurrently or serially. The ongoing Common Agenda for History Museums project in the United States, for instance, is starting by trying to define data content standards, specifically a common data element dictionary (Chapter 16). However, its sponsor, the American Association for State and Local History (AASLH), has reissued a vocabulary which has achieved the *de facto* status of a terminology standard: Chenhall's *Nomenclature* (Chapter 58).

Elsewhere, I have discussed the political and technical relationship between standards efforts (Bearman, 1988). Indeed, I am involved with a committee of the Society of American Archivists that is looking at the entire range of standards activities with which archivists are and could be involved and attempting to define a framework that can govern the commitment of the professional association to these various efforts. Here, I would like to address two broad areas in which terminology standardisation has proved possible and may be beneficial for museums. The first is the processes involved in management of collections, which are similar across types of museums and nations because they reflect the underlying commonalities of curation. The second is the abstract concepts involved in scholarly analysis of holdings which are employed in dialogues that are transnational in scope.

Collections management

An analysis of the information flows in dozens of museums of the Smithsonian Institution conducted from 1982 to 1985 revealed a wide variety of different practices and terms, but an underlying commonality in the ways that not only museums, but also archives and libraries, manage their collections (Smithsonian Institution, 1984). Initially, those of us involved in this effort found these commonalities uncanny. With time, I have come to see them as direct outcomes of the missions of cultural repositories; that is, to collect items of cultural informational value, and to make these items available, across time, to specialists and the general public, in order to enrich our understanding of the world in which we live.

It follows from the mission that all cultural repositories must consider what they want to acquire. They must identify where items they would want to acquire can be found and engage in activities ranging from exploration to purchase to acquire them. They must arrange to assume legal and physical custody of the objects, store them and conserve them. They must make them available for study and display, while maintaining a knowledge of their whereabouts and condition and be able to plan for their future use. They must provide for the cumulation of knowledge regarding the objects in their custody and manage the dissemination of this information through publications, multi-media presentations and exhibits.

Each of these processes in the life of cultural objects derives from the missions of cultural repositories, and while the techniques each organisation employs differ, the underlying requirements of accountability and rational planning assure that each action will be documented according to who initiated, approved and took it, and the resulting status of the item. These commonalities in the underlying process of managing collections provide us with one strategic focus for terminological standardisation.

The data models recently completed at the Virginia Museum of Fine Arts as a product of a cooperative international project with the Canadian Heritage Information Network (CHIN) (Virginia Museum of Fine Arts, 1987), mirror those emerging from the continuing data architecture project at the Smithsonian Institution. When these models are evaluated to identify information that results in actions, we find substantial agreement about types of decisions and the implications, and high overlap in the actual terms used for administrative steps. Since the terminology for administrative actions is not burdened by great emotional investments or hoary intellectual histories, full agreement should not be difficult to achieve when reasons for commonality can be articulated.

Scholarly access

A second focus is provided by the continuities in the cultures of which the museums we represent are a part. As participants in a community of discourse specific to the modern western world, we see the world through frameworks shaped by the humanistic and scientific disciplines this civilisation has fostered. We organise our museum holdings to reflect these frameworks and hire specialists in these disciplines to oversee the intellectual description of the heritage we gather. While there may be other ways to view the artefacts and specimens which populate our collections, we have historically defined ourselves in terms of disciplines which aspire to be trans- or extra-national.

Geologists across national boundaries believe that the same characteristics of rocks are important and that differences recognised in one nation are valid for geology in another nation. Similarly, though they may disagree about the relative importance of particular factors in the development of society, cultural anthropologists in different western nations carry on discourse about cultures using terms and perspectives familiar to their colleagues in other countries. Collectors of military insignia, or fabrics, and of stamps could, likewise, talk across national boundaries, even when the only translation of a technical term from another culture is achieved by adopting the vernacular term from the language of origin.

When CHIN developed its data dictionaries and its physical database architectures, it divided humanities and sciences because the museums holding objects classified into these broad categories of knowledge employed different styles of documentation (Canadian Heritage Information Network, 1985a and b). The Smithsonian Institution has recently adopted a similar implementation strategy while retaining a higher level data view that is integrated. Both found that natural history museums describe objects using an approach that might be called Generic-Specific: they identify the generic, such as species or mineral type, and then describe the item in hand as a member of that class. Cultural history museums, including those whose objects are scientific/industrial artefacts, employ an Attributive approach: they distinguish objects by their provenance, both in the narrow sense of ownership history and in the broadest sense of cultural context. Both types of museums relate the objects they hold to bibliographic entities, reproductions (photographic and otherwise), ideal types (whether these are concrete taxonomic type specimens or abstract style terms with scope notes), and life associations (which may be people and organisations, specific natural events, or even curatorial and collections management actions). And both types of museums attempt to attribute subject descriptors to objects.

What is an object about? What information does it carry? To define an object as *about* something, is to identify its subject, and objects only have subjects in the context of a specific discourse. Thus, the subject of a painting of the refugees from Ar fleeing to Zoar (Isaiah 15–16) from an art historical perspective is described using iconographic language, while its subject to a natural historian may require ecological concepts, and its subject to an anthropologist demands a cross-cultural vocabulary of social crisis.

The challenge to those who would employ terminology standards to clarify communications is threefold. First we must establish languages which enable us to talk within a discipline and within a community. Second we must seek means to communicate across disciplines, bridging the new desert landscape devastated by erosion and the symbolic rape of a culture. And third, we must conduct this conversation across time and language.

Although the problems of communicating across disciplinary perspectives still haunt us, the prospects for communicating across national boundaries within disciplinary frameworks are good. We need not invent, indeed cannot afford to invent, these languages, but we can forge alliances with disciplines to use these languages, indeed to illustrate them concretely, in and with museum objects. Such an enterprise has the potential of benefiting both the disciplines and the museums.

For example, the possibility of creating visual thesauri of art and culture are presented by the timely confluence of the republication of *Nomenclature*, the publication of the *Art and Architecture Thesaurus* (AAT), and the development of CD-ROM technology. Why not create an illustrated thesaurus of art terminology and cultural artefacts, drawn from the collections of many museums? Not only would such a visual thesaurus assist in cataloguing objects, providing the humanities equivalent of a type specimen, but it would permit users unfamiliar with the technical distinctions and terminology of a field to browse, with purpose and success, for terms required to search text databases, and, having identified the appropriate terms, to launch more successful queries.

Implementation of terminology control

Like all other professions, museum professionals observe standards in their work. Conservators follow standard analytic methods, archaeologists follow standards for documenting sites they excavate, and development officers use standard deeds of gift and agreements in accepting donations. These practices are utterly non-controversial, indeed, they are inherent in the very definition of professionalism.

The concept of standards in each of these cases is distinct. Some of these standards, like those followed by the conservator, are methods, techniques and practices known to work, but the conservator is free to employ other methods without approbation. Others, like standards for documenting an excavation, represent consensus reached within one discipline about methods that maintain communication within that discipline, and are enforced by excluding those who do not abide by them from disciplinary recognition, such as publication. Standards such as those guiding the drafting of deeds of gift have a power in law; violating them is likely to render the agreement invalid.

Because the administration of a museum is a complex undertaking, involving many different professions, and because different kinds of museums serve different patrons, we cannot speak about museum standards as a unitary concept. In these proceedings, we really intend to only consider standards for the documentation of museum specimens and artefacts. These standards exist to enhance communication about management of collections within the museum and about the objects themselves within the scholarly disciplines devoted to their study.

These two purposes of documentation standards are discrete and, occasionally, at cross purposes. Both begin by agreeing on the character of the documentation system: are we creating catalogue *raissonné*, inventories and location registers, scholarly analysis of items, or exhibit labels? Agreements at this level of discourse are called information systems standards.

Once the subject of the discourse is established, both standards focus on what we want to say about the subject. If we decide that we want to record information about the physical properties of the objects, is the weight of the object a category of discourse? its external texture? its chemical composition? its optical or magnetic properties? Agreements at this level of discourse are called data content standards.

In order to communicate, further agreement will be necessary. Should chemical composition be expressed by chemical formulae or by common name? Should weight be expressed in English or metric units? (This sounds easier than it actually proves to be: is the English unit called a ton equal to 1 016.06 kilograms, often called a long ton or shipping ton, or is it equal to 907.2 kilograms, often called a short ton except in the United States, Canada and South Africa. By agreeing on English we have ruled out the metric ton, equal to 1 000 kilograms and by agreeing to a measure of weight we ruled out a measure of volume equal either to 40 cubic feet, a freight ton, or 35 cubic feet, a displacement ton.) Agreement at this level is called data value standards and it is to this level of discourse that the concept of terminology control applies.

If we have agreed that chemical composition is to be expressed by common name of the substance, we need to have further agreement that the common name of the substance often referred to as petroleum jelly is petrolatum, that agar-agar will be called agar, or that the substance historically known as Greek fire will be referred to by that name. If we are using common names, we need to decide if ermine coats are to be called ermine or fur and if pumice stones are to be called pumice or stone.

In spite of these examples of the benefits of common vocabularies, museums resist terminology standards. Why? Terminology control has proved to be its own worst enemy. In the process of implementing systems to control terminology, the most avid supporters of greater clarity of communication and exchange of information are frequently alienated. While we might in theory leave this discussion until after agreement has been reached on terminology controls, it is impossible to isolate resistance to the idea of terminology control from experiences or rumours of bad implementations.

The end advanced by advocates of terminology control is greater efficiency of retrieval through consistency in the application of terms in documentation. The costs of imposing such consistency, the investment in developing or adopting vocabularies and the overhead of training, documentation quality controls and vocabulary maintenance mechanisms, are to be repaid in more efficient controls, greater professionalism, and enhanced exhibits, educational offerings, publications and other products.

Despite the obvious intellectual appeal of consistency in application of terminology, museum management has not embraced terminology control as a strategy. It seems reasonable to assume that for terminology control to become a practice within museums, the management of these institutions needs to become convinced that consistency in documentation is necessary for purposes of administrative control. However, it is also evident that this necessary pre-condition is not itself a sufficient condition for terminology control to be implemented or for the expected rewards to result.

Terminology control is resisted by curators and eroded by practices tied to systems implementation that do not make use of its power to achieve the anticipated benefits. Curatorial resistance is usually tied to failure to locate the authority for appropriate terminology in the nexus of practice and disciplinary knowledge from which it must necessarily flow, or to real or imagined impositions of the implementation system on curators. Usually, if the authority for terminology can be given to curators along with responsibility for its consistent application, and the system being employed does not require curators to employ terms that they believe are inappropriate simply because such terms are used elsewhere, curators will be supportive.

One fear often expressed in initial phases of discussions about common terminology is that adoption of common languages will dictate common practices, without respect to the valid differences between institutional practices brought about by the differences in size, setting, purposes, users and holdings referred to earlier.

Nothing could be further from the fact. Common terminology permits us to share information not about the sameness of our practices and holdings, but about their differences. It does not enforce a commonality of views, a uniformity of intellectual perspectives, but makes possible distinctions otherwise denied us. Without common terminology I may describe an item as pewter and you may describe it as a tin alloy and we will not know whether its composition is in fact identical, or whether the difference in our terminology reflects a degree of difference in the proportion of lead and tin. Is the difference between our descriptions a meaningful difference, or just a difference? Needless to say, this same question arises within a repository whether records from different curatorial units read 'pewter' and 'tin alloy', or 'Queen Anne' and 'Victorian'.

Even curators who appreciate this benefit often feel threatened by terminology standardisation. They may have reason. Some, indeed most, implementations of standards impose unnecessary restrictions on users which are ultimately self-defeating. For example, there are two ways to assure that users of synonymous terms will locate materials catalogued by each other. The first way is to insist that all users use only one (often called preferred) term; in this implementation one, or possibly both, users are forced to adopt an alien usage. A second way is to design systems that permit use of either term in cataloguing, and recognise either term in a user query, and can retrieve all usages of both terms while displaying both the original usage and a user note explaining the dual retrieval. The first implementation imposes a restriction on some users and may obscure valid subtleties in usages; the second is transparent to users and preserves the valid distinctions. Both depend on the acceptance of a terminological standard that equates the two terms for purposes of retrieval; the latter recognises that there may be legitimate, if subtle, distinctions between synonymous terms that can be reflected in scope notes, or that differences in usage at the institutional level may have valid bases (such as integration with earlier record keeping systems) that can be reflected in local use notes.

In 1980, when the US National Information Systems Task Force designed a data dictionary for archives and manuscript repositories (Bearman, 1985 and 1987), there was considerable feeling on the task force that certain data elements were necessary for description and should be required. This pressure was successfully resisted. If data is, in fact, necessary it will be recorded, and if certain data elements are not employed, then they must not be necessary, at least for certain purposes. At the time, there was also sentiment in favour of excluding certain elements of information which some archives said they used on the grounds that the task force felt they were irrelevant or tertiary. Once again the pressure was resisted. If data is irrelevant, it will not be recorded by institutions other than those that proposed them. If others did not adopt a useless practice, what harm did it do to include them in a standard, so that those institutions which thought they wanted to use them could use them in a standard fashion? This philosophy of implementation has been called 'descriptive standards', not because it deals with description, but rather in contrast to prescriptive standards, terms often thought to be so intimately related that prescriptive seems redundant to many.

Standards for what?

Identifying arenas in which the development of descriptive standards could fruitfully take place and suggesting how to manage implementation concerns, are necessary preconditions for dialogue about terminology standards. However, only the identification of concrete benefits from specific agreements will support the implementation and maintenance of a terminology standard. Standards are not ends in themselves, but means. So what are museum terminology standards a means to?

If we start within the individual institution, we can readily find reasons to adopt common methods in order to work more effectively and communicate better. However, there is very little on-going inter-museum communication, so museums find few reasons to accept the (admittedly high) overheads of standards development and maintenance.

Museum professionals often contrast their needs with those of libraries which benefit from the cooperative cataloguing of mass-produced objects. They point out that museums and archives hold 'unique' objects for which they cannot share cataloguing. In so doing, they ignore the needs of museums for some information in common: art museums for artist biographies and the histories of art organisations and auctions; natural history museums for taxonomic data and ecological information sources; history museums for databases of events and actors in them.

Museums could also take a lesson from zoos which, through the International Species Inventory System (ISIS), have implemented a worldwide system of information exchange in order to borrow and loan their holdings. Beginning with relatively few elements of information exchanged on paper (although subsequently entered into a central computer), these zoos have built a database that supports an impressive array of functions, and, recently, have constructed a software system for local use based on the prior agreements on terminology and data content. Granted the economic incentives for zoos to find mates for their animals are greater than those for museums to locate appropriate objects for an exhibit, but the adoption of terminology standards was not expensive by any measure. As illustrated by ISIS, terminology standards may come about to facilitate information sharing and/or to share systems development costs on systems. Cost effectiveness is the driving force for both.

It has to be accepted that cultural/ideological values enter into the decisions to adopt standards and many of these factors can help support information sharing projects, especially at their beginning: the desire to share rather than hide knowledge; the benefits of expanded sources of information and wider vistas; the allure of a deeper, richer knowledge; and the opportunity to participate in defining a culture which is emerging in the unification of electronic sources of information. Of course, national policies and funding also play a role. But in the end, the applications and networks in which we participate must support the costs of standards or we will cease to maintain them and the benefits will erode quickly.

Terminology control and the cultural role of museums

Consistency in the terminology used in any given access point in documentation is advanced as a means to more effective information retrieval. Linkage between terminology used in museum descriptions and the language of a discipline and its bibliographic tools is advanced as a means to improve research use of holdings. Increasing the number of access points over which such terminological control is exercised is seen as a means of supporting inter-disciplinary research. Connecting the vernacular to objects distinguished by connoisseurs is perceived as a means of making holdings more accessible to the public. Establishing authorities and vocabularies is a scholarly activity valued in itself, but also for the potential power it exerts over the use of language by others. In sum, terminology control is seen as a means of connecting the museum to its potential users, users who employ other vocabularies as a consequence of either a specialised view or, ironically, their lack thereof.

Thus, when we propose terminology control, it is usually someone's terminology that we propose to adopt. Or we expect to make a terminology that, by being widely adopted, will be a *linqua franca* for some group. The intention is to place our museums in the information seeking path of identified communities of information seekers: be they scientists, hobbyists or schoolchildren.

There is one big attraction on the horizon. Over the next century the civilisation of which we are a part will recreate itself in the electronic medium. We will build civilisational knowledge bases, consisting of texts, images, sounds and electronic representations of three dimensional objects in time and space. The source materials for these knowledge bases are currently the province of museums (and the democratisation of this knowledge which will result is clearly the subject of another paper). Standards will make it possible to unify the disparate sources of our self-understanding into a powerful cultural force akin to the 'World Brain'. Surely museum professionals will be attracted to this enterprise.

II
INTERNATIONAL DEVELOPMENTS

4 INTERNATIONAL DEVELOPMENTS

D. Andrew Roberts
Museum Documentation Association
Cambridge

Section II incorporates papers about the roles of international organisations at the terminology standards and applications levels. These demonstrate the extent of expertise within the broad information community available to be tapped by museums.

The International Organization for Standardization (ISO) and Infoterm work to coordinate and encourage international standards initiatives. ISO itself liaises with national standards bodies such as the British Standard Institute (BSI), American National Standards Institute (ANSI), Deutsches Institut für Normung (DIN) and Association francaise de normalisation (AFNOR).

Axel Ermert demonstrates the relevance of a number of ISO standards to the work of museums, including examples such as country codes and object and conservation term lists. He stresses the role of Technical Committee 46 concerned with information and documentation and its willingness to work with museums through agencies such as CIDOC.

Infoterm is a specialised agency of Unesco's General Information Programme which concentrates on terminology developments, acting as a clearinghouse and information centre. Wolfgang Nedobity describes how it has been involved in developing the theory of terminology and worked with ISO to produce terminology standards. As with ISO, Infoterm is interested in liaising with museums and is aware of the benefit which a museum's input could make to its research.

From a museum perspective, both these organisations have already done significant work that is relevant to museums. However, this has in the past usually been undertaken with minimum consultation or input from the museum community, even when the work is directly concerned with museum interests, such as object name terminology. Museums tend to take second place, far behind the library and (to a lesser extent) archive interests with their strong pressure groups. In the absence of national museum organisations like the British Library or Library of Congress, with their own professionally staffed standards development sections, this situation is inevitable. With limited resources and coordination, museums need to be responsive to standards developments and opportunities and exert influence wherever possible.

One museum organisation that has worked to draw colleagues together and act as a forum is CIDOC, the Documentation Committee of ICOM. A decade ago, I discussed the need for a professional secretariat for CIDOC, to encourage international museum standards developments (Roberts and Light, 1980). In the absence of such an initiative, progress has been painfully slow and CIDOC continues to depend on the commitment of a number of individuals and their organisations. It is now working with ISO to establish museum information exchange standards and in 1987 established a Terminology Control Working Group.

Eleanor Fink describes the initial aims of this Working Group, including encouraging an awareness of the importance of a consistent approach to terminology, surveying practice in individual museums and compiling a basic bibliography.

In a closely related field, the International Committee of the History of Art (CIHA) demonstrates how much is possible with the right mix of expertise *and* resources. With support from the Getty Art History Information Program, a Working Group has been examining automation issues including terminology needs. Marilyn Schmitt outlines its plans and progress, including a historical-geographical system and the development of a multilingual version of the Art and Architecture Thesaurus.

A further example of a cooperative international initiative is the Conservation Information Network. John Perkins concentrates on the information exchange aspects of the Network and particularly its design of a data dictionary.

Finally, Susanne Peters presents a further case study of the work undertaken by the International Councils of Museums (ICOM) and Monuments and Sites (ICOMOS) to develop a common thesaurus. Her account of the problems entailed in bringing together the needs of two international organisations is a useful insight into the pitfalls that lie in wait for the unwary.

---

5 INTERNATIONAL STANDARDS: THEIR RELEVANCE TO MUSEUMS AND MUSEUM TERMINOLOGY

Axel Emert

Secretary ISO/TC 46/SC3
DIN Deutsches Institut für Normung e.V.
Berlin

Standards for museums

The International Organization for Standardization (ISO) is responsible for developing international standards in all fields, including the professional aspects of the work of institutions like libraries, archives and museums. Drawing on the experience of many organisations around the world, these standards have the potential to contribute to the performance of individual museums and to support networking and the sharing of information.

This paper concentrates on international standardisation activity. There is a growing tendency for organisations to use international standards rather than comparable national standards, although it should be noted that many standardisation procedures are currently only defined in national proposals. ISO is made up of national agencies such as the British Standards Institute (BSI), and works with these to develop common resources.

ISO's involvement with museums has been less extensive in the past than might have been hoped. We now hope to redress this situation. One example of closer links is the formal liaison status that now exists between the Documentation Committee of ICOM (CIDOC) (Chapter 7) and the ISO/TC 46 Committee.

Successful standards depend on an effective analysis of the concepts or operations that are being standardised. In the case of museums, we are interested in standards for all aspects of the handling of collections, including administrative information about individual objects. It seems that museum collection information is amenable to harmonisation, and not too different from information processed by other organisations like libraries (see Houghton, 1969). Consequently, we believe there is an overall coherent information community with similar problems and the opportunity to benefit from each other's experiences (International Organization for Standardization, 1983).

Types of standards

Although standardisation is particularly apparent in the field of computerisation, the dependence on standards has existed for many years. A standard can have one or more of the following characteristics (Crawford, 1986, Kindleberger, 1983 and Sanders, 1972):

embody a working method (e.g. tables for transliteration such as ISO 233 for Arabic). These establish a specific procedure out of a number of alternatives;

embody a working method together with a full list of subject contents (e.g. an authority list of country codes);

define a set of requirements;

define a limited range of possibilities out of a wider set of alternatives;

serve as models which can be adapted to a particular application (e.g. the bibliographic data element directory in ISO 8459);

serve as a checklist (e.g. the data elements of an institution, defined in ISO 2146);

define a methodology (such as ISO/TR 9007 which is a powerful description of the architecture and components of an information system).

Standards for documentation

Turning to standards concerned with documentation operations, a useful outline was compiled by Unisist in 1980 (Vajda, 1980). This section concentrates on a brief indication of the remit of ISO/TC 46. Relevant standards for the presentation of information are incorporated in a handbook available from ISO (International Organization for Standardization, 1988). Key subjects include:

ISO 2146, a checklist of the administrative aspects of an institution to be considered when drawing up a directory of institutions;

ISO 8459, a series of bibliographic data element directories;

ISO 5127, vocabulary of information and documentation;

ISO 690, a short description of the content of bibliographic references, detailed versions of which are given in various documents called International Standard Bibliographic Descriptions (ISBD). Other standards like ISO 832 and ISO 4 define aspects of the terminology to be used in these formal descriptions;

ISO 3297 and ISO 2108 define the structure of the ISSN and ISBN series and book numbering systems;

other standards cover apsects of the use of different alphabets, such as filing rules (ISO 7154), transliteration rules (ISO 233 for Arabic, 9 for Slavic-Cyrillic, 843 for Greek, etc.) and coded character sets (ISO 646 defines ASCII, for which ISO 2022 gives extension rules, while ISO 6861 defines the Cyrillic coded character set and ISO 6438 the African coded character set for specialised bibliographic needs).

In the specialised case of computer-based information, a key standard is ISO 2709, the format for bibliographic information exchange on magnetic tape, which defines the form for the arrangement of information. It would be possible to produce a specific application of this for museum use.

ISO 7498 defines the Open Systems Interconnection (OSI) model for electronic information exchange. Other ISO standards expand on the physical specification of the seven layers within this system (see Chapter 9). New standards for information management also build on these principles, such as ISO 8777 on the commands in interactive systems and ISO 10 160/63 on application services.

One subject of particular interest to museums is the standardisation of country names and codes. ISO 3166 covers all states and related entities. Work is now under way to extend this into more depth by providing codes for subdivisions within countries (like BS 6879 for UK counties) and by including historic countries. This type of work involves a great deal of research and cooperation.

Terminology standards

ISO/TC 37 has particular responsibility for terminology standards. General introductions to this subject provide background details (Felber, 1984, Picht and Draskau, 1985 and Rey, 1979).

ISO 2788 and ISO 5964 define rules for developing thesauri. At a more fundamental level, ISO 704 and ISO 860 are concerned with formalising the organisation of any vocabulary list. ISO 6156 defines an exchange format for the transmission of terminology records.

The need to formalise and define the meaning of technical concepts is a fundamental characteristic of any discipline. Basic museum documentation sources such as *Museum registration methods* (Dudley and Wilkinson, 1979) and *Practical museum documentation* (MDA, 1981) illustrate this problem. ISO 5127 is developing an extensive vocabulary for documentation. It will provide the authority for common concepts such as classification, thesaurus, index, authority file and terminology itself. ISO 5127 is designed to define for the first time the extent of the field of documentation as a tool for mutual communication across the information community.

Directly relevant parts of this work include ISO 5127/3 which covers iconic documents, such as drawing, paintings and prints (two-dimensional pictorial documents). ISO 5127/13 is envisaged as defining three-dimensional objects as documents. Links have been made with ICOM and the Reinwardt Academy, Leiden, to support this research.

Existing sources such as the *Dictionarium Museologicum* (Eri and Vegh, 1986) and the ICONCLASS classification scheme (Chapter 43) were consulted, but were found to have a rather different emphasis from that envisaged by ISO.

A further section in preparation (ISO 5127/14) will cover the terminology of the conservation of documents.

ISO is a federation of national standards organisations. In addition to the links between CIDOC and ISO/TC 46, museums should influence standards work by participating in the standards efforts of their national agencies, and in particular the various technical committees relevant to museum needs. ISO will welcome your support in the development of new resources.

6 TERMINOLOGY AS A MANAGEMENT INSTRUMENT FOR MUSEUMS

Wolfgang Nedobity

International Information Centre for Terminology (Infoterm)
Vienna, Austria

Introduction

Infoterm, the terminology centre within the General Information Programme (PGI/UNISIST) of Unesco was established and is sponsored by Unesco within the framework of PGI/UNISIST, on the basis of a contract concluded in 1971. It is affiliated to the Austrian Standards Institute (ON) in Vienna and financed by the Austrian Federal Ministry of Economic Affairs, the Federal Economic Chamber and the Austrian Standards Institute. Infoterm works in liaison with terminology standardising and harmonising bodies; acts as a clearinghouse, documentation and analysis centre for the theory, utilisation and documentation of terminology; and promotes and coordinates terminology work carried out by subject specialists.

Infoterm has carried out a number of projects which demonstrate that well organised terminology can assist documentation specialists and other experts to successfully utilise the multifunctionality of terminology as a management tool. A methodology has been developed which supports the establishment of high-quality multifunctional terminological databases and is now being applied in large enterprises for the control of information flow (Galinski and Nedobity, 1986). Research and management is impossible without access to information. In the sphere of museums, information exists primarily in an accumulated form, embedded in the history of an object. It becomes evident when we try to represent such an object by concepts and terms. Thus, the terminology involved is the first key to information at more complex levels, culminating in a comprehensive information system.

Bergengren criticises the quality of information systems: 'Very few museums have information systems that, as a whole, work satisfactorily. Most museums have some subsystems that are very useful and others that are not. Besides, certain subsystems which ought to be found in the museum are missing. However, the biggest problem is not whether the individual subsystems function, but the fact that there is no coordination of their activities' (Bergengren, 1978). Terminologies can improve this situation, because they act as interfaces between the various modules of a knowledge based system.

The functions of terminology

Terminologies — the specialised vocabularies of specific subject fields, recorded in their conceptual classifications — form one of the bases of:

the representation and structuring of knowledge (conceptual classification of every subject field);

the communication of knowledge and skills (teaching of the subject field, transfer of knowledge);

the conversion of knowledge from one language to another (interpretation, translation);

the presentation of subject information;

the description and condensation of the content of documents (indexing and abstracting);

the search for stored information (thesaurus construction, retrieval languages);

accessing knowledge based systems.

Each function can be activated by a certain combination of data categories in a terminological record, pertaining to a single concept and its surrounding conceptual field.

Tools for information management

Nowadays, the labour force is dominated by the information professions. There are far more people who make their living working with information than with any other economic resource. Museum curators fall into this category, dealing mainly with three types of information:

bibliographic information:

object-oriented (factual) information;

terminological information.

As regards the management of the first two types, tools developed by library and information science are most widely applied. They concern cataloguing, indexing and thesaurus construction. The application of terminological methods to these activities was discussed by Nedobity (1983). A 'vocabulary' has to serve as a basis of these activities, which leads to the third type of information.

There are a number of published vocabularies available to museums, although many museums do their own terminology work based on the content of their collections. In other words, they use only terms that relate to what is in the collections and the vocabulary is built up as the recording proceeds. The kinds of problems that are usually encountered in such a case were described by Orna: 'The most frequent form in which this problem presents itself is that of alternate names for objects, processes, materials, etc. The alternatives may be between common and scientific nomenclatures, between contemporary and earlier names, between names from different cultures, or between general and dialect names or names from different dialects. The choice of the standard term will depend on the nature of the collection, the way in which it is used, and by whom it is used, and on whether there are any existing standards for terminology for the subject matter in question' (Orna and Pettitt, 1980).

Being aware of such problems, terminology scientists have developed a general theory of terminology, comprising the principles and methods to be applied in practical work. The essence of this theory has been laid down in a number of standards of the International Organization for Standardization (ISO) and other standards bodies (Nedobity, 1987).

The following standards have been published by ISO:

ISO 639:1988	Code for the representation of names of languages
ISO 704:1987	Principles and methods of terminology
ISO 1087:1990	Vocabulary of terminology
ISO 1951:1973	Lexicographical symbols particularly for use in classified defining vocabularies (reconfirmed 1984)

ISO 6156:1987	Magnetic tape exchange format for terminological/lexicographical records (MATER)

The following standards are in preparation by ISO/TC 37 'Terminology (principles and coordination)':

ISO/CD 860	International unification of concepts and terms
ISO/DP 10241	Preparation and layout of international terminology standards
WI 10	Concepts systems (development and representation)
WI 11	Computer aids in the systematic preparation of technical dictionaries

Museum documentation systems

Museum documentation supports the physical control of objects (e.g. acquisition, loan, restoration and storage) and the documentation of their significance and content. Such systems can be supplemented by data files concerning the management of finances and personnel of a museum (including statistics on the frequency of visitors, exhibitions, etc.).

Sarasan pointed out the advantages of a computerised system over a conventional system: 'In many manual systems, the network of pointers between files has broken down. Cross-reference files do not interrelate well or may reflect different versions of what should be the same data. Files may be incomplete or infrequently updated. Information searches, therefore, are often incomplete or incorrect. The system is perceived as unreliable. When this point is reached, automation may be the best method available to correct the problems of the manual system' (Sarasan and Neuner, 1983). It is not only the gaining of precision, but also the universal applicability, that justifies the establishment of such systems.

Terminological databases

Terminological databases of a higher degree of complexity (i.e. a structure in which concepts and systems of concepts are sufficiently interrelated) are a solution to problems such as:

- the wealth of information;
- the many forms in which the available information occurs;
- the divergent access systems;
- the multilingualism of subject communication;
- the diversity of user groups searching for information.

The extraction, acquisition and maintenance of high-quality terminological data is expensive and time consuming. In the case of knowledge-relevant data, this work can only be carried out by experts supported by specialists in terminology documentation.

In-house experts are the most economical and reliable suppliers of concept-related information, especially if they are given a tool to facilitate their work. Furthermore, such a terminological database offers access to the various internal and external sources of information and facilitates the assignment of data to the correct conceptual framework.

The computerisation of object documentation

Object documentation is a central activity of any museum and has been computerised in a large number of institutions. The justification for the introduction of the computers is usually based on factors such as:

data can be updated in all relevant records more easily;

indexes can be produced at shorter intervals;

records can be selected and retrieved according to any combination of required data.

Terminological methods can be applied in object documentation at the point of preparing a record to act as a surrogate for the object. Inconsistencies in the presentation of information in the record, for example describing similar objects by different terms, or spelling the same artist's name differently, may lead to failures to locate related objects.

There are different types of terminologies, depending on the type of object, the kind of abstraction for a group/set/class of objects and the type of conceptual system aimed at. With the exception of concepts of single objects being represented by names (which — in analogy to terms — can be codes or other symbols, too) there are basically two types of conceptual systems: those falling under a concept classification (vocabularies, glossaries, etc.) and those belonging to the documentation languages (subject classification, thesaurus, etc.). The latter can be considered as artificial terminologies (nevertheless represented as a rule by natural language symbols, often supplemented by a systematic notation). The others — when represented by linguistic symbols — are used in natural language communication by subject specialists (Budin, Galinski, Nedobity and Thaller, 1988, page 53).

In order to obtain an overview of all the linguistic symbols used in a particular object documentation system, one produces alphabetical or systematic indexes. The seeming simplicity of access through an alphabetical arrangement tempts users just to index and not to burden themselves with classifying, especially since the latter cannot be performed automatically. However, a classified structure helps the user make consistent decisions about where to insert new material and makes users aware of related areas which may also yield relevant items. In many instances, it offers a search alternative to the structure of the collection itself.

From an object database to a user information system

Terminological principles and methods are not only of relevance during recording, but also when designing output facilities, otherwise such a situation as that described by Sarasan may be noted: 'Numerous museums have found themselves with masses of computerised data that are substantially unusable for data retrieval purposes. This realisation is generally made after data entry has been completed' (Sarasan, 1981). It is necessary to consider the requirements of future users right from the beginning, so that effective interfaces can be created for various types of user groups. It is also necessary to monitor the use of the collection, the types of questions that are put and the degree of specificity they demand.

Each user group is accustomed to a different level of the special language used or at least does not necessarily want to learn a special query language. Thus research into natural language interfaces has been launched, allowing the user to select from terminologies suitable from the primary school level to those of subject specialists.

The basis of any user information system has to be a functioning object documentation system. By applying techniques from knowledge engineering, such a documentation system can be extended towards a real knowledge-based system. For example, image processing facilities would be one important addition, as in the visitors' information systems of the Musée d'Orsay and La Villette in Paris, and the Museum of Ethnology in Osaka.

Knowledge- based systems are only useful if they are conceived as interactive advisory systems which are capable of simulating certain situations on request. The idea of using terminologically processed structures as convenient access systems has been widely accepted (Budin, *et al.*, 1988). They centre around a conceptual interface which is appropriate to the mental structures of the users and which allows a smooth transition from the familiar to the novel, from the general to the specific and from detail to an overall picture in a large selection of languages.

---

7 THE WORK OF THE DOCUMENTATION COMMITTEE OF ICOM (CIDOC)

Eleanor E. Fink

Manager, Vocabulary Coordination Group
Getty Art History Information Program
Santa Monica, CA

The International Council of Museums

The International Council of Museums (ICOM), founded in 1946, is dedicated to the improvement and advancement of the world's museums. Embracing museums of every discipline, whether science, technology, natural history, art, history, or archaeology, including zoos, aquaria and botanical gardens, ICOM has over 7900 members, both individual and institutional, in 113 countries. It consists of 75 National Committees and 30 International Specialised Committees and affiliated organisations: groups of professionals representing the leading authorities on a given type of museum, or an activity common to museums such as education, conservation, etc. These committees meet regularly to discuss new developments, familiarise themselves with the latest techniques and make recommendations that are circulated to ICOM members throughout the world. ICOM holds a General Conference and General Assembly every three years, hosted by one of its National Committees.

ICOMs Documentation Committee

The International Committee for Documentation/Comité International pour la Documentation (CIDOC) is one of ICOM's specialised committees. CIDOC holds its meetings every year and every third year with ICOM. The principle objective of CIDOC is to further research and standardisation in the field of museum documentation. This objective is underscored by the impact of the information revolution, which has created a seemingly insatiable demand on museums as primary sources of information. To assist museums in remaining responsive to the needs of those they serve, CIDOC addresses a wide range of documentation issues through the formation and activities of working groups.

Membership in CIDOC is open to any ICOM member. While the membership varies from time to time, it has grown since 1956 (when CIDOC was formed) from eight members representing eight countries to more than 200 members representing 32 countries. The membership reflects various museum interests of countries from both the developed and developing worlds. When required, CIDOC also co-opts members who may not meet the requirements of general ICOM membership, but who have a certain expertise in the museum field. Co-opting ensures that the necessary skills and talents are available to effectively resolve documentation problems.

Prior to its 1987 annual conference, CIDOC consisted of seven working groups engaged in the following activities:

Terminology Working Group. Developing and maintaining a multilingual dictionary of museum terms *(Dictionarium Museologicum)*.

Handbook on the Documentation of Museum Collections Working Group. Preparing a handbook on museum documentation that will provide basic practical guidance to museums on the aims and methods of museum documentation.

Bibliography Working Group. Assisting the UNESCO-ICOM Documentation Centre in compiling an annual bibliography of references to articles and monographs of museological interests throughout the world.

Museum Database Survey Working Group. Researching, compiling and distributing material on automated, collection related documentation systems in museums.

Working Group for Pictorial Archives. Acting as a clearinghouse for information on the computerisation of photo and iconographic archives.

Documentation Centres Working Group. Coordinating activities for national and international museum libraries and documentation centres; concerned with the management and use of museological literature; studying bibliographic standards and the development of thesauri in these centres; examining the possibility of developing a shared catalogue; considering other issues related to documentation centres.

Documentation Standards Working Group. Coordinating the integration of standards projects being worked on by different disciplinary and national committees.

One key area missing among CIDOC's working groups prior to the 1987 conference was terminology or vocabulary control. Although CIDOC contains a working group on terminology, which maintains the *Dictionarium Museologicum*, the aim of that group focuses solely on the technical terms used in the every day operation and management of museum activities, as opposed to the vocabulary entered in a computer system to record or document information about a particular museum collection, object or specimen. Recognising that data is the most valuable component of a computer system and that control of vocabulary is essential to effectively manage data, a proposal to establish a working group on terminology control was presented to the CIDOC Board at the conference and was unanimously accepted. Fourteen conference participants joined the new working group and met to define goals and elect a chairperson.

Some of the points raised in the first meeting were:

there is a critical need to educate people on the meaning of terminology control;

terminology control is a necessary step in the development of a database, not the last step;

consistency and commonality of terminology is important and will continue to be important as technology advances;

commonality of terminology is a communication aid which can lead to data sharing and exchange;

duplication of efforts in developing authority lists should be avoided;

where possible, it is desirable to coordinate efforts with other organisations and groups focusing on terminology control issues.

Based on these points, the group drafted the following statement:

'Consistency and commonality of terminology in museum documentation is a necessary consideration to manage databases effectively and to facilitate sharing and exchange of information among systems. Based on the premise that terminology control is essential and will continue to be important as technology advances, the terminology control group views its primary goal as educational — that is to create an awareness of what terminology control is and its value.'

As goals for 1987–88, the group proposed:

compiling a questionnaire to survey what museums are doing about terminology control, what authority lists have or are being developed;

compiling a basic bibliography of select publications which will be distributed with the questionnaire to assist museums in understanding the meaning of terminology control.

Based on the responses to the questionnaire, the group has proposed as a long range plan the publication of a directory on terminology control. This is to include sample pages of controlled vocabulary lists being used by museums.

---

8 THE TAU (THESAURUS ARTIS UNIVERSALIS) PROJECT OF THE INTERNATIONAL COMMITTEE OF THE HISTORY OF ART

Dr Marilyn Schmitt

Getty Art History Information Program
Santa Monica, CA

In 1983, the International Committee of the History of Art (known as CIHA), meeting in Vienna, appointed a working group called Thesaurus Artis Universalis (or TAU) and charged it with exploring issues of automation as they affected the History of Art. The J. Paul Getty Trust agreed to support the investigations of TAU, since the interests expressed by TAU coincided with the interests of the still-developing Getty Art History Information Program. Made up of major scholars from eight countries,[1] this TAU working group chose Jacques Thuillier of the Collège de France as its Chairman and Henry Millon of the Center for Advanced Study in the Visual Arts as its Scientific Secretary. Under this leadership, TAU has met some 13 times to define in what areas, and in what form, the computer could be used to benefit the history of art.

TAU's areas of interest

Although the initial interest of TAU centred on the treatment of biographical information — with a databank of artists' biographies as the goal — other areas of inquiry soon emerged that placed a concern for biography in a larger context and defined areas of information that contributed to biography. To put it simply, standards for terminology — the collection, structure and use of terminology in automated systems — began to occupy the group.

TAU recognised that many projects had a need for consistent ways to deal with certain categories of information — among them personal names, geographic locations, building and institutional names, object names and dates. If there was to be the exchange of information on an international plane, there would be a value in devising international, even multilingual standards in these areas. Moreover, this international group of scholars recognised that the scholar's voice needed to be heard if the information was to be structured in a way that would be useful to scholars.

It was clear that individual projects seldom had either resources or incentive to develop standards beyond those necessary for their own project. TAU decided to direct its work to the areas that might otherwise receive less attention, for example a survey of

1. Members: John Boardman, Oxford University; Albert Châtelet, University of Strasbourg; Nancy Englander, The J. Paul Getty Trust; Oreste Ferrari, Istituto Centrale per il Catalogo e la Documentazione, Rome; Hermann Fillitz, Kunsthistorisches Museum, Vienna; Lutz Heusinger, Bildarchiv Foto Marburg; Irving Lavin, Institute for Advanced Study, Princeton; Henry Millon, Center for Advanced Study in the Visual Arts, National Gallery of Art, Washington, DC; Serenita Papaldo, Istituto Centrale per il Catalogo e la Documentazione; Myra Nan Rosenfeld, Canadian Centre for Architecture; Hayat Salam-Liebich, Canadian Centre for Architecture; Alfred Schmid, University of Fribourg; Marilyn Schmitt, The Getty Art History Information Program; Oreste Signore, Consiglio Nazionale delle Ricerche, Istituto CNUCE, Pisa; Jacques Thuillier, Collège de France; Ernst Ullmann, Karl-Marx-Universität, Leipzig.

automated projects to find what standards or authorities were in use. For another example, many projects use the Times or the Rand McNally Atlas as a geographical authority. TAU knew of no *historical*-geographical authority that would take into account the changes in geographical names over time. That lacuna seemed a prime area to be addressed by a group particularly concerned with the historical designation of place names.

Finally, the development of thesauri in different countries without reference to each other, and offering no possibility for multilingual bridges to connect them, attracted TAU's attention and concern.

The projects of TAU

TAU's agenda, when formulated fully, came to consist of four projects:

a methodology and data structure for a system to accommodate an international historical-geographical thesaurus;

standards for an international biographical databank of artists;

a methodology for the realisation of a multilingual Art and Architecture Thesaurus;

a survey and an analysis and evaluation of authorities currently used in automated projects in art history.

Each project has followed a different course of development. The original project, to create a model for a biographical database, has worked to reconcile the two great differences in scholarly computing: on the one hand, the belief that structured information, broken into small units, is the only appropriate way to store information in a computer; and, on the other, the conviction that only a full accommodation of textual information can retain the full significance of that information.

Many museums may well have already made a choice between those alternatives, in favour of structured databases with controlled vocabulary. But I can assure you that many banks of scholarly information are being built without those features, not out of oblivion of 'correct database methodology', but in active rejection of the impoverishment that much of the scholarly world believes its information will suffer by being chopped and minced into small pieces that the computer can digest. TAU has sought a solution that will provide both the efficiency of controlled vocabulary in a structured automated environment and, for those who desire it, access to the original language of the text.

The co-directors of TAU's biographical database, Jacques Thuillier of the Collège de France and Lutz Heusinger of the Marburger Index, represent the two divergent positions. The committee hopes to satisfy both views through a multi-level data structure.

The historical-geographical database was developed by two countrymen already committed to the concept of the structured, relational database, Oreste Ferrari of the Istituto Centrale per il Catalogo e la Documentazione in Rome and Oreste Signore of CNUCE in Pisa. Details of their work are presented in Chapter 31. They have developed a flexible concept that allows for the construction of an index and a thesaurus of historical-geographical terms, as well as for a visual component to locate in geographical space the places for which the names stand.

The effort to locate, identify, and represent the myriad authorities that might be used for art-historical information — indeed to define and limit the very concept of authority — has been arduous. Assigned to Deirdre Stam of Syracuse University, with the collaboration of François d'Hautpoul of Paris, the search and the explication have demanded more travel, collection, digestion, and commentary than might have been imagined. The work is still underway and, on completion, may well contain the information most immediately helpful to those who prepare art-historical information for the computer.

The *Art and Architecture Thesaurus* (AAT), supported by the Getty Art History Information Program and under the direction of Toni Petersen (Chapter 56), has long been a candidate for translation from the American English in which it is constructed. Nevertheless, TAU began with an even-handed search for thesauri in different languages that might be mapped to each other on equal terms. After thorough investigation and experiment, the team of Myra Nan Rosenfeld and Hayat Salam-Liebich of the Canadian Centre for Architecture concluded that the AAT, as the most detailed and highly structured example of thesaurus construction, would have to act as the backbone of any multilingual effort, with allowance made to accommodate the differing conceptual structures that terminology in other languages may demand. An experimental translation of portions of the Architectural Components hierarchy of the AAT into French has prompted TAU to place the responsibility for implementation in the hands of the University of Montréal's Department of Linguistics and to seek other financial support to continue this effort.

Meanwhile, meetings have occurred or are planned to pursue the translation of the AAT into Italian, German and Spanish. The difficulties of such a task — of matching words that sometimes cannot mean exactly the same thing, of maintaining the structural links between hierarchies that may take partially different forms, and of ensuring sufficient communication between multi-national teams with different concepts of thesaurus construction — guarantees a long and demanding process for those involved.

The completion of TAU's work

In September 1989, CIHA will hold its triennial international congress in Strasbourg. At the meeting of the general assembly, TAU will present the results of its projects in published or soon-to-be-published form. The intention is that the international organisation will respond by setting in motion biographical and historical/geographical data-collection efforts, as well as thesaurus translation efforts that will adhere to the systems developed or adopted by TAU.

The members of TAU have laboured faithfully to promulgate a concept of automation that takes into account the information needs and assumptions of the scholarly community, a consideration that cannot be said to be universal in the automation world. It will have completed a difficult, multi-national task in basic agreement. The rest will depend on the people who make things happen, who determine the shape of systems, and who collect the scholar's information and return it in a form that one hopes will be recognisable and usable.

9 DEVELOPMENT OF COMMON DATA STRUCTURES IN THE CONSERVATION INFORMATION NETWORK

John Perkins

Projects Coordinator
Getty Conservation Institute
Marina del Rey, CA

Introduction

Technological advances in computing systems and data communications — collectively referred to as information technology — are dramatically changing the way information may be used by a profession (Wilkinson and Winterflood, 1987). Telecommunications erase vast distances by allowing individuals to communicate with one another with speed, convenience and efficiency regardless of location. Computerised databases make available large bodies of information that traditionally have had very limited access.

The Conservation Information Network (the Network) was established by an international conservation community using information technology to generate and provide access to a wide variety of information resources pertaining to the conservation of cultural property (Perkins, Jelich and Lafontaine, 1987). One of the major objectives of the Network was the convergence of disparate bibliographic-oriented activities into a more uniform and coherent process. In this area, the Network's information resources are developed by five contributing institutions from four countries working in an online environment, as well as by an organised volunteer network of individuals who contribute information in a variety of formats. Although there are differing preferences for language, vocabulary and standards, unified approaches are being negotiated.

Over 350 individuals and institutions in 22 countries currently use the databases, electronic mail system and reference publications that collectively make up the Network. Users are encouraged to be contributors generating a two-way flow that enhances the timeliness, scope, quality, collection and dissemination of conservation information. This exchange of information is arguably the single most critical component affecting every aspect of the Network and is the focus of this paper.

Information exchange in an international network

The successful development of a network requires both the desire to exchange information and the ability to connect. For the Network, the ability to connect is made possible by information technology, sufficient financing, a critical mass of expertise and a support infrastructure. The desire is expressed by the contributor's commitment to established objectives and a willingness by the participants to share and exchange information.

In the same way that language, grammar and syntax provide a common basis for communication of spoken or written information, there must be similar structures supporting the exchange of computer-based or machine-readable information. (International Organization for Standardization, 1982a). There is a great deal of effort devoted internationally to the pursuit of standards for information exchange and the results are apparent in efforts such as UNIMARC, an international standard for the exchange of

Figure 9.1 Open System Interconnection model

OSI Layered Architecture

Layer 7 Application
User Application Process and Management Functions

Layer 6 Presentation
Data Interpretation, Format and Code Conversion

Layer 5 Session
Administration and Control of Sessions Between Two Entities

Layer 4 Transport
Transparent Data Transfer, End-to-End Control, Multiplexing, Mapping

Layer 3 Network
Routing, Switching, Segmenting, Blocking, Error Recovery, Flow Control

Layer 2 Link
Establish, Maintain and Release Data Links, Error and Flow Control

Layer 1 Physical
Electrical, Mechanical, Functional Control of Data Circuits

bibliographic information between national bibliographic agencies (Holt, McCallum and Long, 1987), and JCAMP-DX which is a standard for the exchange of infrared spectra information (MacDonald and Wilks, 1988). In an effort to encourage the development of standards, the International Standards Organization (ISO) has been working since 1977 to build a reference model that describes the conditions required for the complete interconnection of systems and successful transfer of information between them (International Organization for Standardization, 1984). This Open Systems Interconnection (OSI) model, shown in Figure 9.1, defines a structure comprised of seven levels that allows protocols to be developed for passing information from one system to another by their mutual adherence to a set of common standards within each level.

The two highest levels of the OSI model are concerned with the way information can be communicated once full physical interconnection has been achieved by the lower levels. It is in the domain of these higher levels that the Network is attempting to implement conventions and procedures that will facilitate information exchange, leaving the job of ensuring compatibility of hardware and the interconnectibility of software to others. The decision to focus on content was taken because conservation professionals are the only ones who can determine the standards for content, whereas other vendors and developers can assist with software compatibility.

Network data dictionary

In the pursuit of collaborative information exchange, the Network's primary focus of activity has been the creation of a data dictionary, a document in three volumes that defines the nature, organisation and structure of the information held in the database (Conservation Information Network, 1987). The dictionary serves as an evolving standard for the description of conservation-related information and it promotes information exchange by suggesting how elements of information can be described

Figure 9.2 A sample data dictionary page

PAUT

FIELD MNEMONIC	PAUT
FIELD LABEL	PUBL AUTHOR
FIELD NAME	Published Author
FIELD DESCRIPTION	This is the field to which author names are entered. It contains the surname and name of author(s). Enter all author names associated with a document. This field is converted for retrieval to the AUT field. PARIS
ENTRY RULES	Enter upper and lower case, using special character codes for accents, the name of author inverted, with comma after surname, as it appears on the piece. If only initials are supplied and full names are not known, enter initials with periods and without spacing between them; if the full information is available elsewhere, enhance between parentheses. If only initials are provided, enter inverted with the initial for surname in the first position, followed by a comma. Names in non-roman alphabets are transliterated in accordance with ISO rules. For Arabic names, determine the elements of the name and enter in the first position the best-known element or combination of elements; give the other elements, if any, after comma. Thai and Chinese names are entered under the first element. Names with articles and prefixes (al, de, l', vom, della, op de, etc.) are entered according to ISO rules. As a general rule, titles (honor, nobility, religious, etc.) such as "Sir," "Dr.," "Prof.," etc. are omitted. For special cases consult UNISIST and AACR2. For more than one author name, enter the names separated by semi-colons with no space. When no name of author is available, indicate that this information has been verified by entering "Anon." to the PAUT. Enter to this field for publication, not to the system-indexed AUT field.
EXAMPLES	Du maine, Jacques;Frohling, M.P. OR Mokhtar, G. OR Ahmed Mustafa Kemal OR Abu Hayyan al-Tawhidi;Ali ibn Muhammad OR Malik ibn Anas OR \46im\88nkova, Eva;Hobinkov\70 Durianov\70,Tatjana
COMMENTS	For online searching it will be important to use the "LOOK" command to retrieve all variant spellings and forms of author names. A standardized author name field may be created as a separate field in which full, or most common forms of author names may be recorded as an authority.
CATALOGUING STD.	AACR2 21.1A1, 22.5D1, 22.4, 22.5, 22.22, 22.26C1, 22.C7 (exception to rule for titles of nobility and terms of honor and address, 22.12); UNISIST A.11
REQUIRED	Essential field for all literature types and levels.
RECORD TYPE	Abstract
DATA TYPE	Alphanumeric
INDEX CLASS	Phrase linked to PAUTAD, PAUTCRY, PAUTCTY, PAUTPC and PAUTST
RANGE SEARCH	No
BREAK CHARACTERS	;
SOURCE	AATA;CAL;CCI;GCI;ICCROM;ICOMOS
ORIGINATING INST.	AATA
SECURITY CODE	7
DATE OF BIRTH	861015
DATE OF CHANGE	880318
PAR NUMBER	148

consistently yet independently of the computer system used. This is important to the Network collaborators, because the same information has to be accommodated in different applications and computer systems. If these different systems have similar data structures because their form has been derived from a common data dictionary, then there is an inherent basis for information exchange between them.

The data dictionary is an integral part of the Network documentation package that is distributed to all subscribers as soon as their user accounts are activated. It is hoped that the data dictionary will be considered a reference tool which can be used for at least three different purposes: contribution of new material to existing databases, building new databases and retrieval of information from the online databases.

For contributors, the dictionary serves as a style manual showing how to enter the required information in the proper form to encourage the creation of clear, consistent, and functional databases. Figure 9.2 shows a typical page from the data dictionary for the bibliographic database. There is a similar page for each unique element of information in the bibliographic database (173 in total). This provides a contributor or database developer with a complete list of all relevant information categories, rules for entering information, the standards used to create the rules and an indication of the importance and use of each element of information.

This kind of information is also useful for building new databases since it provides instructions on how to enter information. The dictionary is helpful because it annotates the data elements, indicating whether each is mandatory, essential or optional for the Network's databases. However, developers are free to choose from the list of elements only those they feel are relevant to their needs.

For searching and retrieval, the dictionary is a supplement to the Users Guide, providing details on where the information is located, how it is structured, what it is called and how it is indexed. This is useful for creating effective search strategies.

Factors influencing the effectiveness of the data dictionary

The existence of a first version of a data dictionary for the Network is indicative of the enormous cooperation among collaborators to produce a mutually agreeable set of standards to organise the information they want to capture. It has come into existence because dedicated groups have committed themselves to its development, based on a commonly understood need (These groups are the Content Review Boards for the Network Databases which provided the technical and structural input and the Network Steering Committee which supported the undertaking at the highest administrative level.)

To date, this document has guided the production of content-compatible databases in at least three countries. These databases have been developed in a mainframe environment using BASIS software, in the MS-DOS microcomputer environment using Advanced Revelation and in Hypercard for the Apple Macintosh, underlining the efficacy of the data dictionary.

Despite this initial success, a more important measure will be the number of compatible systems that exist ten years from now and ten years from then. Towards that end, the data dictionary needed to have other attributes.

An accommodating structure was considered to be extremely important. The dictionary had to have a unified international perspective, yet serve the needs of diverse local systems. While encouraging conformity, it had to be yielding. The dictionary structure had to be immediately applicable to local circumstances, since without that there would be little incentive to continue committing the necessary development resources. Conversely, if there was no convergence of systems, the development of a network would not materialise.

Consequently, the preliminary version had to show results of the negotiation process quickly, yet still be considered a work-in-progress. Continuing evolution of the structure was considered essential and this was to be based on an evaluation of the usefulness of each version as it was produced. The evolutionary perspective was necessary both because information needs are continually changing and because it is impossible to be completely comprehensive in one attempt.

Finally, the structure defined by the dictionary also had to be flexible enough to accommodate existing diverse and comprehensive automated systems yet not be quickly outdated. This requirement underscored the importance of focusing on application and content issues rather than equipment and software concerns.

Conclusion

Although the Network is still working toward the creation of a common data structure, much has been achieved to date. The existence of the unified, online database constructed to the specifications of the data dictionary is facilitating the development of shared records. If this trend continues, it will signal the successful establishment of common data structures in the Conservation Information Network.

10 THE CULTURAL HERITAGE THESAURUS DEVELOPED BY ICOM AND ICOMOS

Susanne Peters

Head
Unesco-ICOM Documentation Centre
Paris

Introduction

Past experience suggests that any work undertaken on an international, non-profitmaking, basis tends to last much longer than was anticipated at the onset and, moreover, the end-product differs considerably from the original concept. This divergence — between plan and reality — should be kept in mind when dealing with all international organisations, but especially with the larger kind. An outline of the events that preceded the compilation of the draft version of the *ICOMOS–ICOM Cultural Heritage Thesaurus* (Anon, 1985), some comments on the organisations which contributed to it, and those factors that influenced it over time, would seem to provide a fairly typical example of this process at work.

Brief historical outline

In the mid 1970s, Unesco investigated the bibliographic resources and needs of the International Council of Museums (ICOM) and the International Council on Monuments and Sites (ICOMOS). It agreed to launch a project with the following objective: 'In order to promote the accumulation of information on the preservation and presentation of cultural property, and in collaboration with international governmental and non-governmental organisations, an international documentation centre will be established by integrating the Unesco-ICOM Documentation Centre with the Unesco-ICOMOS Documentation Centre'. (It must be added here that at the time this was written the ICOMOS Documentation Centre existed in name only.)

Studies and discussions among interested parties carried out during subsequent years pointed to the impracticality of such a procedure and, in 1978, this led to the re-definition of the activities necessary to establish an 'international documentation programme on the preservation and presentation of cultural property'. The programme now had as its goal the development 'into a network of links among various documentation centres, either international, regional or national' and, as a point of departure, envisaged 'a computerised data bank pooling the information available separately to ICOM, ICOMOS and ICCROM'[1] to 'be created within the framework of Unesco's computerized documentation service'.

Measures were elaborated to execute the programme; one major task to be carried out was the production of a single thesaurus for ICOM, ICOMOS and ICCROM. A working document dated 3 July 1978 fixed the deadline for completion of this project as 1 June 1979 . . . . Initially the idea was to create a single structured list of descriptors for indexing

1. ICCROM is the International Centre for the Study of the Preservation and the Restoration of Cultural Property.

and information retrieval, which would combine ICOM's Museological Classification Scheme (based on the AM Section of the Library of Congress classification), ICCROM's mono-hierarchical list of keywords covering conservation, and the terms used for monuments and sites established progressively by ICOMOS.

In 1982 a bibliographic database common to ICOM and ICOMOS was created, and Unesco hired an outside consultant to submit a proposal for the thesaurus project. The database — with the rather confusing name of 'ICOMMOS' — was maintained (and still is) on the Unesco mainframe computer under the CDS/ISIS system and fed with bibliographic entries from both sides, using *home made* descriptors to start with. Meanwhile, back in Rome, ICCROM quietly continued its efforts in automated bibliographic data management begun in 1977; considerable differences in software frustrated all proposals to merge the separate databases, and the plan to incorporate the holdings of all the Centres into a unified database remains an unfinished project.

A similar fate was in store for the proposals to streamline the terminology of the three Centres; although the contract signed by the consultant in 1984, which covered phase one of the project, still required the incorporation of ICCROM descriptors, the contract for phase two only talked about the completion of: 'a thesaurus of keywords relating to the cultural heritage in order to facilitate international access to the computerised data base on the cultural heritage set up by Unesco in 1981–1983', homogenising 'the word lists of the Unesco-ICOM and Unesco-ICOMOS Documentation Centres' creating 'from them a polyhierarchical working thesaurus (8 000 to 10 000 words approximately)'.

This narrower focus made the task of compilation considerably easier, but the streamlining of the two remaining lists of keywords proved anything but a simple procedure; none the less, the draft version of the *Cultural Heritage Thesaurus*, containing around 4 000 keywords, was completed by the end of 1985; but only in print-format! It has been in constant use by the respective documentation centres since then.

Outline of form, structure, current use and future prospects

I was not involved in the initial development of the project and, with the benefit of hindsight, I can now suggest some problems which should have been foreseen — and avoided — from the onset. There is a fundamental flaw in the present structure of the programme: the thesaurus is not available online in combination with the bibliographic database. Whatever the historical reasons, it seems very odd to have created in dBase III a working tool for a database which has a fully fledged thesaurus-subsystem at its disposal within the general software it uses.

There are other systematic problems which emerged during the creation of the joint ICOM-ICOMOS project. As mentioned above, the thesaurus represents a combination of two descriptor lists, one based on a classification scheme (ICOM), the other on an essentially unstructured list of terms used for the description of monuments and sites (ICOMOS). Figure 10.1 illustrates the result. The ICOM classes, I–VII, have been inserted into the ICOMOS classes A–E; that this marriage was not a totally happy one can already be seen from the double employment of geographic areas in II and E, respectively. Moreover, the merger of the two classes has been effected in a less neat way than this table makes us believe. This can be seen from the subsequent detailed list of classes which presents the main concepts occurring under each heading, together with the respective ordinal numerical notation employed by each documentation centre: I–VII are actually placed right in the middle of class C, immediately after ICOMOS' number 344: MUSEUMS AND MUSEOLOGY, and before 345: DOCUMENTATION.

Figure 10.1 ICOMOS and ICOM classes

Main headings

ICOMOS classes are A thru E. ICOM classes are I. thru VII.

A Architecture
B Sites
C Conservation and restoration
I. Generalities on museums
II. Geographical distribution
III. Museum methods and techniques
IV. The collections
V. Special activities of museums
VI. Museum related institutions and activities
VII. Categories of museums and collections
D Deterioration
E Geographic areas and countries

Figure 10.2 Classified arrangement

121.5 Museum charges
UF charges
* Admission fees 120.45
* Artistic property 1.9
* Fees 120.45
* Intellectual property 1.9

Figure 10.3 Alphabetic arrangement

Exhibits
ICOM: 150 154
BT Display
TT The collections
SA Educational exhibits
SA Interpretive exhibits
SA Selection of exhibits
UF Presentation
FR Elément d'exposition

Figure 10.4 Abbreviations and symbols used in the thesaurus

*	Cross-reference	SA	See also
BT	Broader term	TT	Top term
FR	French	UF	Use for

In accordance with established conventions (Austin and Dale, 1981), the *Cultural Heritage Thesaurus* then provides a classified section, followed by an alphabetical presentation of descriptors. At first sight it appears that the *Cultural Heritage Thesaurus* follows closely the *Unesco Thesaurus* (Aitchison, 1977) and, to a lesser degree, the *International Thesaurus of Cultural Development* (Viet, 1980). The classified section (Figure 10.2) uses the devices of UF to indicate preferred terms, and an asterisk (*) for cross-references to terms in other schedules; however, there are no scope notes.

In the alphabetic thesaurus (Figure 10.3) we find again the UF device, and the notations for top term (TT) and broader term (BT); narrower term (NT) and related term (RT) unfortunately are both expressed by 'see also' (SA), and again there are no scope notes whatsoever. Figure 10.4 summarises the range of abbreviations and symbols used in the thesaurus.

It must not be forgotten that we are only concerned here with a print version of the draft: more correctly perhaps the plural form should be used since we are considering print *versions*. The uninitiated — and unwary — user will inevitably be confused when confronted by three adaptations of the *Cultural Heritage Thesaurus*, that is, one each for ICOM and for ICOMOS, and a combined one for both. Such a situation is quite untenable in the long run and needs to be resolved as quickly as possible, preferably through the

Figure 10.5 Problems associated with the numerical notation

The numercial notation is doubly misleading:

a. It presents *both* the ICOM and ICOMOS classification numbers which can easily confuse the user:

Accession Lists
ICOMOS: 347 ICOM: 136.4

b. In the classified list of the ICOM Section, it misleads by occasionally expressing something approaching a hierarchical relationship between terms:

128.51 Fire protection
128.511 Detectors

whereas in most other instances the notation and indentation hint at relationships which do not exist:

122.2 Trade unions
122.21 Directors

online provision of the thesaurus in the appropriate system, which in this case would be CDS/ISIS.

But while the transfer of the thesaurus online would almost automatically eliminate *minor* errors, *major* shortcomings such as overlaps, false relationships and non-adherence to the principles of thesaurus construction will require a certain amount of revision to the draft.

To get an idea of the scope of the remedial action that needs to be undertaken, one should consider the examples in Figure 10.5. In the same vein, departures from the principle of thesaurus construction as laid down in ISO 2788 (International Organization for Standardization, 1974) occur in the alphabetic thesaurus; they need to be picked up and corrected. Two brief examples are shown in Figure 10.6.

Apart from several inconsistencies of this type, difficulties are also encountered with so-called 'new' terminology: words not originally built into the classification scheme and which were grafted on in various places. For instance, computer terms have suffered from this procedure. Figure 10.7 shows how they appear in various sections of the ICOM classified thesaurus: quite at random, it seems.

Most examples given here point up the crucial role of detailed and timely *planning* in the development of specialised terminology. In particular, methodical pre-planning is essential when seeking to integrate disparate sources into a single coherent nomenclature. This work is time consuming and demands a full understanding of the needs and functions of participating institutions. Above all, everyone concerned must be fully convinced that a standardised vocabulary will be of real value to them.

Figure 10.6 Examples of divergence from ISO thesaurus principles

---

ISO 2788 stipulates that the BT-NT relationship should be used only when the NT is a specific case of the BT — e.g. Parrots BT Birds — so:

Armed conflict
    ICOM: BT History of museums
        TT Generalities on museums

is incorrect since not all armed conflict is an aspect of the history of museums. In the second example:

Lavatories
    ICOMOS: BT Non-religious
    ICOM: BT Construction

we see the departure from the established rule that the BT-NT relationship should be between terms which describe the same type of entity. Something like:

Lavatories
    ICOMOS: BT Non-religious areas and spaces
    ICOM: BT Rooms

would seem somewhat more appropriate.

Figure 10.7 Occurrence of computing concepts in the thesaurus

---

a. under *Audiovisual documentation* (2.3)

2.38 Computer networks
Computer systems
Computers
Data processing

b. in the section *Organization and administration* (120–121)

120.1 Computerization
Data banks
Information management
Information networks
Information retrieval
Word processing
*Data processing 2.38

c. under *Cataloguing and classification* (138–139)

138.8 Computerized catalogues
Computerized inventories
Computerized records
Data categories
*Information retrieval 120.1

d. in the section *Display documentation* (156–158)

158.9 Computerized exhibition aids

e. under *Educational services and activities* (170–176)

172.5 Computerized educational aids

f. in the section *Activities for children* (179)

179.35 Computer games
UF Games in museums
UF Play

A strict framework is needed from the outset, but it is in no way contradictory to recommend the conservation of some 'local' conventions whenever possible, provided this does not contravene fundamental principles of thesaurus construction (Aitchison and Gilchrist, 1987). Institutions such as libraries or museums generally serve a relatively well-defined group with distinct requirements; appropriate terminology must reflect these, allowing room for future developments in various directions.

Another vital part of the planning process is the choice of suitable software. As mentioned above, CDS/ISIS contains a thesaurus subsystem. The building of the *Cultural Heritage Thesaurus*, and subsequent vocabulary control, could have been facilitated considerably had it been exploited from the beginning. The most rational and least wasteful choice is a software system which will fulfil all the requirements both now and in the future. The effective incompatibility of the program applied to the *Cultural Heritage Thesaurus* has slowed down the completion of the project.

The attentive reader of this brief outline may well by now have gained quite a negative impression of the *Cultural Heritage Thesaurus* draft, so it is high time to emphasise that it has many positive aspects. It is imperfect, but it is the best tool we currently possess; last but not least, its constant and successful use in the Unesco-ICOM Documentation Centre should speak for itself. The ICOM side of the combined database currently contains over 12 000 bibliographic entries on which we carry out an average of five literature searches a day (not counting the routine searches undertaken by staff) with both recall and relevance of a high standard in most cases.

We are, however, planning to cooperate increasingly with other museum documentation centres, sharing the data and, eventually, the task of data input. The expanded scope for the database makes the systematic changes I have traced above a necessity rather than a luxury. Whereas *we* in Paris might just manage to keep 'fudging' successfully with the draft of the *Cultural Heritage Thesaurus* and get away with it, in order to offer it to the international community as a working tool, it needs to be corrected and improved. We have already come one step closer to this goal: the conversion of an estimated 30 000 bibliographic records into machine readable format — a project financed by the Getty Trust being undertaken by the Unesco-ICOM Documentation Centre together with Saztec Europe Ltd — forces us to look very closely at our descriptors. This is a suitable point of departure for a major revision of the thesaurus draft which, it is hoped, will attract the interest and expertise of specialists in the field throughout the world, and will give the venture a truly international scope.

III
NATIONAL DEVELOPMENTS

11 NATIONAL DEVELOPMENTS

Richard Light

Deputy Director
Museum Documentation Association
Cambridge

The five papers in this session, Chapters 12 to 16, all look at terminology control development at a national level. They offer a wide range of experiences, but there are some common threads that run through all the papers, which probably apply to any attempts to co-ordinate terminology at such a broad level.

First, national initiatives tend only to happen if there is a body with the long-term interest to promote them. This might be a branch of national government (CHIN or the Inventaire Générale), an independent body with a brief to advise museums on such matters (MDA), an academic/research institution (Scuola Normale Superiore of Pisa), or an *ad hoc* working party (Common Agenda for History Museums Data Base Task Force). Without central, stable support it is not feasible to develop agreed terminologies of national significance.

Second, terminology control has to take place within the context of an agreed structure for information. France offers an example, in the Inventaire Générale, where structural control and terminology control have proceeded together in a coordinated manner. Other countries have been less fortunate: UK museums and history museums in the USA have a framework within which to record, but no detailed agreement on vocabulary control conventions. In such situations, the existence of published sources such as Nomenclature or SHIC offers a partial lifeline to museums seeking guidance. The existence of a national data structure at least allows published sources to be used in an agreed context.

Third, terminology control is often seen as an integral part of attempts to computerise museum records and to share museum information. It is widely accepted that the discipline of using a standardised terminology will yield benefits in terms of improved information retrieval within national databases. In the Inventaire Générale, for example, 'former imprecise terms and variant forms have been grouped together as synonyms'. However, it should be noted that this process diminishes the richness of vocabulary that can be used. In Italy, the development of computer-oriented controlled vocabularies is seen as the continuation of a tendency dating from the seventeenth century to produce formal, prescriptive lexicons that do not reflect the variety of actual usage. The Scuola Normale Superiore is actively working to produce the opposite: a lexicon that reflects the richness of art history terminology across different Italian languages and epochs.

Written sources are an essential ingredient in the development of national terminologies. The value of published sources has been noted above. The Scuola Normale relies on primary historical sources (inventories, sales catalogues) for its lexicon. In museums themselves, however, these sources are often lacking. A survey of terminology practice in the UK revealed a surprising number of museums with 'in-house unwritten' conventions, i.e. conventions held in a curator's head! This doubtless applies to many museums outside the UK as well. Until individual museums can document their own practice and thereby state their need for terminology control more coherently, there is little hope for effective support or coordination at the national level.

12 THE STATE OF TERMINOLOGY CONTROL IN UK MUSEUMS

Mike Budd

Advice and Training Officer
Museum Documentation Association
Cambridge

In July and August 1988 the Museum Documentation Association (MDA) carried out a survey of the use of terminology control in the cataloguing systems of UK museums. The survey was built on a pilot study performed in 1987 by Amanda Horsfall, then a student of the University of Sheffield (Horsfall, 1987). This paper outlines the state of terminology control in museums, based on an analysis of responses during the survey.

Terminology survey

The MDA has often been thwarted in its attempts to help museums with documentation problems by a lack of comprehensive, reliable information on the state of documentation practice. Such information is essential, both for strategic planning and the handling of day-to-day enquiries. The position was particularly pressing in the area of terminology control, where there was no clear idea of the approaches being adopted by museums.

It was recognised by both the MDA and the Museums and Galleries Commission that it would be useful to gather information on terminology practice. With background data, it would be easier to make informed judgements on which terminology systems and publications were widely used and might be given a high priority for futher development and support or where new initiatives might be needed. Similarly, it would be possible to provide an improved advisory service by referring enquirers to model museums using particular systems, etc.

As part of a degree project, Amanda Horsfall carried out a pilot survey in Yorkshire and Humberside during 1987. The MDA then designed and revised a questionnaire which was mailed to museums in April 1988. Figure 12.1 illustrates the questionnaire itself. This was supported by a covering letter from the Commission and a brief series of guidance notes. The following analysis concentrates on the main bulk of responses, received by August 1988.

The questionnaire was sent to 1 000 museums, representing a wide cross-section of the museum community, including large and small institutions, in the local authority, national and independent sectors. Of these, 255 institutions returned forms by the closing date, representing 26 per cent of those mailed. While a higher return rate would have been welcome, the level of response is sufficient to give a reasonable level of confidence in the results.

There were also 47 'extra' forms, as a result of a request that museums that have branches or departments that document their collections in significantly different ways should fill out a separate form for each. This attempt to deal with the variation within museums means that the statistics presented refer to the number of museums, plus the number of museum departments or branches with distinct documentation systems.

Retrieval and terminology

As effective retrieval is one of the most important benefits of terminology control, the first part of the survey looked at the retrieval systems currently is use in UK musuems. This, it

Figure 12.1 Terminology control questionnaire

MDA THE MUSEUM DOCUMENTATION ASSOCIATION

Building O
347 Cherry Hinton Road
Cambridge CB1 4DH

TERMINOLOGY CONTROL SURVEY - 1988

Please read the appended "Notes and Guidance" sheet before filling in the form. We would be grateful if you could return the completed questionnaire by 23 May 1988. A reply paid envelope is enclosed.

A. BACKGROUND INFORMATION

1. Name and address of your museum.

Please correct the attached label, if necessary.

2. Your name ______________________ **and post** ______________________

3. Does your institution have branch museums or departments that document their collections in substantially different ways? yes [ ] no [ ]

If no then proceed to question A4.

Please photocopy this questionnaire and make a separate return for each different department or museum. Indicate here which departments or branch museums are covered on this sheet.

____

4. Do you use catalogue cards or forms? yes [ ] no [ ]

If no then proceed to question A5.

a) How many copies of each completed **full** catalogue card or form do you produce? ____________

b) Please name the different orders in which full catalogue cards are kept. (For example in order of accession number, object name, donor, etc)

____

5. Do you produce index cards? yes [ ] no [ ]

If no then proceed to question A6.

Please name the different orders in which the index cards are kept.

____

6. Do you use a computer to store or index object records? yes [ ] no [ ]

If no then proceed to question B1.

Please name the software package(s) used for object documentation.

____

B. USE OF TERMINOLOGY CONTROL

1. Do you use any form of terminology control for your catalogue records? yes [ ] no [ ]

If no proceed to B3.

2. Please fill in the table below - you may tick more than one box if appropriate.

Catalogue Data Item	**Data item not used**	**Type of Terminology Control used**					
		None	In-House Written	In-House Unwritten	External	Published	Description or reference (if published)
a) Simple Item Name	[ ]	[ ]	[ ]	[ ]	[ ]	[ ]	________
b) Full Name	[ ]	[ ]	[ ]	[ ]	[ ]	[ ]	________
c) Classified Name	[ ]	[ ]	[ ]	[ ]	[ ]	[ ]	________
d) Acquisition Method	[ ]	[ ]	[ ]	[ ]	[ ]	[ ]	________
e) Materials	[ ]	[ ]	[ ]	[ ]	[ ]	[ ]	________
f) Place Name	[ ]	[ ]	[ ]	[ ]	[ ]	[ ]	________
g) Production Method	[ ]	[ ]	[ ]	[ ]	[ ]	[ ]	________
h) Production Role	[ ]	[ ]	[ ]	[ ]	[ ]	[ ]	________
i) Other (please specify)							
________	[ ]	[ ]	[ ]	[ ]	[ ]	[ ]	________
________	[ ]	[ ]	[ ]	[ ]	[ ]	[ ]	________
________	[ ]	[ ]	[ ]	[ ]	[ ]	[ ]	________
________	[ ]	[ ]	[ ]	[ ]	[ ]	[ ]	________
________	[ ]	[ ]	[ ]	[ ]	[ ]	[ ]	________

3. Please write any comments or information, which you have been unable to include elsewhere, on additional sheets stapled to this form.

THANK YOU FOR YOUR PATIENCE AND COOPERATION

Figure 12.2 Order(s) in which catalogue cards are kept

	No.	% of respondents
Identity no.	149	50
Simple name	57	19
Classified name	56	19
Donor's name	15	5
Maker's name	15	5
Place	12	4
Other	27	9

was felt, would help us to understand why museums are controlling or not controlling various forms of information. It would also help us to identify the current terminology control needs of museums. As the majority of museums still do not have computer documentation systems, it was decided to restrict detailed analysis of retrieval to manual systems.

The estimated 78 per cent of UK museums with partly or wholly manual cataloguing systems have, in the main, met their retrieval needs in one of three ways. Many keep their catalogue records in identity number order and generate one or more indexes (usually card-based) into this catalogue. This may be regarded as the conventional system. However, the advent of the photocopier has meant that some museums (about 25 per cent of those responding to the survey) make several copies of their catalogue records and use these as index cards. As a further permutation, some museums keep their master catalogue records in a non-identity number order and may or may not combine this with an identity number index.

In the survey, information on retrieval systems was elicited by asking respondents to state the orders in which they kept their index and/or catalogue cards (Figure 12.2).

Fifty per cent of the respondents kept at least one copy of their catalogue cards in Identity Number order. However, a significant minority, 38 per cent, kept either the master or subsequent copies in Simple Name (common object name) or Classified Name (classification) order. This may reflect the contribution of the many small museums in the sample, who frequently find it useful to file catalogue cards under simple object names such as 'bicycle' or 'teapot', so that their catalogue doubles as a simple index. The cards filed in Classified Name order may reflect the importance of taxonomic names in Natural History and, increasingly, of the SHIC classification system in Social History.

By comparison, the proportion of catalogue cards filed in Donor or Maker's Name order was quite low (5 per cent). However, these data items achieve a greater importance in the parallel table for index cards (Figure 12.3).

Although only 55 per cent of the respondents stated that they kept indexes, almost one third, 27 per cent, kept an index in Donor order, reflecting the importance of this data item for answering enquiries and for accountability pruposes. Also 12 per cent held an index in Maker's Name order. As both Donors and Makers could be people or

Figure 12.3 Order(s) in which index cards are kept

	No.	% of respondents	
Identity no.	36	12	
Simple name	22	7	
Classified name	72	24	
Donor's name	82	27	Personal and Corporate Names
Maker's name	36	12	
Associated name	15	5	
Place	43	14	
Storage location	25	8	
Material	10	3	
Other	41	14	

institutions, these statistics underline the importance of investigating terminology control techniques for personal and corporate names.

The responses also suggest that 12 per cent of these museums are using an Identity Number index to access a catalogue stored in a different order. This seems rather unlikely. Perhaps instead this statistic reflects the use of 'Location Indexes' — indexes of object storage location kept in Identity Number order.

Some 24 per cent of museums held Classified Name indexes, second only to the number holding Donor indexes. This is probably for similar reasons to those mentioned previously in the context of catalogue cards. Surprisingly, only 7 per cent referred to having Simple Name indexes.

An appreciable number of museums also held indexes in a geographical 'Place' order, and in 'Storage Location' order. The 'places' involved are typically places of collection (especially in natural history and archaeology), places of manufacture, or places associated in some way with an object's history. In addition, a number of museums appear to be producing 'place' indexes which combine all of these notions of place into one index.

Terminology control

Museums were asked whether they used any form of terminology control on their records. A surprisingly high proportion, 70 per cent, said that they did use some form of terminology control. A possible cause of this high percentage might have been that a number confused MDA syntactical separators with terminology control. However, entries where this was suspected have as far as possible been eliminated from the statistics. This factor is thus unlikely to have caused much over-estimation. A more credible explanation for the high percentage will be developed from the evidence in Figure 12.4.

The intention of this table is to identify which items are currently controlled by museums and using what methods. The data items are listed down the left hand side, divided into two groups. In the top group are data items that were specifically mentioned

Figure 12.4 Usage and type of terminology control by data item (% of museums)

	Controlled	In-house written	In-house unwritten	External	Published
Acquisition method	54	26	26	6	5
Simple name	53	24	20	10	15
Classified name	49	22	10	11	23
Place name	48	25	19	5	7
Materials	42	18	21	5	5
Full name	39	17	18	7	10
Production method	32	12	17	3	4
Production role	28	11	14	2	3
Descriptive concepts	—	16	5	5	4
Personal/corporate name	—	3	2	1	.3
Date/period	—	2	1	0	0
References	—	.3	2	1	1
Permanent location	—	2	1	0	0

on the form. Museums were also encouraged to name any other data items that they might control. Their answers are categorised into the data item headings that appear below the line. One implication is that the lower percentages recorded by the data items below the line may have resulted from the fact that the survey did not specifically mention them.

With the exception of 'Descriptive Concepts', the data item headings in the table have the meaning defined in the MDA Data Standard. Thus 'Simple Name' is the common object name, 'Classified Name' is the category in which the object is placed within a formal classification, and 'Full Name' is the name that might be used by experts to refer to the item. 'Production Role' describes the role a particular person played in the production of the item — examples might be 'painter' or 'blacksmith'. 'Permanent Location' refers to the internal museum storage location of the item. The 'Descriptive Concepts' heading encompasses a number of MDA Data Standard 'Aspects' including 'Condition', 'Completeness', 'Dimensions', together with 'Method of Inscription'.

The methods are listed across the top. The 'Controlled' column indicates the percentage of the museums that said they controlled the data item by any of the above methods. The 'In-house Written' column indicates, for each data item, what percentage of museums controlled recording with an internally generated term list, thesaurus or other written instrument. The 'In-house Unwritten' column gives the same information for museums who felt they did control recording but had not written down the rules they applied. The 'External' column notes the percentage of museums using a 'Written' or 'Published' terminology control instrument that was produced outside the confines of their museum. The 'Published' column records the use of a formally published terminology control instrument.

In each case the percentages relate to the percentage of respondents controlling that particular data item. As museums may control more than one data item, the columns will clearly not add to 100.

Returning to the question on the explanation for the high percentage of museums who employ terminology control, a glance at figures in the column for museums claiming to use 'unwritten' and 'written in-house' controls suggests an answer. It seems that museums are indeed controlling terminology but, with the dearth of published systems, are having to do so by developing their own systems. Some of these are no doubt very good, but many do not even get to the stage of being written down. The fact that they are willing to go to this trouble, indicates the need that is being felt for terminology control.

To understand the percentages in the table, it is better to look at the general patterns rather than treating the items individually. The most obvious pattern is that the extent to which a particular data item is controlled, and the methods by which it is controlled, seem to be determined by the interplay between two main factors: the need to control a particular data item (mainly as expressed by retrieval requirements); and the existence of well developed systems for controlling that item, or the ease of formulating your own.

Thus, the three concepts which are most strongly controlled are Acquisition Method, Simple Name and Classified Name. Each are controlled by about 50 per cent of respondents. As a significant proportion of museums held indices in Simple Name order, the need to control Simple Name probably comes from retrieval requirements. A well developed published system, the 'Hertfordshire Simple Name List' is in common use.

The need for control of Acquisition Method may arise from the legal need to be absolutely clear what gift, loan, etc., mean, rather than for retrieval requirements, as few museums indexed this data item. Because a small number of acquisition terms cover most requirements it is relatively easy to develop in-house controls. The need to control Classified Name is inherent in the meaning of the concept, and widely used published systems for this data item exist in Social History and Natural History.

This approach also helps to explain the balance between the data items for which 'In-house' (written or unwritten) systems are used and those for which 'Published' and 'External systems' are used. In general, if a well developed external system is available people will tend to use it in preference to developing their own system.

Perhaps the most useful question to ask of this table is 'what are the gaps?'. What data items do museums need to control, but are prevented from controlling effectively by the absence of a well developed system? Comparison of the external and published column of this table with the earlier tables on the orders in which catalogue and index records are kept suggests that the most important are: Place names and References; Personal and Corporate Names; Acquisition Method; and Materials and other Descriptive Concepts.

Of these, Acquisition Method is already covered by a term list developed by the MDA. This perhaps just requires further publicity. This leaves Personal, Corporate and Place Names, together with descriptive concepts such as materials, colour, condition, and dimensions as possible foci for national or regional developments. Of course, many discipline specific needs will be hidden by such a broad brush analysis.

Figure 12.5 looks at the main published terminology control systems that are at present in use in the UK. There are few surprises here, but a some figures are worthy of comment. Note for instance the substantial influence of both SHIC and the Hertfordshire Simple Name List. It is no small achievement to have about 12 per cent of museums using one classification system.

Figure 12.5 Published references used for terminology control

	No.	% of respondents
SHIC	36	12
Hertfordshire conventions	18	6
ICOM costume classification	7	2
Natural history taxonomy	6	2
Ordnance Survey maps	6	2
Suffolk guidelines	3	1
Wiltshire conventions	3	1
Other	27	9

In addition, it is worth drawing attention to the laudable efforts of the Suffolk, Wiltshire and Hertfordshire museums who are working towards a homogeneous system of terminology control for most types of data across a group of museums.

One puzzling feature is the low percentage of museums who mentioned the use of taxonomic references for natural history recording. This may be because the use of references to look up species names is so automatic it is not regarded as terminology control.

Conclusion

In conclusion the results of the 1988 UK Terminology control survey indicate that the majority of museums do already control terminology, in some manner, on at least a small range of data items.

However, due to the lack of well developed systems in more than three or four areas, much of this control is on an *ad hoc* basis, in many cases completely undocumented. There is therefore an urgent need for a national initiative in the development of carefully constructed, tested, and documented systems.

13 STANDARDISED VOCABULARIES FOR MOVABLE ARTEFACTS IN THE INVENTAIRE GÉNÉRAL (MINISTÈRE DE LA CULTURE), FRANCE

Catherine Arminjon

Conservateur, Inventaire Général
Ministère de la Culture et de la Communication
Paris

Introduction

The *Inventaire Général des Monuments et des Richesses artistiques de la France* (General Inventory of the Monuments and Artistic Wealth of France) was created by André Malraux, Minister of Culture, 25 years ago. Its aim is to inventory, study and make known all the artistic works in France which make up the cultural heritage outside museums (as distinct from that held in museums).

The inventory is concerned with architecture and the heritage of movable artefacts (tapestries, paintings, sculptures, furniture, secular or religious objects, ceramics, glass, stained glass, costume, etc.). In addition, it studies the architectural, industrial and twentieth century heritage.

Standardisation of terminology

To make a homogeneous study of all these areas and construct such a huge, novel and difficult database, it was clear from the outset that standardised terminology would have to be adopted for the different fields of the history of art. The Inventory therefore began to standardise language and the format of the descriptions, to avoid doubt or error in interpreting texts, unnecessary detail and gaps in some of the data. All this was required by both the public and researchers; the Inventory responded by publishing successively, in the series *Principes d'analyse scientifique* (Principles of scientific analysis), vocabularies for tapestries, architecture, sculpture, secular domestic objects and domestic furniture. The general classification is methodical, and the definitions were made according to function and form. The research carried out was based on museum collections, bibliographies, inventories (whether published or not), enquiries and oral enquiries. This is carried out continuously within the framework of the General Inventory in each of the 22 regions of France.

With computerisation as an aim, unique definitions of terms have been developed in order to allow better control over the data. Terms which will lead to a definition in the vocabularies — which will also be used in the computer based *Systèmes descriptifs* — were chosen with the aim of reconciling former usage and present terminology and providing an unambiguous classification. Homonyms have been eliminated and each term corresponds to one concept.

Former imprecise terms and variant forms have been grouped together as synonyms, with cross-references to the chosen defined term. Regional and vernacular terms have been kept as synonyms, but the study of these is not exhaustive since recording them is the province of linguistic atlases. Computer systems are envisaged to record all the local terms found on the spot, but studying and hierarchically classifying the vocabularies was done according to the name of the function.

The same work has been carried out on technical vocabularies and will give rise to a number of publications on stained glass, metal, wood, painting, textiles, ceramics and glass, following tapestry and sculpture which have already been published.

From vocabularies to *Systèmes descriptifs* for automation

These vocabularies have allowed us to put together thesauri of selected terms collected into two works not yet published, namely *Système descriptif* for Architecture (1978, new edition 1988) (Chatenet and de Montclos, 1989) and *Système descriptif* for Personal Objects (April 1987) (Arminjon, Blondel and de Reyniès, 1987).

These specifications are compatible and harmonise with the ones used within the Ministry of Culture by the *Direction des Musées de France* (Directorate of French Museums), in particular the databases Painting (Joconde) [=Gioconda] and Sculpture (Carrare) [=Carrara]. The database of 'objects mobiliers' in the national museums, which brings together decorative art and folk art and tradition, is pending.

The description and historical study of a work, whether in a museum or outside it (in a church, for example), involves the same criteria for study, except for administrative and museum data.

The *Systèmes descriptifs des objets mobiliers* used by the Inventory, like those used by museums, bring together data on the name of the work; particular designations (relating to usage, history, owner, or local or vernacular terms); titles (different titles can be given to a work at different times or according to successive publications or identifications); structure and form; iconography; size; and inscriptions, marks and hallmarks. There is also historical data, bringing together information on the author or the place where where it was made (when we are dealing with a regional workshop or with a town, Faience de Rouen for instance) or its provenance (places or buildings where the work was sited or displayed) when it is no longer in its original site, and the places it was intended for (which can include the place it was first intended for but where it could not be put). The different stages of its creation are also studied, with vocabulary, appropriate to each domain, the dating of the work (particularly for conserved objects), and its legal status.

Existing vocabularies or lists of controlled terms currently deal particularly with names, materials and techniques, and iconography (in the case of iconography, reference is made to the Garnier system, with some modifications).

For artists (spelling, during drafting, is checked in Thieme Becker and Bénézit) and for places, terms are entered as they stand and corrected afterwards. (The names of the French communes follow the rules of the Dictionary of Communes.) Each heading or field which consists of a word-list or pre-defined vocabulary is duplicated in a second heading based on free text.

The documents of the Inventory are filled in throughout France by the staff of the Inventory. This guarantees the consistency of the documentation from every region, with the aim of having a coherent organisation of all the files.

The documentation of the Inventory is to be placed on microfiche (chosen to allow the possibility of reading text in conjunction with photographs). The microfiche is called automatically by the online database.

This microfiche documentation and the databases 'Architecture' and 'Objects Mobiliers' will be available for consultation in the Document Centres of the Inventory in each regional capital as well as the National Centre in Paris.

14 ART TERMINOLOGY IN ITALY

Professor Oreste Ferrari
Director, Istituto Centrale per il Catalogo e la Documentazione
Ministero per i Beni Culturali e Ambientali
Rome

The themes of art terminology in Italy are linked to the problems stemming from the very long evolution of the Italian language. For a variety of complex historical reasons, this has branched out from the Latin root — which itself was enriched by a number of contributions of very diverse origins — into a multitude of local 'languages', peculiar both to regions and to distinct social classes.

A relative and dynamic linguistic 'unity' existed only in the upper classes and extended to the rest of the country only in connection with national political unification in the second half of the nineteenth century. This can explain the fact that, although a rather widespread philological tradition did exist and ideally can be taken as far back as Dante Alighieri's *De Vulgari Eloquentia*, it is less than 50 years since the task of compiling a real *History* of the Italian language was tackled by scholars such as Giacomo Devoto and Bruno Migliorini.

This difference of 'languages', or rather of lexicons, was always in the minds of writers of art treatises. Giorgio Vasari himself, in the *Introduzzione*... to the first (1550) and second (1568) editions of his *Vite* had attempted to give some sort of systematic order to the arts and crafts lexicon. In view of this, he had also requested the advice of 'professional' men of letters, such as Paolo Giovio and Annibal Caro; it is in fact the elegant Caro himself who, in a letter dated 15 December 1547, advised Vasari to use a terminology 'which contained proper rather than methaphoric or far-fetched terms and current rather than artificial ones'. Vasari declared he welcomed this advice and, in writing his *Introduzzione* of 1550, stated that he was writing 'in the language that I speak, regardless of whether it is Florentine or Tuscan'. It is true, however, that while being fully coherent with his intention of asserting the supremacy of Tuscan, or rather Florentine, art and figurative culture, Vasari with his huge literary production, implicitly asserted the supremacy of the *spoken* Tuscan *language*. Anyway, his source is direct experience, the 'current' use of words that were peculiar both to his art collegues and to artisans.

But if Vasari's behaviour was, so to speak, intuitive, completely different and far more resolved intellectually were the intentions of the famous Crusca Academy which in the very first edition of its *Vocabolario* (1612) ignored the spoken language and based its work on the 'auctoritas' of the words used by the most renowned Florentine men of letters of the fourteenth century onwards (or men of letters from other regions who followed the Florentine custom). In this manner, as Giovanni Nencioni later remarked, 'emerged a selective, somewhat archaic and therefore highly conventional lexicography'.

It was along those same lines that the *Onomastico* was probably planned in the first decades of the seventeenth century by the polygraph Giovan Battista Doni, a work that attempted to be a complete vocabulary in 20 volumes of sciences, art and domestic uses, which was never published and of which the manuscript itself was eventually lost.

Instead, we have to wait for more than a century after Vasari's *Vite* for Filippo Baldinucci to publish in 1681 his *Vocabolario Toscano delle Arti del Disegno* especially dedicated to the Crusca Academicians, which sought to be something similar to a specialised section of the general *Vocabolario* of the Academy.

Although partial and strongly disputed (to the point that in 1744 the erudite Giovanni Bottàri will exhort the Crusca Academy to give 'a plausible beginning to the compilation of the "arts vocabulary"'), Baldinucci's work remains an example of a lexicographic model, even though little employed from a practical viewpoint.

In fact, in the very art treatises special 'languages' persisted which had their roots deeply embedded in the current usage: the most striking example of this is given by Marco Boschini who wrote in Venitian 'language' (more than a dialect).

However, even when Francesco Milizia's *Dizionario delle belle arti del Disegno*, published in Bassano in 1797, triggered off a reaction against the academic and pompous set up of the Crusca *Vocabolario* and, from the spoken language, the names of the trades, art techniques and materials have been retrieved, the result is still decidely conventional and abstract.

Hence the relentless conflict with almost no chance of a dialectical mediation between *historical lexicon* and *conventional lexicon*. However, these particular historical factors have constituted a lexical heritage that should be taken into good consideration in the modern terminology research connected with the history of arts in Italy.

Moreover, this heritage is in danger of perishing not only because modern linguistic unity inevitably impoverishes and simplifies the use of words, but also and mainly because of the almost total disappearance of those groups — artists and artisans — that ensured their traditional use.

Sadly little has been done in modern times to launch an efficient lexical investigation. The new Italian art historiography seems unaware of such a need, among other reasons because it has maintained a certain 'literary' vocation, the taste for an elegant style and the personalised use of words.

Nothing would have been father away from the mentality of an illustrious historian such as Roberto Longhi, who has been rightly defined by André Chastel as a 'genius of the *ekphrasis*', in other words of the oral imagination able to return and interpret the aesthetic equivalence of the figurative imagination. Nothing would have been farther away than to feel the need of consulting a vocabulary which was not that of the *beautiful language* but purely technical.

Not even large systematic undertakings such as the *Enciclopedia Italiana*, the *Lessico Universale Italiano* or, more recently, the *Enciclopedia Universale dell'Arte* were preceded by lexicographic research aiming at recovering the vital linguistic heritage and settling the controversy between the historic lexicon and an ever stiffer, one could almost say bureaucratic, conventional lexicon.

This is why concerns are still acute among the art historians, who in recent times have studied terminology matters and been able to perceive the danger of a final dispersion of the wealthy traditional linguistic heritage.

Two important Seminars held in Cortona (1979) and Pisa (1980), organised by the *Scuola Normale Superiore* of Pisa, the *Accademia della Crusca*, the *Istituto Centrale per il Catalogo e la Documentazione* and *CNUCE* have stressed the complexity of such questions and the need for an overall coordinated study that would, on the one hand help recover the very values of that traditional lexical heritage and, on the other, establish a relationship between the terms on a historical rather than abstract basis.

The work presented at these Seminars and later intensely followed up by scholars linked to Pisa's *Scuola Normale*, under the knowledgeable guidance of Paola Barocchi, had the great merit of tackling the problems of the lexical sources.

For Italian art terminology, these sources obviously consist mainly of historiographic literature which, however, favours the aesthetically more important sectors of artistic production (the *fine arts*, that is to say painting, sculpture and architecture) with limited interest for decorative arts. Conversely, of great importance for the latter are the few existing technical treatises and, above all, the ancient inventories of the patrician families, the testaments, the contracts between clients and artists, the 'memoirs' and the *workshop* inventories of the artists themselves, the reports of 'pastoral visits' or rather the lists of possessions owned by churches or monasteries which were required by the bishops. On the other hand, rather less numerous, compared to what took place in France and in other European countries, are the sales catalogues.

These particular sources are, in terms of quantity, in far greater number than the real historiographic ones. But they present rather peculiar problems due to the fact that, having been compiled without any 'literary' concerns and often by people lacking proper competence, they abound in jargon terms, in words of current and local use, often in inaccuracies and need, therefore, to be evaluated carefully and deciphered, so to speak, intuitively.

On the other hand, decorative arts studies in Italy are not yet as well developed as studies of fine arts or major guilds, and it is not infrequent to come across terms that have not yet been attributed to definite objects. Thus, one often finds *names* without *things*, and, *vice-versa*, one often encounters *things* whose historical *name* has not been identified.

It is this same need of terminological 'assurance', relative as it may be, that has led to the use of computerised technologies for cataloguing archaeological and artistic works, and stimulated the compilation of *Dizionari Terminologici* (Terminology dictionaries) such as those published by the *Istituto Centrale per il Catalogo e la Documentazione* (see Chapters 35, 44 and 45) (Badoni, 1980, Boccia, 1982, de Vita, 1983 and Montevecchi and Vasco Rocca, 1987).

I would like to stress the word 'stimulated', which means that our *Terminology Dictionaries* were not planned exclusively in relation to the use of the computerised processing of archaeological and art history data. I am more and more convinced that a terminological investigation undertaken exclusively, or simply mainly, in relation to computer requirements is a mortified one, carried out only at the instrumental level. For computerised technology, a 'controlled vocabulary' could be sufficient: an accurate but rather concise *authority file*, with a selected number of cross-references to synonyms or equivalent terms.

I personally believe that in art lexical history (this same reasoning could also apply to other disciplines, in particular to humanistic disciplines) there have never been, strictly speaking, synonyms: terms that can be estimated equivalent have always had specific and particular reasons linked to a stylistic moment, a cultural area, or a more or less strongly personalised formal and expressive 'alternative'.

The danger of an *authority file* set up and developed in order to use computerised technology more efficiently is, finally, that of consolidating irreversibly the tendency for a rigorously conventional lexicon.

On the contrary, our ambition has been to identify and keep alive a relationship between a historic lexicon, with all its wealth and semantic relativity, and the 'forcibly' conventional one. In other words, what we want is a modern and accurately verified terminology that would still let us hear the speech of the artists and artisans, patrons and writers of treatises, biographies and city guide-books of the past.

I am by no means in the best position to judge whether we have been able to fulfil our ambition adequately: this judgement lies with the people who will use the *Terminology Dictionaries* and with colleagues in archaeology and history of arts.

---

15 TERMINOLOGY DEVELOPMENTS IN CANADA FROM A CHIN PERSPECTIVE

Stephen H. Delroy

Curator
House of Commons,
Ottawa

Terminology is improving in Canadian museums and galleries, but the rate of improvement is slower than expected given the resources available. The five groups of organisations interested in terminology are museums, museum studies programs, commercial vendors, museum associations and governments. Each group has a different perception of terminology and these perceptions are changing.

The Canadian museum community consists of 1 500 museums holding 30 million objects and specimens. The 10 000 paid staff spend over $200 million annually. Unfortunately, no one knows what proportion is spent on documentation. Canadian Heritage Information Network (CHIN) studies have shown that 1 000 museum staff are involved with the network on a regular basis.

In the past, both small museums and large museums thought of terminology as an esoteric subject. For small museums that meant that it was an expensive luxury that could be dispensed with. For large museums the result was sometimes even worse. Curators and cataloguers attempted the impossible task of exhaustively documenting their collections. Today, terminology has shifted in two ways. Most museums plan their documentation with explicit priorities. Most choose a phased approach and complete inventory level documentation of the entire collection before expanding to other levels. The second shift has been to document other activities beyond collections management. Large museums are computerising their exhibition and conservation documentation. Small museums now often document their memberships before their collections.

This should make museums rethink the purpose of terminology. All terminology standards have to be useful for the activity being documented. Formerly, museums considered a standard good if it improved their access to a person, place, thing, event or concept. Now they must ask if a new standard is an efficient use of resources. Given limited resources, a small gallery may choose to edit the names and addresses of its members before the names and biographies of the artists whose works it has collected.

Other activities aside, there are indications that collections terminology is being improved by Canadian museums. Some 60 museums contribute data online to CHIN's two national databases, one for humanities and one for natural sciences. Although the National Humanities database has grown to 1.2 million records, the number of object names has decreased from 90 000. CHIN users still make about 400 000 edits a month to their data. The national databases have become the terminology standard in Canada as far as the choice of data fields is concerned.

In Canada, there are almost a dozen museum studies programs that lead to a certificate or a degree. Virtually all of them contain courses in documentation. However, there is no consensus on a minimum syllabus for documentation and the computer courses offered sometimes ignore museum information entirely. Most Canadian museum workers have their formal qualification in a museum-related discipline, such as art history, and have gained their museum-specific understanding through informal apprenticeship. As a result, terminology can have a very discipline-specific flavour. More than a little time has been wasted in arguments over data field equivalencies. An art curator may insist that a field be labelled 'artist' while a historian from the same institution may insist on 'maker'.

Commercial vendors are now beginning to influence terminology in Canadian museums. Most of the influence is unintentional. Given the small market there are few specialised vendors of computer systems. The usual result when an unspecialised commercial vendor and a museum discipline specialist come together is a system that misses key collection management fields and does not allow for exception processing. CHIN's major complaint with the specialised vendors is that they seldom allow for the efficient import and export of data.

Canadian museums associations have begun to take a major role in terminology by offering regular and inexpensive training courses, seminars and workshops. Some have also created advice bureaus. Most offer advice in making grant applications for documentation projects. And not least, they lobby governments and, increasingly, corporations to provide more funds for documentation as a core museum function. The difficulty with the provincial museum associations is that they reflect the relative and absolute wealth of their provinces. An association based in a small, poor province may offer virtually no help at all.

Governments have a role second only to museums themselves in terminology, because they provide over 70 per cent of all operational funding. In more and more provinces, funds are tied to the fulfillment of minimum standards, including a collection inventory. The shifting attitude toward museums can be seen in a recent change of jurisdiction. Responsibility for museums has been shifting from government departments of culture toward departments of communications and tourism. Prudent management is now demanded. Museums are increasingly called upon to justify their budgets through visitor statistics and other measures of output. The association with communication is more benign if not beneficial as far as terminology is concerned. Museums which emphasise their role as communicators of content are receiving substantial grants for equipment. Government departments not responsible for museums have also made substantial grants for training. This mix of funding has created an unusual problem as far as documentation terminology is concerned. Some museums have accepted the funds to automate their documentation systems in the hopes of attracting grant money for documentation staff. Some systems are lying idle because museum management saw documentation as an add-on instead of a core activity.

CHIN is a special government case since it offers service rather than funds. Its role in terminology is both reactive and proactive. To be reactive, CHIN has constantly sought new ways of consulting the museum community. The structure of the original databases was created by 19 disciplinary task forces. These field tables were merged to create the two data dictionary structures in 1982. Since then, seven annual users seminars were held to expand the data dictionaries and to finalise the structure of the two national databases. Ongoing disciplinary working groups were created not only to edit the data dictionaries but also to begin standardising terminology at the content level. Museum users have determined which data fields were a priority. Given these priorities, CHIN has conducted research studies on Object Names, Fine Art Object Names, Categories, Materials and Culture in addition to the study already done on condition terminology. Since 1987, almost all the working groups have held regional meetings to discover and solve terminology issues. Increasingly CHIN has found that the electronic mail service available to all client museums can be used by museums to make specific terminology queries, organise meetings and order batch changes and reports from CHIN.

The National Databases have become a terminology barometer. The Fine Art Working Group has been particularly successful in developing and implementing object name standards. CHIN has found that the exchange of documentation is the strongest incentive for implemented terminology standards. The embarrassment factor is quite high for any museum that agrees to a standard and can then be seen as a major culprit. It is in this situation that CHIN takes its most active role. When a museum experiences difficulties in cleaning up its data, CHIN can provide various analytical reports to identify problems as well as running batch changes to free the museum to concentrate on one-off changes. In some instances CHIN has arranged data entry and editing contacts.

At the insistence of its users, CHIN has begun to develop or take on reference databases. An artist authority file coordinated by the National Gallery of Canada has been released. Several recent projects have pointed out the need for an institutional authority file and a bibliographic database beyond that offered by the Conservation Information Network.

Three new developments have considerably improved CHIN's ability to improve terminology. The association with the Conservation Information Network may mean the development of a generic mainframe/microcomputer thesaurus module. The transfer in September 1987 from the National Museums of Canada to the Department of Communications has given increased telecommunications support and resources for testing new technology. Finally, CHIN has entered a pilot project with the Ontario Museums Association to add 150 new online museums in two years. The goal has shifted from trying to automate 95 per cent of the collections in the country to trying to network 95 per cent of the museums.

---

16 RECENT DEVELOPMENTS IN COMPUTERISATION: UNITED STATES MUSEUM INITIATIVES

James R. Blackaby

Curator
Bucks County Historical Society
Doylestown, Pa.

Introduction

Recent developments in the computerisation of collection records in the United States have taken some turns away from past practice, primarily as the result of new hardware and more computer literacy among museum staff and administrators. The large projects running on mainframe computers have not been heard about much lately. There are a few, of course. The US Army museums are working on a project that will provide inventory access to all of their collections, but the Army museums have a willingness to accept uniform standards not found in the general population of museums. The silence from the large systems does not indicate idleness, though. On the contrary, there is more feverish computer activity than ever among American museums. Most of it, however, is taking place on small machines — primarily IBM PCs and their compatibles — using off-the-shelf software — primarily dBase III+, although Rbase and Advanced Revelation have also been mentioned as favoured systems. The quantity and the quality of this effort is difficult to judge. What can be said with certainty is that computers are becoming familiar tools in museums, and the questions one hears about them have to do with how and when computerisation will take place rather than whether or not computers should be used for collections management.

There are many signs of this new found ease with computers. A revised edition of *Nomenclature for Museum Cataloging,* a word list used as a tool for normalising object names in historical collections, was published with little comment (Chapter 58). Its initial publication ten years ago was met with confusion, hostility, and dismay on the one hand and partisan and visionary support on the other. The revised edition elicited no such strong sentiments, though sales have been brisk. An increasing number of users groups have been formed to share ideas about museum applications of computers. Not only are there regularly meeting groups like Compumuse in the Philadelphia region, but the Museum Computer Network, a national organisation, has shifted its focus away from advocating literal computer networks and towards providing a forum for 'networking' and idea sharing. The National Endowment for the Arts and the National Endowment for the Humanities, the two largest federal funding agencies, have devoted more of their funds and more of their attention to questions of documentation and computerisation. National and regional initiatives for reviewing the state of museums and the kinds of things that museums have been doing have included as a matter of course components on computerisation. Finally, there have been many new tools made available to assist museums that are computerising or considering computerisation. The National Parks Service has made its dBase III+ driven collection management program widely available at a nominal cost. The Library of Congress has published its visual materials word lists (Chapters 46 and 51). The Getty *Art and Architecture Thesaurus* will publish its first volume soon (Chapter 56). The MARC format, used for some time as a standard for cataloguing library materials, has been adopted as an approach for dealing with archival materials by the Society of American Archivists, and plans are underway to extend the range of the format to include three-dimensional objects. There is plenty of activity surrounding computer use, even if there seems to have been little in terms of great breakthroughs or super projects.

Many of the recent activities have centred on information analysis and data control. Data dictionaries are beginning to be developed as regular components of registration manuals, and lists of controlled terms are being developed and distributed. The most visible developments have emphasised planning more than implementation, and that planning has tended to emphasise the importance of an organised approach to internal data management with hopes of data sharing on a local, regional, or national level held as interesting goals, but goals somewhere in the distant future. Three major developments are worth noting: the discussions that have begun to be heard about the possibility of data sharing by those who have or use similar applications programs; an overall curiosity about the possibilities of the MARC format; and the data analysis that is being pursued by the Common Agenda for History Museums project.

Networks based on shared software

Perhaps on account of the difficulties that have been experienced by those who have tried to set up data sharing networks among art museums, or because of the problems of trying to organise as many museums as would be necessary for a comprehensive network in the United States, or because experience is showing that one's own house must be in order before sharing can even be considered, there has been little talk of vast networks being set up to solve data exchange needs between museums in the United States. The idea is still appealing in most quarters, and because of long familiarity with standard nomenclature and the relative simplicity of the information that must be shared, some natural history networks have been effectively established. But, for the most part, museums in the United States have looked inward to their own data management needs rather than outward to networks. The principal exception to this can be found in the systems that are being set up for managing the collections of the US Army museums and the National Parks Service. There has also been some discussion by vendors of particular programs about the possibilities of networking that will accrue to those who use their products. These attempts at networking all depend on institutions that are sharing — or are obliged to share — identical applications programs with identical data fields, data dictionaries and standards for describing objects.

The most viable of these efforts has come from the National Parks Service which is in the process of installing its Automated National Cataloging System (ANCS) at its nearly 400 sites. When fully implemented, this system will enable easy communiction among sites because they will have identical software, screens, query systems, and so on. The ANCS system uses IBM compatible PCs running dBase III+ as its basis, though new releases have been written using proprietary dBase III+ compilers. The data collected by the program is based on cataloguing standards, many of which have been in use by the National Park Service for some time. Because of the uniformity that the National Parks Service can expect of its sites and the centralised control of information managing materials such as catalogue cards and worksheets, the ANCS effectively answers the needs for collections management that the Parks Service has set for its sites. Because the program and its associated materials have been developed at public expense, the program and manuals are available to any United States citizen under the Freedom of Information Act at a nominal cost. The Parks Service has made special efforts to make the availability of this program known throughout the museum community, and it has distributed several hundred copies to museums — primarily history museums — outside of the Parks Service. It is too early to know how effectively these institutions have used the ANCS program.

The ANCS program has a necessary rigidity imposed by the fact that it has been written for a system that is in place. Some of the data fields offered by the program are ones that non-Parks Service users might not find useful. Some data fields that individual museums might want or need for their own purposes have, of course, been omitted from the program. Because the ANCS program is supplied in an encrypted and compiled form, program modification is impossible by the user (a benefit for insuring uniformity among Parks Service sites, but a problem for those musems seeking slight modifications). The fact that while Freedom of Information offers the program, the Parks Service cannot, of course, provide support to those who are using it is said to be a problem for some end-users. Whether or not these difficulties can be overcome so that anyone using the ANCS system will have the ability to communicate with anyone else using it remains to be seen. The idea has a certain amount of promise, but the problems associated with it seem difficult to solve.

Much simpler in scope as it is currently configured is the network that has been under development for the US Army museums. Again, because of the uniformity that has determined the kinds of data that have been recorded about collections, the possiblity of effective computerisation is available. Since a primary concern of the Army in the management of its museums is location of property, the programs that they are using emphasise inventory management more than information sharing. The Army system depends on a centrally located mainframe serving a network of nearly 100 museums. While the network is not accessible to museums outside the Army system, the model offered is worthy of notice.

As vendors have placed more programs in museums, the possibility of data sharing has been created because several museums are now using the same applications programs. At the present time, this has simply been offered as a possibility to encourage sales, and no formal systems have been set up. In time, this may be a means to establishing networks.

All of these structures that offer the possibility of networking are based on existing applications programs. In some instances, consideration has been given to how a network using them might operate, but in others, little consideration of how or what might be shared has been given. In any event, the difficulties of either trying to fit existing records management systems to the programs or to find sufficient compatibility between customised programs are significant. Much more careful planning and consideration of information sharing and information management standards needs to precede implementation of these systems.

The MARC format

Developed in an environment free from specific concerns about applications programs, the AMC MARC format used by libraries for the transfer of information has been considered by many museums as the basis for their information management needs and for the possibilities that MARC offers in terms of data sharing with libraries and archives. The sophistication that MARC offers to library cataloguing and management is something that museums have certainly looked at with interest and even envy. The publication of the subject terms for visual materials, the adoption of MARC format as a suggested standard for archive management, and the promise of a sanctioned format for recording three-dimensional figures have brought MARC more clearly to the attention of museums.

Although commercial applications packages utilising the MARC format are available for cataloguing museum objects, consideration of adopting the MARC format for museum objects has been limited to attention to the ways MARC fields map onto data fields used by museums for collections management. A strength of the MARC format is its ability to effectively and efficiently address the problem of cataloguing identical items. Once the MARC formatted entry for John Updike's latest novel has been created, any library that owns that book can simply adopt that catalogue information without having to develop an entry all its own. For museums, the objects that are held are apt to be unique, so these efficiencies are lost, though using the MARC fields may provide some useful standards.

Another strength of the MARC format is its ability to point towards related information — authors and subjects, for instance. Library data management systems depend on such referencing rather than actually developing and storing such data. Museum collections management often requires the extra overhead involved with describing, storing, and even expanding upon such related information. Frequently, that is the primary function of museum collections data management. A museum would normally record information about tools that it had that came from a particular clockmaker's shop, for example, but it would also have ways to collect information about that shop, the clockmaker, and any clocks that it might own that were made there or any clocks held by other collections that were made there. It might even include as a part of its catalogue information about similar clockmakers. While it is possible to record information with this complexity of content with MARC formatted records, the fact that MARC does not utilise relational databases as effectively as other formats might undercut the value that MARC has for managing all aspects of museum collections management. This comes as no surprise. MARC was developed for library needs, not for museums.

The MARC format has evolved out of careful, prolonged analysis of the data that must be collected to catalogue library materials. In some respects, the system responds to museum's needs, but in others, it does not. Before any formal system of identities can be established, though, it will be necessary for museums to follow the very effective model that MARC has offered, and to analyse their information management needs. Relying simply on trying to adopt an existing standard overlooks one of the most valuable things MARC can show us, and it neglects the fact that ongoing needs analysis is one of the strengths of the MARC format. At the present time, the MARC format does not easily collect or manage the wealth of associated and related information that frequently makes museum objects significant. Further analysis of the kinds of data museums collect must be done independently of existing systems for formats before a standard can be described.

The Common Agenda for History Museum Data Base Task Force

Recognising that there was a need to analyse the kinds of information that museums managed and the need to describe some standards that would indicate what information museums — particularly history museums — needed to record about objects,the Common Agenda for History Museums project designated a task force with the

Figure 16.1 The Common Agenda survey. General areas covered by the survey

Management data

Data that is normally recorded or created when an object comes into a collection, and that data that is recorded as a means of relating objects to records or records to objects (including location, valuation, conservation, and documentation data).

- Identifying numbers
- Acquisition
- De-accession/status change
- Monetary value
- Location
- Exhibition/loan
- Legal information
- Care and conservation
- Audio/visual documentation of objects

Descriptive data

Data that can be gathered about an object by observing it or by applying fairly simple research techniques such as discovering an object's name or title.

- Classification
- Material/surface details
- Size
- Inscription/marking
- Decoration
- Production
- Condition

Historical data

Data about the people or organisations that are associated with a particular object. For each of the associations, a number of data elements might be noted: the name of the individual or organisation, their location or address, any particular cultural affiliation, and the dates of birth or incorporation, death or dissolution, and periods of activity that can be discovered for those people and organisations.

- Object history
- Associated people/institutions/organisations
- Associated places/things/events
- Subject associations

responsibility of reviewing current standards and making recommendations. In fact, the task force has two charges: to describe a basic group of data fields that history museums might look to as a standard for describing objects and to suggest a structure for describing the scope of a group of objects or collection within the holdings of a single institution. The first task, standards for cataloguing single objects, is being accomplished through review of published materials, consideration of existing models, and a survey of the field to determine current practice. The second task, scope statements, is being developed through consideration of the data fields for single objects, current models, and a test sampling of institutions. The task force is scheduled to complete its work in the spring of 1989.

One of the more ambitious goals of the task force is to review current data fields being used by history museums, determine the strengths, weaknesses, and commonalities among a wide range of institutional concerns, and present a synthesis of points of view as well as a standard that helps to describe how cataloguing might be done. The primary tool used for this task has been a survey form that was based on an initial gathering of potential data fields from a wide variety of sources by the task force committee itself.[1] This survey was published in the summer of 1988 as an insert in *History News,* the publication of the American Association for State and Local History, the principal sponsoring agent for the Common Agenda project (Anon., 1988). While the publication of the survey was intended primarily to be eductional — to indicate to the field the kinds of things that the task force was considering — the results of the survey were interesting none the less.

The survey offered a list of data fields that history museums might use as part of their cataloguing process, and asked respondents to indicate which of those fields they actually utilised, which they informally utilised,and how important they felt the data for that particular field was. The list of data fields was divided into three types of data: management data, descriptive data and historical data. Within these three broad areas, more limited groups of related data fields were listed, and respondents were invited to add any other data fields they recorded that were related to these sub-categories. The survey was accompanied by a data dictionary that provided definitions for each of the fields mentioned in the survey. The general scope of the survey is outlined in Figure 16.1. A typical group of entries is shown in Figure 16.2 (the square boxes were for indicating whether or not the field was recorded and the curly brackets were for indicating the importance placed on recording the field). Figure 16.3 then gives the definitions that were applied to the different fields.

An analysis of the responses to the survey has led the task force on to developing a draft version of a model for effective collection management. This model will be published in 1989.

---

1. The Common Agenda Data Base Task Force includes the following members: James R. Blackaby, Curator, The Mercer and Fonthill Museums, Doylestown, PA, Chair; Marguerite d'Aprille-Smith, Adjunct Editor, Getty Art & Architecture Thesaurus, Williamstown, MA; Ann Hitchcock, Chief Curator, National Parks Service, Washington, DC; Kim Igoe, Director, Museum Assessment Program, American Association of Museums, Washington, DC; Ron Kley, Museum Computer Network, East Winthrop, ME; Carol Schull, National Register of Historic Places, National Parks Service, Washington, DC; Jane Sledge, Office of Information Resource Management, Smithsonian Institution, Washington, DC; Kathy Spiess, Assistant Registrar, National Museum of American History, Smithsonian Institution, Washington, DC.

Figure 16.2 Common Agenda survey entry for 'classification'

Descriptive Data

Data that can be gathered about an object by observing it or by applying fairly simple research techniques such as discovering an object's name or title.

Classification

[ ] { } Systematic Classification System Used?
If so: [ ] { } Internal System
[ ] { } Published System: ________________

[ ] { } Preferred Object Name
[ ] { } Alternate Names

[ ] { } Identifier [ ] { } Date
[ ] { } Title/Proper Name (including product name/pattern)
[ ] { } Alternate Title
[ ] { } Names of Parts (for multi-part objects such as sets)
[ ] { } Description
[ ] { } Style
[ ] { } Number of Items in Group
[ ] { } Unit of Measurement
[ ] { } Other (specify): ________________

Figure 16.3 Common Agenda data definitions for 'classification'

Descriptive Data

Data that can be gathered about an object by observing it or by applying fairly simple research techniques such as discovering an object's name or title.

Classification: *Data identifying objects in relationship to one another.*

Systematic Classification System Used: if a formal classification system such as *Nomenclature* is used or if a formal internal classification system is used, it should be noted here.
Preferred Object Name: a formal indexing or identifying term that is "preferred" by a systematic classification system.
Alternate Names: this can include the local, informal names that an object is known by that may or not be included as a part of a formal classification system.
Identifier: the person who determined an object's name.
Title/Proper Name: the formal title or product name for an object – usually given by the maker or manufacturer.
Alternate Title: an alternate to the formal title, often assigned by popular agreement.
Names of Parts: for recording multi-part objects such as sets.
Description: a narrative word picture of an object.
Style: classification based on the aesthetic qualities of an object that relates its decoration or form to other objects, events, or movements.
Number of items in group: along with a description of the unit of measurement describes bulk items or sets of like things.

The other project of the task force has been to establish some data fields that would allow institutions to indicate the scope of their collections. In the survey, this took the form of a very simple set of data fields that gave the opportunity to indicate type of object in particular sub-collections, any historical or geographical similarities that related the objects in that sub-collection, and the size of that sub-collection. The responses from the survey indicated that such a simple model was effective, and a more comprehensive single sheet form that can be filled out for as many sub-collections as an institution finds useful is being prepared by the committee. It will be tested by a limited group of museums in early 1989, and the format will be published.

The goal of the task force is to provide tools that will enable individual institutions to manage their collections more effectively, that will enable a set of standard fields to be identified for those institutions that would like to work towards information sharing, and to provide a structure for complex queries about groups of objects in collections that might not be apparent from the more generalised listings found in museum directories. The tools that the task force is developing are not software or system specific — indeed, they do not even depend on computerisation. They do intend to bear clear relationships to existing systems and formats — such as the Nomenclature lexicon and the MARC format. They are being developed out of consideration of need and practice, and on that account, it is hoped that they will have more universal application than more limited approaches to data management and sharing have had.

Conclusion

The recent developments in the United States have represented small steps taken with growing awareness of the difficulties of really trying to develop effective systems for managing an individual institution's data as well as sharing that data with others. Slowly, though, museums are getting a clearer view of what kinds of data they need to record, and why or how they need to record it in order to lead to the information and the knowledge that their collections potentially offer. While some of the steps and some of the solutions will continue to be false steps and problematic solutions, the long term gains in understanding how to manage data in museums will be significant. The next few years will continue to provide incremental improvement of the techniques and sophistication required for sound data management and data sharing.

IV
INSTITUTION-WIDE INITIATIVES

17 INSTITUTION-WIDE INITITIATIVES

Peter Wilson

Head of Gallery Services
Tate Gallery
London

Those of us who have the relatively simple task of overseeing documentation in single-discipline museums such as art galleries, where terminology issues between object classes still seem complex enough (my own organisation agonised for some while over the difficulties of using the term acrylic when it could refer to a sheet of ICI Perspex or some paint from a tube supplied by an artists' colourman!) can hardly begin to appreciate the difficulties which beset those charged with the planning and implementation of a documentation initiative in a large multi-disciplinary museum. The less fortunate majority will be only too familiar with these difficulties. The following four papers review progress on such initiatives in large but different museums. They help to identify problems and offer useful experience.

The four museums are the long-established and very large British Museum, the specialised but none the less diverse collections of the National Maritime Museum in London, the relatively recently amalgamated from separate museums National Museums of Scotland and finally the Smithsonian Institution. This last is in no way the least: even the most complex organisation can draw comfort from the example of the Smithsonian, an organisation whose constituent museums occupy a substantial part of the centre of a capital city and beyond. For the Smithsonian Institution, terminology control needs to cover a range of object types, just for example from a beetle to a spaceship!

All these papers bring fresh insights and approaches to bear on our common problem. The pragmatism and calm with which daunting tasks can be tackled can be an inspiration to us all.

18 INSTITUTION-WIDE INITIATIVE AT THE BRITISH MUSEUM

Alison Allden

Collections Data Management Section
The British Museum
London

Introduction

The initiative of the title was that taken by the Collections Data Management Section of The British Museum to establish both the will and the mechanism for introducing and maintaining institution-wide terminology control throughout the Museum (comprising ten, in many respects autonomous, antiquities departments). This was to be introduced for the computerised inventory database and, moreover, would have to be applied retrospectively to the 600 000 records already on the computer.

There was a catalyst for this initiative: the acquisition in 1988 of a new computer system. This comprises a PRIME supermini 9955 MKII, running the Information database management system, consisting of a specially developed application called &Magus which has been built by Ampersand Systems Ltd using the &Pace applications generator. This provided the opportunity to consider carefully, when defining the operational requirement and systems analysis and design, the extent and types of terminology controls desirable.

Terminology control strategies

After an assessment of the use made of the inventory database over the preceding five or more years, together with the accumulated experience of the Section in compiling records in response to curatorial requirements, it was proposed the terminology should be managed in two main ways.

Natural Language. There is provision for information to be entered in certain sections of the record without restricting or controlling the vocabulary, i.e. using 'natural language'. One example is the ability to provide a free-text description of each object. Thus, the record for each object accommodates highly specialised vocabulary and detail which has been recognised as advantageous for high precision retrieval (Lancaster, 1986 and Bulaong, 1982). Sledge (1988) emphasises the desirability of retaining the richness of language, and reports that the use of free-text or 'natural language' may in fact provide for greater contextual compatibility between different institutions' databases, in a way that locally controlled terminology cannot.

Certain free-text fields, for example Description and the 'Curator's Commentary', will also be word indexed — bar a stop-word list — thus providing for more efficient retrieval on their content.

Controlled Vocabulary. This will be managed at two levels. First, there will be simple data validation word lists or code lists for fields with limited contents, such as 'Acquisition method'. These lists can be used as a check at input, as well as providing the mechanism for automatic code expansions. Some of the fields controlled in this way will be indexed. Where not, retrieval will be possible using string searches, and the authority lists may be viewed easily for guidance.

Second, fully interactive thesauri will be developed for use in certain fields, such as Object Name, People/Institution Names and Materials. These will provide vocabulary control, with the facility for on-screen term selection during data entry. In addition, every field for which a thesaurus is identified will be indexed, and so the system will then utilise the thesaurus to provide supplementary interactive support on retrieval. In this way it will be possible to opt for high precision recall using specific terms, or less precise but broader recall, by utilising the term relationships set up in the thesaurus.

Development of museum thesauri

The responsibility for the construction and maintenance of the thesauri will lie principally with the Collections Data Management Section in collaboration with the curatorial staff.

The structure of the thesauri follows closely, in design and approach, the latest British and International standards. It allows the control of synonyms and the recognition of broader, narrower and related terms, as well as the inclusion of scope notes and the definition of top terms. The thesaurus is constructed on a step by step basis for the expression of hierarchical relationships, although at retrieval the full hierarchy can be recovered.

In one respect it is unusual. While recognising both 'preferred terms' and their synonyms or equivalents as 'non-preferred terms', it is none the less possible to enter the latter as index terms into the database. This is in recognition that in the museum environment the semantic need for a particular term in a particular context, though exceptional or idiosyncratic or personal, should be admissible. However, there are penalties, because, apart from its identified preferred term, a non-preferred term can have no other thesaural relationships. It can, of course, be selected when the preferred term is specified in retrieval.

Other features of the thesaurus include the facility to 'force' a term at input, when necessary. This will then be flagged as a temporary term until it is agreed and accepted. Thesaurus construction and maintenance is assisted wherever possible by the computer, for example in setting up reciprocal relationships.

In addition to these means of vocabulary control and indexing, the database has been designed to provide for more precise post-coordination at retrieval. This incorporates a global record structure for the museum, to provide for cross-department or database searches. In this way, combined with the terminology controls, a fully compatible information resource for the museum as a whole is considered achievable and institutionally desirable.

To be able to advance our initiative, it was necessary to assess the resources available, measured in staff time and expertise. Priorities had to be identified in the context of the inventory project, particularly with reference to the programme for installing the new system and the transfer to it of 600 000 records from the batch processed database files. It was only then possible to plan a programme for establishing institution-wide controlled terminology. This needed to satisfy the requirements of every department, for the range of objects held and indeed the range of documentation that would be encountered.

The initial step was to educate ourselves, by organising seminars and seeking advice, assistance, models and publications. In addition, professional affirmation was sought for our plans to construct word-lists and thesauri. This process of education, communication and contribution to wider initiatives will continue in the future.

It was important to consult the raw material inherent in the accumulated vocabulary of 600 000 records, compiled from a wide range of documentation, providing what Lancaster describes as 'literary warrant'. The fact that these records had been utilised for about five years gave the vocabulary, with its recognised strengths and weaknesses, considerable 'user warrant'. In addition, there were the card indexes that had been compiled for each departmental scheme (currently six out of the ten departments are being computerised). These provided a system of manual vocabulary control, and incidentally demonstrated the duplication of effort that a single system would help to avoid.

The simple validation word lists, incorporating limited vocabulary, could be compiled relatively easily, by comparing and rationalising terms or codes already used. In the future these can be conveniently updated through a menu option on the new system.

The priority subject thesauri were identified as being those for the data types common to all the current records, namely:

geography/place-name details;
object names;
materials;
techniques;
people/institution names (in particular with reference to acquisition details).

Personal and institution names had already been subject to some structured cross-department research and control. The new record structure will act as an information-based thesaurus as far as synonyms or pseudonyms are concerned, since associated

Figure 18.1 Control of personal names

a. Associated Names as entered into a record

ASSOCIATIONS				
Name *[II]	[Regulus, Marcus	] [	] (	)
AKA Ass Name	[Reghulo, Marcho	] [	] (	)

b. Acquisition details as entered into a record

REG NO [1883,0218.39		]	SCREEN 4	PRN [MCA3664]
ACQUISITION DETAILS				
Acq Name * [P]	[Mulgrave	] [Earl of	] (	)
AKA Acq Name	[Mulgrave	] [Rev	] (	)
Acq Hist	<			>
Acq Year	[1883]			
Acq Notes	<			>

AKA Also known as II Named in inscription and portrayed P Purchased from alternative names can also be recorded (Figure 18.1). However, all names will be corrected to achieve consistency, and the thesaurus will be compiled automatically in the first instance from the data already in the database. From then on, it will act as a check on input and be refined as necessary.

In view of this background, it remained to tackle the first four vocabulary areas mentioned above. Collections Data Management Section team members were formed into Terminology Working Parties. They would draw on their own experience and expertise, but more vitally would act as go-betweens to consult with relevant curatorial staff throughout the museum.

For the most part the empirical approach (Lancaster, 1986) to thesaurus construction was adopted, by virtue of the vocabulary contained in the 600 000 records already compiled. Any bias resulting, revealed by the terms required by other areas of the collections not yet computerised, will be rectified in subsequent years. However, the vocabulary from the records compiled for the departments of Ethnography, Egyptian Antiquities, Oriental and Japanese Antiquities, Coins and Medals and Medieval and Later Antiquities provides a useful cross-section on which to base this thesaurus development work.

In the case of the *Geography Working Party,* the aim to achieve consistent geographical input is not so simple, when having to allow for one object found in 'a certain grave, in a site on a farm, near a village, in a parish, of a county of England' and another from a 'range of mountains' or 'some country that no longer exists or has drastically changed its boundaries'.

The search for an established structured world-wide thesaurus that could be adopted was not successful. Guidance and gazetteers were sought through many organisations including Aslib, Unesco, oil companies, The British Library and recommended publications. (Following the terminology conference, further possible sources for assistance will now be pursued.)

Realising the complexity of associating place-names through a thesaurus, initially only preferred and non-preferred names will be identified to provide a validation list. The record structure automatically groups associated place-names and a code with each indicates its status: town, country, etc. (Figure 18.2). This status code also indicates

Figure 18.2 Control of geographic names
Geographic details as entered into a record

```
.................GEOGRAPHY/FIND-SPOT DETAILS.................
* [F] Place      [C  ]   [Norway                ]  (          )
                 +E      Oppland fylke
                 +M      Lom sogn
                 +0      Lyngved
                 +
                 +
Geog Notes       <                                            >
```

C Country E Province M Parish O Village F From

Figure 18.3 Control of materials terms
Sample entries from materials thesaurus

Term ABACA	Type P Created 21OCT88 By DBM
Scope Notes	The palm Musa textilis in family Musaceae which furnishes manilla hemp; also the name for its fibre
Preferred Term	
Broader Terms	VEGETAL
Narrower Terms	
Related Terms	KOFFO MANILLA HEMP
Non-Preferred Terms	

Term ALUMINIUM	Type P Created 15SEP88 By LDJ
Scope Notes	
Preferred Term	
Broader Terms	METAL
Narrower Terms	
Related Terms	BAUXITE
Non-Preferred Terms	ALUMINIUM FOIL SILVER PAPER

Term AMBATCH.	Type P Created 14DEC88 ByBMA
Scope Notes	Aeschynomene elaphroxylon, family Leguminosae. Wood used for instance by Nilotic Sudanese for rafts and floats
Preferred Term	
Broader Terms	WOOD
Narrower Terms	
Related Terms	
Non-Preferred Terms	

archaic place-names — these may be integrated with current place-names or form a separate group if there is no identifiable common ground, but will appear in the thesaurus as any other place-name.

Having established this system for recording place-names, the Working Party has been able to spend most of its time trying to check more obscure geographical references, particularly for the Ethnographic and Oriental material, from which tribal and cultural terms are being extracted to be stored in appropriate fields in the new record design. In addition, when possible hierarchies are being identified for recorded place-names. It is anticipated that before too long the thesaurus will be enhanced to contain the continent: country relationship, but it is likely to be some time before full hierarchies are constructed.

The second Working Party has dealt with the terminology for both *materials and techniques thesauri* (Figure 18.3). The scientific and technical aspects of this terminology required, in this case, the adoption of a top-down approach for establishing the primary thesaural relationships. The Working Party was also mindful of the quality of the source material and the requirements of the average user, so that highly developed material science or technical thesauri were not considered appropriate end products.

The Working Party proceeded to identify, and insert into the hierarchical structure, preferred and non-preferred terms from the vocabulary already used, supplemented when necessary to maintain the hierarchical relationships. It took advice from the Museums' conservation and research laboratory scientists to ensure 'correctness', and consulted with natural scientists at Kew Gardens and the Royal Zoological Society, in particular to corroborate some very obscure ethnographic materials.

As a result, two workable thesauri, pertinent to the level of information held in the collection database, have now been established. In time these will complement the more specialist conservation and research laboratory controlled terminology that is under development (see Jones, Chapter 87).

The third Working Party had perhaps the widest ranging vocabulary to be built into a *thesaurus for object names*, covering both two- and three-dimensional objects (Figure 18.4). An attempt to adopt a top-down approach, to try and impose a hierarchical structure for the task, proved untenable, even with reference to other relevant hierarchically structured word-lists. It became clear that a bottom-up term by term approach would have to be the starting point, concentrating on the listings of one or two departments at a time. Through this reiterative process, taking in a different department each time, rules could be developed and judgements refined in the light of newly introduced terms.

Like the other Working Parties, initially a wordprocessed alphabetical file of terms was used as a working list in which the preferred or non-preferred status was recorded and

Figure 18.4 Object names
Extract from object names term list

CROZIER	CUFF	CUSHION-COVER
CRUCIBLE	CUP	DAGGER
CRUCIFORM BROOCH	CURFEW	DAGGER-SHEATH
CRUET		

other thesaural relationships noted as they became apparent. In addition to scope notes which would be included in the thesaurus, this list recorded essential notes for the edits that would be necessary to bring the terminology in line for transfer to the new system.

Certain fundamental rules, for example as regards punctuation and plurals, were determined from the start. Other rules were established as problems were resolved, often thematically, for example on how to deal with models or natural remains. One difficult area that had to be resolved was how to deal with parts of objects, identified where possible as narrower terms of the whole. In addition, foreign terms proved to require more than simply identifying English equivalents as preferred terms. The extent of their integration into the thesaurus was considered on an individual basis.

Gradually a structured thesaurus is emerging, with curatorial collaboration, frequent reference to the Oxford Dictionary, standard reference works, other available word-lists and lessons learnt from Book X of Plato's *Republic*.

Future research

Having adopted this hybrid system (Lancaster, 1986) for terminology control, it is also necessary to look at the resource implications for maintaining it in the future. The primary role of the Collections Data Management Section is to furnish the Museum with a computerised inventory. However, the current concern is with the total number of object records on the computer rather than the number of terms in the thesauri.

The process of implementing a new database system created this opportunity to spend time on rationalising our terminology control. However, that 'development of thesauri should be based on firm research evidence of how they have been used in practice, and with mechanisms to ensure that their creation and maintenance make economic sense' (Dubois, 1984) is advice that should be heeded. Currently, there is negligible experience of the use of fully integrated thesauri and databases in a museum context. This would be a useful area of study and assessment. The success of the thesauri so far developed for the British Museum will be carefully monitored and the commitment to their further development at this stage has to be guarded.

Any method of vocabulary control must allow for symbiotic growth with the database, and should not become proscriptive. This must be understood at its inception and adoption. It is hoped that a workable and useful level of terminology control has been identified, which will enhance the database, but need not make such demands that it deflects from the goal of compiling an inventory that one day will total over 6 million records.

19 PROGRESS WITH TERMINOLOGY CONTROL AT THE NATIONAL MARITIME MUSEUM

Paul Pelowski

National Maritime Museum
Greenwich, London

Introduction

The National Maritime Museum offers an interesting example of terminology control development, as the four classic stages of terminology control are clearly discernible:

The Traditional approach. The approach taken from the time of the inception of the Museum in 1937 up until 1971. In effect no systematic approach. Terminology was dependant on the choice of individual curators — with or without discussion.

The Pre-input thesaurus. From 1971 until 1975 considerable work was carried out on a thesaurus named MATELOT (Maritime Thesaurus Edited List of Terms). It was intended to cover the general range of maritime subjects and the Museum's collections in particular. Based on the Engineers' Joint Council Thesaurus of Engineering Terms, it included the usual referral format and symbols ('use', 'used for', 'broader term', etc.). A curatorial committee sat periodically to discuss and edit the term lists, which were compiled from Museum information indexes. The thesaurus was automatically generated from the edited lists of terms on an Imperial War Museum computer. The project reached the letter F before it was abandoned, seemingly in recognition of the vastness of the undertaking and its ever-increasing drain on staff resourses.

Word list checking for individual projects. After the introduction of computerisation for documentation to the Museum in 1974, the approach was one of project based standardisation of input data and the gradual generation of simple authority lists from input data. Wordlists were produced in each project, preferred terms chosen and recorded, the records edited and re-edited as necessary. In some cases the resulting authority lists formed part of project manuals. Generally the lists were not made available for reference to curators outside of the immediate project areas. Feed forward from one project to another was not systematic.

Centralised terminology control. In 1984 a new department called the Information Project Group was set up, primarily to examine the Museum's documentation and information needs and to attack the large backlog of Museum cataloguing. Radical by-products of this were the establishment of a central standards unit for research and development of data standards, the standardisation of terminology across all cataloguing projects and the application of our computer technology to terminology control.

The current approach

Many curators have a popular conception of the dreaded museum THESAURUS, an all-consuming beast, ready to eat up time and resources. Actually the poor monster has been kept on a sensible diet and contained by our gradual, cumulative and pragmatic approach to terminology control.

Of course there is not a single all encompassing thesaurus, but various types of terminology control.

We have written style guidelines and conventions for simpler concepts such as date, place and personal name, and we have started to broadcast these beyond specific cataloguing projects to the Museum at large in a Museum Documentation Manual. Some short lists of standard terms are also incorporated in the Manual.

We have evolved some fixed lists of terms which may be displayed on screen and machine verified at the time of input. This happens in such cases as 'Method of Acquisition'. Computer held registers are maintained for certain centrally allocated codes and numbers: unique item numbers for museum objects, record photograph numbers, collection names, etc.

Fully structured authority lists are being developed for a number of the data categories of our multidisciplinary Management Record. To date we have worked in the following areas:

Common Name (i.e. 'simple name' of the object);

Design Name;

Dossier Name;

Events;

General Subject Concepts;

Part Name (i.e. detachable parts of the object);

Person and Organisation;

Personal Titles and Honours;

Physical Properties (including material, support and method of production);

Place Name;

School;

Vessel Name;

Vessel Type.

Some lists are small (School has 20 terms); some are huge (Personal Name runs to many thousands). They are in various stages of research and preparedness.

We download terms from each cataloguing project that we come to — Flags, Firearms, Oil Paintings, etc. — into the relevant authority list database. There we work on individual terms using a modification of our homegrown data entry and editing software (STEER) and a special purpose authority list record structure.

The full record structure is quite large and complicated but basically it follows the standard thesaural approach as outlined in British Standard BS5723, with broader terms, narrower terms, related terms, scope notes, etc. (British Standards Institute, 1987). Subsets of the full record are used for particular authority lists.

The authority list user index

The main product derived from the full authority list is the user index. With this product, we set out to provide easy access to the standard form of a term, complete with its hierarchical relationships to other terms, useful cross-referencing to and from other terms, unique identification of the term (through definitions, dates, classification, etc.), and guidance on the use of the term.

Figure 19.1 shows typical entries from the Physical Description Authority List User Index. The full information about a term is given in the main entry for that term, i.e.

Figure 19.1 Example of entry in the National Maritime Museum's Physical Description Authority List User Index

alloy, copper	(material: metal: alloy, copper) Alloy consisting of mixture of copper with other metal or non-metallic elements. Use the broader term alloy when the precise nature of the alloy is uncertain. Authority: Cottrell, 527–8.
aluminium	(material: metal: aluminium) Very light and malleable metal. Use only when use the materal is identified as aluminium, otherwise use the broader term metal. Authority: OED.
copper alloy	See: alloy, copper
material	Outermost Term. The physical material from which an object is made. Authority: common usage.

- inorganic
  - carbon
  - silicon
  - stone
- metal
  - alloy, copper
  - alloy, iron
  - aluminium
  - copper
- organic
  - bone
  - bristle
  - leather
  - shell

metal	(material: metal) Any of large class of chemical elements such as gold, lead, etc; crystalline when solid and often dense, fusible, malleable, opaque and lustrous. Use only when the material is identified as metal but it is not clear which particular metal is present. Authority: common usage.

- alloy, copper
- alloy, iron
- aluminium
- copper

where it appears as the lead term in the index's main A–Z sequence. Full information is not repeated where the term is simply listed at the second and third levels of the index. Second and third level listings of terms under broader terms are internal search aids only, designed to bring conveniently together terms otherwise scattered throughout the main sequence of the index. See 'aluminium' as a full entry compared to its appearance in the lists of terms under 'metal' and under 'material'. Simple cross references are provided from non-preferred to preferred forms of terms where there is inversion of the natural word order. Hence we find entries such as, 'copper alloy See: alloy, copper'.

Structure and use of the user index entries

As the example shows, the index term is given on the left hand side of the top line and the rest of the first line shows its relationship to its broader terms. The broader terms are shown in round brackets as a simple hierarchy, usually in the order of general to specific.

In the main entry this is followed by data which helps us uniquely to identify the term. Such data can include definition or classification of the term where this is appropriate ('very light and malleable metal . . . ') and other explanatory data and guidance on when the term should be used ('when the material is identified as aluminium, otherwise use . . . ').

Finally we include the authoritative reference source from which we obtained our preferred form and further information about the term. These are usually reliable published sources; in the absence of published sources we turn to the most reliable unpublished sources that we can find. Sources are quoted in the index entries in a short form (usually author name only, or short title).

More complex relationships between user index entries

Where the leading term is an alternative, non-preferred version this is stated, with 'Alternative Term' at the beginning of the second line. More rarely, we use 'Alternative Outer Term' to provide pointers to other broader terms by which the term might be known: 'Historical' for historical versions of the term, 'Variant' for variant spellings, and so on.

Where necessary, index entries will include referral from non-preferred to preferred terms using 'see also'. 'See also' references are provided also to other terms of equal weight and related interest.

Wider use of the authority lists

A number of lists which have been researched and thesaurally structured are already used for machine checking of project data. However, it has always been envisaged that authority lists would have a life of their own, as reference tools at the point of data input, independent of the Documentation Manual although complementary to it. Ultimately we aim to make the terms used in many data categories standardised throughout the Museum, so that we have a link connecting all the relevant information and nothing significant is lost in information retrieval.

It is obviously our aim to achieve the maximum possible degree of standardisation between projects, and ultimately between departments.

Other developments

Two other interesting areas of development are described below.

The use of KWIC indexing in the Museum Records Acquisition Data Project

In essence a cataloguing project, the Acquisition Data Project involved the extraction of acquisition data from thousands of Museum paper files and slips to make produce computer held records of Museum acquisitions, together with useful indexes and listings.

A mass of rough and unstructured descriptive data was recorded along with acquisition dates, donors, acquisition numbers, etc. It was recognised that in the long term this descriptive data would be redundant, since full master records would be made

Figure 19.2 Example of an entry in the National Maritime Museum's KWIC index for the Museum Records Acquisition Data Project

Two	MODELS of the motor ship John E. Hyde	XBC2033
10 ship	MODELS of Tilbury Contracting	XBC1159
6	MODELS, rigged 4-masted barque	XBC1190
Book,	MODERN EUROPEAN HISTORY 1789–1945	XBC0510
Book, The	MODERN SYSTEM OF NAVAL ARCHITECTURE, by	XBC2760
9 drawings of the Hussar,	MODESTE and other ships, by Robert	XBC2955
chart cylinder, all belonged to Mr	MOFFETT'S grandfather coxwain-master	XBC2520
by Fairfields (Glasgow) Ltd Livadia,	MOISE, St Augustine, Abdel Kader, Isaac	XBC0631
Drawings of vessels by H B	MOLESWORTH, USA 1901–02	XBC2522
Engraving by J	MOLINEUX of the Dutch and English Fleet	XBC0036
Map of the world by H	MOLL ca.1730, a view of ye General	XBC2810
Relics of the German battle cruiser	MOLTKE and papers captured at the	XBC2857
removed from the German cruiser	MOLTKE by Francis Neville Halsted	XBC1317
	MOMENTO presented by crew on Naval	XBC0614
gale or squall, by Parr after P	MONAMY and F Swaine	XBC0648
7 engravings by Canat after P	MONAMY published 1746, Fresh gales	XBC1114
of Appledore, 4 of Bideford, 2 of St	MONANCE, 1 of Glasgow, 3 of Pittenween	XBC0324
Tapestry picture of HMS	MONARCH, 1842	XBC1354
training on HMS Excellent, HMS	MONARCH at Portsmouth ca.1870 and an on	XBC2821
Midshipman's logbook of HMS	Monarch kept by A C Willes Watson	XBC2544
2 models of passenger liners	MONARCH OF BERMUDA 1931 and Strathmore	XBC1232
wages . . run away with sums of	MONEY	XBC0512
Flag Officers of the Fleet . . prize	MONEY, dated 26 Jan 1709	XBC0512
Photocopy of calculation of prize	MONEY for La Prothee, 1780	XBC1137
Book,	MONITORS OF THE US NAVY 1861–1937, by E	XBC2319
buttons of 1891–1901 type, 3	MONKEY jacket and 2 waistcoat buttons	XBC1078
Lt-Cdr A F Inglefield consisting of	MONKEY jacket, blue trousers and	XBC2045
undress sword belt, dirk belt,	MONKEY jacket of commander, cap of	XBC0480
blue waistcoat with RNR buttons,	MONKEY jacket of lieutenant RNR, frock	XBC0094
worn by D P Simson comprising,	MONKEY jacket of Radio Officer, pair	XBC1015

for all items, and unique item numbers would link the object, inventory and master records.

However, the descriptive data would be useful for the detective work necessary to piece together the acquisition data, and to some degree it was important to retain the original wording of descriptions. What we needed was a quick and simple system which allowed the input of data as found and the generation of practical indexes.

For this project we chose to produce our own program for the generation of KeyWord In Context (KWIC) indexes. Using this approach each word in the text is compared with the words in a stoplist of terms unsuitable for indexing purposes. When a match with the stoplist occurs the text word is rejected, but if no match is found the word is designated as a lead term for indexing purposes, the rest of the accompanying text rotated so as to show the keyword always 'in context'. Our program would align keywords in the centre of the page, to facilitate easy scanning, and include a citation of the record in which the description occurred (Figure 19.2).

Obviously the aim in stoplist production is to anticipate terms which would not be helpful as lead terms. Therefore, words with any possible index value to the user community at large are excluded from the stoplist.

We have included in our stoplist, for example:

purely syntactical terms — articles, prepositions, pronouns, etc.;

quantative adjectives — 1, 2, 3, and one, two, three, large and small, early and late, 1st, 2nd, and first, second, etc. Also qualifications such as circa and its abbreviations, c, c., ca., etc.;

titles and honours, including ranks;

other terms of dubious use as index terms — corner, flyleaf, good, obverse, etc. Common sense decisions were made.

Again our approach was pragmatic, growing our own stoplist from the input data in a similar way to our gradual generation of authority lists from input project data.

The KWIC approach was found to be cost effective in this case, being fast at input although somewhat more labour intensive at the search stage; index entries were generally sensible, the paper indexes were bulky but not unmanageable, the key terms were usefully left 'in context'.

Changes made to *Nomenclature*

We are building our object classification (or simple name of the object) for the Common Name Category of our Management Record on the basis of *Nomenclature for Museum Cataloguing* (Blackaby *et al.*, 1988) (see Chapter 58). R. G. Chenhall — the originator of the system — was aware of the scheme's inevitable incompleteness for individual museums. The first edition (1977) included advice on how users might develop in-house versions of the system for their own purposes.

We have always viewed *Nomenclature* as a useful starting point only, recognising that it would be limited in what it could do for us without alteration and extension. The process of 'customising' it for our own use is well under way. To date we have done the following:

American spellings have been anglicised whenever they have been met with, e.g. 'armor' becomes 'armour';

similarly, American expressions have been changed, e.g. 'balance scale' becomes 'weighing scale';

some superficial changes have been made for the sake of brevity, in particular the shortening of 'transportation' to 'transport' in such cases as 'water transport' and 'water transport accessory';

the scheme has been extended to include non-man-made objects and natural phenomena where they are represented on or by Museum objects. New major categories added have all come from our Ships' Badges Project:

animal — for all animals (including inner level classification terms such as: bird, fish, insect, and reptile);

animal, mythological — for animals which are unlikely to have ever existed, e.g. dragon, sea-monster, wyvern, etc.;

figure, human — for representations of the human form, — including those in particular costumes or poses, e.g. man, cavalier, cossack, warrior, etc.;

figure, mythological — for representations of human (or near human) mythological figures, e.g. gorgon, witch, sphinx, etc.;

natural features — for geographical features and phenomena of the natural world, e.g. iceberg, volcano, aurora borealis, etc.;

plant — for all ranks of flora (including to date the inner level classification terms: bush, flower and tree);

finally, perceived gaps in the existing scheme have been filled with our own classification terms, e.g.:

security device: key;

tobacco users t&e: cutter, tobacco.

---

20 SOME ASPECTS OF A STRATEGY FOR TERMINOLOGY CONTROL IN THE NATIONAL MUSEUMS OF SCOTLAND

John Burnett

Head of Documentation
National Museums of Scotland
Edinburgh

'Scotland small? Our multiform, our infinite Scotland *small*?' *Hugh MacDiarmid*

Introduction

The National Museums of Scotland (NMS) was formed in 1985 by the amalgamation of two venerable institutions: the National Museum of Antiquities of Scotland (NMAS) and the Royal Scottish Museum (RSM). The collections of the NMAS date from 1780, when a hoard of late Bronze Age metalwork, found on the outskirts of Edinburgh, was presented to the nascent Society, and identified with confidence as 'A quantity of Roman arms' (Stevenson, 1954). Problems of organisation of the collections have been with us from the beginning. One notable later quirk was the classification in the nineteenth century of an electric catfish as industrial object: the curator of industry was deemed to be the only one who understood electricity.

The great age of the institution, and the fact that the RSM was run for much of its life not as a museum but as three or four museums under one roof, has left us in a position where the existing documentation, though fairly complete, is very diverse. We estimate that our central database, when complete at the end of 1994, will contain about 600 000 records, representing 3.6 million objects, and covering every field of human and natural history except botany. It is highly desirable to achieve at least an internal standardisation of these records, particularly in fields such as place-names and personal and corporate body names, which are of interest to the whole museum.

It is also essential to have a view of how we are going to organise subject retrieval from our database.

The remainder of this paper discusses four components of our approach: the importance of thinking about the users of our documentation; the assessment of effectiveness of the subject retrieval which we provide; the way in which a short description of the object forms a vital part of each catalogue record; and the integration of dialect and Gaelic terms into our database. The first two of these issues concern users, the second two concern the way in which data is organised in a record.

The users of the data

We do not expect to have a single classification system or thesaurus for the whole of the NMS, but rather to use the most suitable techniques for subject retrieval for each of our user groups. For example, our curators of Scottish archaeology are anxious to create a sophisticated research tool by building up a thesaurus of terms relating to the description of their objects, terms which as far as possible exclude any indication of the supposed function of each object. This approach is by no means an obvious one. It is, for example, the opposite of that taken with the second largest archaeological collection in Scotland, in the Hunterian Museum, where subject retrieval is effected through a classification based on function (McKie, 1980). The topic of archaeological classification is, of course, one which has a large theoretical literature.

For industrial history a much simpler and more general thesaurus will be used to allow basic retrieval to take place. It will be based on, if not identical to, the Science and Technology Object Thesaurus (STOT) (Chapter 57). SHIC (Chapter 59) is more apposite for certain curators' purposes, and we look forward to using it on many parts of the collections which will also be served by STOT. The two types of subject access will complement one another. SHIC and STOT both categorise objects — at least in part — by their function, though one uses social function and the other technical function. This is clearly different from the descriptive approach being taken by the NMS archaeologists, and from the descriptive approach of the ICOM costume classification (Chapter 61) which we also expect to use for certain collections. Another variable, perhaps most clearly exemplified by our draft archaeology thesaurus and SHIC, is that different areas will be treated with different degrees of detail.

In the areas where a thesaurus is applicable, we intend to apply the British and International Standards for thesaurus construction. The one substantial object-related thesaurus — the *Art and Architecture Thesaurus* — demonstrates amply the virtues of applying high standards (in the sense of pursuing excellence) and standards (in the sense of having a piece of high-quality work which a large number of museums will use).

A more difficult question is that of drawing together the documentation of our disparate collections in such a way that members of the public can use it. We look forward to tackling this issue in one or two years' time — once we have a clearer idea of the ways in which the public will want to use the data, and when we have a better understanding of a number of techniques which are approaching maturity, such as hypertext.

Curatorial use of the object data will change as the database grows and as the curtators begin to perceive the opportunities it creates. We cannot have a closely defined long-term policy on terminology: as the needs of the curators evolve we must be as sensitive as possible to their changes.

Evaluation of record quality and retrieval performance

The primary users of subject retrieval systems in museums are the curators. As I have already said, we do not really know what they want, or think they want, or what they need. We certainly do not know how user demand is affected by automation. The more mature study of the use of catalogues in libraries has produced some surprising results. For example, quarter to a half of library users do not use the catalogue; known item searching — that is, searching for items which had been identified before the user approaches the catalogue — accounts for the largest proportion of catalogue use, and it increases as the educational level of the user rises (Hancock, 1987). A recent writer on online subject access added, 'entering an information system, getting a feel for it, and figuring which terms to search on are complex and subtle processes' (Bates, 1986). Curatorial searching of object databases is likely to be equally unpredicatable, and we will have to be aware of this. We have not been able to study searching in another large multi-disciplinary museum which has given its curators online access to collections data. It is therefore essential that we keep these issues in mind over the next few years.

We should therefore have some view of methods which might be used to assess the quality of subject retrieval. The cost of building a large database is substantial, both in terms of the cost of hardware and software, and of the cost of the staff time involved. If

Figure 20.1 The relationship between factors which control the performance of a subject retrieval system

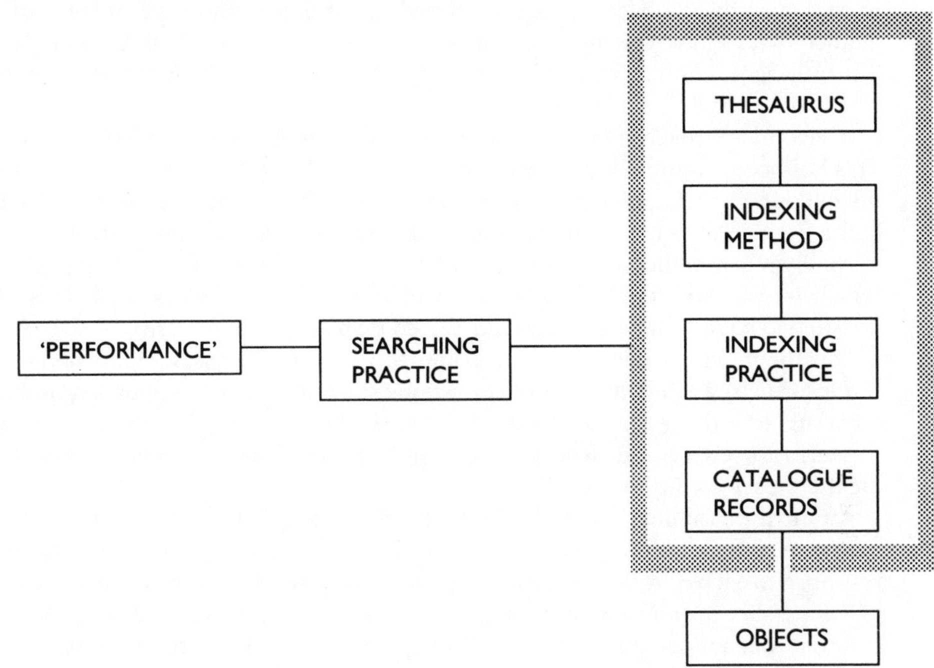

we are to be certain that we are doing the work efficiently we must have some way of assessing the effectiveness of the product.

The different factors involved are somewhat complex, and Figure 20.1 attempts to illustrate the relationships between them. 'Performance' is defined as the extent to which subject retrieval meets the users' need to find objects — a very slippery idea which I do not propose to tie down more precisely. The other five factors may affect performance. The thesaurus may fail through being insufficiently complete, or through not addressing the subject of the collection, through having an inappropriate level of detail, or for other reasons. Even if the thesaurus was perfect, the wrong indexing method applied to it (say, the assigning of only one term to each record from a thesaurus designed for post-coordinate indexing) would lower the level of performance. Similarly, a sound indexing method can be vitiated by poor indexing practice, which might be caused by the defective knowledge of the person carrying out the indexing or by the fact that only a proportion of the records have had thesaurus terms assigned to them. The terms are normally allocated to each record on the basis of the content of that record: if the record is not a fair and full description of the object then it will not be possible to select the best and most specific terms from the thesaurus. Finally, performance will be reduced if the searching practice is not adequate. This may be due to its being too complex for the user to grasp it fully, or because it is so time-consuming that the user is disinclined to employ it correctly, or for a number of other reasons.

How can the effectiveness of subject retrieval be assessed? One possibility is to question the users to attempt to find out whether they are satisfied with the service they are receiving. If this is going to be done, it should be started before automation takes place, so that there is a base line for assessing changes in performance. Since curators are likely to be concerned about performance, they are likely to be interested in cooperating in such a study. Perhaps the biggest drawback of this method is that users of a service almost always have inflated ideas about the level of service which they ought to have. The number of curators available to participate in a survey is likely to be too small to allow conclusions to be drawn with any statistical validity.

A second approach is to look at properties of the method of terminology control itself. This has been attempted for thesauri by the Bureau Marcel van Dijk, but the results were not encouraging (Lancaster, 1986). For example, one of the measures suggested was the 'richness ratio', the ratio of non-preferred to preferred terms in the thesaurus, and it was normally recommended that this should exceed 1. This arbitrary figure is a rule of thumb which is derived from an examination of thesauri which work well. It is obviously possible to have a high richness ratio caused by badly-selected terms.

Thirdly, it may be possible to make limited but objective assessments of the quality of the records by asking very simple questions such as — what proportion of the records have subject indexing terms allocated to them?; How often is each term used in the index? (if a term is used too often it ceases to be useful for retrieval); How many of the terms used are the most specific ones available?

A fourth possibility, which has been used in document retrieval, is to set up a trial database, and define a set of questions, and a set of documents which should be found in response to each question. A series of retrieval strategies can then be tested against each of the questions, and the results quantified. It would be possible to do this on a sample of records from a museum collection, although one should be wary of the amount of work involved. In comparing manual and automated retrieval the differing time taken to produce results would also have to be taken into consideration. If this method is applied to a standard terminology, such as a thesaurus, it tests two distinct things: the quality of the thesaurus itself, and the quality of its application to the body of data. It is certainly possible to have a well-constructed thesaurus which has been applied ineptly.

Importance of the short description

Although we believe that the most effective way of creating a thesaurus and applying it to a collection is to input the raw data, and to use the data itself to create the thesaurus, we still recognise that it is very highly desirable to have a clear view of the method which is going to be used to create the thesaurus. In particular, this may have an effect on the initial record structure, and on the way in which the data is entered in that structure.

The fields in a record which are used for subject retrieval do not exist in isolation from the rest of the catalogue record. This is obviously true in a trivial sense: at least some of the indexing terms will be derived from descriptive material elsewhere in the record, or related in some way to it. Many museums include in their record structure a Short Title (or Brief Description) field, which is a summary in about ten words of what the object is and why it is interesting. In the Science Museum in London this is the exact equivalent of the traditional Inventory Description — the formal statement of the nature of the item for which the Museum is responsible. In the National Army Museum an identical field evolved through the Photographic Caption, which had been conceived as the caption which would have been written for a photograph of the object, whether or not such a photograph existed. Short Title data, so useful in subject retrieval, exists for only a

igure
0.2 The relationship between the short description of an object and the sources of subject information

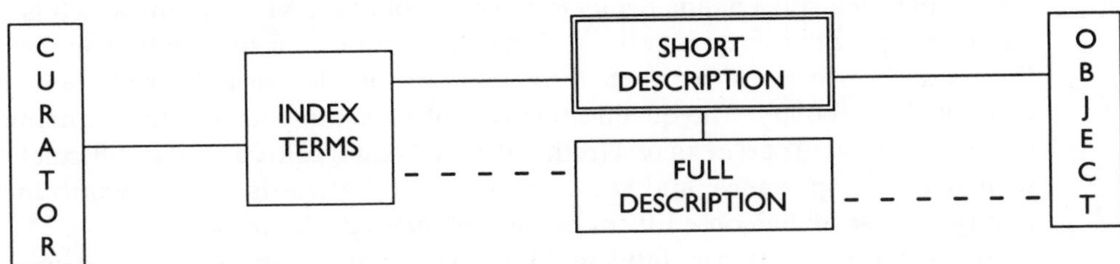

proportion of NMS collections, and it is thus having to be extracted from data in other fields of the records at the time when data capture takes place.

Two Short Titles for objects in the NMS collections are:

Gold lunula from Auchentaggart, Dumfriesshire

Seal of the Cathedral Chapter of Brechin, inscribed S. CAPITVLI. SANCTE. TRINITATIS D' BRECHIN, 14th century

What is the use of the Short Title? Consider the process of finding the object or group of objects which are relevant to an enquiry. The curator makes an initial search based on index terms. This will typically produce a number of hits. It is possible at this stage to examine full catalogue records,but probably rather time-consuming. It is more effective to use the Short Title for each object, either by examining the Short Titles directly, or by carrying out a free-text search on them. At that stage the enquirer is likely to want to see the objects themselves. The relationships between the concepts being discussed are illustrated schematically in Figure 20.2.

For all kinds of retrieval — place-name, owner's name, or whatever — the Short Title is of vital importance. It provides a brief and immediately intelligible summary of what the object is, who made it or used it, and perhaps where it came from. It may be compared to the title-page of a book. Since it is in free text, it is sensitive to peculiarities of naming and use (such as trade names and dialect words and obsolete spelling) in a way that a controlled language never can be. The Short Title provides a way of resolving tensions or ambiguities in the relationship between the actual object and the formal terminology which has been used to index it.

If the Short Title is used in conjunction with other fields which are controlled by a thesaurus, it will be much easier to introduce new words in the Short Title than in thesaurus-controlled fields, since updating the thesaurus will require a curatorial decision (probably at a senior level) and also a decision by the documentation specialists. Much less formality is needed in changing a Short Title.

English, Scots and Gaelic

Apart from English, there are two languages in use in Scotland: Scots and Gaelic. Both were more widely used in the past than they are now. Many names for objects in our collections come from these languages: Scots words such as Jougs and Crusie, and Gaelic words such as Quaich and Clarsach. There are also English nouns which have different meanings in Scotland — most dramatically the Maiden, known to the rest of the world as the Guillotine.

There is much geographical variation in the Scots language, and objects relating to farming and to domestic life often have different names depending where they were made and used. If we are to retain contextual information about our collections, a sensitivity towards these words is needed. A concern with these terms can also be taken to be a part of a concept analogous to the concept of literary warrant which is used in librarianship, with two qualifications. Literary warrant is the justification on the basis of the frequency of use of terms in a body of literature for selecting indexing terms to use in a controlled vocabulary. The qualifications about museum data are, firstly, many of the dialect words were part of an oral (rather than a literate) culture, so it is difficult to assess their relative importance; and secondly, some of the words may be worth including purely because of their obscurity or because of their very local use.

Fortunately our database software (Minisis) has a multilingual thesaurus, and we will use this to handle the two additional languages. Most of the Gaelic and Scots terms will occur in the English-language thesaurus at the most specific level of naming. For example, Clarsachs will be a narrower term of Harps. Although most of the Gaelic and Scots words will be names of objects, some will be more general, such as the Scots Plenishings (for Furniture). Our present intention is to use the multilingual facilities in Minisis to isolate the Scots and Gaelic words so that they are accessible through a route which is not cluttered up with terms from other languages. We see the benefit of the extra effort required to create this multilingual thesaurus, in addition to using the same words in the general thesaurus, as being justified by the opportunities it offers for research.

Afterword

One final piece of context, which may be taken to illustrate how trivial the problems are of data management. The glory of the National Museums of Scotland is a small reliquary. As a specimen of ninth-century metalwork it is exquisite. It was probably made to hold relics of the most famous of the early Christian saints in Scotland — St Columba, founder of the Abbey at Iona. On the greatest day in Scots history, in June 1314, it was carried at the head of the Scots army marching to Bannockburn. It is difficult to conceive a single object with a more remarkable combination of aesthetic, religious and political significance. This, in Gaelic, is St Columba's Brecbennoch.

21 SMITHSONIAN STRATEGIES FOR TERMINOLOGY CONTROL: A PEOPLE-DEPENDANT PROCESS

Jane Sledge

Office of Information Resource Management
Smithsonian Institution
Washington, DC

Introduction

The Smithsonian Institution's 14 museums and the National Zoo are the world's largest museum complex, holding some 135 million objects and specimens in trust for the 'increase and diffusion of knowledge among men.' The collections represent broad-ranging interests on, under, and beyond the earth, with ancient and contemporary Asian, African, North and South American art and cultural objects, as well as core samples from below the oceans and rocks and meteors from strange corners of the universe. The Smithsonian even stores some of its objects on the moon.

In the midst of this diversity, a 'strategy for institutional terminology control' is a misnomer. Terminology control is carried out through an emphasis on strategies to promote communication and understanding. These strategies build the context in which data standards, thesauri, vocabulary lists, authority files, coded values, and other traditional forms of terminology controls develop. An enquiry into the overall organisation and context of Smithsonian information precedes the creation and use of appropriate terminology within individual data fields. The word 'control', as in exercising authority, having a dominating influence over or holding in restraint, is not part of the Smithsonian vocabulary. Precision, tenacity, perseverance, vigilance, and opportunity better describe the work.

The institutional strategies are multidimensional. That is the strategies are not linear: one strategy does not stop where another starts. A single strategy supports or uses other strategies; everything is interwoven. The strategies for communication and understanding are:

- teamwork;
- data standards;
- an information architecture methodology;
- creative attitudes;
- management committed to long-term solutions.

In discussing information strategies, there is often an unspoken assumption that the strategies are for a particular system using particular software and hardware. While the Collections Information System (CIS) is a rubric which incorporates collections-related information, it does not necessarily mean a single system. CIS encompasses information from the following Smithsonian museums:

- Cooper-Hewitt Museum of Art and Design;
- Freer Gallery of Art;
- Hirshhorn Museum and Sculpture Garden;

National Museum of African Art;

National Air and Space Museum;

National Museum of American Art;

National Museum of American History;

National Museum of the American Indian

National Museum of Natural History;

National Portrait Gallery;

Arthur M. Sackler Gallery;

National Zoological Park.

Within these museums some six million automated records exist on different hardware and software, including the SELGEM batch computer system operating on a Honeywell mainframe, Wang networks in the National Museum of American History and the National Museum of American Art, a variety of microcomputer applications, and, since 1986, a new online system using INQUIRE on an IBM mainframe. This last facility is gradually replacing SELGEM. Given this variety of equipment, the phrase 'insurmountable opportunity' might seem like an appropriate description for the desire to develop integrated systems using institution-wide data standards. Past experience suggests that such a task is not impossible as the strategies noted above seek to gradually enrol staff to establish common objectives.

Teamwork

The chief strategy to enrol staff in common objectives is teamwork. The Smithsonian concept of teams is as multi-dimensional as its strategies. At the Smithsonian the concept of teamwork is not exclusive or competitive, as an individual can be a member of several teams at the same time, all moving towards the same large objectives. Teamwork serves as a means of broadening support, interest and understanding for CIS. This is important given the Smithsonian's size. Teamwork provides a context for widespread staff participation in discussions to provide insight about the different requirements the CIS must support. The focus is on information rather than on particular systems or terminology. Teamwork acknowledges the importance of distinctions without implying that one point of view is more important than another. Understanding the distinctions between terms and ideas provides a rich context in which to organise information. For example, the CIS must support both the analytical vocabulary of the conservator (i.e. methyl methacrylate copolymer resin) and the vernacular vocabulary of the cataloguer (i.e. acrylic resin) when recording the material composition of the object.

Data standards

Teamwork and data standards are not usually synonymous. A commonly held view of vocabulary or terminology control concedes this area of research to discipline specialists. The Smithsonian uses teamwork in the area of data standards to create an environment to support synergetic relationships between discipline specialists and information specialists. Precise data element definitions and formats result from the interaction provided by teams of information specialists and discipline specialists.

The rule book for data standards is a *Data Administration Standards Manual*, which defines formal guidelines for the definition and use of data elements to ensure

Figure 1.1 Example of data element documentation, Smithsonian Institution

```
CS1                                                        PAGE      2
           D A T A   C A T A L O G  2           REPORT DATE-      01/19/88
                                                REVISION NUMBER-        86
             E N T R I E S   R E P O R T        LAST REVISION DATE- 01/19/88
                                ART DATA   -   D R A F T


 CATALOG NAME                       TYPE
 ------------                       ----
  CDE-ADDRESS                       ELEMENT



                         CONTROL

           STATUS=PROPOSED

                         CLASSIFICATION

           CIS
           MIS
           MAIL
           NMAA
           NPG
           HMSG
           FREER
           CHM
           NMAFA
           SACKLER
           LIBRARY
           ART


                         DESCRIPTION

           IDENTIFIES THE REASON WHY AN ADDRESS IS MAINTAINED TO
           ACCOMMODATE A PERSON HAVING MORE THAN ONE ADDRESS.

                         ORIGIN

           DEPARTMENT=STANDARD                        GENERATED=NO

                         VALUES

           VALUE=R   RESIDENCE
           VALUE=T   TEMPORARY
           VALUE=V   VACATION
           VALUE=B   BUSINESS
```

consistency and continuity in systems design and implementation (Smithsonian Institution, 1986). The underlying tool supporting the *Standards Manual* is an automated data dictionary (Data Catalog 2) under the control of a data administration group in the Office of Information Resource Management (Toney, 1988). The data dictionary consolidates and organises all information used within CIS and other Smithsonian systems. The CIS data dictionary now holds about 1 200 individual data elements. Figure 21.1 is an example of the data element documentation. This is a page from the data dictionary which documents 'CDE-ADDRESS', a field used across several Smithsonian systems: collections, bibliographic, mailing, etc. The Classification category lists the different users of this field. All the fields in the data dictionary use a three letter code to start the field name, to identify the type of data the field will hold: a code (CDE), a count (CNT), a flag (FLG), an identifying number (IDN), a location identifier (LOC), a measurement (MEA), a name or term (NAM), a date or time (TME), or a piece of text (TXT). The data dictionary also holds alternate names for the same field, so that the user can apply a shorter or a more familiar name to a date element, and alias names for mapping data to a physical application. The data administration group builds the ground for positive communication among the people who develop and the people who use the data standards.

Information architecture methods

Data standards and teamwork are not enough: they do not solve all the problems. Automating a poorly organised and maintained manual system without solving the causes of the problems will result in automated systems with the same problems occurring at an even faster pace. Stafford Beer noted:

> '... again we are concentrating on slicker ways of doing things rather than what we do. What is the use of the ever-faster, ever slicker, more nearly perfect implementation of rotten plans? ... The question which asks how to use the computer in the enterprise, is, in short, the wrong question. A better formulation is to ask how should the enterprise be run given that computers exist. The best version of all is the question asking what, given computers, the enterprise now is.' (Beer, 1972)

Information architecture, the third strategy, provides an opportunity to study what we do and the information we need to get the job done. In planning for automation using the information architecture project, museums and offices have the opportunity to research and understand how business is done and to develop long-term plans for improvement and change.

The success of information architecture depends upon the strategies of teamwork, creative attitudes, and project management committed to long-term solutions. Within the Smithsonian many projects, including the information architecture project, compete for resources. While participation in the information architecture project is voluntary, there is an increasing number of museums, offices and people who consider information architecture a lifeboat in the complex sea of computer technology.

The information architecture project has two distinct components: functions (what is done) and data. Using facilitated workshops, the functional component first produces models which describe what the Smithsonian does now, not the best way or ideal way in which things 'should' be done. Figure 21.2 is a simplified piece of the functional business model 'Provide Physical Care For Collections', a diagrammatic description of the components of the provision of physical care. In addition to functional business models

Figure 21.2 Functional business model

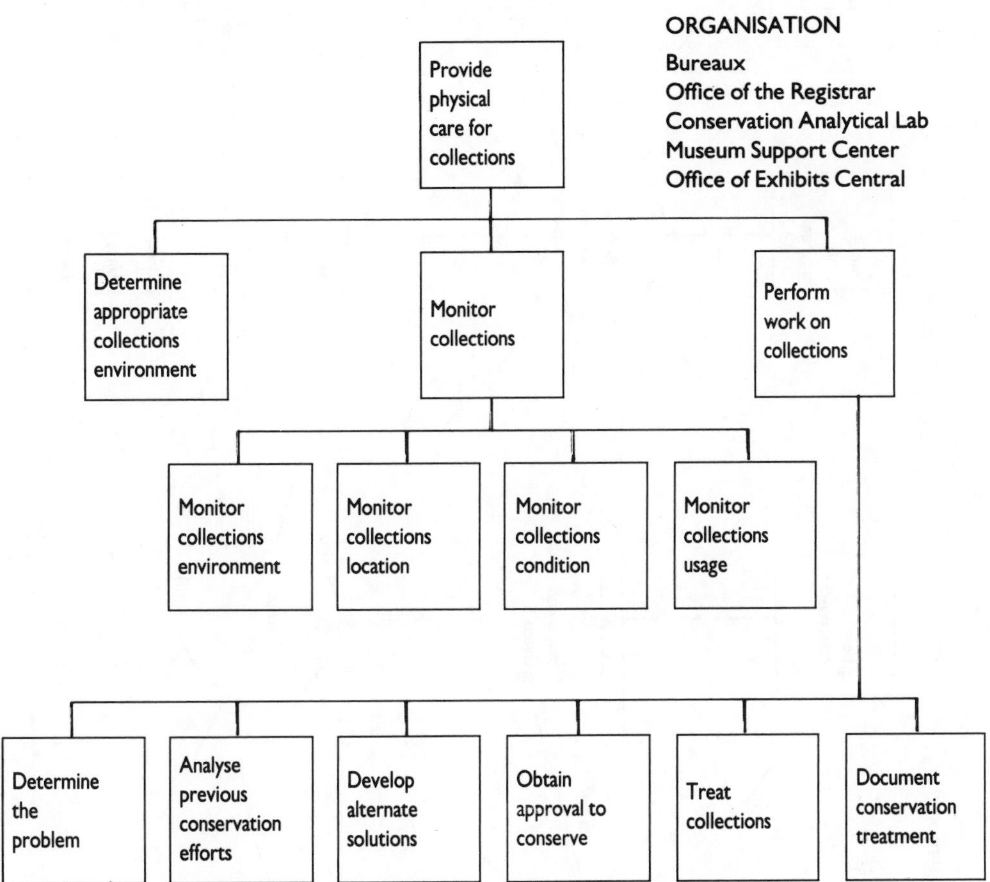

reviewing a single function, information usage models show how the different functions interrelate to accept, create and store information. Figure 21.3 is a simplified companion information usage model to 'Provide Physical Care for Collections'. The information usage models document Smithsonian functions. This includes the sources and destinations of information outside the Smithsonian and the stores of information maintained or used by the Institution such as catalogues, curatorial files, and even staff knowledge and experience. Understanding what is done provides an opportunity to reconsider and evaluate better means of achieving objectives. This is documented in a second set of future business models.

Within the realm of CIS, functional analysis raises questions about the interconnections between collections management, research, and communications or public programmes. These three collections-related functions are the subject of an in-depth study by the National Museum of American History. The project has strong management commitment and the active involvement of over 100 staff in 'facilitated' workshop sessions. Another functional analysis project within the Museum Support Center, a major off-site storage and conservation centre for Smithsonian collections, studies

Figure 21.3 Simplified information usage model

Object care reference materials
Knowledge and experience
Move collections
Manage public programs
Contract for required conservation
Plan space
Determine appropriate collections environment
Smithsonian objects
Perform work on collections
Manage resources
Manage research
Collections information files
Collections condition files
Monitor collections
INFORMATION USAGE MODEL
PROVIDE PHYSICAL CARE
FOR COLLECTIONS
Collections location files
Internal audit track
Plan to move objects
Determine method of disposal
Plan collections

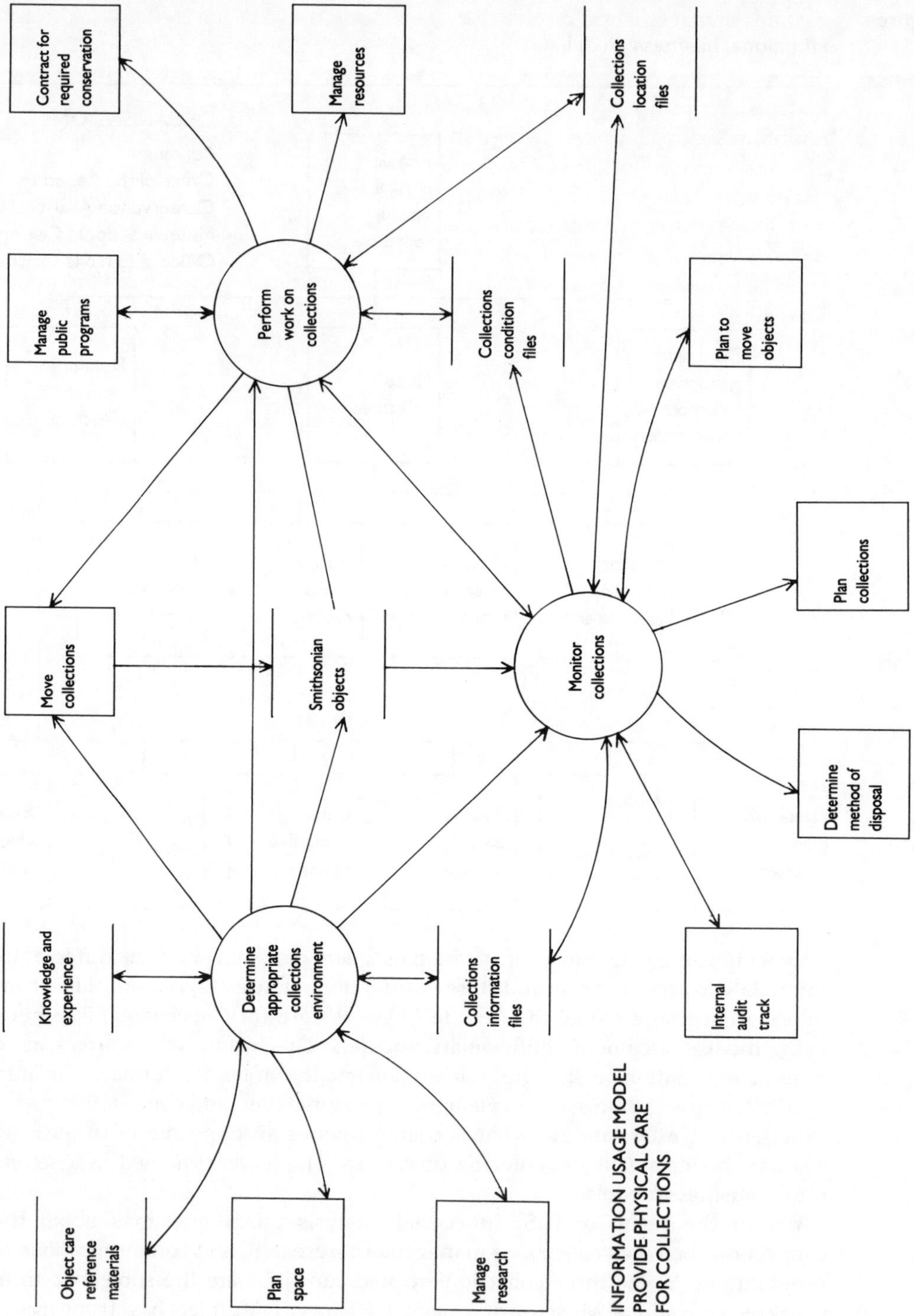

facilities management requirements. It is important to tie the facilities for object storage and exhibition to the physical care requirements of the object. Smithsonian objects have different lighting, humidity, temperature, access, and risk management requirements to match with the capabilities of our facilities. Through the information architecture project, multidimensional thinking relates all areas of activity which will use CIS data, not just the obvious one of collections management.

The other major part of the information architecture project, data modelling, identifies and defines the data required by the Smithsonian and the relationship between groups of data known as entities. An important distinction separating the data modelling phase from the functional analysis phase is that there are no actions or functions in data modelling. The diagrams say nothing about who does what with what information. This separate study of the data, without consideration of functions or automated systems, serves as a blueprint for the data required for CIS. Information architecture provides a development and testing ground for data structures.

Facilitated workshops produce data models identifying entities (persons, places, things, concepts and events) of interest to the Smithsonian. Data models re-shape opinions about the organisation of data for storage and retrieval. Through the identification of data entities, each data element receives a 'home' : a place where it fits into the data structure. The model enables the identification of shared data opportunities, or overlaps with different areas recording the same data in different systems, turning potential conflicts into opportunities.

An example of such an opportunity recently occurred when the Smithsonian Office of Membership and Development considered extending their commercially purchased system to track donors of major gifts to the Smithsonian. The Office requested access to pertinent information held in CIS. The Membership and Development Office and CIS have the opportunity to use the same data standards to track donors, be they donors of cash gifts and in-kind services or donors of objects to the collections, and eventually to integrate the information. Information architecture promotes consistent development of common data standards across all Smithsonian systems to further the possibility of system integration. The ideal is to store one piece of data once in a given system and provide accountable access.

With Pat Reed, Data Administrator and a key member of the data administration group, managing the data modelling project, the art community took primary responsibility as a test user group for data modelling. Rachel Allen refers to the results of this work in Chapter 92. The initial project identified the major groups of data needed by art-related users of CIS to support what they do.

What is so valuable about data modelling? Data modelling re-shapes ideas of data structures by allowing users to see how to express more with less. An example of this is the development of the idea of roles and role players. In a study of the fields needed to support the various roles of people in regard to objects, the existing SELGEM records held: artist, engraver, lithographer, calligrapher, printer, founder, poet, sitter, source, lender, borrower, etc. The data elements describing people marked a tendency to confuse data values (the contents of fields) with data elements (the names of fields).

The advantage of the structure proposed in the data model is that the name of a particular role player occurs only once in the role player's file. A role player entity links to one or more roles (by combining the role player and the role) as often as necessary, with each occurrence containing links as required to objects, events, or geography, etc. The role file expands as necessary to include new roles as new data values are identified. The extension of this concept to other entities such as materials (i.e. what role — medium, support, mount, base, etc. — does a particular material play in the construction of the object) is now being tested. Tests are conducted by taking component pieces of the model and inserting data into the relevant fields to determine whether the results of queries provide the answers expected. It occurs to the data modelling team that the idea of roles and role players might also extend to natural history to note predator-prey, host-parasite, symbiotic, and pollinator relationships among specimens.

Most important here is the structure in which to store data. Data modelling provides a structure which organises and groups data elements together. Relationships are specified between groups of data. The relationships among data groups are as important as the data elements within the data groups. The systematisation of museum information depicts a complex network of associations between people, objects, time, geography, style and motif, etc., as noted by Janet Stanley in her discussion of African art data and thesauri (Chapter 53). When the data modelling team began its effort members realised, from collective past experiences, that they had previously tried to control individual pieces of data and terminology without a framework within which to understand, build and test associations. The data modelling effort provides a tool in which to organise and classify data types.

While the concept of role player is significant to the data model, a second major form of data structure was also influential throughout the model. The form organises different but similar pieces of data which would have once been separate fields into a single field. This concept is exemplified by Pat Reed's development of a new data structure for audio-visual technical information depicted in Figure 21.4. Among other things, she created a repeating data group containing a field called 'technical descriptor' to name the type of audio-visual qualitative feature — playback speed, sound type, noise reduction, bias, etc. — and a second field to identify the value or term in the field. The data modelling team realised that there is no end to the various kinds of technical descriptors or features needed for audio-visual materials, and that there is no way to specify all the fields in advance. Creative thinking and judicious design work increased the capability to hold data while maintaining integrity and retrievability. This concept easily applies to a

Figure 21.4 Audio-visual technical descriptors

Playback speed

Values: 1–⅝, 3–¾, 7–½, SP Mode, LP Mode, SLP Mode

Sound type

Values: Monophonic, Stereophonic, Quadrasonic, Hi Fidelity, Silent

Noise reduction

Values: Dolby, ANRS

Bias

Values: High, Medium, Low

hierarchial organisation of 'geographic place types': continent, country, state, province, city, suburb, neighbourhood, etc., with the second field holding the associated value of place-name.

Creative attitudes

Teamwork, data standards and information architecture methods require support from the fourth strategy: creative attitudes. Without a creative attitude the information architecture project might never have begun. The creative attitude is exemplified by a characteristic feature of the data modelling meetings. Data modelling workshops are difficult because there are no ready answers. The data modelling process requires an investigation into the nature of our data rather than a supply of ready answers. Participants put forward opinions, seek information from colleagues, admit they do not know the answers, and struggle to discover what is unknown. The result is that participants discover things 'they didn't know that they didn't know'. David Nicoll writes:

> 'The meaning of knowledge comes from the context; all "facts" are relational and contextual. We are finding that what counts in a multiplex world is willingness and ability to find those perspectives — social, psychological, historical, spacial, etc. — that provide the most functional interpretation of our situation. We are teaching ourselves to let go of our drive for the ideal form and to find value in a universe that is made up of multilayered, interpenetrating levels of diverse reality.' (Nicoll, 1984)

Terminology control is more than a prescribed list of terms or vocabulary to be used in a given field. At the Smithsonian, staff inquire into the interaction between the individual recording the data and the data itself. There is no 'ideal form', everything is shaded by the social and cultural context of the recorder. This aspect became clear in the discussions of the different types of role players: individuals, organisations including governmental organisations, and cultural groups. The data modelling team confronted a tendency to relegate the first peoples of North America to 'cultural groups' rather than to acknowledge tribal nation status. The concept of a cultural group is now encompassed by organisations, formal and informal.

Management committed to long-term solutions

Supporting the development and use of data standards and information architecture methods requires a creative attitude from Smithsonian management. Management must have an extraordinary commitment to contribute resources and patience to produce and carry out long-term widespread solutions to manage our information resources. Managers have problems: not enough money, not enough space, not enough staff, not enough time and too much work. Managers expect automation systems to solve problems and to produce immediate benefits. Neither automation by itself nor terminology controls will solve the problems of mis-attributed information, incomplete information, missing information, out-of-date files, a lack of storage space, or a backlog of uncatalogued items (Sarasen and Neuner, 1983). The ultimate computer, in which problems go in and are immediately solved, does not exist.

Conclusion

The Smithsonian has unavoidable constraints. Data must be migrated from the older computer system (SELGEM) to CIS. Staff at the Smithsonian do not live in an ideal world as hardware, software, and data constraints prohibit immediate use of many of the ideas formulated through the information modelling studies. The state of Smithsonian data does not now support easy conversion to relational database structures. Rachel Allen discusses later the use of transition databases as an interim strategy to provide a development and data clean-up laboratory to bring us closer to relational systems (Chapter 92). By making dreams into plans, plans will eventually turn into reality.

The Smithsonian is a large bureaucracy with competing priorities. People often ask: 'How will the Smithsonian manage to turn its dreams into reality?' A recent article noted that an organisation really contains two organisations, one with articulated goals and the other, lying quietly under the surface, which actually determines what will happen in the long-run. This second organisation is called the 'organisational unconscious'. If change is imposed without obtaining agreement from the unconscious, or if change ignores other underlying, unspoken commitments, then it will be thwarted.

> 'We hear a lot about people resisting change, but this is often resistance to change that others impose upon them without their participation in its development. Most of us are eager to participate in changes that we create ourselves, particularly when we share that creative activity with others.' (Allen and Kraft, 1984)

The institutional strategies of teamwork, data standards, information architecture methods, creative attitudes, and management committed to long-term solutions involve staff in the process of creating and stating their own requirements for information structures, context and use. Specific field-level terminology controls will eventually result from this effort. Given the nature of the enquiry, it is expected that how we think of terminology controls today may not be how we think of them in the future.

V
CONTROLLING PERSONAL AND CORPORATE BODY NAMES

22 CONTROLLING PERSONAL AND CORPORATE BODY NAMES

Dr Leonard D. Will

Acting Head of Research and Information Services Division
Science Museum
London

Proper names of people and corporate bodies might be thought to be relatively straightforward compared with the complexities of subject terms. People generally have a 'correct' name, as recorded on their birth certificate, and corporate bodies usually have a 'correct' name under which they do business.

Unfortunately things are more complicated: changes of name, variant forms of name used simultaneously or successively, differences in fullness, additions to names, nicknames, pseudonyms, unknown names, identical names for different people, and language and transliteration differences, all make it difficult to decide what a person's name is; and corporate names bring in the additional problem of subordinate bodies in complex hierarchical structures, often with historical and geographical ramifications. Even when a 'correct' name is determined, there are still many problems in deciding how that name is to be used, either for indexing purposes or when simply displaying it as part of the information in a record of a museum object.

Two stages are necessary in standardising a vocabulary, whether of names or anything else. First we must define the rules we are to apply, and secondly we must compile an authority file showing the results of applying these rules to specific cases, so that once a decision on a form of name is made it will be applied universally. If there is good reason to change a decision, then it should be possible to make the change in one place and have it take effect automatically throughout the system rather than having to change each occurrence individually. These ideals are seldom put into practice, but they are what we should aim at in the long term. As with subject indexing, we must recognise that a name is just a label to allow us to identify and retrieve items related to a particular person or body, and that to do this efficiently it is often more important to achieve consistency than pedantic correctness, which may often be a matter of unresolved argument.

This problem has been recognised and addressed for many years in the field of documentation and library cataloguing. The primary key to most publications is the name of the author, and the second edition of the *Anglo-American cataloguing rules* (AACR2) (Gorman and Winkler, 1988) deals exhaustively with the choice and form of names. Before embarking on new projects to devise rules for recording names in museum records, we must think very carefully whether there is a real necessity to use something other than AACR2. As with the IBM PC, there are overwhelming advantages in using the same standards as everyone else, even though there may be some things about them which we do not like.

An early booklet on museum documentation (Roberts, 1976a, pages 23–25) includes a diagram of a museum's databases split into a 'relational' structure, with separate files to hold information about objects, biography and bibliography. The intention was that these should be linked so that related information could be combined for retrieval without its having to be stored in more than one place. Modern online computer systems give us the capability to implement this structure in a much more comprehensive way than was possible a decade ago, linking many different files within and outside an organisation, on all types of computer. It would be possible to devise such a structure while using different forms of names in each file, but the advantages of simplicity and efficiency all seem to lie with standardisation.

The six papers in this section address these questions. The first four are primarily concerned with the names of artists, one deals with titles of regiments in the British Army, and the last describes an index of corporate names of art museums and galleries. The predominance of art in these papers does not mean that this is simply a concern of curators of art objects: almost every item in a museum collection has some names associated with it, and the same problems arise whether we are recording production, association, acquisitions or loans.

The major name authority file which has been compiled by the International Repertory of the Literature of Art (RILA), as described in Chapter 23 by Gillian Lewis, is a significant resource for the whole art museum community. As the Library of Congress name authority file was one of the primary sources drawn upon, these two files should be compatible, allowing users to choose headings from either of them without conflicts. The RILA *Verification Manual* seems very comprehensive, and would be of value to many other users if it were made generally available, but the sample contents page shows that it covers many topics which are also dealt with by AACR2, and it would be reassuring to know whether the compilers of these two manuals are working closely together. There may be need for two publications with different emphases for different applications, but we must ensure that the underlying rules and principles are the same.

In developing the use of computers to do the bulk of the work of identifying variant forms of name, Dr Marilyn Schmitt and her colleagues have produced a valuable tool to help achieve the consistency for which I am arguing. Automation makes it more practicable for a limited number of professional staff to clean up a large file by applying their expertise to the final judgements rather than to the initial grouping.

I cannot help feeling, though, that the Getty Union List of Artist Names, described in James Bower's paper, is dodging the problem by presenting a group of alternative names in a 'neutral matrix' without showing one as a preferred form. Certainly modern computer systems should be able to retrieve an item directly in response to a request for a non-preferred form, but I hope that the system will show clearly which forms are most in accordance with standard rules; without this, a great deal of unnecessary professional time has to be spent in every institution deciding which one to use, and different choices will still be made and variant rules developed. It may be that we shall not record names at all when cataloguing on a computer, but just the 'Getty cluster number'; we shall still have to decide what to print when the name is to appear in a catalogue.

Robin Dowden describes the practical application of many of these points in an account of the work at the National Gallery of Art, Washington, DC. There they have established an authority file of names which can be linked with other databases as required. Headings are in accordance with AACR2 and in conformity with the existing authority lists of the Library of Congress and RILA where possible, and while direct access from non-preferred forms is available, the preferred form will be indicated. This is surely the right way forward.

British regimental titles provide a very different and very complex set of headings, whose arcane mysteries seem to prevent the use of alphabetical entries at all. Boris Mollo shows how the National Army Museum has found it better to use a classification system.

As with all classifications, though, an index is still needed to translate the name which the enquirer brings to the system into the classification code, and unfortunately we do not know how the problems of alphabetical entry in the index are dealt with. Perhaps browsing through the classified listing is the only way in.

Finally, Dr Colum Hourihane describes the experience of the Witt Computer Index in recording corporate names for museums and galleries. They have devised their own rules, re-inventing some differently-shaped wheels in the process. Inversion of personal names at the start of corporate names is intuitively attractive, but there are too many cases where the inversion is not obvious: for example, what should we do with the 'Mary Rose Ship Hall and Exhibition', 'Lady Stair's House', and 'Tam O'Shanter Museum' or the 'Hewlett Packard Company'? AACR2 says that the main entry should be in the direct form, with references from inverted forms where required. There is room for much discussion, but the retrieval problem will become of less importance as more intelligent computer systems allow us to match names regardless of the order in which we input their component words.

23 AUTHORITY CONTROL AT RILA

Gillian H. Lewis

Associate Editor
RILA International Repertory of the Literature of Art
Sterling and Francine Clark Art Institute
Williamstown, Mass.

Introduction

The *International Repertory of the Literature of Art* (more familiarly known as *RILA*) is a bibliographic service of the Getty Art History Information Program. It is an abstracting and indexing tool for current publications in the field of art and is published twice a year. *RILA* covers world-wide literature on Western art from Late Antiquity (fourth century) to the present and includes all types of print publications. Each issue of *RILA* is divided into two sections: a classified section giving bibliographic citations and abstracts of the contents and a detailed index that provides many access points to each bibliographic entity (Figures 23.1 and 23.2). The various names and subjects that make up the index are subject to authority control and what follows is a brief description of *RILA*'s experience in developing controls over personal and corporate names.

In addition to discussing *RILA*'s past and current practices, there will be some consideration of the future. Authority work, along with other aspects of *RILA* work, will be considerably affected by its merger with the *Répertoire d'Art et d'Archéologie* (the *RAA*), scheduled to take place in 1989. This paper will cover the history of authority work at *RILA*, the *RILA Verification Manual*, our procedures for verifying names, the automation of the *RILA* authority files, the part the authority files will play in the processing of bibliographic records in the future for the *RILA*/*RAA* merger, and the effect of the merger on future authority work.

History

The history of verification at *RILA* is tied closely to the history of the publication and has grown and developed along with it. *RILA* first published a demonstration issue in 1973 and regular production began with the 1975 volume. Publication of two issues a year began with the 1976 volume and continues at this time. We have also published two cumulative indexes, each covering five volumes and five years. A record of the verification research for the names in the demonstration issue was not always retained, but the names were each placed on a 3 × 5 inch card. These cards became the nucleus of our card authority file which has now grown to 102 catalogue card drawers containing well over 100 000 names. The file consists of personal names, corporate bodies, geographic names, buildings and other structures, works of art, conferences and manuscripts. Subjects consist of approximately an additional nine catalogue card drawers containing around 7 000 terms.

Names were at first recorded on plain cards with cross references and brief source information added on the face of the card. Later a card was designed which could function as a work card during verification procedures and as the authority card that is filed into the authority file. *RILA* verifiers use the same card for every type of name and record their research findings and any needed references in pencil directly on to the front and back of these cards. Cards can be revised and updated as necessary.

Figure 23.1 Classified section in *RILA* subject index

MEDIEVAL ART: 59 Artists and architects

On an illuminated manuscript of Jacob van Maerlant's *Rijmbijbel* (i.e. an adaption in Middle Dutch verse of Peter Comestor's *Historia Scholastica*), dated 1332 and signed by Michiel van der Borch (MS 10 C 21, Rijksmuseum Meermanno-Westreenianum, The Hague). Reproductions of all illuminations.

1600 [CAVALLINI, P.] BOSKOVITS, Miklós. **Proposte (e conferme) per Pietro Cavallini** [Proposals (and confirmations) concerning Pietro Cavallini], *Roma anno 1300: atti della IV settimana di studi di storia dell'arte medievale dell'Università di Roma "La Sapienza" (19-24 maggio 1980)* (RILA 13 119) 297-329. *43 illus.* In Italian.
Chronology and attributions.

1601 [CAVALLINI, P.] BRANDI, Cesare. **Pietro Cavallini**, *Roma anno 1300: atti della IV settimana di studi di storia dell'arte medievale dell'Università di Roma "La Sapienza" (19-24 maggio 1980)* (RILA 13 119) 13-16. In Italian.
Discusses questions of chronology and influence, particularly the influence of Byzantine painting of the Palaeologian period and of Giotto.

1602 [CAVALLINI, P.] POESCHKE, Joachim. **Per la datazione dei mosaici de Cavallini in S. Maria in Trastevere** [On the dating of Cavallini's mosaics in S. Maria in Trastevere], *Roma anno 1300: atti della IV settimana di studi di storia dell'arte medievale dell'Università di Roma "La Sapienza" (19-24 maggio 1980)* (RILA 13 119) 423-431. *7 illus.* In Italian.
Compares the medallion with the Madonna and Child in the donor mosaic of S. Maria in Trastevere, Rome, with that in the mosaic over the tomb of Boniface VIII (by Arnolfo di Cambio) formerly in Old S. Peter's. Argues that Cavallini's mosaic post-dates the tomb; that is, the S. Maria in Trastevere cycle must have been completed after ca.1296.

1603 [CAVALLINI, P., SCHOOL] CARDILLI ALLOISI, Luisa. **Affreschi cavalliniani presso il Laterano** [Cavallini school frescoes near the Lateran], *Roma anno 1300: atti della IV settimana di studi di storia dell'arte medievale dell'Università di Roma "La Sapienza" (19-24 maggio 1980)* (RILA 13 119) 449-456. *10 illus., plans, elevations.* In Italian.
On the fresco cycle decorating the oratory of S. Margherita in a tower of the Aurelian wall between S. Giovanni in Laterano and S. Croce in Gerusalemme, Rome. Attributes the frescoes to followers of Cavallini in the first half of the 14th c.

1604 [CIMABUE] CORDARO, Michele. **L'abside della basilica superiore di Assisi: restauro e ricostruzione critica del testo figurativo** [The apse of the upper church at Assisi: restoration and critical reconstruction of the pictorial cycle], *Roma anno 1300: atti della IV settimana di studi di storia dell'arte medievale dell'Università di Roma "La Sapienza" (19-24 maggio 1980)* (RILA 13 119) 119-125. *8 illus.* In Italian.
In the light of recent restorations, considers the effect of losses and repainting on the attribution and identification of scenes in the apse frescoes of the upper church of S. Francesco, Assisi. Attributes some of the ornamental painting in the apse to the workshop of the Northern Master. Discusses problems of identification of individual scenes and figures in Cimabue's *Life of the Virgin* cycle, particularly the standing figure to the right in the *Dormition of the Virgin*, here identified as S. Paul.

1605 [CIMABUE] WHITE, John; ZANARDI, Bruno. **Cimabue and the decorative sequence in the upper church of S. Francesco, Assisi**, *Roma anno 1300: atti della IV settimana di studi di storia dell'arte medievale dell'Università di Roma "La Sapienza" (19-24 maggio 1980)* (RILA 13 119) 103-117. *7 illus., diags.* In English.
Following the campaign of restoration in the choir and crossing of the upper church (1979), analyzes the sequence of the mural paintings: the work carried out under the Northern Master in the upper part of the north transept, the *Four Evangelists* by Cimabue and his workshop in the crossing vault, followed by their work on the lower walls.

1606 [CONSOLO] CRISTIANI TESTI, Maria Laura. **Consolo: il Maestro del busto di Innocenzo III e i collaboratori negli affreschi del S. Speco di Subiaco** [Consolo: the master of the *Bust of Innocent III* and fresco painters in Sacro Speco, Subiaco], *Roma anno 1300: atti della IV settimana di studi di storia dell'arte medievale dell'Università di Roma "La Sapienza" (19-24 maggio 1980)* (RILA 13 119) 403-411. *12 illus.* In Italian.
Contrasts the style of the painter of the *Bust of Innocent III* and related works with that of Consolo (Magister Conxolus) and his assistants in the fresco decoration of the lower church (late 13th and early 14th cs.).

1607 [DUCCIO DI BUONINSEGNA] SMART, Alastair. **A Duccio discovery: an early *Madonna* prototype**, *Apollo* CXX/272 (Oct 1984) 226-237. *18 illus. (1 col.).* In English.
Attributes a previously unpublished *Madonna and Child* of the *glykophilousa* type in a private collection to the young Duccio (ca.1280-1285). Discusses stylistic connections between Cimabue and early Duccio. Identifies the new painting as the prototype of the Pératé *Madonna* by a follower of Cimabue (ca.1285-1295; Louvre, Paris) and of the Oberlin *Madonna* by a follower of Duccio (ca.1285; Allen Memorial Art Museum, Oberlin).

1608 [DUCCIO DI BUONINSEGNA] WALKER, Richard W.; BARKER, Godfrey. **Getty fails to acquire Duccio**, *Art News* LXXXIII/8 (Oct 1984) 21-22. *1 illus.* In English.
Describes the struggle between the J. Paul Getty Museum, Malibu, and the City Art Gallery, Manchester, to acquire the *Crucifixion* by Duccio formerly in the collection of the Earl of Crawford and Balcarres, and sold at auction in 1976. The City Art Gallery succeeded in matching the purchase price offered by the Getty.

1609 [FRANCESCO DI NERI] KREYTENBERG, Gert. **Das Pollinigrabmal im Bargello und der bildhauer Francesco Sellaio** [The Pollini tomb in the Bargello and the sculptor Francesco Sellaio], *Antichità viva* XXIV/1-3 (Jan-June 1985) 112-117. *9 illus.* In German; summary in English.
Examines the style and chronology of the tomb of Cione di Lapo Pollini (Bargello, Florence), for which a date of either 1313, inscribed on the tomb, or 1348, the year of his death, has been suggested. Proposes an attribution to Francesco di Neri and a date of ca.1370. The execution of the tomb so long after the death of Pollini may be explained by the Pollini family's desire to demonstrate visually their patronage of S. Maria della Scala (the original location of the tomb, now called S. Martino della Scala) at that time. Discusses other works by Francesco di Neri. *(Antichità viva)*

1610 [GADDI, T.] ESMEIJER, Anna C. **L'*Albero della vita* di Taddeo Gaddi: l'esegesi "geometrica" di un'immagine didattica** [The *Tree of Life* by Taddeo Gaddi: the geometric exegesis of a didactic image]. Edam; Firenze: Istituto Universitario Olandese di storia dell'arte, 1985. 26,[11] p. *10 illus., diags.* In Italian. [Translation of: *Lignum Vitae: een visueel-exegetisch leerbeeld "more geometrico" gedemonstreerd.* Assen: Van Gorcum, 1981].
Analyzes the composition of Gaddi's fresco in the former refectory, S. Croce (now Museo Dell'Opera di S. Croce), Florence, concluding that the artist applied a theological geometry, based on S. Bonaventura among others, in order to resolve the problems of exegesis. Notes the significance of Gaddi's work for the development by Florentine artists of decorative programs in refectories in the 15th c.

1611 [GIOTTO] BATTISTI, Eugenio. ***Body language* nel ciclo di San Francesco ad Assisi: una introduzione al problema**, *Roma anno 1300: atti della IV settimana di studi di storia dell'arte medievale dell'Università di Roma "La Sapienza" (19-24 maggio 1980)* (RILA 13 119) 675-688. In Italian.
Analysis of the gestures in the *Scenes from the Life of S. Francis*, upper church of S. Francesco, Assisi, by Giotto or one of his assistants.

117

RILA subject index

SUBJECT INDEX

castles, Swedish *(continued)*
Skokloster, 17th-19th cs., 2702
castles, Swiss
towers, 12th-13th cs., 1023
Vaud, Gothic revival, 19th c., **2872**
Castres (FRA), Musée Goya, painting, Goya, F.J. de, *Company of the Philippines*, 3633
catacombs, *see also* **Early Christian catacombs**
catacombs, Italian
Abruzzo, Early Christian, 794
Chiusi, Catacombe di S. Caterina, **852**
Morlupo, Cimitero ad vicesimum, **4th** c., 855
Rome, Catacombe di Generosa, 4th-9th cs., 853
—— Catacombe di S. Callisto, 4th-5**th** cs., 844
—— 17th c., 1707
—— 4th-5th cs., 337
catafalques, Italian, Modena, Este family, 17th-18th cs., 1730
catalogues
Great Britain, furniture, *Cabinet-makers' London book of prices*, 2069, 3233
—— furniture, 18th-19th cs., 3243
—— prints, 17th-19th cs., 1934
Netherlands, Hope, J., collection, **1959**
catalogues raisonnés
Algardi, A., sculpture, 2156
and connoisseurship, 177
Barocci, F., painting, 2181
Bastien-Lepage, J., 3363
Bega, C.P., 2190
bibliographies, 11
Bilivert, G., 2209
Carracci family, prints, 2258
Cavael, R., 3435
Coter, C. de, painting, 2291
Dove, A.G., 3526
Drewes, W., prints, 3528
Fischer, Fritz, illustrated books, **4565**
Francillon, R., 3589
Giovanni di Pietro, 2363
Haden, F.S., 3654
Hoffmann, J.F.M., architecture, **3676**
Kertész, A., photography, 3707
Lobo, B., sculpture, 4709
Louis, M., painting, 4713
Perugino, painting, 2517
Poussin, N., painting, 2551
Redon, O., prints, etching, 3906
Rembrandt, painting, 2575
Schaefer, C.F., prints, 3969
Venne, A.P. van de, painting, **grisaille**, 2686
Victors, J., 2700
Ward, J.Q.A., sculpture, 4081
West, B., 4086
Wright, Joseph, 2716
Catalonia (region, ESP)
art, Medieval, **648**
painting, 12th c., 1342
—— 20th c. (1980s), 4358
views, illustration, Parcerisa y **Boada, F.J.**, 3865
Cataluña (region, ESP), *see* **Catalonia (region, ESP)**
Catania (ITA), S. Agata (cathedral), architecture, Vaccarini, G.B., façade, 2680
catechisms, Italy, illustration, 16th c., **1971**
Catena, Vincenzo di Biagio, Italian painter, ca.1470-1531, influence on Bello, M., 2194
cathedrae, Italian
Bernini, G.L., 1456, 1491
Vassalletto family, 1643
cathedrals, *see also* **Anglo-Saxon cathedrals; Armenian cathedrals; Carolingian cathedrals; Early Christian cathedrals; Gothic cathedrals; Medieval cathedrals; Romanesque cathedrals**
Holy Roman Empire, 10th-14th cs., **924**
cathedrals, British, 257
Canterbury, Christchurch, 6th-11th **cs.**, 771
Dunblane, 13th c., 845
Iona, cathedral, 12th-16th cs., 1021
Peterborough, 13th c., 816
Worcester, cathedral, 11th-15th cs., **875**
cathedrals, early Netherlandish
Hertogenbosch, 's, S. Jan, 13th-15th cs., 701
Liège, S. Lambert, 12th c., chancel, **900**
cathedrals, French
Bayeux, Notre-Dame, 13th c., 1005
Coutances, Notre-Dame, 13th c., 895
Paris, Notre-Dame, 1085
—— Notre-Dame, 13th c., 589, 918
Reims, Notre-Dame, 13th c., 925
—— Notre-Dame, 9th c., 783
technology, 12th-13th cs., 1006
Thérouanne, 12th-15th cs., 753
—— 14th c., adjunct buildings, 754
cathedrals, German
Altenberg, 13th c., 813
Bremen, S. Peter, 899
10th-14th cs., 924
cathedrals, Italian
Otranto, SS. Annunziata, 12th c., 914
Pisa, cathedral, 12th-13th cs., 789
Spilimbergo, S. Maria, 13th-15th cs., 865
cathedrals, Russian, Echmiadzin, cathedral, 4th-5th cs., 992
cathedrals, Spanish, 203
cathedrals, Swiss
Bern, S. Vincent, 13th-16th cs., 871
Geneva, 4th-5th cs., 761
Catherine de' Medici, queen of France, 1519-1589, entry into Paris (FRA), (1549), 1748
Catherine II the Great, empress of Russia, 1729-1796, patronage, pottery, Wedgwood ware, 3246
Catherine of Alexandria, S., manuscript illumination, early Netherlandish, 13th c., 1306
Catherine of Aragon, queen of England, 1485-1536, marriage celebrations, 2391
Catherine of Siena, S., 1347-1380, art, 15th-16th cs., 328
Catherine-wheel windows, *see* **rose windows**
Catholic Church, *see also* **Byzantine Rite; papacy**
and Reformation, bibliographies, 18
France, opposition to theater, 17th-19th cs., 1785
—— property, secularization, 18th c. (1790s), 3546
iconography, painting, Veronese, 2695
Switzerland, Assens, S. Germain, 1860
use of religious images, 16th c., 1971
Catholic Reformation, *see* **Counter-Reformation**
Caucasus (region, SUN), *see* **Kavkas (region, SUN)**
Caulfield, James, viscount Charlemont, *see* **Charlemont, James Caulfield, viscount and earl of**
Caulfield, Patrick, British painter, printmaker, b.1936, and Hodgkin, H., 4634
Caus, Salomon de, French architect, physicist, engineer, ca.1576-1626, influence of gardens, Italian, Pratolino, Villa Demidoff, 1755
Cavaceppi, Bartolomeo, Italian sculptor, restorer, 1716-1799
sculpture, *Portrait Bust of a Cardinal*, Minneapolis (MN, USA), Minneapolis Institute of Arts (attributed), 2266
terra cotta, *Flora*, Berlin (DEU), Staatliche Museen Preussischer Kulturbesitz, Skulpturengalerie, 2266
Cavael, Rolf, German painter, printmaker, 1898-1979, 3435
cavalcades, *see* **festivals**
Cavalier Calabrese, *see* **Preti, Mattia**
Cavallini, Pietro, Italian painter, ca.1250-ca.1330, 1219, 1600, 1601
influence on Giotto, 1615
monuments, tomb of Matteo d'Acquasparta, Rome (ITA), S. Maria d'Aracoeli, lunette fresco (attributed to Cavallini, P., school), 1621
mosaics, Rome (ITA), S. Maria in Trastevere, 1602
painting, *Last Judgment*, Rome (ITA), S. Cecilia in Trastevere, 1319
—— Rome (ITA), S. Cecilia in Trastevere, 681
Cavallini, Pietro, school
monuments, tomb of Matteo d'Acquasparta, Rome (ITA), S. Maria d'Aracoeli, lunette fresco (attributed), 1621
painting, Rome (ITA), Oratorio di S. Margherita (attributed), 1603
—— *S. Lucy*, Grenoble (FRA), Musée de Peinture et de Sculpture (attributed), 1267
Cavallino, Bernardo, Italian painter, 1616-1654/56
painting, *Lot and His Daughters*, Toledo (OH, USA), Toledo Museum of Art (attribution discussed), 1932
—— *Triumph of Galatea* (art market), 1932
Cavazzoni Zanotti, Giovan Pietro, *see* **Zanotti, Giampietro**
Cavedone, Giacomo, Italian painter, 1577-1660, drawing, Paris (FRA), Musée national du Louvre, Cabinet des dessins, 2267
caverns, *see* **caves**
caves, *see also* **grottoes**
caves, Greek, Santorin, 532
Cavour (ITA), S. Maria (Benedictine abbey), church, architecture, 11th c., 801
Cazes, Pierre Jacques, French painter, 1676-1754, decoration, Versailles (FRA), Hôtel de Ville, 1877
Cebej, Anton, Yugoslav painter, 172[illegible] 1774, painting, Slovenia (YUG), 1945
Cecchino de' Salviati, *see* **Salviati, Francesco**
Cecilia, S.
iconography, 16th-17th cs., 2445
sculpture, Maderno, S., 2445
celebrations, *see* **feasts; festivals; rites and ceremonies**
Celle, Pierre de, French, bishop of Chartres, theologian, ca.1115-1183, monuments, tomb, Lèves (FRA), Benedictine abbey, Notre-Dame de Josaphat, 1209
Cellini, Benvenuto, Italian sculptor, goldsmith, author, 1500-1571, 2270
drawing, *Young Man Dressing*, Milan (ITA), Ambrosiana, Biblioteca (attributed; subject proposed as Narcissus), 2269
forgeries, Vasters, R., 4071
writings, treatises on goldsmithing, 2268
Cellole (Campania, ITA), S. Marco, painting, Medieval, 1224
Celmins, Vija, American artist, b.1939, iconography, 4510
Celtes, Conradus, *see* **Celtis, Conrad**
Celtic manuscript illumination, *see* **Hiberno-Saxon manuscript illumination**
Celtis, Conrad, German humanist, poet, 1459-1508
influence on Burgkmair, H., the elder, 2311
writings, *Amores*, illustration, Dürer, A., 2311
cements, mortars, and plasters, *see also* **masonry**
Great Britain, Brixworth, All Saints, 8th c., 746
cemeteries, *see also* **Anglo-Saxon cemeteries; Carolingian cemeteries; catacombs; Early Christian cemeteries; Frankish cemeteries; Germanic cemeteries; Lombard cemeteries; Medieval cemeteries;**

Verification Manual

The purpose of the *RILA* Name Authority file is to ensure consistency and accuracy in the published product, by standardising and controlling the use of names in the indexes. The file is intended to record *RILA*'s established standardised version and the variant forms and spellings of names. It is also meant to preserve a record of the references that have been made from headings that have not been used to those that have been used. The manual is designed to help build the Authority file as smoothly and consistently as possible. It is a set of rules with examples and exceptions and is similar in many respects to a cataloguing manual.

The writing of the *Verification Manual* was an ambitious attempt to organise the many *RILA* rules which had been formulated and written down over time but which were not always easily located (Figure 23.3). Developed for house use, it is especially useful for training purposes and to answer questions. In 1987, it was completely revised in order to try to reflect future policy for the *RILA/RAA* merged publication. It is still not complete and we are gathering items and revisions to include in a new edition. As we continue to set policy and conduct tests, we make editorial changes which have an effect on verification practices and on the manual. We are fortunate to have some very experienced staff members who know not only what our policies are, but also what we did in the past and, more importantly, the reasons we had for changing policy. They provide a crucial sense of history for the organisation and valuable support for the authorities work.

The *Manual* is organised with general information first followed by chapters on personal names, geographic names, corporate bodies, buildings and other structures, references, and titles of works of art. Appendixes contain sample verification cards, lists of national, cultural, and geographic designations, biographical descriptors, secular and ecclesiastical titles, and architectural, corporate, geographic, and art descriptors, as well as lists of abbreviations, and rules for capitalisation.

Verification procedures

Verification is the process of determining the existence of a person or other entity, and of establishing the form that should be used for the heading. It also involves determining the relationships of the heading to any other headings, and establishing the necessary connecting references.

Verification usually involves consulting a number of bibliographic sources, which can include not only the traditional reference sources — biographical dictionaries, encyclopedias, directories, gazetteers, etc. — but also any monographs, periodical articles, and museum and exhibition catalogues which may contain information about the person or entity being established. Preference is given to art historical literature, and because *RILA* uses many vernacular forms of names, preference is given to sources published in the language of the person or entity under consideration.

Information uncovered in the course of research is frequently contradictory or ambiguous and interpretation must therefore be left to the individual judgement of the verifier. It is sometimes necessary for the verifiers to consult together or with the *RILA* editor who produced the indexing and abstract. The Authorities Editor has to render a decision when there is a lack of consensus or a difference of opinion.

The verification process begins once abstracts have been completed and the editor has proposed index entries. These are checked against the Authority file by the verifiers and edited to conform to previously established entries, or the Authority file is corrected and

Figure 23.3 *RILA* verification manual

CONTENTS

updated in the light of new information, which may be drawn from the publication in hand. This process allows for continuous maintenance and updating of the existing file based on new information found in the current literature. Care must be taken, however, to ensure that new information is generally accepted.

Any proposed index entries that are not found in the file are then researched to determine the form that the headings should take and the references that should be made.

An important aspect of the verification process is the determination of appropriate sources. The *Verification Manual* contains a bibliography that is intended as a guide to suitable reference sources that are available in the library in which we conduct most of our research. The bibliography is neither exhaustive nor exclusive and is subject to on-going revision.

General reference sources, such as dictionaries, encyclopedias and directories, are useful but are often not sufficiently specialised. National biographical dictionaries are authoritative sources for the establishment of names, as are the *National Union Catalog* from the Library of Congress and authority files available on fiche and on the bibliographic utilities such as the Research Libraries Information Network (RLIN) and the Online Computer Library Center (OCLC). Sources in the language of the subject, even when not scholarly, are useful for establishing entry elements and for orthographic policies. A variety of sources are consulted and different approaches tried in order to solve a verification problem.

An important aspect of verification is the recording of sources so that the research trail is well-documented. It is useful to record not only where information was found, but also where it was not found. Relevant information from each source searched is recorded so that it can be used to establish an entry heading. This procedure also makes it possible to see the pattern of agreement and disagreement among different sources and makes it possible to reconsider verification decisions when necessary without replicating every step. This information is useful later when weighing the importance of new evidence or at any time when re-evaluation is necessary. Bibliographic citations should be precise and accurate but abbreviations can be used for standard sources and page numbers can be omitted if the information is easily accessible.

Authority records are subject to revision and/or augmentation as new information is received. A history of the revisions to each part of a name including the nature of the changes and the reason for the change is recorded. If for example, a date is changed because of new evidence, the record will indicate this and cite the source of the new information, rather than merely giving the new date.

RILA verifiers devote differing amounts of time to the researching of names. Some names are found quickly and easily and there is no disagreement about the form they should take. Others are complicated by numerous versions or confusions in dates and still others cannot be found at all. Many names take only a few minutes to research satisfactorily but others can take a great deal longer and involve some extensive reading and consultation. Verifiers typically complete the research on several hundred authority records a month, with the number dependent upon experience with *RILA* practices and sources as well as skill.

Personal names

Entries for persons are categorised as artist or non-artist. Because artist entries are especially critical to *RILA*, verification of artist entries is somewhat more stringent than

igure 3.4 Biographic record illustrated in the *RILA* verification manual

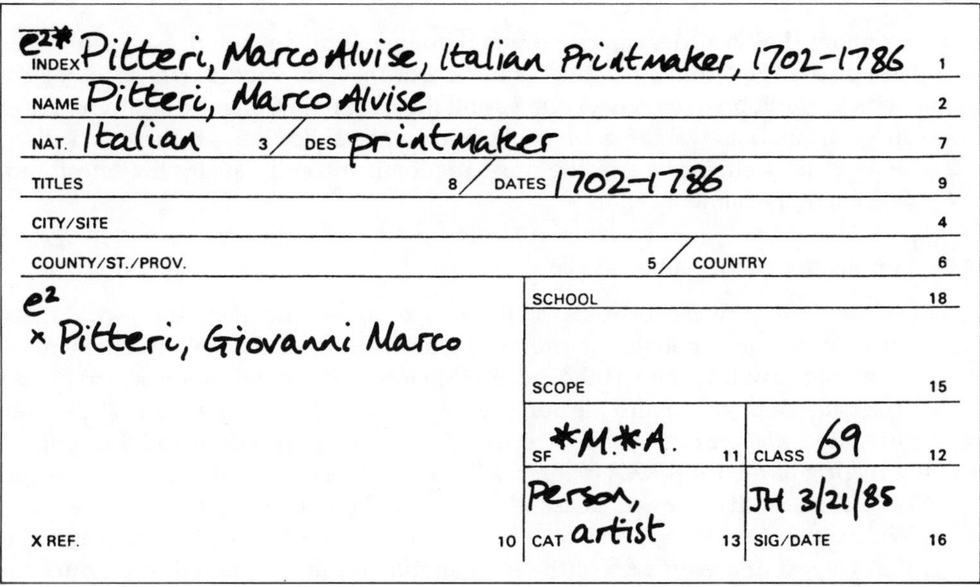

e²* INDEX Pitteri, Marco Alvise, Italian Printmaker, 1702-1786 1
NAME Pitteri, Marco Alvise 2
NAT. Italian 3 / DES printmaker 7
TITLES 8 / DATES 1702-1786 9
CITY/SITE 4
COUNTY/ST./PROV. 5 / COUNTRY 6
e²
× Pitteri, Giovanni Marco
SCHOOL 18
SCOPE 15
SF *M.*A. 11 CLASS 69 12
X REF. 10 CAT Person, artist 13 SIG/DATE JH 3/21/85 16

HISTORY 17
✓ WITT (Marco Alvise [Giovanni Marco], 1702-1786)
✓ TB (= WITT, engr, etch, metal-cutter)
✓ Bolaffi (Marco, 1702-1786)
SOURCES 14

* Indicates *RILA* vol. no. where used

that of non-artist entries. Artist entries are confirmed ideally by two or more sources, preferably of different types. Non-artist entries include many categories, for example, historical figures, religious leaders, patrons, sitters for portraits, collectors and scholars. One source which does not conflict with the document being indexed is generally sufficient for verification of non-artists.

Traditionally *RILA* has provided very full information about a person. In addition to the name we may also supply numeration, an alternate name in parentheses, one or more titles, a qualifier, nationality, biographical descriptors and dates (Figure 23.4).

Dates may include a combination of birth, death, and activity dates and may be qualified by before, after, circa or a date range.

Corporate bodies

Corporate body entries can be extremely complex and difficult to establish, especially in the case of government entities and bodies that are subordinate to other corporate bodies. Traditional reference sources and the Library of Congress authority file are used in verification as well as guidebooks and local publications. If there is a discrepancy among the sources we use the most predominant and usually the latest and fullest version of the name.

Automation of the Authority file

RILA's Authority file consists of the single large card file discussed above. When operations were automated at *RILA* the preferred terms and cross references from this file were made available on its inhouse microcomputer. To obtain sources and histories and to see all headings the card file must be consulted. Names in the file can be looked up by the editors and entries can be corrected by the Authorities Editor and the verifiers.

As part of the *RILA/RAA* merger, *RILA* will be assuming all the authority work at its offices in Williamstown, Massachusetts. Bibliographic forms will be created in Williamstown, in Paris, and in our European centres. With publication planned for four times a year and with each of the merging publications expected to produce the same number of entries as they have in the past, it is expected that authority work will at least double. Instead of doing the verification work for 10 000 bibliographic records annually, it is anticipated that we will be working on 20 000 records. As the two publications currently overlap in their coverage, the elimination of duplication will result in increased coverage of Scandinavia, Eastern Europe and South America. These are areas which *RILA* has not covered in depth in the past and for which we have not completed much authority work. Some of this authority work may present special problems, especially as we will be dealing with a larger number of bibliographic records for which we do not have hard copy of the article or monograph being indexed. We will be dependent upon the editors to supply us with as much pertinent information as possible.

Not only will the amount of verification increase with the merger, but some of our methods will change also. In the spring of 1987, work was begun on the design of microcomputer-based authority files for the *RILA/RAA* merger. By the autumn of 1988 all the files were designed and installed in the *RILA* offices and the authority file data had been divided among them. Instead of one large authority file there are now five: personal names, geographic names, corporate bodies, conferences and works of art. The geographic and the corporate body files, although separate, are linked.The record for each corporate body contains fields for the geographic location. The geographic file can be searched from the corporate body file and once the appropriate place name is selected it can be inserted into the corporate body record.

We used the computer system to divide the Authority file. We are now in the process of keying in the sources and the history which is contained on the card for each name and checking that each name is correctly parsed into its respective fields with each element entered into a separate field. In the process we are finding names which need to be revised to bring them into conformance with current policy or to make them compatible with the needs of the merger, as well as the names for which no verification was recorded. We are also entering all new names added to the Authority file since our original data load. Once we have entered all our data into the automated files, the card file will become obsolete.

Our authority files are currently mounted on three Compaq Deskpro 386/25 computers each of which has a 300 Mb hard disk and a tape utility with 135 Mb capacity. These computers are fast and powerful and the tape utility enables us to back up our files on tape in one operation, an important consideration when dealing with a large quantity of data. Leasing rather than owning these computers has permitted us to upgrade already to more powerful machines with greater memory. In late 1988, each of these machines contains data that cannot be accessed from other machines, but we intend to link them into a network. Networking will enable us to access all of the authority files from any authority work station and in the future will also permit the editors to consult the authority files from their work stations while they are preparing bibliographic records.

Authority work will serve a dual function with the new *RILA/RAA* merged publication. In addition to controlling terms, it will also be the means of supplying a translation. While the bibliographic or classified portion of the publication will be in either English or French, with approximately half the records in each language, the subject index portion of the publication will be divided into an English and a French index, the one a translation of the other. Any term or name that will appear in the index must go through thesaurus processing in order to provide the terms of the other language. In order to pass thesaurus processing, which will be done prior to publication in Paris, every term must find an exact match in one of the authority files. In addition to doing the authority work in Williamstown, the office will be preparing new authority tapes to be sent to Paris each month for processing. For the past several months we have been testing this processing and we have found that problems can involve the authority records, the bibliographic records, or the programs that handle the processing. Our difficulties are compounded by the distances and time differences between Santa Monica, California, where the computer systems work is conducted in the Getty offices, Williamstown where all the authority work will be done, and Paris where the publication work will be accomplished.

Merger and effect on future authority work

In addition to the increased amount of verification that will be created, the *RILA/RAA* merger will also have an impact on the form of names as we increasingly move towards the use of the vernacular. In the future, our general rule for personal names and corporate bodies will require the vernacular name most commonly used by scholars in the field, as found in the literature. There are exceptions to this rule, especially for early names for which the choice of vernacular is in doubt and other names for which the vernacular is not commonly known. In those instances when the well established English-language version of the name is chosen over the vernacular, the name will also be verified in French.

Conclusion

This has been a brief overview of the ways in which *RILA* authority files have developed over the course of our history and a glimpse into the future. Although we are in the process of moving from a card file to an automated system, which will change the way in which our authority data is stored, it is unlikely that our research methods will change significantly. We have developed written policies and we attempt to follow them consistently. We hold staff meetings to discuss problems and we amend our policies as needed. All names are subject to revision if they come up for use again, but as a good percentage are used only once we expect a large amount of new verification with every issue. With the expansion of our verification responsibilities, *RILA*'s authority files will grow even more quickly and will become more far-reaching. It is an exciting if formidable challenge.

---

24 THE MUSEUM PROTOTYPE REVISITED: MATCHING ARTISTS' NAMES

Dr Marilyn Schmitt

Getty Art History Information Program
Santa Monica, CA

In 1983, the J. Paul Getty Trust assembled a consortium of eight US museums for an ambitious purpose: to develop cataloguing standards for museum objects and to establish the core of a system for centralised cataloguing.[1] After three years, the Museum Prototype Project, as it was called, discontinued its work as an active consortium, having assembled eight separate databases of paintings records. These databases were generously lent to the Getty Art History Information Program to be used for experimentation in the merging of data.

The eight databases offer certain advantages as experimental material. They span a considerable range of information, from the Middle Ages to the present and from most European countries as well as North America. The records are a manageable number, just under 12 000. Despite the fact that they were entered according to the same data structure and program and under the reconciling eye of Willoughby Associates during their rapid data entry, the differences in the ways data are expressed — between and even within museums — offer a vivid picture of the variety and lack of standards that can characterise museum data.

Description of the 'tool'

We began at the logical beginning, with artists' names. What we have almost completed is a 'tool', a set of algorithms that address most of the problems that commonly arise from variations in the composition of artists' names. Our intention is that it should be a great aid to authority work, though not a substitute for authority work.

Although there has been work done on reconciliation of names, but none that we know of reaches either the complexity or the 'cleanliness' of these algorithms. (By 'cleanliness' we mean the efficiency of correct matching of names and the low level of false matches.) We believe our work is distinctive in its comprehensive coverage of numerous problems, from simple to complex.

What do these algorithms, or comparison techniques as we also call them, do? First, they operate on two main fields: the Last Name, which was seen as the indexing name (whether it came first, as in Rembrandt van Rijn, or last, as in Jean-Auguste-Dominique Ingres); and the First Name, which contained all names not in the Last-Name field. Databases with a different or more complex data structure can be mapped to this simple breakdown, as we are presently doing with the very complicated name list of the International Repertory of the Literature of Art (RILA) (Chapter 23).

---

1. Participating museums: The Art Museum of Princeton University,the Boston Museum of Fine Arts, the J. Paul Getty Museum, the Solomon R. Guggenheim Museum, the Hood Museum of Dartmouth College, the Metropolitan Museum of Art, the Museum of Modern Art, and the National Gallery of Art.

The algorithms begin with the precise manipulations of characters similar to those in many spell-checking devices. The stripping of upper case, punctuation marks and hyphens further promotes this simple matching of characters.

Another group of algorithms performs string comparisons, though in a more complicated way than much string comparison work does. If initials have been substituted for names, even in an erratic way (as in William Seitz, William C. Seitz, or William Chapin Seitz); or, if a first name is excluded entirely (as in, simply, Matta versus Roberto Sebastian Antonio Echaurren Matta), the computer is instructed to ignore these large chunks of diversity.

Moving to still more difficult and unusual string comparisons, the techniques adjust for the inclusion of names within names, as in Hilaire Germain Edgar Degas versus simply Edgar Degas; or the extension of names, as in Francisco de Goya and Francisco de Goya y Lucientes.

Where all else fails, a set of what are called approximation algorithms find cases, for instance, in which one-third or more of the words in the first-name and last-name fields match. This helps especially with the transposition of names (as in Eugène Louis Boudin and Louis Eugène Boudin). It also reconstitutes diversely indexed names (for example Roger van der Weyden, which may be indexed under R, V or W). This last correction of diversely indexed names allows us to respect different cultural conventions of filing: For example, Antonello da Messina may be indexed under Antonello, Da, or Messina, depending on the country, institutional custom, or personal preference of the indexer. The word approximation algorithm joins all versions together.

To 'sweep up' after all these comparison techniques have done their work, a character approximation algorithm matches percentages of characters without regard for order or structure. This technique finds matches that cannot be found by other means, but it also matches names that have no intellectual relationship to each other.

The essential role of authority work

The approximation algorithms bring us to the issue of verification and authority work. If one distinction of most of these algorithms is their precision — that is, precisely refined restrictions that eliminate inappropriate matches — nevertheless, as we proceed from the more minute character corrections via the more gross string comparisons to the relatively crude approximation algorithms, the false matches do increase.

Even in the simpler techniques, only a human being can decide whether Joan Brown and J. G. Brown are the same person; or know that Tintoretto, Domenico Tintoretto, and Jacopo Tintoretto are most certainly different people; or know what to do with John James Audubon and John Woodhouse Audubon.

Make-up of the team

What we have, then, is a tool, a labour-saving device, but not a panacea. Its elaborate structure results from a diverse group of experts working in an empirical manner on real museum data. The Project Manager, who has maintained, with me, the direction of the project and overseen the decision-making, is an art historian, Susan Siegfried. A Systems Analyst, Robin Garcia, kept the project organised and oversaw database (as opposed to programming) functions such as report generators and the preparation of data for processing. Aaron Gross, the Programmer, designed the algorithms. An Authority Analyst, Julie Bernstein, working from a printout of the 6 000 names, had, before and during the programming, distilled the principles by which names failed to match. She then pitted herself against the computer to analyse the results of the algorithms. The dialogue between the Programmer and the Authority Analyst, refereed by the art historian/Project Manager and the Systems Analyst, was crucial to the refinement process. Two other art historians, James Smalls and Guy Wheatley, are presently verifying the matches and resolving authority problems. We believe the project could not have achieved what it has without this full mix and balance of experts.

Character of the information

Our elaborte effort to accommodate complex as well as subtle differences bespeaks a recognition that the world of art-historical information is full of variation. Our effort has been to recognise and to accommodate the differences that affect the construction and development of artists' names across time and space, for those variations themselves contribute to the study of the information.

Future plans

The steps remaining to be done include the streamlining of the package of algorithms to speed processing; the development of collocation routines; and the testing of the package against other name data from Getty projects.

We would hope to make this work available to institutions and projects that might find it useful. We would be very much interested to hear about potential use as well as about the form such dissemination might take. We are not in a position to become vendors or supporters of this software; rather we think in terms of publishing the code itself, and even of making the C-Languge programs available on tape for those with facilities to adapt it. The community's response will help us to decide our future course.

25 THE GETTY UNION LIST OF ARTIST NAMES

James M. Bower

Technical Information Specialist, Vocabulary Coordination Group
Getty Art History Information Program
Santa Monica, CA

Introduction

Control of personal names has been an ongoing task for many projects of the Getty Art History Information Program since their inception. Although the projects which constitute the Art History Information Program (AHIP) are very diverse, one primary area of commonality is the documentation of works of art, and of the people who create them. As the number and scope of AHIP projects has grown, a proportionately larger effort has been spent on the common task of researching, documenting, and applying these personal names.

Recognising the apparent redundancy of this labour-intensive and time-consuming research, the leaders of several AHIP projects began to investigate the possibility of pooling their separate artist authority files into a common resource to be shared by all. The five projects involved at this exploratory stage were: the Avery Index of Architectural Periodicals and the International Repertory of the Literature of Art (RILA) (Chapter 23), two of the principal abstracting and indexing services for art and architecture literature; the Witt Computer Index, an automated index of American paintings represented in the photographic archives of the Witt Library at the Courtauld Institute of Art; the Census of Antique Works of Art Known to the Renaissance; and the Provenance Index, a Getty project which documents the ownership and sale of European and American paintings. Eventually, two more projects expressed interest in collaborating on a merged union name list: the Foundation for Documents of Architecture (a consortium of institutions concerned with scholarly documentation of architectural drawings), and the Photo Archive of the Getty Center for the History of Art and the Humanities.

A merged database of artist names would offer its users two attractive features: first, its cumulative nature might minimise the expensive redundancy of name authority research performed by each contributor; and second, it would promote uniformity and compatibility among diverse projects using disparate computer systems as a first step toward potential long-term integration.

Vocabulary Coordination Group research

With these goals in mind, selected fields from the artist authority records of the five original contributing projects were merged in late 1986. The resultant database of about 50 000 names and cross-references, along with 'core' data elements of National School, Life Dates, and Artist Role, were presented, with a rudimentary browsing mechanism, at a meeting of AHIP project heads in February 1987 (Figure 25.1).

As the project heads considered this newly minted union list of artist names, they determined that the first step in its further development should be the design of an extended data format. This became the first task of the Vocabulary Coordination Group,

Figure 25.1 Sample display from Union Name List Browser (prototype, 1986/87)

```
            #================================================#
            | UNION NAME LIST BROWSER -- FORMAT 1 OF 3  |
            #================================================#
#============================================================================#
| Blackbeard, Bill, American author, 20th c.                              R |
| Blackburn, Ed, American painter, b.1940                                 R |
| Blackburn, Edmund, American ceramist, b.1947                            R |
| Blackburn, Henry, British journalist, 1830-1897                         R |
| Blackburn, James, 1803-1854; Australian architect                       A |
| Blackburn, James, Australian architect, 19th c.                         R |
| BLACKBURN, Joseph, American painter, op.1725-1778                       W |
| Blackburn, Joseph, British active in U.S. painter, act.1754-1763 %CA 18th %S   P |
| Blackburn, Joseph, British painter in USA, act.1754-1763                R |
| Blackburn, Michael, British painter, b.1950                             R |
| BLACKBURN, Morris A., American painter, 1902- %PB born-Philadelphia,PA.  W |
| Blackburn, Robert, American painter, printmaker, b.1921                 R |
| Blacker, Catherine, British sculptor, 20th c.                           R |
| Blacker, Catherine, see from Blacker, Kate                              R |
| Blacker, Kate, see Blacker, Catherine                                   R |
#============================================================================#
```

founded later that year with the charge to help coordinate the development and application of proper name vocabularies in Getty projects.

Design of the extended data format began in November 1987, with the collection of artist authority database specifications from each of the (now) seven participating projects. Working from these varied authority formats, the Vocabulary Coordination Group sought to identify those data elements relevant to a 'union' environment, and translate them into a conceptual structure for the merged database. This process resulted in the identification of four distinct types of data elements common to all seven authorities:

Names, the core of each file, recorded in both preferred and non-preferred forms according to the method of the individual project, and at varying levels of atomisation: that is, some projects recorded only the full name, while other separated names into smaller pieces — surname, forename, middle names, and titles;

Biographical data, including fields for nationality or school, life dates and roles captured for the first, experimental database, plus many other fields used to document biographical events and relationships;

Bibliography, meaning published or documentary sources from which the names and biographic data were established;

'Local' data fields such as sort names and processing data which were useful in the contributors' local systems, but which lost relevance in the context of a merged database.

The conceptual model built by the Vocabulary Coordination Group from these four data types represents a great enhancement over the first, experimental database in both quantity and quality of the data it supports. Quantity was improved by combining many

Figure 25.2 Union List of Artist Names — cluster display (prototype, 1988)

■■

---> Search = CORBUSIER

Cluster 7931	**Contributor**	**Brief Citation**
JEANNERET, Charles Edouard (French, La Chaux-de-Fonds, CH. 1887 - Roquebrune-Cap-Martin, F. 1965) CORBUSIER, Le	WITT	
Le Corbusier (1887-1965; architect, draftsman, author, mathematician, Bundesrepublik Deutschland, France) Jeanneret, Charles Edouard Jeanneret-Gris, Charles Edouard	FDA■	MEA
Le Corbusier (French architect and author, 1887-1965) Corbusier Jeanneret, Charles Edouard Jeanneret-Gris, Charles Edouard	AVRY■	LCNA
Le Corbusier (French architect, painter, 1887-1965) Corbu Jeanneret, Charles Edouard Jeanneret-Gris, Charles-Edouard Le Corbusier (Charles Edouard Jeanneret)	PHOA■	MEA
Le Corbusier (French architect, theoretician, 1887-1965) Corbusier Jeanneret, Charles Edouard Jeanneret-Gris, Charles Edouard	RILA■	
Le Corbusier (La Chaux de Fonds, architect, draughtsman, writer, theorist, 1887-1965) Jeanneret-Gris, Charles-Edouard	CENS■	
Le Corbusier (Charles Edouard Jeanneret) (French, 1887-1965) Charles Edouard Jeanneret Corbusier Jeanneret, Charles Edouard Le Corbusier	PROV	RILA

■■

■ AACR2-compatible form of name

specific biographic elements left unused in the first merged file into a flexible construct of relationships and events defined by combinations of related persons, places, and dates. Quality was improved by linking the *individual* names from the separate authority files into *clusters* containing multiple preferred and variant names for each artist (Figure 25.2). Formation of these clusters, we hope, can be largely accomplished with the use of name matching algorithms developed elsewhere within AHIP. These algorithms are similar to those used by library vendors to perform batch authority conversions, but are highly tailored to the distinct characteristics of artists' names (see Chapter 24).

Presentation of clustered names to users of the database presents a difficult conceptual problem. While the Union List of Artist Names is composed of data from Getty authority files, the list itself is *not* an authority file in the traditional sense: that is, there is no single bibliographic, pictorial, or object collection for which the Union List of Artist Names controls access points or descriptive elements. To elevate any one form of name to

igure
5.3 Union List of Artist Names — search display matrix (prototype, 1988)

```
---> Search = GENTILESCHI

4 clusters                                                      A C F G P R W

Artemiggia -- see Gentileschi, Artemisia
Artemiscia Gentoleschi -- see Gentileschi, Artemisia
Artemisia -- see Gentileschi, Artemisia
Artemisia Gentilesca -- see Gentileschi, Artemisia
Artemisia Gentileschi -- see Gentileschi, Artemisia
Artemitia Gentilesca -- see Gentileschi, Artemisia
Artemizia Gentilesca -- see Gentileschi, Artemisia
Artimisia -- see Gentileschi, Artemisia
Gentileschi                                                           P
Gentileschi -- see Gentileschi, Artemisia
Gentileschi -- see Gentileschi, Orazio
Gentileschi, Artemisia                                              G P R
     (Italian painter, 1593-aft.1651)  [G]
     (Italian painter, 1593-after 1651)  [R]
     (Italian, 1597-aft. 1651)  [P]
GENTILESCHI, Artemisia Lami (Schiattesi?)                                 W
     (Italian, 1597-p.1651)
GENTILESCHI, Francesco                                                    W
     (Italian, 1599-p.1665)
Gentileschi, Orazio                                                 G P R W
     (Italian artist, 1562-1647)  [W]
     (Italian painter, 1563-1639)  [G,R]
     (Italian, 1563-1639)  [P]
Horace Gentileschi -- see Gentileschi, Orazio
Lomi, Artemisia -- see Gentileschi, Artemisia
Oratio Gentileschi -- see Gentileschi, Orazio
Orazio Gentileschi -- see Gentileschi, Orazio
```

KEY			
	A	=	Avery Index of Architectural Periodicals
	C	=	Census of Antique Works Known to the Renaissance
	F	=	Foundation for Documents of Architecture
	G	=	Getty Center Photo Archive
	P	=	Provenance Index
	R	=	RILA
	W	=	Witt Computer Index

primary status would compromise the integrity of all names in a cluster. Thus, the Union List of Artist Names does not represent any name as the 'established Getty name'; it attempts instead to present the clustered names in a set of neutral matrix displays that will show to each user the similarity or variety of usage for all name forms associated with a single artist (Figure 25.3). The projects would then determine for themselves, according to their own criteria, whichever form of name is appropriate for use in their local authority file.

Typically — in libraries, at least — name authority work is performed according to prescribed rules and methods, the purpose of which is to determine the most authoritative form of a name. Over time, an authority file clearly reflects those criteria used in the formulation of its names, and systems using different criteria are likely to establish dissimilar names. The Union List of Artist Names, however, is not intended as an authority file, and thus can retain all of the names established according to the distinct and varied methods of its contributing projects.

Avoiding the bias of any *single* method, then, allows representation of a *multiplicity* of methods, and their resultant names, not limited to those adopted by Getty projects. Names from any authority system to which the data model can be mapped become candidates for inclusion in the Union List.

By corollary, the ability to *export* artist names to other authority systems is, in concept, limited only by the necessity to identify and isolate name forms that satisfy the criteria for authoritativeness established by the target system.

Future collaborative opportunities

Thus far this paper has sought to establish the *possibility* of the Union List adapting to multiple authority standards, but what about the *desirability* of doing so? The inclusion in the Union List of a non-Getty name from an external authority is desirable when it satisfies the need of a Getty project; for example, to catalogue a new painting or index a *catalogue raisonné*. By extension, dissemination of Getty names may be desirable when another authority system is used to control access to information of use to Getty projects.

Take, for example, the collections of the Library of Congress, which are rich in works *of* art and works *about* art. Description of those materials is done in accordance with Anglo-American Cataloging Rules, which are also used to determine forms of names entered into the Library of Congress Name Authority File, now containing nearly two million personal names. This authority file has accumulated names over many years and has been influential around the world because of the Library of Congress' distribution of cataloguing records, originally on printed cards and now on magnetic tape. Together, the richness of the Library's art holdings and the size of its authority file make it reasonable to suppose that many of the artist names likely to be used by Getty projects would already be represented in the Library of Congress Name Authority File — and that the Library of Congress could be a candidate source of names for the Getty Union List.

This assumption has been tested by comparing 800 sample names from two Getty contributors against the Library of Congress Name Authority File, available on the Research Libraries Information Network (RLIN). Four hundred names were randomly chosen from the RILA and Photo Archive authority files, to represent both the bibliographic and visual collections controlled by these projects. With some overlap among the sample name sets, the total test sample included 787 artist names.

Each name was searched in the Library of Congress Name Authority File; if a matching record was found, the match was characterised as an exact, close, recognisable, or possible match. Unmatched names were then searched again, in the bibliographic databases of the RLIN network, to discover if the name had been applied *without* control.

Only 20 per cent of the sample — one out of five Getty artist names — had *any* matching name in the Library of Congress Name Authority File. More interesting is the fact that 182 names — more than 25 per cent of the Getty names without Library of Congress correlates — were found used in RLIN bibliographic files without supporting authority records. Thus, on balance, it seems most promising for the Library of Congress to adopt Getty artist names, in order to control materials of mutual subject interest.

Returning to an earlier point; if the capacity to export names depends on the ability to satisfy the recipients' rules for establishing names, then the ability to disseminate artist names to the Library of Congress depends on the ability to provide names consistent with the Anglo-American Cataloguing Rules. A comparison of the revised Anglo-American Cataloging Rules (Gorman and Winkler, 1988) with the RILA manual for name verification has shown that the similarities outweigh the differences. Thus, the long-term possibilities for interchange of Getty artists names with those of external, widely-applied authorities such as the Library of Congress Name Authority File seem very promising.

Conclusion

Compilation of the Getty Union List of Artist Names has been undertaken principally as a means of fostering — without *enforcing* — consistent use of artist names among projects of the Getty Art History Information Program, and of eliminating redundant effort in the labour-intensive research of name authority control. The development of a conceptual data model unencumbered by arbitrary and universal designations of preferred and non-preferred names has allowed multiple integral Getty authorities to be successfully merged. In turn, those authorities can be mapped — to the extent that resources, systems, and programme interests warrant — to external name authorities embodying non-art historical methodologies which may control access to bibliographic, pictorial and object collections of great parallel interest.

26 THE DEVELOPMENT OF AN AUTOMATED ARTIST FILE AT THE NATIONAL GALLERY OF ART

Robin Dowden

National Gallery of Art,
Washington, DC

Introduction

In 1982 the National Gallery of Art began the task of compiling information on artists represented in the collections. The project entailed determining preferred and variant forms of artists' names and recording data pertaining to artists' biographies. This information would then be entered into a computer-based information retrieval system which would provide the Gallery with a mechanism for ensuring the consistent application of name headings and a means for collocating records for objects executed by the same artist. Initially the task seemed relatively simple: working from a card catalogue alphabetised by artist name, the names and basic biographical information for artists represented in the prints and drawings collection would be obtained. This file would be compared to a list of objects sorted by artist name pulled from the Gallery's existing computerised inventory system, in which information on all objects, excluding graphic arts, had previously been entered. A master artist file would thus be created, and the first step in the Gallery's effort to create an integrated online catalogue would be completed.

Within a fairly short period, the problems associated with creating an artist file became apparent. Because an assessment of the Gallery's records revealed that they were not a reliable source of artist information, the decision was made not to enter artist data directly from original records, but to formulate standards for determining form of name and procedures for documenting the authorities or sources consulted. The current file contains information on approximately 7 000 known artists in 9 300 records. This paper describes the procedures established in 1982 for controlling artists' names, the structure of the file as it exists today, and significant changes affecting name that will be implemented in the Gallery's new Art Information System scheduled for release in 1991.

Background and development of a computerised collections information system

The National Gallery of Art has in its collections roughly 68 000 objects: 62 000 graphic works including prints, drawings, photographs, and illustrated books; 2 800 paintings; and 2 500 objects classified as sculpture and decorative arts. Objects are divided among nine curatorial departments on the basis of object class (e.g. painting, sculpture, graphic art) and period.

The office of the Registrar is responsible for maintaining records on the entire collection. The initial plans for computerising this information stemmed from discussions with staff from the Detroit Institute of Arts (DIA) which took place at the 1979 Museum Computer Network (MCN) conference. At that time, the DIA was the only art museum in MCN using an online computer system to track the location of its art objects. Based on a study of the Detroit system, data processing personnel at the National Gallery developed the museum's first art system, the primary purpose of which was to improve the accessibility of information related to the location of the Gallery's art objects, and thereby expedite periodic physical inventories of the collection. Working from records maintained in the office of the Registrar and from published summary catalogues of portions of the collection, basic information on all objects, excluding graphic arts, was entered in an NCR system in 1980–81.

In 1982, with the procurement of an IBM mainframe computer, the Gallery prepared an information processing plan that detailed the development of an expanded art information system. Of the modules proposed in the 1982 plan, the file for recording information about persons related to the collections in the roles of artist/maker and source was the first developed and populated. The first version of the entire Art Information System was released in July 1983.

Retrospective conversion of manual records was completed in 1987, enabling the Gallery to switch from manual files to an online catalogue and realise the benefits and potential of an automated collections management system.

Artist file structure

The National Gallery artist authority file comprises two inter-related files: a computer file where validated artist data is entered, and a manual file where the sources consulted in establishing this information are documented. Each record in the computer file includes fields for recording artist name (entered last or index name first); nationality; place(s) of birth, death, and activity; birth/death or active dates; and sex (Figure 26.1). A remarks field is used for recording additional names by which an artist is known, which are to be concatenated with the preferred name in the generation of label copy or artist display name. The remarks field is also used for cross-reference notations in records established under an artist's non-preferred form of name.

Figure 26.1 Online authority record

```
                                                              AADDINQ1 3.0
                                 ARTIST INQUIRY
     ______________________________________________________________________
     NUMBER: 0013100       NAME: Greco, El
     ______________________________________________________________________

           GENDER: M


            DATES:              flag   START              flag       END
                                       1541                          1614


           COUNTRY: ESP    SPAIN
       NATIONALITY: Spanish
     PLACE OF BIRTH: Candia, Crete
     PLACE OF DEATH: Toledo
       ACTIVE PLACE:
           REMARKS: (Domenikos Theotokopoulos)
      ALSO IN NAME/ADDRESS SYSTEM: N

     ______________________________________________________________________
                                 PF15 = RETURN
```

Figure 26.2 Manual authority record

```
Grèco, El
     x: Theotokopoulos, Domenikos
     x: Theotocopuli, Domenico
Spanish, (Candia, Crete) 1541 - (Toledo) 1614

Brown, Jonathan et al. El Greco of Toledo, 1982 (NGA
   exhib.) Domenikos Theotokopoulos, Candia 1541-
   Toldeo 1614
NGA Lib. (AACR2-LC)  Greco, Spanish, 1541?-1614
   x: Theotocopuli, Dominico
   x: Theotokopoulos, Domenikos
   x: El Greco
RILA Authorities 1-11/1  Greco, El
   (Domenico Theotocopuli), Greek in ESP, 1541-1614
T.-B.XXXIII.4  Theotocopuli, Dominico
   Domenikos Zeotokopoulos; El Greco), Crete 1541 -
   Toledo 1614
```

Each artist record in the computer file is rendered unique through the assignment of artist identification numbers. Artist numbers are seven digits in length. The first six digits are unique to an individual or group, and the seventh digit identifies the master or preferred record (always zero), or 'alias' record (values 1 through 9) assigned to alternate names or the artist's preferred name followed by an attribution qualifier. Examples of attribution qualifiers are 'attributed to', 'follower of', and 'style of'. The artist number provides the link between artist and object records.

Artist authority information (the sources consulted in establishing an artist record), is recorded on index cards or worksheets organised by artist name in manual files (Figure 26.2). Modelled on the National Gallery library authority file, each authority record cites at the top verified headings and subheadings. Sources consulted are recorded at the bottom of the card/worksheet, identified by standard abbreviations. If any variations from the established form at the top of the authority record are found in the sources consulted, this information is noted to the right of the particular source. If none of the standard reference sources index the name being established, alternate sources (e.g. monographs or unpublished material) may be used. Whether a primary reference or alternate source is used, the authority citation should provide the facts necessary to both identify and/or reconsider the verification decisions at a later date.

Verification process

Prior to the Gallery's decision to computerise its object catalogue, the museum did not have specific rules or guidelines to standardise the form or content of collections data. Like many museums converting from manual to computerised systems, automation accentuated the inadequacies of past documentation practices in virtually every area of museum documentation.

Standards for establishing artist name were no exception. The work of a single artist could be found under various headings in the Registrar's artist file, as was also the case in the files maintained by the curatorial departments. Lacking a standard authority, the museum's curators consulted a variety of published sources, from general encyclopedias to scholarly journals, when either reviewing or adding artist information. While the Gallery had relatively strict formal procedures designed to ensure that new artist information was recorded in the central catalogue maintained by the Registrar, the degree to which such procedures were followed varied among curatorial departments. Documentation of the sources consulted in establishing artist information was equally inconsistent.

In 1982 having determined that the artist information in Gallery records would be subject to a verification process prior to computerisation, rules were formulated and external sources of artist information were evaluated. In so doing, we determined that the Gallery already had two artist name authority files: one maintained by the library and the other by the Photo Archives. While neither file was totally adequate for our purposes, we consulted the library file with some frequency and in large measure based our rules for verifying artists' names on theirs.

The rules governing the selection of artist name and entry element are derived primarily from the second edition of *Anglo-American Cataloguing Rules* (AACR2) (Gorman and Winkler, 1988). In general, AACR2 specifies that preference is given to the name by which a person is most commonly known from reference sources issued in his or her language or country of residence or activity. This may be the person's full or partial given name and surname, nickname, initials, or other appellation. Cross-references are supplied whenever the name of a person or corporate body is known or reasonably known under a form not used as the primary heading. To determine if AACR2 forms had been established, we consulted the Gallery library's authority file. In instances where the library had not established a name heading but it was considered probable that an AACR2 form had been established by the Library of Congress (LC), we searched the LC authority file available through the Online Computer Library Center (OCLC) network. Whether or not the AACR2 form was found, additional sources were consulted. Aside from requiring additional information not included in AACR2 forms of names as established by the Library of Congress, we defined the principle of common usage as locating at least two non-conflicting sources.

In preparing a verification bibliography, a list of authoritative sources was obtained from the library cataloguing section. This bibliography was augmented by sources that we found useful, the most significant being the *International Repertory of the Literature of Art* (RILA) (Chapter 23). As a bibliographic service funded by the J. Paul Getty Trust, RILA was seen as a means of tapping into new artist information as published in current art history literature. In addition, it was felt that applying RILA's name authorities could prove advantageous should the Getty Trust play a major role in the development of international standards for sharing art related information. RILA has become the one source that all names added to the Gallery artist file are checked against. In a ranking of published sources, it is considered the final authority. Given that the library only establishes artist headers based on the acquisition of monographs, compounded by difficulties in gaining access to OCLC authority files, consultation of the library authority file is limited to well-known artists.

During the 1982 project, proposed artist information that differed significantly from the entry found in existing Gallery records was submitted to the curator for review. In general, we found that curatorial staff did not dispute the chosen forms. When there was disagreement, the form and information considered the most accurate by the curator became the preferred form. Today this verification process is still in effect. When a new artist is added to the file, the curatorial department provides the cataloguers with biographical information and its choice of artist name. The entry is then verified and documented according to the process outlined above. Revisions to the curatorial form are reviewed with the curator, and changes are made as necessary. Similar procedures are followed when updating artist information. As an additional means of keeping the database current, we hope to implement a procedure of checking Gallery records against the RILA Authority File once the latter is made available online.

Changes/future developments

Since the conversion of essential information on all Gallery objects into machine readable form, the needs and desires of the Art Information System users have expanded. These needs, coupled with continuing technological advances, have shown that the existing system requires significant modification to address immediate user requests or provide a foundation for future development. Recognising that the limitations encountered stem primarily from the software on which the system is based, the Gallery did a requirements study which made clear that a relational database management system would provide a better structure for the art system. A prototype of the central object and person databases is now under development. This portion of the prototype was scheduled for completion in August 1989, and it is intended that the production system will be implemented during early 1991.

The new system will incorporate a number of features that will significantly change not so much the procedures for controlling names as the format of the data and the means by which information is obtained from the system in a name-based query. For example, the person authority file will not be dependent upon the use of preferred terms. In the current system, variant forms of name refer the user to the preferred form. As in a manual system, the user must exit the file and re-enter the file under the preferred form of name to access the artist information and/or related records. In the new system, the fields corresponding to name are repeating. An artist may have an unlimited number of names that will be classified according to type (e.g. nickname, pseudonym, variant spelling and preferred). Each of a person's names is equivalent to others in that they all refer to precisely the same entity. The name authority number will be used to link different forms of name, so that a user searching under either a preferred or a variant form will be led to everything by this artist included in the catalogue. Thus, a query under an artist's nickname (e.g. Canaletto) or true/full name (Giovanni Antonio Canal) will achieve the same results. The display will indicate to the user the Gallery's preferred form as well as the other names by which the artist is known or recognised.

One of the more exciting challenges in the development of the new system will be the attempt to remove some of the literalness of the computer. As we all know, retrieval of data that exactly matches a text string, including diacritics and case, is fairly straightforward. The problem arises when the user omits an accent, changes a case, or mis-spells a word. In the new system, we hope to provide a function that will map a string into a value using a phonetically based algorithm. Working like a spelling checker common in word processing software, the system will supply the user with a list of possible values when an exact match is not found.

Since the Gallery has relatively few objects for which the artist is considered a corporate body, the additional complexities involved in controlling corporate body names have not been a significant issue in the creation of the artist file. In the existing system, these records are not distinguished from those representing an individual or personal name. In the new system this will become more of an issue, as artists are merged in a person database with the names of organisations or groups related to objects in varying roles (e.g. production, ownership, etc.). To accommodate the special requirements for describing corporate bodies, new fields will be added. In addition, a person-part table will be created that will allow us to express the relationships between higher and subordinate bodies by linking subdivisions of a corporate body to a parent body.

In the new system, a field in the person record will be used to categorise record type: the three types identified at present are individual, corporate body and anonymous. The last is a particular issue relative to art object databases. For anonymous artists where a specific hand is not identified and the artist is labelled by locale and date of object, the National Gallery does not create unique artist records. For example, there is one artist record for 'Anonymous Venetian 16th Century'. All objects classified as Venetian school and executed in the sixteenth century by unknown artists are associated with this one artist record. These records will constitute the type 'anonymous' records in the new system. In the case of an anonymous artist whose specific hand is recognised but whose name is unknown and therefore assigned (e.g. Master E.S.), the artist is treated as a named artist. Finally, for anonymous artists identified by their relationships to the work of a known artist (e.g. Follower of Raphael), the artist is considered in the Gallery's existing system as an alias of the known artist. In the new system, this relationship will be treated differently. Attribution qualifiers will be entered in the table linking artist and object records. Each anonymous artist of this type will in effect be individualised, although there will not be an actual record in the person database for each appellation composed of a name and qualifier.

Among the many data elements being added to the Gallery's new artist file will be a field for recording the source notes now maintained in manual files. In recent years there have been several instances when the National Gallery has shared its artist file with other institutions developing collections management systems. Once we are able to substantiate artist information with the authority data, it will be a far more useful source for others interested in creating similar files. While the primary objective of the systems developed at the Gallery is directed toward the support of the museum in the administration of the objects in its care, the prospect of sharing art information electronically with other institutions is one that we welcome.

---

27 MANAGING BRITISH REGIMENTAL TITLES

Boris Mollo

Formerly Research Fellow
National Army Museum
London

The National Army Museum has worked, with the help of the MDA, for ten years on the development of its computer cataloguing. It has recently set up the &MAGUS system.

In considering the control of personal and corporate body names, the National Army Museum uses such names in the following areas:

acquisition	donor
production	name
	service
association	name
	service
	place
	event
	concept

For the syntax of personal and place-names, MDA data standards are followed and in our experience have proved effective. For concept terms we have had thesauri in use for some years but have been awaiting a validation facility, which is available on &MAGUS, before producing a more strictly defined version for the computer, particularly as &MAGUS includes a facility for broader and narrower terms. This leaves two areas which are vital to us for retrieval purposes and for which we have had to develop our own control lists:

REGIMENTAL TITLES	in the production and association groups, in the field SERVICE
CAMPAIGN NAMES	in the association group, in the field EVENT

This paper deals with the first of these. The regimental system has been a vital feature of the British Army for over 350 years. It is a system which came under severe threat in the 1960s, but which fortunately has survived and is now the envy of many other armies. The British regiment acts much as a family and, like a family, has its own, often complicated, family tree which takes into account raisings, disbandments, amalgamations, attachments and detachments. A clergyman, The Revd J. B. M. Frederick, has produced a two-volume book on regimental lineage which does no more than list every change of title. So we are dealing with a complicated and emotive subject. Woe betide the National Army Museum if we get so much as a comma wrong in the particular title of a particular regiment at a particular date.

This preamble indicates what we are faced with when we come to the problem of indexing regimental titles. It is important to be able to retrieve references to a particular regiment at any period of its history but a normal alpha-numeric system finds it difficult to cope when both the regimental number and title change a number of times in its history.

Furthermore, we often have the situation where a query cannot be given a definite answer, only leads or indications. For example, if information was sought about the saddlery of the 11th Dragoons in 1760 and none were available, any details of the saddlery of the 10th or 12th Dragoons, who were similarly equipped, would be of value. There may also be items which we can identify as dragoons, but not the precise regiment and so any indexing system must be able to cope with partial identification.

Since no alphanumeric indexing system for regiments has ever proved satisfactory, military historians and researchers have become used to searching for regiments in their order of precedence. The system dates from the time when regiments were continually being raised and disbanded and the battlefield ability of a regiment was closely equated with its age. In the line, older, more experienced regiments took precedence, i.e. the critical positions at the end of the line, while newer regiments were positioned in the middle, supported on either side by the older. From early days, precedence was laid down officially, as the order in which regiments are found in the Army List and fortunately it has remained reasonably consistent.

Under these circumstances, we decided to opt for a system of codes which followed this precedence order for the following reasons:

it would provide a consistent identifier for a unit regardless of its changes of title;

it would enable searches to be made and reports written in the quirky precedence order;

it would allow searches to be made on a wider basis than on individual regimental titles.

Since the National Army Museum is primarily concerned with the British Army, we chose the three-figure digits 100–199 for its subdivisions. For our next major responsibility, the Indian Army, we chose 200–299. Thereafter, our database on any one particular country is much smaller and so we adopted a country code system.

Figure 7.1 Subdivision of fields for British Army

100–109	Army in General
	Higher formations
	General staff
	Bodyguards
110–119	Cavalry
	Armoured corps
120–123	Corps (of senior precedence)
130–139	Foot guards
	Infantry
140–149	Specialist Infantry
150–159	Corps, departments, schools
160–169	Pensioners, associations
170–189	Auxiliary forces
190–199	Other services (RN RAF)
	Civilian organisations

Figure 27.2 Subdivision of fields for Indian and other armies

.01	Higher formations, armies	.27	Pioneers
.02	Higher formations, corps	.28	Signals
.03	Higher formations, divisions	.30	Guard infantry
.04	Higher formations, brigades	.31	Line infantry
.05	Army staff	.32	Local infantry
.06	General officers	.33	Reserve infantry
.07	Staff officers	.34	Veteran battalions
.08	District staff	.37	Light infantry
.10	Guard cavalry	.38	Rifles
.11	Heavy cavalry	.44	Mounted infantry
.12	Light cavalry	.50	Corps
.13	Irregular cavalry	.51	Women's corps
.15	Camel corps	.52	Military schools
.16	Armoured corps	.53	Officer cadet schools
.20	Artillery	.54	Staff colleges
.21	Horse artillery	.55	Arms schools
.22	Foot artillery	.56	Junior leaders regiments
.23	Heavy artillery	.57	Boys' regiments
.24	Mountain artillery	.60	Unattached list
.25	Engineers	.63	Pensioners
.26	Sappers and miners	.99	Unidentified

We then subdivided 100–199 into ten areas (Figure 27.1). For the Indian and other armies, we adopted a slightly different approach. We start with a code to identify the country, followed by a standard code to identify the arms of service based on that used in the British Army sector (Figure 27.2). After the Indian Army we have chosen four further subdivisions to suit the way in which we need to retrieve the information.

3. xxxx Foreign troops in British pay (where xxxx represent the first four letters of the country of origin)

4. xxxx Colonial Forces

5. xxxx Foreign Armies

6. xxxx British troops in foreign pay

We have developed the coding system to suit our own particular needs. It would need adaptation for use in a regimental museum because we seldom go into greater detail than the regimental name, whereas the regimental museum would have greater need to identify battalions and companies. On an international level, the general principles could still be used, replacing our particular system of country codes by an internationally recognised code such as UDC with the subsequent subdivisions used as I have described.

It has worked for the National Army Museum. The curators found that it took some getting used to, particularly getting all the letters and full stops in the right place, but once familiar with the logic, the error rate has dropped right off. The important thing is that we can now get consistency which we never could when relying on the full title. Online searching is much easier using just the code and date and it enables us to produce logically ordered reports and indexes. Validation will in due course allow the curator to enter just the code and date leaving the computer to supply the full correct titles for the date, right down to the last comma and bracket.

---

28 THE WITT COMPUTER INDEX: EXPERIENCE IN CORPORATE NAME DEVELOPMENT

Dr Colum Hourihane

Senior Assistant, Witt Computer Index
Courtauld Institute of Art
London

Introduction

The Witt Computer Index was started in 1983 under the aegis of the Getty Art History and Information Program and is based at the Courtauld Institute of Art. The initial pilot project was a computerised catalogue of approximately 60 000 images of works of art in the American School of the Witt Photographic Library. These images vary in date from the early 1900s, when the photographic collection was started by Sir Robert and Lady Witt, to the present, and come from a variety of sources such as exhibition and sale catalogues.

Developing a museum authority file

Through inputting the information on these mounts, we now have an authority file of approximately 1 200 museums distributed throughout the world. When starting this project we acquired a collection of reference works for museums. It was hoped that they would give us a formalised and controlled structure for our indexing. However, we found that they were uniformly organised on a geographic basis. To those of us who did not know where the Timkin Museum of Art, the Wadsworth Atheneum or Parrish Art Museum were, such an approach posed many problems and long searches.

The quality of the information on the Witt mounts varies, some recording nothing more than the institution name. The standard geographical format in the reference works was usually hierarchially structured, working from state, department or area to the more localised city, village or town. Some included an alphabetical index of institutions which was always an invaluable starting point, but which was by no means an obligatory feature.

Instead of providing a clear cut format, these books showed the gaps and the divergences that exist when controlling museum names. Discounting the formats employed in bibliographic sources, where prefixes, such as 'The', 'Museum of' and 'Gallery of' are ignored for ordering purposes, yet printed in front of the institution name, a wide divergence exists. For example, the Solomon R. Guggenheim Museum is listed under different forms in three standard reference books: in *The Official Museum Directory for the United States* (American Association of Museums, 1985) it is listed under S as The Solomon R. Guggenheim Museum; in the *American Art Directory* (1984) it is indexed under G, but as the Solomon R. Guggenheim Museum; and in *The International Directory of Arts* it is listed under New York and G, as Solomon R. Guggenheim Museum.

Similarly the Art Institute of Chicago is indexed under A, as Art Institute of Chicago and under C, as Art Institute of Chicago. These are single entries with no cross-references and historial variants are never listed. The classifications do not appear to be governed by any inherent rules and because these lists are in paper format there are less of the stringent demands that a computer requires. The first word in a computer index is the word under which the institution will be filed, while on paper this can be prefixed by any number of words and still filed under the same letter.

We approached the problem with an awareness of what was absent and what was desirable to a public who were not necessarily either geographers or librarians. Our authority was developed on a combination of the established formulae, a need to encompass the variety and complexity of our material which could not be catered for by the existing structure and a wish to staisfy the needs of the public and specialist user who would eventually be using the database.

We opted for a cross-referencing system similar to library practices whereby one label is preferred and it's variants are cross-referenced to it as a 'see under'. In our system the preferred status is indicated by the presence of a cross at the end of each label. All of the variants go towards the preferred and *vice versa*. This latter element is unlike standard library practices where the non-preferred terms go only to the final classification and not *vice versa*.

We abandoned the restrictive geographic prefix as our primary control but decided to encompass it under a cross-reference. Our criteria for preferring and for controlling our institution labels was to opt for the unique, identifying and most recognisable word in the relevant name and to file it under such. It was felt that words such as 'Museum of', 'Art Gallery of' and 'Art Institute of' were not sufficiently unique for classification purposes. For example the Tate Gallery is classified in our database as Tate Gallery but variants of it are listed under London, Tate Gallery and National Gallery of British Art, the name by which it was founded in 1897, and National Gallery, Millbank, London, the name by which it was known in 1920. All of the historical and geographic variants direct the user to the preferred label and *vice versa*.

We have certain guidelines in structuring specific labels. Where a geographic element was inherent in the museum name, the specificity of the computer and our practice of inverting the most important word elsewhere lead us to putting the place in a primary position. This will avoid the confusion referred to above where The Art Institute of Chicago could be possibly filed in two areas. In our system the Museum of the City of New York is filed under New York, Museum of the City of and The Art Institute of Chicago is filed under Chicago, Art Institute of. This has the secondary effect of grouping all the museums in a particular place together where geography is found anywhere in the label.

Our practice of inverting the construction of a personal name where a museum name had a personal name in it, was an application of our standard practice for personal names. We have avoided the confusion discussed above where Solomon R. Guggenheim Museum was filed under S and G and New York. In the Witt Index it is filed under Guggenheim, Solomon R. Museum, the name by which the museum was known since 1952; as well as New York, Solomon R. Guggenheim Museum; and Guggenheim, Solomon R. Museum of Non-Objective Painting, the name by which the museum was founded in 1939. Similarly The Cecil Higgins Art Gallery is filed under Higgins, Cecil Art Gallery and the Amon Carter Museum of Western Art under Carter, Amon Museum of Western Art.

Unique labels such as The National Gallery of Art, Washington, have remained as such in our system but are cross-referenced under geography to Washington, National Gallery of Art.

The practice of cross-referral proves invaluable where the museum was part of a larger institution. Where we did not want to lose the association between the university or centre and the respective museum it was possible to have a variant such as Harvard University, Fogg Art Museum, redirecting the user to the preferred label Fogg Art Museum.

One of the major advantages of the Witt library is the archival material which has been gathered since its' inception. Many mounts record older forms of museum names and some museums such as the Kaiser Friedrich Museum which have long disappeared as separate enteties, but whose collections have been dispersed. We are interested in the history of ownership and as such the histories of institutions from their formation to the present. When we went to standard texts we could find no mention of the John Herron Art Institute, the name by which the Indianapolis Museum of Art was known up to about 1967 and yet it was found on several of our mounts as a perfectly valid name. It was as if the museum had completely vanished in the mid 1960s when we consulted these books. The advantage of the Witt system is that such variants are cross-referenced to present day names. The inclusion of these variants adds up to the creation of a robust authority file whereby all of the possibilities can be included.

The approach we have used in structuring our institution authority is unique and innovatory but it is hoped will be of benefit and use to other projects and researchers.

VI
CONTROLLING GEOGRAPHIC DESCRIPTIONS

29 CONTROLLING GEOGRAPHIC DESCRIPTIONS: WHERE IS MERRYHILLS?

Martin Norgate

Documentation Officer
Hampshire County Museums Service
Winchester

Once upon a time I lived at Merryhills Cottage No. 1; just where is that? Half an hour fussing through bookshelves in my study provided some answers, given below in fairly controlled keywords; I should provide the clue that Merryhills is in Scotland.

Merryhills / Pool of Muckhart / Clackmannan / Central

using modern local authority areas, ending with the district and region (equivalent to a county in England); this answer alludes to the old county of Clackmannanshire.

Merryhills / Muckhart / Perthshire

using old local authority areas, ending with civil parish and county; terms that are still valid and useful in local history research.

Merryhills / Rumbling Bridge / by Kinross / Kinross-shire

the postal address, where the post town was in a neighbouring county. In practice, the county name at the end was redundant, not needed by the postal service.

Merryhills / Rumbling Bridge / Kinross / KY13 7PX

with the postcode added to the fairytale address the mail was routed, more slowly, via Kirkcaldy, in the neighbouring county of Fife.

The four descriptions of the location Merryhills involved four different counties in central Scotland: perhaps a rather satisfying confusion!

Other administrative descriptions of the location of Merryhills, a 'village' of 4 houses with a population of 16, use various other geographical units:

Muckhart / Alloa (primary/secondary school catchments)

Fife Water Authority

South East Caledonia Area / North of Scotland Hydroelectric Board

Kinross and South Perthshire Constabulary

Central District / Perth and Kinross Public Health Service

North District / The Scottish Court

Fossoway (telephone exchange, no doubt the lowest element of some sort of hierarchy in a network)

Devon / Forth (river catchment; an even smaller unnamed stream ran into the Devon which flowed into the Forth)

Venicones (ancient British tribal area)

Murray OR Douglas (overlapping Scottish clan areas)

I do assure you that the keywords I have quoted are fact, I haven't made them up.

In strictly defined language, so you can look it up on a map, Merryhills is located at:

NT 0157 9991 (national grid reference, UK Ordnance Survey)

56°10′54″N, 3°35′09″W (latitude and longitude)

Where is it? is not a simple question. The answer depends on why you are asking and for when the answer must be true. The partitioning of a country's land surface is not fixed; different organisations are differently arranged, borders move from time to time. The subsets are not always disjoint, areas can overlap, indeed they may not be at all well defined or have well drawn borders — our doctor belonged to one health board, our district nurse to another.

Added to all this sort of thing is the likelihood of variant spellings, with not much authority for right against wrong. Many of Scotland's place-names are Gaelic and even those in English are in a broad Scots vernacular — the doric speech which in our area was probably some species of lallans, the lowland speech of the borders. When place-names were gathered by the Ordnance Survey in the mid-nineteenth century some of the transcriptions were made by English surveyors, who misheard and got them badly wrong. Similar problems have occurred in the mapping by Europeans of foreign lands.

The four papers that follow report on projects that have explored or run into the difficulties of controlling place-names, problems that we gloss over in everyday usage, but which cause havoc in a computer database. Two papers explore more general problems of terminology control: validation on entry; updating; posting of cross-referals between terms; use of cross-referals in searches; what data should be included with a term; and so on. One paper reports on a project to provide access to the geographical data through graphics, maps, rather than words — on the face of it, an attractive idea. I think I still need the words as well!

30 THE RLG GEOREFERENCE INFORMATION NETWORK

Larry Carver

Library Map and Imagery Laboratory
University of California Santa Barbara
Santa Barbara, CA

The need for a national geoinformation network

Accessing bibliographic records of spatially referenced information is difficult because few databases or library catalogue systems allow for searching these materials in a way most users request them — by the specific area of the earth's surface the item represents. Compounding the problem is the amount of geographic data being generated; the lack of a systematic method of describing the diverse group of materials that can be spatially referenced; and the wide disbursement of collections among academic, corporate, private and governmental organisations. In many cases, the only access to these data repositories is via an 'Old Boy' network.

Recognition of these needs, as well as the access problems within the Map and Imagery Laboratory, led the University of California Santa Barbara Library administration to investigate the feasibility of creating a national geographic information system. The Research Libraries Group (RLG), a consortium of research libraries and an acknowledged leader in the development of national databases, was approached to determine its interest in directing such a project. RLG was indeed interested in the enterprise and has assumed the leadership role.

Project planning

A planning group was convened to identify the current status of those systems either planned or implemented, to determine the complexities of such an undertaking, to evaluate the interest in inter-organisational cooperation and to outline an achievable set of goals. Issues discussed were:

- Key problems faced by researchers in finding spatially referenced data;
- cataloguing standards for geographic data;
- the practicality of linking existing databases;
- the problems associated with controlling large masses of data;
- whether such a system could improve the university community's ability to obtain and use this data;
- the identification of material formats that should be included.

The meeting was attended by representatives from National Space Science Data Center (NSSDC), National Aeronautics and Space Administration (NASA) Head Quarters, Jet Propulsion Laboratory (JPL), United States Geological Survey — Reston (USGS), National Oceanic and Atmospheric Administration (NOAA), University of Michigan, Stanford University and the University of California Santa Barbara.

A task force was set up by RLG to construct a requirements definition for a geoinformation management capability and a grant proposal was written. The proposal was submitted to the W. M. Keck Foundation who awarded $200 000 to start the project.

The grant provided monies to establish a working task force, to hire a systems staff headed by Dr Cecil Block, and to construct the external system design (Block 1987, 1988a and 1988b). This work is now complete.

Project objectives

The goals of the completed RLG research and development program are:

- to create a national computer-based geographic information network that may be searched by a variety of geographic access points;
- to develop a research level information resource dedicated to cataloguing, managing and accessing spatial data;
- to develop a graphics interface between the user and the database that will allow for differing levels of interest and expertise;
- to provide an information resource which is of significant value to any discipline which can benefit from access to geographic data.

Scope

The database will document materials and information which refer to an area of the earth, oceans or atmosphere. At a later date, planetary infomation will be included.

Figure 30.1 Selecting general region of interest

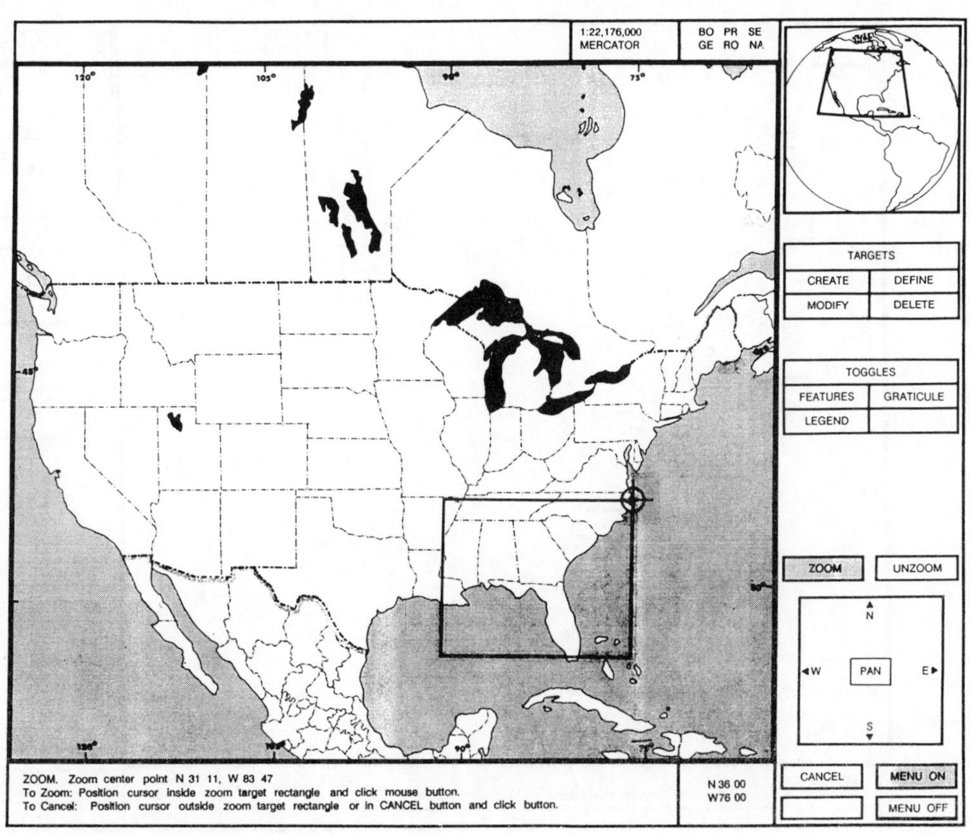

The system will contain records describing the data. Records for the following types of materials have been identified for inclusion:

remotely sensed data and imagery;

cartographic materials;

photographic materials;

numerical and statistical data;

books, reports, and other types of spatially referenceable materials;

The database will also contain ancillary data. Some examples are descriptions of imaging instruments, techniques used to gather or process data, assessments of data quality and the type of formats available.

Selected system features

The system will provide the user with a powerful geographic searching package.

At the heart of the system is the graphic user interface. Two levels of interface will be provided: a simplified menu-driven implementation allows novice or infrequent users to use the system with a minimum of training; more experienced users will have access to the full range of features and options by way of the command language.

Figure 30.2 Selecting specific area of interest

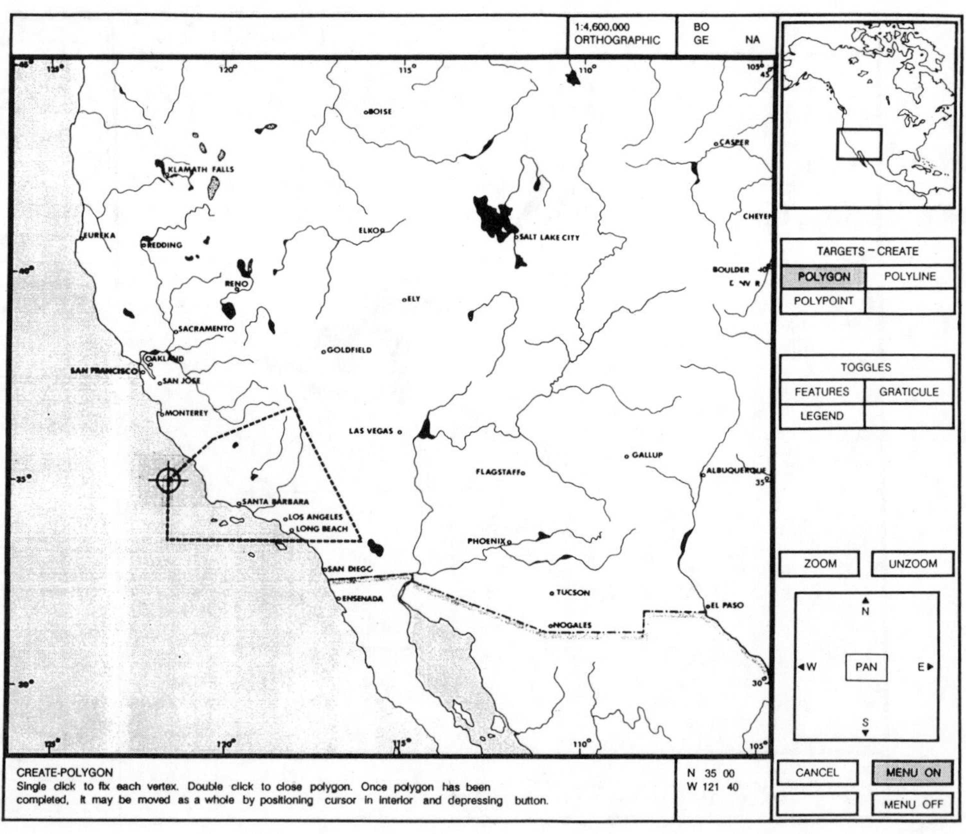

In addition to the graphics component, there will be a text component for both search entry and the display of results. A user can enter queries and other commands at the keyboard as customary; and, in addition can use an interactive cartographic display to indicate geographic search targets by drawing polygons, circles or paths on a background map of the region of interest (Figure 30.1).

The user will be able to pan across a global map zooming to higher or lower magnifications until the region of the earth's surface being studied is sufficiently well resolved to start the search (Figure 30.2).

In conjunction with geographic location, searches can be conducted on such attributes as scale, temporal coverage, or subject, to name but a few possibilities. The search may also be restricted to materials of one or more types.

The text window will allow scrolling through retrieved records, which may be displayed in several formats. The graphics window will display the 'footprint' or geographic coverage of each of the items in the search result as polygons, circles, or paths superimposed on the background map. Each footprint is numbered and cross-referenced to the text display; a small graphics symbol at the centre point of each footprint represents the type of material in question (e.g. a filled square denotes a map, a filled circle a photograph, etc. (Figure 30.3).

Figure 30.3 'Footprints' of spatial data types on specific area of interest

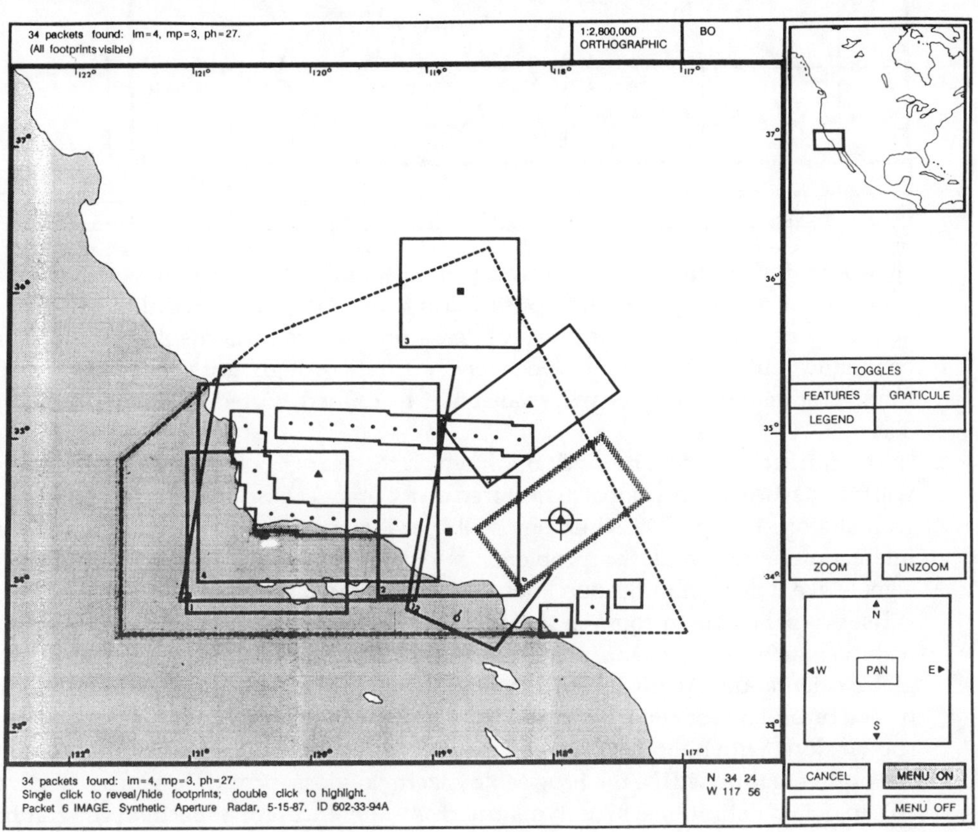

Figure 30.4 Background features turned 'ON'

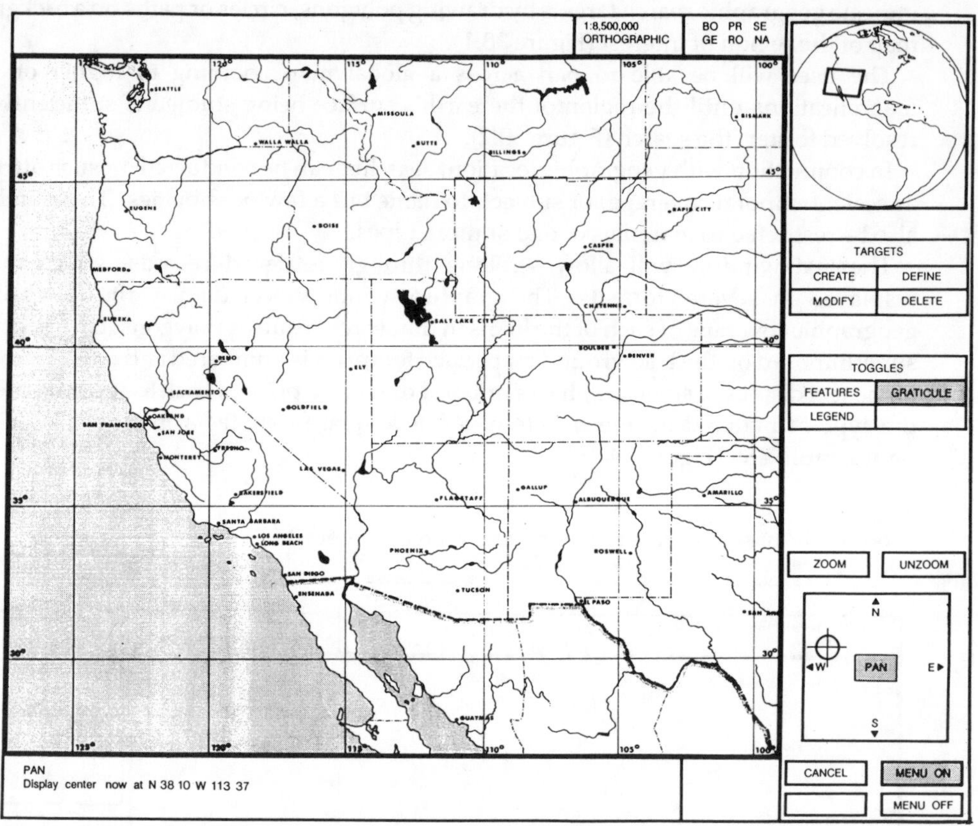

Each footprint can be queried directly by positioning the cursor over the symbol at its centre point and clicking the mouse button; the footprint is highlighted and a brief summary of that item's attributes appears on the graphics display. Various display commands enable the user to selectively suppress or highlight groups of footprints by number or material type. Search results may be refined, sorted, saved or printed (Figure 30.4).

The cartographic background, upon which the search polygon or point is overlayed, will take its form from a global map stored on a Compact Disc device attached to each user workstation. Using CD technology will provide the station with fast graphic screen interactions and avoid the problems associated with transmitting complex graphic signals over telecommunication lines to a remote database.

Users will be able to zoom in to larger map scales showing more detailed geographic features, such as rivers and secondary roads, or zoom out to smaller scales for better global orientation. At any time during the search the background feature classes may be turned on and off for better screen clarity. In Figure 30.4 the latitude and longitude grid is shown along with boundaries, water features, and major place-names.

Another feature will be the browsable gazetteer, glossary and thesaurus. Users will be able to obtain definitions, synonyms and cross-references for a specified geographic area or subject entry. A geographic name authority database has yet to be selected; however, it will probably be one of those identified in the Getty study, *Geographic Name Authority Survey* (Weller and Fink, 1987). Users will also be able to easily translate latitude and longitude to the Universal Transverse Mercator grid or to a geographic name and *vice versa*.

Eventually, a series of online directories will be available. They will provide information about the location and scope of specialised collections at other institutions and selected government agencies.

For those who have large data collections of graphic or remote sensing information, a high speed data input sub-system is being designed. The workstation, consisting of digitiser and graphics components, will be used to establish coordinates for those materials that have none printed on them. For example, the system will determine the boundaries or footprint of an object, and attach the bibliographic identifiers and descriptors to each item record. This will greatly increase the speed of database building and record editing.

This GeoReferenced Information Network will solve many perplexing data handling problems and provide a powerful geographic bibliographic information searching package.

---

31 A CASE STUDY FOR HISTORICO-GEOGRAPHICAL AUTHORITY

Oreste Signore and Rigoletto Bartoli

CNUCE
Istituto del CNR
Pisa

Introduction

This paper describes work on an historico-geographical thesaurus, carried out by the TAU group (Chapter 7) of the *Comité International d'Histoire de l'Art*, funded by the Getty Art History Information Program.

Historico-geographical authority

The problem of defining an historico-geographical authority may be illustrated by the following example:

the locality presently known as Sezze has belonged to:

Stato della Chiesa from *I don't know when between Xth and XIth century* up to *year 1404*;

Regno di Napoli from *year 1404* to *year 1414*;

Stato della Chiesa from *year 1414* to *year 1870*;

the locality presently known as Sezze was named:

Setia from *year 382 BC* to *XIth century*;

Castrum Sitiense from *XIIIth century* to *some unknown year, but probably up to a period that may be estimated to lie between the XVIth century and the XVIIth century*;

Secia from *year 1478* to *(I may guess) XVIIth century*;

how was it named when it was belonging to Regno di Napoli?

may I have a map showing the evolution of Regno di Napoli with localities with the historical name? (i.e. may I produce an historical atlas?).

It should be noted that the two pieces of information (administrative belonging and historical name) are completely independent, and may be obtained from different sources in different times. A link between them may only be established on the basis of the *time*.

The time coordinate

The 'time' coordinate is something that is always present, as a lot of information is dependent on the time. Many concepts are time dependent: not only names of places, or administrative boundaries or ecclesiastical jurisdiction, but also some other information that, at first glance, seems to be invariant, such as watercourses, lakes (artificial ones may be born, others may be dried), roads, marshes, etc.

The traditional fuzzy dates

Scholars are used to expressing dates in a fuzzy way, as they typically use expressions like:

- in the XIth century;
- before the Ist century BC;
- after Ist century AD;
- *circa* 853;
- between 88 BC and 80 BC;
- in the mid of VIth century;
- may be estimated as VIth century.

However, even if dates expressed in this way are meaningful to scholars and easy to specify, they:

- are language dependent;
- do not permit sorting;
- do not permit searching on the basis of exact years or intervals of time.

In other words, this traditional format does not allow different information to be combined on the basis of the period to which it applies.

The extended format syntax

During a meeting in Paris organised by the French Ministry of Culture in 1986, it was agreed to express every date in three possible ways:

- as a simple date;
- as an interval ($Date_{min}$–$Date_{max}$);
- as an interval, with indication of a probable date: $Date_{prob}$ ($Date_{min}$–$Date_{max}$).

The first form is the correct one for a date known with certainty. The second is used when the scholar is not able to determine a probable date between the minimum and maximum date. The third case comes up when, together with a probable date, there is present conflicting information, but from a reliable source.

The preferable forms are, obviously, the first and the third. There are, however, numerous cases where it is not possible to suggest a probable date, in that any hypothesis would have little substantiation. Similarly, there exist cases in which it is not scientifically correct to guess at limits for a date qualified as *circa* (about).

We have investigated methods of formalising a syntax for recording information about dates in Italian. It should be possible to devise similar rules for other languages.

After several attempts at formalisation, it has been considered opportune to use a series of conventions to represent, in the most natural way for the scholar, the possible forms to give to dates. On the basis of this convention, every date is expressed in one of the forms recorded above, where $Date_{prob}$, $Date_{min}$–$Date_{max}$ all have the same format, which can be one of the following:

- a number, preceded by the expression *anno* (if the date is known with certainty) or the expression *circa* (if it is approximate);
- a roman numeral preceded by the expression *sec.* or *inizio* or *metá* or *fine*.

They will be followed by the expression *aC* or the expression *dC* (or nothing) depending if the date is before or after Christ. In the case in which the date is merely hypothetical, and is recorded only for the purpose of avoiding inconsistent answers, the expression is followed by *'(?)'*. The expression *oggi* indicates the present year.

The coded format

In a database approach, processing and sorting of dates can easily be done if dates are stored as signed numbers: the dates before Christ will be recorded as negative numbers.

As each date is expressed (in the extended way) as a string of characters, with a well defined syntax, the basic problem has been to translate every date in a set of fields, which contain, in a coded way, the same information that is contained in the extended format. Each date is therefore split into several fields, whose meaning and structure are explained in Signore, Campari, Magnarapa, Ferrari, Grita and Papaldo (1988) and in Signore and Bartoli (1989).

Figure 31.1 Present toponym data form

```
Code          ___-__-___
Coordinates   ____________

Regione __    Provincia __
Comune        ______________________________________
Frazione      ______________________________________
Localita'     ______________________________________
```

Figure 31.2 Historical names form

```
Code  ___-__-___
Historical name     _________________________

           probable          minimum           maximum

From       ________          ( _______      -  _______)

To         ________          ( _______      -  _______)

References:
    Code     ___________        detail    ___________
             ___________        detail    ___________
             ___________        detail    ___________
             ___________        detail    ___________
```

At the query stage, all the processing is performed using only the coded format, while the user interacting with the system perceives only the extended format. This approach has been selected as the most efficient for database query processing.

Data collection forms

The plan for collecting and recording data in order to construct a historical-geographical authority must be based on the present administrative division of the territory under examination.

In a specific case, that is, the situation in Italy today, the record has been defined at the level of the municipal entity. Be it on paper forms or on the screens for data entry, the record format adopted is modular, presenting a form relative to the Present toponym data and analogous forms for the History (Figures 31.1 to 31.4).

Forms are filled out again for every addition or variation of the data previously recorded, always maintaining unchanged the data which does not vary.

The same type of form is used both for the information relative to the municipal centre and for that relative to various territorial entities. For every municipality, one begins with the information about the municipal centre and then that relative to the territory that belongs to the municipality. For every centre or territorial entity we proceed by supplying first that data relative to the Present situation on the appropriate form, and then the series of forms relative to the History.

The forms may be compiled in arbitrary order, as the correct temporal sequence will be established by the dates management algorithm.

The form structure is reflected in the database structure, as physical tables or logical views.

Figure 31.3 Historical administrative data form

```
Code ___-__-___
Hist. pol. status ______________________________

              probable          minimum             maximum

From          __________        ( _________    -    __________)

To            __________        ( _________    -    __________)

References:
     Code          _____________       detail     ______________
                   _____________       detail     ______________
                   _____________       detail     ______________
                   _____________       detail     ______________
```

Figure 31.4 Ecclesiastical jurisdiction data form

```
Code  ___-___-___
Ecclesiastical jurisdiction  ______________

              probable          minimum             maximum

From          ________       ( ________     -    ________)

To            ________       ( ________     -    ________)

References:
    Code        ____________          detail    ____________
                ____________          detail    ____________
                ____________          detail    ____________
                ____________          detail    ____________
```

Present toponym data

The data regarding the present situation refers to both the administrative circumscription and to the geographic identification by means of geographic coordinates. While the part relative to the identification data has a general validity (with the exception of the particular conventions regarding the way to codify the geographical coordinates), the part concerning the political-administrative data must be structured in a different way for different countries. Data must be drawn from official records, from census reports and from administrative and/or military maps.

Each locality is identified either by the code or by the geographic coordinates. As a consequence, the two fields are dependent one on the other. This choice has been dictated by the fact that a code may be made more easily understandable than a geographic coordinate. A different code structure, in agreement with the ISO standards, may be easily adopted.

History

The historical data is to be drawn from bibliographical research and from historical maps, if necessary enriched by on site investigation and by archival research.

The forms may be completed and entered in arbitrary order, be it in respect to the type of information or the chronological order. The code and date will permit the information to be ordered in the correct sequence.

It is therefore possible for research to proceed from one text to another, rather than conducting an exhaustive investigation locality by locality. Incoherent data may be reported on different forms, with the indication of the bibliographic source and chronological limits.

In all forms, the chronological span is expressed by a beginning date (*From*) and an end date (*To*). Both dates are expressed in the extended format syntax.

Conclusions

The case study

At present, only the region Lazio is covered, with province of Latina in full (31 *Comuni* and 269 *Località*), other provinces partially. In total, 738 localities are covered, with 2 676 notices and 3 543 references to sources. This data was collected by G. Grita, with advice from O. Ferrari and S. Papaldo (ICCD, Rome).

Output of the system

A set of application programs can produce various printed indexes of high quality (see Papaldo and Signore, 1989). The following indexes are presently available:

Topographical index (Figure 31.5) where for every *Comune*, and for each *frazione* or *località*, all collected data, in chronological order and with indication of source, are reported, grouped by:

historical names;

ecclesiastical jurisdiction;

historico-political situation;

historical names index where, for each historical name, the time span and the corresponding present toponym are reported;

ecclesiastical jurisdiction index where, for each diocesi, present toponym names, accompanied by the historical names assigned in the period where they were belonging to the diocesi, are reported;

historico-political situation index (Figure 31.6) where, for each historico-political situation, present toponym names, accompanied by the historical names assigned in the period where they were belonging to the historico-political situation, are reported;

sources.

Ad hoc queries may be satisfied using the query language of the database management system (SQL/DS). Some parametric queries have been defined.

In addition, maps showing historical administrative or ecclesiastical entities, together with historical names of localities, may be easily produced. This work has been supported by I. Campari and C. Magnarapa (CNUCE, Pisa).

Outstanding problems

Even if the general approach appears to work very well, especially for dates management, there are some outstanding problems for which we envisage some possible solutions:

for unlocalised toponyms, a possible solution is to give coordinates with uncertainty, specifying them as a rectangle, or as a circle. In both cases, the structure of the database should be modified. The preferable solution seems to be the second (supplying centre and radius);

linear elements (rivers, roads, lake boundaries) could be digitised together with a date (from–to), so allowing the choice of the correct data depending on the date the historical map is referring to;

Figure 31.5 Example entry from topographic index

Topographic index

SEZZE (288-00-000)

Coordinate: 33TUF381961

Nomi storici

- SETIA
  Da anno 382 a.C.
  A sec. XI
  Referenze
  - EAA, VII,230
- CASTRUM SITIENSE
  Da sec. XIII
  A (sec. XVI (?) - sec. XVII (?))
  Referenze
  - SILVESTRELLI 1940, I,123
- CASTRUM SITINUM
  Da sec. XIII
  A (sec. XVI (?) - sec. XVII (?))
  Referenze
  - KEHR 1907, 128
- SECIA
  Da anno 1478
  A sec. XVII (?)
  Referenze
  - FRUTAZ 1972, II,tav. 17 VII 5
- SEZZA
  Da sec. XVI
  A sec. XVII (?)
  Referenze
  - FRUTAZ 1972, II,tav. 45 XVII 4
- SEZI
  Da anno 1556
  A sec. XVII (?)
  Referenze
  - FRUTAZ 1972, II,tav. 40, XVII 2 a.
- SEZZE
  Da sec. XVII
  A oggi
  Referenze
  - FRUTAZ 1972, II,tav. 68 XXV 1

Giurisdizione ecclesiastica

- DIOCESI DI SEZZE
  Da sec. VIII
  A anno 1039
  Referenze
  - ANNUARIO CATTOLICO, 203
  - EC, XI,2013
  - KEHR 1907, 127
  - LANZONI 1927, I,147
- DIOCESI DI PRIVERNO SEZZE
  Da anno 1039
  A anno 1217
  Referenze
  - ANNUARIO CATTOLICO, 203
  - EC, XI,2013
- DIOCESI DI TERRACINA PRIVERNO SEZZE
  Da anno 1217
  A anno 1967
  Referenze
  - ANNUARIO CATTOLICO, 203
  - EC, XI,2013
- DIOCESI TERRACINA LATINA PRIVERNO SEZZE
  Da anno 1967
  A oggi
  Referenze
  - ANNUARIO CATTOLICO, 203; 501

Condizioni storico-amministrative

- COLONIA LATINA
  Da anno 382 a.C.
  A fine I a.C.
  Referenze
  - RE, II A, 2;1924
  - ZACCHEO PASQUALI 1972, 51
  - ZACCHEO 1985, 64; 216
- LATIUM VETUS
  Da anno 382 a.C.
  A (fine I a.C. - inizio I d.C.)
  Referenze
  - ZACCHEO PASQUALI 1972, 53

Topographic index 1

- REGIO I LATIUM ET CAMPANIA
  Da (fine I a.C. - inizio I d.C.)
  A fine III
  Referenze
  - DE ROSSI 1980, 28
- MUNICIPIUM
  Da fine I a.C.
  A sec. V
  Referenze
  - RE, II A, 2;1925
  - ZACCHEO PASQUALI 1972, 54 - 55
- PROV. CAMPANIA
  Da fine III
  A (sec. VI - sec. VII)
  Referenze
  - COARELLI 1982, 334
- DUCATO ROMANO
  Da sec. VIII
  A sec. IX
  Referenze
  - LOMBARDINI 1876, 42
- STATO DELLA CHIESA
  Da (sec. X - sec. XI)
  A anno 1404
  Referenze
  - SILVESTRELLI 1940, I,122
  - ZACCHEO 1985, 216
- REGNO DI NAPOLI
  Da anno 1404
  A anno 1414
  Referenze
  - ANGELINI 1976, 228
- STATO DELLA CHIESA
  Da anno 1414
  A anno 1870
  Referenze
  - ANGELINI 1976, 26
- REGNO D'ITALIA
  Da anno 1870
  A anno 1946
- REPUBBLICA ITALIANA
  Da anno 1946
  A oggi

SEZZE loc. LE MURACCIE (288-00-001)

Coordinate:

Nomi storici

- GRANARI D'AUGUSTO
  Da anno 1804
  A fine XIX (?)
  Referenze
  - ZACCHEO PASQUALI 1972, 126 n. 2

SEZZE loc. MONTE TREVI (288-00-002)

Coordinate: 33TUF397954

Nomi storici

- CASTRUM TREBARUM
  Da sec. XIV
  A sec. XV
  Referenze
  - ZACCHEO 1985, 96

SEZZE loc. ZENNETO (288-00-003)

Coordinate:

Condizioni storico-amministrative

- TENETO
  Da sec. XIII
  A sec. XVII (?)
  Referenze
  - MARTINORI 1933-1934, II,425

Topographic index 2

Figure 31.6 Example entry from historico-political index

Historico-political index

REGNO DI NAPOLI

Da (anno 1266 - anno 1282) A anno 1816

- **CAMPODIMELE**
  - **CAMPO DI MELE**
    Da fine XV
    A sec. XIX
  - **CAMPODEMELE**
    Da anno 1497
    A sec. XVII (?)
  - **CAMPODIMELE**
    Da sec. XIX
    A oggi
  - **CAMPU DE MELE**
    Da fine XI
    A sec. XV (?)
- **CASTELFORTE**
  - **CASTELFORTE**
    Da sec. XV
    A oggi
  - **CASTELLOFORTE**
    Da sec. XV
    A sec. XVII
  - **CASTRUM FORTE**
    Da (sec. XI - sec. XIII)
    A sec. XV
- **FONDI**
  - **FONDI**
    Da sec. XVI
    A oggi
  - **FUNDI**
    Da sec. IV a.C.
    A sec. XVI
- **FORMIA**
  - **BURGUM DE MOLA**
    Da (anno 1120 - anno 1124)
    A sec. XVI (?)
  - **BURGUM MOLE**
    Da (anno 1120 - anno 1124)
    A sec. XVI (?)
  - **CASTELLONE**
    Da (sec. XIII - sec. XIV)
    A anno 1872
  - **CASTELNOVO**
    Da sec. XII
    A (sec. XVI - sec. XVIII)
  - **CASTELNUOVO**
    Da sec. XII
    A (sec. XVI - sec. XVIII)
  - **FORMIE**
    Da sec. XV
    A sec. XVI (?)
  - **MELA**
    Da inizio XIX
    A anno 1861
  - **MOLA**
    Da anno 915
    A anno 1861
  - **PHORMIE**
    Da anno 1511
    A sec. XVII (?)
- **GAETA**
  - **CAIETA**
    Da sec. XIV
    A sec. XV (?)
  - **CAJETA**
    Da sec. I
    A sec. XVIII
  - **CASTRUM CAJETANI**
    Da sec. VIII
    A sec. XIII (?)
  - **CASTRUM GAETANI**
    Da meta' XIII
    A sec. XV
  - **GAETA**
    Da sec. XV
    A oggi
  - **GAETTA**
    Da sec. XV
    A sec. XVII
  - **GAJETA**
    Da sec. X
    A sec. XV (?)
  - **KASTRI KAIETANI**
    Da anno 866
    A sec. XIII (?)

Historico-political index 3

  - **KASTRO GAETANO**
    Da anno 867
    A sec. XIII (?)
- **ITRI**
  - **ITRI**
    Da sec. XV
    A oggi
  - **ITRJ**
    Da sec. XV
    A sec. XIX (?)
  - **ITRO**
    Da sec. XV
    A sec. XVII (?)
  - **ITRUM**
    Da sec. XII
    A sec. XV (?)
  - **YTRO**
    Da anno 1491
    A sec. XVII (?)
- **LENOLA**
  - **ENOLA**
    Da inizio XVII
    A sec. XVIII (?)
  - **ENULA**
    Da sec. XI
    A sec. XV (?)
  - **INOLA**
    Da sec. XI
    A sec. XV
  - **INULA**
    Da sec. XI
    A sec. XV (?)
  - **LENOLA**
    Da fine XV
    A oggi
  - **LEULA**
    Da meta' XVI
    A sec. XVII (?)
  - **SENOLA**
    Da anno 1770
    A sec. XIX
  - **YNOLA**
    Da fine XI
    A sec. XV (?)
- **MINTURNO**
  - **TRAETTO**
    Da sec. XVI
    A anno 1879
  - **TRAIETTO**
    Da sec. XVI
    A sec. XVIII (?)
  - **TRANSIECTUM**
    Da anno 1039
    A sec. XVI (?)
  - **TRIECTUM**
    Da anno 1049
    A sec. XVI (?)
- **MONTE SAN BIAGIO**
  - **CASTRUM MONTICELLI**
    Da sec. XVI
    A sec. XVIII (?)
  - **MONTE OCELLO**
    Da sec. XI
    A sec. XIX
  - **MONTECALLI**
    Da sec. XVI
    A sec. XVII (?)
  - **MONTICELLI**
    Da sec. XI
    A sec. XIX
  - **MONTICELLI DI FONDI**
    Da sec. XVI
    A anno 1862
  - **MONTICELLO**
    Da sec. XI
    A anno 1862
  - **MONTICELLO DI FONDI**
    Da sec. XVIII
    A anno 1862
- **SPERLONGA**
  - **CASTRUM SPELONCAE**
    Da sec. X
    A sec. XVI (?)
  - **CASTRUM SPELONCHE**
    Da sec. X
    A sec. XVI (?)
  - **CASTRUM SPELUNCE**
    Da sec. X
    A sec. XVI (?)
  - **CASTRUM SPELUNGA**
    Da sec. X
    A sec. XVI (?)
  - **SPELUNCA**
    Da sec. I d.C.
    A sec. XVI
  - **SPERLONCA**
    Da sec. XVI
    A sec. XVIII (?)
  - **SPERLONGA**
    Da sec. XV
    A oggi
  - **SPERLUNGA**
    Da anno 1504
    A sec. XVIII (?)
- **SPIGNO SATURNIA loc. SPIGNO SATURNIA SUPERIORE**
  - **CASTRUM SPINEI**
    Da sec. X
    A sec. XIII

Historico-political index 4

physical data may be useful for defining hypothetic boundaries, as all data are collected as points, and it seems to be incorrect to rely on present boundaries. An approach similar to that adopted for the linear elements may appear feasible, but it is difficult to establish at which level of detail we have to store information. Also, it is not definite where to guess boundaries, as some concepts may be not well defined. Typically, what we have to consider to be a mountain, that could have probably determined a boundary between two different administrative entities? (Webster's dictionary defines a hill as being lower than a mountain and a mountain as being higher than a hill!);

the upward-downward extension to countries in one direction, and to towns and streets in the other, appears possible, but costly, and would require an in depth historical research. The cost/benefit ratio of a similar extension should be carefully evaluated.

---

32 DEVELOPING AND USING A GEOGRAPHIC NAMES THESAURUS FOR A MULTIDISCIPLINARY DATABASE

Maryse Rahard

Institut de l'Information Scientifique et Technique
Centre National de la Recherche Scientifique
Paris

This paper reviews the experience of the *Institut de l'Information Scientifique et Technique* (INIST), established in March 1988 by the *Centre National de la Recherche Scientifique* (CNRS).

Since 1972, the Centre de Documentation Sciences Humaines (CDSH) has created and managed a database in the human and social sciences, FRANCIS. This has now grown to 1.2 million bibliographic references, divided into 20 files ranging from philosophy to art and archaeology, sociology and economics. Some of them concentrate on information concerning the present, others offer an historical point of view. All of them need vocabulary specific to their subjects, but some terms are used by every file: all of them use subject terms, geographic place-names, personal names and abstract concepts for indexing.

We therefore faced the difficult task of indexing our files in a manner which would allow users to carry out interactive updating and searches, whether or not they were subject specialists.

We had to create search tools, but in order to do that we first had to create indexing tools and use them as authority files to control the input. It is evident that authority files should ideally predate the creation of a database. But when FRANCIS was launched, there was no experience anywhere of online multidisciplinary searching. So we had a lot of problems settling in and, like gifted pupils, we suffered from a lack of maturity. We wanted to show the development of terminology, calling on several years' practical experience to fix *a posteriori* a vocabulary which had been tested empirically.

One major drawback to this approach was the use over time of different terms to describe identical concepts. Removing past errors from a database is nearly as expensive as creating a new one, but leaving ambiguities leads to significant omissions ('lower recall') when searching. We regularly have to decide whether we are going henceforth to use the 'correct' term (which may become obsolete in a year's time), despite potential correction costs and the incorrect entries already in the database; or whether we should continue with our errors in order to be self-consistent. Of course we chose the former approach, but not without difficulty.

There were also problems caused by the multidisciplinary nature of the database. 'Perception' has different meanings in education and in civil administration: both are equally correct. What does one do in a multidisciplinary database? Certain terms can only be searched for within a given subject area: specialist searchers are informed of the areas which have their 'own' vocabulary.

Despite these problems, it is possible to establish vocabulary lists of terms which apply to the whole FRANCIS database, and that is the first task we set ourselves. We decided to tackle proper names, which ought by definition to be well-defined and easily managed.

The project chosen was a place-name thesaurus, which we thought would be easy to standardise and arrange hierarchically. How naïve we were!

Since the thesaurus would have to be used for both indexing and searching, we envisaged the following steps of work:

listing terms in current use;

finding authoritative sources to fix standards;

creating links between terms already in use and preferred terms;

translating the whole into English.

Starting from current practice required a comprehensive inventory of the different ways in which each place-name could have been entered. This revealed that indexers have fertile imaginations, even when indexing place-names! For instance the Federal Republic of Germany was indexed in ten different ways:

Allemagne RF

Allemagne (République Fédérale)

Allemagne (RFA)

Allemagne de l'Ouest

Allemagne Fédérale

Allemagne FR

Allemagne occidentale

Republique fédérale allemande

Republique fédérale d'Allemagne

Allemagne RF was chosen because it was the most frequently used, the shortest, and the most precise.

It was of course necessary to prepare a printed thesaurus containing 'Use for' references to other terms which might be used for searching. Later, variant terms might be linked by computer software at search time.

The previous example concerned different ways of expressing the name concept: other choices were more difficult. Should one choose 'Shenyang' or 'Chen-yang', 'Mer des Caraibes' or 'Mer des Antilles'?

Each such case was resolved using authoritative sources: atlases like the *Atlas Universel* (edited by *Selection du Reader's Digest* and *Le Monde*), dictionaries like the *Robert* dictionary of proper names, and official lists like that of economic regions for France produced by the Institut National de la Statistique et des Etudes Economiques (INSEE). Finally, geographers from CNRS were consulted.

The *Times Atlas* was used when translating terms into English. The translation itself was not without ambiguity; for instance:

Mexique in French corresponds to Mexico in English;

Mexico in French is to be translated as Mexico City in English.

The main question when working on a geographic vocabulary is the relationship between space and time. As we saw, some FRANCIS files cover the historical aspect of their subject rather than the present. Now a geographic concept can only have a precise meaning if related to a date. Some town names have changed: Istanbul cannot be used instead of Constantinople or Byzantium, although all three of them were in the same place. And in some countries like Poland, frontiers moved so many times through history that the links between specific provinces or towns and the broader term 'Poland' have to be decided by historians rather than geographers.

The fact that FRANCIS contains files which have a historical perspective, and others which do not, pose problems for searching which we have not yet overcome. Take for example, the Austro-Hungarian Empire, the Low Countries, Cyprus or Palestine. Concepts like Latin America did not exist during the periods covered by archaeology: but a search in FRANCIS on all references to a particular country ought to include archaeological finds, which form part of its cultural heritage. Certain aspects of this space-time conundrum remain unresolved, pending more powerful computing facilities.

Other difficulties we encountered are less fundamental and we solved them empirically, sometimes only provisionally, in order to facilitate indexing and searching. They concern:

the number of levels of narrower terms: theoretically it's unlimited; is it or is it not useful when searching the broader term Europe, to retrieve automatically the name of a French village of 1 000 inhabitants on which a sociological investigation was performed, or a small valley studied from the physical geography point of view? We thought the number of narrower terms to be taken into account was to be specified by the searcher according to their needs: for instance the region may be the lowest level for a search on a continent, the town for a search on a region;

international institutions which are not properly speaking geographic terms but are often a search subject: for instance, European Economic Community (EEC), Organisation of Petroleum Exporting Countries (OPEC) or Council for Mutual Economic Assistance (CMEA). We decided to add such institutions and their member countries where this would facilitate searching;

informal, social, cultural, ethnic, religious, economic or political groupings of countries. Once more we were empirical: authorities were consulted and we established lists; these should be used with caution. By consulting the printed thesaurus, the user can see the coverage of these concepts in FRANCIS. They may use them as given, modify them, or create new groupings.

We do not pretend to be the only authority; we wanted to offer a useful product without losing all notions of vigour. That is why we kept the French way of expressing geographic descriptions. To facilitate searching we input the term as found in French dictionaries and added under 'English translation' the form used in English speaking countries (either in English or in the original language).

Having completed the work of preparing the thesaurus, we turned to the computing aspects of the problem. An automated thesaurus should offer:

automatic conversion of terms to the preferred form;

control of the indexing vocabulary during data entry, and the automatic posting of broader terms for certain specific terms to reduce the work of indexers;

global searches on all terms specific to a broader term, such as all the countries in a continent or region.

The last task, never ended, is the updating of such a work: tedious but necessary! As we have seen, place-names change with time. New countries are created, others change their name when becoming independent, single countries split into several, or several may merge into one. Federations of states are created; political organisations like EEC take on more and more member states. We have to maintain and update our product to keep it reliable.

Documentation is a work in progress and we have to integrate any evolution in our field as well as any advance in automation and computer science. In the last 30 years we have seen revolutionary changes in the methods and principles of information management. But otherwise, where would be the challenge?

---

33 GEOGRAPHIC NAMES DATA BASE

Gretchen Kuhn
National Geographic Society
Washington, DC

Introduction

The Geographic Names Data Base (GNDB) is an automated names system that serves as a readily accessible central reference file of geographic names and associated data as used by the National Geographic Society (NGS). The need had been recognised by the Society for a more effective means of spelling and checking geographic names for articles and maps as well as to provide uniformity in names usage. Using the existing mainframe computer system and some addition of terminals, the system's capability of storing, managing and retrieving geographical names provides online access to cartographers and researchers throughout the Society.

The requirements for the system were devised from discussions with personnel from the Society's divisions who would be anticipated users and an examination of current functions within the divisions. Essentially the objectives of the system were to create an online database containing several hundred thousand names as well as pertinent information about the name. Access to the database through computer terminals allows users to select from a search list any variation of a particular name and be shown a display of information stored about that name. As the system's primary function is to serve as a spelling checker and 35 per cent of the geographical names from the NGS World Atlas require diacritics, an essential feature was that the system clearly display accents on the screen.

The system requirements study and design of the GNDB were completed by IBM. As the software was written and implemented by the staff in our Computer Center, programming requirements for enhancements can continue to be fulfilled within the Society as needed. Mid 1984 the Geographic Names Data Base became operational, allowing initial input of names and associated data, file maintenance and display of information at terminals. Additional programming completed at a later date released features that expand the use of the system for research and production needs.

For the initial data load, the selection of geographic place-names and features for the database will follow the approximately 150 000 names index of the National Geographic Atlas of the World (Fifth Edition). As the Atlas coverage corresponds to present day, official usage, the index (source list) reflects that name policy orientation and consequently prescribes the focus of name research for GNDB. Historical names of information about the history of a name is not part of the research effort nor is it retained in the database.

Structure of database

Each name in the GNDB has a detail information screen with associated data, known as the *Name Detail Screen* (Figure 33.1). First, the geographic name appears with the proper part of the name (for example, Cambridge) and is followed where necessary by the generic (examples, Ard, Loch; D'Iberville, Mont; Georgia, Strait of). The use of the comma indicates the official name usage and spelling would be Loch Ard, Mont

Figure 33.1 GNDB name detail screen

NGS — GNDB

GEOGRAPHIC NAME DETAIL INFORMATION

UPDATE PATH (INSERT) USAGE

....

(1) NAME ..../......./.......

(2) NAME ..../......./.......

BASE LOCATION .... ABBRV. NO. STATUS PERM

FEATURE DESCRIPTOR POPULATED PLACE .... MAP GRID .... MAP SIZE ....

COORDINATES ..../............ ..../............ ..../............

POPULATION (1) .... POPULATION (2) ....

ELEVATION METERS .... FEET .... SOURCE NGS WORLD ATLAS............

NAME CLASS .... DATE ENTERED ..../......./....... DATE OF LAST UPDATE ..../......./.......

COUNTRY/CONTINENT/OCEAN TERRITORY/REGION/SEA

==

==

FUNCTION | PA1–MAIN MENU PA2–OFF 13–RETURN
KEYS |
| 21–HELP

==

D'Iberville, Strait of Georgia. However, for indexing purposes the specific part of the name is followed by the generic. This rule of indexing, followed by the NGS World Atlas Index and official gazetteers, eliminates considerable search time on thousands of Lake . . . or Mount . . . , etc.

Although the system functions as a spelling checker and has the capability to display high resolution diacritics, the name is first shown as it would appear on a map but, without accents. This is for computer reasons and also for usage purposes. If the name has accents, then the accented version follows on the next line with the accurate spelling and display of accented characters.

Additional fields of information known as associated data are included with each name and pertain to geographic information or a particular cartographic function for the Cartographic Division and its map production. The basic geographic data elements include a *Base Location* for the name that is either a political or physical location. If the feature crosses boundaries and is located in more than one location, the Base Location will be the largest entity that encompasses the feature. For example, the Rhein River has Europe as its Base Location with additional locations for the countries through which the river flows.

Describing the type of feature is a field of information known as the *Feature Descriptor*. This system-specific list is made up of five generalised categories including political, physical, cultural, hydrographic and undersea feature descriptors. Several examples from each category, respectively, are: *political* country, commonwealth, province; *physical* summit, plateau, cape; *cultural* archaeological site, battlefield, national park; *hydrographic* stream, lake, gulf; *undersea* undersea canyon, reef, fracture zone.

Coordinates are provided to function largely as a location reference and not for plotting purposes. One to three sets of coordinates may be given. In the case of large features crossing country boundaries — for example, the Nile River — a first set of latitude and longitude establishes the mouth. A second set of coordinates is chosen as an arbitrary middle point and the last set would be an (end) point or source. Coordinate measurements are taken from official gazetteers or hand measured from large scale maps.

Population figures are also provided where available and are referred to in the map-making process to determine townspot sizes and cut-off for inclusion on varying scales of maps. In the case of large, metropolitan cities, the city proper and the metro area figure may be given. We also give populated ranges for countries where compiled, census material is not available and the only source to determine population figure is by carefully comparing townspots on official maps to the legends.

Elevation, given in meters and feet and with automatic conversion from one to the other when entering data, is given for singular summits or ocean floor depressions.

As name policy decisions throughout the world result in new names being added or updated in the database, the *Source* is an important field indication the reference material from which the spelling was taken. As the Atlas is our initial reference, and most names have not changed from the last publication, it remains the most frequently referenced source for name spellings within the GNDB. If examination of research materials yields another decision, however, the Source field indicates the reference from which the new name was taken. This field is system specific, allowing only sources from an authorised list to be entered into the system.

To differentiate between place-names with various spellings in the GNDB, one of four classifications is provided in the *name class field*. A *standard* is a native spelling, accented where appropriate and represents the greater percentage of names in our base. For example, København (Denmark), Wien (Austria) and Napoli (Italy) represent standard spellings in our GNDB classification system. *Conventional* indicates a translated, anglicised version so that Copenhagen, Vienna and Naples are examples of conventional names. The two remaining classifications, used less often, are variant and former. A *variant* is a non-official or other spelling of the feature. Cusco is a variant to the preferred usage of the standard name Cuzco in Peru. In keeping with the emphasis on current names in the Atlas coverage, *former* names are used very infrequently. However, an example would be Hierro (Canary Islands) with the former name Ferro.

Certain relationships between the geographic name and conventional (anglicised) translations, variant or former spellings known as *alternate* spellings are also kept in the base. To indicate these relationships on the screen to the user, the name to which all alternate names are related is called the primary. An alternate names category is also provided on each name detail information screen to show if alternate names are available. For example, the name detail information screen for the Nile (river) has a 'yes' marked by the alternate names category. These alternate names can be accessed as an alphabetised list on the screen (for example: Albert Nile; Damietta; Jebel; Nil, Bahr el; Rosetta-Victoria Nile) and then each alternate name accessed individually with its associated data (location, feature descriptor, coordinates, etc., as described above).

Name verification

The Geographic Names Data Base research staff is responsible for researching all data and refers to the Society's map and book library for official maps, atlases and gazetteers to verify or suggest changes in spelling. Names usage in the United States is based on the official decisions of the US Board on Geographic Names, a Federal body authorised to establish and maintain uniform geographic name usage. To assist in all decisions, particularly non-US content, our staff Geographer maintains communication with international committees, organisations and country contacts concerned with place-name verification.

To date, approximately 100 000 names reside in the NGS Geographic Names Data Base. The availability of source material to support the research effort has been one of the most critical factors in deciding research priorities. North America, Central America and South America are near completion, as well as coverage in Europe, the Middle East and Australia. The approximate one-third remaining of the NGS World Atlas index will be our next research horizon.

VII
DISCIPLINE DEVELOPMENTS: ARCHAEOLOGY, ANTHROPOLOGY AND ETHNOGRAPHY

34 DISCIPLINE DEVELOPMENTS IN ARCHAEOLOGY, ANTHROPOLOGY AND ETHNOGRAPHY

Jennifer Stewart

Curator of Archaeology
City Museum and Art Gallery
Bristol

Background

Like several other disciplines discussed in this publication, archaeology, anthropology and ethnography are extremely broad-based subjects in both time and place, covering as they do the whole of human history prior to industrialisation and every part of the globe colonised by humans. This vastness of subject matter is further complicated by the size and bulk of collections: in archaeology, for example, one medium-sized excavation can generate several hundreds of boxes of artefacts, photographs and paper records.

Trying to systematise or make sense of these collections exercised the minds of several great Victorian archaeologists and anthropologists, such as General Pitt-Rivers, Sir Leonard Woolley and Sir Flinders Petrie. Looking back at their pioneering work, conducted often without the aid of electric light and certainly without the use of word-processors or computers, one is envious of the simplicity of their systems and the clarity of their thought. (Mowat notes that the Blackwood system used at the Pitt-Rivers Museum, Oxford, is now a much-treasured museum object in its own right.) These innovative systems of terminology control and classification often formed the basis of computerised progeny, as in the Blackwood system just mentioned. Despite this basis, late twentieth century documentation still faces many new, and not-so new, problems.

Problems in archaeological terminology control

It would appear from the papers and the discussions in the workshop that two main types of problem can be isolated: those relating to the general management and direction of systems and those problems specific to the internal workings of a system.

Management and direction of systems

One fundamental aspect reiterated in the final discussion at the conference was the fact that museums are faced with an elemental dictonomy: preservation versus assessibility of collections. We must preserve objects in our care, in perpetuity; within reason we must make these self-same objects available to the public. Documentation can act as a buffer between the conflicting stresses caused by the twin needs of preservation and accessibility, providing us with information about the collections, without unnecessary handling of the objects. (If documentation acts as a buffer, to continue the analogy, then terminology control acts as the lubricating fluid for the documentation system.)

The second major problem encountered in the session was a variety of terms used to describe systems — lexicons, glossaries, dictionaries, thesauri, authority files, classifications and cross-referenced alphabetical indexes — but these did not necessarily mean the same thing to each participant. Actual examples from the systems discussed in the following Chapters would in fact show them to be hybrids of several approaches. (This may not be a problem for future systems, which most participants suggested would be of a similar construction, that is, a poly- or multi-hierarchical system, sometimes combined with 'add-on' cross-referencing glossaries or thesauri for individual needs.)

The third main area of discussion was an underlying anxiety about the cost, time and purpose of the current diverse systems. The cost element was not necessarily for the hardware or software, but the staff costs and time in setting up and maintaining the system. In discussion, one person quoted a staff cost of £1 million for a team of 15 people to work on a five-year project — the size of a project most large provincial or national museums may need to tackle their documentation or terminology problems.

The purpose of terminology control systems was occasionally in dispute: to aid in the care and management of collections and archaeological sites, as suggested by Welsh, Mowat, Aberg and Chadburn, or as an aid to researchers, as in the view of Skinkel-Taupin and Badoni. This illustrates another basic problem, that of training — not only for the makers and users of systems but also to elevate certain aspects of documentation such as terminology control which in many institutions was accorded a low status. In addition, training, or more accurately, educating, museum authorities to reconsider documentation as a core activity in the management of collections, was seen as a long term and continuing need.

The fourth management problem, as yet not satisfactorily tackled in the literature, is that of how to reconcile various inherited systems of documentation, including terminology control. For example, museums in Britain have an inheritance of over 100 years if not 150 years of complex, incomplete and often conflicting systems of accessioning, cataloguing and indexing. Deciding whether to recycle parts of the existing systems or to start afresh can be one of the most important decisions to face a collections manager, but for this there is as yet little training or guidance apart from that given by the MDA. It is not a decision to be taken hastily, but requires time, consideration and expertise. Unfortunately, the current 'headlong rush into computerisation', as one participant called it, does not always allow time for consideration. Nor will computerisation solve the problem of how to tackle incomplete and complex records or, more importantly, how to finance the staff to input the records in the first place. This problem is further compounded in Britain with the demise of government-funded, short term work projects, such as the Manpower Services Commission, which leaves in its wake a landscape littered with half-finished projects or completed projects which can no longer be maintained.

Specific problems

The main problem faced in the internal workings of archaeological terminology control involve those of identification, hierarchy, term redundancy, multi-functions and synonyms.

Identification

Assigning a name to objects is a primary aim of documentation and one of the basics of terminology control — is the object fashioned by nature or by human hands? If by human hand, incompleteness of the object due to ancient or modern damage can also make identification difficult. Lack of an identification can mean that an object, and therefore its information, languishes in some 'dustbin' category.

Hierarchy

Several authors mention this problem: Chadburn cites the example, when discussing site-type terminology, of a dovecote which may be a building type in its own right or may be subsumed within a larger architectural complex, with the retrieval problems which that subsequently brings. As Welsh noted, efficient searching is difficult in some hierarchical systems if one wants a general grouping of objects, for example those used for skiing if the individual items are recorded separately under 'equipment', 'sport' and 'footware'.

Term redundancy

As with identification, redundancy of terms depends more on the knowledge of the cataloguer than on the efficacy of the terminology control system. Like costume, object names in particular follow fashions: the Victorian word 'celt' no longer has currency in archaeology, being replaced now by one of the 'axe' terms, but the use of the now-redundant term may be of interest.

Multi-functions

A system based on the function of an artefact can cause problems in archaeology where the use is unknown, so it is consigned to an 'unknown' or 'miscellaneous' section. In anthropology, this problem is further compounded by the multi-functionality of certain objects, an amuletic finger-ring being both 'religious' and an 'ornament'.

Synonyms

Mowat in her paper gives a classic example of the problem of synonyms in anthropology: that of the terms 'bracelet', 'armlet', 'bangle', 'armband' or 'wristlet'. In the computerised Pitt-Rivers system, these items would all be entered in the 'arm ornament' section.

The way ahead

It would seem that the problems of the management and direction of systems can probably be solved or at least alleviated if, in the age of accountability, documentation and terminology control are view as a core activity in the management of collections, on a par with conservation, with the necessary funds assigned to it. However, the funding of staff to input records may remain a fundamental problem.

The specific terminology problems of synonyms, hierarchy and term redundancy could be catered for in a poly-hierarchical system as described by Welsh, which allows access at all levels while showing the interrelationships of the different terms. However, queries in the identification of the object will remain a discipline problem. Here the work of curatorial and finds groups, at least in Britain, may be of help. For example, the excellent data sheets produced by the Finds Research Group 700–1 700 which describe and illustrate a type of artefact could also be the vehicle to discuss and comment on the variety of terms to name that type of object. This type of intellectual 'networking' could also be applied to joint terminology and cataloguing problems, as in the recording of personal and corporate names, geographic names, dates (numerical and period), names of materials and descriptions of object condition. Here the MDA and in particular its Terminology Working Party have made a start on the multi-disciplinary discussion of common terminology problems.

35 TERMINOLOGY DICTIONARIES: MATERIALS FROM THE LATE BRONZE AGE AND THE EARLY IRON AGE

Franca Parise Badoni

Istituto Centrale per il Catalogo el la Documentazione
Ministero per i Beni Culburali e Ambiental
Rome

Examining card indexes and other documentation produced in recent times, has underlined the fact that frequent vaguenesses and lack of homogeneity in the denominations of the catalogue 'objects' were the result of conditions that deeply affected both archaeological and art history disciplines.

The most important factor affecting the value of these records is the vagueness and lack of homogeneity which, apart from a few exceptions, are already present in the basic information tools, or rather in modern archaeological literature.

The need emerged to supply precise standards for certain historical periods, through the publication of specific terminology dictionaries. The following remarks constitute a somewhat more explicit restatement of the topics dealt with in the Introduction to the first such Terminology Dictionary (Badoni, 1980). This takes advantage of the experience gained during the time elapsed since its publication in Florence in 1980.

Before illustrating the *Dizionari Terminologici de Materiali dell'eta del Bronzo finale e della prima eta del Ferro* (the Terminology Dictionary for materials from the late Bronze Age and early Iron Age), it should be stressed that as regards Archaeological Heritage, even if the criterion should obviously extend to all the Cultural Heritage, the need for a terminology codified in a uniform manner should not mean robbing of its originality the historical context relating to the archaeological materials. Cataloguing must not be limited to a correct description of these materials, but must be the result of their scientific processing. In other words, card indexes referring to the materials are not sterile lists of the individual archaeological items, but must reflect the critical evaluation of the objects as part of a specific cultural and historical background. Thus card indexes represent the first phase of a scientific assessment of the materials.

The publication of *Dizionari Terminologici de Materiali dell'eta del Bronzo finale e della prima eta del Ferro* must be considered as a stage in the attempt to create a common language defining the archaeological materials, especially the prehistoric and protohistoric ones. These are more difficult to encompass because of the non-standardisation of the production, which accounts for the lack of a consolidated terminology tradition.

Besides the need to achieve a homogeneous terminology, which is the indispensable condition for data processing, it was observed that utilising the same terms regardless of the chronological and cultural position of the corresponding materials gave rise to a number of difficulties.

As a first example of terminology processing, a certain chronological period was chosen between the end of the Bronze Age and the beginning of the Iron Age (twelfth to eighth century BC), in order that the suggested terms could stem from a direct typologic analysis and not from abstract contructions that might lack significance. For certain regions it was deemed advisable to go beyond the eighth century BC limit, because of the presence of cultural facies which indicated the uninterrupted continuity of their typological features from the early Iron Age to the following centuries.

During the period examined, in most cases Italian culture shows a remarkable degree of homogeneity, especially as regards the technical level of production of the various classes of materials.

The criterion upon which the whole work was based was that of supplying a series of simple terms, usually of current use, most of which were normally adopted in archaeological literature. The choice of the terms was not based on the function of the objects, which can vary for analogous forms even in the same context, and is anyway rather difficult to pinpoint, but on morphological characteristics which offer a series of objective elements.

The general criteria adopted are obviously similar for all classes of materials; however, some objective differences do exist, in particular between crude ceramic and metallic materials, which are reflected in the terminology and descriptive criteria adopted.

Crude ceramic, which in this period is almost exclusively hand-made, is a strictly local production probably mainly domestic. Standardisation is therefore always relative and limited to individual cultural environments. Over more extended areas, such as the Italian peninsula, one can find at the most a vague homogeneity of form. Bronzes, on the other hand, are mainly the result of specialised processing which implies the circulation over very vast areas of both raw materials and the models for manufacturing the objects. The degree of standardisation of the production is therefore much greater and is shown in the dissemination of the same types — besides closely related forms — in diverse and distant cultural environments.

This greater homogeneity of metallic materials is reflected in the unitary typological classification works already existing or in the press, mainly for some classes of bronzes originating from the whole or from very extended parts of Italy, in the series of *Prähistorische Bronzefunde*. A similar work on crude ceramic would be totally deprived of interest from a methodological viewpoint.

Therefore, as regards the terminology adopted in the Dictionary, the indications concerning ceramic are limited to a general morphological definition of the different forms accompanied by very detailed examples taken from materials belonging to the main protohistorical complexes of the whole of Italy, to which reference is made for the different forms in a specific bibliography.

For most of the bronzes, a more accurate type of classification for homogeneous classes is given within a particular form without further apportioning into types. For some of the most important bronzes already included in the series of *Prähistorische Bronzefunde*, the terminology and descriptive criteria are obviously those already adopted in these classifications.

In some cases, examination of the materials of a certain context has underlined the difficulties inherent in the choice between two terms for a form with characteristics on the borderline between one and the other definition. Since it is, at any rate, advisable that cataloguing be preceded by the scientific study of the materials, it seemed wise to let the choice of the more adequate term among those indicated (or, if necessary, the adoption of an unforeseen term) originate from the overall typological classification of the materials of the complex.

The use of diminutives or augmentatives is recommended only in cases in which an element of typological specification can be identified in the size.

igure
5.1

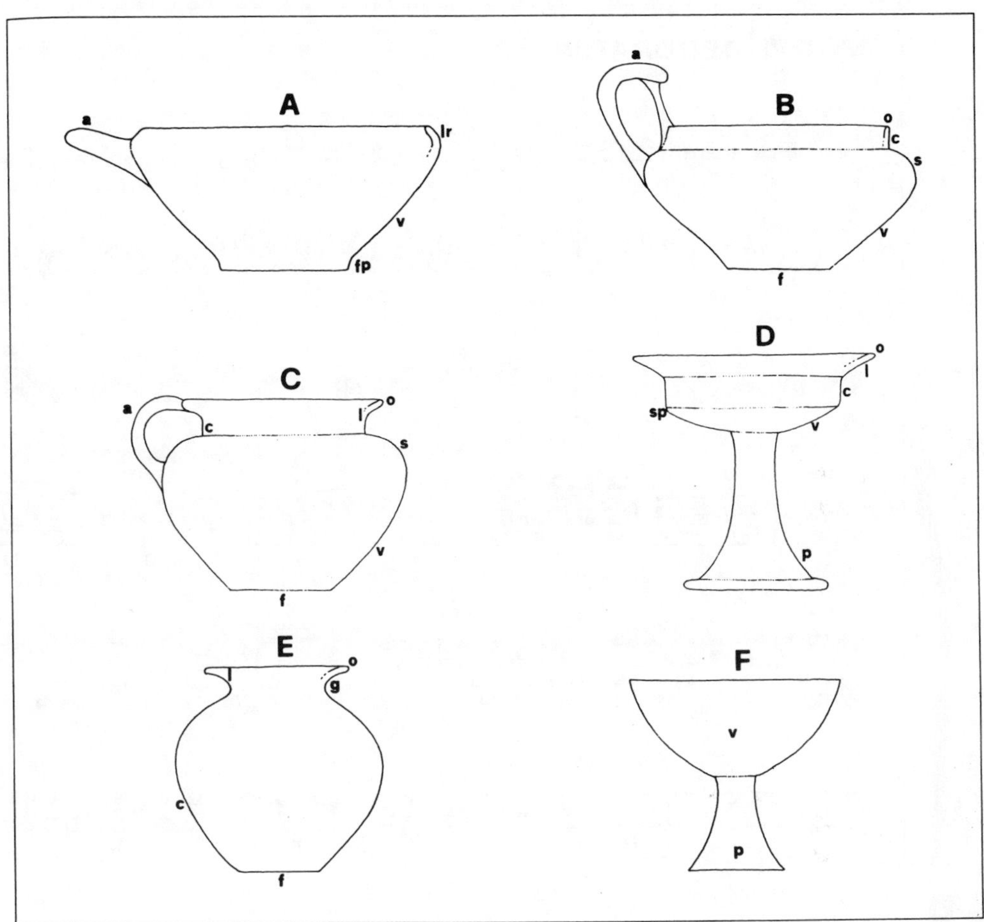

1. Schema esemplificativo degli elementi costitutivi del vaso:
A) a. ansa; lr. labbro rientrante; v. vasca; fp. fondo profilato.
B) a. ansa; o. orlo; c. colletto; s. spalla; v. vasca; f. fondo.
C) a. ansa; c. collo; o. orlo; l. labbro; s. spalla; v. ventre; f. fondo.
D) sp. spigolo; o. orlo; l. labbro; c. collo; v. vasca; p. piede.
E) l. labbro; o. orlo; g. gola; c. corpo; f. fondo.
F) v. vasca; p. piede.

25

Figure 35.2

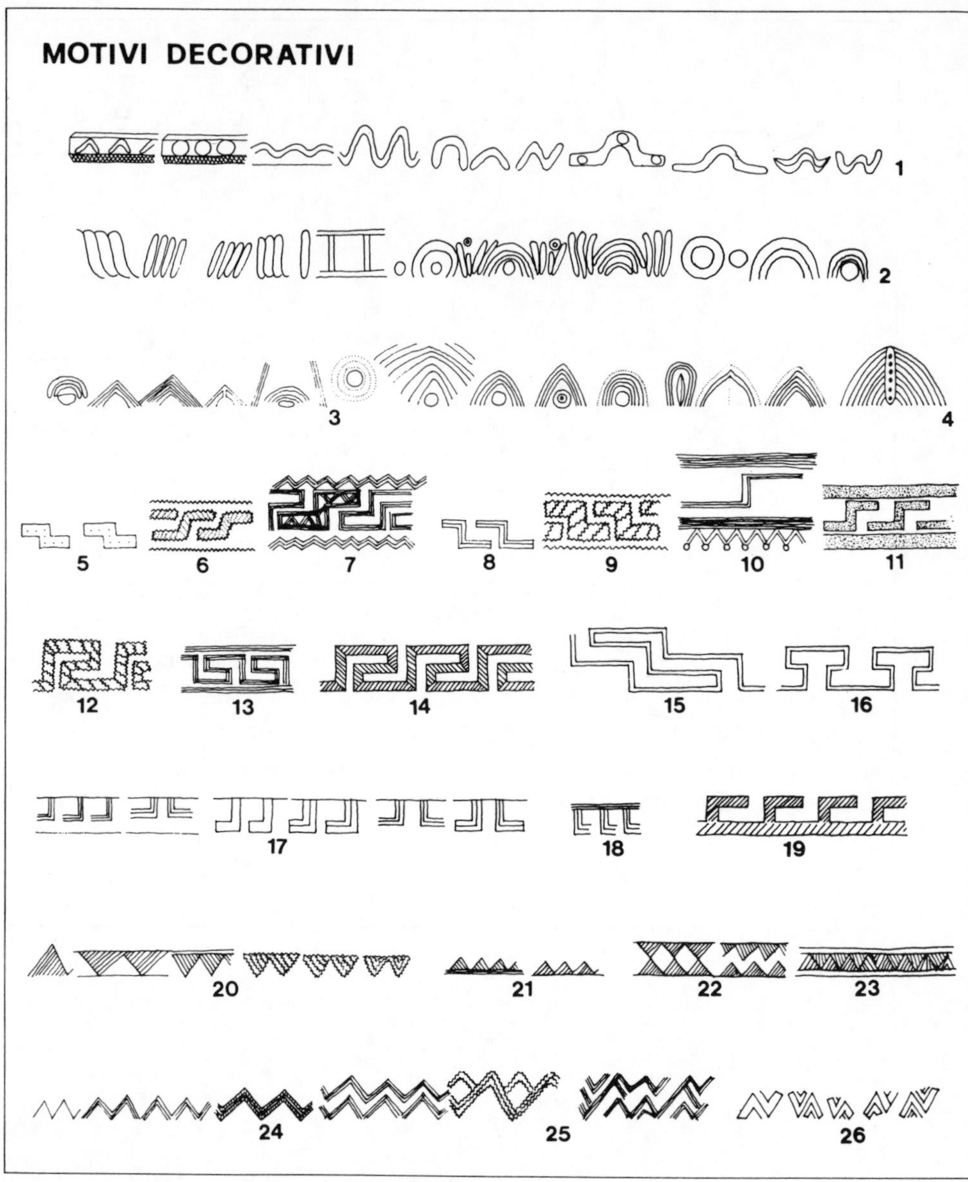

12. Motivi decorativi.
Motivi decorativi applicati (1-2).
Motivi decorativi incorniciati da incisioni e solcature (3-4).
Motivi decorativi incisi dipinti e applicati. Meandro a scala (5-11).
Meandro continuo (12-16).
Motivi a L incisi (17-19).
Motivi a triangolo (20-23).
Motivi a zig zag (24).
Motivi angolari (25-26).

36

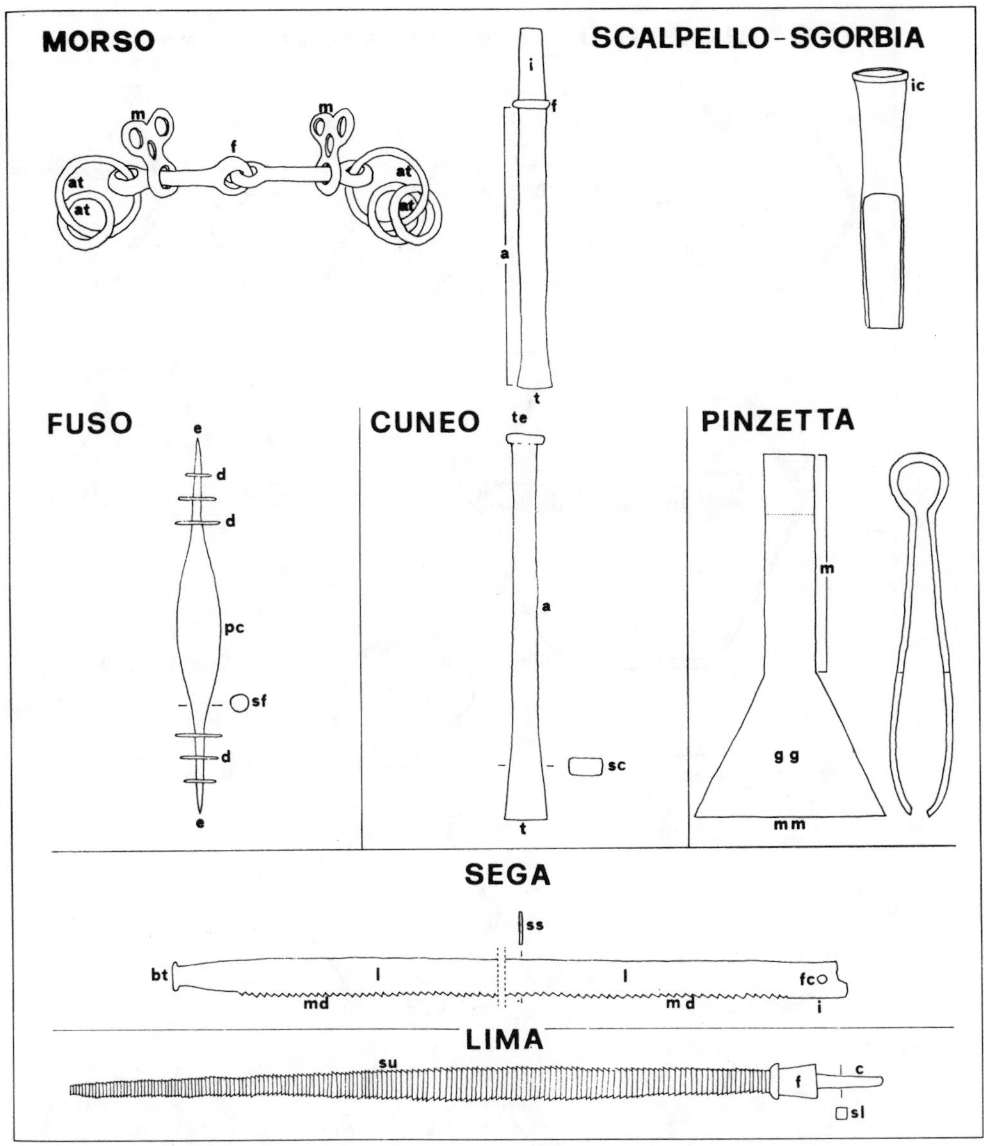

21.
Morso: f. filetto; m. montante; a. anello; t. tirante.
Fuso: pc. parte centrale; e. estremi; d. dischi; sf. sezione.
Cuneo: te. testa; a. asta: t. taglio; sc. sezione.
Pinzetta: m. manico; gg. guance; mm. margini.
Sega: l. lama; md. margine dentellato; i. immanicatura; fc. foro per chiodo; bt. bottone terminale; ss. sezione.
Lima: su. superficie d'uso; f. fermo; c. codolo; sl. sezione.
Scalpello, sgorbia: i. immanicatura; f. fermo; ic. immanicatura a cannone; a. asta; t. taglio.

45

Figure
35.4

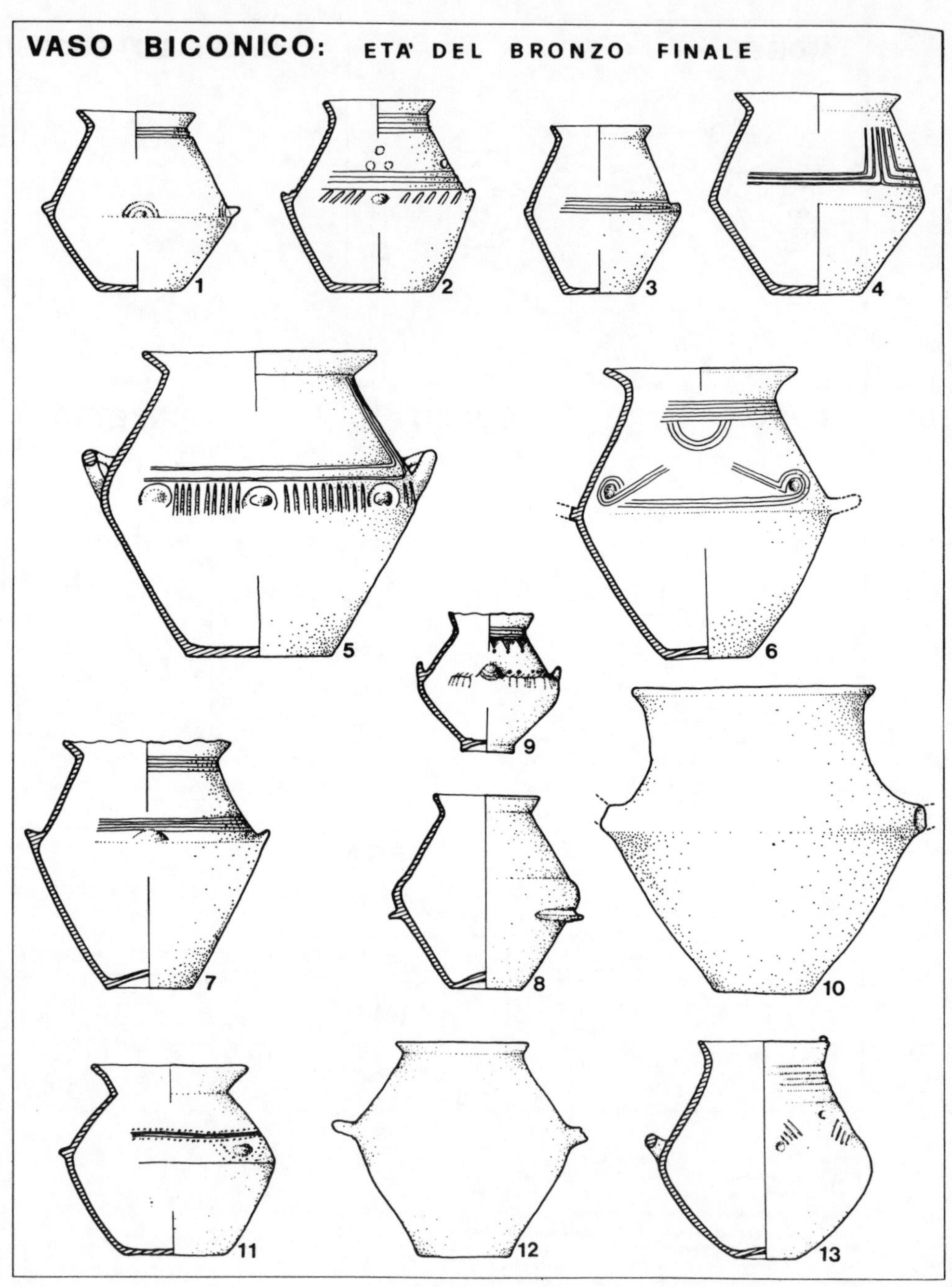

Tav. XII

120

'igure
5.5

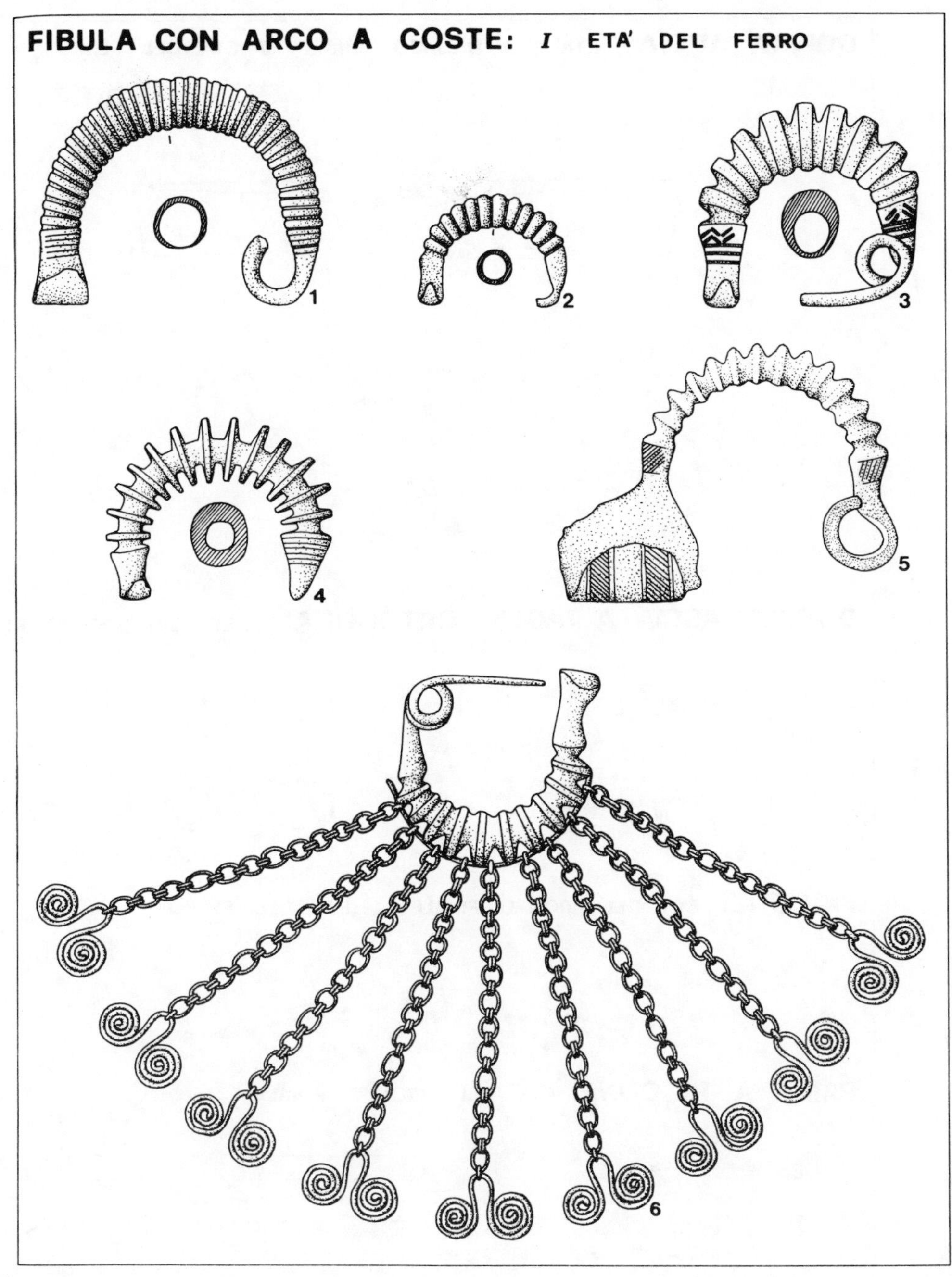

Figure 35.6

DOPPIA ASCIA: ETA' DEL BRONZO FINALE– I ETA' DEL FERRO

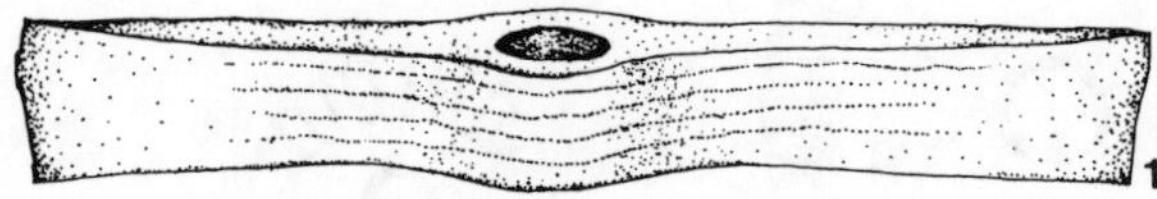

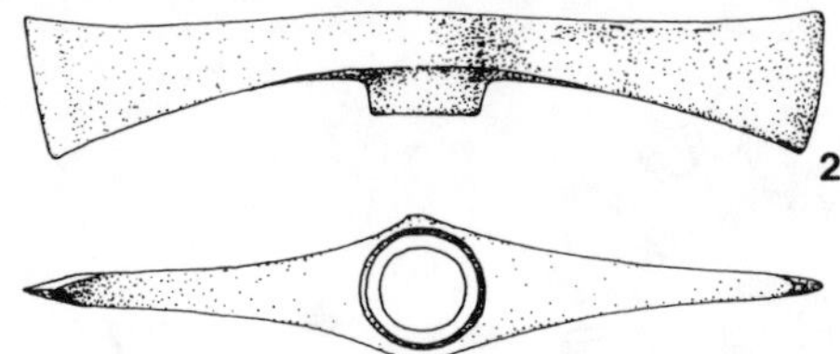

DOPPIA ASCIA A TAGLI ORTOGONALI : ETA' DEL BRONZO FINALE

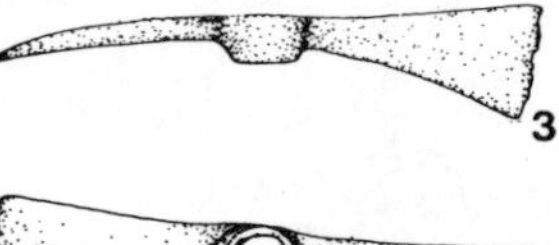

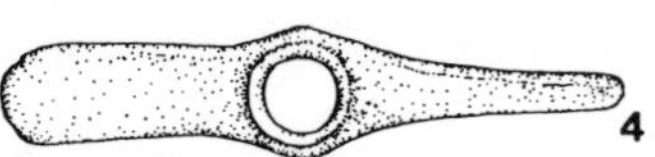

PICCONE: ETA' DEL BRONZO FINALE– I ETA' DEL FERRO

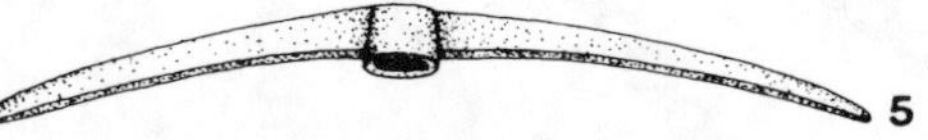

PANE A PICCONE: ETA' DEL BRONZO FINALE

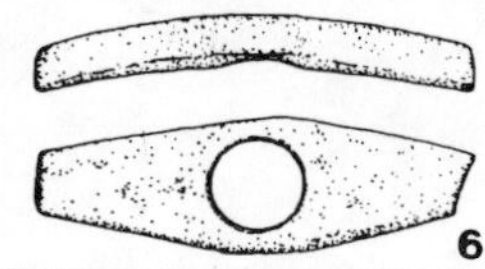

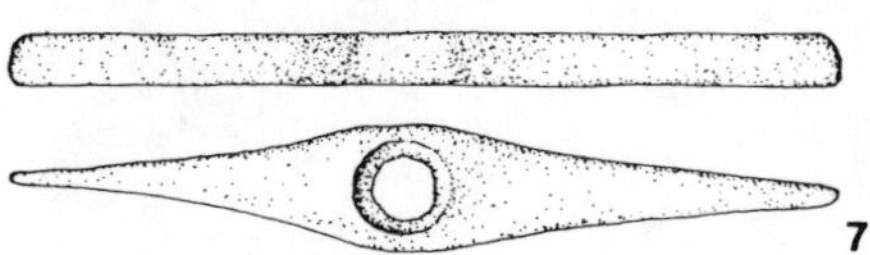

Tav. XCIX

207

For the individual forms belonging to the various classes of materials the following elements are supplied as scientific and didactic cataloguing tools:

terms to designate the form and its definition, dividing ceramic into open and closed forms;

indication and designation (illustrated by a sketch) of the components of every form and order to be adopted preferably in the analytical description (Figures 35.1 to 35.3);

tables containing detailed examples of the forms with samples taken from publications of all the Italian material, organised for indicative purposes according to typological and chronological criteria (Figures 35.4 to 35.6).

The Dictionary also contains guidelines for the preparation of the catalogue card index of the late Bronze Age and early Iron Age materials.

---

36 THE NATIONAL MONUMENTS RECORD ARCHAEOLOGICAL THESAURUS

F. Alan Aberg

Principal Investigator
Royal Commission on the Historic Monuments of England
London

Introduction

The National Monuments Record (NMR) Archaeological Thesaurus appeared in a draft form in 1986 (Royal Commission on the Historic Monuments of England, 1986). It is intended as a manual to serve the internal needs of the Royal Commission on the Historical Monuments of England (RCHME) for the archaeological terminology used in recording. It provides the vocabulary to assist indexing and retrieval, and, although in draft form, has been made available to organisations with parallel requirements. After two years it is now possible to review its use at a stage when computerisation of the record is far more advanced, and the range of terminology and retrieval need is better understood.

The Royal Commission was established in 1908 'to compile an inventory of the Ancient and Historical Monuments . . . of the people of England'. Its terms of reference as given in the Royal Warrant have changed to take greater account of the sites and monuments of the eighteenth and nineteenth centuries, to accept responsibility for the depiction of antiquities on Ordnance Survey maps, and to offer a growing public archive through the National Monuments Record. The latter was created in 1963 as successor to the National Building Record, but with an enlarged Archaeolgical Section. It acts as a government and public repository for relevant records of sites, excavations and research. The retrieval needs for such a comprehensive record therefore embrace every type of archaeological monument in England, and include many historic buildings as well.

Requirements

The national record lists 127 000 sites and buildings in the computerised data bank held at the Royal Commission's Southampton office, and is a growing, changing index of the archaeological sites of England. It was created originally by the Ordnance Survey to provide accurate antiquity information for map depiction, a service that it still performs, and increases annually as the result of fieldwork carried out by recording teams at regional offices in cities such as Exeter and Newcastle. Records are also added from other sources through collaborative projects with local authorities, such as Somerset County Council, government departments, and by the staff at Southampton abstracting records from a search of relevant monographs and journals. The increase in the Southampton record each year is substantial: in 1987–88, for example, 2 698 new sites were added, 2 345 were amended and a further 2 155 were checked without any change being made. In addition 12 083 references were added from the literature search.

The retrieval terms range across the whole spectrum of archaeological monuments from adits' to 'watermeadows', and also takes in terms such as 'country house' and 'conservatory', which overlap with the requirements of the building records of the NMR. For the post-medieval and industrial periods the national records include 'coalmines', 'textile mills' and other monuments, and the vocabulary has to be comprehensive to embrace these more recent archaeological sites. The thesaurus also has to include a range of archaeological objects, since many archaeological sites have been destroyed by development or agriculture, and are known only by the finds made at that time. Despite the lack of adequate information to designate a typology or classification for such monuments, they are included in the record on the basis that further research might in the future give more precision, and for the monument the find, or finds, is used as a description. Terms representing ornaments, pottery, implements, etc., are therefore necessary for the Southampton record.

The London office of the archaeological record also has its own special demands for terminology to be considered in the compilation of a thesaurus with the NMR. The public archive includes a large collection of historic photographs of monuments, taken between 1857 and the present, and the titling of the photographs may describe details of excavations and use structural terms not needed for a general classification of sites. Since 1978 the Archaeological Section has also compiled a computerised index of all archaeological excavations in England, which totals some 30 000 sites, and this provides retrieval by period, site type, excavator's name, finds, surviving archives, etc. The standardisation of terminology between these records and the Southampton index was, therefore, essential to cross relate any computer search, and a thesaurus was obviously necessary. Other records within the London archive also need a controlled vocabulary during computerisation, and these may include specialised indexes with their own terminology. The Council for British Archaeology's Implement Petrology Index uses geological terms for the description of stone axes; and the catalogue of the Medieval Village Research Group archive includes documentary terms relating to the historical records for these settlements. The word lists for those indexes extend therefore into narrower fields of interest than the general records, which may justify a specialised response.

Compilation

The thesaurus of archaeological terms was begun in 1978, in cooperation with a working party of local authority archaeologists from the Wessex area, and subsequently in consultation with other interested organisations. It was eventually completed internally, and produced for internal use and external guidance in 1986, based on the need outlined above for standardisation in the use of language within the NMR. It was also hoped it would serve as a guide to others seeking the retrieval of records from the NMR, and as a model and list of terms if other comparable records required an archaeological thesaurus for their own purposes. In the past, documents produced as internal record manuals have often been requested by other organisations engaged in comparable record keeping, and it was decided to circulate the draft thesaurus so that the information was immediately available to a wider audience.

The compilation of the thesaurus was based on a number of word-lists available from internal and external sources:

the archaeological record at Southampton had a series of descriptors produced at different times for the recording duties of staff, and these included most of the types of archaeological monuments found in Britain and a limited number of objects;

in 1974–75, the Council for British Archaeology produced a generic list of terms which was drawn up by a Working Party on Archaeological Records. This included both a list of terms and a classification to provide a structure for archaeological record systems;

local authority manuals drawn up by the Archaeology officers of the County Councils were also consulted whenever available, since the functions of these record systems in a local and regional context are closely comparable with the NMR. Many of the manuals include word-lists and in some regions, e.g. the West Midlands, the local authorities have worked together to produce common terminology;

the indexes and classification systems used in a number of specialist subjects, e.g. pottery, were consulted, and the indexes of the national archaeological journals were checked to ensure that a comprehensive vocabulary was achieved.

It was decided that the thesaurus needed to include some terms for the rest of Britain, and archive or foreign terms were added when they are frequently found in archaeological literature. The result of compilation went beyond the immediate retrieval needs of the NMR and produced a list of approximately 3 500 terms, in which it was clear immediately that objects formed an overwhelming majority. Many of the object terms never occur in the records, and the thesaurus faced the problem of delays in production, if all the descriptions were incorporated from the beginning. It was therefore decided to limit the range of objects included in the first draft, and to produce initially a thesaurus that incorporated all the site typologies needed, with only a selection of the object terms. The resulting thesaurus, therefore, has only 1 633 descriptors at present, pending revision to include the others that rest in a reserve index.

Thesaurus structure

As adopted for use,the NMR thesaurus in its draft form comprised three sections. An alphabetical list of descriptors forms the first part, and this is followed by two classified sections, one for sites and the other for objects. The alphabetical section displays the inter-relationship of terms (Figure 36.1).

Hierarchy in the draft thesaurus was defined as distinguishing between sites and objects, and had no other function. The classification was adopted to assist communication by directing retrieval to the broadest category of terms that share common attributes, e.g. Ceramics, although it was recognised that the introduction of a classification meant problems in the assignment of terms into the rigid structure thus created. A typical entry appears in the alphabetical section in the form shown in Figure 36.2. 'Use' does not

Figure 36.1 Term relationship in NMR Thesaurus

HR	Hierarchy
CLS	Classifications
BT	Broad Term. When the descriptor is a general term for which there is a group relationship
NT	Narrow Term. A specific or narrow term falling within a group relationship
RT	Related Term. One or several typological descriptions that relate to the entry term, which may assist in a search of the databank
USE	This indicates a descriptor which is the preferred entry term when a synonym occurs
UF	Use For. A descriptor which is a synonym, but is not an entry term

Figure 36.2 Example from NMR Thesaurus

CAIRN

HR	ARCHAEOLOGICAL SITE	UF	KERB CAIRN
CLS	FUNERARY-BARROW	NT	CAIRN CIRCLE LONG CAIRN RING CAIRN ROUND CAIRN
BT	BURIAL MOUND		
RT	CAIRNFIELD CHAMBERED CAIRN		

appear unless one of the other descriptors in the alphabetical list is the preferred entry term.

Revision

After three years the thesaurus is being revised to take into account the experience arising from use in the NMR. Computerisation in the office has made considerable strides during this period, and public enquiries involving the computerised records are frequent. Staff examination of the thesaurus and practice in its use can also be taken into consideration, so that a general revision is planned.

The word-lists generated from the computer show that the record incorporates a considerable number of terms not present in the manuals previously accepted as being comprehensive. The new terms have been added by recorders who have felt the need to introduce new terms in the period since the Royal Commission introduced the thesaurus, and the additional type descriptions will greatly enlarge the present list. Typological terms will also need to be compared with those used by English Heritage for the Monument Protection Programme, so that both government bodies conform in this subject, and the question of a combined thesaurus has already been discussed. Objects will, however, be retained, and if the thesaurus is extended it may include a large selection of object types as deemed appropriate from the many excluded in the draft.

The introduction of new terms will be the appropriate moment to examine the structure of the thesaurus, and to improve on its present ordering. A suggested new ordering has been put forward, so that the terms may be recast to follow a pattern which will clarify the preferred entry term, and provide more careful definitions in the scope notes. The expansion of synonyms and homonyms will be looked at, and a rigorous pursuit carried out on the related term references.

Consideration is also being given to recasting the thesaurus into a polyhierarchical format to replace the present classification adopted in 1986. The latter was a very late attempt to assist searches, but in practice it has not been used as much as the alphabetical list, and a hierarchical approach which will provide multiple classifications may afford more assistance in tracing relationships.

Computer applications may, as they are refined, require revision of thesauri in the light of the improved data control they provide. Vocabulary control to meet user requirements for indexing and retrieval, as was stated at the beginning of this assessment, is a primary requirement for record management. The draft Archaeological Thesaurus fulfilled that requirement, and the revised form will, it is hoped, eliminate the problem and extend the scope of what was produced in 1986.

37 TERMINOLOGY CONTROL AND THE SCHEDULED ANCIENT MONUMENTS RECORD

Amanda Chadburn

Records Office
English Heritage
London

Introduction

This paper reviews the terminology control used in recording ancient monuments, and more specifically, that used for recording the Scheduled Ancient Monuments (SAMs) monitored by English Heritage.

English Heritage (also known as the Historic Buildings and Monuments Commission for England) was set up in 1984 by an Act of Parliament, and its duties include securing and advising on England's architectural and archaeological heritage, and promoting the public's knowledge and enjoyment of it. The organisation took over many of the functions which used to be the responsibility of the former Inspectorate of Ancient Monuments and Historic Buildings of the Department of the Environment (DoE). More specifically, duties include identifying nationally important buildings and ancient monuments as candidates for legal protection (historic buildings are protected by the Secretary of State for the Environment by 'listing'; ancient monuments by 'scheduling'). Amongst other duties, it also monitors applications to change the use or form of these legally protected sites, monuments and buildings.

The current system

There are about 13 000 SAMs in England, and in order to carry out its responsibilities regarding them, the DoE set up a computerised record in 1980. The record is now run by English Heritage, and the main input to the record is from data collected by Field Monument Wardens, employees of English Heritage, whose task is to visit and monitor the physical condition of these protected archaeological sites.

The wardens' report on each visit to a SAM, entering data on a record form called the AM107 (Figure 37.1). Some of the data on SAMs collected by the earlier government organisations responsible for their protection (the DoE and Ministry of Works), is incorporated into the AM107s. The SAM record is more fully described elsewhere (Booth, 1988). English Heritage has recently set up a computerised mapping system complementary to the SAM record, to map the physical extent of the SAMs (Clubb, 1988).

The software package currently in use for the SAM record is Superfile, a package which allows data entry, editing and output via a flexible screen form. It can run on a wide variety of microcomputers, and allows long passages of text to be entered into a record which may also contain structured data. Any field of information as shown on the AM107, or any combination of them, may be searched using Superfile, although as the text fields are not indexed, searching them is very slow.

The data in the AM107 (and thus in the SAM record), can be divided into three types: controlled, structured and free text. In certain fields, controlled vocabulary is used because it allows rapid, thorough, and global searches of data. (A global query would be something like 'find me all the round barrows in East and West Sussex which are under

Figure 37.1 The AM107

Historic Buildings and Monuments
Commission for England

Ancient Monuments Record Form

01 Site number	02 Cross reference		03 G.R number
04 County	05 County number	06 Local Authority	
07 Parish	08 NGR	09 Height OD	10 File number

11 Site Name

12 Description

13 Site type/Period-general/Period-specific/Form

14 Proportion of Site Scheduled/Survival within Scheduled Area/Condition	15 Area
16 Land Class. on site	17 Land Class. around site
18 Site Status	19 Area Satus

20 Owner(s)

21 Occupier(s)

22 Legal Action

23 Works File

24 Site Management

Site number

25 Assessment of Importance of Monument

26 Scheduling Procedure

Date / /19 /Recommended/IAM, ...

/ /19 /(Approved (Not Approved/PIAM, ...

/ /19 /Review by Scheduling Policy Branch

/ /19 /Review by Head of Territorial Branch

/ /19 /(Recommended (Not Approved/Ancient Monuments Board

/ /19 /Notices Sent

/ /19 /Monument included in Schedule

Other Comments:

28 Monument not scheduled, de-scheduled because:

28 Archaeological History: Event/Name/Date

29 Visits: Name/Date

30 Sources: Source Type/Collection/Author/Date/Title/Other

31 Date of Compilation, Updating (For Office Use Only)

rough pasture'.) If there was no vocabulary control, the SAM record would need to be searched and read through manually, record by record, to attempt to answer global queries. In fact, answering such queries without vocabulary control would be extremely difficult, as there would be no direct method of comparing like with like. For our purposes and needs, this latter approach is clearly impractical.

Controlled vocabulary is currently used in the following fields of information (which are also shown in the AM107 (Figure 37.1)):

04 County

06 Local authority

13.1 Site type

13.2 Period general

13.4 Form

16 Land classification on site

17 Land classification around site

18 Site status

19 Area status

28.1 Archaeological event

30.1 Source type

Vocabulary control is achieved in these fields through the use of glossaries which are held within the database; words which are not glossary terms cannot be entered into the database. Other fields which contain structured data may also be searched for such items as personal or corporate names. Numeric controls are in force in certain other information fields.

New requirements

Although computing was already established in a number of archaeology museums, the SAM record was a pioneer as a management record in the UK when it was first set up in 1980. Enormous changes in the field of computing, and the knowledge that there will soon be a huge increase in the number of SAMs, has necessitated a review of our current systems and working practices

English Heritage is currently undertaking the Monuments Protection Programme (MPP), a review of sites of archaeological and historical interest, which aims to increase the number of Scheduled Ancient Monuments, and to iron out some of the imbalances which are apparent in the current Schedule of Ancient Monuments (Darvill *et al.*, 1987). Some imbalances in the SAM record can be seen in Figure 37.2. As part of the MPP, a new SAM record is planned.

There are a number of requirements and objectives for the vocabulary for this new record, which mainly relate to the site-type terminology and period terminology. These requirements include having vocabulary for site-type which allows complete and accurate retrieval, and which fully describes the monument in question; and also using terms which are going to be flexible enough to meet the needs of long-term record keeping. Terminology is not static: changes in the interpretation of monuments will occur with academic research, terms will go out of vogue, monuments will be reclassified, and so on. If the record is to remain academically credible, it is vital that the

Figure 37.2 Archaeological site types in the SAM Record up to September 1988

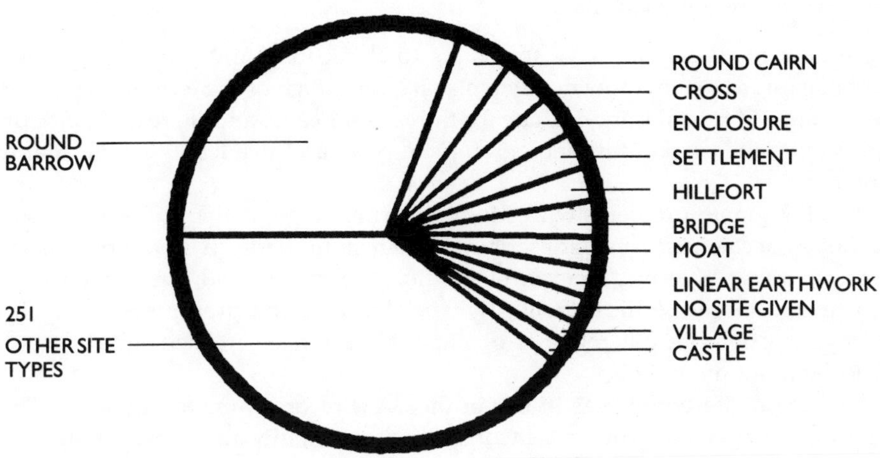

new vocabulary does not fossilise the new record into the classification and terminology of the 1980s.

The MPP will evaluate monuments by adopting a classificatory approach to site-type terminology. The monument class is the level of definition at which groups of monuments are defined and described, and at which evaluation takes place in the case of single monuments. Descriptions for all the main classes of monument are currently being written, so as to standardise the evaluation process. The terminology which results from this Monuments Descriptions exercise, may not be the most suitable for retrieval or record-keeping purposes. However, the retrieval vocabulary which is developed must directly relate to the monument descriptions. There is a clear need for some sort of thesaurus here.

The thesaurus must also relate to the various requirements of users of the SAM record who may not be directly concerned with the MPP classification, and additionally relate to other record systems, especially the county-based Sites and Monuments Records (SMRs) and those of the Royal Commission on the Historical Monuments for England (RCHME). Local records such as the SMRs will be 'trawled' for nationally important sites during the course of the MPP, and sites which are selected from them will be evaluated. There must therefore be a way of linking the vocabulary used by SMRs with the monument descriptions terminology of the MPP.

In addition to the MPP, RCHME has produced a thesaurus in use for the National Monuments Record (Royal Commission on the Historical Monuments of England, 1986) described in Chapter 36. It is important that the terminology of the new Record of Scheduled Monuments relates to the RCHME thesaurus, because, like the SMRs, the National Monuments Record and the National Archaeological Record will be 'trawled' for information during the course of the MPP. Although the RCHME has different vocabulary requirements from English Heritage (for example, the RCHME needs vocabulary to describe portable artefacts), the two organisations face similar problems regarding site-type vocabulary, and are currently working together in the hope of reaching common ground.

Site-type and period vocabulary

These new requirements have forced us to think long and hard about our current vocabulary and system, now nearly ten years old. Much of the terminology currently in use in the SAM record is inadequate for these new needs, and there are major problems especially in the current terminology for site-type, and to a lesser extent, that used for period.

One of the main problems with site-type terminology, is that there is no established vocabulary or classification for describing British monuments. It is possible to call a round barrow by range of terms, for example: tumulus, burial mound, barrow, tump, mound, or to give it a more specific term like twin bell barrow. This presents obvious difficulties for anyone attempting a regional or national search of archaeological records for a particular monument type.

The current site-type terms in use in the SAM record, numbering some 270 words, suffer from three main problems: inconsistency, ambiguity and duplication.

Figure 37.3 Examples of the current word-structure in the SAM Record

AP Site (unclassified)
Unclassified site
Non-antiquity

House (domestic)
Gatehouse
Earth-house

Figure 37.4 Currently allowed entries in the Period-specific field

Option		Entry
Specific dates	e.g.	1234 AD
Century dates	e.g.	C5 C5BC C5bc (for C14 dates)
A date range	e.g.	C5–C8 1527–8 1527–1528
Suggested terms	e.g.	Beaker Trajanic Celtic Palmerstonian

Inconsistency is apparent throughout, such as when classification by form is mixed with classification by function (e.g. Chambered round barrow with Chipping floor). Legal terms such as Manor are mixed with non-legal terms; foreign words are mixed with English words; and some regional variants are allowed, whereas others are not.

Duplication exists as some terms can be classified under a number of terms, for example the last phase of Waylands Smithy (a Neolithic megalithic long barrow) could be classified in the SAM record as a Megalithic tomb, Tomb, Chambered long barrow, or Long barrow, all of which would be correct. However, there may only be a single term suitable for classifying other monument types.

Ambiguity arises in the use of such terms as Hospital, which can be used to classify monuments in the medieval and post-medieval periods with differing functions.

In addition, terms are structured differently, and are presented in a variety of ways (Figure 37.3).

As well as problems with the actual terminology, the requirements for quick and accurate retrieval of site-types cannot be fully met because of a number of other difficulties.

The current wordlist for site-type is not cross-referenced in any way, so that a search for 'Barn' would produce incomplete results without knowing that 'Tithe barn' is also allowed. This factor makes global searches very difficult at present, unless the user is familiar with all the available options.

In addition, no guidance is given as to how to find the correct keyword. Someone trying to find all the scheduled mines would have to know that (amongst other terms) Coal mine, Gold mine, Flint mine and Copper mine are all allowed. Similarly, someone searching for all scheduled ponds would have to be aware of all the available glossary terms, including Decoy, Dew-pond, Fishery, etc. (Note that a computer search for all ponds would not be successful using the wildcard option of *pond*, which would allow retrieval of any terms which include the word 'pond').

There are some monuments, such as dovecotes, which can be SAMs in their own right, or can be part of larger monuments such as priories or manorial complexes. At the moment there is no mechanism of retrieving all dovecotes as they could be classified under the 'umbrella' term of a larger monument.

The main problem in the period fields is the terminology used for describing a specific period or date. Controlled vocabulary is *not* used, and a variety of data can be entered in this field, including dates relating to a culture such as the Beaker Period, and calendar dates, as can be seen in Figure 37.4. The lack of tightly controlled data in this field makes global retrieval virtually impossible, and the mixture of calendar dates with words is extremely undesirable.

Possible options for the future

There are several main ways in which site-type vocabulary is currently being controlled in records such as SMRs and national archaeological records, and which provide useful comparative approaches when devising vocabulary for the new Record of Scheduled Monuments. These are more fully described elsewhere (Chadburn, 1988).

One option is not to use controlled vocabulary at all. Some SMRs have taken this approach, and simply use any terms or any natural language which they feel is appropriate. The current SAM Record and most SMRs do, however, use controlled vocabulary, displayed as a simple alphabetical list of words, not cross-referenced in any way (the 'wordlist' approach).

The problems inherent in both these approaches have already been discussed with reference to the current SAM Record. Neither approach will be used in the new Record of Scheduled Monuments, as they would not allow speedy, accurate and full data retrieval which English Heritage requires.

One possible approach (rarely used in SMRs) which we could take in future, is to produce an index of archaeological terms. Indexes, generally fully cross-referenced alphabetical lists of terms including keywords and alternative terms, give guidance to a correct entry term (or the 'preferred term' or 'keyword') and also guidance to related words, by instructions such as *use, use for, see also,* and so on. Indexes have the advantage of flexibility over thesauri, in that they are not tied to a structure or classification.

Another possible approach (again rarely used by SMRs) is to produce a thesaurus of archaeological terms, a thesaurus having been as defined a 'a list of words organised by the ideas they express' (Royal Commission on the Historical Monuments of England, 1987). Thesauri are similar to indexes in that they provide guidance to keywords through cross-referencing. However, they are not simply alphabetical cross-referenced lists, as they are organised by topics which provide another level of guidance for a user. For example, archaeological site-type terms might be organised into topics such as industrial, domestic, and ritual. The Architectural Thesaurus (Royal Commission on the Historical Monuments of England, 1987) organises terms into hierarchies and sub-hierarchies by form, function and building complex. Of course, thesauri may also be displayed in a simple alphabetical format, rather like an index, although generally the underlying classification scheme would be displayed alongside too.

One drawback, with thesauri is that they are time-consuming to construct, although a good thesaurus is an invaluable aid to analysis and retrieval. Another is that the classification system has to be one which is, or will be, generally accepted by users. We have already noted the considerable drawback of having no established vocabulary for archaeological site-type in the UK.

As these two latter approaches would both provide an acceptable level of guidance and retrieval to the new record, it has been decided that English Heritage will need to produce an index or thesaurus to meet its new vocabulary requirements. The first stage, a literature search for currently used archaeological site-type terms, has already been undertaken, and much material analysed. The next stages will include grouping terms into topics, and developing relationships between the terms. It will be decided whether a classificatory scheme is necessary, or whether an index will suffice for the needs of the Record of Scheduled Monuments (RSM), *after* the grouping exercise. It has been seen that imposing a classificatory system upon archaeological site-type terms is not particularly successful (Royal Commission on the Historical Monuments of England, 1986) and if a classification is needed, it will be developed from the groupings into which the words fall: a 'bottom up' approach, rather than by starting out with a rigid classification.

---

38 AN APPROACH TO TERMINOLOGY FROM THE PERSPECTIVE OF ARCHAEOLOGY, ANTHROPOLOGY AND ETHNOGRAPHY

Dr Peter H. Welsh

Director of Research/Chief Curator
The Heard Museum
Phoenix, Arizona

Introduction

The terminological challenges faced by anthropology museums are similar to those of all museums with broad-based collections. Our purpose in developing terminological systems is to be able to find objects in our collection that meet the criteria of complex queries. The terminology we use must be meaningful for all types of objects — from pot shards to paintings and from biological specimens to buildings — as well as all the photographic and documentary evidence relating to those objects.

This paper will focus on a successful approach to the terminology problem now in use by a growing number of museums and archives in the United States. This approach employs an automated lexicon approach that permits the rapid development of a complex structure among words and phrases (see Figure 38.1). This system handles such thorny terminological issues as ambiguous meanings, multiple encompassing terms and synonyms. Because this approach to terminology is at the heart of the collections management database systems with which it operates, many of the data fields that previously proliferated for dealing with specific classes of terminology — such as material, construction or design — can be replaced with fields such as 'description' and 'subject' more commonly associated with manual systems.

Having crossed the threshold into the automated age, we constantly find new and expanded ways to make use of data that we have available to us. One of the reasons that we see so much promise for future applications of our database has to do with the approach we have taken to the terminology problem. Five basic principles have guided the approach to terminology control described in this paper. While making no claims for their uniqueness, they can be summarised in five short phrases:

terminology control is for finding things;

terminology is a system — not a list;

names are not identities;

authority should not hinder accuracy;

use the words you have.

First of all, we must be clear in our purposes for trying to establish a terminological system. Is it to be a collections management tool, a research tool, or both? We must also clarify how broad we envision the applications of such a system to be. Do we see it as transcending a single collection to embrace all things, or is it to be a finding aid for a single collection at one institution? What will be the structure of the vocabulary: alphabetical, hierarchical or something else? Is control of names sufficient, or do we need vocabulary control to describe attributes of an artefact beyond just its object name?

Figure 38.1 The basic lexicon structure

7, 8 PARENTS	GRANDPARENTS	
1 TERM	12, SISTERS	
17-DISPLAY TERM		
5 PFD TERM		
15, SONS		4 ILLEGAL
	10 REMARKS	

The basic structure of the approach to terminology described in this paper can be seen here. The screen depicted in this figure is part of the ARGUS Collections Management System developed by Questor Systems of Pasadena, California.

Though the field tags may at first seem idiosyncratic, they are not incompatible with standard thesaurus terms. PARENTS are broader terms, SONS are narrower terms, SISTERS are equivalent but non-preferred terms; a PREFERRED TERM (PFD TERM) is the term among a group of equivalent terms that is linked to broader and narrower terms; terms tagged as ILLEGAL are ambiguous and require the use of one of their PARENTS; REMARKS are Scope Notes; DISPLAY TERMS enable the user to convert a TERM to upper and lower case for use in screens and reports; and GRANDPARENTS are, intuitively, the PARENTS' PARENTS.

In working with this system, the TERM is the centre of activity, and this screen is used to view and define a TERM's relationship to other TERMS. Several actions are allowed: a new TERM may be created to serve as a PREFERRED TERM or a PARENT; if the TERM is a PREFERRED TERM one or more PARENTS are assigned; if the term is not preferred, a PREFERRED TERM is assigned; if the term is ambiguous, specific PARENTS are assigned and the term is declared ILLEGAL; REMARKS about usage can be made, and a DISPLAY TERM can be created.

Several important features should be noted. SONS are developed only by determining that a term is part of a larger class. If X is a PARENT of Y, the Y is a SON of X. The system does not allow a user to assign SONS to a term, only PARENTS. Similarly, and applying the same logic, a user is not allowed to assign SISTERS to a term, only PREFERRED TERMS. These rules prevent proliferation of unnecessary terms, and allowing the system to be built only from the 'bottom up' forces users to look for connections. A critical aspect of this approach is that the system is by necessity truly poly-hierarchical. Users are encouraged to assign more than one PARENT to a term.

Among its many obvious advantages for terminology development — which permit us to approach the polysemy of natural language — poly-hierarchy has another, less obvious, feature. This system does not use the concept of a related term. We have found that a logical and effective approach to related terms in a poly-hierarchical environment is simply to note that related terms share a parent.

Terminology control is for finding things

In museums we employ our catalogue records in two distinct ways. One way is to retrieve information about a specific object, usually by looking it up under its catalogue number. On finding the card, we can read the information recorded there to learn about the object. What is it? What culture or period is it from? What is it made of? We want the words used to be accurate and reasonably descriptive, but we are not concerned whether they have any structured relationship to the terms describing other items in the collection. We are far more interested in how well the terms describe the item in question, and in how well they convey the historical or collection information augmenting first-hand examination of the piece. Structured vocabulary control is irrelevant for this use of the catalogue record.

However, there is another extremely important use of the object record file. That is to find objects which meet a set of specified criteria but whose catalogue numbers are *not* known. In this case objects are found in catalogue records by looking under one or more terms used to describe them. Without confidence that objects can be found using the catalogue, we are forced to go to the collection area and rummage for objects, an activity all museum professionals want to minimise. The need to increase the quality of searching, and decrease the amount of rummaging, makes terminology control imperative.

Terminology is a system — not a list

It is critical to recognise the difference between terms and terminology. Terms are those words or phrases that have a precise meaning. Terminology is best thought of as the terms in systematic relationship to one another. No matter what terms we use, we can recognise certain types of relationships among them.

A fundamental type of relationship among terms is inclusion. Inclusion is a distinction of practicality which incorporates both true hyponymy — described by the relationship: X is a kind of Y — as well as part-whole relationships (Lyons, 1977, pages 291–305). While the concept of inclusion glosses over some distinctions that are important from the point of view of theoretical semantics, it satisfies our need to find things in our collections. For instance, although the relationship between 'chair' and 'furniture' is hyponymic — a chair is a kind of furniture — and the relationship between 'chair leg' and 'chair' is part-whole, in conducting a search for 'furniture' we would probably be interested in knowing that there were 'chair legs' as well as 'chairs' in the collection.

Arranging terms in this kind of relationship produces a hierarchical system in which more generalised terms encompass a number of more specific terms. Inclusion is a powerful tool for grouping terms, since searching for a general term captures all of the specific terms under it. We are comfortable with the idea that a general term can encompass a number of more specific terms. However, a simple hierarchy that places terms in only one larger class is unsatisfactory for lexicon development because it does not adequately reflect the reality of how terms are used.

The problem of a simple hierarchy can be illustrated with a group of terms taken from the widely used terminology developed in *Nomenclature* (Blackaby, Greene and the Nomenclature Committee, 1988). Suppose I was interested in finding all objects used for skiing in a collection. I might look for skis, poles, boots, and goggles. In *Nomenclature*, SKI, SNOW is classified as 'Sports Equipment'; BOOT, SKI is classified as 'Clothing–Footware'; POLE, SKI is classified as 'LTE (Land Transportation Equipment) — Human-powered'; and

GOGGLES (GOGGLES, SKI is not a term) is classified as 'Personal Gear'. I have no disagreement with any of these individual classifications, each is reasonable and justifiable. Viewed from the perspective of the functional assemblage, however, the system offers little hope of efficient searching. Working in an environment that permits a term to be part of only one higher order group forces decisions that lead to unsatisfying classifications.

Preferable, then, are poly-hierarchical systems that allow terms to be part of more than one class, permitting all things having to do with skiing to be linked together, and also allowing each element in the skiing assemblage to be connected to those other reasonable and justifiable groupings to which it might belong.

Another kind of relationship among terms is 'equivalence'. We have devised different procedures for handling the different degrees of equivalence that terms can have. Synonyms are the most closely related terms. We handle those by deciding on a preferred term to which other terms point. The preferred term is linked into the hierarchy of terms. The idea of a preferred term is important, because it is also used for those terms which are not, precisely speaking, synonyms. An archaic, colloquial, or regional term may point to a term which will be made part of the hierarchical system. Sometimes it is difficult to decide whether to make a term a sister or a son of another. The determining factor has to do with whether the non-preferred term can act as a non-redundant heading for other terms. In actual use, a non-preferred sister term is simply a terminological dead end. It points to its sister term, and to nothing else. When a preferred term is used in a search, all of its non-preferred sisters are offered for inclusion.

More distantly connected terms — often called related terms — are handled by our system in one of two ways. The first, and most common way, is to give the two terms the same 'parent' term. For example, Hopi and Zuni Indians are both classified as 'Western Pueblo'. Their relatedness is revealed by stepping up through the hierarchy of terms and seeing that Hopi and Zuni are both sons of Western Pueblo. In some cases it may be that the parent connecting related terms is at a more general level than the parent that connects two other terms, but poly-hierarchy makes no demands that all parents should be equally broad. The difference between this relationship and inclusion is that the two terms are compared in relation to a third higher-level term. Inclusion is a relationship between a general and a specific term. When the relatedness that connects terms is so distant that assigning a common parent seems forced, REMARKS (Scope Notes) can be used to direct a searcher to another section of the lexicon.

To summarise, inclusion defines the vertical 'dimension' of our system and equivalence defines the horizontal 'dimension'. There is a third form of relationship with which we must deal in our systems — that is the relationship of ambiguity. The classic case of ambiguity is what we have come to call the 'Crow Problem'. The tribe of Indians called Crow is certainly different from the bird called crow. We had to devise a way to make sure we did not confuse the two terms. Our solution is to make the term 'Crow' 'illegal'. The word cannot be used. When someone enters 'crow' a prompt appears on the screen which says that he or she must enter a more precise term: 'Crow Indian' or 'Crow, bird'. We also apply this technique to the instances in which towns in different states are given the same name, as in Las Vegas, Nevada and Las Vegas, New Mexico. 'Las Vegas' alone is an illegal term.

Names are not identities

As we work with a terminological system with its various dimensions of relationships, we may lose sight of the fact that we must go beyond a system for a single characteristic of a museum specimen. A great deal of attention has been devoted to the names we call things, but equivalent systematic effort must be devoted to thinking about the multiple characteristics of an object — its identity. This concept of identity is an analytical approach similar to what others have called 'faceted classification' (Foskett, 1959), and which in other disciplines has been called 'distinctive feature analysis' (Lyons, 1977, page 232), 'componential analysis' (Goodenough, 1956), or 'compositional analysis' (Eco, 1979, pages 91–120).

Our primary purpose in striving for vocabulary control should be to detect identities rather than to list names. To clarify this distinction, we can think of our everyday system for naming and identifying people. The concept of identity used here derives from notions of social identity developed by Goodenough (1965) and Keesing (1970). In the United States, each of us has, with few exceptions, one and only one name. ('Name', as used here refers to the combination of First, Middle, and Last names by which we introduce ourselves.) In the context of social life, however, we each have numerous identities. We have professional identities (curator, anthropologist, administrator), familial identities (husband, father, brother, son), and even impersonal identities (shopper, driver, stranger). Each of these identities can be described on the basis of a set of criteria, none of which requires that our name be known, yet few of these identities are discernible from our name alone.

We can think of objects in the same way. Each has a name, but each also has numerous identities. When we search for objects we usually want to find those items which have a specific kind of identity. To accomplish this we include in our search some of their descriptive attributes. In particular, terms describing material, construction, decoration, design, function, as well as the subject matter of paintings and photographs quickly become critical to a system designed for searching the catalogue. It is our belief that the utility of vocabulary control is that it can greatly aid our search for identities in collections and thus we need to think beyond simple naming. We take a basic premise, therefore, that vocabulary control must not be limited to a single descriptive category.

Suppose, for instance, we were interested in finding all silver cups made in Philadelphia, Pennsylvania, that were in our collection. In addition to needing to have the object terms structured so that we could find cups of all types, we also need to have a structure for materials terms and geographical terms. Without such an approach we will have made little headway in seeing more deeply into our collections.

Unfortunately, in the recent revision of *Nomenclature*, the important distinction between names and identities has been dismissed. The authors suggest that they had to make a decision among possible filtering systems — materials, country of origin, age, style, and so on — but 'function was chosen as the most useful' (Blackaby, *et al.*, 1988, pages 1–3). Indeed, original function is a useful and critical filter for dividing things into groups. *Nomenclature* is a useful tool, but its limitations are directly related to the intentions of its authors who conceived it to be a tool to aid collections managers, not as a tool to aid those who seek deeper understanding through finding new relationships. To quote:

> 'Of course, for the . . . historian, color, date, use, provenance, and so on are the most interesting data fields. For purposes of collections management, however, identifying an object as a SPOON from the classification "Food Service T&E" is more important than knowing that it is part of a set, that it is made of silver, that it dates from the eighteenth century, or that it was used by Thomas Jefferson.' (Blackaby, *et al.*, 1988, page II–1)

Arguing for greater concern for identities is arguing for more depth in our understanding of how objects can reveal themselves to us. Names are undeniably important, and deserve attention, but virtually every descriptive field has its own set of conceptual and content-oriented problems. For some categories, like geographical provenience, we can draw on an elaborate and specific terminology which has been developed outside museums. While the terminology and structure of other categories — design, for instance — is much more fuzzy, all descriptive categories appear to share some common structural principles. We must turn our attention to the whole spectrum of characteristics that are embodied in material culture.

Authority should not hinder accuracy

Authority lists are different from terminology systems. In order to appreciate this difference, it is worth considering at some length exactly how authority lists are used.

First of all, we must remember that no authority list, as just a list, provides assurance that a word is used correctly. Only the expertise of the cataloguer ensures correct word usage. There is a difference between the things correctly described by the words 'fresco' and 'oil on canvas', just as there is between 'horse' and 'elephant'. Having a word in an authority list does not keep it from being used incorrectly.

If we are concerned with correct word usage for cataloguing, and conversely, with appropriate word comprehension by a user of the catalogue, then an authority list must be expanded to become a dictionary or glossary. That is, if the cataloguer and the user have a reference book of terms and definitions, then the authority list assists in the cataloguing and comprehension process. In this context, then, we have greatly expanded the idea of a simple list of authorised terms to address the much more difficult problem of assigning meaning(s) to the terms used.

We must also remember that in some cases, the wrong term may be right. There are archaic terms that can be appropriate in an historic sense when we may be just as interested in what they *used* to call it, as we are in what we call it now. This same issue can be expressed in words which have regional applicability — is it a 'fiddle' or a 'violin'? Furthermore, there may simply be colloquial terms that people may want to use in a search, such as 'USA', 'Coke', or 'T-shirt'. None of these terms may be preferred for actual cataloguing, but they must be part of any worthwhile authority list. Clearly, there must be different types of terms in an authority list.

Some might argue that one purpose of an authority list *is* to reduce the number of words used, thereby making it easier for users to learn the meanings of the allowable words. This is true at one level, for if synonym-like words are eliminated, there are fewer terms to remember. But such a decision has a cost. To the extent that it prevents using more descriptive or appropriate words (specific terms, relevant slang, etc.), then such an authority list would become a detriment.

The idea of a more *appropriate* term opens another area of concern. Proper or appropriate use of terms will vary depending on the expertise of the cataloguer, and the needs of the user. It may be perfectly adequate for cataloguing purposes to describe an object as a 'painting' when it could be more accurately described as an 'oil painting on canvas' or even an 'oil painting on gessoed linen canvas'. Athough the descriptions become progressively more specific, none of them are incorrect. Yet, for someone attempting to determine whether the painting is a forgery, the terms 'oil', 'canvas', and even 'gesso' and 'linen' are hopelessly vague. The chemical or microscopic constituents of the oil and the canvas would need to be discussed in order for a determination of authenticity to be made. However, the descriptive words that would be derived from such an analysis might very well be considered much too detailed for many other legitimate uses of the catalogue. Reflection will show that virtually every aspect of a catalogue record has a degree of specificity or detail which makes it such that no catalogue record can be all things to all people. Any word detailed enough for a curator making an attribution is probably far too specific for a collections manager looking for an 'oil painting'.

What then is the role of an authority list in cataloguing and searching? Cataloguing presents one type of problem. Which term among several 'correct' possibilities should be chosen from the list? While being more specific is generally desirable, a cataloguer can only be as specific as our confidence in our assessment of the material allows. Sometimes we can be sure it is X, but not to which subclass of X it belongs.

In other cases, our expertise exceeds that of the authority list. 'Mimbres Style II' is very real, but very few people can identify it. No authority list is likely to have the term. Yet it is correct, and in fact is more correct (in the sense that more specificity is desired) than any term on any authority list. Is the curator to be denied using what he or she deems to be an appropriate term?

The authority list really becomes necessary for searching. In a search for oil paintings on canvas, if both 'paint' and 'oil paint' are authorised terms, then a search needs to look in both categories: under 'oil paint' because I am looking for oil on canvas, and also under 'paint', to allow for the possibility that the cataloguing of an oil work was not done to the level of specificity in which I am interested.

It quickly becomes apparent that it is in searching that authority lists become critical. A catalogue record that is simply being read can have a very loose terminology with minimal problems. It may use 'pants' or 'trousers', or 'Mimbres' or 'Mimbres Style II'. Some terms may not be the best possible, some may not be specific enough for current purposes, but no serious harm is done (remember we are not discussing actual errors).

But as soon as we try and look up an object by using these terms, things are very different. Without an authority list, we do not know what terms have been used, which are not allowed, or which terms are available for searching. From a curator's point of view, authority lists are not to make cataloguing correct (they can not do it); they are not to make cataloguing consistent (consistency is in the eye of the beholder); they are so I and others can find the things.

Use the words you have

If we agree that it is necessary to have controlled vocabulary for useful object descriptions, we can examine the process by which the actual corpus of terms used might be developed. There seem to be two fundamental approaches.

The first way is to approach the problem abstractly and think of all the possible terms that might be encountered in a particular terminological domain, such as man-made objects, or art and architecture. An advantage of this approach is that once the terminological structure has been applied, and after preferred terms have been agreed upon, subsequent cataloguing and searches can be accomplished simply be looking up the correct term in the thesaurus. Moreover, the resulting standard list can be used in a variety of institutions, thereby facilitating information transfer.

The drawbacks, of course, are significant. First, someone must invest enormous amounts of time finding and evaluating terms that may never be used. Second, the institutions which adopt such a system may have to undergo a large amount of recataloguing in order to bring their records into line with the standard, something many institutions may have neither the time nor the resources to implement. Third, as has been recognised in regard to *Nomenclature*, standardisation involves a long-term commitment to system maintenance. Without such maintenance to respond to new terms or new thinking about the relationship of terms to each other, the system soon loses its place as a standard.

An alternative approach to thesaurus development is to modify and restructure the actual set of terms that have been used to describe objects in an existing collection. The main advantage is that the corpus of terms already exists simplifying or eliminating entirely the difficult decisions about what to include and what to exclude. In addition, by making liberal use of preferred terms and synonyms, most of the original terminology can be retained, reducing the number of changes required in the original system. Such an approach is particularly important for vocabularies which have no standard lexicon (such as design motifs). In this case it is still possible to proceed effectively and efficiently because the basic vocabulary, flawed as it may be, already exists in the collection records.

The primary drawback to this approach is that an institution might spend time and effort working out the structure of a terminological system only to find that another institution has previously accomplished this task. They have 'reinvented the wheel' when, had they had access to the other institution's terminology, they might have needed only to make minor modifications to the structure and add the terms that were particular to their collection.

It turns out that these two approaches to developing lexicons are not as different as they first appear, and a combination of both methods seems to be the optimal solution. While it seems neither possible nor, in fact, desirable to achieve consensus on the specific terms we use to fill our lexicons, there is some likelihood that standards can be established at higher levels of categorisation. It seems pointless to expend energy and intellect on arguments about how to classify a Swiss Army knife. A far more productive effort, it seems, would be to establish agreement on the more general qualities of material things.

For example, we can take advantage of the work already invested in object names. We can select the appropriate higher-level categories of systems such as *Nomenclature* or the *Art and Architecture Thesaurus*. These logical categories provide the overall structure to the lexicon. The collection's existing descriptive terms can be incorporated into this framework using many synonyms and multiple parents. By only dealing with the terms actually occurring in the collection records, and by using synonyms and preferred terms, the original content of the records can be retained. The result is a structured system compatible with others at general conceptual levels, yet unique at the most specific levels.

Conclusions

Terminology is an extraordinarily powerful tool for bringing order to our understanding of museum collections. Language, the words by which we know what something is — and is not — serves us as so much more than a device for counting the cups in our cupboards. Yet, as we try to use language to convey ideas expertly expressed in a non-linguistic medium, we struggle with the frustrations of adequate representation. As we go further and attempt to construct controlled and computerised terminologies using exotic-sounding and authoritative approaches like faceted descriptions, poly-hierarchical thesauri, and authority lists, we risk making a fetish of the process and losing sight of the real reason for our efforts.

Museums curate the physical products of human expression whether overt expressions, such as painting and sculpture, or subtle expressions, such as the artefacts of daily life. In all of these media we can detect the expression of what we might call statements. Rarely, however, do they pose a question. That function — enquiry — is reserved for language. The more refined our language for enquiry gets, the more effective and penetrating our questions can be.

I have great affection for a phrase coined by the anthropologist Gregory Bateson which helps preserve my perspective on this problem. He talked about the 'differences that make a difference' (Bateson, 1979, page 110). Terminology — language — is about differences and about resemblances. By concentrating on the differences that make a difference, we can find appropriate levels of discrimination and begin to ask the more interesting questions.

---

39 TERMINOLOGY AT THE PITT RIVERS MUSEUM: THE PRAGMATIC APPROACH

Linda Mowat and Elizabeth Edwards

Pitt Rivers Museum
Oxford

Introduction

We are pleased to give this paper on what is happening to terminology at the Pitt Rivers Museum, as we have been making quiet but definite steps forward during recent years in the documentation and retrieval of its fine collections. Our 'pragmatic' approach may not necessarily appeal to terminology purists. It is, however, an attempt to find an accurate, consistent and workable corpus within the considerable constraints imposed by a major historical collection, existing documentation systems and very limited resources, both human and financial.

The Blackwood system

The Classification of Artefacts in the Pitt Rivers Museum, Oxford was devised by the anthropologist Beatrice Blackwood in the course of the Second World War (Blackwood, 1970). During these years the original catalogue entry for each of the quarter million or so artefacts in the collection was duplicated on to two 3 × 5 inch index cards and filed according to Region and Subject. Remarkably, the war lasted long enough for this project to be completed. The Classification, which was published in 1970, refers to the Subject Index.

Beatrice Blackwood's classification might be regarded today as a little eccentric. Her subject categories range from artefactual groupings such as Tools and Textiles to specific artefact types such as Combs and Netsuke; and from materials such as Barkcloth and Ivory to concepts such as Death and Religion.

Probably today no one would produce quite such a diverse classification; but we have to remember that Beatrice Blackwood was working without the benefit of computers. We should also bear in mind that her classification was tailored specifically to the archaeological and ethnographic collections of the Pitt Rivers Museum, and that as a means of providing information about that collection it works very well. Its versatility is demonstrated by the fact that it was adopted, with certain modifications, by several other museums with ethnographic collections.

Developing a computer-based object thesaurus

Our decision to begin computerisation in 1986 was a step towards reducing the labour-intensity of managing a truly enormous card index. The database we are using is Cardbox Plus, which has excellent indexing facilities and is easy to use for those, like ourselves, with little grounding in computer science. Separately designed data entry forms are in use for archive photographs and museum objects. Figure 39.1 is a specimen printout of a museum object record: the two fields of most relevance to this discussion are those for Object NAME and CLASSification.

igure
9.1 Specimen museum object record

```
.ACCNO: 1985.50. 227              .NO: 1      .DATE:              .DIM: L 30 MM
.BOOKNO: HILDBURGH NOTES VI 10     .ARCH/ETH:E .

.CONT: EUROPE          COUNTRY:  ITALY                          .CON: WATER-DAMAGED.  CLEANED AT PRM 1988.
.REGION: ROME
.GROUP:
                                                                .DOC: HILDBURGH DOC
.NAME: HORSE-SHOE-NAIL  FINGER-RING  AMULET        NATNAME:
.CLASS: ANIMALS  TOOLS  ORNAMENTS  RELIGION

.PROCESS:                    .MATERIAL:  IRON  METAL    .COLOUR:
                                                        .BLACK    .RELCOLLS:
                                                                  .ILL: PHOTOCOPY

.COLLECTOR: HILDBURGH, W.L.                             .COLL: 1910          .LOC:  OG
.DONOR: WELLCOME INSTITUTE                              .ACQ: LOAN 1985      .REC: LMM 1988 5

 Horseshoe nail bent into a ring.  Amulet against the Evil Eye.
```

As Blackwood's Classification was already in existence and of proven efficiency, being indeed a unique and treasured museum object in itself, we could see no advantage in abandoning it. However, the transition to computerisation provided an opportunity to streamline it a little. Figure 39.2 lists the old and new classifications for objects, showing the various groupings and dispersals of categories that have been made. Some of the retained categories may still seem a little quaint to the uninitiated: RINGS of unknown use, for example. Easy enough to dispense with if there were no such objects in the collection, but certain dustbin categories seem to be essential.

The beauty of the new system of course is that an object can now have as many names and classifications as are necessary, without the need for typing and filing duplicate index cards or, as usually happened in practice, making an arbitrary decision as to which classification was most appropriate. Such decisions, whereby a priest's head-dress, for example, might be filed under INSIGNIA rather than CLOTHING or RELIGION, led to the cumulative frustration of successive generations of documentation assistants. The trouble with ethnographic artefacts is that so many of them are multi-functional. Now, however, such frustration is a thing of the past, and a recently acquired amuletic horseshoe-nail-finger-ring can be classified painlessly and instantaneously under RELIGION, ANIMALS, TOOLS and ORNAMENTS.

The decisions that have to be taken now concern terminology of object names. With the card index it was immaterial whether something was a bracelet, a bangle, an armlet, an armband or a wristlet: all could be found in the same box of cards. Now a choice has to be made — ARM ORNAMENT in this case — and stuck to. Each time a new object name is chosen — always with reference to Blackwood for guidance — it is entered in a separate thesaurus database together with its possible classifications and notes concerning its use. An up-to-date printout of the thesaurus lives next to the computer, and is routinely consulted when entering data.

Blackwood's Classification included sub-classifications in some cases, resulting in a hierarchy of terms: hats, wigs and headcloths would all come under the sub-classification HEADGEAR for example. Cardbox Plus Version 3, with which we set up our system, did

Figure 39.2 Comparison of Beatrice Blackwood's original classification with the version currently in use

Beatrice Blackwood	Computer classification	Notes
Agriculture and Horticulture	Agriculture	
Amulets and Charms		*See* Religion
Animalia	Animalia	
Animals – Domestic	Animals	*Includes* Harness
Arctic Exploration	Arctic Exploration	
Bags and Pouches	Bags	
Barkcloth	Barkcloth	
Basketry	Basketry	
Belts, Girdles & Sashes	—	*See* Clothing
Boxes	Boxes	
Carvings not otherwise classifiable	Carvings	
Casts	—	*See* Reproductions
Ceremonial Objects	Ceremonial	
Chains	Chains	
Clothing	Clothing	*Includes* Belts & Accessories
Clothing Accessories	—	*See* Clothing
Collections	—	*Retrievable by donor*
Combs	—	*See* Ornaments *or* Toilet
Cradles & Baby-Carriers	Cradles	
Currency	Currency	
Dance Gear	Dance	
Death	Death	
Deformation, Artificial	Deformation	
Divination	Divination	
Dwellings & Buildings	Dwellings	
Fans & Flywhisks	Fans	
Figures not specified as Religious	Figures	*Religious and secular*
Fire-making	Fire	
Fire, Prevention of	—	*See under* Fire
—	Firearms	
Fishing	Fishing	
Food and Drink	Food	
Forgeries	—	*See* Reproductions
Geology	Geology	
Harness & Riding Gear	—	*See* Animals
Head-Hunting	Headhunting	
Head-Rests	Headrests	
Hunting	Hunting	*Excluding* Weapons
Insignia	Insignia	
Ivory Objects not otherwise classifiable	—	*Retrievable by material*
Knives	Knives	
Lighting — Lamps	Lighting	
Lighting except Lamps	(Lighting)	
Locks and Keys	Locks	
—	Marriage	
Masks	Masks	
Mats & Mat-Work	Mats	
Materials (unusual)	—	*Retrieve by material*
Medals & Medallions	Medals	

Medicine	Medicine	*Includes* Surgery
Metallurgy	Metallurgy	
Musical Instruments, Automatic	Music	*Separate classification*
Musical Instruments, other than automatic		
Narcotics	Narcotics	
Navigation	Navigation	
Netsuke	—	*See* Ornaments
Ornaments, Personal	Ornaments	*Includes* Netsuke *and* Combs
—	Paints	*Includes* Dyes
Photographs & Pictures except Prints	Photographs Pictures	*Separate classification*
Photographs (Prints)		*See* Photographs
Physical Anthropology	Physical Anthropology	
Pigments	—	*See* Paints
Plants	Plants	
Pottery	Pottery	
—	Punishment	*Includes* Torture
Religion	Religion	*Includes* Amulets & Witchcraft
—	Reproductions	*Includes* Casts, Fakes & Forgeries — *not models*
Rings of Unknown Use	Rings	
Scientific Apparatus	Scientific Apparatus	
Spectacles	Spectacles	
Staves & Sticks	Staves	
Stools	Stools	
String, Rope & Cord	String	
Surgery	—	*See* Medicine
Techniques	Techniques	
Textiles	Textiles	
Time Indicators	Time	
Toilet Apparatus & Cosmetics	Toilet	*Includes* Combs
Tools, Unhafted	Tools	
Tools other than Unhafted Implements		
Torture	—	*See* Punishment
Toys & Games	Toys	
Transport	Transport	*Except* Navigation
Trays	—	*See* Vessels
Unidentified Objects	Unidentified	
Vessels except Pottery	Vessels	*Except* Pottery. *Includes* Trays
Weapons, Defensive	Weapons	*Except* Firearms *and* Knives
Weapons, Offensive		
Weddings	—	*See* Marriage
Weights & Measures	Weights	
Witchcraft	—	*See* Religion
Writing & other means of Conveying Information	Writing	

Figure 39.3 Specimen page from the object thesaurus

```
ADZE                 NOTES:              CLASS: TOOLS
AMULET               NOTES: FORM?        CLASS: RELIGION ?ORNAMENTS ??
ANCHOR               NOTES:              CLASS: NAVIGATION
ANIMAL-FIGURE        NOTES: IF TOY,      CLASS: FIGURES  ?RELIGION
                     TYPE TOY-ANIMAL.
                     INCLUDES REPTILES
ANIMAL-HEAD          NOTES:              CLASS: FIGURES ?RELIGION
ANVIL                NOTES:              CLASS: TOOLS  ?METALLURGY
APPLE-CORER          NOTES:              CLASS: TOOLS  FOOD
APRON                NOTES: RITUAL?      CLASS: CLOTHING   ?RELIGION
ARMLET               NOTES: USE          CLASS:
                     ARM-ORNAMENT
ARM-ORNAMENT         NOTES: USE FOR      CLASS: ORNAMENTS
                     BRACELET, BANGLE,
                     WRISTLET, ARMLET
ARMOUR               NOTES:              CLASS: WEAPONS
ARROW                NOTES:              CLASS: WEAPONS
ARROW-HEAD           NOTES: IF IN        CLASS: WEAPONS
                     DOUBT USE
                     PROJECTILE-POINT
ASTRALAGUS           NOTES: PURPOSE?     CLASS: ANIMALIA  ?TOYS
AWL                  NOTES:              CLASS: TOOLS
AXE                  NOTES:              CLASS: TOOLS
BABY-CARRIER         NOTES:              CLASS: CRADLES
BACK-ORNAMENT        NOTES:              CLASS: ORNAMENTS
BACKSTRAP-LOOM       NOTES:              CLASS: TEXTILES
BADGE                NOTES:              CLASS: INSIGNIA  ORNAMENTS
BAG                  NOTES: FUNCTION?    CLASS: BAGS  ?NARCOTICS
BALANCE              NOTES:              CLASS: WEIGHTS
BALL                 NOTES:              CLASS: TOYS
BALL-COURT           NOTES:              CLASS: TOYS  RELIGION
BANGLE               NOTES: USE          CLASS:
                     ARM-ORNAMENT
BANJO                NOTES:              CLASS: MUSIC
BANNER               NOTES: FOR WHAT?    CLASS: INSIGNIA  ??
BARKCLOTH-BEATER     NOTES:              CLASS: BARKCLOTH  TOOLS
BARK-PAPER-BEATER    NOTES:              CLASS: TOOLS  BARKCLOTH
                                         WRITING
BARK-SPECIMEN        NOTES:              CLASS: PLANTS  ?MEDICINE
                                         ?BARKCLOTH  ?WRITING
BASKET               NOTES: FUNCTION?    CLASS: BASKETRY  ??
BEAD                 NOTES: TRADE?       CLASS: BEADS ?CURRENCY
BEAD-STRING          NOTES: TRADE?       CLASS: BEADS  ?CURRENCY
                                         ?ORNAMENTS
BEADWORK-SPECIMEN    NOTES: USE ONLY     CLASS: BEADS
                     IF FUNCTION
                     UNKNOWN
BEATER               NOTES: FOR WHAT?    CLASS: ?TOOLS  ?FOOD ?BARKCLOTH
BEHEADING-KNIFE      NOTES:              CLASS: KNIVES  HEADHUNTING
BELL                 NOTES: FUNCTION?    CLASS: MUSIC  ??ANIMALS  ?DANCE
                                          ?RELIGION
BELLOWS              NOTES:              CLASS: TOOLS  FIRE  ?METALLURGY
BELL-PAD             NOTES:              CLASS: MUSIC  DANCE  CLOTHING
BELT                 NOTES: SEE ALSO     CLASS: CLOTHING  ??
                     WAIST-ORNAMENT
BELT-BUCKLE          NOTES:              CLASS: ORNAMENTS  CLOTHING
BETEL-NUT            NOTES:              CLASS: NARCOTICS  PLANTS
BIBLE                NOTES:              CLASS: WRITING  RELIGION
BIRD-BOLAS           NOTES:              CLASS: WEAPONS
BIRD-FIGURE          NOTES: IF TOY,      CLASS: FIGURES  ?RELIGION
                     TYPE TOY-BIRD
BIRD-HEAD            NOTES:              CLASS: FIGURES ?RELIGIONN
```

Figure 39.4

Terms used to date in WEAPONS classification

ARMOUR	NOTES:	CLASS: WEAPONS
ARROW	NOTES:	CLASS: WEAPONS
ARROW-HEAD	NOTES: IF IN DOUBT USE PROJECTILE-POINT	CLASS: WEAPONS
BIRD-BOLAS	NOTES:	CLASS: WEAPONS
BLADE	NOTES: OF WHAT?	CLASS: ?KNIVES ?WEAPONS ?TOOLS TOOLS
BODY-ARMOUR	NOTES:	CLASS: WEAPONS
BOLAS	NOTES:	CLASS: WEAPONS
BOOMERANG	NOTES:	CLASS: WEAPONS
BOW	NOTES: FUNCTION?	CLASS: ?WEAPONS ?MUSIC ?TEXTILES
CLUB	NOTES:	CLASS: WEAPONS ?DANCE
DAGGER	NOTES: SEE ALSO KNIVES	CLASS: WEAPONS
GROIN-GUARD	NOTES: ALSO TYPE ARMOUR	CLASS: WEAPONS
HARPOON	NOTES:	CLASS: WEAPONS ?FISHING
HARPOON-HEAD	NOTES:	CLASS: WEAPONS ?FISHING
HARPOON-LINE	NOTES:	CLASS: WEAPONS ?FISHING
HELMET	NOTES: ALSO TYPE HEADGEAR	CLASS: CLOTHING ?WEAPONS
PROJECTILE-POINT	NOTES: IF NOT DEFINITELY AN ARROWHEAD	CLASS: WEAPONS
QUIVER	NOTES:	CLASS: WEAPONS
SHEATH	NOTES: FUNCTION?	CLASS: ?KNIVES ?WEAPONS
SHIELD	NOTES: FUNCTION?	CLASS: WEAPONS ?DANCE
SLING	NOTES:	CLASS: WEAPONS
SLING-STONE	NOTES:	CLASS: WEAPONS
SPEAR	NOTES: USE FOR LANCE, JAVELIN	CLASS: WEAPONS
SPEAR-HEAD	NOTES:	CLASS: WEAPONS
SPEAR-THROWER	NOTES:	CLASS: WEAPONS
STRANGLING-CORD	NOTES:	CLASS: WEAPONS STRING
SWORD	NOTES:	CLASS: WEAPONS
SWORD-CLUB	NOTES:	CLASS: WEAPONS
THROWING-CLUB	NOTES:	CLASS: WEAPONS
THROWING-SPEAR	NOTES:	CLASS: WEAPONS
THROWING-STICK	NOTES:	CLASS: WEAPONS
WEAPON	NOTES:	CLASS: WEAPONS
WRISTGUARD	NOTES:	CLASS: WEAPONS

not include sufficient fields to devote one to sub-classifications, but the problem was circumnavigated with an ALSO TYPE command in the thesaurus. Thus HAT, WIG and HEAD-CLOTH are all entered with the term HEAD-GEAR, and by selecting HEAD-GEAR, all these object names are retrieved.

Figure 39.3 is a specimen page from the object thesaurus. It expands gradually as records are entered, and is still subject to occasional alteration and improvement as necessary. Listings of object names within each classification can be produced, though it should be stressed that the range of classifications is not always rigid. Shields are sometimes used for dance; fans are somtimes used or fires; many types of clothing and ornaments have religious significance, etc. Figures 39.4–39.6 illustrate the object name

Figure 39.5 Terms used to date in DANCE classification

BELL	NOTES: FUNCTION?	CLASS: MUSIC ?ANIMALS ?DANCE ?RELIGION
BELL-PAD	NOTES:	CLASS: MUSIC DANCE CLOTHING
CLUB	NOTES:	CLASS: WEAPONS ?DANCE
COSTUME	NOTES: FUNCTION?	CLASS: CLOTHING ?RELIGION ?MARRIAGE ?DANCE
DANCE-STICK	NOTES:	CLASS: DANCE STAVES
JINGLE	NOTES:	CLASS: MUSIC ?DANCE
MASK	NOTES: FUNCTION?	CLASS: MASKS ?RELIGION ?DANCE ?TOYS
PADDLE	NOTES:	CLASS: ?NAVIGATION ?DANCE
SHIELD	NOTES: FUNCTION?	CLASS: WEAPONS ?DANCE

Figure 39.6 Terms used to date in FISHING classification

FISH-HOOK	NOTES:	CLASS: FISHING
FISHING-SCOOP	NOTES:	CLASS: FISHING
FISHING-BOAT	NOTES:	CLASS: FISHING NAVIGATION
FISHING-LINE	NOTES:	CLASS: FISHING
FISHING-NET	NOTES:	CLASS: FISHING
FISHING-SPEAR	NOTES:	CLASS: FISHING WEAPONS
HARPOON	NOTES:	CLASS: WEAPONS ?FISHING
HARPOON-HEAD	NOTES:	CLASS: WEAPONS ?FISHING
HARPOON-LINE	NOTES:	CLASS: WEAPONS ?FISHING
KITE	NOTES: ?FISHING	CLASS: TOYS ?FISHING
LURE	NOTES:	CLASS: ?HUNTING ?FISHING
NET	NOTES: FUNCTION?	CLASS: ?HUNTING ?FISHING

lists produced so far for the classifications, Weapons, Dance and Fishing, giving an indication of the degree of overlap of terms.

Terminology control of the ethnography photographic collection

We are also involved in a major project to document, catalogue and index the photographic collections, which comprise an estimated 70 000 images. This is being developed in parallel and inter-related with the terminology and indexing of the object collections. This project is being discussed in this section rather than as a visual representation problem, because of the way we perceive the collection at the museum and the way in which it has always been used and, one suspects, will continue to be used.

From the very beginning in 1884, the archive collections at the Museum have had a dual role. First, they represent what can best be described as the 'non-three-dimesional' in the traditional museum sense, recording the intellectual context in which the collections developed. Second, they are part of the Museum's documentation system, adding to the body of knowledge about a whole class of objects, rather than specific objects (such material has always been treated directly as 'related documents'). In addition, some of the material has been collected because of its intrinsic historical value. Such collecting has been a conscious policy of the Museum since its foundation, and rather than an *ad hoc* mass of ephemera, the archive collection itself is highly structured and as such is not without historiographical interest.

Despite the fact that the photographic collection was widely acknowledged as 'important', its cataloguing and retrieval were lamentable, and although accessioning continued, the collection was largely ignored from the 1930s on. However, over the last five years we have made serious attempts to remedy the situation and the photographic collection has been brought once again into the mainstream of the museum's activities (Edwards, 1989). Thus it seemed logical when developing a retrieval system and related thesaurus that the object and archive collections should be seen as integrated parts of a whole. Although at present they are on two separate databases, we are very much aware that the research potential lies in the ultimate amalgamation of the two. So this is our overall long-term strategy.

Concerning terminology, Blackwood's classification was again the starting point (Blackwood, 1970). Like the object collections, we use her terms or the revised edition of her terms wherever possible. The photographic collection takes its lead in terminology from the objects rather than *vice versa,* although we do discuss the desirability of terms (e.g. the arm ornament question) whenever possible. However, photographs present rather different problems which can be attributed to two basic and not unrelated features. First, the size of individual collections, especially modern collections, means that in practical terms catalogue entries often refer to a series of photographs or even a whole album rather than single images. The massive amount of detail which can occur in a photographic image can become unmanageable. To catalogue a photograph by Roger Fenton, Henry Peach Robinson or Henri Cartier Bresson as a fine art object presents one set of problems, to cope with 2 500 technically third-rate but ethnographically interesting images from someone's fieldwork in New Guinea in 1930 is another. Second, there is perhaps a fundamental difference between objects and photographs when it comes to description. The object record is a record of the physical object itself: in the context under discussion, the photographic record is a description of the content, not the photograph as a physical object. The latter requires a different set of specialist terminology, which is, of course, part of the full record of any photograph, but for documentary photographs in a museum of ethnography the content is paramount.

Consequently the photographic collections require a system and terminology general enough to be accurately applied over a wide range of material, but specific enough for useful retrieval in a reseach context at a variety of cataloguing levels from a whole collection down to single images (Figures 39.7 and 39.8). The terms chosen are those that are generally 'sought', accurately describe a class of objects and are unambigous. Although much of the terminology we use is common to both objects and photographs, bearing in mind that we view photograph and object collections as integrally related, the way in which terminology is structured, the relationship between terms, is somewhat different, but not, we hope, contradictory. Although many terms stand exactly as in the

Figure 39.7 Photograph record for a single image

```
PITT RIVERS MUSEUM  PHOTOGRAPHIC ARCHIVE RECORD CARD  ===== SINGLE IMAGE
..........................................................................................................
. NO.B54 6 E            . CONT.N AMERICA                                . PHOT.BELL, C.M.           . DA.1880    .
. P/F.1/PR              . COUNTRY.USA                                   . EXP.                      ............
....................... REG/STL.PLAINS                                  ............................. PROC.ALB.PR .
. TYPE.PORTR            ................................................ MM.144 X 101 PR.DOMED     .            .
. PERSON.PRETTY-EAGLE   . GROUP.CROW                                    .                           .            .
.                       .                                               ..........................................
.                       .                                               . CON.GOOD                               .
......................................................................... INSRC."[illeg. name]" [PR.L.LH]. "ABSAROKA" .
. DESCR.FULL-FACE 1/2L PORTR OF PRETTY EAGLE. SHIRT DECORATED WITH BEADWORK,  . [PR.L.RH]                    .
. HAIR AND ERMINE PENDANTS. ABALONE SHELL EAR ORNAMENTS, BEAD NECK ORNAMENT.  ...............................
. HAIR BRAIDED, FRONT SHORT & STIFFENED WITH BUFFALO GREASE. FEATHER IN HAIR. . DD.TYLOR E.B.    D.    ME.DON .
......................................................................... REL.COL.COLL.XI MISC (PHOTO.LIST 71]  .
. CLASS.CLOTHING ORNAMENT BEADWORK TOILET                               . DOC.SENT BY POWELL [BAE] 1885. NAA?. SRDF. [EE .
. NAME.SHIRTS EAR-ORN NECK-ORN HAIR-DRESSING                            . 1987/1]                                .
. EVENT.                                                                .                                        .
. IDEA.                                                                 .                                        .
..........................................................................................................
```

Figure 39.8 Photograph record for a series of images

```
PITT RIVERS MUSEUM  PHOTOGRAPHIC ARCHIVE RECORD CARD === SERIES OF IMAGES
..........................................................................................................
. NO.BB B1 41 - 50      . CONT.N AMERICA                                . PHOT.BROWN, J.D.          . DA.1926 6  .
. P/F. 10/PR            . COUNTRY. USA                                  . EXP.                      ............
....................... REG/STL. ARIZONA SW                             ............................. PROC.BRO.PR .
. TYPE.                 ................................................ MM.147 X 93               .            .
. PERSON.               . GROUP.HOPI PUEBLO APACHE PIMA                 .                           .            .
.                       .                                               ..........................................
.                       .                                               . CON.FAIR                               .
......................................................................... INSRC.                                 .
. DESCR. SPORTS DAY AT PHOENIX INDIAN SCHOOL. SWIMMING,SHOT PUT, AMERICAN       .                              .
. FOOTBALL, LONG JUMP. I UNIDENTIFIED GROUP OF INDIANS AT SCHOOL [STAFF?].2    ...............................
. GENERAL VIEWS.                                                        . DD. BLACKWOOD      D.      ME.     .
......................................................................... REL.COL.BB MS                          .
. CLASS. RECREATION                        •                            . DOC.[EE 1986/8]                        .
. NAME.                                                                 .                                        .
. EVENT. SPORTS-DAY                                                     .                                        .
. IDEA. ACCULTURATION                                                   .                                        .
..........................................................................................................
```

object collections (e.g. BASKETRY, INSIGNIA, POTTERY and PHYSICAL ANTHROPOLOGY), many other terms which are class names in the object records are treated as full names in the photographic collection thesaurus, subsiduary to a broader heading (e.g. CRADLES which constitute a class of objects are a sub-class of CHILD-CARE, and FANS are a sub-class of CLOTHING OR DOMESTIC OBJECTS). This arrangement does not upset the basic purity of the terminology, in that the same terms are accepted as sought terms throughout the institution ensuring consistency, but it does allow classification at a fairly general level. This facility is essential where one is indexing series of images, for however desirable it might be to index down to the last coconut on the tree, it is not practicable (Figure 39.9).

Figure 39.9 Illustration of a record for a series of images

```
PITT RIVERS PHOTOGRAPHIC ARCHIVES - BROAD CLASSIFICATION OF A GROUP OF PHOTOGRAPHS
.........................................................................................................
. NO.BB A2 1-5              . CONT.N AMERICA                           . PHOT.BLACKWOOD          . DA.1925 7 25 .
. P/F.2/PR 5/NEG (X)        . COUNTRY.CANADA                           . EXP.                    ..............
........................... REG/STL.ONTARIO LAKE-OF-THE-WOODS NORTHEAST ......................... PROC.BRO.PR  .
. TYPE.                     ........................................... MM.55 X 81              . NITR.N       .
. PERSON.                   . GROUP.SAULTEAUX-OJIBWA                   .                         .              .
.                           .                                          ..........................................
.                           .                                          . CON.GOOD                               .
...................................................................... INSRC.                                  .
. DESCR.GENERAL VIEW OF BERRYING CAMP (1), DRYING FISH (1), STRETCHING .                                        .
. MOOSE-SKIN (1), BIRCH BARK TEPEE WITH MAN HOLDING BABY IN BABY CARRIER (1). ...................................
. PEOPLE.                                                              . DD.BLACKWOOD        D.        ME.       .
...................................................................... REL.COL.BB MS.                          .
. CLASS.SETTLEMENT SHELTER FOOD-STORAGE SKIN-DRESSING CHILD-CARE GATHERING . DOC.FULL LIST & ACCOUNT OF THE VISIT SRDF. PR. .
. NAME.TEPEES FISH-DRYING CRADLES                                      . OF BB-A2 5 AT C1/3/26e. [EE 1986/7]     .
. EVENT.                                                               .                                        .
. IDEA.                                                                .                                        .
.........................................................................................................
```

Further photographs may show activities to which material objects are connected. Being able to index fairly broadly co-locates photographs of activity and material culture. This broader approach to classification is also in line with the type of enquiry made of the collection. In the planning stages of the project we analysed the enquiries made of both the object and photograph collections over recent years. In the case of the photographic collection the vast majority of approaches, even from those with extremely specialist interests, was by geographical region and then perhaps by broad subject (Australian weapons, African agriculture, etc.), rather than for a specific object.

The precise description of specific objects, including native names, etc., is placed in a text description and is not used for retrieval. The only way to retrieve photographs of very specific items is to structure the search in such a way as to yield the most specific shortlist possible: for example, a Kora from Mali would be indexed under MUSIC (Classification term) — STRINGS (Full Name) — MALI (Country) and a glance at the text descriptions would identify all photographs of Kora. This may not be ideal, but it works. The description of the image content is thus reduced for indexing purposes to a series of keywords which are entered in the appropriate field according to the importance in the content of an image or series of images. The Full Name is not a true full name in quite the way it is in the object collections but a more specific keyword which relates hierarchically to a term in the classification field above, thus the collection can be searched on two levels. Like an object record, more than one term can be applied to the subject of a photograph if necessary. Furthermore, broad classification terms and full names can exist in a one to many relationship. For example, for a photograph of a barn:

Classification: Shelter — Agriculture

Full Names: Barns- Fodder Storage

All these terms are inter-related when describing a barn.

The thesaurus is controlled by an authority file which gives the Classification terms and the Full Name dependant upon it (Figure 39.10). A Full Name must never be used without the appropriate Classification term in order to maintain the structure of

Figure 39.10 Authority File — hierarchical order

CLASS NAMES	Upper case
Full names	Lower case with capital
Unacceptable terms	Lower case

Sheep	enter HERDING in Class
Shell Money	enter CURRENCY in Class
SHELTER	
Shields	enter WEAPONS in Class
Shifting-Cult[ivation]	enter AGRICULTURE in Class
Ships	enter BOATS in Class [use only for European ships]
Shirts	enter CLOTHING in Class [upper garments, no front opening]
Shoes	use Footwear
Shops	enter TRADE in Class
Shrines	enter RELIGION in Class
Silver	enter METALWORK in Class
Singing	enter MUSIC in Class
Sitars	enter MUSIC in Class
Skin-Containers	enter DOMESTIC-OBJ and/or TRANSPORT in Class
SKIN-DRESSING	
Skirts	enter CLOTHING in Class
Sledges	enter TRANSPORT in Class
Slings	enter CHILD-CARE or WEAPONS as applicable in Class
Smoking-Pipes	enter NARCOTICS in Class
Snake-Charming	enter RECREATION in Class
Spears	enter FISHING, HUNTING or WEAPONS in Class as used
Spear-Throwers	enter WEAPONS in Class
Spinning	enter TEXTILES in Class
sport	use RECREATION
Standards	enter INSIGNIA in Class
Stations	enter TRANSPORT in Class
Stone-Cults	enter RELIGION in Class
Street-Ent[ertainers]	enter RECREATION in Class
STREET-LIFE	
Strings	enter MUSIC in Class
Sugar	enter INDUSTRY in Class
Sweathouses	enter SHELTER in Class
Swords	enter WEAPONS in Class
Tattoo	enter DEFORMATION in Class
Temples	enter RELIGION and SHELTER in Class
Tents	enter SHELTER in Class
Tepees	enter SHELTER (USA — Plains only) in Class
TEXTILES	
Theatres	enter DRAMA in Class
Tigers	enter ANIMALS in Class
Tillage	enter AGRICULTURE in Class
Timber	enter INDUSTRY in Class
TOILET	
tombs	use Graves: DEATH
TOOLS	
Totem	enter INSIGNIA in Class [*use singular*]
Totem-Poles	enter INSIGNIA in Class
Town-Walls	enter SHELTER in Class
Tracks	enter COMMUNICATIONS in Class
TRADE	
trails	use Tracks

Figure 39.11 Authority File — dictionary order

FURNITURE (*see also* DOMESTIC OBJECTS)
  CHAIRS

GATHERING
  DIGGING-STICKS (*see also* AGRICULTURE)

GEOLOGY

GRAPHIC ART
  DECORATION (*when on another classified object*)
  PAINTINGS
  PETROGLYPHS (*incised*)
  ROCK-PAINTINGS
  SAND-PAINTINGS

HARNESS (RIDING & DRIVING GEAR) — *all animals*
  SADDLE-BLANKETS

HERDING
  CAMELS
  CATTLE
  GOATS
  RANCHING
  REINDEER
  SHEEP

HISTORY — *use only for specific major events*

HUNTING

INDUSTRY
  COAL-MINING
  FISHERIES
  PLANTATIONS
  SUGAR
  TIMBER

INSIGNIA
  STANDARDS
  TOTEM
  TOTEM-POLES

jewellery — *use* ORNAMENT

MAGIC (*use with* RELIGION)
  AMULETS

---

information. There is also in the authority file a list of terms in dictionary order (Figure 39.11), which includes not only the acceptable indexing terms but also other related sought terms which are unacceptable with their acceptable synonym, such as:

Hats — use CLOTHING: Headgear

Bracelets — use ORNAMENT: Arm-Orn

Like the object thesaurus, it is kept to hand so terms can be checked at input. It is continually added to. Photographs require a vast range of indexing terms and so we are building on to Blackwood's Classification to include terms which do not commonly featured in ethnographic classifications (e.g. Fish Canning Factories, Sugar Plantations or Colonial Administration). This process is not as *ad hoc* as might appear. In order to maintain a logical framework to terminology we turn to other authorities such as *SHIC*, the *Outline of Cultural Materials* or indeed the *Bliss Bibliographical Classification* (second edition) which is used in the Museum's library, all of which have useful and logical structures and ennumeration of phenomena. (SHIC Working Party, 1983, Murdoch, *et. al.*, 1987 and Mills and Broughton, 1984). Existing terms are also constantly under revision as good and logical reasons for using one term rather than another present themselves. Each case is discussed on its merits. There are indeed some outstanding differences to be resolved, reflecting not so much inconsistency in the system but rather pin-pointing the difficulties of trying to integrate the terminology for needs which can only be described as 'the same yet very different'. For example, the object thesaurus states DWELLINGS whereas the archive thesaurus would prefer SHELTER, this being a broader term better suited to a particular need, not all structures or buildings being dwellings, not all dwellings are structures, for example caves.

In addition to large geographical and tribal thesauri which are shared by both object and photographic collections, smaller thesauri, specific to either the object or photographic collections are being developed. For example, the names of materials from which objects are made and the processes by which they are manufactured; or the concepts (e.g. acculturation, power structure) embodied in a photograph or events and happenings (e.g. sacrifices, funerals) depicted in it.

Growing a thesaurus organically in the course of work on the collections is proving more satisfactory than having it laid down rigidly in advance. Every object, every group of photographs, poses a new problem. Anomalies may not become apparent until the database contains a substantial number of records. By constant application of the new terminology to day-to-day cataloguing work, mistakes can be corrected as they occur and we continue to learn by experience.

---

40 SHAPES AND THEIR NAMES IN GREEK POTTERY

Claire Skinkel-Taupin

Musées royaux d'Art et d'Histoire
Bruxelles

The terminological situation

Many terms, having been in use for more than a century, have acquired an authority that makes them accepted without a reassessment of their significance or value in the light of late twentieth-century knowledge.

In fact, problems appear from the words 'Greek pottery' on. The term 'Greek' has both a geographical and a chronological meaning: it covers Greece itself and the parts of the Mediterranean area under Greek influence and/or occupation during the Hellenic and early Hellenistic periods. 'Pottery', in this context, usually means vases (which can roughly be defined as containers), although a few other objects have been included in the group in as much as they have been decorated by vase-painters; 'pottery' also covers both the fine, often painted wares and the common or kitchen wares, which have been long disdained.

This case study is a practical exercise in terminology. It is concerned with a vase of the Greek and Roman Department of the *Musées royaux d'Art et d'Histoire* in Brussels (Skinkel-Taupin, 1984). It is an unusual piece, made in Southern Italy around 400 BC (Figure 40.1). But its body (and that of the four miniature vases perched on the lid) is of a shape frequently met in the Greek world. In the context of Attic pottery of the Classical period, it is called 'lebes gamikos of type 2' (i.e. nuptial lebes with low foot) by Beazley (1956); in the Boeotian context of late black-figure it is termed 'stamnos-pyxis' by Ure (1927). Trendall (1967) uses the 'lebes gamikos' label for Southern Italian red-figured vases of this shape, although they have no relation to the nuptial ritual. In other contexts the same shape can be found labelled 'crater', 'stamnos', 'pyxis', 'lebes', 'stamnoid pyxis', etc. . . .

This bewildering array of labels is the situation facing Greek ceramologists once they step out of a few specific and well studied fields.

The root of the problem seems to lie in the fact that, for many years, Greek vases have mainly been studied for their painted decoration. The richest field, from that point of view, is that of the Attic black- and red-figured vases of the Classical period. In this specific context, the shapes are clearly structured, often designed for a definite use. It is also a context for which there are enough documents to know, in some cases, both the name of the shape and its use at that period, so that terminology has not appeared as a problem.

But once one steps out of this chronological context, even if staying in the geographical context of Attica, this labelling system breaks down. For the Geometric period, when shapes were not yet so clearly structured, the same shape can appear under the name of 'amphora', 'crater' or 'lebes'. Moving down towards the end of the fourth century, a time when potters tried to renovate their repertory by creating hybrids, one is faced with a treasure-trove of fancy labels, ranging from the pseudo-antique to the nonsensical. And outside the Attic context, the situation is even worse.

Thus it must be admitted that Greek ceramology is in urgent need of a drastic overhaul.

Figure 40.1

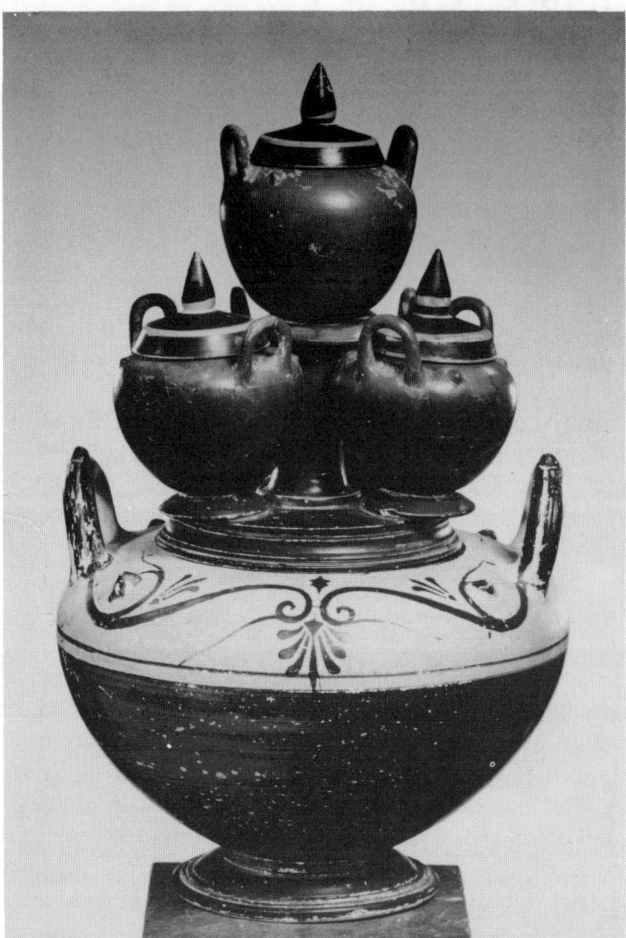

Problems in terminology: the Greek vase of the *Museés royaux d'Art et d'Histoire*, Brussels

Towards a solution: A terminology based on a meta-analysis

The goal is a terminology in which each label is applied to one shape and one shape only, but to that shape whatever its stylistic, geographic or chronological context.

To achieve this, a new terminology is needed, based on definitions that are both discriminant and open. Discriminant because, to be of any use, the terms must refer to specific shapes, not to big classes such as 'drinking vessels'; open because they must allow for variants at the level of elements that are regarded as secondary, so that the term can accept the modulations of a shape through the whole range of Greek pottery.

Such definitions must be the result of a structural and hierarchical analysis of the shapes: structural in that it takes into account all the elements of the structure that makes the shape, hierarchical because it organises those elements according to their discriminatory power.

Defining the vase on which the case study was based according to the type of meta-analysis outlined above, the discriminant elements are that it is a closed shape, mounted on a low foot, with a medium-sized aperture and that it has two upright handles horizontally implanted between the mouth and the joining of the shoulder to the body; the open elements are the fact that the aperture is often surrounded by a low neck but may have no neck at all, that the profiles, both of the shoulder and the body, vary considerably and that the foot follows the general pattern in fashion at the time and the place of the potting of the vase.

This definition readily admits some of the labels encountered earlier for this shape: the Attic 'lebes gamikos with low foot', the Boeotian 'stamnos-pyxis', the Southern Italian red-figured 'lebes gamikos' and many pyxides (or boxes). It excludes other labels, such as 'stamnos' (upcurving handles implanted below the shoulder-body joining, wide aperture with higher neck), the 'lebes' (no handles, no foot, wide mouth with large lip) and the column- and volute-craters' (upright handles but linked to the protruding lip that crowns the high, cylindrical neck). It also shows that the shape is well known, often since the Geometric period, in numerous productions centres of the Greek world, having been used as a handy container for anything from human ashes to cosmetics.

The shape thus defined should be labelled. To keep within the scholarly tradition, taking into account its many uses and its most striking feature, it may be called 'pyxis with upright handles'. But the naming of the shape is a minor problem, which could even be shelved by replacing names by a numerical or alpha-numerical code.

What is essential in the present situation, when attempts are already made to put Greek pottery in databases, is the working out of a meta-terminological frame into which the vast amount of material existing and still being excavated can be fitted so as to be more easily handled and studied in a broader context. I hope that the very theoretical outline I have sketched will meet some of the fundamental requirements for the making of this frame Greek ceramology needs.

VIII
DISCIPLINE DEVELOPMENTS: FINE ART, ICONOGRAPHY AND VISUAL REPRESENTATION

41 DISCIPLINE DEVELOPMENTS IN FINE ART, ICONOGRAPHY AND VISUAL REPRESENTATION

Jennifer Hirsh

Advisory Officer
Museum Documentation Association
Cambridge

The following chapters describe terminology developments in the fields of fine art and visual representation. In these disciplines developments would appear to be broader based and more international in scope than in other subject areas. The chapters represent areas as diverse as African Art, Twentieth Century War and Ecclesiastical Furnishings. The need and use of terminology control and thesauri are seen more as an access aid to users, mainly art historians, but also increasingly publishers and the media, than the care and management of collections.

The dilemma which has had to be faced in museums is whether there already exists a thesaurus that is adequate for their own special needs and therefore allows them to use the same terminology as other institutions, or whether they must create their own thesaurus and thus possibly partially re-invent the wheel.

Various authors comment on the difference between the practical approach of constructing termlists as needed using real terms, as opposed to the theoretical approach of devising a thesaurus of ideal terms before cataloguing commences. The transition from database building to database use is discussed by a number of authors and indeed some have used existing databases as the primary source for building thesauri. The use of computers has facilitated this, though by no means all the authors discuss the use of thesauri in automated systems. Automated use of terminology lists allows vocabulary 'frequency of use' lists to be analysed, thus providing feedback to the developers of the lists themselves. The thesaurus for Ecclesiastical Furnishings was constructed at the same time as the indexing was being done for the Dictionary.

The trend is moving away from the traditional 'medium' and 'style or school' classification to subject based. This in itself can pose challenges as with non-representational art. African Art, often regarded as ethnography, does not fit readily into terminology for western art styles. The Art and Architecture Thesaurus excludes iconographic terms and may need areas in which to put highly specialised classifications. The alphanumeric coding system of Iconclass allows the generic and specific to be described and used within a single code and can be a means of communication across language barriers.

Various problems emerge, such as the difficulty of expressing negatives in a thesaurus, for example, 'no windows' (though Iconclass appears to resolve this by the use of repeating a code, for example, the single code expressing 'Hope' and the double code 'Despair'). Another problem to be faced is that of removing from documentation staff the responsibility for moral and political judgement, as at the Imperial War Museum.

Van de Waal thought in 1954 that it should be possible to put into a consistent classification all the subjects which man has succeeded in portraying. The following chapters indicate how far this thought has been put into practice, a third of a century later.

42 NAMING, DEFINING, ORDERING: AN EVOLVING AND NEVER-ENDING PROCESS

Helene E. Roberts

Curator, Visual Collection, Fine Arts Library
Fogg Art Museum, Harvard University
Cambridge, Mass.

Introduction

Naming (onomasiology)

The philosopher W. V. Quine noted that there is in humans a marked proclivity for 'breaking reality down somehow, into a multitude of identifiable and discriminable objects to be referred to by singular and general terms' (Quine, 1969, page 1). Humans have, in plainer language, an incurable disposition to name things. Naming is, of course, an ancient activity. It was first manifested by Adam's naming the animals in Genesis (Figure 42.1), and it is one that is still very active in the modern world. If anyone doubts this fact, try a literature search under 'Onomasiology', the modern name for naming. Such a search would show that naming is not an arbitrary activity, but one fraught with many philosophical, psychological and linguistic ramifications. My favourite philosophical commentary comes from the seventh-century Spaniard, Isidore of Seville, who

Figure 42.1

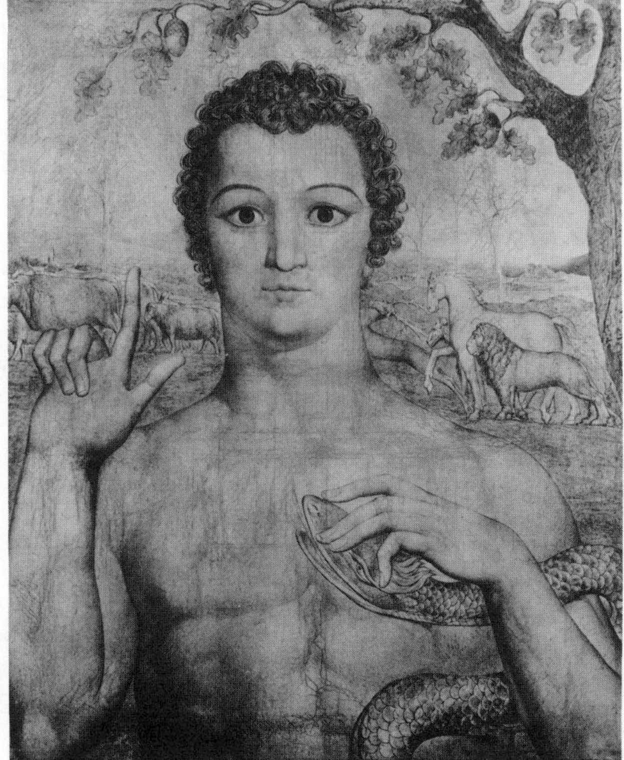

NAMING. William Blake, *Adam Naming the Animals*

With acknowledgement to The Stirling Maxwell Collection, Pollok House, Glasgow Museums & Art Galleries

thought the essence of the object or creature named should be expressed in the sound of the word. The appropriateness of a word is usually only realised in retrospect: witness the farmer who declared that the pig is well named because it is such a filthy beast.

Defining (lexicography)

Defining words, or, in its more modern academic term, lexicography, also has a long history. Perhaps the first 'dictionaries' could be found in ancient Sumaria where clay tablets full of words helped young scribes learn their trade. These words were, however, arranged in like groups. Curiously enough, alphabetisation of sequences of words was not common until 1600, well after the invention of printing. Organisation by some thematic order was the rule.

Ordering (taxonomy)

The ordering of things is usually broken into two parts, the making of categories and the creation of a hierarchy or system of superordinate and subordinate terms. The idea of entities being ordered in a great single hierarchy or Chain of Being culminated in the Renaissance. The merest speck of matter began the chain leading to larger inanimate objects up to lowest living creatures (the oyster) to the highest mammals (the lion or elephant). Man provided the link between earth and heaven with its nine ranks of good and bad angels. The highest, the cherubim and seraphim, connected the chain to the throne of God Himself. The Renaissance had the Great Chain of Being; we have progressed to the Art and Architectural Thesaurus.

Not all taxonomies are so neatly ordered as these two. Michael Foucault describes a Chinese encyclopedia in one of Jorge Luis Borges's works which divides animals into categories, including:

> '(a) belonging to the Emperor, (b) embalmed, (c) tame, (d) suckling pigs, (e) sirens, (f) fabulous, (g) stray dogs, (h) included in the present classification, (i) frenzied, (j) innumerable, (k) drawn with a very fine camelhair brush, (l) et cetera, (m) having just broken the water jug, (n) that from a long way off look like flies.' (Foucault, 1970, page XV).

The rather disorderly world of nature, concepts and events does not always fit into the neat orderly hierarchy of a contrived thesuarus, but despite the occasional skewing of reality, the ordering of things is necessary to gain an understanding of the world around us and to be able to communicate about it.

According to interpreters of Genesis, Adam gained mastery over the animals by naming them. In a sense the activities of naming, defining and ordering, give a mastery, or at least a greater sense of mastery, over the world. Through these activities one can see relationships between things and can compare and contrast their characteristics. One can begin to make order out of chaos.

Ordering the fine arts: The past

Medium: Pliny

As soon as people began to think about works of art and to write about them, it became necessary to name them, to define them and to order them. Some of the concepts and principles of artistic organisation devised by the ancient world are still with us today. In the first century AD, the Roman polymath, Pliny the Elder, included the arts in his *Natural History*. He had collected anecdotes, stories and opinions about artists and works of art from a wide variety of sources. When he came to present them to the public,however, it was within a structure divided according to the materials of which they were made and the techniques used to make them. The category of 'medium' is one that still provides the basis for the organisation of works of art, representations of works, or books about them, in museums, libraries and visual collections.

Style and schools: Vasari

The great Renaissance art historian, Giorgio Vasari, kept Pliny's distinction according to medium in his *Lives of Painters, Sculptors and Architects,* first published in 1550, but concentrated on moulding his descriptions of the lives and works of various artists so that improvements in their respective style and technique would constitute a pattern of progress, one that went from crude beginnings toward a perfection only achieved in his own age. Artists were linked to each other because they built on what their predecessors had done. Vasari tells the story of artists' lives within a structure which traces the influence between forerunners, masters and followers. These ascriptions, of course, advance as time passes and as superseded masters become forerunners and as the most progressive of their followers become the new masters, only, in time, themselves to be superseded, until perfection is reached. In his large collection of drawings, the *Libro di Disegni,* Vasari organises the artists and their works in a manner that demonstrates this onward march, each artist improving in the mastery of technique on what has gone before (Figure 42.2).

Figure 42.2

ORDERING BY STYLE AND PERIODS. Filippino Lippi, *Five Studies (and Portrait).* From Vasari's *Libro di Disegni*

With acknowledgement to The Governing Body, Christ Church, Oxford

The influence of Vasari was both immediate and long lasting, affecting not only the organisation of art, but concepts relating to it, and the teaching of its history. We have inherited his pattern of organising works of art by schools and by artists and of linking works of art to each other through style and technical improvement and influence. The organisation in itself has merit, it has served us well for 400 years. Once a method of ordering works by medium, school and artist became widely adopted, it became self-perpetuating, making the way people think about works of art rigid and inflexible. Once museums, art libraries and visual collections all become organised by media, school and artist, one might well think that a natural order in the world is being reflected, rather than a contrived man-made one. The Vasarian method, however, has its flaws: it tended to create a narrow enclosed world of art, concentrating on style, feeding off itself, immune from outside influences.

Figure 42.3

ORDERING BY ICONOGRAPHIC SUBJECT. The Goddess Fortune. From Bernard de Montfaucon, *Antiquite Explained and Represented in Sculptures*, London, 1721–22, vol. I, Pl. 89

The alternate tradition: Iconography

The next way of ordering art evolved in the seventeenth century, a method that was based on *ut pictura poesis*, a tradition that emphasised the equivalency of poetry and painting. It was concerned with the study of the subject depicted rather than the style and technique of execution. Bernard de Montfaucon, for example, in his *Antiquity Explained and Represented in Sculptures*, arranged his collection of images, not according to their style or technique, but according to their subject or iconography (Figure 42.3). Iconography has rarely replaced style and school or artist as the primary classification scheme for works of art, but it has become the basic concept used to index works of art. Although works remain ordered on the shelf, that is, classified, according to the Vasarian categories, a separate index can provide other means, most commonly by subject, of accessing materials. Other contributions will describe various systems which have been developed in order to index subject matter in works of art.

Analysis of visual images: The present

Today significant changes are taking place in the discipline of art history. Art historians are beginning to question these traditional models for ordering the arts that arose from Pliny and Vasari. They are also questioning the romantic conception of the work of art as a mysterious product of artistic genius. Their interest has shifted to subject content and beyond to the whole context of the work of art. Emphasising the many different aspects of works of art, art historians are breaking down the enclosed world of stylistic influence to study the relation of works of art to historic events and economic forces, to psychological phenomena and sociological findings, and to linguistic analysis and philosophical theories. There is a shift from examining the work of art as an aesthetic object to examining it as a historical document, as a process, and as a language.

In preparing this paper, I thought it might be interesting to examine some recent writings about works of art and assess how a database using existing indexing systems might have helped these art historians and writers from other disciplines to locate visual materials relevant to their books. The art historians I have chosen are not, of course, the sole arbiters of the direction of art history in the future, nor have I been able to include all the important new art historians. Furthermore the examples that I have chosen are those that are interesting from the point of view of this paper, and may be peripheral to the art historians' main argument.

Art as an historic document

The new art history

An early sign of discontent with the traditional approach to art history came from T. J. Clark in a 1974 essay in the *Times Literary Supplement*. Clark called for art historians to take into account those realities of society which affect the production of art. It was not Clark's intent simply to add one more consideration to the art historians' way of analysing art, he wished to change completely the way people thought about art.

> 'It ought to be clear by now that I'm not interested in the social history of art as part of a cheerful diversification of the subject, taking its place alongside other varieties — formalist, 'modernist', sub-Freudian, filmic, feminist, 'radical', all of them hot-foot in pursuit of the New. For diversification, read disintegration.' (Clark, 1974)

A significant number of art historians have taken this charge, and have rallied under the banner of 'The New Art History'. Although not covering all the current approaches to art

Figure 42.4 ART AS HISTORIC DOCUMENT. Edouard Manet. *The Bar at the Follies Bergere*
With acknowledgement to Courtauld Institute Galleries, London (Courtauld Collection)

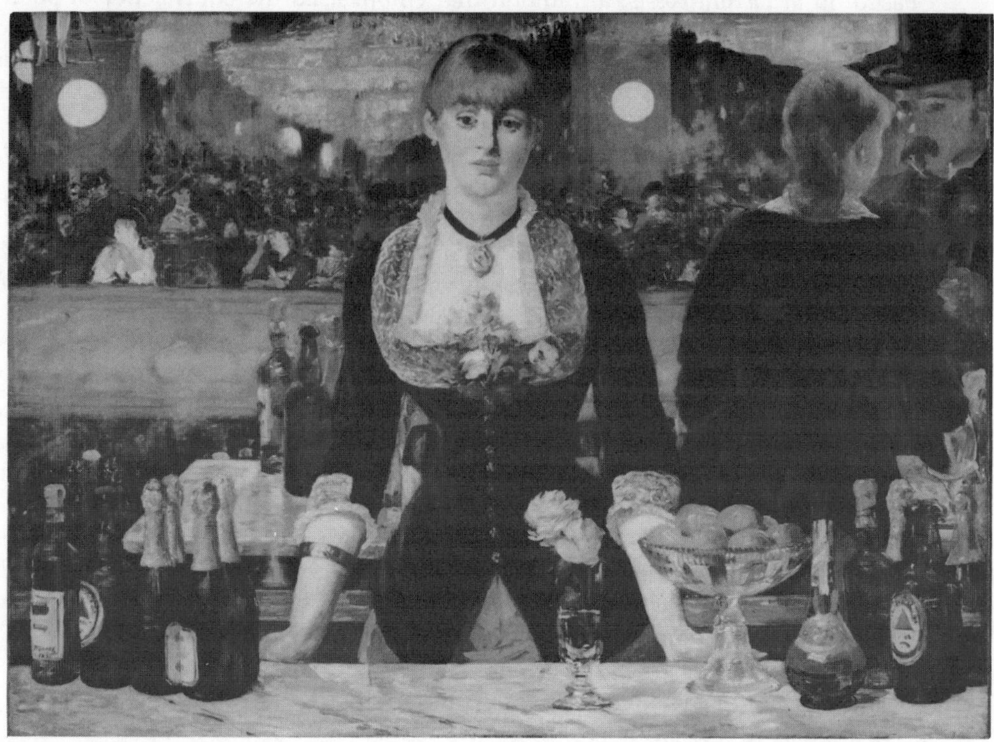

history, the term 'The New Art History' has been applied to those art historians calling themselves Marxists, feminists, structuralists, post-modernists or deconstructionists. The term has this broader usage, but it is also more narrowly associated with a group centred around the periodical *Block*. Inspired by T. J. Clark, their view sees 'art as intimately linked to the society which produces and consumes it, rather than something mysterious which happens as result of the artist's genius' (Rees and Borzello, 1988, pages 4–5). The feminists in this group are particularly interested in showing 'how gender relations of dominance and subordination are legitimised and reproduced across the whole range of social and cultural practice' (Bird, 1988, pages 35–36).

The single-mindedness of traditional art history is sometimes exaggerated in the current rhetoric, as is the innovativeness of the new art history. But for the purposes of this paper, let us ask if the current ways of classifying and indexing works of art largely based on traditional art history will answer the needs of this new art history? If not, how can they grow as the discipline of art history changes?

One of the concepts frequently used in the new art history is that of 'class'. T. J. Clark in *The Painting of Modern Life; Paris in the Art of Manet and His Followers* (1985), for example, in describing the background of Manet's painting *Bar at the Follies Bergere* analyses the ambience of the scene (Figure 42.4). It takes place in a new kind of popular establishment called concert cafes. These cafes developed not only a new kind of entertainment, but a curious group of patrons, cutting across some of the usual class distinctions and reflecting some new elements in society. Clark uses much written evidence to describe this ambience, but also a few paintings, primarily by Degas. Before Clark left Harvard, I asked him if it would have been a help to have had an index that would have enabled him to find all the paintings of concert cafes or even the broader category of cafe scenes. He said it would have been wonderful, but doubted if it could be done. It could have been done, of course, and done using our present indexing systems. We have not, unfortunately, sufficiently indexed our holdings, either individually or cooperatively.

The new art history not only emphasises class, but also gender. In addition it includes art forms sometimes excluded by traditional art historians. The change in terminology from 'minor arts' or 'decorative arts' to 'material culture' also indicates this new view. Lisa Tickner, one of the *Block* group, in *The Spectacle of Women; Imagery of the Suffrage Campaign, 1907–14* (Tickner, 1988), describes the artists and craftspersons who were responsible for designing and executing the posters, postcards and banners used by the suffragettes, describes the use of these images made by the various suffrage groups for their activities, particularly their processions, and analyses the content and implications of the images of women used by the suffragettes and by the anti-suffrage groups. She treats art as a historic document, that is, as evidence in assessing the activities of the suffrage campaign; as process, that is, in seeing how the imagery grew out of a specific set of political concerns and how it was used in furthering these concerns; and as language that is, as a way of communicating specific ideological beliefs.

What could better indexing have done for Lisa Tickner? It probably could have identified materials as suffrage or anti-suffrage. One poster, for example, which was used as an illustration, might be identified as a suffrage poster, as a poster related to the Reform Bill of 1912 and the debate in the House of Lords, instead of — as would be likely in most collections — being identified as a lithographic poster designed by Mary Lowndes. Indexing might also identify when the imagery is militant or constitutional, whether it depicts women as victim or aggressor, and include the figure of justice and the concept of injustice. The use of banners, posters and postcards also brings up the fact that paintings and sculpture, and not the so-called minor arts, are the usual candidates for subject indexing. Yet, increasingly the importance of needlework, pottery, glassware, popular art, magazine illustrations, costume, jewellery, even kitsch and souvenirs, as historical documents and carriers of political and social messages, are being recognised.

Other disciplines' use of art

It is not only art historians who consider works of art as historical documents. Historians are increasingly turning to visual materials to support their historic analysis. The historian Simon Schama, for example, in his book, *The Embarrassment of Riches; an Interpretation of Dutch Culture in the Golden Age*, uses a total of 314 illustrations, all but a few of them works of art. He of course uses works of art that depict historical events, but he also uses them to illuminate moral and religious attitudes, domestic arrangements, child-rearing practices, and a host of other aspects of Dutch society. Certainly the general location and actions of the scenes can be indexed, if the more subtle of the symbols and interpretations cannot. Interestingly enough, Schama cites Henri van de Wall as 'the seminal work on Dutch prints and other imagery as a source for the history of mentality', and the *Decimal Index to the Art of the Low Countries* (DIAL), using van de Wall's ICONCLASS subject classification as 'the indispensable guide for historical research in Dutch Art' and the 'first resource for any historian investigating social motifs in Dutch culture' (Schama, 1988, page 656).

Schama, in many of his illustrations, focuses, not on the main theme of the painting, but on significant details to make his point. In Joachim Beuckelaer's painting, which most people would have indexed by its title, *Christ in the House of Martha and Mary*, for example, it is not the depiction of the Biblical story taking place in the background of the painting which captures Schama's interest, but the 'Rabelaisian pleasure of troweling on great heaps of comestible matter' implicit in the piles of food which dominate the foreground (Schama, 1988, page 155).

Other authors also concentrate on the significant details as well. Margaret R. Miles, for example, in *Image as Insight; Visual Understanding in Western Christianity and Secular Culture* (Miles, 1985), concentrates on the emotional expressiveness shown by figures on the periphery of the central scene. Joseph, in Pietro Cavallini's mosaic of the *Nativity*, in Santa Maria in Trastevere, Rome, sits disconsolate, agonising that he cannot provide a better shelter for his family. The central theme of Giotto's *Slaughter of the Innocents* in the Arena Chapel is supposed to be the killing of the children, yet, as Miles points out, they are piled up like cord wood in the foreground, while the focus of the painting is on the hostility between the men and women in the background. Should the painting be indexed under the category 'gender hostility'?

The historian Diana Owen Hughes also looks away from the main subject of paintings. In her *Representing the Family*, in *Art and History* (Hughes, 1988), she concentrates on the role dogs play in portraits. She observes that Van Dyck, for example, depicts the rites of passage of the future Charles II from child in skirts playing with an average sized animal to adolescent in pants resting his controlling hand on a giant mastiff. Do indexers include rites of passage as a category?

Art as a process

Perspective

Psychology and psychoanalysis are used to measure the process by which the artist arrives at his composition. Margaret A. Hagen, a perceptual psychologist, in *Varieties of Realism; Geometries of Representational Art*, believes that 'all successful pictures make available to the beholder the same kind of visual information as does the ordinary environment', and that 'all art is governed by geometrical principles' (Hagen, 1986, pages xi and 1). She provides diagrams to analyse works according to the plane of figures: frontal, profile and lateral; and according to options of station points and perspective: metric, similarity, affine, and projective. These kinds of analyses are, of course, measurable and indexable, but they might be the sort of analysis that one day can be done by a computer.

Psychological interpretations

In his psychoanalytical study of Michelangelo, Nathan Lietes speculates about Michelangelo's relation with his mother from the many figures of *Madonna and Child* made by Michelangelo which show them seeming to avoid contact with each other (Lietes, 1986). Rarely do Michelangelo's figures look at each other (Figure 42.5). But this is not proof unless the author compares Michelangelo's *Madonna and Child* to the norm of the period. Such a comparison could be made if an indexed database were available that would enable the author to see whether or not a Madonna who ignores her child is very unusual or is a common trait among other artists. Some of the present indexing systems do indicate the relation of figures to each other, but perhaps not in the exact way that researchers would wish. The relation of the Madonna and Child is also a theme central to

Figure 42.5

ART AS PROCESS. Michelangelo, *Madonna and Child*. Florence, Museo Nazionale

the work of Judith Kristiva and of Leo Steinberg, although each deals with different artists and uses their information for different purposes, Steinberg to show the sexual nature of Christianity, and Kristiva the language of gesture.

Art as a language

Considering works of art as a form of language, and applying the techniques of linguistics and literature to them, is another apparent trend in art history (Figure 42.6). A few scholars trained in literary criticism have created a new area between art and literature. Norman Bryson, for example in *Vision and Painting: the Logic of the Gaze,* challenges the concept that the work of art is a record of a perception of the world (Bryson, 1983, pages xiii–xiv). A painting, he asserted, is 'a production, rather than a preception of meaning'. In his view a painting consists of 'codes of recognition' which the viewer transforms into his own meanings. Those constructing a comprehensive index of art will have trouble with this no-man's land, a land lying somewhere between art history and literature, a land mined with theory and laced with obscurities, a land of fascinating complexities. Indexers confronting such a land will have to go beyond the themes and the objects in a painting to analyse a host of associations and the methods by which these are communicated.

Gesture

Hopeful constructors of art indexes must deal with the gesture as an important way in which meaning within paintings are communicated. Gestures, sometimes directly and

Figure 42.6 ART AS LANGUAGE. Giotto. *The Presentation of the Virgin at the Temple*. Padua, Arena Chapel.

easily understood, are at other times more obscure and require knowledge of some code. Moshe Barasch, *Giotto and the Language of Gesture*, indicates how gestures elucidate the meaning of Giotto's art and identify the sources from which they were taken (Barasch, 1987). Do we have an adequate taxonomy of gestures to index them?

Narrative

Two other authors, Wendy Steiner and Richard Brilliant also treat art as a language, but instead of studying gesture, analyse the narrative structures. Wendy Steiner, also from English literature, in *Pictures of Romance; Form against Content in Painting and Literature*, describes the presentation of more than one temporal moment as being the essence of narrative. In Sassetta's *Meeting of St Anthony and St Paul*, for example, St Anthony is depicted in three different incidents on his journey. She also takes her analysis into twentieth-century art, finding the use of narrative techniques in the works of pop artists

(Steiner, 1988). Richard Brilliant, in *Visual Narratives: Story Telling in Etruscan and Roman Art*, diagrams the placement of figures in the Arch of Septimus Severus to plot the flow of the story and the action (Brilliant, 1984). Would the addition of a taxonomy of narrative techniques to present indexing systems, and the application of them to indicate which works of art illustrate their use, be of help to scholars?

Analysis on non-representational art

Non-representational art poses the greatest challenge to those searching for a comprehensive indexing system for all the arts. It is an area that has eluded any categories other than identification by artist, title, media, dimensions and date. Broad stylistic terms, such as Cubism, Futurism Suprematism, Abstract Expressionism, Minimalism, or Earth Works, may be used, but there are problems of vagueness in definition, and these categories still define a very large number of works. The works themselves are largely distinguished one from another by formal qualities, rather than those of subject content. Subjects, when they exist, are usually irrelevant or not memorable as identifying characteristics. In order to index non-representational works of art, some kind of formal criteria is needed. Such criteria, even when formulated, would be difficult to teach to a variety of indexers. This is one area where the computer might be able to accomplish a task beyond human capacities.

Experts have developed techniques whereby the computer is taught sets of 'picture grammars' by which it can identify stored images that contain the elements in that grammar. Architects, for example, have created shape grammars for a variety of entities including landscapes, buildings, architectural drawings, furniture designs and window patterns. These forms, of course, lend themselves easily to schematisation. Other researchers, however, have been able to extend the use of similar techniques to paintings. Joan and Russell Kirsch have taken the Ocean Park series of some 140 paintings by Richard Diebenkorn and constructed a grammar or algorithmic program for them. The computer can now recognise the other paintings in the *Ocean Park* series, and, in fact, created a new painting that conforms to the series. Even the artist recognised the computer's creation as a plausible painting. Diebenkorn's *Ocean Park* series was composed mainly of straight lines, an easier situation to represent in a computer analysis. Joan and Russell Kirsch have now tried a more difficult task, analysing the shape grammar of Joan Miro's series of 23 gouaches called *Constellations*. By analysing the shapes in the series, represented here by one example, *The Beautiful Bird Revealing the Unknown to a Pair of Lovers*, the Kirschs came up with a set of prototype shapes. The computer scanned the series for these prototypes; a combination of computer graphics and manual tracing produced the actual shapes. The program allows for size and shape variations. To validate the choice a simulated Miro was created in the computer. The Kirschs assert that 'at this time, it appears to us that serious fine art is too rich and varied to allow a mechanical discovery of its structure' (Kirsch and Kirsch, in press). They point to a future, however, where, as computers build up an accumulation of pictorial grammars, they will be able to make analysis of paintings. Information valuable to connoiseurship and aesthetic analysis will be generated, and improvements in data storage and formal analysis can be anticipated.

New subjects in museum exhibitions

The change in the direction of the discipline of art history in the last decade has been dramatic and sudden, a change that art museums have been slow to reflect. Nevertheless museums are beginning to adapt to the new forces as well. The great majority of museum and gallery exhibitions still concentrate on the works of a single artist or closely related group of artists. Consideration of art as historical document, a social process or a language is beginning, however, if sometimes only in the text of the catalogue. The 1982 Tate Gallery exhibition of the works of Richard Wilson, although conventional enough in its choice of paintings and in the hanging, was accompanied by David Solkin's catalogue whose Marxist interpretation of eighteenth-century landscape painting stirred controversy. Changes in attitudes helped to make the Manchester City Art Galleries exhibition, *Hard Times, Social Realism in Victorian Art* (1987), possible. As Julian Spalding, the Director of the Manchester City Art Galleries admitted in the preface to the catalogue:

> 'The fact that we can stage it now is partly due to the Post-Modernist Movement in art, which has freed us from some of the narrower dogmas of Modernism and is exploring once again figurative subject matter and earthy tonalities. There is also the New Art History which places greater emphasis on its social context than on the individual's aesthetic experience. Realist art, particularly when it has a political dimension, is everywhere being re-assessed.' (Treuherz, 1987, page 7)

Once the attention is shifted from the work of an artist to the context of society, and from style to figurative and representational subject content, the helpfulness of the traditional classification by media, school and artist, lessens, and the importance of having an alternative indexing system which deals with subjects, objects and themes, becomes evident.

Also appearing in museums is another kind of exhibition, that which treats art from different cultures comparatively or which compares art with nature or science. The exhibition *Primitivism* at the Museum of Modern Art in New York compared the forms of traditional ethnic art with European painting and sculpture. It also dealt with the historical influence of primitive art, and, less successfully, with the essence of primitivism captured in contemporary art.

Another exhibition, in the Mathildenhöhe, Darmstadt, gathered together a number of different works on the theme of *Symmetry*. Not only was the idea of classical symmetry explored, but parallel ideas, inversions and mirror images. The symmetry of science and nature was compared with that found in art. The exhibitions at the new Musée d'Orsay, Paris, especially in the *Dossier* series, investigates the historical context of works of art in great detail. A new exhibition at the Museum of Modern Art, New York, will compare the genres in high and low art, showing how the same theme might be treated in each genre. In all these instances a database of indexed works of art could have provided many more examples, and perhaps even some new insights.

A recent exhibition at the Musee Picasso centred on one painting, Picasso's *Demoiselles d'Avignon*. The mammoth catalogue of over 700 pages included illustrations of approximately 1 300 studies, sketches and related works (Musée Picasso, 1988). This exhaustive treatment of a single work brings out several questions for the indexer. Could (or should) an indexer identify works related to other works? studies? influences? How far should an indexer go in noting various aspects of a work? The setting of *Demoiselles d'Avignon* is a brothel; in fact the original title was *The Philosophical Brothel*. Should this painting be retrieved from a database if the user asks for paintings of prostitutes? of African masks? How far should an indexer go in reflecting interpretations of works of art? The facial features of the women in *Demoiselles d'Avignon* have been interpreted as representing the ravages of syphilis and expressing Picasso's fear of it. Is syphilis an appropriate indexing term for this painting? The stoney stare of the women have also been interpreted as Medusa heads revealing Picasso's fear of castration. Are 'Medusa' and 'castration' appropriate indexing terms? These interpretations might be welcome information to a student or scholar, but how useful would they be without a citation to the textual description of the theory? Where should the line be drawn between indexing of visual aspects of the work of art and the indexing of texts and criticism about the work? Can they be successfully integrated?

That there are more museums and art galleries than ever before, with more visitors than ever before, is well known, but why large numbers of people are coming to art exhibitions is less clear. Explanations range from the speculation that art has become a yuppie status symbol (Robert Rosenblum) or that it provides 'self-recognition and a sense of identity' (Joseph Veach Noble) to 'the hope that art will provide the moral and spiritual resources traditionally offered by religion and philosophy' (Mark Stevens). Whatever the reason, it seems clear that a large part of the audience viewing works of art do not know much about what they are looking at, and that they are searching for some kind of meaning. Patterson Williams of the Denver Art Museum asserts that 90 per cent of the visitors rarely talk about formal qualities. The less visitors know about art, the more they want to see recognisable subject matter. 'Museums have failed to capitalise on the boom in attendance', Sherman Lee asserts, 'passing up opportunities to draw parallels between art and the viewers' lives' (Virshup, 1988).

Conclusions: The task ahead

If the direction of art history is any indication, and if art museums are going to fulfil their visitors need for meaning, subject indexing should become more valuable than ever. What can the indexer make of this bewildering explosion of new approaches to art history? Can the indexing of images ever keep up with it? Can an indexer be so subtle, so flexible, that all aspects of the work of art will be captured? Certainly not everything can be done through indexing. It would not even be desirable. Subject indexing can do so much to provide a better access and understanding of works of art, but it cannot, nor should it try to, replace the historians interpretive and critical analysis.

'Where is wisdom we have lost in knowledge?
Where is the knowledge we have lost in information?'

asked T. S. Eliot long before the information explosion (Eliot, 1934, page 107).

Eliot's scepticism notwithstanding, the works of art are still there. They still constitute the basic information bearing entity of art history. Indexers are not increasing their number, but are putting the information they bear in some kind of order, so that instead of a chaotic sea of unrelated and unordered works, it will be possible to arrange these works in different ways, comparing and contrasting their characteristics, seeing them in relation to each other. From such a capacity comes knowledge, perhaps even wisdom, a capacity for knowing and judgement that leads to greater mastery of the ever-increasing number of works of art in the world.

The need for subject indexing is being recognised by art historians as well as librarians and visual resources experts. As one art historian interviewed in the Getty Art History Information Program *Object — Image — Inquiry; The Art Historian at Work,* confessed, 'the difficulty of searching for subject matter almost forces me to do monographic work, to deal with one artist at a time' (Schmitt, 1988, page 147). Another art historian in the same source agreed, for him 'the great dream is images indexed by a reasonable efficient subject index' (Schmitt, 1988, page 103). 'Reasonably efficient' is what indexers should look to as a goal. If the indexer could guide the user to a managable number of images it would be sufficient. In the ordering of artistic knowledge, endless searches through random sources is the Serbonian bog to be avoided. The goal to find the one single answer to a request is too ambitious, and perhaps not desirable. The advantages of browsing and serendipitious discovery are too great to be foregone. An indexer's time might better be spent increasing the amount of materials covered rather than the fineness of the indexing profile. As art historians and museum exhibitions use a greater number of materials outside the canon of great works, the number of images of interest greatly increases. Art historians and curators are not interested in all works of art, including banners, postcards, photographs, videos, baseball cards and all kinds of ephemera. They are interested in the images of science, nature and journalism. They are rapidly becoming visual historians instead of art historians. Visual historians conceive of images as not only connected to each other through artistic genesis and stylistic influence, but imparting historical information, embodying social processes, and conveying a whole range of meaningful signs.

The whole discipline of art history, and all its adjunct activities in museums, libraries and visual collections, has in the past been ordered according to the Pliny/Vasari concept. Today's visual curators and librarians are witnessing the unravelling, the literal deconstruction, of that concept. The Pliny/Vasari use of media, school and artist no longer fulfils the function of placing objects in an order that reflects the mental categories that art historians now increasingly use to analyse and interpret works of art. Yet there is no universally accepted system of ordering to replace it. Even the most radical of art historians still know the old order. But will this be true of the next generation of art historians, those raised on the new art history or those who come from other disciplines?

How are those of us who have large collections of materials (works of art, books and visual collections), going to meet this challenge? Given the size of our collections, reclassification seems impossible, nor has another viable system for classification yet emerged. The alternative tradition of subject indexing, on the other hand, has the flexibility, and with the computer, the means, of providing a multitude of categories, of ordering information about works of art in a variety of ways. With improvements and expansions here and there, existing indexing systems can gain the comprehensiveness demanded by the broader approaches of new art historians.

Unfortunately not enough subject indexing has been done, nor has that which has been done, always been shared. Futhermore art historians seem largely unaware of the existing indexing projects and of the use that could be made of them. It means that much more indexing needs to be done, and that work given more visibility in the art historical world. Given the enormous number of works of art in the world, it is an enormous task, and one that would profit by close cooperation. Adams's job of naming is far from complete. Let's get on with it.

---

43 AN INTRODUCTION TO ICONCLASS

Dr Catherine Gordon

Project Director, Witt Computer Index
Courtauld Institute of Art
London

Introduction

In the five years since I first began working with the ICONCLASS iconographic classification system, I seem to have been frequently asked a similar series of questions about the system: what it is and how does it work, how easy or difficult is it to learn, or to use, how effective is it in answering a typical or even a more obscure subject enquiry? I hope that this paper may provide answers to at least some of the questions which seem to have come up again and again in many individual discussions.

You may perhaps have seen ICONCLASS in a library context as a set of books, or have read an article about the system, you may have perused a few pages of one of the published volumes, or you may have sought the answer to a subject enquiry by using one of the services which has applied the ICONCLASS system, such as the subject indices to the Marburg fiche, the DIAL postcards, or the published Iconographic indexes to Hind and Bartch.

But ICONCLASS's value and strength as a successful system for classifying the content and subject matter of fine art material, lies above all in its underlying broad philosophy and logical structure. This perhaps is not so easily understood or so quickly recognised from a brief exposure to the system. I would therefore like to present some of the basics of the ICONCLASS system.

History

ICONCLASS is an iconographic classification system (Van de Waal, 1973–85) developed over a period of 40 years since the Second World War at the University of Leiden by Professor Henri van de Waal and an editorial team which, since van de Waal's death in 1972, has been directed by Leendert Couprie. Despite the fact that ICONCLASS is a Dutch system, from its inception it has been designed in English, and English remains the common language for its use within a variety of international projects.

ICONCLASS has been designed to satisfy the classification requirements of *visual* material — I stress visual — as Henri van de Waal wrote in 1968, 'the material offered for consultation should always be visual — any other reference — either verbal or by means of codes — can never be more than the first stepping stone' (Van de Waal, 1968, preface page 14). ICONCLASS provides a means of describing what we can *see* as well as what we can *know* or can *interpret* in images. ICONCLASS offers a tool for the classification of images: in particular it deals with that body of material which is depicted or protrayed in works of art and it has in some areas a natural, although not exclusive, bias towards Western art.

ICONCLASS consists of a series of hierarchically arranged alpha-numeric codes or notations, each associated with an English text description in a printed system. This system has been published as a series of 17 volumes over a 12 year period from 1973 to 1985: these 17 volumes are made up of the seven System Volumes and three Alphabetical

Index Volumes which make up the ICONCLASS system proper. These are accompanied by seven Bibliography Volumes which constitute an application of the ICONCLASS system and provide an art historical bibliography, with a particular focus on books and articles of iconographical interest.

ICONCLASS is therefore a traditional publication in book form, not a computer software system. It can be purchased from the Royal Netherlands Academy of Arts and Sciences either complete or in sections, or even as individual volumes, like any other book. As with all quality reference books, it is expensive, but it is also to my knowledge, the largest, the most comprehensive and the most sophisticated visual subject indexing system available. It is also one of the few systems of subject classification for images which was designed and consciously planned for universal application, separate from any very specific focus of interest, and independent of its use within any particular visual collection.

Although ICONCLASS is not a computer system, Van de Waal was aware from the early 1950s of the potential value of computer application of the system. Since its publication ICONCLASS has been applied to a variety of computer generated databases in various international projects which run on a variety of hardware and software. At the same time, it also continues to be used as a filing and retrieval method in a series of image collections which are manually arranged according to ICONCLASS notations. It has also served as the organising principle for various publications concerned with iconography.

In November 1987, an international group of ICONCLASS users met in Los Angeles. The report of this workshop discussion, including descriptions of a variety of projects which apply ICONCLASS, has been published as a special issue of *Visual Resources* (Gordon, 1988).

Basic structure

ICONCLASS notations are presented as a series of decimal codes which have a hierarchic structure reading naturally from left to right. The main divisions are capable of unlimited subdivision, unlike hierachic systems such as those used at the Slide and Photographic Archive of the National Museum of American Art or the British Art Center at Yale, which have just primary, secondary and tertiary levels. Subdivision to nine or ten levels is common in the published ICONCLASS system and the use of five or six levels is routine. The first two characters of an ICONCLASS notation are digits and the third character is always a capital letter, thus permitting 25 subdivisions at the third level of the hierarchy. Subsequent subdivision is by decimal numbering. The alphabet is reduced to 25 rather than 26 characters because J is not used. The numbers used are 1 to 9, normally excluding the number 0 (zero) which is used only rarely, when it is assigned a particular meaning within ICONCLASS notations.

The fundamental divisions of the ICONCLASS hierarchy are represented by the numbers 1 to 9, each of which stands for a primary topic. Numbers 1 to 5 are general/universal topics and numbers 6 to 9 are special, or what I would call text-based topics. The simplicity and breadth of concept conveyed by each of the major divisions was indicated by van de Waal's statement of 1954 when he wrote 'I thought that it should be possible to put into a consistent classfication all the subjects which man has suceeded in portraying' (Van de Waal, 1955).

The divisions are:

1. Religion and Magic
2. Nature
3. Human Being, Man in General
4. Society, Civilisation, Culture
5. Abstract Ideas and Concepts
6. History
7. The Bible
8. Literature
9. Classical Mythology and Ancient History

Division 1: Supernatural/Religion/Magic: includes saints and devils, Madonnas and clerics, Judaism and Buddism, Theology and the Ocult, but not representations of Jacob's Dream or The Good Samaritan because these are narratives within the Biblical text, and therefore fall into Division 7.

Division 2: Nature: includes landscape, wild animals and plants, the seasons and weather conditions, the sun and the moon. It also contains city views which when regarded broadly, are a form of landscape, albeit not totally 'natural'.

Division 3: The Human Being/Man in General: includes man as a biological creature, anatomy and the nude, the parts and postures of the human body, ways of dying and sexual relationships, racial types and the ages of man.

Division 4: Society/Civilisation/Culture: includes transport and agriculture, housing and furniture, clothes and industrial activities, art and education, government and trade, still life, child care, marriage and burial rites, hunting and children's games. It also includes some of the 'tamed or domesticated' animals: horses in transport and cattle in agriculture.

Division 5: Abstract Ideas and Concepts: includes abstract or allegorical portrayals of Contemplation and Fortune, of Patience and Rumour, of Wisdom and Folly. It also enables you also to describe the manner of the depiction, such as a 'personification of an abstract concept represented by a female figure, partially clothed with wings'. Division 5 does not contain Greed as a Deadly Sin or Temperance as a Cardinal Virtue, which are covered within Division 1 as aspects of specifically Christian theology.

Division 6: History: includes the dating of historic events and all portraiture, whether identified or not, because all real persons are accepted as being 'historical'. History, however, starts in Division 6, from the Reign of Constantine (306–337 AD). All Biblical and Classical history is carried in Divisions 7 and 9. The date of the Battle of Waterloo would be carried in division 61 A, while the nature of the event — a battle — would be classified within Division 45 H, War being part of Society, Civilisation and Culture.

Division 7: The Bible: includes all narratives from The Bible, and also some apocryphal stories, legendary extensions of biblical themes and a certain amount of non-biblical narration relating to the lives of the Apostles.

Division 8: Literature/Tales and Sagas: includes all depictions from non-biblical and post-classical texts, such as Arthurian legend and Shakespeare, Dante and Tennyson, fables, tales, and proverbs, together with characters from such literature.

Figure 43.1 Page from Index Volume illustrating the entry for 'school'

school

school
St. Augustine taken to school by his mother Monica 11 H (AUGUSTINE) 21
St. Cassian teaching, seated amidst schoolboys 11 H (CASSIAN) 41
St. Cassian's pupils kill him with their iron styles 11 H (CASSIAN) 68
Jewish school 12 A 82 : 49 B 2
child and school (~ games and plays) 43 C 74 2
school festivity 43 C 74 21
games at school 43 C 74 23
riding-school, manège 46 C 13 11
place or institution of education and training of the artist, e.g.: academy of art 48 B 14 1
building ~ education, tuition KEY (+1) to 49 B
scholastic education, tuition 49 B
elementary school; class, form 49 B 2
school-building 49 B 2 (+1)
the Christ-child brought to school by Mary 73 B 73 4
Paul preaching in Tyrannus' school 73 F 22 34 22
Phaedra, in the temple of Venus, unobserved watches Hippolytus training in the gymnasium; possibly in frustrated passion she jabs the leaves of a nearby myrtle-tree with a hairpin 95 B (PHAEDRA) 21 1
school board
school board, board of directors KEY (+91) to 49 B
school outing
school outing 43 C 74 22
schoolmaster
see teacher
schooner
sailing-ship, sailing-boat (with NAME) 46 C 24 (...)
Schulklopfer
'Schulklopfer', synagogue-knocker, a man who summons members to synagogal services 12 A 34 22
schuttersfeest
meeting of citizen soldiers (Dutch: 'schuttersfeest') 45 B 54 (+26)
Schutzmantel
Mary protecting mankind against the plague, e.g. by hiding people under her cloak; 'Pestbild' 11 F 34
Mother of Mercy, 'Mater Misericordiae', 'Schutzmantelmadonna', 'Schutzmantelmaria' 11 F 62 4
saint (with NAME) protecting devotees with cloak, 'Schützmantel' see 11 H and 11 HH (...) 11 9
Charlemagne protecting devotees with his cloak 11 H (CHARLEMAGNE) 11 9
St. Ursula protecting the eleven thousand virgins with her cloak 11 HH (URSULA) 11 9
schwärmen
contemplation of the moon, 'schwärmen' 24 B 62
Sciagurataggine
Infamy; 'Sciagurataggine' (Ripa) 57 AA 92
Sciapodes
'Scopodes', 'Sciapodes', i.e. beings with one leg 31 A 44 12
science
Church (and Religion) vs. Philosophy and Science 11 P 16 6
war and science 45 A 14 3
allegory of arts and sciences 48 (ALL.) : 49 C 0
education, science and learning 49
aspects of science in general 49 C
symbolic representations, allegories and emblems ~ science, 'Scientia'; 'Scienza', 'Studio' (Ripa) 49 C 0
science versus worldly temptation 49 C 01
science and technology 49 E
cupids together with attributes of the arts, sciences, etc. 92 D 19 16 4

1204

Division 9: Classical Mythology and Ancient History: includes classical literature and mythology, events and people from classical history: the Gods of Olympus, the Trojan Wars, the Muses and Metamorphoses, the activities of Greek and Roman deities and the lives and deaths of classical heroes.

These nine divisions represent the bedrock of the comprehensive logic of ICONCLASS. The understanding and regular recollection of these few fixed primary access points is an important prerequisite to examining the variety and subtlety of all subsequent subdivisions in ICONCLASS.

Index/Bibliography

It is also necessary to bear these nine divisions in mind in order to fully benefit from the Alphabetical Index and the Bibliography Volumes of ICONCLASS, because both these sets of volumes are organised and internally ordered in accordance with the decimal notations.

The word 'School' can be readily looked up in the Alphabetical Index (Figure 43.1) under S where you will find a series of references to the term as an indexed keyword appearing within a variety of notations. Within the various entries the references are ordered according to the 1 to 9 sequence. An example of the consequence of this is that specific appearances of the word 'school', as in 'St Augustine taken to school by his Mother' — which falls within Division 11 H (Saints) — or a particular occurrence of the term 'school', as in the phrase 'riding-school' — which falls within the Division 46 C 13 (animal mounts) — take precedence in the printed Index over the main entry for 'school' which falls within 49 B (scholastic education/tuition). This code, by its decimal placing, appears further down the page.

Similarly, the Bibliography Volumes of ICONCLASS are arranged according to the nine main divisions and within each volume are ordered by their decimal notation. For example, literature on the Symbols of the State, such as Flags and Banners will be found listed in Volume 4 under the notation 44 A 3 (Figure 43.2). You could have located this reference under the term 'Flag' in the Alphabetical Index, which applies equally to the Bibliography Volumes as to the System Volumes themselves.

Development of the notations

I will now describe some of the structured components which make up the basic form or shape of an ICONCLASS notation. Although the Alphabetical Index provides immediate and simple access to ICONCLASS notations it is, like any keyword indexing system, restricted in its choice of terms and limited by the vagaries of natural language. The alphabetical index should not be used as a substitute to understanding the structure of the System. At the Los Angeles workshop, it was emphasised that the Alphabetical Index should be seen as being of value for user access, while those engaged in the indexing procedure needed to understand the logical structure of the ICONCLASS System. This is best discovered by examining the notations themselves as presented in the System Volumes.

A completed subject classification as given to any single image may consist of a series of ICONCLASS notations, some presented in combination. These notations are made up of primary subdivisions, queues and auxillaries such as key numbers, structural digits, double letters and specific titles or words.

The coded structures of ICONCLASS are only bewildering at first. The ICONCLASS system may seem to lead to apparently odd international conversations in which people

Figure 43.2 Page from Bibliography Volume, illustrating the entry for flag'

44 A 3 flag, colours

44 A 3 flag, colours
Cartari p. xlii s.v. Fahne – Henkel-Schöne 1486, 1550 – Lurker, Symbolkunde 305, 529 s.v. Kleidung und Insignien – RDK VI 1060 s.v. Fahne; VI 1168 s.v. Fahnenbuch – Ripa s.v. Età del Ferro – Saffroy, Nos. 12615-12821

A. Rabbow, Visuelle Symbole als Erscheinung der nichtverbalen Publizistik, Münster i.W. 1966 (diss.)

K. Sierksma (ed.), Flags of the world 1669-1670. A seventeenth century manuscript, Amsterdam 1966

W. Smith, The bibliography of flags of foreign nations, Boston (Mass.) 1965

C. Gottlieb, The pregnant woman, the flag, the eye. Three new themes in 20th century art, *JAAC* 21(1962-1963)177

P. Wentzcke, Die deutschen Farben. Ihre Entwicklung und Deutung sowie ihre Stellung in der deutschen Geschichte, Heidelberg 1955

H. Wescher, Die Fahne, *Ciba-Rundschau* No. 83(1949)3076

H. W. O. F. Neubecker, Fahnen und Flaggen, Leipzig 1939 (with bibliography)

H. Meyer, Kaiserfahne und Blutfahne, *Zs. Savigny-Stiftung f. Rechtsgesch., Germanistische Abt.* 51(1931)204

E. Waldmann, Lanzen, Stangen und Fahnen als Hilfsmittel der Composition in den graphischen Frühwerken Albrecht Dürers, Strassburg 1906 (Stud. z. dtsch. Kg. 68)

44 A 31 banner, standard
Praz 1964, 100, 107 (~Cupid); 188

L. H. Loomis, The oriflamme of France and the war-cry 'Monjoie' in the 12th century, Fs. Belle da Costa Greene, Princeton 1954, 67

H. Meyer, Sturmfahne und Standarte, *Zs. Savigny-Stiftung f. Rechtsgesch., Germanistische Abt.* 51(1931)204

H. Meyer, Die Oriflamme und das französische Nationalgefühl, *Nachr. Ges. Wiss. Göttingen, Philol.-hist. Klasse* (1930)95

G. A. Desjardins, Recherches sur les drapeaux français. Oriflamme, bannière de France . . . , Paris 1874

44 A 4 decorations, honours
Henkel-Schöne 220 – RDK IV 1164 s.v. Eisernes Kreuz; V 123 (~emblems) – Ripa s.v. Religione di S. Lasaro e S. Mauritio; Stabilità

B. Heydenreich, Ritterorden und Rittergesellschaften. Ihre Entwicklung vom späten Mittelalter bis zur Neuzeit. Ein Beitrag zur Phaleristik, Würzburg 1960 (diss.) (with bibliography)

44 A 5 symbols of particular nations, states or districts
Saffroy, Nos. 12822-12868

W. Deonna, Histoire d'un emblème: la couronne murale des villes et pays personnifiés, *Genava* 18(1940)119

America

E. Lehner, American symbols. A pictorial history. Intr. by R. Butterfield, New York [1957]

127

Figure 3.3 Page from System Volume (volume 2)

25 F 2 mammals

25 F 23	(continued) TIGER, WEASEL, WOLF dog 34 B 11 cat 34 B 12
25 F 24	hoofed animals with NAME between brackets, e.g.: ⊕ ANTELOPE, BISON (bonasus, aurochs), BOAR, ⊕ CAMEL, DEER, DROMEDARY, ELK, GAZELLE, GIRAFFE, GNU, HIPPOPOTAMUS, IBEX, MUSK-DEER, ONAGER (wild ass), ORYX, QUAGGA, RHINOCEROS horse 46 C 13 14
25 F 25	trunked animals with NAME between brackets, e.g.: ELEPHANT ⊕ ivory 25 F 25 (ELEPHANT) (+ 33 4)
25 F 26	rodents with NAME between brackets, e.g.: BEAVER, HARE, MOUSE, MUSK-RAT (musquash), ⊕ RABBIT, RAT, SQUIRREL, WOMBAT cat and mouse 34 B 12 1
25 F 27	swimming mammals with NAME between brackets, e.g.: DOLPHIN, SEAL, WHALE ⊕ ambergris 31 A 51 41 (AMBERGRIS)
25 F 28	flying mammals with NAME between brackets, e.g.: BAT ⊕
25 F 29	other mammals not meant or mentioned above with NAME between brackets, e.g.: ARMADILLO, HEDGEHOG, MOLE, PORCUPINE ⊕
25 F 3	birds ⊕ wings of a bird 25 F 3 (. . .) (+ 34 2) ⊕ feathers of a bird 25 F 3 (. . .) (+ 35 2) ⊕ bird (singing) 25 F 3 (. . .) (+ 49) ⊕ egg of a bird 25 F 3 (. . .) (+ 91) ⊕
25 F 31	groups of birds birds as house animals 34 B 13 birds as garden animals 34 B 23

22

Figure 43.4 Page from System Volume (Outline)

25 D	rock types; minerals and metals; soil types
D 11	precious stones
D 3	mining
D 4	fluids and gases
E	historical geology
25 F	animals
F 2	mammals
F 3	birds
F 4	reptiles
F 5	amphibians
F 6	fishes
F 7	lower animals
F 8	extinct animals
F 9	monsters
FF	fabulous animals
25 G	plants
G 2	products of plants, fruits
G 3	trees
G 4	plants and herbs
G 41	flowers
G 5	lower plants
G 6	extinct plants
G 7	language of flowers
GG	fantastic and fabulous plants
25 H	landscapes
H 1	landscapes (temperate zone)
H 2	waterscapes
H 21 3	river
H 23	sea
I	city view, landscape with man-made constructions
I 1	city
I 2	village
K	landscape (non-temperate zone)
K 1	(sub) tropical landscape
K 2	polar landscape
K 3	exotic landscape
L	allegories of cities
M	Seven Wonders of the World
N	fictitious countries
26	meteorological phenomena
A	clouds
B	rain
C	winds
D	frost
E	thunderstorm
F	good and bad weather
G	mirage
29	surrealia

involved in indexing naturally speak of images of angels fighting as 11 G 3, or of the crucifixion as 73 D 6, or they find themselves asking each other if this is a 25 H or a 25 K 1 (a temperate or tropical landscape). ICONCLASS is not a language, but I have found it a satisfying intellectual structure, as well as a ready means of communication across language barriers.

The extensions of the notations beyond the basic divisions, which appear after the capital letter, and which are referred to as 'queues', are not arbitrarily assigned numbers, but have their own elements of internal logic. Each additional number carries its own meaning in a hierarchically ordered position within its primary division (Figure 43.3). For example, within the division 46 C (traffic and transport), all notations initiated by 46 C 1 relate to transport on land, those which begin 46 C 2 are transport on water, and those which start with 46 C 3 are transport in the air. Journeys into space will be 46 C 4.

Having selected the primary access point from the numbers 1 to 9, you choose the appropriate numbered System Volume. Each System Volume is then preceded by an *Outline* (Figure 43.4) which gives a useful overview of the subdivisions covered by that Volume. Once you have located the subdivision which you want, you can then turn to its appropriate extension within that same book.

It is, of course, not necessary to establish the one code or notation which encompasses all you wish to describe. Any single image can be assigned any number of ICONCLASS notations which satisfy however much or little you recognise within an image. Various projects have found that four notations are an average, while some images require only one and others many more than four.

Within the ICONCLASS system of notation there are a variety of structured components, such as combined notations, key numbers, structural digits and the use of words, each of which is recognisable and meaningful.

Combined notations

The ICONCLASS system is very comprehensive, but it does not attempt to supply an individual notation for every imaginable situation. For example, while it does provide a generic code for performances with trained animals (43 A 37 4), and further subdivisions provide for performances with monkeys, elephants, bears, lions and tigers, horses, dogs, dolphins, seals and fleas, should you require to classify a circus performance which included trained camels you would use the structure of a combined notation. The code 43 A 37 4 (performance with trained animal) would be followed by a colon and then by the notations 25 F 24 (CAMEL), for animals, mammal, hoofed, of the specific type Camel.

Inclusion of proper names

This example introduces another of the structural elements of an ICONCLASS notation: the inclusion within many notations of specific words, names or titles which are presented within parentheses. The use of this type of structure is regularly indicated in the printed system by the phrase 'with NAME between brackets'. Such a structure permits both the generic and the specific to be described and retrieved within the compactness of a single code. This naming of names, in English, appears at many points in the ICONCLASS hierarchy: for the species of birds and the sitters of portraits, for the identity of saints and characters from Greek legend, for the names of rivers, mountains and towns, of red indian tribes and monastic orders. But significantly each term is always contained and controlled by its presence within a hierachic structure, which always begins on the left with a generic subdivision. This means that there is no way to confuse or conflate WASHINGTON as a man or a mountain, or AJAX the Greek warrior with AJAX the British cruiser.

The various word lists as presented in the printed form of ICONCLASS are, of course, simply offered as samples: there could be no attempt to list a form of the name for every potential portrait sitter or identified piece of topography. In the area of subject classification ICONCLASS offers a conceptual framework into which such controlled terminology can be placed. It remains the responsibility of any project using ICONCLASS to maintain consistent control on such inserted terms.

Doubling of capital letters

At various points of the third level of ICONCLASS hierarchies, the option to double the captial letter is introduced. This doubling permits a broad shift in categorisation to be conveyed to all notations within such a subdivision. For example, where an identified male portrait would be preceded before the sitter name by the code 61 B 2, an identified female portrait will be preceded with the notation 61 BB 2. In other instances this doubling of the capital letter may allow for a shift from indoor to outdoor activity, such as meals taken indoors or outdoors, or from the real to the fabulous, as in animals and fabulous animals. In Division 5 the doubling of the letter may express the positive and negative variants which can convert Hope into Despair.

Key numbers

There is a further auxilliary structure available in ICONCLASS, known as Key numbers. These are found listed at the back of each System Volume (Figure 43.5). When placed in brackets at the end of a code, they function rather as qualifying adjectives or phrases, adding a particular meaning as appropriate within the subdivision. These key numbers are distinguished by being preceded by a plus sign +. An example is the code 25 F 23 (LION) (+46), where the presence of the +46 conveys within the overall subdivision 25 F (animals) the concept sleeping, so we have a sleeping lion, whereas a similar notation 25 F 23 (LION) (+67) would represent that the lion was stuffed, the +67 itself being a subdivision of the +6 key number indicating dead. Another example of a notation with key numbers would be 11 HH (+3 +5) from the main Division 1 Religion which would indicate a female saint depicted with angel/s and with donor/s.

Structural Digits

Certain notations share a type of extension which is called Structural Digits. These can be found for example in the categorisation of saints. Every saint, and the particularly famous events of their life and death has a place within the system, or the option for creating one. They also share certain characteristics which tend to go with sanctity, such as the ability to perform miracles or to suffer martyrdom. This shared 'lifestyle' is reflected by the use of consistent codes. All saintly temptation is encompased by the structure 11 H or HH (inset of saints name) 35, all miracles by 11 H or HH 5, all finding of relics by 11 H or HH 81.

Conclusion

I hope these various examples of the use of combined notations, text insert, key numbers and structural digits may have given some idea of the subtlety of classification which ICONCLASS offers, as well as an insight into the internal logical mechanisms of the system. The ICONCLASS structure is a working tool and it can permit new notations to igure 3.5 Page from System Volume (Key numbers)

KEY to 25 D 11

+1 precious stones used symbolically
+11 'lapidaria'

KEY to 25 D 3

+1 coal
+11 brown coal, lignite
+2 stone with NAME
  e.g. MARBLE
+21 gravel and sand
+3 other minerals (add NAME
  or apply system)

KEY to 25 F and subdivisions

+1 animals used symbolically
+11 bestiaries, 'Physiologus'
+12 heraldic animals
+13 animals as attributes
+14 animals in caricature
+15 ornamental variants
  fabulous animals 25 FF
+15 1 symmetrically placed
+15 2 partly joined
+15 3 partly interlaced
+15 4 symmetrically placed, divided by a (human) figure or an object

+2 sex and age; propagation
+21 young
+22 male
+23 female
+24 very old

+3 anatomy of animals

+31 skeleton

+32 trunk
+32 1 sexual organs
+32 11 male sexual organs
+32 12 female sexual organs
+32 2 buttocks
+32 3 entrails, internal organs
  excreting +45 9

+33 head
+33 1 skull
+33 2 antlers; horn
+33 3 ears
+33 4 fang, tusk
+33 5 snout, jaw, beak, nib
+33 6 tongue

+34 limbs
+34 1 claws, paws
+34 2 wings
+34 3 tail
+34 9 track, trail

+35 external appearance
+35 1 skin, fleece, hide, fur, leather
+35 2 feathers
+35 3 scales

+36 shell, snail-shell, etc.

+4 animal behaviour

+41 birth
+41 1 from an egg
+41 2 brooding; hatching
  egg +91
+41 3 'larva', grub
+41 4 'pupa', chrysalis

+42 feeding and care of young
+42 1 nest, den, burrow
  bird's nest 25 F 3
  (+42 1)
+42 2 'educating the young', playing with young
+42 9 killing own breed

+43 courting and mating
+43 1 courting
+43 2 mating

97

be devised for unforseen subjects as long as indexers are familiar with the System and are knowledgeable in art history.

But ICONCLASS also allows classification where we lack knowledge. This is a very important aspect of the freedom and breadth of the ICONCLASS system. Where a specific narrative or topic is not recognised, it is still possible to classify what is seen. In more traditional systems, what cannot be identified may not be able to be filed, but as R. H. Fuchs wrote in a memorial essay on Henri van de Waal 'ICONCLASS transcends this difficulty and permits the filing of unidentified images simply by classifying them according to what is actally *seen* — therefore it can operate not only as a filing system but also as a precise instrument for iconographic classification' (Fuchs, 1972–73).

Other qualities which we should recognise in the ICONCLASS system are that it is free from the constraint or limitations of natural language, or the demands of standardised vocabularies and it has the value of compactness, whether on computers or any other form of storage, as a single notation can encompass an entire event which otherwise occupies an entire sentence of description.

Finally, lest my enthusiasm mislead you into thinking that I claim ICONCLASS as the ultimate precision tool or scientific implement rashly imposing the demands of its ordering system on the imaginative world of the fine arts, I should like to refer to just one more notation which reminds us just how our understanding is tempered by our vision. The notation 25 H 22 and its subdivisions represent a canal with its accompanying locks, gates and sluices. This code resides within the overall subdivision which categorises all that is natural in landscape, rather than that which is man-made. Henri van de Waal was Dutch and the ICONCLASS system displays, the personality, the tolerance, and in this case, the particular vision of his homeland.

---

44 TERMINOLOGY DICTIONARY OF ECCLESIASTICAL FURNISHINGS

Dr Sandra Vasco Rocca

Istituto Centrale per il Catalogo e la Documentazione
Ministero per i Beni Culturali e Ambientali
Rome

The *Dizionario Terminologico della Suppellettile Ecclesiastica* (Dictionary of Ecclesiastical Furnishings) (Montevecchi and Vasco Rocca, 1987) is the fourth volume of a collection put together by the *Istituto Centrale per il Catalogo e la Documentazione* regarding cataloguing methodologies and their controlled application.

This series was set up in response to the various scientific requirements stemming from the cataloguing of cultural heritage (see Chapter 14). Texts focus on the search for the accurate definitions of art objects through the study of lexical changes relating to their morphologic, stylistic and functional variations.

This volume deals with a very broad and complex material, such as the furnishing pertaining to the Roman Catholic rite. The choice of the subject matter was dictated by a number of factors and by a particularly favourable circumstance. In the cataloguing project in Italy, a large part of the research carried out until now relates to the huge patrimony conserved in places of worship or under the supervision of the church, a patrimony that is still alive and effectual in its multiple aspects: liturgical, devotional, historical or, generally speaking, socio-cultural. We were dealing with a field often unexplored because of the vastness and qualitative disparity of the evidence, which did not always rise to the level of artistic facts but was in many cases modest and almost serial, though representing a significative documentation of a community life focused on a liturgical practice. The sector urgently required careful attention, mainly for practical reasons inherent in the preservation of a heritage threatened on many sides, including difficulties of control and protection, the volume and fragility of the materials, the expanding market and, last but not least, the progressive disuse of some of the instruments, particularly as a result of applying the guidelines stemming from the Second Vatican Council of 1963.

What was proposed, therefore, with particular relevance in this specific case, was the concept of knowledge as a basis for protection, not only on the part of whoever owns the object, but also of whoever is in charge of it, that is even within the context of juridical competences of a civil and ecclesiastical nature.

Besides the need to tackle a field of major importance within the context of the census and cataloguing of art history items, we were also confronted with the need to supply a correct and homogeneous terminology based mainly on a greater conceptual awareness of the 'catalogued' item for the different classes of material.

The subject matter involved different kinds of aspects — liturgical, historical, artistic and lexical — which were to be assembled into a comprehensive framework for cataloguing purposes.

The present volume should be considered as a contribution aiming to give a scientific order to a theme that has rarely been tackled or, especially in Italy, has been tackled in a rather limited way. Historiographic tradition is based on French and German inventories

Figure 44.1

Illustration from Rohault de Fleury, 1888, VI, tau. D111

Figure 44.2

4070. — Encensoirs divers.
D'après O. Wulff, *Altchristliche und Mittelalterliche Bildwerke*, pl. XLIII, XLVI, XLVII.

Illustration from Cabrol-Leclercq, 1922, V, coll 29–30

such as the works of C. Rohault de Fleury, F. Cabrol-H. Leclercq (Figures 44.1 and 44.2) and, most importantly, J. Braun, who sets out his work on the study of the Latin inventories and on the typological classification of the strictly 'sacred' furnishings. The major Italian reference remains the *Enciclopedia Cattolica* (1948–54), a general source of great practical usefulness.

Aware of the fact that it was impossible to deal with the matter without bearing in mind the complexity of the context into which this particular sector of 'applied arts' falls, an effort was made to focus on the historical evolution of ecclesiastical furnishings. This was done in parallel with the motivations that, in one way or another, have conditioned their specificity without neglecting the lexical and classification aspects also required for the automatic processing of the documentation.

The matter has been subdivided into seven sections following a classification by functions: altar fittings, sacred vessels, sacred clothes and coverings, liturgical objects, processional objects, ecclesiastical insignia and devotional items. Hangings and furniture have been omitted as they will form part of a second volume.

Figure 44.3

Pomo Scaldamani, fifteenth century, Tesoro di S. Pietro, Rome

Within the seven subdivisions, which in some cases overlap (on this subject, see Chapter 45), the individual objects are examined. For each of these is provided, besides ethymological and lexical data, a brief history of their use and possible typological evolution.

Each element has been analysed along closely interrelated lines, linked to the lexical, liturgical and art history aspects, with a standardised nomenclature concerning the object itself and its components, and a general typological classification, wherever the variety of the forms was sufficiently defined to make this possible. In fact, the correct recognition of the function can lead back to the exact terminology. The knowledge of the ecclesiastical norms, according to the period, may suggest details for the right chronological reference, while the analysis of the symbolism and iconography contribute to the appropriate classification and dating.

The treatment of the entries is therefore divided into etymon, translation in the major European languages, definition, liturgical function and typological development, even though for these last two aspects a clear distinction is not always possible in that they are closely intertwined, especially in the case of specimens pertaining to the oldest tradition. In accordance with these general criteria, instead of following the classical alphabetic indexing, the Dictionary is set out according to objects interrelated by functions, with a criterion similar to that adopted for the vocabulary *Principes d'analyse scientifique. Objets civils domestiques* (1984) prepared for the *Inventaire général des monuments et des richesses artistiques en France.* We have also included items for which direct evidence is lacking, or which, due to the extreme rarity and peculiarity of their use, it will be very difficult to encounter in the course of a normal cataloguing (Figure 44.3).

Of course, it is not always possible to achieve an unequivocal degree of definition given the very nature of the materials dealt with. In many cases recognition and, hence, classification of the piece remain problematic, not only as far as the origin itself of the sacred furnishings is concerned (derived from the civil one), but also, very often, because of the appearance of forms of adaptation not easily classifiable, especially when the object is not intact or has more than one function. During the first phase of tension between pagan and Christian art, there are in effect only few motives to have changed or to have been assumed with a different meaning from the emerging religion, while the objects remained the same as regards forms and structures: such is the case of the ciborium, the dyptich and the chalice itself. If in the Christian religion the process of stabilisation of different cult fittings had ended in the seventh century — and for clothes in the twelfth

Figure 44.4

Figure 44.5

Ostensorio-reliquiario, fifteenth century, Cividale, Museo archeologico

Reliquiario: calice e patena, fifteenth century, Chiesa dei S Cosma e Damiano, Rome

century — phenomena of re-use have arisen later within the same kind of furnishing; thus, the ostensory does not originate with its own physionomy but from the use of other containers, while it is not infrequent to find compound objects with different functions (Figure 44.4), or objects whose original function underwent a process of 'sacralisation'.

Regarding this last case, I can quote the example of the so-called 'Adaptation reliquaries' or rather containers of different provenances, in which the introduction of relics has led to a new qualification, both as regards function and linguistic definition. This can be seen in the eucharistic set with chalice and paten of SS Cosma e Damiano in Rome (fifteenth century), re-adapted to become a reliquary (Figure 44.5). It is obvious that in such cases a definition should be worked out that reflects both the *facies* reached historically and the original qualification of the piece or assembled pieces, with a progression in one or the other way according to the feature one wishes to stress. In the work process, initial support was sought from the main historical sources on the subject, from *Liber Pontificalis* to the encyclopaedic works of the nineteenth century, among which stands out the *Dizionario di erudizione storico-ecclesiastica* by G. Moroni (1840–79), supplemented by the consultation of the printed inventories, in particular the one related to the Avignon papal seat published in 1944 by H. Hoberg, and an investigation carried out in the Roman State Archives regarding the Agostinian fund. As far as the divergencies that may arise between historical lexicon and conventional lexicon are concerned, it should be borne in mind that in our work the lexicon always refers to a present and generalised use of the vocablulary, with practical and operational purposes that are, hence, different from the glottologic and philosophic ones from which one cannot albeit totally prescind.

The definition of the lexicons presented some difficulties of a different nature according to the subject dealt with and the level of 'lemmatisation' which, departing from the object, involved on the one hand the typological classifications, and on the other the nomenclature of the component parts with the possible typologies.

Regarding a few categories of fittings having already undergone a linguistic stabilisation with classic roots codified and handed down by the ancient ecclesiastical language, the choice of the lemma came almost automatically because of the exact correspondence between the Italian and the Latin definitions, whether as a direct deduction or as a straight translation of the term.

Greater perplexities arose, on the other hand, in selecting the lemma for different less formalised and official context, or of a medieval origin or which could present cases of synonymity or, again, where the word had acquired a variety of meanings. For all these problems, thanks to the advice given by the Department of Romance Studies of the University of Rome, a case by case solution was studied which obviously implied a margin, however small, of discretionary power.

The basic criteria was to define a lexicon as appropriate as possible in relation to the theme and to avoid compound forms, except in cases in which an additional specification to the primary lemma represented the sole alternative for distinguishing instruments that were different from the civil ones only because of the 'ritualisation' of their function, and also in order to eliminate possible confusions with future lexicons and thesauri.

A supplement containing the new standards for cataloguing this type of material according to the requirements of automatic data processing is now expected to be published.

---

45 THESAURUS FOR ECCLESIASTICAL FURNISHINGS

Dr Benedetta Montevecchi

Istituto Centrale per il Catalogo e la Documentazione
Ministero per i Beni Culturali e Ambientali
Rome

As the study of computerised methodologies has now demonstrated, a thesaurus — the group of descriptors of a given subject-matter, arranged according to different types of relationships — represents a fundamental support for the setting up of a databank, for verifying and up-dating the latter and for a more efficient and satisfactory question–answer relation.

At the same time therefore as the *Dizionario Terminologico della Suppellettile Ecclesiastica* (Dictionary of Ecclesiastical Furnishings) (Montevecchi and Vasco Rocca, 1987) (Chapter 44) was being prepared, and while the indexing criteria of the historical and artistic objects were being gradually finalised, the terminology collected to compile a thesaurus was organised so that it would not only serve as a basis for the automatic research of documentation, but also supply the elements needed to give a scientific order to a subject-matter that lacked logical reference structures. In fact, the compilation *a priori* of a thesaurus ran the risk of creating a product that could not stand up to practical testing. On the other hand, an operation carried out with a thesaurus entirely set up *a posteriori* could entail problems of a different nature stemming from an inadequate approach and a theoretical framework. Thus it became necessary to work on both approaches, taking into account both practical and theoretical requirements, and starting to define a thesaurus put together according to hierarchical and taxonomic ramifications, open to further implementation according to the level sought by the researcher.

A first layout of this work was presented at the seminar *Automatic processing of Art History Data and Documents* held in Pisa in September 1984 — an international seminar in which were compared both the methodologic lines and the general problems connected with applying data processing methods to the history of art. Its second and more detailed compilation was prepared for the seminar *Automazione dei Dati del Catalogo dei Beni Culturali* held in Rome in June 1985 and organised by the *Istituto Centrale per il Catalogo e la Documentazione.* On this occasion a booklet was published that consisted of the print-out of the thesaurus and a series of schematic illustrations representing a selection of the figures that were to accompany the texts of the *Dizionario Terminologico* (Montevecchi and Vasco Rocca, 1985; Vasco Rocca and Montevecchi, 1985). Once the research for the compilation of the volume came to an end it was possible to start the revision, correction and completion of the thesaurus the contents of which now reflect those of the Dictionary itself, except for some slight editorial differences (Montevecchi and Vasco Rocca, 1989).

A flexible indexing methodology of the objects pertaining to the sector of the artistic heritage, classifiable as Ecclesiastical Furnishings, was imposed by the need to back up the system of automatic information retrieval with a support based upon the relations existing between the terms of the databank that users, whether experts or not, could utilise in order to orientate and improve research. The databanks used by the *Istituto Centrale per il Catalogo e la Documentazione* are in fact created by the information contained in or deduced from the text of the document written in natural language, without making use of different keys to identify the terms. The large number of data, the different terminologies adopted to indicate the same concept and the very flexibility of the natural language nevertheless have an impact on the question and answer dialogue, so that the system is sometimes unable to give as accurate and exhaustive an answer as the user may expect. Therefore, the thesaurus plays the role of an auxiliary tool integrating the automatic data research system, since it creates a network of relations on different levels — linguistic and conceptual — which helps and guides the user in the course of their questioning. It supplies the list of the terms used in compiling the card index and identifies the lemmas selected for the standardisation and computerised input of the documents. For example, if in a query on the object 'thurible', the user requests the synonym 'censer' and that word does not appear on the records present in the databank, after consulting the thesaurus the user will find that the term 'thurible' is given as the keyword to be utilised for the research. The user will also be supplied with the network of relationships concerning the object in question and the level at which it is placed in the logical structure of the thesaurus. Besides this kind of cross-reference connected with queries on an individual object, the thesaurus represents a support for the research itself, in the sense of a reasoned index, as it supplies the lists of terms that link up with categories and groupings. Thus, if the user wishes to carry out a study on sacred vessels, they need only ask for that definition to get the list of objects forming the category and from which they can pass on to the following classifications.

The general subdivision of the matter reflects that of the *Dizionario Terminologico della Suppellettile Ecclesiastica,* with the relative internal classifications, albeit with slight divergencies due to obvious schematisation requirements. The thesaurus of Ecclesiastical Furnishings finds its place within a broader structure that summarises the subdivisions according to which artistic matter can be apportioned. This has as its broadest grouping five primary classes: Painting, Sculpture, Architecture, Applied Arts and Popular Arts and Traditions. Although the Ecclesiastical Furnishing thesaurus often encroaches on some of these primary classes, the one from the topic in question — that is to say the Applied Arts class — is distinguished in particular. Within its context four sectors emerge: Clothes, Arms, Furniture and Musical Instruments. Furniture has been divided into mobile and fixed; mobile furniture includes fittings and furnishings divided in turn into civil and ecclesiastical, thus reaching the field where the thesaurus fits in.

The material forming the Ecclesiastical Furnishings has been subdivided into seven main categories following a general classification by functions: altar fittings, sacred clothes and coverings, ecclesiastical insignia, devotional objects, liturgical objects, processional objects and sacred vessels. In this phase of the work, liturgical vestments and ecclesiastical fittings were omitted as they will form the subject of a second dictionary — in the process of preparation. In the present structure of the thesaurus they would come under the headings Clothing and Ecclesiastical Fittings. In some cases the seven subdivisions appear accurately detailed — as, for example, the sacred vessels — while in others they show a certain degree of encroachment and changeability which has required an internal cross-reference network to overcome a certain amount of awkwardness in the distinctions. One example is an object like 'altar candlestick', incorporated in the category of altar fittings and, in a more restricted manner, in the chapter Eucharistic Celebration. It also appears in the Liturgical Objects category in the paragraph Liturgical Lighting Objects.

The structure of the thesaurus is based on a system of hierarchical relations, much the same as the methodological organisation used in taxonomy, with a classification that goes from family to genus, species and finally individual with its range of alternatives. According to a logical vertical descending scheme, the system goes from main categories (families), including various groups of objects or subcategories (general) which have been gathered together following typologies (species) that can in turn be further subdivided according to the different alternatives.

To give an example, the Sacred Vessels main category includes three large subcategories: Sacred Vessels for Holy Communion, Sacred Vessels for Holy Oils and Reliquaries. This last subcategory gathers together a large number of typologies, including that of the 'anthropomorphous reliquaries' in which can further be identified alternatives such as the 'bust', or 'statue', or 'sculptural group' reliquaries. However, it should be stressed in this connection that the object discussed, though pertaining to the subcategory of Reliquaries within this specific thesaurus, represents at the same time an evidence that can be linked to other artistic sectors and also fall into the primary classification Sculpture.

To give a more complex example, a 'painted ex-voto' belonging to the 'Devotional objects' category can also be incorporated in the primary classifications bearing the headings Popular Arts and Traditions and Painting. Therefore, each specific thesaurus is part of a broader network of thesauri, different in size, logical structure and purpose, which meet at the top with the large primary classes into which the artistic matter has been apportioned.

Besides this 'broader' horizontal relational system which extends to the primary classes, the thesaurus uses a network of more direct relations that can be linguistic, structural or have a complementary function. The linguistic relationships are linked to the flexibility of the natural language and include synonymity, lexical variations, some dialectical differences (mainly for the popular devotional objects whose terminologic definition is less connected with the national language), archaic and obsolete alternatives, abbreviated forms and compound expressions.

The structural relations concern the cross-references between an object and its specific parts which can also be found and classified as separate finds since they are sometimes of a different material or go back to different epochs (tabernacle/tabernacle door; pastoral staff/pastoral staff curl).

Finally, the relations based on complementary connections are those that link objects used for the same function and can be defined by the expression 'set for ablutions, incensing, etc.' (in this case the whole list of objects likely to be found in a set are quoted, even if one object excludes the other, such as the cruet-stand with respect to the cruet-tray or the baptismal shell versus the baptismal cup, or between objects one or more of which act as accessories for others (incense-boat/incense-spoon; pastoral staff/pannisellus).

As regards the data processing aspect, studied by R. Bartoli and O. Signore of CNUCE (Pisa), the complexity of a thesaurus that uses some related terms not provided for by international standards, and possible future developments, mainly as regards graphic interfaces and the addition of images, have made it advisable not to resort to the traditional approach adopted by documentation systems but to favour instead an approach that relies on databases.

In such an approach there are no limits to the number and type of preselected related terms. The user can choose any term they wish and then find in succession all the related terms.

In order to ensure maximum independance of the system adopted for the implementation, a totally 'neutral' input format has been defined in which the data to be introduced is limited to the minimum. The present thesaurus includes around 800 keywords, synonyms and alternatives.

Relationships between descriptors have been defined through their name, their identifier represented by a symbol, their characteristics (symmetry, transitivity) and the existence of an opposite.

Among the objects forming the thesaurus of Ecclesiastical Furnishings the following relations have been identified:

'broad term' (BT) with its opposite 'narrow term' (NT);

'primary key' (PK) with its opposite 'has as primary key (KP);

'has as accessories' (ACC) with its opposite 'is accessory of' (IAO);

'general typology' (TOP) with its opposite 'specific typology' (TYP);

'has as component part' (CPT) with the opposite 'is component part of' (CPO);

and finally 'see also' (SA), this last relation being characterised by the symmetry feature.

In other cases the opposite indicates a relation of reversibility between the descriptors (if A is the 'broad term' for B, B is the 'narrow term' for A; for example, Sacred Vessels for Holy Communion is the BT for chalice; chalice is the NT for Sacred Vessels for Holy Communion). Symmetry corresponds to a relationship of equivalence (if A refers to B, B refers to A; for example, for the Liturgical Objects pertaining to the Acoustic Call typology, reference is also made to the Musical Instruments subdivision within the primary class of Applied Arts, the same as in the subdivision Musical Instruments where there will be a reference to Liturgical Objects for Acoustic Call). Finally, transitivity indicates a relation of reflection between different terms (if A is synonym of B and B is synonym of C, A is synonym of C; for example, 'canon' is synonym of 'altar-card' as 'altar-card' is synonym of 'secreta-table', it follows that 'canon' is synonym of 'secreta-table').

Besides representing a basic support for databank research and establishing the network of relations for every indexed object, the thesaurus acts as a practical guide for a more accurate wording of the index cards, offering the indexer the list of the keywords to use in the course of their work.

It remains understood that, although keeping the suggested structure, the thesaurus could be implemented on the basis of possible new acquisitions or for further description needs.

---

46 CONTROLLED VOCABULARY FOR INDEXING ORIGINAL AND HISTORICAL GRAPHIC MATERIALS

Elisabeth Betz Parker

Prints and Photographs Division
Library of Congress
Washington, DC

Introduction

The Prints and Photographs Division of the Library of Congress is responsible for the collecting, care, documentation and reference service of all types of still images: original photographs and negatives, fine prints, historical and popular prints, posters, and artistic, documentary and architectural drawings. Our holdings number nearly 15 million images covering a broad span of topics and time periods. With this kind and amount of material and the variety of access which is desired, the Division has characteristics in common with libraries, archives and museums.

There has been an absolute boom in the picture 'business' in the United States! From the time of our Civil War centennial in the 1960s, more and more TV documentaries, historical studies, exhibits and coffee table books are being produced for an increasingly visually oriented public. Thus, in the last 15 years, institutions with pictorial collections have had a marked increase in the number of researchers and reference requests.

Each month, the Prints and Photographs Division responds to more than 1 500 queries and an average of 650 persons consult the collections. Research questions vary considerably in content, depth, and complexity but, on the whole, subject queries predominate. This is partly because our pictorial collections are 'unknown', that is, they are essentially unique or unpublished and the researcher does not arrive with a citation in hand. It is also because our collections are primarily documentary in nature and thus of subject interest.

Building subject access

In response to increased demands, we made a concerted effort to build an extensive manual subject index. The purpose of the index was threefold: to provide a central point through which the various collections and formats in the Division's custody could be searched by subject, no matter where the material was physically located; to make searching for pictures more flexible and independent of staff memory, influence, and availability; and to protect the collections from wear and tear by enabling one to pinpoint subjects without having to handle many pictures unnecessarily in the process of browsing.

By the mid 1970s, the card file had grown to some 67 000 entries. But with so much material and so many possible subjects, both staff and researchers could not use the index effectively.

What could be done to facilitate subject access?

By 1978, it was obvious that we first needed a record of what headings had been applied to the Division's collections. Over the course of two years, the subject terms were copied onto 3 × 5 inch cards. Whenever possible, these headings were reformulated to be in synchronisation with the *Library of Congress Subject Headings* (LCSH) list, the most widely used source of standardised subject access terms in American libraries. None the less, many terms remained idiosyncratic because of our extensive manual files. For example, our subdivision practice was highly specific and unlike that found in book cataloguing: names of wars were subdivided by the compound heading Parades and Ceremonies; building types were subdivided by Interiors and Exteriors; and the term Industry was subdivided by particular types of industries. Since we *never* believed we could automate, much less integrate our records with those of the rest of the Library of Congress, it did not seem to matter if our policies about the terms and their application only met immediate, local needs. My objectives were the following: to create a list that was as internally consistent as possible, that provided the cataloguer with a controlled vocabulary and patterns for establishing new terms, and that enabled researchers to plan a search strategy for material in our collections.

The typed list, completed in 1980, was christened *Subject Headings Used in the Library of Congress Prints and Photographs Division*. Having been created on the basis of actual cataloguing rather than from a theoretical construct, we could immediately apply it. And because the list represented a wide range of subjects and formats, it happened that the terms could also be used in other libraries, historical societies, archives and museums with similar holdings. Clearly, people were interested in doing so, for hundreds of copies were requested.

Within a few years, the list became impossible to maintain with the rapid growth of the manual index and changing research demands. We also were uncomfortably aware of its undesirable quirks. Two developments then gave us incentive to bring subject access in line with bibliographic standards. The American National Standards Institute (ANSI) *Guidelines for Thesaurus Structure, Construction, and Use* provided a model for subject lists and how they should function. We also obtained a thesaurus software package that would enable us to construct an extensive automated subject headings file and to update it readily.

In 1983, the enormous task of upgrading our old subject headings to the current standard was begun. To indicate its revised format and status, the new list was called the *LC Thesaurus for Graphic Materials: Topical Terms for Subject Access* or LCTGM (Parker, 1987).

Principles affecting picture cataloguing

In book cataloguing, titles are assigned a limited number of subject headings which apply to the work as a whole. Generally, the subject can be determined by examining the title of the book, the table of contents and by scanning the text. Literary warrant helps provide new terms to establish for the subject list.

Subject cataloguing of pictures is less straightforward. Pictures certainly *do* have features in common with textual materials, and in many cases the same indexing conventions can be applied. But pictures, unlike books, often come without written identification. After all, when pictures are made their purpose and subject are known, so why bother to describe them? Pictures also obviously rely on their subject being conveyed nonverbally — it is just often difficult to know what it is as time goes by and the context is lost. Even the date of creation and the creator's underlying intent may be no longer possible to determine.

Because pictures usually do not supply words expressing their subject content, the *cataloguer* must determine the 'who, what, where, when and why'. The picture must be analysed and any caption and accompanying documentation examined in order to determine both the most salient concrete aspects (what the picture is *of*) and any apparent themes or authorial intents (what the picutre is *about*). The point of view — which affects the depth of indexing and specificity — varies depending on whether a single item is being catalogued or a group of items. The focus changes from a greater degree of specificity with the single item to a more general one with a collection.

Other factors affect the choice of terms and the amount of indexing. The picture cataloguer must also consider the following: the nature and intended use of the collections, the prominence of a subject within an image or in the context of a collection, the relationship of the material being catalogued to other holdings, and staff expertise. A final consideration is whether or not the material adequately represents a particular subject to warrant being indexed.

The nature of pictures then, requires cataloguers to take an active role in the indexing process. Similarly, researchers must take an active role in approaching the indexing terms. Both cataloguers and researchers therefore need guidance from the subject cataloguing tool.

The *LC Thesaurus for Graphic Materials*

The encyclopedic LCSH list is an obvious candidate for large, documentary pictorial collections. Why should we have another list, especially since we have begun to enter automated records into the Library of Congress integrated automated catalogue? If not LCSH, then why not the *Art and Architecture Thesaurus* (AAT) or any other existing lists related to visual materials.

Available lists are, on the one hand, too narrowly focused, technical, and detailed *or*, on the other hand, too general in terminology to serve for the retrieval of pictures in large collections.

LCSH, for example, with more than 171 000 terms established primarily in the course of cataloguing textual, monographic length material, confounds the picture cataloguer trying to choose among the myriad terms that seem to overlap, or to determine how to apply various terms when the material being catalogued provides no words on which to hook its access.

AAT, as another example, provides terms that can be used to index pictures of the built environment, but lacks terms for people and activities, everyday objects, events and places sought in many picture collections, and also lacks abstract concepts which are represented by such pictorial material as allegorical prints, cartoons and posters. Lists geared to textual materials lack terms for concepts that are primarily visual in nature and terms that are too specific to be the subject of a book but frequently a subject sought in pictures. Examples are Mushroom clouds; Hammer and sickle; Ship of State; Moonlight; Interiors; and Corn husking. Lists created for general purposes also lack useful techniques that would enable the indexing to reflect pictorial aspects of the materials being catalogued; LCSH, for example, attaches the phrase 'in art' to existing terms (as in 'Bullfights in art') which, for us, implies a value judgement regarding the aesthetic qualities of images not necessarily appropriate when the subject matter is being presented in a documentary form. Lists of terms for art movements, artistic styles, themes, or iconology are not appropriate for the vast majority of our collections and intent. In some cases, lists contain the kind of idiosyncracies we were trying to avoid or they are not structured according to the ANSI standard.

It is really *not* so much that the terms in lists such as LCSH or the AAT are wrong, as that the lists do not really provide the necessary guidance for application in picture cataloguing or an appropriate relationship structure within a universe of terms relevant to general collections of pictorial materials.

Indeed, it must be emphasised that terms in the *LC Thesaurus for Graphic Materials: Topical Terms for Subject Access* (LCTGM) are mostly taken from LCSH, AAT and the *Legislative Indexing Vocabulary*, with LCSH as the predominant source because of its broader scope. Words (and their definitions) are also found in such publications as *Webster's Collegiate Dictionary* and the *Encyclopedia Americana*. Preference is given to the form found in standard thesauri so that compatibility in terminology is maintained to the degree possible. Regardless of a term's source, it is incorporated into LCTGM and *its* structure.

The goals for our subject list remain essentially the same as those in 1978, with a greater consciousness of a world in which cataloguing records are being shared and research is crossing over more disciplines and formats: to create a list that is internally consistent, provide the cataloguer with a controlled vocabulary and guidance in its application, and provide the researcher with a means to plan a search strategy for material in pictorial collections. These objectives are achieved more readily now because we have gained experience with picture retrieval through catalogues and because thesaurus construction standards exist. Patterns of application are made more evident through public notes and cataloguers' notes that are directly associated with the terms. The thesaurus structure and a rich entry vocabulary lead both cataloguers and researchers to the indexing terms. By following thesaurus construction standards we can avoid idiosyncracies that were in our old list and eliminate anomalies. The standards also help us to develop a structure for exploiting the capabilities of automated retrieval systems. (Institutions with manual files should not be scared away by this: general guidance on how the thesaurus can be adapted to a manual system is given.)

When LCTGM was published in 1987, subject cataloguing in the Prints and Photographs Division had generated approximately 3 500 terms and 2 500 cross-references from non-preferred terms. More than 550 terms and cross-references have subsequently been added in the course of cataloguing and will be in the next edition.

Descriptive terms for graphic materials: Genre and physical characteristic headings

Some pictorial materials are important as much for their artefactual value as for their subject content. The distinction between topical terms and genre or physical characteristic terms is critical in describing such materials, since researchers often wish to see *examples* of portraits' or of 'daguerreotypes'. At first glance one might think these terms also belong in a list of subjects. Genre or form and physical characteristics terms, however, do not represent what pictures are *of* or what they are *about*. Rather, they exemplify categories of material and name the physical objects themselves. A Daguerreotype (a physical characteristic), for instance, may be a Portrait (a genre) of an unnamed child (the subject). A Stereograph (a physical characteristic) may be about infidelity (a subject) when it shows a man and woman kissing (subject) while her husband looks at stereographs (now a subject).

As is true with the subject list, the terms of graphic arts, photography and design can also be used most effectively when presented within the structure of a thesaurus which establishes relationships and guides users. For this purpose, *Descriptive Terms for Graphic Materials: Genre and Physical Characteristic Headings* (GMGPC) was developed and published in late 1986 (Zinkham and Parker, 1986). GMGPC was designed to provide terms for access to *categories* of media and formats rather than to enumerate terms for indexing every conceivable aspect of graphic materials. With more than 500 terms and 290 cross-references, it is thus primarily useful for large, general pictorial collections.

Conclusion

We have come a long way since 1978 in our ability to serve the public's desire for pictorial materials. Together, these thesauri provide a means for predictable search strategies, which can result in interesting and exciting finds whether pictures are being sought as illustrations for books, as evidential documents in social, political, historical, and cultural studies, for thematic and artistic exhibits, to create sets for films and plays, to reconstruct historic buildings, or for pure pleasure.

---

47 THESAURUS OF BUILDINGS

Yolande Morel-Deckers and Wilfried Janssens

Koninklijk Museum voor Schone Kunsten,
Antwerp and
Koninklijk Instituut voor het Kunstpatrimonium
Brussels

Background

With the same linguistic background, organisations with parallel interests in Belgium — more precisely, Flanders — and the Netherlands find it valuable to work together. One aspect of this collaboration is a thesaurus of buildings being developed by three organisations:

for the Netherlands: *MARDOC/IMC*, a foundation located in Rotterdam, conducting research on registration methods and applications in the field of computerising museum collections;

for Belgium: firstly *the Koninklijk Instituut voor het Kunstpatrimonium* in Brussels (Royal Institute for the Artistic Patrimony), a state institution charged with the scientific research, stocktaking and preservation of the Belgian artistic patrimony (one aspect of which is supervising the very extensive collection of photographs (750 000 items) on this artistic patrimony and making it accessible as much as possible); and secondly a rather coincidental partner, the Ministry of the Flemish Community, which took the initiative of launching a temporary but massive survey of about 30 Flemish museums from 1979 to 1982.

The contacts that already existed between these three institutions were formalised in early 1985. It was then agreed to collectively develop a thesaurus of buildings. This project was partly subsidised by the *Nederlandse Taalunie* (Dutch language union), an organisation established in 1980 with the aim of coordinating the Dutch language and literature policy in the Netherlands and in Flanders.

Since 1985, six people (historians and art historians) have been working on this thesaurus on a part-time basis: MARDOC/IMC, Maritiem Museum Prins Hendrik, Rotterdam (Jeanne Hogenboom, Jan Van de Voort); Koninklijk Instituut voor het Kunstpatrimonium, Brussels (Yves Fremault, Wilfried Janssens, Raf. Van de Walle); Ministerie van de Vlaamse Gemeenschap, Koninklijk Museum voor Schone Kunsten (Royal Museum of the Fine Arts) Antwerp (Yolande Morel).

Function and aim of the buildings thesaurus

The buildings thesaurus has the purpose of being an aid to institutions supervising data on buildings. This includes institutions that really supervise buildings — such as monuments or the industrial patrimony — and institutions merely supervising data on buildings — such as collections of architectural drawings, photographs, prints and paintings depicting buildings or literature on buildings in ethnographical and/or historical collections. It may be used for registering documentation at well as for museological registration and retrieval.

The development of the thesaurus and its users

The thesaurus of buildings contains terminology on man-made buildings in the broadest sense of the word, including non-permanent constructions, based on the description in *Nomenclature* (Chenhall, 1978): the definition of 'structures': 'artefacts originally created to serve as shelter from the elements or to meet some other human need in a relatively permanent location'. This thesaurus of buildings is not a linguistic thesaurus, but a piece of documentation, implying that relations established between terms are not always totally correct at the language level, as they mainly serve a practical purpose: describing documents dealing with this linguistic aspect and making it easier to retrieve them. This implies that two categories of people use the thesaurus: some recording the data and others retrieving it (and consequently the part of the collection involved).

As the compilers were unable to determine in advance which collections would qualify to be made accessible or what questions would be asked, no limitations were imposed as far as time and place are concerned. When developing the thesaurus of buildings, they used two equivalent approaches. As a matter of fact, it may be necessary — from a documentary point of view — to put different concepts on the same level instead of arranging them in a list.

The first approach consists of a functional classification of buildings. This classification was used when developing MARDOC's general thesaurus. This work was partly based on *Nomenclature* and the thesaurus of buildings fits in. The building's original function is the criterion. This way, the main classes (include) religious-, funerary- and commercial-buildings.

The second approach considers the buildings from a typological point of view. Here, the architectural type is the criterion. The classes include churches, crypts, chapels and baptisteries.

Both approaches are interwoven and form a network of descriptions with logical relations for the thesaurus' users (Figure 47.1). This makes a functional as well as a typological approach of the terms possible. Those who asks the question selects the 'way in' themselves. The 'farm' concept, for instance, can be approached in various ways: *functionally*: industrial building, residential building, animal shelter, storage facility, etc.; *typologically*: barn, pile barn, etc.

Contrary to mono-hierarchic classifications, a thesaurus may have one or more broader terms, by which it becomes much more flexible than a classification. Question patterns of different user groups and/or a systematic subdivision from several angles can be taken into account within this framework. Although the compilers treated as many descriptors as possible on a pre-coordination basis, it is impossible to exclude post-coordination. In the historical-cultural field, most question patterns consist of three elements: subject, time aspect and geographic aspect. This was taken into account when compiling the thesaurus. Time and place indications were clearly distinguished from the thesaurus of buildings and — where necessary — they must be used in post-coordination.

The terms were collected by both deductive and inductive methods, although the latter method was applied much more frequently. Terms from specialist literature were gathered and divided according to one or more classification systems. Afterwards, they were processed, meaning that synonyms were grouped, preference terms were indicated, relations with other terms were described and homonyms were distinguished.

Figure 47.1 Example from buildings thesaurus

```
         TCAT n
              bww
         SN   Bouwwerk bestemd om aan mensen en dieren beschutting te
              bieden of zich te verbergen
              bron: Van Dale
         BT   bouwwerk
         NT   schuilplaats[gebouw]
PT    schuilplaats[gebouw] (F)
         TCAT n
              bww
         SN   Gebouw ingericht om aan mensen of dieren beschutting te
              bieden of zich te verbergen
              bron: Van Dale - KIK - MARDOC
         BT   schuilplaats[bouwwerk]
              gebouw
         NT   schuilkelder
              schuilkerk
              opvanghuis
              refugehuis
              schuilhut
              afdak
NT    schutdeur
         USE  sluisdeur
PT    schuttersdoelen (F)
         TCAT n
              bww
         SN   Verenigingsgebouw en oefenplaats van het schuttersgild.
              bron: Van Dale
         UF   schuttershof[gebouw]
              doelen[schuttersgebouw]
         BT   gildehuis
         NT   kloveniersdoelen
NT    schuttershof[gebouw]
         USE  schuttersdoelen
PT    schuur (F)
         TCAT n
              bww
         SN   Eenvoudig,in beginsel houten gebouw zonder verdieping,uit
              vier wanden en een dak bestaand en inwendig niet of weinig
              betimmerd,als bergplaats i.h.b. agrarisch gebouw als berging
              van de veldvruchten en landbouwgereedschappen.
              bron:Summa Encycl.
         BT   agrarisch gebouw
              opslaggebouw
         NT   tas[schuur]
              mendeur
              dorsvloer[schuur]
              schuurreed
              tas[schuurruimte]
              schuurtype
              hooizolder
         RT   veestal
              boerderij[gebouw]
PT    schuurreed
         TCAT n
              bww
         SN   Doorrit in een schuur.
              bron: KIK - MARDOC
         BT   schuur
              gebouwdeel
PT    schuurtype (T)
         TCAT n
              bww
         SN   Soort van schuur.
              bron: KIK - MARDOC
         BT   schuur
         NT   bergschuur
              zolderschuur
              Brabantse schuur
              dwarsschuur
              tiendschuur
              wagenberg
              graanspijker
              paalschuur
NT    scierie
         USE  zagerij[gebouw]
PT    scriptorium (F)
         TCAT n
              bww
         SN   Middeleeuwse schrijf- en verluchtkamer, in kloosters vaak
              met de librije verbonden.
              bron: Haslinghuis, 1986
         BT   culturele ruimte
              werkruimte
              klooster[gebouw]
PT    seinbrug (F)
         TCAT n
              bww
         SN   Bij de spoorwegen, brug voor seininstallaties.
              bron: Van Dale
         BT   communicatiebouwwerk
              spoorwegbouwwerk
PT    seinhuis(F)
         TCAT n
              bww
         SN   Gebouw van waaruit seinen worden bediend
              bron: Van Dale
         BT   communicatiegebouw
              verkeersgebouw
PT    seinmolen(F)
         TCAT n
              bww
         SN   Watermolen die aan andere molens seinen moet geven, b.v.
              dat het maalpeil bereikt is.
              bron: Van Dale
         BT   communicatiegebouw
              waterradmolen[gebouw]
              molen naar functie[bouwwerk]
NT    seintoren
         USE  semafoor[stellage]
```

Here, the international standard ISO 2788, was taken into account. (ISO, 1974). This standard offers guidelines for developing mono-lingual thesauri. The main indications are:

aim and structure of the thesaurus;

the subject-field covered;

the main sources from which terms were collected;

the chosen form for presenting the terms;

declaration of abbreviations;

the method selected for alphabetising the data;

user's manual;

information on updating;

the number of descriptors and non-descriptors.

All terms in the thesaurus of buildings are mentioned separately. For each term it is indicated whether the term involved was determined as a description (i.e. as a term to be preferred for a certain concept, from now on: PT) or the term is not to be preferred and only indicates the preference term, consequently (NPT).

For each descriptor determined, links with other terms are made: with more general concepts (broader term, BT), with more specific concepts (narrower term, NT), etc. Each term is also defined or described (scope note, SN), preferably by specialists.

In order to help enquirers use the thesaurus, an extensive user's manual was added. At first sight, a question from the public may sometimes seem very general, but — when examined more closely — it may turn out to be very specific. This implies that the question must be translated into the index language of the system, of the thesaurus. That is why we mean the whole series of explicitly indicated relations, leading the user to the right descriptor(s) almost automatically, when we refer to a user's manual in this context.

Computerised use of the thesaurus of buildings

Since 1984, MARDOC/IMC has had a Prime 2250 minicomputer and the Adlib package at its disposal. This package includes a thesaurus module with extensive possibilities. After some time, the lack of such a computer in Brussels was compensated for by the Prime and Databasix firms, providing the Belgian collaborators with the required hardware and software for free. At this point in time, the thesaurus of buildings consists of the following main divisions:

building;

part of building;

ornamentation;

architectural styles (to be developed).

The plan is to introduce the thesaurus of buildings, consisting of about 3 500 terms, to the general public in 1989. It will then be available in a printed and machine-readable form.

48 BUILDING BRIDGES: PLANNING AN INTERNATIONAL NETWORK ABOUT ARCHITECTURAL DOCUMENTS

Dr Vicki Porter

Project Manager
Foundation for Documents of Architecture
Washington, DC

Project goals

In 1983, a dozen archives, museums and research institutions from Europe and the United States began to meet regularly, as the Architectural Drawings Advisory Group (ADAG).[1] These institutions had in common the need to give researchers access to their collections of architectural drawings and related material. Since the development of standards for the scholarly cataloguing of such material lagged behind other media, it seemed an appropriate time to strive for a broadly-based consensus in the field. If achieved, these standards would be the foundation for a computer network to give researchers consistent and reliable access to collections across all participating museums, or at the very least through local catalogues.

From its inception, ADAG wanted to create standards that were consonant with scholarly practice and interest. After all, the resulting network of information was not intended for member institutions' internal collection management, but for researchers. In this paper I will focus on some key steps we took while preparing the way for a scholarly information network. I will also outline some of the unsolved problems — we call them challenges — that remain in our path.

Defining the problems

First, in order to make sure scholars' needs were considered from the very beginning, ADAG included among its diverse members scholars as well as curators, librarians and archivists. Now, reading the minutes of early meetings one is struck by the fact that each of these professional groups employed a specialised vocabulary not necessarily understood by the others. For instance, librarians would use the terms 'access points', 'headings', 'authority control', 'statement of responsibility', and 'indexing' in very specific ways, but it seems these notions were foreign to most participating archivists, curators and scholars. Meanwhile, scholars uncovered inherent contradictions in commonly-used art-historical concepts, such as 'artist' and 'provenance'. And archivists struggled to communicate their different interpretations of some of these same terms and

1. Participating institutions include: Royal Institute of British Architects, London; Royal Library, Windsor; Graphische Sammlung Albertina, Vienna; Canadian Centre for Architecture, Montreal; National Archives of Canada, Ottawa; Ecole Supérieure des Beaux-Arts, Paris; American Institute of Architects Foundation, Washington, DC; Avery Memorial Library, New York; Cooper-Hewitt Museum, New York; The Library of Congress, Washington, DC; National Archives of the United States, Washington, DC; National Gallery of Art, Washington, DC; Bildarchiv Foto Marburg, Marburg.

concepts, notably 'provenance'. While it was tempting to set aside these ambiguities, ADAG decided to persevere in arriving at a consensus.

To avoid being caught in an endless webb of words with multiple, even contradictory meanings, ADAG needed a way to focus debate and define concepts to ourselves and to technical consultants. Adopting a method introduced to us by Professor Oreste Ferrari of the Italian Catalogo project, ADAG began to define key concepts using a graphic entity-relationship model. By first concentrating on common definitions of major concepts, rather than terminology, these diagrammatic models made it easier for our diverse members to communicate. In short, we could begin to *see* the forest and the trees — we concentrated on defining entities or major areas of interest before we worried about their attributes. For example, we agreed to concentrate on describing drawings or images, and only secondarily to concern ourselves about the structures therein depicted.

After we agreed on our essential focus, we then turned to defining attributes of the entities: titles, dates, names, methods of representation, purpose, locations — these are examples of attributes, not entities. We tried to define them first by what entity they described, and whether they could repeat, be contradictory, be absent, and so on. Next, we defined the possible sources of information for attributes — the object itself, a scholar, documentation, or bibliographic sources, for example.

It was only at the next step in defining our standards that we turned to the issue of terminology. Since few pre-existing authority lists for names of buildings or geographic places, for example, seemed appropriate, ADAG realised it would have to build its own authority lists, based on the drawings themselves, scholars' knowledge and printed sources (Figure 48.1). Thus, we now have ancillary or supporting files for entering

Figure 48.1 Sources for ADAG authority lists

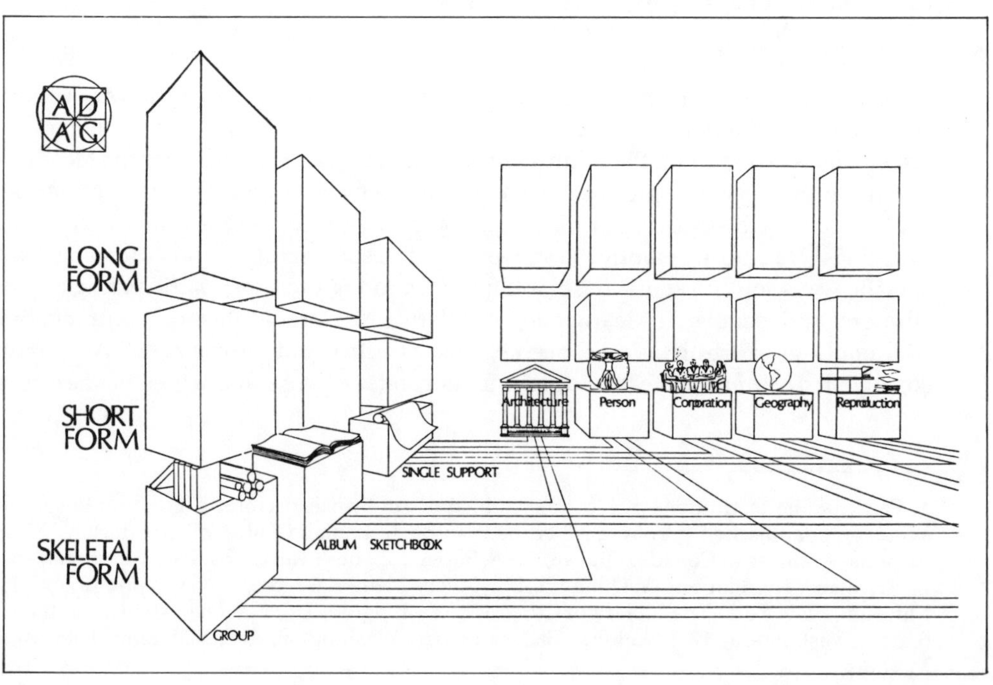

information about the following entities: architecture, people, corporations, geography and reproductions. In these files we can record minimal building histories, biographies, variant names and other information that will in itself be important means of scholarly access or retrieval.

Building flexible standards

Because we have an international membership, we needed a flexible standard for proper names. We decided not to privilege any given version of a name, be it that of a person or of a geographic place. A contributing institution may use any version of a name, in any language, and that name will be linked to all the other names for that entity through our expanded authority files. Moreover, an institution may use one name for a particular drawing, and another name for the same entity in the record for another drawing. For example, there are two drawings made by the same person in our database, but they were signed differently: Jeanneret in one, and Le Corbusier in the other. While the database links the two names as one person, the respective records may have the approprate inscribed name for the artist. While the technical implementation of this capability presented definite challenges, we hope that this terminological flexibility will better reflect scholarly practice.

For data fields that use generic terminology — terms like 'splayed arches' or 'bird's eye perspectives' — we are working toward a parallel flexibility in our use of the Art and Architecture Thesaurus (AAT) (Chapter 56). In close coordination with AAT staff, we are planning ways in which to submit non-English terms when needed. We also hope to explore the implications of using what AAT calls non-preferred terms, when they are warranted.

So far, I have sketched the successive stages of ADAG's approach to formulation of standards, starting with the definition of entities, their relationships to each other, then defining the attendant attributes, followed by agreement on the sources used or generated for terminology. A step remaining in ADAG's work is to codify the format of that terminology: that is, syntax, order and punctuation. While we have some general guidelines, we will explore this area in the coming months. In the relative hierarchy of important issues, however, we believe that this is less crucial an area for standardisation than the previous issues.

Testing the standards

As ADAG progressed in its work, some members wanted to pool resources to construct this scholarly network, testing and refining the standards that ADAG had articulated. For these purposes, in 1986, five institutions from ADAG founded a non-profit public corporation, called the Foundation for Documents of Architecture (FDA). It retains ADAG as its advisory group, but is governed by an autonomous Board of Directors, whose President is Henry Millon, Dean of the Center for Advanced Study in the Visual Arts, at the National Gallery of Art, Washington, DC. To date, member institutions are in the United States and Canada.[2] The FDA has a central staff of seven; each member institution contributes at least one full-time cataloguer to the project.

2. FDA participating institutions include: Canadian Centre for Architecture; National Archives of the United States; National Gallery of Art, Washington; National Archives of Canada; The J. Paul Getty Trust.

For the purposes of testing and implementing ADAG's standards and considerable technical requirements, one of FDA's members, the Getty Art History Information Program, is developing custom-designed software on hardware from Sun Microsystems. So far, the software is in the preliminary development, testing and debugging stage, and its scope satisfies only part of ADAG's requirements. The system as installed at FDA headquarters in Washington is limited to data entry functions, and has no scholarly retrieval capabilities to date. However, it features several functions I outlined for enforcing ADAG's 'flexible' standards. We have 23 000 AAT terms linked to the cataloguing system, so that terms entered in each AAT-controlled field are checked automatically against the applicable AAT hierarchies. Cataloguers may create candidate terms to AAT; they may also use non-preferred AAT terms. Our ancillary files for architecture, people and others are automatically linked to one another so that the computer puts in one logical place all the information about a person (variant names, birth and death dates, locus of activity, and more), for instance.

In summer, 1988, FDA began a three-year experimental phase of what we hope will become a long-term, viable service to scholars. In this first phase, we had several intermediate goals. Each member institution sent a cataloguer to FDA's Washington office for mutual resolution of remaining issues; as a result, we hoped to achieve several goals at once: training of cataloguers using ADAG's standards; de-bugging of and adding new features and fields to FDA's system; building a deeper mutual understanding among members; and drafting the cataloguing manual, which will eventually be published. In addition, the FDA is conducting a comparison of its standards with those of the library community in order to identify areas that might be barriers to the exchange of data with institutions that conform to such standards as the International Standard Bibliographic Description and the Anglo-American Cataloguing Rules. In this comparison, we anticipate the highest level of data exchange with outside bibliographic databases without sacrificing art-historical nuance.

In the second year of the experimental phase, FDA cataloguers will return to their home institutions to begin full-scale online cataloguing and orientation of colleagues to the FDA system. We also hope to continue adding capabilities to the system, including retrieval suitable for scholarly needs.

In the third year of the experimental phase, the FDA will sponsor an outside review of the database to determine whether the scholarly community finds it valuable and worth continuation. A separate review will evaluate the long-term viability of the technical approach taken. Assuming favourable reviews, the FDA would continue developing its database, adding members, improving the system when necessary, and distributing its database to subscribers.

Some typical conceptual problems for the future

While the FDA has devoted much time to planning because of its potentially wide scope, we have recently begun to implement these plans. In so doing, we are excited by the prospects of tackling the many interesting but thorny problems that inevitably escaped us in the planning phase. In broad brush, let me finish by describing a couple of these challenges.

FDA will need to explore the implications of our current practice of conflating the notions of indexing and describing drawings. We have guidelines for a thorough description of the objects, along with more conceptual evaluations — mostly fielded and vocabulary-controlled, with an eye towards retrieval, of course. But how will these

Figure 48.2 Example from FDA system

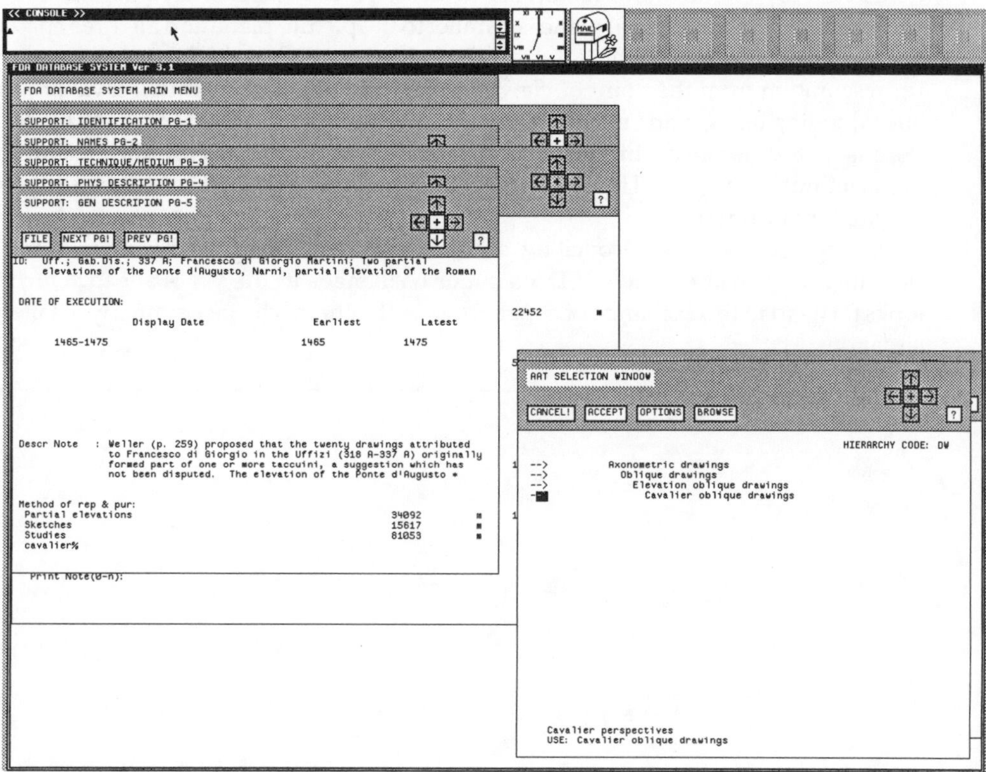

descriptions relate to indices — especially printed ones — where like concepts are supposed to appear together?

For example, we have envisioned a database in which contradictory opinions could be recorded and retrieved. If a drawing's subject is controversial, the values in the subject field might include conflicting opinions: for example, 'church' ; 'villa'. Yet a drawing that has two subjects might be identically indexed: that is, the entry would read: 'church' ; 'villa'. We currently have no mechanism for distinguishing such cases. A related problem is that in indexing or describing a drawing using AAT terms, we currently have no way to make a negative. One may say 'domes' or 'windows', but not 'no dome' or 'no windows' in cases where the unusual feature of a drawing's subject is the omission of an expected feature. Some have suggested that we use the positive term even when we mean the opposite: 'windows' when there are no windows. Yet this may be very misleading to a scholar, and is definitely not descriptive of the image. Moreover, most AAT terms are plural; therefore, Michelangelo appears as 'draftsmen', not 'draftsman', for example. By using AAT, we gain the ability to search for all 'draftsmen', but lose the ability to describe each one as a 'draftsman'.

Finally, there are problems as well as strengths inherent in the diversity of FDA's contributors and future users. A specialist defines concepts and terminologies more narrowly than a generalist. Indeed, the syndetic structure of FDA's database was optimised to enable users to broaden and narrow their searches. But the problem of making a large database for users of widely diverse interests is not entirely solved by data structure (Figure 48.2). For example, the term, 'cavalier oblique projection', is used generically by architectural historians to describe drawings of any period in oblique projection where the vertical plane is parallel to the picture plane and all three spatial axes are drawn in the same scale. But one military historian defined the same term as a representation from the point of view of a man on horseback — thus, 'cavalier', the last such drawing being made no later than 1914, when cavalry ceased to be used in warfare. Because of differences in focus among the two disciplines in this example, the architectural historian will have a better chance of finding what he or she wants than does the military historian.

Finding methods for reconciling such differences among art historians and other potential users will be one of FDA's major challenges in the years ahead. Our project looks forward to the exchange of experiences with others who face similarly 'challenging' situations.

---

49 'THE ABSENCE OF A SYMBOL INDICATES PAPER' — IMPROVING ON AN *AD HOC* OBJECT DESCRIPTION SYSTEM AT THE TATE GALLERY

Peter Wilson

Head of Gallery Services
Tate Gallery
London

In 1967 the Tate Gallery published its first complete inventory of the collections: *The Collections of the Tate Gallery*, which has always been known within the Gallery as 'The Concise Catalogue' after the opening words of the foreword. The Concise Catalogue attempted to list, on a single-line-per-item basis every work of art in the Tate Gallery Collections. The inventory was typed and the typescript, with suitable cutting and pasting, was presented as camera-ready copy to the printer. The foreword of the time recorded that 'The direct-copy technique . . . permits much freer correction and more frequent editions . . .'.

A number of compromises about the information recorded were made in order to support the single line entry practice, most notably that the medium and support description were abbreviated to a two-part 'code' consisting of one or more upper case letters (for medium) and a group of lower case letters (for support). Thus Oc denoted 'oil on canvas' which is the established way of describing a painting made with oil (or oleoresinous or resinous or similar paint) applied to a (probably) primed canvas stretched on a wooden stretcher. It is clearly unlikely that any printed catalogue would aspire to such a clumsy description, but it is equally clear that established practice does not provide the basis for a systematic description. The terms used had been quite serviceable in their original context but did not provide a comprehensive way of recording the object type, the materials used or the techniques employed. The shortcomings of the *ad hoc* approach become even more apparent when considering other abbreviations which included C for colour print, D for drawing (regardless of medium), K for mobiles or kinetic (moving) objects, M for monochrome engraving, R for reliefs, and S for sculpture — all of these being descriptive, of object type rather than of the materials or manner of creation.

The second part of the code, the 'support' — a term really only appropriate for two dimension art — included these abbreviations: m for metals (except bronze), s for stone (or marble) and z for bronze. The most problematic abbreviation of all was that 'The absence of a (lower case) symbol indicates paper'! This convention, depending upon how it was interpreted, meant that it would be possible to believe that every item in the collection might contain paper or alternatively that it was impossible to record the presence of paper when any other 'support' was present.

The lack of consistency in the nature of the information being conveyed by the upper and lower case parts of the code appears to have been of no great concern to any of those who used the Concise Catalogue's first seven editions, nor did it in any way hamper the ingenuity of the cataloguer charged with the description of the less conventional works of art which a museum of contemporary art collects. The eighth edition had added a symbol for paper, the Greek pi, and there had been a number of other 'enhancements' of the system in the intervening years, most of which had only served to confuse matters further. M had been extended to cover any monochrome print, unless it was a lithograph in which case an L was added, or a woodcut or other relief block print (MP) or an intaglio block print (MI) and, of course there were colour versions of these CL, CP and CI. The 'kinetic photograph' (KF) had been invented for cinema films but a new symbol X had been added for video tape. There were also a small number of entries which had abandoned the conventions altogether:

RvπbWall which was used to describe a complex contemporary work by Jannis Kounellis 'Untitled' of 1979 which consists of a design for a drawing to be executed directly onto an appropriately coloured (white) gallery wall by the exhibit installer, together with other wall-attached elements including stuffed birds impaled on arrows.

DWall used to describe two similar 'wall drawings' by the American artist Sol LeWitt, 'A Wall Divided Vertically into Fifteen Equal Parts Each with a Different Line Direction and Colour, and all Combinations' (1970) and 'Six Geometric Figures (+Two) (Wall Drawings)' (1980–81).

China used for a 'pop art' work by Roy Lichtenstein: 'Set of Dinnerware Objects: Dinner Plate, Soup Dish, Salad Plate, Side Plate, Saucer, Cup' (1966).

It was by this stage clear that the simplicity of the original intention had been lost and that a better system was needed.

Shortly after the eighth edition was published the Gallery began to consider computerising its inventory record and the Concise Catalogue became the basis for this exercise. The original typescript method of production had been superceded in 1977 for the sixth edition and we immediately turned to the computer typesetting master tape as a quick method of establishing a database. This proved to be very much more difficult than anticipated as the printer had treated the tabulated inventory as a series of columns and so there was no direct relationship between inventory number, title and other details. Fortunately, an alternative source of machine-readable information was found in a dBaseIII file which had been created by Tate Gallery Publications for the production of labels for photographs of works of art. This database had been keyed in by an untrained typist and there were many errors and one or two design errors: for instance, the title field had been entered upper case. An account of the project to clean up this data does not belong here. What is significant for this paper is that the database file allowed us to analyse the way in which the medium/support coding had been applied. We found that there were about 470 different grouping of letters, the vast majority of which had only been used a very few times. Ninety-two of the abbreviations referred to prints and a further 55 described reliefs (that is 'sculptural' works of art intended to be displayed on a wall rather than on a floor or a plinth). There were 87 groupings for sculpture.

It rapidly became clear that if we wished to classify the collection in a pragmatic way (by object type, principally for collections management purposes) this could easily be done:

painting

sculpture

relief

unique work of art on paper

editioned work of art on paper

film, video

leaving only a very small number of works of art unclassified: these were generally objects such as those which are works of art consisting of a number of components, which are put together according to the artist's instructions for each display. The works by LeWitt and Kounellis fall into this category. This kind of work is generally known as an installation.

The new broad 'object type' term was explicit in the encoded abbreviations for some categories:

sculpture — S

relief — R

editioned works on paper — C, M

film, video — KF, X

and implicit in certain combinations of abbreviations:

painting O/A/T + c/w/b

unique works on paper — π (except where C & M are used)

In addition, the abbreviation conveyed either information about the technique or process used in the object's making such as the method of printmaking:

I for intaglio

L for lithograph

P for plaster or other moulded material (i.e. a modelled sculpture, not case)

or simply recorded one or more of the materials used.

Figure 49.1 Relationship between recording concepts

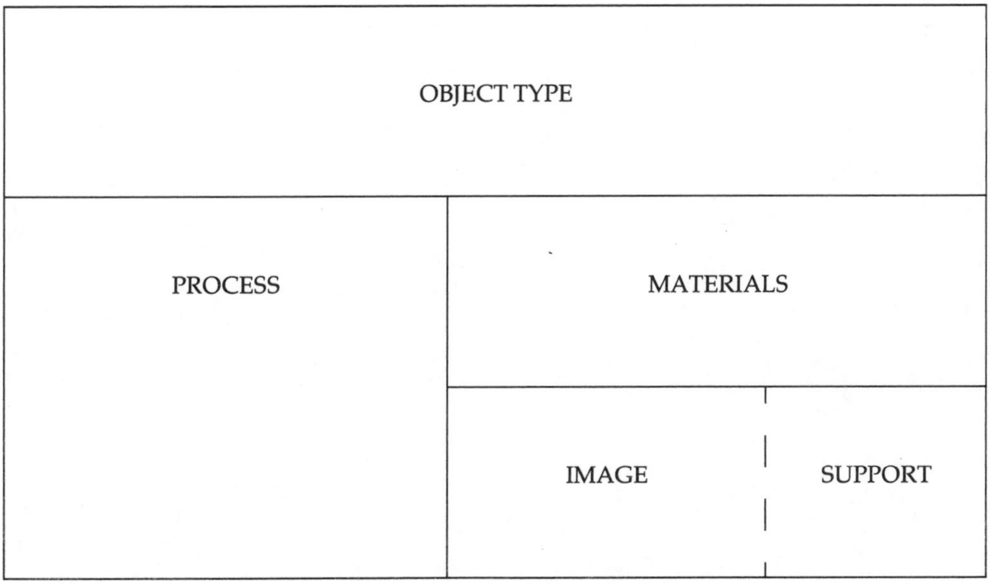

<table>
<tr><td colspan="3">OBJECT TYPE</td></tr>
<tr><td rowspan="2">PROCESS</td><td colspan="2">MATERIALS</td></tr>
<tr><td>IMAGE</td><td>SUPPORT</td></tr>
</table>

In the case of most of those object types thought of as two dimensional (paintings, unique works of art on paper) the material making the image is recorded with the upper case part of the code whilst the support is recorded in the lower case part. For remaining types (including editioned works of art on paper or prints), the upper case part indicated the object type or the process, whilst the lower case part gives the principle materials.

A new classification scheme could be developed from the existing information (Figure 49.1).

The ninth edition of the Concise Catalogue will be published late in 1990. It will be sent to the publishers in electronic form, probably as a Postscript file output from Ventura Publisher. Entries are no longer subject to the constraint of a single line and the information will include the object type followed by a tidied up and simplified version of the former abbreviation, omitting the redundant part of it but still combining information about process or making with information about materials. The Tate Gallery expects to have developed simple and concise lists of terms descriptive of process and materials to replace the abbreviations in time for the tenth edition in 1992.

---

50 VISUAL RECORDS FROM THE TWENTIETH CENTURY: SOME TERMINOLOGY APPLIED BY THE IMPERIAL WAR MUSEUM

Roger Smither

Keeper, Department of Information Systems
Imperial War Museum
London

Introduction

The Imperial War Museum, which was originally founded at the end of the First World War to record the role of the British Empire in that conflict, has had its terms of reference adjusted as the century and its wars continued. It is now expected to cover all aspects of any military operations since August 1914 in which Britain or other members of the Commonwealth have been involved. Living up to these terms of reference, and especially to the implications of the phrase 'all aspects', is a challenging task, and requires the Museum to handle a wider range of materials than those that constitute the typical concerns of most other mseums.

The Museum has, of course, its collections of three-dimensional exhibits, although even these have their special characteristics: since the Museum is basically a museum of the twentieth century, the exhibits are products of modern mass production more often than unique artefacts. To do justice to its terms of reference, however, and to cover the conflicts of a century that has given birth to such phrases as 'total war', and the 'war for men's minds', the Museum is dependent on far more than its range of conventional exhibits. In all, the Museum has seven collecting departments, broadly defined by the material collected. In addition to exhibits, these departments cover printed books, documents, sound records, film, photographs and art.

It is the three last departments, with their very large collections (27 000 items in the film collection, 68 000 in the Art Department and a daunting five million photographs) that provide the background to an Imperial War Museum contribution to discussions of terminology for fine art, iconography and visual representation.

Although the Museum houses a major national collection in each of these areas, it is not the intention here to discuss the Museum's approach to standard terminology problems. The Imperial War Museum faces little that is unusual in the naming of artists and others responsible for creating the items in its collections, or in describing the provenance, storage, conservation or history of those items. The problems are those encountered by other museums, and the solutions are similarly recognisable: only the subject matter of the works concerned is likely to be different. Attention will instead be focused on two specific problems where the Museum's experience is thought to be less universal without, it is hoped, being unique. These involve issues of identification and description, and of intention.

Identification by reference between items

Identifying archival film

One of the major problems for curators of modern collections is to evolve procedures to cope with the identification (and, to some extent, the description) of items that inhabit the uneasy limbo between museum object, archive document and library volume which is the traditional realm of 'audiovisual' or 'non-book' material. Many items in this category combine characteristics of both the unique artefact, which curators have traditionally expected to describe fully in documentation, and the 'published' item, which librarians commonly expect to document primarily by the transcription of readily accessible data (such as that found on a title-page). The concerns of film archivists may be used to introduce and illustrate some of the resulting difficulties.

Film manages to be simultaneously an extremely international and an extremely parochial medium: a point that is bound to cause difficulties for those involved in sharing or exchanging information on film (Smither, 1987). A very large proportion of the screen time of most countries of the world (including both cinema and television screen time), is occupied by products of other nations and different cultures. At the same time, those products are normally shaped by the cinema distributors or television broadcasters to local circumstances and audiences. 'Foreign' soundtracks are routinely subtitled or dubbed; cuts are made by censors to accord with local political or moral requirements or susceptibilities; other adjustments will be made to ensure the film or programme will fit with schedules, with the needs of advertisers and with the appetites of audiences.

In all the processes just outlined, no part of a film is sacred. By far the most vulnerable parts of a film, however, are its title and credits sequence, precisely those parts on which (because of their superficial resemblance to a title-page) traditional librarianship practices would expect to place the heaviest reliance. Film titles are changed to increase their attractiveness for the local audience, or to remove unfortunate nuances which may not travel as well as the visual material does.

It should not be overlooked that more mundane factors also affect the form in which films — the 'same' films — enter archives around the world. Film is an extremely vulnerable medium, and every projection or viewing carries with it the danger of damage. Films that are much used will tend to get shorter as damage occurs and is repaired. Thus, even films that carry the same title and share a similar provenance may prove, on examination, to have substantial differences. Therefore, although 'film' may be considered to be a 'published' medium, the copies of films in the vaults of archives are all likely to have at least some of the characteristics of the unique artefact.

For these and other reasons, film archivists have evolved a code of practice that seeks to describe the copies of a film, which are physically held, primarily in terms of the version of the film that was originally made. The main retrieval key will be the original release title in the country of origin and 'statements of responsibility' may be derived from research rather than from the item itself. The copies are then described in terms of their adherence to or divergence from this original (which may, of course, no longer exist anywhere, let alone in the archive cataloguing its copies) (Fédération Internationale des Archives du Film, 1979; Harrison, 1988).

The Imperial War Museum, which is a member of the International Federation of Film Archives (FIAF), has adopted this principle in so far as it applies to the Museum's film collection. In practice, the scope is not comprehensive, as much of the collection is held in the form of unedited (and so 'unpublished') record footage. The Museum has also found it useful to adopt a similar approach in the documentation of the rest of its pictorial or 'non-book' collections, which are as already noted largely the product of mass production processes.

This approach consists of designating one example of an item as a standard specimen, and then of identifying and describing the other examples of that item in the collection by reference to that one. A terminology has been evolved to reflect the degree of proximity of specimens to the selected standard: this moves outwards from a 'Model' to one or several 'Secondary Models' and/or to 'Specimens'. Its workings can be described and illustrated by reference to the famous (or notorious) 'Lusitania Medallion'.

On 7 May 1915, a German submarine sank the British transatlantic liner *Lusitania,* a controversial act which did much to swing American public opinion against the Germans at that stage of the First World War. The celebrated German medallist, Karl Goetz, was moved to produce as a private enterprise a satirical medallion recording, among other things, the German claims that the *Lusitania* was a legitimate target because she was carrying armaments as well as passengers and that the American and other civilian passengers had been warned by advertisements in the New York press of the risk of U-boat attack, but that Cunard had dismissed such warnings (Dutton, 1986). These claims explain the two captions on the medallion 'KEINE BANNWARE' (no contraband) and 'GESCHÄFT ÜBER ALLES' (business before everything). In his first effort, Goetz got the date wrong and recorded the sinking as having taken place on '5 MAI 1915'. The Imperial War Museum has one example of this first issue medallion, which is consequently catalogued as the Museum's 'Model' in a record which contains a full description (Figure 50.1).

Goetz's medallion presented the British with an unintended propaganda opening on which they were not slow to capitalise. To begin with, they successfully blurred the distinction between Goetz's private medallion and an officially state-struck medal, to convey the impression — echoed in some respected history books to this day — that it

Figure 50.1

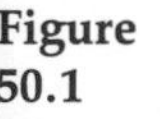

Reverse of Goetz's 'Lusitania medallion' — death does brisk business at the Cunard ticket office. (Imperial War Museum negative number QS1867)

Figure 50.2

Obverse of the second edition of Goetz's 'Lusitania medallion' with the corrected date. (Imperial War Museum negative number QS1866)

was the German state that had produced a medal to honour what much of the world perceived as an atrocity. A propaganda sub-plot was built around the wrong date, which was used to suggest that the sinking had been long-planned and the medal struck in advance, only to be wrong-footed by events. The British produced large numbers of a replica of Goetz's medallion which were sold in a box with a page of text making the British propaganda point. The Museum's prime specimen of this British issue is therefore described as a 'Secondary Model' to the Goetz original: Goetz's design is not described again, but the significant difference (the spelling of the controversial date with a British 'Y' not the German 'I' in 'MAI') is recorded, and full details of the accompanying box are also provided.

Goetz attempted to undo some of the damage by producing a second issue of his medallion with the date corrected to '7 MAI': an example of this medallion is also recorded as a 'Secondary Model' to the first issue: once more, only the divergent detail is noted in the description. The Museum's third 'Secondary Model' is an example of the British replica in bronze rather than the usual iron: this is recorded as a secondary model to the British replica, and is thus a kind of tertiary model (though the term is not used) to the German original (Figure 50.2).

All the Museum's additional examples of these medallions — which include one of the Goetz second issue, and almost 20 of the British replica — may then be described simply as additional 'Specimen's. No description is provided in the catalogue entry for a 'Specimen' of its design, materials or dimensions (or of the accompanying material, in the case of British replicas, beyond a statement of its presence or absence): description is restricted to statements concerning those aspects which are unique to each example, namely condition and completeness (Figures 50.3 to 50.5).

Figure 50.3 A schematic representation of the Museum's holdings of 'Lusitania Medallions'

IWM MODEL/SECONDARY MODEL/SPECIMEN DESIGNATIONS.

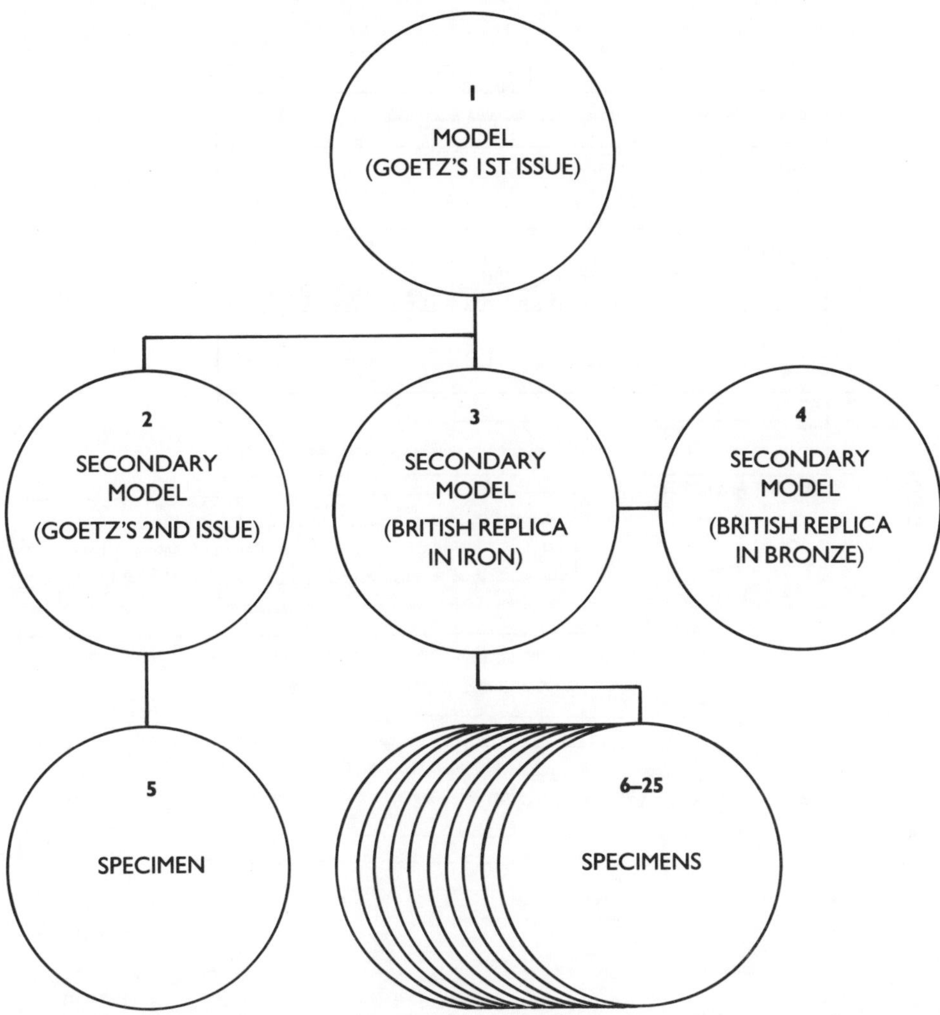

The full hierarchy of terminology used in 'description status' statements throughout the Museum also includes the terms Original, Experimental, Variant, and Modification which are used in appropriate contexts (which do not often include visual records, though they are commonly found in exhibit collections) to note 'one-off' items which are unlikely to be useful as points of reference for other specimens. The practice of relating the description of mass-produced items to a hierarchy of model specimens is found to save time, effort and computer storage space as the task of cataloguing collections progresses.

Terminology for political intentions

The other dimension of terminology practice to be discussed here is the one named earlier as 'intention'. This label is not entirely a happy one, but it attempts to suggest a

Figure 50.4 Lusitania Medallion: Catalogue entry for 'Model'

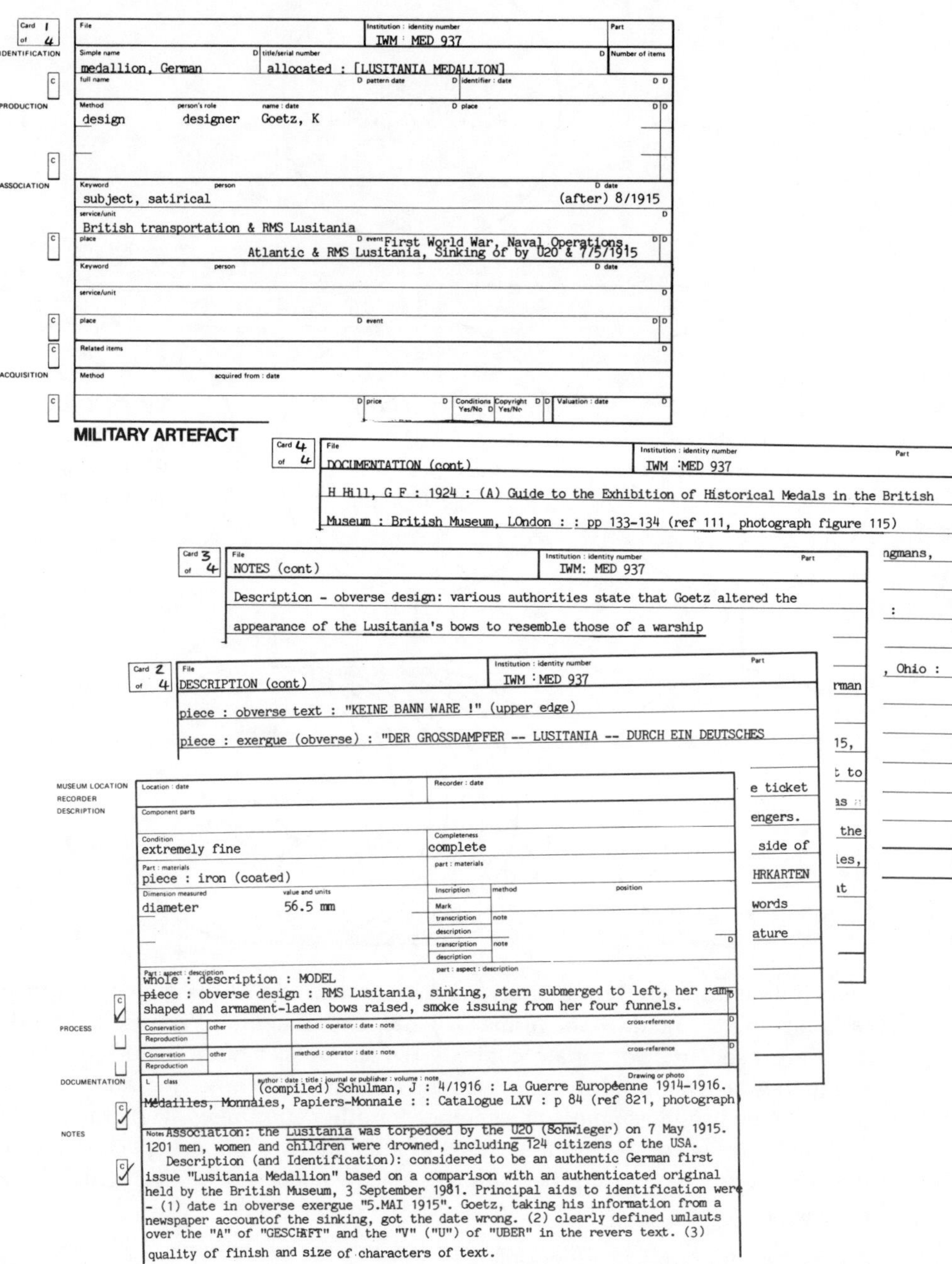

MILITARY ARTEFACT

Card 1 of 4
IDENTIFICATION — Institution : identity number: IWM : MED 937
Simple name: medallion, German — title/serial number: allocated : [LUSITANIA MEDALLION]
PRODUCTION — Method: design — person's role: designer — name : date: Goetz, K
ASSOCIATION — Keyword: subject, satirical — date: (after) 8/1915
service/unit: British transportation & RMS Lusitania
event: First World War, Naval Operations, Atlantic & RMS Lusitania, Sinking of by U20 & 7/5/1915

Card 2 of 4 — DESCRIPTION (cont) — IWM : MED 937
piece : obverse text : "KEINE BANN WARE !" (upper edge)
piece : exergue (obverse) : "DER GROSSDAMPFER -- LUSITANIA -- DURCH EIN DEUTSCHES

Card 3 of 4 — NOTES (cont) — IWM: MED 937
Description - obverse design: various authorities state that Goetz altered the appearance of the Lusitania's bows to resemble those of a warship

Card 4 of 4 — DOCUMENTATION (cont) — IWM :MED 937
H Hill, G F : 1924 : (A) Guide to the Exhibition of Historical Medals in the British Museum : British Museum, LOndon : : pp 133-134 (ref 111, photograph figure 115)

MUSEUM LOCATION / RECORDER / DESCRIPTION
Condition: extremely fine — Completeness: complete
Part : materials: piece : iron (coated)
Dimension measured: diameter — value and units: 56.5 mm
Part : aspect : description: whole : description : MODEL
piece : obverse design : RMS Lusitania, sinking, stern submerged to left, her ram-shaped and armament-laden bows raised, smoke issuing from her four funnels.

DOCUMENTATION: (compiled) Schulman, J : 4/1916 : La Guerre Européenne 1914-1916. Médailles, Monnaies, Papiers-Monnaie : : Catalogue LXV : p 84 (ref 821, photograph

NOTES: Association: the Lusitania was torpedoed by the U20 (Schwieger) on 7 May 1915. 1201 men, women and children were drowned, including 124 citizens of the USA.
Description (and Identification): considered to be an authentic German first issue "Lusitania Medallion" based on a comparison with an authenticated original held by the British Museum, 3 September 1981. Principal aids to identification were - (1) date in obverse exergue "5.MAI 1915". Goetz, taking his information from a newspaper accountof the sinking, got the date wrong. (2) clearly defined umlauts over the "A" of "GESCHAFT" and the "V" ("U") of "UBER" in the revers text. (3) quality of finish and size of characters of text.

Figure 50.5 Lusitania Medallion: Catalogue entry for 'Specimen' (British Replica)

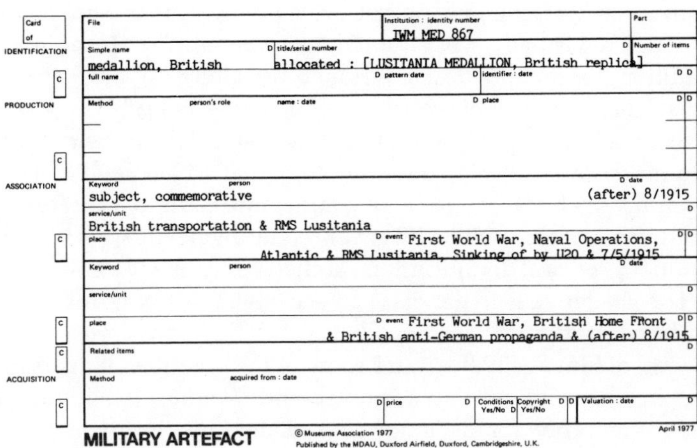

Card of

IDENTIFICATION

File | Institution : identity number: IWM MED 867 | Part

Simple name: medallion, British | D | title/serial number: allocated : [LUSITANIA MEDALLION, British replica] | D | Number of items

full name | D | pattern date | D | identifier : date | D D

PRODUCTION

Method | person's role | name : date | D | place | D | D

ASSOCIATION

Keyword: subject, commemorative | person | D | date: (after) 8/1915

service/unit: British transportation & RMS Lusitania | D

place | D | event: First World War, Naval Operations, Atlantic & RMS Lusitania, Sinking of by U20 & 7/5/1915 | D | D

Keyword | person | D | date

service/unit | D

place | D | event: First World War, British Home Front & British anti-German propaganda & (after) 8/1915 | D | D

Related items | D

ACQUISITION

Method | acquired from : date

D | price | D | Conditions Yes/No | D | Copyright Yes/No | D | D | Valuation : date | D

MILITARY ARTEFACT © Museums Association 1977 Published by the MDAU, Duxford Airfield, Duxford, Cambridgeshire, U.K. April 1977

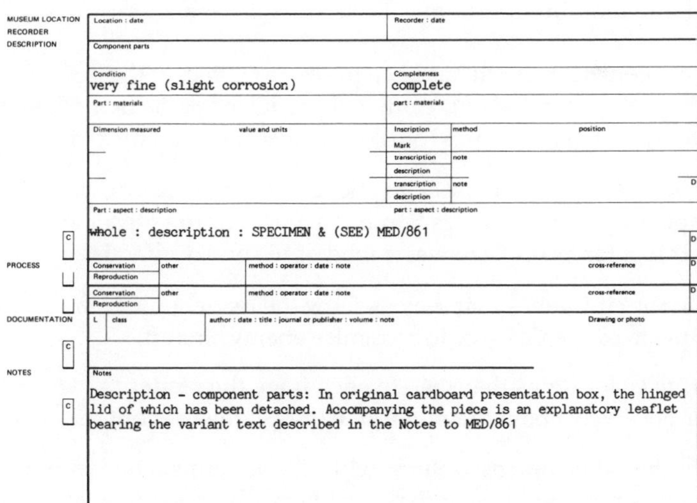

MUSEUM LOCATION
RECORDER
DESCRIPTION

Location : date | Recorder : date

Component parts

Condition: very fine (slight corrosion) | Completeness: complete

Part : materials | part : materials

Dimension measured | value and units | Inscription | method | position

Mark

transcription | note

description

transcription | note | D

description

Part : aspect : description | part : aspect : description

whole : description : SPECIMEN & (SEE) MED/861 | D

PROCESS

Conservation | other | method : operator : date : note | cross-reference | D
Reproduction

Conservation | other | method : operator : date : note | cross-reference | D
Reproduction

DOCUMENTATION

L | class | author : date : title : journal or publisher : volume : note | Drawing or photo

NOTES

Notes

Description - component parts: In original cardboard presentation box, the hinged lid of which has been detached. Accompanying the piece is an explanatory leaflet bearing the variant text described in the Notes to MED/861 problem of documentation likely to be widely encountered in museums with modern (and perhaps especially modern military) collections. In a recent article (Wood, 1987), it is suggested that 'our national military museums must perforce be the most political of museums'. The author points out that every item in a military museum's collection has an inescapable political dimension: for example, a British soldier's shako worn in the Punjab in 1848 by its very existence implicitly raises the issues of the 'rightness' of British Imperialism, and of that Imperialism's own longer-term effects. A museum cannot simply display items without addressing the issues suggested by their history, since even a decision to say nothing may be open to a political interpretation. Such resonances, of course, attach to virtually every item in the Imperial War Museum's collections.

In addition to the political overtones attaching to ordinary exhibits in military museums, there are whole classes of items, especially in the textual and visual collections, that were openly and avowedly political from their creation. Such items will require a museum to develop a terminology that will expand conventional descriptors: the Museum's Art Department, for example, must add to its list of portraits, landscapes, abstracts and so on terms that will cover recruiting posters, proclamations by an army of occupation, or satirical denunciations of the enemy like the Goetz medallion considered earlier. The challenge is to generate an acceptable list of terms, a list that will itself not prove to be controversial.

The world of film again illustrates some of the potential dangers in this area. FIAF has been seeking for some time an approved and standard list of film genres. The attempt progresses smoothly for as long as consideration is given to slapstick, westerns, romances, musicals, epics and the like but reaches deadlock when spy films and other thrillers come under discussion: a piece that will be recognised as harmless entertainment by one side of the Iron Curtain — for example the early 'James Bond' film *From Russia With Love* — will have a very different aspect on the other. The question of overt political intention in art or film collections is capable of raising similar, if not identical, issues.

The Museum's approach has been to seek to reflect in the documentation, in a neutral vocabulary, the intention of the original producers of the item. First, therefore, there are added to our list of item types (portrait, landscape, etc.) further types such as:

canvassing: for items that seek to encourage the reader or viewer to *do* something, for example to buy war savings bonds, to enlist, or to vote a particular way; or *not* to do something, for example to waste food or to spread rumours;

instructional: for items that seek to show the reader or viewer *how* to do something, for example to eat healthily or to recognise enemy aircraft;

propaganda: for items that seek to encourage the reader or viewer to *think* something, either positively about their own side or negatively about the enemy.

Second, the Museum associates with these terms and with their more common equivalents a number of secondary qualifiers which aim to give, though still in a neutral vocabulary, a more precise indication of the intention. Several of these secondary qualifiers are quite straightforward — for example 'canvassing, war savings' or 'canvassing, recruiting' or 'canvassing, charity'. Others may require some definition:

commemorative: this term generally implies a historical or retrospective air: applied to a portrait medallion, for example, it would imply that the subject is dead;

inflammatory/inspirational: one or other of this pair of terms is commonly associated with the designation 'propaganda' to indicate whether by its tone the propaganda seeks to incite the viewer to dislike an enemy or to cherish their own side;

satirical: this term generally implies that the intention of the item is to make a point by humour or ridicule, as in the case of the 'Lusitania Medallion'.

Terminology such as that just outlined is intended to produce a set of descriptors that are intentionally bland, and that will allow a cataloguer to describe in neutral terms the character of an item: thus, a 'Troops Out' poster denouncing the Army's role in Belfast, a British depiction of a murderous Uhlan in Belgium in 1914, or an anti-semitic Nazi caricature from the Second World War, might all be described as 'propaganda, inflammatory' leaving to those whose job it is to use the material in exhibitions the responsibility of addressing the historical resonances of the items. The traditional impartiality or objectivity of the cataloguer is occasionally hard to sustain when confronted with overtly political material, but it is felt that the Museum's documentation staff have enough to occupy them, without acquiring the responsibility of moral or political interpretation as well.

Conclusion

The ideas outlined in this paper are still in the process of development and refinement: the solutions to be finally adopted will not necessarily be exactly those described here, but we are convinced that something along these lines is required in the Museum itself and is likely to be needed by other organisations handling similar types of collections. The alternatives all threaten either to generate excessive quantities of documentation or enmesh documentation staff in problems they do not need to add to an already heavy workload.

51 THE MARC FORMAT FOR VISUAL MATERIALS AND THE APPLICATION OF STANDARD TOOLS FOR CATALOGUING

Elisabeth Betz Parker

Prints and Photographs Division
Library of Congress
Washington, DC

The Library of Congress Prints and Photographs Division holds some 12 million still images, including photographic prints and negatives, fine prints, historical prints and pictorial ephemera, posters, and artistic, documentary, and architectural drawings. The materials represent many time periods and subjects. Each month, the Division receives more than 1 500 queries and provides reference service to an average of 650 visitors consulting the collections. People seek pictures for many different reasons: for example, illustrations for printed and audiovisual products and for exhibits, visual evidence from which to make sets for films and plays, to use in reconstructing historic buildings, or to complement and support other primary sources such as manuscripts. People also come for the pure pleasure of looking at images.

Most queries relate to depictions of people, places, topics, or themes. But some researchers want the pictures of a particular creator or collector. And increasingly requests are made for examples of a particular genre or form (such as editorial cartoons or landscapes), or examples of a production process or physical format (such as lantern slides or lithographs). Often questions involve a combination of these aspects.

Our need to control rapidly expanding collections, to serve the ever-growing numbers of researchers and their evermore sophisticated research needs and — at the same time — to preserve the materials for future researchers has fuelled our desire to provide efficient indirect access to our holdings through catalogue records and finding aids. Indirect access has actually long been provided in our reading room through numerous card indexes and catalogues, *but* because they are scattered, in varying states of completeness, and complex, a member of the reference or curatorial staffs must usually be called upon to make good use of them.

Automated access offers the prospect of a more effective, centralised means of retrieval. Automation brings an added incentive for us to standardise our catalogue records and cataloguing practices, for it is well known that consistency is vital to computer retrieval, especially in online databases. It should come as no surprise — situated as we are at the Library of Congress — that we are inclined toward library cataloguing standards. Although the general library cataloguing code does not address the preliminary issues of arrangement in pictorial collections, certain principles about description and indexing already exist, and they offer us incalculable savings in time and intellectual effort when we are trying to develop our own.

In order to package the catalogue record so that library computer software can recognise and take advantage of it, we use the MARC Format for Visual Materials, one of a family of machine-readable cataloguing formats.

We have discovered that people who are new to library cataloguing systems become confused by the terms MARC and MARC format (Crawford, 1984). This is not surprising, since they can refer to several different things. MARC format stands for a structure made up of fields, tags and indicators (Library of Congress, 1988). It can also refer to the set of instructions that explains the use of each field and subfield. And, often, cataloguing operations are referred to as MARC cataloguing, as if the format somehow determined the record content. This last is not the case. The content, that is the catalogue record itself, is created first — preferably in accordance with a cataloguing scheme — and *then* coded in the MARC format. We can liken the catalogue record to a letter and the MARC Format to the standard-sized envelope into which we slip it so that the post office will accept it and deliver it expeditiously. Although data compiled according to practically any scheme can be coded, the MARC formats were developed with the characteristics of Anglo-American cataloguing conventions and international standards for bibliographic description in mind and therefore relate most closely to the specific tools discussed below.

If the MARC format is the envelope, then the second edition of the *Anglo-American Cataloguing Rules* (AACR2) is a tool that helps us to construct the 'letter': the catalogue record (Anglo-American Cataloguing Rules, 1988). It is a general cataloguing code that sets forth a standard pattern for catalogue records, regardless of the material being described. By following the pattern, we gain the advantage of familiarity. Whether our records appear only in the card catalogue in our reading room or in the Library of Congress integrated bibliographic database, it is important for the data to be expressed in a manner familiar to library users, both researchers and staff. These rules also lay out international conventions for punctuation that are recognisable not only to cataloguers but to computers as well.

Chapter 8 in AACR2 deals with graphic materials, primarily those that are commercially produced and currently available. However, it does not adequately address the range of situations one encounters when dealing with original items and historical collections. For that reason, it was important for the general pattern to be presented (and in some instances extended) in such a way as to give guidance to cataloguers attempting to create more specialised descriptions of visual materials. At the same time, it seemed useful to examine and adapt library cataloguing and retrieval techniques to the needs of picture control and access. Thus, in 1982 the manual *Graphic Materials: Rules for Describing Original Items and Historical Collections* was published to supplement AACR2 (Betz, 1982). (Other specialised manuals have also been published for cataloguing rare books, manuscript and archival collections and motion pictures). The graphic materials guidelines have helped clarify the often hazy distinction between description and subject and other indexing access to pictures. The manual's subtitle spells out its coverage of conventions for describing original items such as an engraving by Rembrandt, as well as collections such as a group of photographs by Mathew Brady's studio of Civil War soldiers or an unpublished album of chromolithographs. The manual provides guidance in expressing the number, size and kind of images involved, the date of execution, as well as suggesting the forms, sequence and phrasing of notes in a consistent way.

Even more important for retrieval than consistency in descriptive conventions is consistency in the words used as access points. The Anglo-American rules guide us in formulating proper names for persons, corporate bodies and places as headings, and we then rely on authority files to ensure that the headings will not have to be formulated anew each time we use them. To make sure that the headings in our records are consistent with those used to index records for books, serials, maps, etc., we consult the Library of Congress Name Authority File (Library of Congress, 1977–). If the name does not appear in the file, we formulate the needed heading according to AACR2 rules and submit it to the central file; therefore, our name authority records become available to cataloguers at the Library of Congress and institutions having access to the LC authority file tapes or microfiche.

Name authorities help catalogue users to retrieve all of the material related to a particular person, corporate body or place. Controlled vocabulary is equally helpful in retrieving material by topic or theme and by genre or form and physical characteristic. To this end, the *LC thesaurus for Graphic Materials: Topical Terms for Subject Access* (Parker, 1987) and *Descriptive Terms for Graphic Materials: Genre and Physical Characteristic Headings* (Zinkham and Parker, 1986) were developed and are now accepted standard sources for index terms (see Chapter 46).

It is important to see these publications as an array of tools that can work together in the standardisation of picture cataloguing. We and other institutions holding pictorial collections have come to realise that standards not only can serve local applications but also can facilitate dissemination of information about our collections. With standardisation, researchers' increasingly sophisticated and complex demands for access to pictorial collections can be met more effectively by our ability to take advantage of centralised, online access. Adherence to standards that have been worked out for describing materials and for communicating the descriptions creates the potential for us to share information about our holdings beyond the Library of Congress. Our records can be distributed to subscribing institutions and networks via computer tapes, for the MARC format allows computer to computer communication of cataloguing data and is used by libraries and networks throughout the United States and, in variant forms, in other countries.

It is extremely encouraging to see parallel developments in England, France, Italy, and Spain, where there are published or draft cataloguing rules patterned after the AACR2 and the manual *Graphic Materials,* as well as versions of the MARC format (for example, Biblioteca Nacional, 1988, Bibliothèque Nationale, 1987, Istituto Centrale per il Catalogo Unico, 1986 and Sheridan, 1986). This movement will help us to cooperate in the further development of tools and guidelines for cataloguing graphic materials and will help researchers to retrieve information about our valuable resources across international boundaries.

52 THE DYNAMICS OF DATA CONTROLS AT THE HISTORIC NEW ORLEANS COLLECTION

Rosanne McCaffrey Mackie

Director of Systems
The Historic New Orleans Collection
New Orleans, Louisiana

Introduction

Instituting data controls is a dynamic process which cannot be accomplished overnight, but must be planned and then nurtured as a computerisation project evolves. At the Historic New Orleans Collection (THNOC), we planned from the beginning of our project to maintain internal consistency and to recognise data distinctions through a combination of software features and the compilation of a data dictionary. Other controls are constantly created and defined within the atmosphere of our database management system. This approach has been employed with success in managing our collections and continues to become more refined with time. As automation has proceeded, staff interest in creating and maintaining standards has increased. They now better understand the nature of data and are able to make more informed judgments and decisions on specific data issues; at the same time, the quality of our database improves.

THNOC background

The Historic New Orleans Collection is a regional history museum and research centre focusing on New Orleans, the State of Louisiana and the southern United States around the Gulf of Mexico. It emphasises the accessibility and use of its holdings to the public through three research divisions which administer the permanent collections: the Curatorial Division is responsible for visual materials, including over 200 000 photographs, prints, paintings, drawings, maps, films and three-dimensional objects, the Manuscript Division contains over 8 000 linear feet of documents, family papers and other written material, and over 8 000 reels of microfilm, and the Research Library houses publications and printed matter of over 30 000 books and 20 000 pamphlets.

In 1985, after a number of years of investigation and planning, the decision was made to begin computerisation with the Curatorial Division. Large photographic and other collections were being acquired and an efficient means of tracking the items through all of the collections management activities was needed to contain the backlog. In addition, we wanted to continue the in-depth item level cataloguing our patrons desired, because a significantly increased number of outside researcher queries each year has added to the demands on the collections and the staff.

Hardware/software features

To this end, the Historic Collection has developed a large-scale integrated information system, called FACETS, to provide automated access to data and to streamline collections management functions. FACETS is based on the concept that pictorial material is made up of different kinds of visual data and that these data, or 'facets', require different retrieval approaches to optimise their accessibility. Designed by Willoughby Associates,

Ltd, and the prototype for their QUIXIS package, it is being implemented on a Hewlett-Packard 3000 series 42 minicomputer around the MINISIS database management system.

MINISIS allows for the definition and creation of databases without requiring computer programming and offers a number of features ideal for museum automation projects which provide many data controls, such as:

a relational file structure;

full text indexing;

variable-length fields;

repeatable field values;

sub-fielding;

global change;

immediate file updating;

foreign character handling.

Information is retrieved through a sophisticted query system which permits free-text, keyword, Boolean, comparison and date searches. It can also do wild card searching, adjacency searching, presence/absence searching and range searching.

Thesaurus

The system supports a multilingual online thesaurus to further enhance the quality of data retrieval. It can search on synonyms, broader, narrower, related and forbidden terms, as well as performing automatic translations from other languages. A subject thesaurus is a feature we expect to implement in the future; it will be created from actual data in the database and thus contain real rather than ideal terms. We expect to take advantage of existing external authorities, such as the Getty Trust's Art and Architecture Thesaurus project and the Library of Congress graphic materials thesaurus, to broaden its scope.

It will be particularly helpful to allow us to maintain the historical integrity of archaic terms, regional differences and richness of language in our indexed descriptions of objects, which follow a basic uniformity of style and format, but not of terminology. A linked vocabulary mechanism is also being considered to keep the thesaurus from becoming static. It will permit the system, over time, to accommodate multiple philosophies and views to supplement those of the initial designers and developers.

Visual facets

Another planned highlight of the FACETS system is the concept of visual facets with differential retrieval. This process is an attempt to divide visual information or facets, such as 'people, places, events and dates depicted', into separate entities, just as non-visual information is split into data fields such as Artist, Title and Date of Execution. Then the distinctive nature of each can be exploited to enhance retrieval. For instance, 'Place Depicted' might be initially entered as '533 Royal Street' but with global editing, it could later be accessed by various hierarchical levels such as 'French Quarter', 'New Orleans', 'Orleans Parish', 'Louisiana' or 'Southern United States'.

The idea of 'associated' facets and terms can also be handled in the same fashion as 'depicted' ones, without the confusion of what is visible in an image and what is not. For example, a photograph of a storefront might have the 'Associated Person' term of the proprietor's name, even though the owner himself may not appear in the picture. Although some of this information might also be contained in the indexed description, a faceted distinction yields better reporting and sorting capabilities.

Strategy

We have planned but have not yet created our systematic thesaurus, nor have we incorporated all of the specialised visual and associated facets beyond the pilot project into a majority of our online records. The reason is at the heart of this paper's topic: that the dynamics of data controls lead to various priorities being realised and different needs evolving at different times. At the Historic Collection, we determined that implementing some of these features, after they had been planned, was not essential to the *initial* phases of our database, especially with free-text search capabilities thus far giving us a satisfactory percentage of hits from queries. We instead chose to put the available resources into adding some large photographic collections to the database and will proceed with the thesaurus and other facets as budget allows and as the growth of the database makes the need more pronounced.

Determining the best strategy for particular museums and specific collections within them is the most important step in constructing an evolutionary database. In New Orleans, we realised that a rapid retrospective data entry scheme would let us gain immediate control over our insitution's collections if the information was captured with speed and accuracy from the existing documentation and if the structure allowed easy access to the data.

Database construction began with an analysis of the museum's records and the data in them. We became aware that the same data had different uses for different applications and the problem was how to manage it all. Decisions had to be made as to what fields should first be included, how they were related and what form the data was to take in each field. These elements comprised the data structure. A good understanding had to be gained of the attributes of data, of the physical constraints placed on collection data by the retrieval system, and of the functions and importance of different types of data to meet the museum's objectives. All of these considerations were not independent, but highly interrelated, and affected the initial design as well as the continued success of the system.

Data dictionary

In order to facilitate data retrieval and to guide initial data entry and ongoing cataloguing, FACETS was planned to combine the powerful features of MINISIS with terminology controls. This began with the compilation of a data dictionary (now in its third draft) created to address specific data entry conventions through syntax and vocabulary controls. Each page of the data dictionary details a single data field by name, field tag, mnemonic, maximum length, attributes (such as alphanumeric, repeatable, indexed by word), description, conventions, examples and comments.

Syntax controls designate the exact form of wording when recording data; vocabulary controls limit the content of the data field. For example, one syntax control we currently maintain is to record all individual artist names with last name first; one type of vocabulary control is that dates of location changes entered must be after 1982, the date of our last inventory, or they will not be accepted by the computer.

Other specific conventions have been evolving as staff experience in querying and using the system has developed. At the Historic Collection, many of these issues were not easily discussed a few years ago; now they are the concern of many. The data dictionary is an evolving document that reflects the growing interest in creating and maintaining internal standards that is apparent once automation begins.

Vocabulary frequency lists and controlled vocabularies

Information entered must conform to the data controls agreed upon at the onset of the database construction, but this is not to say that all vocabulary terms were determined from the beginning. Standardising terminology in a database is much easier to accomplish *after* automation than before. It is virtually impossible to pre-determine the content of controlled vocabularies or authority lists and be completely thorough and accurate. Controlled vocabularies are far more effective if built from the language of the source documents and from the terms commonly used by those who do the querying.

With today's sophisticated computer technology, post-coordinate system methodology is the preferable approach. The data is entered as it appears in the existing museum source material and then reviewed and altered if so desired. Vocabulary frequency lists are generated for each data field which record the number of postings or occurrences of each term. These lists are than analysed, not only to catch and correct typographical errors, but to check and maintain internal consistency. Errors which are caught or preferred spellings desired are corrected with global change capabilities. Terms which appear very infrequently are scrutinised to determine acceptability of usage.

We have become aware of the fact that certain data fields accommodate controlled vocabularies or authority lists, while others do not. Fields such as Artist/Maker Name benefit from such structure to facilitate sorting and searching without the problems of name variants, pseudonyms or abbreviations, which are better placed in a separate artist/maker authority file with additional biographical information. Other data fields, such as Title, do not, since they should include whatever wording was designated by the artist at the time the object was created. Now that the Historic Collection has over 60 000 records in the FACETS database and the staff is more familiar and more expert on data issues, we are beginning to concentrate on the examination and careful upkeep of our controlled vocabulary lists.

Controlling data entry

Data entry was first completed on the core curatorial holdings of about 50 000 items which had some sort of existing documentation. Data was taken from copies of accession ledger books, worksheets or handwritten cards — whatever was available — using specific data entry strategies to exploit repetitions while also interpreting the information into discreet data fields. Since that time, numerous additional data entry projects have been undertaken on specific collections which had no written records and which required rapid data capture before Willoughby Associates could perform their 'rapid data entry' strategy.

Charles Franck Collection

One such example was the Charles L. Franck Collection of 15 000 negatives and photographs of New Orleans architectural and city views from 1900 to 1955. It had no existing source documents, so we first analysed the collection and then created a worksheet format to facilitate basic registration of the negatives by quickly capturing data with as much controlled vocabulary as possible. Within given fields, the acceptable options were all preprinted and the staff simply circled the correct choice for that field.

For example, within the field of Medium, the negatives were all 'safety' or 'nitrate' film, so an easy designation of one or the other could be circled. This same procedure worked well for dates and dimensions.

The negative worksheets were then photocopied and sent off for data entry. We created only the 7 500 worksheets for the negatives, and then the records for the 7 500 photographs were generated from them, since much of the data from the modern prints was shared with that from the original negatives. By providing one sheet listing the data fields particular to all of the prints, we were able to maintain consistency and hasten the data entry phase for those items.

Clarence Laughlin collection

Our latest and most ambitious data entry project is the Clarence John Laughlin collection of surrealist experiments and architectural images of Louisiana and western United States. The photographs and negatives number about 42 000 items, acquired in two different years from two different sources. All items needed to be assigned museum accession numbers and to be linked to the only documentation existing, a set of index cards created by Laughlin himself based on his approximately 17 000 unique negative images.

We surveyed the collection and determined that the best stategy was to create composite worksheets for prints made from the same negative for each of the two accession groups and to incorporate information from the photographer's original index cards without unnecessary transcription. The sheets contained preprinted data shared by all the objects, such as the Source of that accession group, and the acceptable terms for the Lead-in, Medium and size or Dimensions fields. As much handwritten capture of information as possible was eliminated using the multiple choice method, and to foster accuracy, the accession numbers were also preprinted and only the final digits of each had to be added.

The composite worksheets were generated in six months by one full-time and two part-time people with minimum effort and error. All were photocopied in preparation for data entry. Additional strategies will be imposed at the data entry phase to maintain consistency and control. For instance, the approved ranges of years in the Date of Execution fields have been limited so that no values earlier or later than those pre-determined will be accepted by the computer. The keying and data conversion will be completed in about five months time; afterwards the records will be immediately accessible in the database and vocabulary lists will be produced to provide instant feedback for proofing and updating.

Conclusion

The Historic New Orleans Collection has applied a combination of software strategies and data controls to its automated FACETS system for collections management and to its data entry procedures. Additional controls are evolving as staff knowledge and awareness of the need for internal standards increases.

Project goals have been to optimise the accessibility of visual items by making data retrieval more precise and consistent. Thus far computerisation has had a great impact on the processing of records and information; it has the continued potential to open up new avenues of discovery through search capabilities previously impossible using manual methods.

53

AFRICAN MATERIAL CULTURE AND THE ART AND ARCHITECTURE THESAURUS: CHALLENGES TO THE AAT

Janet L. Stanley

National Museum of African Art Library
Smithsonian Institution
Washington, DC

Introduction

To find African art in an art museum is a relatively recent occurrence. It is also largely an American phenomenon. In Europe, objects of African material culture reside in museums of ethnography where the object is viewed as a product of a particular culture and people. In an art museum, the object is selected and exhibited for its visual and aesthetic qualities.

However, the requirements for documenting African art are the same whether in a museum of art or a museum of ethnography. This means that art museum cataloguers must probe a little more deeply than usual practice into history, use, meaning and symbolism of an object to fully document it. This is especially true because the primary access point, namely the individual artist or creator, is usually absent in cataloguing African art.

Documentation at the National Museum of African Art, refers to three activities: cataloguing of objects in the collection; cataloguing of visual images in the photographic archives; and indexing of bibliographic materials in the museum library. The concern in this paper is with the subject cataloguing, that is, the vocabulary used to describe objects, images and written literature. Although these tasks are handled by different departments and different individuals within the museum, the body of material is the same: African material culture.

The demands on indexing vocabulary, however, are varied. Describing a single object out of context is straightforward (even if not always simple). In photographs one finds many more types of objects represented than are actually owned by the museum. Moreover, field photographs may depict objects in context, and this requires a more sophisticated set of indexing terms to express the relationships between objects and settings. Bibliographic indexing requires even more sophisticated and complex terms which move into realms of concept, idea, belief and social process.

In a 1986 paper on African art and the Art and Architecture Thesaurus (AAT), describing this author's work in developing African vocabulary for incorporation into the AAT (Stanley, 1986), several assumptions were made which had informed and guided the advice given to the AAT. Now — three years later — these assumptions deserve to be re-examined. This revisionist approach comes from new currents in the field of African art history itself — a field that is still very young — and from a more sober and reflective analysis.

In applying AAT to the cataloguing and indexing of African material culture, we are challenged to rethink Western categories and modes of description. Although the AAT is intended as a global vocabulary — and several of the hierarchies are yet to be fully developed — it is problematic whether it can ever fully accommodate cataloguing and indexing of African material culture within a museum context, without some local restructuring or expansion of categories. This is not an indictment of the AAT: on the contrary, it is a testament to our growing understanding of African art history and to new thinking in the art history community generally. This is itself in a period of ferment, as it begins 'to recognise the 'Other' in our own European past, and therefore the necessity of taking into account a greater range of context to explain [and to document] the production and nature of art forms' (Adams, 1988, pages 89–90).

Using examples of African art objects, I will examine three problem areas: the validity of African ethnic group as the basis of AAT Styles and Periods terminology; the danger of misrepresentation in disregarding indigenous categories and terminology; and the importance of iconographic terms for African material culture.

Style and periods

What is 'style' in the African context? Does the concept of the unitary style period as applied to European art history transfer to African ethnic groups?

The concept of 'tribal style' dominates the field of African material culture, both in the museum world and in the literature. Labelling objects by tribal origin began with ethnographic museums and has become the primary nomenclature. Ethnographers first equated language and culture, then culture with art object. They then turned this reasoning around and concluded that people who made certain objects must belong to the designated language/culture group. Objects were freeze-framed within a particular cultural context. Yet language-art style correlates are not reliable. While language may be one vehicle for differentiating styles (e.g. Akan-speaking peoples), it is not the only one, nor the most important.

The use of ethnic name as a style designator presupposes that a given object type is everywhere made by that ethnic group; that the distribution of that object, say a particular mask, coincides with the distribution of that ethnic group; and that the tribal 'style' is consistent and unchanging over time.

These presuppositions are wrong for a number of reasons:

eithnic group boundaries in Africa are not, nor were they in the past, fixed and unchanging. The imposition of ethnic boundaries and definitions is a product of the colonial period (Kasfir, 1984);

they deny the historical reality of cross-cultural contacts, long-distance trade and migrations, or what we call today in the African art community 'open frontiers';

they assume a 'given' or fixed artistic reality, a set of identifiable objects, assigned to a culture: the one tribe/one style syndrome (Kasfir, 1984);

they deny individual artistic creativity, innovation and borrowing, and perpetuate the mindset that views African art as timeless and static.

Bascom (1969, pages 102–10) offers a 'style' topography which illustrates both the complexity of 'style' in African art and the pitfalls of assuming a single tribal style. His topography includes:

Style periods. Styles have evolved over time, although in most cases in Africa we lack data about this evolution. Consequently, we also lack a terminology to distinguish time periods in the same way that 'Renaissance' is distinguished from 'Baroque' in the European context.

Local substyles. Within ethnic groups there may be a variety of distinguishable styles.

Multiple subtribal styles. Within ethnic groups the variation in styles may be so great that there are really several quite different unrelated styles.

Individual styles. Conventional wisdom has it that African art is created by anonymous artists. Yet, more and more, the hand of individual artists and workshops can be identified within any style tradition.

Regional styles. Regional styles are those which cross ethnic boundaries linking stylistically objects made and used by different peoples. These styles are often associated with a social institution, such as a cult or secret society, which likewise cuts across tribal boundaries.

Blurred tribal styles. Through acculturation and borrowing and copying of design elements and forms, styles may no longer conform to older identifiable styles.

Craft styles. Pottery, basketry or weaving styles may create different styles based on medium or technique.

Tribal styles. Tribal style remains the dominant concept in classifying African art and cannot be wholly abandoned.

Many African art objects in museums have little or no documentation. Attribution is made on visual examination and comparison with objects of known provenance. Collection data that does exist in museum files may be quite inaccurate or vague as to by whom or where an object was made. For example, masks form the Cameroon Grassfields, collected by German colonial officials in the market town of Kom, appear in German museum records as originating from Kom, whereas in fact, they may have been made quite a distance from that place in a style that is not typically Kom.

Vansina (1984), arguing against ethnic group as a style designator, goes so far as to contend that the ultimate stylistic attribution of objects ought to be the village or workshop, or at least the social institution with which objects are associated regardless of ethnic identification.

There is justification for doing this. Let us look at the social institution of the *gelede* masquerade in this context. *Gelede* is a Yoruba masquerade, but not all Yoruba-speaking people have *gelede.* It is concentrated in south western Nigeria and southern Benin. Here the classification must be broken down further by geographical locale: Egbado *gelede,* Ketu *gelede* and so forth. But the institution of *gelede* also has spread to the Fon people in Benin, to former slave communities in Sierra Leone, and even to the New World. Therefore, one might say that *gelede* constitutes a 'style' regardless of whether it is Yoruba, Fon, Sierra Leone or whatever.

Gelede is more accurately thought of as a spectacle because it involves not only sculpted wooden masks — and there are many varieties of *gelede* masks both in form and function — but also costume, music and musical instruments, songs and oral traditions, dance. There are also *gelede* shrines and sacred storage spaces. So *'gelede'* as a style designator may apply to a whole range of objects, activities and beliefs.

The assumption that international art styles apply to contemporary African art is also open to question. Do modern paintings and sculptures by Africans really fit into Western twentieth-century art styles as outlined in the Styles and Periods hierarchy of the AAT? Is it accurate to categorise an African painting, say, as Surrealist in order to give it a label intelligible to Westerners? Is Surrealism part of the African artistic experience? To say African Surrealism' is even more meaningless. Perhaps we should identify the art school or workshop — e.g. Oshogbo, Poto Poto, Cyrene — and let it go at that and stop trying to force these works into Western art styles.

Indigenous categories and terminology

Most classification schemes ignore indigenous categories, in part because their architects are unaware of them or because they are unconvinced of the importance of incorporating them. They may feel that unfamiliar African categories need to be 'translated' into terms that Westerners understand. Conversely, they are unconcerned with how poorly the Western categories 'fit' African realities.

The *gelede* example illustrates the inappropriateness and irrelevance of generalised Western categories to particular objects from other cultures. *Gelede* masks fall into two broad categories — the nocturnal *efe* and the daytime *gelede* — which are differentiated both by form and function. Within the *efe/gelede* categories, there are whole series of performance masquerades distinguished by appearance and sequence in the performance (see Drewal and Drewal, 1984). They all have different names in Yoruba which translate into English as 'sweeper', 'fire carrier', 'fire extinguisher', 'Great Mother' and so on.

What becomes difficult from a cataloguing and indexing point of view is dealing semantically with these categories. How do we capture in words the 'sweeper' or *Arabi Ajigbale* in Yoruba ('the one-who-sweeps-every-morning') who appears early in the *efe* night performance to 'sweep', literally to clear the marketplace. Assuming one decides to label this mask type '*gelede* sweeper masks' or even use its Yoruba name '*Arabi Ajigbale*', it is clear that we are going beyond terms that are likely or legitimately to be found in AAT.

Masquerades are known and recognised by appearance and by how they act. Among the Igbo of Nigeria, for example, masquerades can be grouped into several descriptive categories to which, in turn, specific masks might be assigned (Onyeneke, 1985):

masquerades that whip people or hurl objects and show athletic exuberance;

dancing masquerades;

singing masquerades;

satirising, gossiping masquerades which make revelations in order to correct faults;

jesting and joking masquerades which portray the wisdom of the elders;

masquerades of extraordinary power, which are ferocious and fierce;

queenly/princely, venerable masks noted for beauty, grandeur, costliness or size;

non-visible masks (e.g. bull roarer).

In writing about Dan face masks (Fischer, 1978) delineates two basic groups: feminine mask types, *gle mu* with beautiful faces, oval outlines and narrow slit eyes, which act in a gentle and mild manner; and masculine masks, *gle gon*, with pentagonal outlines and tube-like eyes which act in vigorous aggressive and fearsome ways. All the large and zoomorphic masks are also defined as belonging to this second group. But he goes further and identifies 11 major face mask types among the Dan all of which have distinctive indigenous names (Fischer, 1984, pages 11–98 and 1978, pages 21–23):

deangle 'smiling mask' associated with the circumcision camp;

tankagle the entertaining masquerade;

gunyega the racing masquerade or 'house' spirit mask;

zakpai ga fire prevention or fire-extinguisher mask;

bagle the dancing and pantomiming mask;

bugle the war masquerade;

kagle the hooked-stick masquerades which take animal forms such as a cow, goat, bird, monkey, antelope;

glagben the stilt dancing masquerade who wears raffia wickerwork over his face instead of a wooden mask;

Masquerades representing illness and disease, or 'flaw-finding masquerades';

Figure 53.1

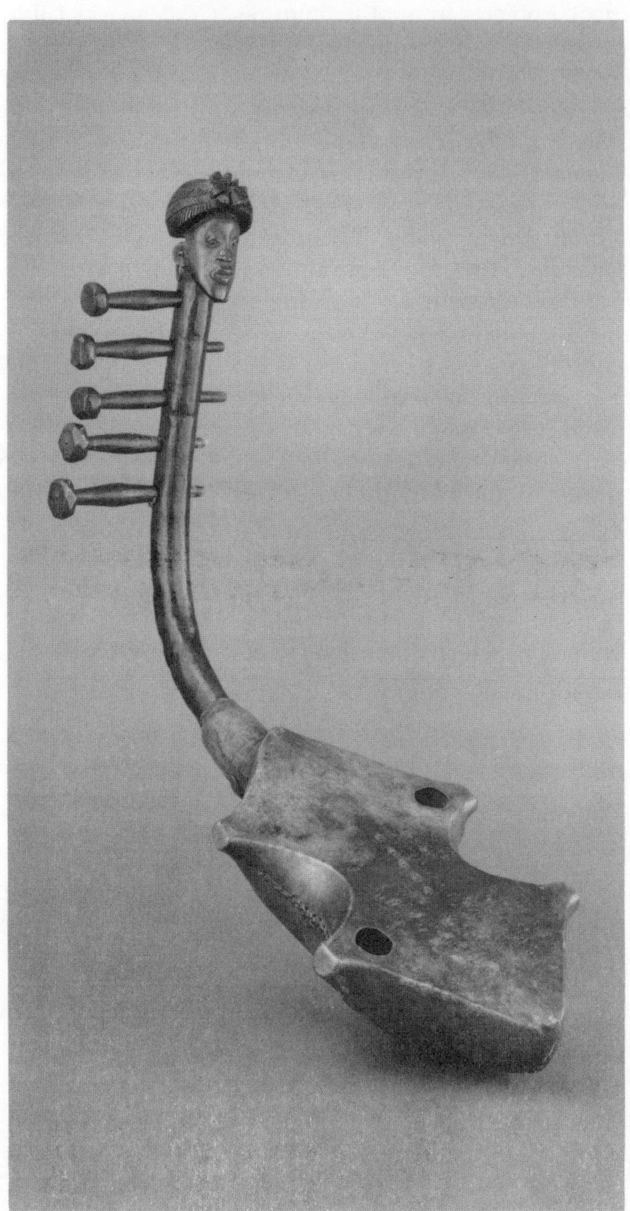

Zande harp

Photograph by Jeffrey Ploskonka
National Museum of African Art
Eliot Elisofon Archives
Smithsonian Institution

gagon the bird masquerade, literally 'masculine maskers' have wooden faces with beak-like features.

glewa the judgement masquerade, literally 'large maskers' or 'important maskers' often named *won pu·gle* literally 'judging maskers'.

Although it has never been explored fully, perhaps there are within these seemingly idiosyncratic and highly descriptive categories certain recurring mask types. Fire-extinguisher types occur in Dan masks and in Yoruba *efe/gelede*.

General functional categories such as 'initiation masks', 'funeral masks' or 'entertainment masks' must be assigned with caution, since masks may be used on different occasions and perform different functions. Moreover, our present very incomplete knowledge precludes our assigning only one of these terms to any mask.

While form categories such as 'face mask' or 'helmet mask' appear more reliable in that the form of a mask is known and unchanging, these terms too may be inadequate. As we have seen with the Dan mask categories. 'Dan face mask' applies to at least 11 distinct mask types.

Basketry as a class of museum objects present both simpler and more complex considerations. Simpler because basketry techniques (coiled, plaited, etc.), forms and uses (storage, transportation, winnowing, etc.) are universal. The complexity comes because technique, form and function are not consistently linked so as to distinguish distinct classes of baskets (Odak, 1988). Rather they are mixed and matched across ethnic group. Added into this mix are myriad indigenous names for particular baskets. These names may reflect form, function, technique or material.

Classifying African pottery into general categories such as 'ritual' or 'domestic' ignores the fact that these terms are *not* absolute and that an object (such as a pot or basket) may shift from one category to another. Such rigid classification completely overlooks 'how the makers and users of the object perceive and categorise them' (McLeod, 1984, page 365).

African art objects (unlike Western art objects) may also have gender designations which must be expressed as an intrinsic attribute (Figure 53.1). Masks, as we have seen, may be male or female. Akan female drums, for example, are distinct from other kinds of Akan drums and constitute a distinct class of objects. Berber tents clearly distinguish women's side of the tent from men's side of the tent, just as we distinguish living rooms from kitchens as architectural components. Yet the concept of 'woman's side of a tent' is not an easily translatable one, and it is certainly not the kind of term the AAT wants to deal with.

Iconography

The importance of iconographic terms for African material culture, particularly zoomorphic or anthropomorphic terms, can hardly be overstated. Although the AAT excludes iconographic terms, a case could be made that to fully catalogue African objects, one needs terms which reflect the 'subject/content' of the object, where the 'subject/content' defines a distinct class. Archetypes, such as 'male and female couple', 'the rider (equestrian)', 'mother and child' (Figure 53.2), or 'the stranger', are dominant and recurring in African art. A 'Dogon primorial couple', for example, is a distinct and recognisable class of sculptural objects, and the use of the word 'primordial' reflects the cosmological meaning of this object to the Dogon.

Figure 53.2

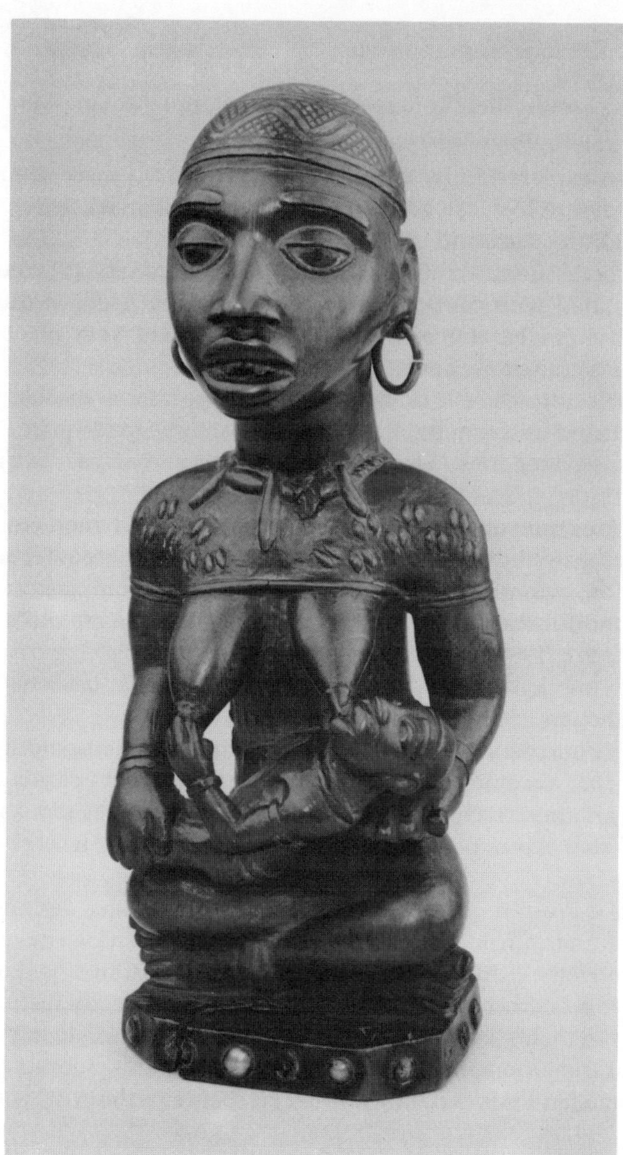

Mother and child, Yombe

Photograph by Jeffrey Ploskonka
National Museum of African Art
Eliot Elisofon Archives
Smithsonian Institution

Akan goldweights provide another excellent example of the vital importance of iconography in classifying certain objects. Roughly, goldweights might be classed as geometric or figurative. But this dual classification, while obvious and irrefutable, is not very helpful. For a museum collection with hundreds of goldweights, this hardly begins to sort them out. The multiplicity of forms depicted in goldweights is as broad as the Akan universe. Moreover, the dozens of recurring forms — e.g. a bird in a trap, two crocodiles with one body — are all associated with Akan symbolism and proverbs. An iconographic classification of goldweights has yet to be developed, although Garrard in his monumental study of Akan goldweights (1980, pages 195–210) discusses their form and symbolism at length. He has also codified their indigenous names based on their actual weight in grams (Garrard, 1980, inserted table). It is unlikely, however, that the AAT would ever incorporate such an indigenous iconographic schemata into its hierarchies. What the AAT can provide is the broader classification structure onto which we can hook these highly specialised classifications. It is left to individual museums, such as the National Museum of African Art, to develop and apply these specialised areas of classification.

IX
DISCIPLINE DEVELOPMENTS: SOCIAL HISTORY, DECORATIVE ART, MATERIAL CULTURE, SCIENCE AND TECHNOLOGY

54 DISCIPLINE DEVELOPMENTS IN SOCIAL HISTORY, DECORATIVE ART, MATERIAL CULTURE, SCIENCE AND TECHNOLOGY

Stuart Holm

Advice and Training Co-ordinator
Museum Documentation Association
Cambridge

A total of 16 papers from these related disciplines are incorporated in this section. This diversity reflects a growing level of awareness and concern over the need to control terminology more effectively in these areas. Despite all this activity, when the achievements to date are weighed against the scale of the problem, one can easily feel overwhelmed. If delegates attending this part of the conference were prone to such feelings in the isolation of their own museums, then the sharing of problems, ideas and above all achievements by the speakers should have done much to dispel this gloom. With a packed programme there was little time for formal discussion but the ideas put forward in these papers must have helped sustain many subsequent informal discussions in the conference bar and elsewhere.

A major problem is the enormous breadth of material which comes into the care of curators working within this loose grouping of diciplines. The grouping is a practical one, with many curators finding themselves responsible for material right across all these fields but, as Burnett suggests (Chapter 55), it is a vast territory incorporating 'all modern artefacts which do not fall into the highly specialist area of fine art'. Not surprisingly, some of the more successful of the projects described in the following chapters have succeeded because they were targeted at well defined subsets of this range of modern artefacts, such as scientific instruments (Chapter 57), lighting devices (Chapter 64), costume (Chapter 65) and architecture (Chapter 68). Most of those described here took some account of developments beyond their immediate boundaries, but some other projects on this scale do not. Whilst they successfully address short-term needs, they could be storing up future problems as the need grows for integrated systems which operate across all areas of modern history.

Broader based systems such as the *Art and Architecture Thesaurus* (AAT), the *Science and Technology Object Thesaurus* (STOT), *Nomenclature for Museum Cataloging* and the *Social History and Industrial Classification* (SHIC) (Chapters 56–59) can bring their own problems. They require massive investment of time and expertise, can be slow to develop to a useful level and need maintenance and ongoing development. Unless more outside investment is forthcoming, such as that provided for *AAT* by the Getty Art History Information Program, few such systems seem likely to emerge. Burnett (Chapter 55) suggests that during the nineteenth century in particular, major developments in terminology control occurred through the desire of industry and commerce to boost trade. As museums in many parts of the world begin, for better or for worse, to view their collections and associated data as a marketable resource, investment in developing tools which facilitate that 'trade' may seem more attractive.

Mention of terminology control outside the museum world raises another source of possible inspiration. Contemporary industry is developing new classifications and thesauri to handle an exponentially increasing mass of data about its products. Because we are dealing with modern artefacts, these tools may also serve at least some of the retrieval needs of the social history, industrial or decorative arts curator. This rich resource has already been tapped. For example, *STOT* (Chapter 57) is based on the British Standards Institution's *Root* thesaurus, parts of *SHIC* (Chapter 59) are closely based on the Central Statistical Office publication *Standard Industrial Classification* and *AAT* (Chapter 56) uses the *Medical Subject Headings* thesaurus as a structural model. Delroy (Chapter 70) wisely cautions against wasting time 'inventing yet another system'. If systems developed within the museum community do not fit the bill, the outside world may provide at least a partial answer without the need for re-inventing the wheel.

In view of the substantial investment involved in setting up terminology control systems, they need to be applicable to as wide a market as possible. The use of illustrations to clarify the scope of a term (Chapters 60, 61 and 67) has sometimes been introduced to help overcome differences in dialect, but could equally facilitate the crossing of national boundaries. Skilful use of this feature might increase the viability of a terminology control product by extending its potential market and also open up the possibilities for international databases accessible to those who do not speak one of the more dominant languages.

Several authors refer to the distinction between 'functional' and 'contextual' approaches to terminology control (e.g. Chapters 59, 69 and 70). Opinions may differ slightly, but the consensus appears to be that the traditional curator's 'functional' approach may not always match changing demands for information about museum collections. Rider (Chapter 69) points out that 'the number of visitors interested in a bottle . . . is far exceeded by those interested in drinking'. Delroy (Chapter 70) also points us towards 'the user point of view . . . examining what museums require rather than what the opposing principles offer'. He warns us that the needs of the public or the museum guide who interprets the exhibits should be given equal consideration to those of the specialist. Vanns (Chapter 59) reminds us that such diverging needs can be met by the use of complementary systems running in parallel.

Taken as a whole these papers give much food for thought. They describe achievements but also pose problems and question traditional values. Some problems may recede as improved computer techniques become available, but computers need to be fed the right information and terminology control will surely have an increasing role as museum data becomes accessible to a wider audience.

55

AN INTRODUCTION TO TERMINOLOGIES FOR DECORATIVE ART, SOCIAL HISTORY, AND THE HISTORY OF SCIENCE

John Burnett

Head of Documentation
National Museums of Scotland
Edinburgh

Introduction

It is impossible within the context of a short paper to discuss all of the terminologies which have been used, and are being developed, for the very wide range of material which can be loosely described under the headings of decorative art, social history, and the history of science and industry — in other words all modern artefacts which do not fall into the highly specialist area of Fine Art. Instead, I will make two approaches towards the subject. The first is to examine some of the detail of the history of subject retrieval in museums, and the second is to discuss some of the properties of existing theasuri with a view to clarifying the ways in which different solutions can be applied to different problems.

Historical discussion

The history of the establishment by institutions, rather than individuals, of collections for research and teaching begins in the late sixteenth century in the universities of Padua and Leiden (Schupbach, 1985).

Although there were collections at Oxford and Cambridge, the most important institutional cabinet of curiosities in seventeenth-century England was that of the Royal Society of London. One of the leaders of the Royal Society's research was John Wilkins (1614–72), the first Secretary of the Society. Wilkins crops up in many phases of mid-seventeenth-century life. He was successively head of an Oxford college and a Cambridge college — probably a unique achievement. Despite being Oliver Cromwell's brother-in-law, he was appointed Bishop of Chester after the restoration of King Charles II. The great spectacle of his age was the Great Fire of London, and the manuscript of one of his books was burnt in it.

The book in question was *An essay towards a real character and a philosophical language* (1668). It was an attempt to evolve an artificial language which would enable him to express philosophical thought (including what we would now call scientific ideas) more effectively. Its cultural background is interesting. The English Civil War took place during Wilkins's lifetime, and in it codes and ciphers were used extensively. Wilkins himself wrote a book about them. There was also a widespread European interest in the similar problems of producing an efficient shorthand. For many centuries Latin had functioned as a universal language in Europe, but Wilkins criticised it for being irregular, lexically redundant, and grammatically complex (Robins, 1979, pages 114–17). From this we can see that Wilkins's aims were at least partly practical. He was attempting to organise language so as to simplify communication.

Wilkins's new language was based on an analysis or classification of things and ideas which might be of interest to science. Of particular importance for the future was the classification of animals and plants with which he was helped by two other Fellows of the Royal Society, John Ray and Francis Willughby. They first produced a classification which was bound by Wilkins's requirement that for his practical purposes species should be grouped into nines (the arbitrary nature of, say, parts of the Dewey classification are echoes of the same difficulty). Then they developed more satisfactory classifications based on morphology. Stuart Piggot has argued that it was as a result of Ray and Willughby's demonstration of the effectiveness of classification in promoting understanding of the natural world that antiquaries started to classify artefacts (Piggot, 1976, pages 102, 118).

I will now move forwards 200 years, and look at some aspects of the Great International Expositions of the nineteenth century. It is quite clear that these events were intended to make money — either directly, by making a profit on their operation, or indirectly, by improving the prestige of a nation and establishing a better trading position for it. The individual exhibitors were normally firms who were anxiously seeking orders. The international exhibition is the precursor of the trade fair. With such a clear economic background, it was essential that information on the exhibits should be made available as effectively as possible.

On one occasion, at Paris in 1867, the exhibition itself was laid out on entirely rational principles. The arena was an oval. Segments of it were allocated to the various nations. Areas at an equal distance from the middle were allocated to particular subjects — raw materials, manufacturing, etc. The number of objects available to fill each space varied wildly, and the plan was not repeated (Allwood, 1977, pages 42–43).

No cataloguing or indexing system exists in itself: it exists in relation to some exterior purpose. Like language, they are instruments for thinking; just as the early Royal Society believed that languages could be created which made thinking clearer, catalogues and indexes can be built to make it easier to find information and objects. That was a nineteenth-century discovery.

Information about the objects on display in the international exhibition, was provided by published catalogues. These usually ran to several volumes, and were not only arranged in the administrative classes which had been set up by the exhibition organisers, but were also indexed. The historical importance of this indexing must be stressed.

In Britain at least, the national museums which were founded in the 1850s were consequences of the Great Exhibition of the Works of Industry of All Nations, held in 1851. Where the Great Exhibition had paid lip service to education, the museums were overtly educational. It was also overt that the museums were instruments of public instruction for the ultimate economic benefit of the state. It was perhaps because of this economic background that they had a good record in the nineteenth century of publishing catalogues which were well laid out and indexed.

A rather unusual case is the Special Loan Collection of Scientific Apparatus, which was assembled in London in 1876. It is without question the finest collection of material on the history of science which has ever been assembled in one place. I mention it here because parts of its classification of objects display some very modern traits (Great Britain. Science and Art Department, 1877). For example:

Measurement

Of length — Standard yard, metre, etc.
Comparator for standards of length (sight and touch)
Gauges, measuring wheels, steel tapes etc.

	Micrometers and verniers
	Cathetometers
Of area —	Planimeters etc.
Of volume —	Standard gallon, litre, etc.
	Pipettes, burettes
	Meters for gas, water, etc.
Of angles —	Divided circles, theodolites, clinometers, goniometers, etc.

The classification then analyses in a similar way the measurement of mass, density, time, velocity, momentum, force and work. This is very similar to the analysis of measurement provided by the British Standards Institution's *Root Thesaurus* (British Standard Institution, 1988). Its clarity derives from the use of concepts at higher levels of generality, rather than the names of types of object.

Closely related to the exhibition was the tradesman's showroom: in the nineteenth century, shops became exhibitions in themselves. Vendors were anxious to provide information about their wares, and their catalogues were often sophisticated devices for doing this. In 1874, the scientific instrument maker, Luigi Pasquale Casella of London, produced a catalogue with a good index, in which we find:

Barometer,	Agricultural	157
	Marine	136 to 140
	Miners'	146 and 147
	Standard	1 to 15

As in the case of Negretti and Zambra, Casella has presented his catalogue with the instruments for each market collected together. His index gives access through the types of object. It should be noted that book indexes of any kind are very rare before the first half of the eighteenth century (Knight, 1979, page 18), and only become common in the second half of the nineteenth century.

What we can see in Casella's catalogue is a recognition of the need to provide subject access by more than one route, a recognition that different users have different information needs.

The modern idea of a hierarchical information retrieval thesaurus dates from the late 1940s, a product of the continuing growth of documentation in science and technology. The early work in developing the concept of a thesaurus, and in implementing them in practice, was mostly done in manufacturing industry and engineering (Roberts, N., 1984).

Throughout this historical discussion, I have emphasised the importance of economic pressures in generating new methods of effective subject retrieval. One conclusion to be drawn from this is that we should look closely at modern methods of subject retrieval which are being developed in areas where the economic imperative is rather more evident than it is in museums: for example, indexing and abstracting services such as *Engineering Index* and *Physics Abstracts*. My other conclusion is that systems became effective for retrieval when retrieval became their specific goal, rather than the much looser aim of organising things or ideas.

Classification: Pragmatic and theoretical

One of the founders of ethnology, and of the eponymous museum in Oxford, was the English General Augustus Pitt Rivers. Before his collections were first exhibited to the public in 1874 as part of the Bethnal Green Museum, he drafted a system for classifying objects. The aim of his classification was '. . . to trace the succession of ideas. This is the distinctive difference between my collection and most others which I have seen, in which the primary arrangement has been geographical . . . both systems have their advantages and disadvantages'. He argued that a museum should use both, and went on: 'Human ideas as represented by the various products of human history are capable of classification into genera, species, and varieties, in the same manner as the products of the vegetable and animal kingdoms, and in their development from the homogeneous to the heterogeneous they obey the same laws' (Lane Fox, 1874).

Pitt Rivers is here making two important points. Firstly, he is arguing for more than one route of access to each object. Secondly, he proposes that ideas should be placed in a hierarchy, with the objects subordinate to ideas. This is the method, already mentioned, which was used in the Special Loan Collection of Scientific Apparatus only two years later. It can be contrasted with the method of seeking general terms for groups of objects, which had previously been the usual way of arranging artefacts. Pitt Rivers was working from the more general to the more specific, from the top down, as against the traditional method of working from the bottom up.

The manifestation of Pitt Rivers's ideas in his museum, however, looks curious to modern eyes. His own theory was not applied completely. The first seven headings in the classification are these:

Agriculture and horticulture
Amulets and charms
Animalia
Animals — domestic
Arctic exploration
Bags and pouches
Barkcloth
(Blackwood, 1970, pages 27–28)

The modern purist will react to this with criticisms, such as: there is a confusion between concepts ('Arctic exploration') and things ('Bags and pouches'); one category ('Animals — domestic') should be subordinate to another ('Animalia') rather than having an equal status; and the categories do not appear to be mutually exclusive. Consider another example:

Metallurgy
  Apparatus
    Anvils
    Bellows
    Fuel
    Lamps, miners'
  Cire perdu process
  Goldsmiths' tools
  Metal objects, specimens of
(Blackwood, 1970, pages 45–46)

The purist will again note categories ('Apparatus' and 'Goldsmiths' tools') which are not mutually exclusive; in addition, there is no single quality of metallurgy which accounts for its subdivision, and two of the subdivisons of Apparatus ('Fuel', and 'Lamps, miners') are not genuinely metallurgical apparatus.

I have commented in some detail on the Pitt Rivers classification because, despite its apparent shortcomings, it has worked in the Pitt Rivers Museum for many years. It illustrates the importance of a pragmatic component in any institution's thinking about subject retrieval. (Details of its current application are given in Chapter 39.)

The properties of thesauri

The ideas lying behind the construction of classifications and thesauri are, to this author at least, by no means straightforward. Sir Arthur Eddington, the great Cambridge cosmologist, is reputed to have begun an ostensibly popular wireless broadcast on the theory of relativity with the words, 'Consider a four-dimensional billiards table . . . . Discussion of the theory of subject retrieval makes me feel that I am listening to a similar broadcast.

In an attempt to clarify the issues involved in subject retrieval, I will discuss a number of properties of different methods of retrieval. This is not, as I have indicated in the discussion of the Pitt Rivers classification, an area in which it is possible to think of right and wrong: it is more appropriate to think of different solutions being more or less applicable in different situations.

Emphasising objects or ideas

Thesauri and classifications which provide subject access to documents normally consist almost entirely of concepts. A thesaurus of objects inevitably has the names of many types of objects in it. Thesauri for objects vary in the proportion of concepts which they contain, and in addition they vary in the approach which was used to establish the structure of their hierarchies. Some thesaurus builders start from the most general terms and work down to the most specific ones: these are usually concept-based thesauri. If the constructor begins at the most specific level and works from the bottom up, seeking broader and broader groupings, then the thesaurus is object-based.

The ICOM costume classification (Chapter 61) is an example of the object-based approach. It standardises the recording of types of garment without considering their function: its aim is to simplify the vast range of clothes which have been devised by examining first, the part of the body they covered, and second their morphology. SHIC (Chapter 59), in contrast, is idea-based. For example (SHIC Working Party, 1983):

Domestic and family life
  Hobbies, crafts and pastimes
    Music
      Played instruments
        Bagpipes
          Brass
            . . .
      Mechanical
            . . .

In general, idea-based classifications are more likely to be successful, though the ICOM costume classification is a notable exception. In an idea-based thesaurus, the clear organisation of general concepts makes it easier to establish the correct position for each term in the structure. This may be particularly important when after some time it becomes necessary to add new terms. Idea-based structures tend to be more flexible. This results in them being more likely to be of use to a range of institutions with varying collections and not entirely similar aims. An object-based thesaurus is more likely to be able to serve only the institution by which it was generated.

Pre-coordination or post-coordination

Many object names embody more than one idea, indeed it is often the conjunction of the ideas which defines the object. A carpenter's rule is both an instrument for measuring length and a tool used by a carpenter. In a pre-coordinated index the terms often express compound concepts such as the carpenter's rule. In a post-coordinate system, the terms are reduced until each one expresses only one concept — such as woodworking and measurement of length. The indexer and the user who seeks to retrieve items then have to perform in their minds the same analysis of complex concepts into simple ones. Automation, which makes Boolean searching much easier that it can reasonably be in a large manual system, has increased the importance of post-coordination.

Linked to the issue of pre- and post-coordination is the question of the number of routes that are needed into an object. For no theoretical reason, classifications tend to be applied in such a way that each object has only one place. In outlining the scope of the *Nomenclature* system, Chenhall is explicit about this. He believes that a single 'original function' can be assigned to every object (Chenhall, 1978, page 8), though he admits that some objects, such as a tray bearing a Coca-Cola advert, may have duplicate functions. This is to introduce the curator as a major factor in determining the way in which the indexing language will be used. Less constricting is the open admission of SHIC that one object may have to be indexed under several headings.

In considering the number of indexing terms which can be assigned to each item, a distinction has to be made between the number of terms which can be assigned, and the number of different factors which have been used in defining the indexing vocabulary. Both *Nomenclature* and SHIC are based on single factors: *Nomenclature* on original function and SHIC on social context. *Nomenclature*, however, allows only a single object name, whereas SHIC permits several classifications to be used. With complex objects there are manifest advantages in being able to provide several routes of subject access. A polyterpic table can be treated as a table, as a games table (backgammon, cribbage, etc.), as a zograscope and as a camera obscura. Rather than thinking 'What is interesting about this object', it may be more helpful to ask instead 'What sorts of people are likely to be interested in it?'. In the case of the polyterpic table the answer may include furniture historians, social historians, art historians and historians of science.

Hierarchical or flat

The concept of hierarchy is implicit in the idea of a thesaurus, but there are circumstances in which a list of terms with no structure may be the best way to control a vocabulary. An authority list of terms for acquisition method is an obvious example.

The *Hertfordshire name list* is an unstructured list of terms for subject retrieval (Hertfordshire Curator's Group, 1984). It contains about 2 000 preferred terms, and one of its notable virtues is its large number of non-preferred terms — 'a rich lead-in vocabulary'. Whilst such a list may be a useful starting point for developing a thesaurus, it is doubtful whether it can actually be said to provide subject access.

Nomenclature (Chapter 58) has a fixed hierarchical structure with three levels; object names occur only at the lowest level. One result is the two more general levels do not allow room to subdivide complex subjects, and therefore a large number of object names can be grouped together. For example, 'Electrical and Magnetic Tools and Equipment' contains 51 object names; various of them might be regarded as measuring instruments ('Ammeter', Galvanometer', 'Fluxmeter'), as components ('Resistor',. Capacitor') or pieces of apparatus ('Oscilloscope'); and there are some object names which could be treated as subordinates of others, such as 'Thermoammeter' and 'Ammeter'. These properties of *Nomenclature* make it inappropriate for large museums. If, however, it is regarded as a list of headings from which a smaller general museum can extract object names and fit them into a framework, then its clarity outweighs many disadvantages.

An interesting variant on *Nomenclature*'s structure is illustrated by the *Zoological Record*. It has two levels of defined categories, and a lowest level which is a short free-text phrase. In a museum record, that phrase might be a short description of the object.

The best example of a hierarchical thesaurus for artefacts is the *Art and Architecture Thesaurus* (Chapter 56). This admirable work follows the most modern thinking about thesaurus construction — one of the few artefact terminology projects which does so. In particular, the principles on which it is built relate closely to the International Standard on thesaurus construction (International Organization for Standardization, 1986).

Internal or general

Lenore Sarasan has recently made the challenging observation that 'ours is not a standards-oriented community' (Sarasan, 1988). Most museums find it difficult to standardise their own internal terminologies, without any thought of having standards which are common with other institutions. However, as it becomes more and more clearly perceived that museum documentation is an extremely time-consuming activity, museums are realising that if someone else has created an adequate classification system for a subject area, they may well be best to adopt it. One of the strengths of SHIC is that it was based in part on the British Government's Central Statistical Office *Standard Industrial Classification* (Great Britain. Central Statistical Office, 1981). Not only did the *Standard Industrial Classification* provide the starting point for SHIC, by giving a professional analysis, but it was far more than a starting point. Unfortunately such helpful classifications do not exist for most subject areas. When the Science Museum (London) began to analyse the problem of subject retrieval for the Wellcome Collection of historical medical artefacts, the obvious place to begin was the MeSH thesaurus used by *Medline*, the vast bibliographical database. It proved to treat hardware cursorily, and to contain no obvious slots into which historical names could be placed.

Now that there is an established concern over terminology, there will be more lists of terms available, and inevitably *ad hoc* standards will arise. In Britain, SHIC is already used by many museums, and it is predictable that the *Art and Architecture Thesaurus* will become very important in its own area. These two publications differ in one vital respect. If a standard is to be maintained there must be a mechanism for maintenance — a responsible authority or committee. The working party which produced SHIC became passive after it had produced its classification, and if a means of updating SHIC is not found it will become outdated. As more time passes it will become less and less useful. AAT, however, has a staff which should be able to develop it and maintain it, thus strengthening its position as a standard.

It is also possible to refer to outside authorities as a method of standardisation. The *Hertfordshire name list* tries to accept the definitions of the *Shorter Oxford Dictionary*, and the National Museums of Scotland uses for parts of its collections *The Concise Scots Dictionary*.

Controlled or open-ended

It is essential that a museum subject retrieval system should allow for change and in particular for expansion. *Nomenclature*, for example, is fixed at its two higher levels, but allows the creation of new object names. SHIC includes rules for adding terms at its lower levels, and below them.

If a general standard is to be maintained, it either has to be something which can only be altered by some accepted mechanism, or something which contains a fixed core, plus peripheral parts which can be created or altered by users.

Historical purity

Documentation is in general a pragmatic activity, but this begs the question of how pragmatic one should be in constructing a thesaurus. The practical approach is taken by the *Hertfordshire List*: 'In many cases no arbiter exists to determine the 'correct' name of an object, and the main consideration has simply been to ensure that we all use the same name for it.' (Hertfordshire Curators' Group, 1984, page 2.) However, it is possible to take pragmatism too far. I once drafted a thesaurus and applied it to a group of objects. A colleague examined it for a long time, then said 'The sugar is in the jar marked salt'. The terminology in the thesaurus had so far simplified the complex area of medical history which it was attempting to handle, that it bore little relation to the reality it was supposed to handle. There is little point in creating a secret language which is intelligible only after the user has been trained in its eccentricities. Yet it is impossible to devise a terminology which is completely sensitive to the vagaries of historical usage. Each case has to be decided on its merits. A further discussion is given in Chapter 57.

Manual system or one involving software

We must distinguish between the creation of standard terminologies and the application of those terminologies to real data. The amount of labour involved in the second of these activities should not be underestimated, particularly in a system which allows more than one subject term to be assigned to each record. It is unlikely that a museum whose collections number more than a few thousand items and whose records are held in manual form, could find the labour to support the assignment of thesaurus terms to all of its catalogue records and the creation of a card-based subject index. Such a museum would certainly save time if it were to use database software, so the question of a manual index based on a thesaurus will not be considered further here.

Online subject retrieval requires the searcher to have a greater range of skills than is required for manual retrieval. It should be borne in mind that in many libraries the searching of large databases is carried out by the libraries on behalf of the enquirer, so that the enquirer is isolated from these skills. So few museums have given their curators online access to large databases describing their collections that it is difficult to know how great the problems will be in the museum context.

Method of construction

The method of thesaurus construction which is generally recommended in the library community is to study the way in which terminology is deployed in a body of literature, and to extract terms from it. Subsequently a structure can be built up from an understanding of the subject matter and through dialogue with specialists.

There now follows a warning based on personal experience. If a museum is building up a retrospective database it can either create a classification system before it starts, or after it has finished. When working on the documentation of the Wellcome Collection (1978–84), the following situation arose. New catalogue cards were being written for the entire collection, in the knowledge that data capture would only begin when most of the records had been written. After about 10 000 records (about 10 per cent of the final total) had been generated, I began to prepare a hierarchical thesaurus. This was a waste of time for a number of reasons.

The boundaries of the subject that had to be covered were not certain. I had no knowledge of the thesaurus software which the Museum was one day going to buy. Since there was no subject access to the catalogue cards (the computer was going to do that — later), there was no way of looking at related records with a view to refining their indexing. As my ideas evolved, it was not possible to find catalogue records which had already been examined once, with a view to altering the terms assigned to them. I could not test the effectiveness of the approach I had adopted until the data was available online. I can only plead youthful enthusiasm. There is little doubt that the best approach is to build the thesaurus after the data has been input.

The management of thesaurus production

The construction of a thesaurus is a time-consuming process. We must not only be aware of the need for a practical attitude in creating an instrument for retrieval which actually works in practice. We must also be aware that too much detail, or an over-scrupulous care over detail, will increase the work content in the preparation of the thesaurus to the point where the thesaurus is never finished. A statement made by Mary Piggott, one of the clearest of modern thinkers on cataloguing in libraries, is relevant here: it is necessary 'to accept cataloguing as a practical means to an end and not an end in itself, just as one takes the London Underground from Waterloo Station to Piccadilly without first studying transport engineering — but not without first taking a look at the map of the Underground system' (Piggott, 1988, pages 139–40). The same is true of thesaurus construction.

I will end with a gloomy thought. We have no methods for costing the construction of classifications or thesauri. We have no agreed methods for assessing their effectiveness. Given that we are contemplating projects which will take years of the time of highly skilled staff to bring them to fruition, are we really being professional about this?

56 CONSTRUCTING A LANGUAGE OF THE ARTS: THE ART AND ARCHITECTURE THESAURUS

Toni Petersen

Director
Art and Architecture Thesaurus
Williamstown, Mass.

Introduction

When the idea for the Art and Architecture Thesaurus (AAT) was first proposed in 1979, the representatives of almost all the known automated indexing projects in the field of art history could be assembled in one room. An actual meeting took place at that time, called by Dora Crouch, an architectural historian, and Pat Molholt, a librarian, from Rensselaer Polytechnic Institute in Troy, New York. At that meeting an overriding need for a controlled vocabulary was seen as the first objective toward solving the problems of automating art history information. This turned out to be a relatively radical conclusion, for none of the three of us sent away to investigate the problem (the two named above and myself) could have foreseen the difficulties, time and cost that would be involved.

The target was a controlled vocabulary for the consistent representation of information about subjects, by making decisions as to which are the preferred ways of referring to concepts, bringing together synonyms of the preferred terms, by noting other relationships such as broader and narrower terms, and by distinguishing among homographs. The call for such a vocabulary came not from the scholarly community of art history, but from the producers of art history databases, some of whom, coincidentally, were also scholars. The purpose of such a vocabulary was to lighten the burden of indexers and cataloguers and to bring about the most comprehensive retrieval of information possible on a particular topic, by linking together terms whose meaning is related.

In the course of constructing the AAT, other aspects of the purposes of a controlled vocabulary began to be revealed. Information scientists acknowledge the shift in the last decade from information retrieval by trained intermediaries using rigidly controlled language, to the natural language processing of documents and user queries, mapping those queries through a semantic network — a network which depends upon the linguistic organisation of knowledge in a particular domain, in other words, a well-structured thesaurus. I will be describing the development of the AAT, and some of the techniques we chose to construct a controlled vocabulary in the 1980s that will serve the needs of the new information retrieval systems of future decades.

There are two kinds of controlled vocabularies: those generated within an organisation, which I will call internal, and those generated outside the user's organisation, or external. The internal vocabulary, for instance, the subject headings of an abstracting and indexing service like *RILA (International Repertory of the Literature of Art)* may be controlled — that is, there may be policy directed toward consistency in the building of the vocabulary — but it will probably not be standardised. What makes a controlled vocabulary also a standard is that it is shared by a community of users who agree to maintain it in a way that is satisfactory to all.

An external vocabulary is independent of any particular indexing or cataloguing project, and must provide for a wide range of environments. Its independence is important, for it must do more than reflect the indexing policies and vocabulary needs of any single user. Art history databases run the gamut of book and periodical indexes, image collections such as photographs, slides and drawings, and museum object catalogues. Building a vocabulary that would fill the needs of such different indexing systems required drawing up an agenda to gain the support of these constituencies. From the beginning, the AAT set its sights on becoming the standardised vocabulary for these varied constituencies. Based on our perception that there was a need for a comprehensive, standardised vocabulary in the field of art and architecture, we envisioned the AAT as a hinge that would bring together terms for the description of objects, images of them, and literature about them.

Elements in a standardised vocabulary

We identified some basic factors characterising the elements of the standardised vocabulary we wished to build:

it would be constructed using standard thesaural conventions, such as those outlined in the American National Standards Institute's *Guidelines for thesaurus structure, construction and use* (1980);

it draws on terminology that is current, that is warranted by use in standard literary sources, and that is validated by the scholarly community. If possible, it incorporates already existing authority lists that may be enhanced or modified;

it is responsible to its constituency, and takes cognizance of the needs of that constituency in the depth and scope of its presentation;

the data comprising the thesaurus must be available in machine-readable forms lending themselves to a variety of automated systems, including relational databases;

the necessary financial commitment must be available, not only to build the original vocabulary, but to maintain it over the long term;

there must be commitment among the user group and the maintaining organisation that the vocabulary will not be changed arbitrarily. Although change is inevitable, it should be planned for and promulgated with the agreement of the user community.

The AAT: hierarchy development

The AAT and its staff of 12 is situated in Williamstown, Massachusetts. Begun as a federally funded grant project, it has been since 1983 an operating unit of the Getty Art History Information Program. Eventually, when the Getty Art Center in Los Angeles is completed sometime in the mid-1990s, the AAT will, with all the other Getty entities, move into it.

The construction of the thesaurus has proceeded in a series of phases since its first development grant was awarded in 1980. The first phase, after a period of research into thesaurus construction methods and a search for existing terminology lists in the field, concentrated on the construction of a set of architectural terminology.

This first phase also incorporated the conceptualisation of a structure for the entire thesaurus that would cover all aspects of terminology in the fields of art and architecture. We first examined published thesauri available at the time and we became convinced that the most desirable model was the Medical Subject Headings Thesaurus (MeSH) 'igure 6.1 Art and Architecture Thesaurus facets and hierarchies

APPENDIX A.

Projected *AAT* Hierarchies

AAT Facets and Hierarchies

ASSOCIATED CONCEPTS FACET
- Associated Concepts

PHYSICAL ATTRIBUTES FACET
- Design Attributes
- Design Elements
- Colors

STYLES AND PERIODS FACET
- Styles and Periods

AGENTS FACET
- People and Organizations

ACTIVITIES FACET
- Disciplines
- Functions
- Events
- Processes and Techniques

MATERIALS FACET
- Materials

OBJECTS FACET

Built Environment
- Settlements, Systems and Landscapes
- Built Complexes and Districts
- Single Built Works and Open Spaces
- Building Divisions and Site Elements
- Built Works Components

Furnishings and Equipment
- Tools and Equipment
- Measuring Devices
- Hardware and Joints
- Furniture
- Furnishings
- Personal Artifacts
- Containers
- Culinary Artifacts
- Musical Instruments
- Recreational Artifacts
- Armament
- Transportation Artifacts
- Communication Artifacts

Visual and Verbal Communication
- Image and Object Genres
- Drawings
- Paintings
- Prints
- Photographs
- Sculpture
- Multi-Media Art Forms
- Communication Design
- Exchange Media
- Book Arts
- Document Types

developed by the National Library of Medicine (1988) for the indexing of medical literature. The well-articulated hierarchical, or 'tree', structures in MeSH give access to arrays of terms conceptually arranged to display genus-species relationships. By proceeding up or down the branches of the hierarchy, both indexer and researcher have immediate access to siblings of a particular term, and to all broader and narrower terms within that same family. In practice, the AAT trees contain many more levels of indention than MeSH trees, owing to the fact that MeSH is restricted to seven levels, and the AAT has much deeper levels of specificity, sometimes reaching as many as 16 or 17.

Once settled on the necessity to build tree-like hierarchies, it was an obvious next step to name the different trees that would be required to hold the various categories of information in the AAT. Naming the trees led to placing them in a particular order, which more or less began with the most abstract concepts and proceeded to concrete, finished names of object types (Figure 56.1).

This task of classifying the hierarchies was our first painful excursion into the representation of the knowledge domain of art history. Classification of AAT terms is on two levels: the representation of concepts on the term level, and the organisation of the thesaurus at the classification, or facet, level. One of the major premises used in building the AAT vocabulary, touched upon earlier, was that we would gather terms from existing subject lists, merging and arranging them into hierarchies. What sounded simple was actually very complex. At the term level, we found that the major lists we had assembled presented concepts in different ways. Only rarely did they provide single concepts in prescribed thesaurus fashion. Most often they combined concepts into pre-coordinated headings configured in several different ways. One would give a complex term in natural language order, like 'Wooden floors'. Another would provide this same concept in inverted order, 'Floors, Wood', or use cryptic faceting codes, like 'Floors: Wood: Firehouses'.

The problem of whether to keep these combinations of terms, known as pre-coordinated terms, or to separate them into single concepts, became, and has remained, one of the more difficult issues that we have faced. We had, for example, identified a hierarchy called 'Materials' and another called 'Built Works Components'. Would we list in the first all the materials used in the construction of architecture, like 'Stone', and also enumerate all occurrences of that material in combination with terms in the Built Works Components hierarchy, like 'Stone walls', 'Stone arches', 'Stone vaults', and so on? We made what seemed like a radical decision at the time, but one which reflects the fact that the AAT is heavily used in automated indexing catalogues and indexing projects. We would 'decombine' all such complex terms into single concepts, following the rules of most thesaurus construction manuals, and allowing for more effective automated combinations of single concepts. This does not mean that there are no multiword terms in the AAT. The key was the developing of guidelines for what constituted unbreakable, single concepts.

The next step was to decide how to organise these decombined terms. The AAT is composed, on the one hand, of terms for abstract concepts related to art, like 'Harmony', 'Renaissance', 'Circular' and 'Printmaking', which are not necessarily in noun form, and on the other, very concrete names of object types like 'Arches', 'Bungalows' and 'Architectural drawings', which are in noun form. Developing hierarchies of genus-species relationships in the latter case, where real objects are concerned, is relatively simple. The problem becomes more difficult when developing hierarchies for more abstract terminology. In the 'object type' hierarchies, we are able to follow similar

Figure 56.2 Example of a hierarchy

```
                                          Jul 6, 1988 - 10:43:01    Page 1
                               Drawings (DW)
1  Drawings *SLB
2    <drawings by method of representation>
3      Composite drawings *S
3      Cutaway drawings *S /Cutaways *S
3      <drawings by method of projection>
4        Orthographic drawings *S /Orthogonal drawings *S /Orthogonal projections *S /Orthographic projections *S
5          Plans *S /Plan diagrams *S /Plan drawings *S
6            <area plans>
7              City plans *S /Town plans *S
7              Site plans *S /Layout drawings *S /Local plans *S /Location plans *S /Plot plans *S
                         /Regional plans *S /Site layouts *S /Vicinity plans *S
8                Block plans *S
8                Grading plans *S
8                Landscaping plans *S
9                  Planting plans *S /Planting diagrams *S
7              Traces (Area plans) *S
6            <building plans>
7              Floor plans *SL
8                Ground plans *S /Ground plots *S
8                Typical floor plans *S
7              Foundation plans *S /Masonry plans *S
7              Framing plans *S
7              Piling plans *S
7              Reflected ceiling plans *S /Reflected plans *S
7              Utility plans *S
8                Electrical plans *S
8                HVAC plans *S /Heating and cooling plans *S
                         /Heating, ventilating and air conditioning plans *S
9                  Heating plans *S
8                Plumbing plans *S
6            Ichnographic plans *S /Ichnographies *S
6            Key plans *S
6            Master plans *S
6            Partial plans *S
7              Half plans *S
5          Elevations *SB /Elevation drawings *S /Orthographs *S
6            Exterior elevations *S /External elevations *S
6            Interior elevations *S /Internal elevations *S
6            Laid-out elevations *S

                                          Sample Figure 2
```

arrangements of sub-groupings under categories like 'by form', 'by function', and 'by location or context'.

Each term is examined for its primary characteristic. For example, we recently received the suggestion for the term 'Lathhouses', which is a structure used in landscaping, made of strips of lathing. It could be categorised by function, but in this case it would be too limiting a placement, for it would then only indicate a type of greenhouse. We chose to classify it by form, acknowledging that the material used in its construction gives it a particular form. Lathhouses now may be used for any number of functions. Abstract terms are classified with much more difficulty. These hierarchies tend to be more shallow than the object type hierarchies, where we routinely develop ten or more levels of indention. In the Abstract Concepts hierarchy, for example, the major section 'Formal concepts in art', contains just one level of indention, with a list of terms under it like 'Harmony'. (See Figure 56.2 for a sample hierarchy listing.)

Of course, organising terms into hierarchies limits their classification to broader and narrower terms, synonyms and variant spelling lead-in terms. Building a network of related terms, the next step in this process, takes on additional significance, especially for the representation of domains of knowledge, for the choices of relationships become significant elements in presenting the collective experience in a particular subject field. In a sense, one builds alternate hierarchies from the paths made by related terms. For example, in the Built Works hierarchy, all single architectural structures are classified within their genus-species relationships: 'Chapel' is a type of 'Church', as is a 'Cathedral'. The architectural elements making up the parts of these structures reside in a different hierarchy, Built Works Components. But through related term references, one may be able to construct the parts of the whole. 'Pews' and 'Pulpits' will point to 'Chapels' and 'Churches' and other religious structures. We have just begun to build this particular feature into the AAT, feeling that we needed a large body of terminology in place before we could develop these relational paths.

The AAT: facet classification

The decisions to develop a classified system of facets ushered in the second phase of development, which has occupied us for the last three or four years. The latter, developing the AAT facets, is the second level of term organisation referred to earlier, and has had the most far-reaching implications for the future of artificial intelligence applications in natural language processing . For us as we began this task, however, it simply meant trying to make some order out of disorder.

The first job was to define the facets which emerged from the rather loose early categorisation of hierarchy names. Following classification theory, facets became the broadest categories by which to organise art and architecture terminology as fields of knowledge. We define facets as mutually exclusive categories in which to collect terms that share common characteristics.

Faceting circumvents the repetitiveness of having to enumerate all combinations of terms into more complex concepts. Facets also provide the context in which terms are to be used, and can lead to semantic parsing of the language of a field. An example can be found around a succession of terms relating to different aspects of the activity of drawing. Membership in different facets is based on the type of term used. 'Drawing' is the activity itself, and is in the Activities facet; 'Drawings' and all types of drawings, are in the Objects facet; drawing materials, like 'Paper' and 'Ink' are in the Materials facet; 'Pencils', instruments with which to draw, are also objects in the Objects facet, but a style of drawing will be in the Styles and Periods facet, and the persons executing the drawing, like 'Draftsmen' will be in the Agents facet. We began to think of facets as ways of providing building blocks to reconstruct complex concepts when desired — to bring back 'Stone walls' when needed in a particular indexing situation.

The AAT: review and distribution plans

The remainder of the second phase, which is now ending, saw us completing those sets of terms in the first six facets that are necessary adjuncts to the description of object types in the seventh facet. Here again, the AAT has evolved a working method that is different from other thesauri. As each hierarchy is drafted, a scholarly review team is assembled. The purpose in doing this is twofold: we want to be certain that we have chosen the proper terms as used currently in the field by working scholars which will validate our work for the end user community. We also expect the review team to evaluate the structure of each hierarchy, since it should mirror the way each area within art history structures itself. These review teams have added immeasurably to the richness and completeness of the hierarchies by their active conceptualisation of the hierarchy branches and trees, and by their insistence on a measure of comprehensiveness to the terminology in each hierarchy.

Eighteen of the projected 36 hierarchies have been completed, and work has been started on the remaining two object type sections yet to be developed: Visual and Verbal Communication, and Furnishings and Equipment. The 18 completed hierarchies form a package ready to be published that, while missing these two areas, provides a comprehensive vocabulary for those who are indexing or cataloguing architectural information. Three volumes are projected for publication that will contain terminology for architecture, descriptive (or modifying) terms, and terms that name the forms of materials: Document Types, Drawings, Visual Genre, and Photographs.

Distribution of these sections of the AAT in machine-readable formats will occur in tandem with the published volumes. Direct-dial access into the AAT database in Williamstown may also be possible. In addition, we are arranging for the AAT to be mounted on a number of available networks, such as the Research Libraries Information Network (RLIN), and perhaps DIALOG, and we will be working out agreements with software vendors, allowing them to provide the AAT as a mounted authority file in their systems.

AAT user community

Almost from the beginning, we have been all too aware that the world could not wait until 1988 or 1990 or 1993 before it had those portions of the AAT it needed. The AAT, or vocabularies like it, are critically needed for automation projects, and in the field of art, automation of collections and the building of art information databases have been escalating exponentially since that first meeting of art database producers almost a decade ago. We have taken it as our mandate not to withhold the AAT from those projects that have expressed a clear need for it. Thus, a growing group of AAT users has developed, providing reciprocal benefits on both sides. In exchange for periodically receiving draft printouts of newly completed hierarchies, those who enter into this user relationship have been sending us valuable feedback on how the vocabulary is being used and where problems in its use arise. They also are encouraged to send us new candidate terms for inclusion in the hierarchies, and these candidate terms quickly go through the normal AAT editorial process and are incorporated. We then publish periodic updates that list all new terms and changes to old terms in the distributed hierarchies. This process is the beginning of the long-term maintenance system to which we are committed.

There is a wide diversity in those projects currently using the AAT. They undoubtedly mirror the types of institutions comprising the eventual AAT user community. They also mirror the fact that since we have as yet little terminology available for some areas within art history,the first users of the AAT tend to be those that are handling architectural and archival information. Periodical indexes like the *Avery Index to Architectural Periodical,* and projects for the cataloguing of architectural drawings, like AVIADOR at the Avery Library of Columbia University (Figure 56.3) and the Foundation for Documents of Architecture project at the National Gallery of Art in Washington, are representative early users. Archives and other collections handling documents and records are also interested in the AAT. There is an especially strong contingent of slide and visual material collections that have begun to use it.

Such standardisation as the AAT is attempting to provide does not come cheaply. One can imagine the resources required to establish a staff of 12 and a work schedule that is in

Figure 56.3 Sample record from the AVIADOR project, in the RLIN system

```
ID:NYDA87-F95         RTYP:c      ST:s    FRN:        MS:         EL:          AD:03-06-87
CC:9554  BLT:km       DCF:a     CSC:d     MOD:        SNR:        ATC:         UD:03-06-87
CPR:xx      L:eng               INT:?                 TEQ:?     TYPE:k        MEI:1
PC:q        PD:1943/1953        RUN:???               GPC:?                   ACMP:?????
MMD:        OR:      POL:      DM:       RR:          COL:        EML:         GEN:   BSE:
COM:g  FMD:    OR:    CL:    PRS:    SEP:    MDS:    WD:    SSP:
COM:k  FMD:    OR:    CL:    PRS:    SSN:
COM:m  FMD:    OR:    CL:     PR:    SEP:    MDS:    WD:    KS:   ARV:
COM:v  FMD:    OR:    CL:     VF:    SEP:    MDS:    WD:    KS:
RMD:   OR:   SPD:   SND:   GRV:   DIM:   WID:   TC:   KD:   KM:   KC:    RC:
COM:a    SMD:     OR:    CLR:   MPHY:          TREP:         PRD:          PL:
COM:d    SMD:     OR:    CLR:   MPHY:          TREP:
040      NNC$cNNC$egihc
043      n-us-az$an-us-nv
100 1    Ferriss, Hugh,$d1889-
240 10   Hoover Dam (Ariz. and Nev.)
245 10   Crest of Boulder.$h[graphic]
260      $cSep 14.
300      1 drawing :$bcharcoal on tracing paper on board ;$c50.8 x 38.0 cm. (2
       0 x 15 in.)30.7 x 23.3 cm. (12 1/8 x 9 1/8 in.)
500      Preliminary for "Hoover Dam, Arizona-Nevada Line" #49, Power in build
       ings/by Hugh Ferriss, 1953.
650  7   Architectural drawings$xAmerican.$2aat
655  7   Perspective drawings.$2aat
655  7   One-point perspectives.$2aat
691  4   Arizona.
691  4   Nevada.
697 24   Hoover Dam (Ariz. and Nev.)
755      Charcoal drawings.$2aat
799 43   The Hugh Ferriss collection.
789      $iNYDA.1000.001.00010.
```

its seventh year and looks ahead to several more years of active construction, plus a permanent maintenance activity. To this must be added a commitment to construct a vocabulary that can be mounted and used in the standardised formats for cataloguing the literature of art, and in the case of museums and visual resource collections, the objects of art. This latter commitment requires that the AAT have a User Services staff that keeps abreast of current technologies and cataloguing codes; that provides help for those who need it in applying the AAT in their systems; and that may even assist in the design of indexing systems. I can say with confidence that the founders of the AAT had little sense of what they were getting into! But I can also say that it has been a privilege to have participated in this very creative and interesting venture, for knowledge bases like the AAT will form the building blocks of future artificial intelligence applications for scholarly research.

57 TWO RELATED THESAURI: FOR TECHNOLOGICAL ARTEFACTS, AND SCIENTIFIC INSTRUMENTS

John Burnett

Head of Documentation
National Museums of Scotland
Edinburgh

Introduction

The purpose of this paper is to give a brief account of two closely related thesauri which are being prepared on a collaborative basis by groups of curators in the United Kingdom. The Science and Technology Object Thesaurus (STOT) is an initiative of the Science and Industry Curators' Group, formerly the Group for Scientific, Technical and Medical Collections. The Scientific Instrument Thesaurus (SIT) is being drafted by a working party set up by the Scientific Instrument Commission of the International Union of the History and Philosophy of Science. In many ways, SIT will be a subset of STOT. Both will be based on the British Standards Insitution's *Root* thesaurus (British Standards Institution, 1988), and will have a hierarchical structure of terms.

There is no tradition of sound classification in science museums which can be used as a starting point for new thesauri. One leading British institution divides its subject matter in a way which reflects its administrative structure before the First World War. Another uses a basic division into 12 categories because its filing system has 12 drawers. The Dutch museum of the history of science, Museum Boerhaave in Leiden, uses the Universal Decimal Classification with some success. It was chosen because it could be used to handle the Museum's important library and archive collections.

The two stimuli for the construction of STOT and SIT are the availability of information technology and the existence of the *Social History and Industrial Classification*, SHIC (SHIC Working Party, 1983) (Chapter 59). Both STOT and SIT are intended to make use of the flexibility which the computer allows, whilst at the same time having terms at the higher levels of classification which are suitable for manual systems. SHIC has demonstrated the value of a classification system which has been clearly thought out. However, many curators in science and industry museums also find that its rigorously social approach to the contexts in which objects were used is at variance with their need to be able to identify items which are technically similar, but which would be separated widely in SHIC. Thermometers (meteorological, clinical, chemical, etc.) are one example. Stationary steam engines, which were used as sources of power in a very wide range of factories as well as in agriculture, are another.

As far as possible, STOT and SIT are following the ISO 2788, *Guidelines for the Construction of Monolingual Thesauri* (British Standards Institution, 1987 and International Organization for Standardization, 1986). The structure of the drafts which have already been produced is very similar to that used in the *Art and Architecture Thesaurus* (Chapter 56). It has to be said that scientific and technical material is notably difficult to classify. Historians of musical instruments have accepted for many years the analysis of von Hornbostel and Sachs, *Systematik der Musikinstrumente: ein Versuch* (1914). The real world of science and industry does not allow such brevity, and clarity is a distant goal.

Scientific and Technological Object Thesaurus (STOT)

The number of names in a Western language which have been applied to technical objects is vast, far larger than the comparable range of names for, say, items of decorative art. The goal we have set ourselves is to make objects findable, and not, like Noah, to name every beast in sight. We make a clear distinction between terminology for retrieval and for description. One premise in the construction of STOT is that any obscure, bizarre or local terminology can be used to *describe* items, but that the description is quite separate from the controlled use of the terms for retrieval.

Root was created to provide a method of subject retrieval for British Standards. It contains 12 000 descriptors and 5 500 non-descriptors. It is now available in machine-readable form, and also in French; there are plans to extend it to other languages. Standards by their nature deal with very specific topics. *Root* is therefore good at handling specific topics but less effective with more general ones.

The selection of headings at the highest level in thesauri and classification systems is to some extent arbitrary. For example, *Root* has a single heading for Agriculture, Forestry and Fisheries. The objects associated with these industries are so different from one another that we intend to separate them into three individual headings.

Root is constructed for post-coordinate indexing, that is, complex ideas are built up by combining simpler ones at the time of indexing or retrieval. This is an approach to subject retrieval which has been used by information scientists in a wide range of applications. The difficulty is that it is not an approach which is in the least familiar to the curator. In a large museum the diesel engines which come from railway locomotives will probably be in a different part of the collections from diesel engines from electric power stations. When attempting to define solutions to information retrieval problems, the solutions have to be intelligible to the users and acceptable to them. Theory and pragmatism collide at this point.

Hierarchical thesauri have in the past been developed on the supposition that they are chiefly concerned with organising concepts. One key principle is that one term cannot be subordinate to another unless the ideas are generically related — in other words, Linear Measurement is a legitimate subdivision of Measurement, but a ruler is not a form of Linear Measurement, and so should not be used as a subdivision of it. Many thesauri consist mostly of concepts, and do not have to address this issue. *Root*, however, allows the names of objects to occur in the same hierarchy as concepts, and we are following its example.

A particularly difficult issue with technical material is the existence of components. Indeed, some need not be handled separately. It may be safe to index an aircraft fuselage simply as an aircraft, if nobody is interested specifically in finding fuselages. Another part of the catalogue record can explain the absence of the wings. Consider, however, the case of a diesel engine from a railway locomotive. *Root* would use two separate terms for it — 'Diesel engines' and 'Railway locomotives'. 'Diesel engines' are found at the bottom of the following hierarchy:

Prime movers
  Internal combustion engines
    Compression-ignition engines
      Diesel engines

Experiments are at present being carried out to determine the most satisfactory way of dealing with this problem.

STOT is not intended to name every possible type of scientific or technological artefact. In library classification the concept of literary warrant has proved useful: a term or idea has to occur with a certain level of frequency in the literature of the subject being studied before there is a real benefit from entering it in a thesaurus. Rarely occurring terms can be replaced for indexing purposes by a more general term. In the same way, STOT will not contain a detailed analysis of (say) all the different types of electrocardiographs, since even specialist museums have only a handful of them.

Scientific Instrument Thesaurus (SIT)

The idea that there is a group of objects which can be related to one another under the general concept of scientific instruments is a twentieth-century one. In the past, terms such as philosophical, optical, mathematical or precision instruments were used, along with more specific terms which indicate the instruments' use, surveyors' instruments, for example. However, the pragmatic approach is to accept the modern analysis of science set out in *Root*, and then to tackle historical problems at a more specific level.

SIT is initially intended to cover instruments in use before 1830. The number of different types of instrument which had been devised increased very rapidly in the middle of the nineteenth century because of the rapid growth of scientists' understanding of electricity, magnetism and physical optics, and because of the development of science teaching, particularly in schools. The task of listing all of the instruments in use in the nineteenth century would be very large, and it is not possible to contemplate the even larger project of listing all the instruments which have been developed in the twentieth century.

Root's lack of historical perspective does produce problems. Many important words are absent: Alembic, Astrolabe ... Zograscope. Historically speaking, 'Navigation' is assuredly not a part of 'Computer and Control Technology'. Some terms, whose use is today unambiguous, had in the past other meanings: 'Pyrometer' is an example. The earliest slide rules do not slide.

As an example of the kind of tangle which history has left us, consider that simple surveyor's instrument the walking wheel or surveyor's wheel, also known in the past by its current name, the 'Perambulator'. These three terms are synonyms. Three other words have, however, been used in the past for the same object: waywiser, pedometer and hodometer. All three have also been employed with two other meanings — a device which can be attached to a carriage wheel which measures how far it has travelled, and the same as the modern pedometer, which counts the number of steps made by a walker and may present this as a distance walked. Confronted with this potential for confusion it is rather relaxing to settle on preferred terms, and start writing scope notes.

Then, however, one chances on one of the later editions of William Leybourn's *The Compleat Surveyor* (1653), in which he describes a new instrument, with semicircular scales, the scales numbered in both directions, and fitted with a siting vane. This instrument is announced on a secondary title-page: 'The Compleat Surveyor shewing How to take Heights, Distances, and to Survey all manner of land by a semi-circle: which (to distinguish it from the theodolite, circumferentor, peractor or other graduated instrument:) I call: The perambulator.' Fortunately, no example of this instrument is known to survive.

This does point another, and completely separate, need in science museums. There are so many interesting problems raised by the naming of scientific instruments — there is a whole book on the naming of the telescope – that it is desirable to have a dictionary of names. Whereas the thesaurus must be prescriptive, the dictionary can be descriptive. A hand-blown X-ray tube may be treated as (I quote the words of a scientific glassblower) 'an envelope of glass entirely surrounded by profanity'.

The structure of the section of SIT which deals with Thermometers is given below as an example of the way in which *Root* is being reinterpreted.

Thermometers
(by design)
Liquid thermometers
Alcohol thermometers
Mercury thermometers SN Mercury-in-glass thermometers
Toluene thermometers
Metallic thermometers
Resistance thermometers
(by purpose)
Maximum thermometers
Minimum thermometers
(by scale)
Celsius thermometers
Fahrenheit thermometers
(by function)
Brewers' thermometers
Chemical thermometers
Meteorological thermometers

Resources and future developments

It is important that both STOT and SIT are constructed within a fairly short timescale, and this is one reason for using *Root* as a source. The example of SHIC, based on a classification of types of work which was produced by a British government agency, is valuable. *Root* is the product of a large quantity of thought by highly skilled information specialists. We see it as a sound starting point, which saves much labour.

A concern in many scientific and industrial museums is the quality of cataloguing, and there is a deeper concern with the comparatively small amount of research which is being produced on objects in the collections. At present many curators believe that it is more desirable to direct resources towards improving the quality of the research being carried out, and to base this on a subject indexing of the collections which does not go into great detail.

These two thesauri are under active development. Progress will be reported in the *Newsletter* of the Science and Industry Curators' Group, and in the Annual Reports of the Scientific Instrument Commission. Anyone who is interested in these two projects, and who does not receive either of these two publications, is invited to contact the present author.

58 THE REVISED *NOMENCLATURE FOR MUSEUM CATALOGING*: AN OVERVIEW

James R. Blackaby

Curator
Bucks County Historical Society
Doylestown, Pa.

Nomenclature for Museum Cataloging is a controlled and structured list of terms used to name man-made objects for the purposes of indexing general collections. It is a classifying system based on common usage drawn from the experience of many North American museums. *Nomenclature* first appeared in print in 1978 after several years of development under the general direction of Robert Chenhall and the Strong Museum (Chenhall, 1978). In 1985 the Strong Museum convened a meeting of experienced *Nomenclature* users to review the word list and structure taking into consideration the years of field experience that had led to a wide range of suggested modifications to the book. In 1988, the *Revised Nomenclature* appeared (Blackaby, Greeno and the Nomenclature Committee, 1988).

In both editions, *Nomenclature* has two main interrelated components: a hierarchy based on the mediating role that objects play between people and the world — how things function — and a list of preferred object terms for the purposes of indexing. *Nomenclature* is based on American English, and the terminology that it uses in the word list and to describe the hierarchy is drawn from common usage in general historical collections. On that account, the system tends to be more usefully applied to such collections, but that is only on account of the fact that it intends no more than broad distinctions between kinds of objects to enable indexing. It is not a guide to all names for all things, and it does not intend to provide a basis for varietal or regional subtleties. The hierarchy reflects the whole array of functions that objects might have, and on that account, it does not provide particular emphasis on areas such as objects of cultural importance that might better reflect the museological significance of artefacts. Within the structure of *Nomenclature* objects of art function to communicate, and so are placed on a plane with other objects that communicate — documentary artefacts, for instance — even though museums value art, and might prefer to see it elevated in importance. The hierarchy itself uses language common to Western tradition for the naming of its classifications, but the definitions that delineate those classifications indicate that they are not limited to those artefacts connotated by the classification name. The classification Glass, Plastics, and Clayworking Tools and Equipment (T&E) includes all the artefacts used for the production of things made from processed inorganic substances such as glass and plastic. Included in this definition, though not noted in the classification name might be artificial pearl-making equipment, artificial turf-making equipment, and so on. A problem of working with a system that relies on natural language is distinguishing clearly between the indexing and classifying language used by the system and the language that is necessary to record for purposes of cataloguing. This distinction is generally liable to lead to confusion in natural language classifications.

Formal taxonomies for recording the natural sciences avoided the confusion between names with local significance and terms for purposes of classification by employing artificial linguistic constructs. Plants use Latin terminology, so what might be called a 'Tomato' (pronounced with either a hard or soft a) in English and a 'Tomate' in French, or even a 'Beefsteak' or 'Burpee Big Boy' or 'Burger Boy' to name some varieties, all share the common Latin term *Solanum Lycopersicum*. *Nomenclature* and other classifying systems and thesauri for man-made objects rely on natural language for indexing terms, so there is apt to be confusion between the potentially rich and evocative object names of local usage — 'Kitchen Match', 'Ohio Blue Tip', or 'Insurance Match' — and the focused, limiting language used for indexing — 'MATCH'. The index terms are important as tools, but they should not be used in place of the local object names for purposes of historical study.

Another significant difference between the taxonomies for the natural sciences and systems such as *Nomenclature* that use natural language is the relation between the terms used to describe the hierarchic structure that distinguishes groups of similar things and the object terms themselves. In the natural sciences, the object term is derived from its location in the hierarchy. For the tomato, *Solanum* indicates the general family in the hierarchy that includes tomatoes and related plants. *Lycopersicum* indicates the particular species. There is no such necessary connection between the classification 'Woodworking

Figure 58.1 Objects sharing the same noun from the same classification

Object term	Classification
PLANE, JACK	Woodworking T&E
PLANE, JOINTER	Woodworking T&E
PLANE, MITER	Woodworking T&E
PLANE, MODELING	Woodworking T&E
PLANE, MOLDING	Woodworking T&E
PLANE, PANEL	Woodworking T&E
PLANE, PLOW	Woodworking T&E
PLANE, RABBET	Woodworking T&E
PLANE, RAISING	Woodworking T&E

Figure 58.2 Nouns with a less uniform relationship

Object term	Classification
PIN, POLITICAL	Personal Symbol
PIN, PRIMING	Armament
PIN, PROLAPSE	Animal Husbandry
PIN, ROLLING	Food Processing T&E
PIN, SAFETY	Textileworking T&E
PIN, SCATTER	Adornment

Tools & Equipment' and the object term 'PLANE, MOLDING' or the classification 'Furniture' and the object term 'TABLE, DRESSING'. It may be that a number of objects sharing the same noun may all be in the same general classification as in the series of terms taken from *Nomenclature* shown in Figure 58.1. The fact that all of these terms belong to a single classification, however, is simply a matter of alphabetic and linguistic happenstance. Most planes are used for woodworking. Other nouns have less uniform meaning, as Figure 58.2 indicates. Even where the noun for a group of objects has a similar meaning, the terms may not fall into a single classification, as Figure 58.3 shows.

The relationship between object terms based on natural language and any classification system is complicated by the fact that identical objects can occasionally be classified in more than one place. A 'LATHE' for example might be classified as either Woodworking T&E, Metalworking T&E, or even Glass, Plastics, Clayworking T&E.

Figure 58.3 Nouns with similar meaning but in different classifications

Object term	Classification
TABLE, DISPLAY	Merchandising T&E
TABLE, DRAFTING	Drafting T&E
TABLE, DRESSING	Furniture
TABLE, ETCHING	Printing T&E
TABLE, EXAMINATION	Medical & Psychological T&E
TABLE, GAME	Furniture
TABLE, GARDEN	Furniture
TABLE, IMPOSING	Printing T&E
TABLE, IRONING	Maintenance T&E
TABLE, KITCHEN	Furniture
TABLE, KNEADING	Food Processing T&E

Figure 58.4 Terms associated with Forestry T&E

ADZ, MARKING
AUGER, RAFT
AX, BARKING
AX, FELLING
AX, MARKING
AX, SPLIT
AX, TURPENTINE
BAR, TOMMY
BRIER
BUCKET, SAP
etc. etc.

The effect of this complexity is that there is and cannot be any necessary relationship between object terms derived from natural language and any classification system based on analysis. This is useful to bear in mind in the construction or use of any list of terms within a hierarchy. The relationships described have validity, but only in so far as they are based on consensus. For a system such as *Nomenclature*, then, terms associated with classifications are simply agreed upon as commonly used for the functions that are described for that classification. By mutual consent and arising out of common usage, the terms associated with the classification Forestry T&E include those illustrated in Figure 58.4. Others might be added; others might have been used. These are the agreed upon preferred terms that help to index. Their inversion helps to organise them into like groupings in an alphabetic list (all of the axes come together here); and it also helps to remind the cataloguer that these are artificially chosen indexing terms to be used exclusively for cataloguing. The index term 'AX, FELLING' might refer equally to an object called a 'Maine pattern felling ax', a'double-bitted Willamette ax', or even to a 'felling ax'. Each of these names is a specific, historic word of local usage that is identified by the generic indexing term 'AX, FELLING'.

While the relationship of the object terms to the classifications may be informal, and the inclusiveness of the lists a subject for interpretation as well as expansion, the classification scheme of *Nomenclature* attempts to be rigorously logical. The usefulness of any hierarchy is a function of its ability to test an entire population by the same standard, and to organise that entire population into smaller groups. Successively lower levels in the hierarchy are created by describing filters through which the entire population must pass. The validity of any hierarchic structure is dependent on the clarity with which these filters are formed and the rigour with which all items are tested by those filters.

Nomenclature begins with the population of all man-made things. The first filter that divides these is one that describes the function that people use objects for to affect the world around them. Some objects passively intervene or mediate between people and the world, some actively intervene or modify the world, and some simply serve as a means to comment upon the world. Some objects cannot be classified at all, not because they lack function, but because they cannot be identified. Each of these sub-sets can be further broken down into what are termed 'Categories' in the *Nomenclature* system.

Figure 58.5 Major categories

Function	*Nomenclature* Categories
Mediate Intervene Passively	Structures Furnishings Personal Artifacts
Act Upon/ Modify Actively	T&E for Materials T&E for Science & Technology T&E for Communication Distribution & Transportation Artifacts
Comment Upon	Communication Artifacts Recreational Artifacts
Unknown	Unclassifiable Artifacts

Each of the *Nomenclature* categories is created as a component of this filtering process. The objects that actively modify the world, for instance, are divided into categories based on the reasons they were created to modify. Some categories of things were created in response to particular materials. Some were created to join ideas and materials. Some were created simply to convey ideas, and others were created to convey materials without usually modifying them. These distinctions provide the categories of Tools and Equipment for Materials, Science & Technology, Communication, and Distribution & Transportation. *Nomenclature* distinguishes ten such major categories (Figure 58.5).

The categories are further broken down into classifications, again relying on the use of a uniform system of filters. The category Tools and Equipment for Materials is divided into classifications organised by various kinds of materials. The matrix in Figure 58.6 indicates the way the category is further divided into parts.

Other materials classifications cut across this simple matrix — Food, Painting, Paper, and Textiles — but these materials are significant enough to be included as independent classifications. An opportunity to list additional materials is offered in the classification for Other T&E for Materials. The other nine categories are organised into classifications that are similarly divided. A complete listing of *Nomenclature* classifications is provided in Figure 58.7.

The overall structure of *Nomenclature* is intended to be fairly rigid. Most museums will be able to relate the structure to their collections without modification, and this fact insures a degree of internal uniformity of information management as well as the potential for sharing with other institutions. Because many general museums organise their collections with some kind of subject index, the *Nomenclature* structure serves to provide a normalized format for such an index that is relatively intuitive. But, where the structure is intended to be rigid, the word list itself is intended to allow for a certain amount of flexibility.

The word list is not and should not ever be a list of all names for all things. In fact, from the point of view of cataloguing, the more limited the word list, the more valuable it is apt to be. The word list simply provides a suggested group of terms that might be used for indexing. An institution that only has one lathe or three boats may find 'LATHE' and 'BOAT' sufficiently precise for the purposes of indexing. Of course, that the lathe is a 'Jacobson slide-rest, treadle-operated machine lathe' will be recorded as a part of the catalogue entry, as will 'Chesapeake Bay trawler' for one of the boats. These more specific names, however, are not generally useful for purposes of indexing an entire collection.

Figure 58.6 Subdivision of Tools and Equipment for Materials category

	Botanical	*Zoological*	*Inorganic*
Raw Materials	Forestry	Fishing & Trapping	Mining/Mineral Harvesting
Cultivated Materials	Agriculture	Animal Husbandry	Stoneworking/ Masonry
Processed Materials	Woodworking	Leather, Horn, Shellworking	Glass, Plastics, Clayworking

Figure 58.7 The *Revised Nomenclature* Classification

Category 1: Structures

Building
Building Component
Site Feature
Other Structure

Category 2: Furnishings

Bedding
Floor Covering
Furniture
Household Accessory
Lighting Device
Plumbing Fixture
Temperature Control Device
Window or Door Covering

Category 3: Personal Artifacts

Adornment
Clothing
  Clothing — Footwear
  Clothing — Headwear
  Clothing — Outerwear
  Clothing — Underwear
  Clothing — Accessory
Personal Gear
Toilet Article

Category 4: Tools & Equipment for Materials

Agricultural T&E
Animal Husbandry T&E
Fishing & Trapping T&E
Food T&E
  Food Processing T&E
  Food Service T&E
Forestry T&E
Glass, Plastics, Clayworking T&E
Leather, Horn, Shellworking T&E
Masonry & Stoneworking T&E
Metalworking T&E
Mining & Mineral Harvesting T&E
Painting T&E
Papermaking T&E
Textileworking T&E
Woodworking T&E
Other T&E for Materials
  Basket, Broom, Brush Making T&E
  Cigar Making T&E
  Lapidary T&E
  Wigmaking T&E

Category 5: Tools & Equipment for Science & Technology

Acoustical T&E
Armament T&E
  Armament — Firearm
  Armament — Edged
  Armament — Bludgeon
  Armament — Artillery
  Armament — Ammunition
  Armament — Body Armor
  Armament — Accessory
Astronomical T&E
Biological T&E
Chemical T&E
Construction T&E
Electrical & Magnetic T&E
Energy Production T&E
Geological T&E
Maintenance T&E
Mechanical T&E
Medical & Psychological T&E
Merchandising T&E
Meteorological T&E
Nuclear Physics T&E
Optical T&E
Regulative & Protective T&E
Surveying & Navigational T&E
Thermal T&E
Timekeeping T&E
Weights & Measures T&E
Other T&E for Science & Technology

Category 6: Tools & Equipment for Communication

Data Processing T&E
Drafting T&E
Musical T&E
Photographic T&E
Printing T&E
Sound Communication T&E
Telecommunication T&E
Visual Communication T&E
Written Communication T&E
Other Communication T&E

Figure 58.7 *continued*

Category 7: Distribution & Transportation T&E

Aerospace Transportation
- Aerospace Transportation — Equipment
- Aerospace Transportation — Accessory

Container

Land Transportation
- Land Transportation – Animal Powered
- Land Transportation — Human Powered
- Land Transportation — Motorised
- Land Transportation — Accessory

Rail Transportation
- Rail Transportation — Equipment
- Rail Transportation — Accessory

Water Transportation
- Water Transportation — Equipment
- Water Transportation — Accessory

Category 8: Communication Artifacts

Advertising Medium
Art
Ceremonial Artifact
Documentary Artifact
Exchange Medium
Personal Symbol

Category 9: Recreational Artifacts

Game
Public Entertainment Device
Recreational Device
Sports Equipment
Toy

Category 10: Unclassifiable Artifacts

Artifact Remnant
Function Unknown
Multiple Use Artifacts

Relying on the more generic *Nomenclature* terms for indexing allows access to less easily normalised names, and it enables grouping of similar objects with dissimilar names for purposes of data retrieval or interpretation.

Following the model of the natural sciences, *Nomenclature* terms tend to be binomial—a single noun modified by a single adjective. Varietal terms are discouraged in favour of more easily retrievable generic ones, and for that same reason trade names, colloquialisms, regional variants, and most foreign language terms have been removed from the word list. Similarly, synonyms are not included in the word list. *Nomenclature* depends on providing a single index term that will lead to a group of related objects which may, in fact, have a number of local or varietal names. There is not, of course, anything sacred about the rule of thumb that limits *Nomenclature* to binomial terms. Some binomial terms reflect varietal specificity and for some a single noun is sufficient. Individual collections will discover how specific their own applications will need the terms to be: specialised museums often need more terms; general museums may not need so much detail.

Nomenclature terms generally omit information that would be normally carried in another field. Names of materials, on that account, are prohibited from being used as modifying adjectives, as are names indicating style or place of origin. 'Staffordshire Platter', 'Bone China Platter', and 'Queen's Pattern Platter' would all be inappropriate for use as indexing terms. Similarly, modifying words such as 'pair' or 'set' are not normally included as part of an index term. Indeed, all index terms are written in their singular form. These conventions allow for the addition of terms, but they hang on to the fact that the purpose of *Nomenclature* is to provide some generic index terms that will lead the researcher on to the more specific information that they may be seeking. This distinction is noted as a particular concern in the *Revised Nomenclature*. Institutions felt, quite rightly, that by relying exclusively on index terms and formal classification names too much important information was being lost. 'MATCH' as an entry under the classification 'Temperature Control Device' has a flatness that does not reflect either the local name or the human activity associated with the object — 'Barn Burner' and 'Arson'. By utilising *Nomenclature* terms and classifications, a standard is achieved that allows institutions to retrieve data without resorting to the addition of all names for all things and all terms for all human activity.

Though *Nomenclature* is no more than a simple word list arranged by classification and alphabetically, it has served general museums — particularly historical museums — very well for more than ten years. The revised edition clarifies some of the definitions in the first edition, provides an updated introduction and bibliography, and encourages retention of local names as well as index terms, but it maintains the fundamental idea that was the basis of the original edition. The care that went into the original concept for *Nomenclature* and the fact that it was generated from the field by those who worked regularly with collections has contributed significantly to its utility. Though there may come a time when more sophisticated tools become available, *Nomenclature* will continue to be a valuable tool for many, many museums.

---

59 THE SOCIAL HISTORY AND INDUSTRIAL CLASSIFICATION (SHIC)

Michael A. Vanns

Assistant Curator (Documentation)
The Ironbridge Gorge Museum
Ironbridge, Telford, Shropshire

In the 1970s, many young curators were helping to bring a greater degree of professionalism to British museums. The creation of the Information Retrieval Group of the Museums Association (IRGMA) was part of this trend, aimed specifically at raising standards in the recording of museum objects. Their theories were based around systems that could be computerised. The result of their work was a highly structured 'data standard', extracts of which were used as the basis for cards for the recording of individual objects. Every aspect of an object's history could be recorded in a systematic way, for the eventual production (via computers) of useful indexes. Many took to this 'scientific' approach with some zeal, but it very soon became clear to folk life and social history curators that without ready access to computers, completed IRGMA cards were of little use unless filed manually in some useful order. A classification system was needed. Some social historians were already familiar with such systems. However, up until then they had been mainly classifications of personal curatorial convenience. Terms were added to indexes as the curator needed to have access to objects to which the terms applied. Very little 'intellectual' thought was brought to bear on these 'classifications'. The Social History and Industrial Classification (SHIC) was to be different.

A Working Party was formed in 1980 to look into the possible production of a social, folk life and industrial classification. Only one member of the eight strong team was a committed MDA man (IRGMA's successor)! The formation of the group coincided with a change of emphasis in museums away from 'folk life' — mainly agricultural and rural collecting — to 'social history' — urban, industrial and very often contemporary collecting. This was reflected in the make-up of the Working Party. Five of the members worked in open-air museums, all aiming to reconstruct a past environment with streets of houses, shops and factories, filled with the artefacts of everyday life. Two members had worked with the Kirk collection at York, the pioneer of contextual museum displays in this country. Another member worked for the Centre for English Cultural Tradition and Language, University of Sheffield. As a result, the Classification the Working Party created managed to look beyond the intrinsic nature of objects, and beyond the arbitrary collections of 'musical instruments', 'coins', 'archaeology', to a view of objects in their social environment or context, and pictorial material, archives, tape recordings, etc. as reflections and indicators of this environment. The pivot of the classification system that emerged from three years of discussion, was this fundamental one of context.

Their Classification was a hierarchical framework into which all human activity was intended to fit. The Classification was not based around objects or their description, but around the social, commercial and industrial activities in which objects performed definite functions. This approach demanded a perception of a social mechanism, and after much debate it was decided that human life could be categorised into four main areas: Community Life, Domestic and Family Life, Personal Life and Working Life.

(These were not new ideas; classifications using similar terms were in use at Beamish and Tamworth.) These four main areas were further divided into appropriate activities, and these in turn subdivided as far as was felt desirable. It was a firm intention of the Working Party not to divide life down to object level. Many similar objects would appear in many disparate parts of the Classification according to where and by whom they were used in society. Object names, therefore, only rarely appear as SHIC headings. The strength of the Classification was that it crossed museum departmental and discipline boundaries and looked at all objects in the way in which the society that produced and used them did. The Classification could be used whether a museum had adopted MDA recording conventions or not. Its numerical coding could work in manual or computerised indexing systems. Perhaps in their more heady moments, the Working Party saw SHIC as the UDC of the museum world!

The *Social History & Industrial Classification* (SHIC Working Party, 1983) was launched at the Science Museum on 29 February 1984, and introductory seminars followed at Leeds,

Figure 59.1 Outline of the SHIC classification scheme

SUMMARY

SUMMARY OF PRIMARY AND SECONDARY HEADINGS

1. COMMUNITY LIFE
   - 1.0 GENERAL
   - 1.1 CULTURAL TRADITION
   - 1.2 ORGANISATIONS
   - 1.3 REGULATION AND CONTROL
   - 1.4 WELFARE AND WELLBEING
   - 1.5 EDUCATION
   - 1.6 AMENITIES, ENTERTAINMENT AND SPORT
   - 1.7 COMMUNICATIONS AND CURRENCY
   - 1.8 WARFARE AND DEFENCE
   - 1.9 OTHER
2. DOMESTIC AND FAMILY LIFE
   - 2.0 GENERAL
   - 2.1 ADMINISTRATION AND RECORDS
   - 2.2 HOUSE STRUCTURE AND INFRASTRUCTURE
   - 2.3 HEATING, LIGHTING, WATER AND SANITATION
   - 2.4 FURNISHINGS AND FITTINGS
   - 2.5 CLEANING AND MAINTENANCE
   - 2.6 FOOD, DRINK AND TOBACCO
   - 2.7 MEDICAL
   - 2.8 HOBBIES, CRAFTS AND PASTIMES
   - 2.9 OTHER
3. PERSONAL LIFE
   - 3.0 GENERAL
   - 3.1 ADMINISTRATION AND RECORDS
   - 3.2 RELICS, MEMENTOES AND MEMORIALS
   - 3.3 COSTUME
   - 3.4 ACCESSORIES
   - 3.5 TOILET
   - 3.6 FOOD, DRINK AND TOBACCO
   - 3.7 MEDICAL AND INFANT RAISING
   - 3.9 OTHER
4. WORKING LIFE
   - 4.0 GENERAL
   - 4.1 AGRICULTURE, FORESTRY AND FISHING
   - 4.2 ENERGY AND WATER SUPPLY
   - 4.3 MINERALS AND CHEMICALS
   - 4.4 METALS AND METAL GOODS, ENGINEERING, ETC
   - 4.5 OTHER MANUFACTURING INDUSTRIES
   - 4.6 CONSTRUCTION
   - 4.7 TRANSPORT AND COMMUNCATIONS
   - 4.8 DISTRIBUTION; HOTELS AND CATERING; REPAIRS
   - 4.9 OTHER WORKING LIFE

Figure 59.2 Example of an object with four classifications, each of which is used as the basis for a separate index entry

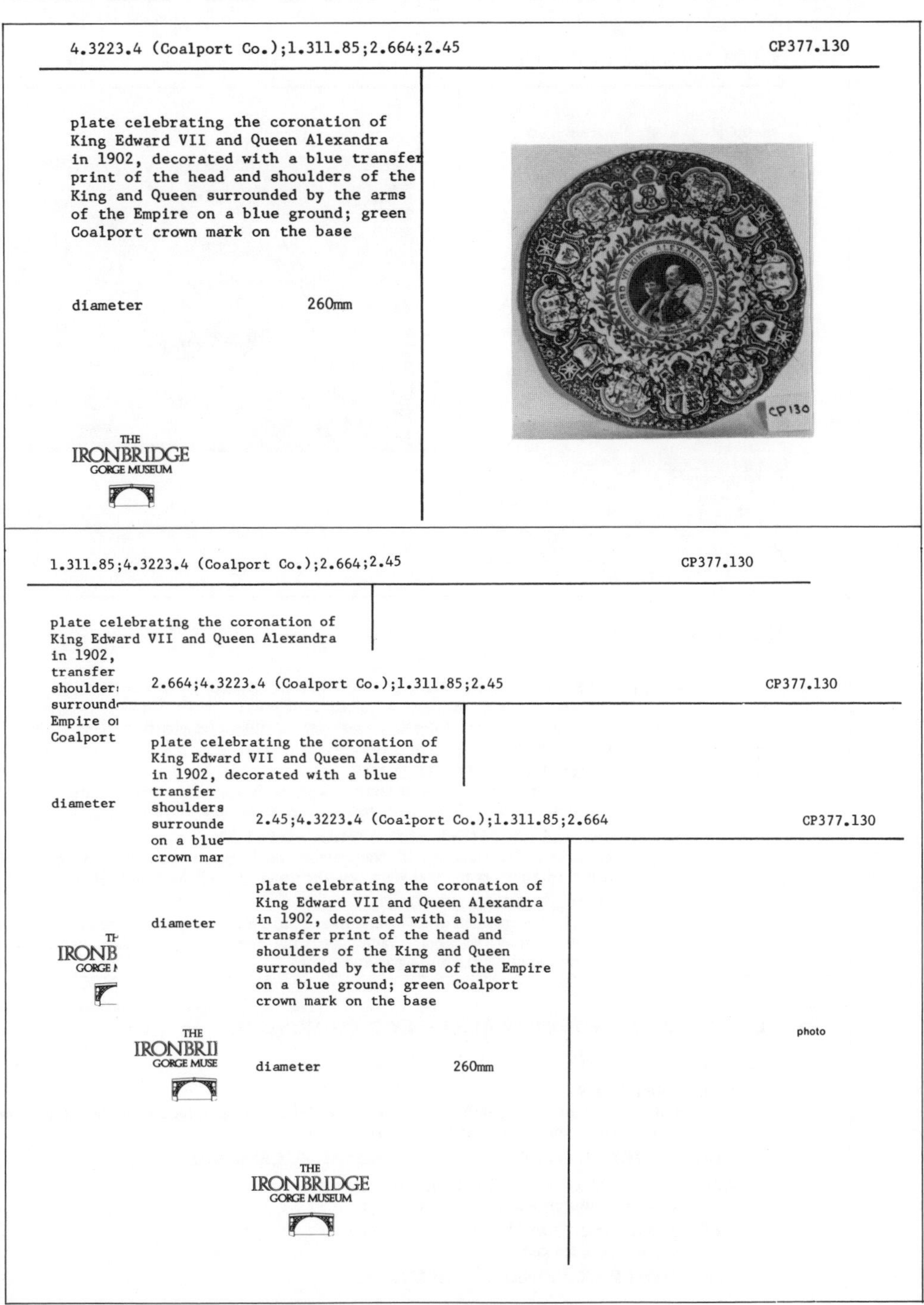

4.3223.4 (Coalport Co.);1.311.85;2.664;2.45 CP377.130

plate celebrating the coronation of King Edward VII and Queen Alexandra in 1902, decorated with a blue transfer print of the head and shoulders of the King and Queen surrounded by the arms of the Empire on a blue ground; green Coalport crown mark on the base

diameter 260mm

THE IRONBRIDGE GORGE MUSEUM

1.311.85;4.3223.4 (Coalport Co.);2.664;2.45 CP377.130

plate celebrating the coronation of King Edward VII and Queen Alexandra in 1902, transfer shoulder surround Empire o Coalport

diameter

TH IRONB GORGE

2.664;4.3223.4 (Coalport Co.);1.311.85;2.45 CP377.130

plate celebrating the coronation of King Edward VII and Queen Alexandra in 1902, decorated with a blue transfer shoulders surrounde on a blue crown mar

diameter

THE IRONBRI GORGE MUSE

2.45;4.3223.4 (Coalport Co.);1.311.85;2.664 CP377.130

plate celebrating the coronation of King Edward VII and Queen Alexandra in 1902, decorated with a blue transfer print of the head and shoulders of the King and Queen surrounded by the arms of the Empire on a blue ground; green Coalport crown mark on the base

diameter 260mm

THE IRONBRIDGE GORGE MUSEUM

photo

Figure 59.3 Index card and extract from SHIC classification scheme

4.3223.71 (Coalport China Works) 1982.1002

group portrait of workers at Coalport China Works.

photograph 1895-1905
photographer, H. J. James

height	153mm
width	201mm

THE IRONBRIDGE GORGE MUSEUM

WORKING LIFE

4.3221 EARTHENWARE TILES (NON-STRUCTURAL)
Includes the manufacture of glazed earthenware tiles, tiled hearths and fireplace surrounds, unglazed decorative tiles (e.g. encaustic), tessellated pavement tiles, etc.
For roofing tiles, plain quarry tiles, etc see 4.3211.

4.3222 CERAMIC SANITARY WARE
Includes the manufacture of sanitary ware of fireclay and vitreous china.
For glazed fireclay drainpipes, angles, bends, elbows and traps see 4.3211.

4.3223 DOMESTIC CHINA AND OTHER POTTERY
Includes the manufacture of ceramic ware for the preparation and serving of food and drink, ceramic ornamental ware, and the decorating of china and earthenware.

4.3229 OTHER CERAMIC GOODS
Includes the manufacture of insulators and other electrical ware of ceramic materials, and the manufacture of other ceramic goods not elsewhere specified, including those for laboratory, industrial and agricultural uses.

MANUFACTURING INDUSTRY ACTIVITY SUBDIVISION

.7 PEOPLE

.71 PERSONALITIES
Includes material relating to people of note connected with the company, such as the chairman, a leading light in a new venture or a character from the shop floor.

.72 OCCUPATIONAL COSTUME AND PERSONAL ACCESSORIES

.721 OCCUPATIONAL COSTUME
Includes uniforms and protective clothing.

.723 FOOD CONTAINERS
e.g. snap tin, tea can.

.729 OTHER PERSONAL ACCESSORIES

Figure 59.4 Index cards and extracts from SHIC classification scheme

4.3211.4 (Hathernware);4.862 1981.257

public house, Bradford Street,
Birmingham, (terra cotta by the
Hathern Station Brick & Terra
Cotta Works, Leicestershire)

photograph 1900-1905
photographer, T. Lewis

height 241mm
width 294mm

4.862;4.3211.4 (Hathernware) 1981.257

public house, Bradford Street,
Birmingham, (terra cotta by the
Hathern Station Brick & Terra
Cotta Works, Leicestershire)

photograph 1900-1905
photographer, T. Lewis

height 241mm
width 294mm

THE
IRONBRIDGE
GORGE MUSEUM

photo

Figure 59.4 *continued*

WORKING LIFE

4.32 MANUFACTURE OF NON-METALLIC MINERAL PRODUCTS

4.321 STRUCTURAL CLAY PRODUCTS AND REFRACTORY GOODS

4.3211 STRUCTURAL CLAY PRODUCTS

Includes the manufacture of clay building bricks, unglazed clay floor (quarry) and roofing tiles, chimney pots, clay pipes, conduits and similar structural clay products. Also includes glazed fireclay drainpipes, angles, bends, elbows and traps.

For glazed tiles see 4.3221; for fireclay sanitary ware see 4.3222.

4.3212 REFRACTORY GOODS

Includes the manufacture of heat-resisting products such as magnesite, silica and high-alumina bricks and shapes, fireclay and graphite crucibles, gas retort and kiln linings, steel moulders' composition and radiants for gas and electric fires.

MANUFACTURING INDUSTRY ACTIVITY SUBDIVISION

.3 PRIMARY OPERATION/PROCESS/ETC

.4 PRIMARY OPERATION/PRODUCTS

.5 PRODUCTION/SERVICE-RELATED OPERATIONS

.51 RESEARCH AND DEVELOPMENT

Includes product design (e.g. drawing office). May include prototype construction and testing where this is separately identifiable from routine product testing - see .54.

.52 JIG, GAUGE AND TOOL PRODUCTION

Includes any material relating to the production of jigs, tools and machinery for use within the company.

.53 BUYING

WORKING LIFE

4.86 HOTELS AND CATERING

4.861 RESTAURANTS, SNACK BARS, CAFÉS AND OTHER EATING PLACES

4.8611 EATING PLACES AND COFFEE BARS

Includes eating places, both unlicensed and licensed to provide alcoholic liquor with meals, but not normally providing regular overnight accommodation, and where any entertainment provided is incidental to the provision of meals. Coffee bars and ice cream parlours are included.

For hotels see 4.865; for night clubs, licensed clubs, etc see 4.863; for catering services operated by railway companies see 4.721.4141.

4.8612 TAKE-AWAY FOOD SHOPS

Includes fish and chip shops, sandwich bars and other premises supplying prepared food for consumption off the premises.

4.862 PUBLIC HOUSES AND BARS

Includes establishments wholly or mainly engaged in supplying alcoholic liquor for consumption on the premises, where the provision of food, entertainment or overnight accommodation, if any, is subordinate.

For off-licences see 4.8424.

Bristol, Nottingham and Edinburgh. The MDA agreed to act as the sales outlet for the two volume classification, and by 1988 it was estimated that over 350 museums had purchased copies in 22 countries. Later that year, an MDA survey into terminology control in UK museums found that 12 per cent of all respondents had adopted SHIC, making it the most widely used museum classification system in the country.

A summary of the main classification shows its organisation in four primary groups (Figure 59.1).

Examples of index cards organised by SHIC and used at the Ironbridge Gorge Museum Trust have been included to illustrate just one way in which the Classification is being implemented (Figures 59.2–4). All accessions at Ironbridge up to 1985 are recorded on MDA-type cards stored in accession number order (after this date they are entered onto computer using MDA's MODES software). Eight inch by five inch index cards are then produced and stored in SHIC order in two main indexes, for objects and pictorial material. In general the subjects of photographs, drawings, paintings, etc., are classified, not the objects themselves. Every index card has a space for a photograph of the item. Figure 59.2 has four classification numbers, needing therefore, four index cards for cross-reference purposes. Figures 59.3 and 59.4 show both the index cards (one and two cards and classifications, respectively) and the relevant entries in the classification scheme. Multiple classification numbers are not unusual, but due to lack of staff time, often only one index is filed away under what is considered the most important SHIC code. Obviously with computers, retrieval on a number of Classification codes would be relatively easy. Many of the difficulties encountered by SHIC users could be overcome if more than one Classification number was allocated per item.

The Classification was never intended to stand alone as the only way for curators to organise their index cards. A museum object could be usefully classified according to SHIC to group it with other objects in a social or commercial context, but also put into a terminology list in alphabetical order to group it with objects of the same name. SHIC could be used alongside other classifications specifically tailored for specialist collections. Unfortunately this has been overlooked by many curators, who in a desire to make SHIC serve all their information retrieval needs, have spent much time and effort modifying the Classification to suit themselves. Getting hold of and vetting these modifications proved impossible for the Working Party. Once SHIC had been published, they were unable to maintain the same enthusiastic cohesion as before, and although there was one very lively addition to the group after 1983, the Working Party eventually broke up. The entire project had been funded privately, and if the Classification is to be reprinted (as stocks are now low), then a new group will have to be formed to achieve this.

---

60 DEVELOPING NOMENCLATURE FOR ETHNOLOGICAL MATERIAL: REPORT FROM A NORWEGIAN PROJECT

Jon Birger Østby

Curator
Norsk Folkmuseum
Oslo

Introduction

In Norway there are two official Norwegian languages beside Lappish, and there are a lot of dialectal synonyms and variants of words.

Let me give an example: I suppose that you all know the type of butter churn that is shown in Figure 60.1. For the dasher handle, I have registered the following synonyms and variants in Norwegian:

kinnekors, kinnekross, kinnekynnel, kinnestav,
kinnestokk, kinneås, kinnstav, kinntre, kinntydul, kinntyl,
kinntyryl, kjednestav
kjernastav, kjernestang, kjernestake, kjernestav
kjernetvåre, kjernetvårell, krossing,
stapper, staukar, staukestav
toroll, turull, tvirel, tviril, tvorel, tvurell, tvurull,

Figure 60.1 Butter churn with dasher handle; for the latter 37 synonyms and variants have been registered in the project

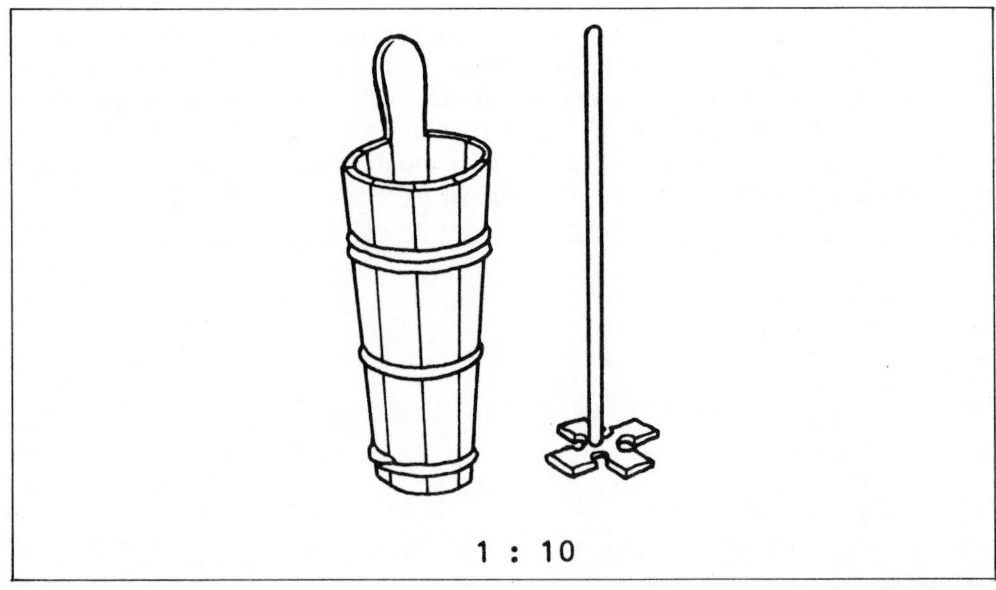

tvørel, tvåre,
tyl, tyril, tørel, tøril, tørvel

These were 37 terms for one single item. There are objects that have more than 90 synonyms and variants.

This situation creates particular problems in data processing. In order to handle this problem, a pilot project was set up to develop nomenclature for selected groups of ethnological material. The initiative behind the project was taken by the museum association 'Norwegian Museums of Art and Cultural History' (NKKM), and I was leader of this project. The project was to carry out a method for developing nomenclature for ethnological material and to present nomenclature for some selected groups of objects that should serve as a model for the continuing work on nomenclature in Norway. In cooperation with an advisory group, four groups of objects were selected:

flatware;
drinking vessels;
appliances for milk and butter;
boxes — chests — trunks.

When selecting these four categories of objects, we tried to single out groups that are well represented in museum collections. At the same time, it was desirable to find groups of objects that could give experience with nomenclature work on objects of different types from various milieus and periods.

The last group, 'Boxes, chests and trunks', has been selected to provide experience with a more general type of object. This list comprises mainly principal types that have the same function. It has been made to see how such general surveys of terms could function as a preliminary help for cataloguing. This was by far the most difficult list to make, and the least successful.

These four publications (Østby, 1982, 1983, 1984 and 1985) are meant to be models for the continuing work on nomenclature, and we are now working to get a permanent position for someone to continue this work.

The lists are based on extensive registration of terms, all of which have been computer processed. In my registration I also bore in mind its usefulness in other fields of research, both in museum and lexicographical work. The Norwegian Lexicographical Institute has obtained a set of copies for use in their work with dictionaries, and the registrations are also used by museum colleagues doing research in some of these fields.

Sources

The nomenclature is to comprise objects that are still in use or have been used in Norway in the period since the Reformation (1537). In this work it has been necessary to exploit varied source materials. It is an extensive operation to make the object categories and the lists of synonyms as complete as possible. It is always difficult to decide how much time should be spent on looking for 'new' types of objects and 'new' terms. The frequency of such findings usually dwindles considerably when a certain amount of time has been spent on studying source materials. Therefore, it is important to end this work in proper time, otherwise a whole lifetime could be spent on one single group! The lists will never be complete anyhow, and they will have to be supplemented in later editions.

Literature

In nomenclature work it is natural to start by orienting oneself in the existing relevant literature. It is considerably easier to set up nomenclature for groups that are well covered in literature, and it is always useful to see how different authors have structured the object material. Literature usually gives a good introduction to the terms applied, often with proper and useful definitions.

Museum catalogues and collections

When literary studies had given a survey of the selected group, I went on studying museum collections. Studies of exhibitions and stored collections are a vital basis for the registration of types and variants. However, the terms used in the museum catalogues often seem to be inconsistent and poorly documented. The quality of the cataloguing varies greatly, and it is often impossible to find the documentation for the terms used. One may often wonder whether the term has accompanied the object, whether the term stems from the dialect of the registrar, whether it is a term that has been coined or whether the term has beeen found in literature.

However, there are exceptions to this general impression. In some Norwegian museums admirable work has been done to collect terms used in the area where the object was found. Catalogues in such museums have been highly useful, especially when it comes to documenting various meanings of older terms, such as the Norwegian terms 'kanne' and 'krus'. These terms are often used as synonyms for 'tankard', though originally the term 'kanne' referred to tankards made of wood or metal, whereas 'krus' was used about tankards made of ceramics or glass. This has been clearly documented in some older and accurate museum catalogues.

In the work with nomenclature on drinking vessels, an experiment was made of sending questionnaires concerning terms to a selection of museums. Thirty-one institutions spread all over the country were initially contacted over the telephone. All of these promised to fill out the lists, but still six years later — only 50 per cent of them have done so. In the answers I have received, I found very few types or terms that had not been documented in other sources. This might have been different if the questionnaire had asked for information on groups less documented in literature. However, the conclusion must be that the staff in museums are so loaded with other types of work that one cannot count on much assistance in this type of research. Therefore it is important to visit museums yourself to make your own studies of catalogues and collections.

When the lists were finished, the manuscripts were sent to selected museums in all counties, and we received a lot of comments to be considered before the lists were printed.

Dictionaries

A number of Norwegian and foreign dictionaries have been used. A general problem is that most dictionaries are ordered alphabetically, and not thematically. Some Norwegian dictionaries, expecially dialect dictionaries, have therefore been systematically perused to register all relevant terms. This has been very time-consuming, but fortunately for me we do not have too many voluminous dictionaries in Norway! Nevertheless this work has given a good number of terms that I would not have found otherwise. By coordinating the registration of terms for several categories it has been possible to save time. Dictionaries have also been of good help in working with definitions.

Questionnaires

Different questionnaires sent out by other institutions have been used. The quality of the answers varies, but especially the older material has been an important source. Without the questionnaires for a broad Norwegian research on mountain summer dairying from the 1930s, it would have been very difficult indeed to make a good list on appliances for milk and butter. The structure of different questionnaires has also been a considerable help in my own structuring of types.

Price lists and pamphlets

Price lists and pamphlets from retailers and manufacturers are a good source on types and terms in present use. Older price lists are highly useful in nomenclature work, but they may be hard to find in libraries. But producers and retailers have given me a lot of help in finding useful material of these types.

Interviews

Interviews, for example with restaurant personnel, have been a good source of information on terms and use of flatware. Besides, retailers have given orientations of current articles and their terminology, and often older personnel can also give worthwhile information on types that are no longer sold, and producers may offer additional information on terms for the different parts of objects.

The publications

Each NKKM publication consists of five parts:

General information on how to use the publication.

Illustrations showing standard terms for different parts of objects. This is meant to be a help for the description (for example, Figure 60.2).

The nomenclature itself, with standard terms in both the official Norwegian languages (Figure 60.3).

In principle the standard terms are to be unambiguous. This is one of the reasons why we have worked with groups of objects and not with single objects. In order to obtain a terminology as consistent as possible, it is important to see the consequences that the choice of a standard term for one object have on terms for related objects. It is also important to try avoiding standard terms that are too general and terms that may convey different meanings.

For some objects I have not been able to find Norwegian terms at all. In such cases terms have been translated from other languages, preferably Danish or Swedish, and in a few cases we have found it necessary to coin new terms. We have preferred terms that are in active use in a modern language, terms that can be used in both the two official languages, terms that are used widely around the country and terms that are self-explanatory.

For each term there is a classification code for *Outline of Cultural Materials* (also known as the Murdoch Classification System) (Murdock, *et. al.*, 1987). This system is now being used by several Norwegian and Swedish museums.

There is a definition, and there is a short description of construction, materials and use.

There are drawings of one or more typical objects. We had a discussion as to whether we should use drawings or photos, but we found that drawings are more expressive and easier to reproduce.

There are references to other types of objects that are similar and a list of registered synonyms and varieties of synonyms.

Figure 60.2 Examples of illustrations showing standard terms for different parts of objects

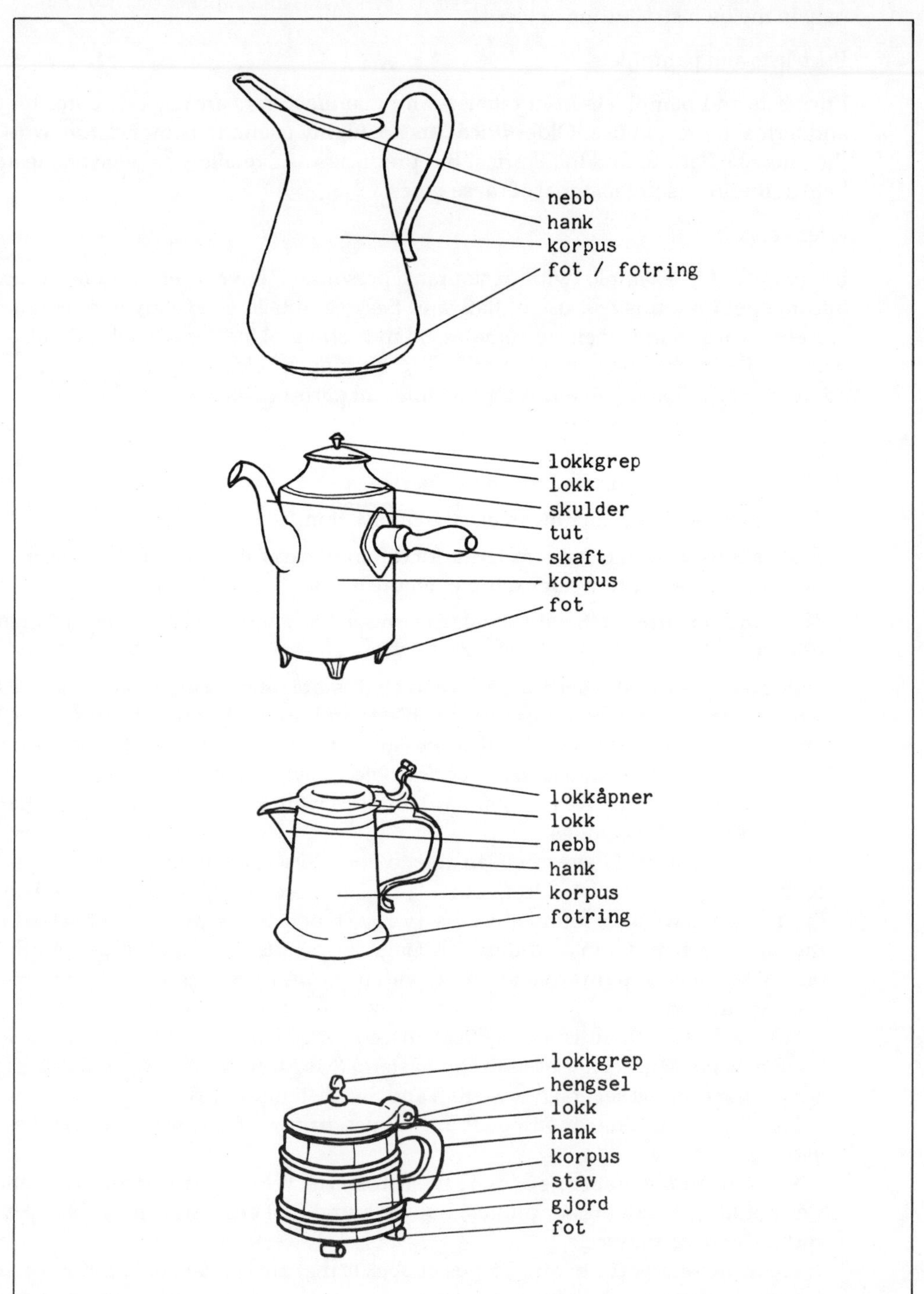

igure 0.3 Sample page from the dictionary of drinking vessels and containers, presenting standard terms for objects, classification code, definition, description, illustrations, references to other types of objects that are similar and registered synonyms and varieties of synonyms

[+]KAFFEKOLBE [x]KAFFIKOLBE

Klass: 272

Kolbe som brukes til tilbereding og servering av kaffe, te eller tevann. Kaffekolber brukes helst i forbindelse med traktemaskiner. De er laget av glass, men de har ofte hank eller lokk av annet materiale.

Jf. [+]kaffekule [x]kaffikule

Synonymer: kolbe, tekolbe

[+]KAFFEKULE [x]KAFFIKULE [1]

Klass: 272

Kar til koking og servering av kaffe. Kaffekuler har en kuleformet kolbe av glass. Når kaffen skal serveres, plasseres kolben i en metallbeholder. Beholderen er foret med tekstil, og den har hank og åpning for tuten.

Jf. [+]kaffekolbe [x]kaffikolbe

[1]Fra svensk, kaffekula.

MUGGE

Klass: 272 264 271 273

Skjenkekar for forskjellig slags drikke og saus. Mugger har nebb og hank i siden. Betegnelsen brukes bare om kar uten lokk. Mugger kan være laget av glass, keramikk, metall eller plast.

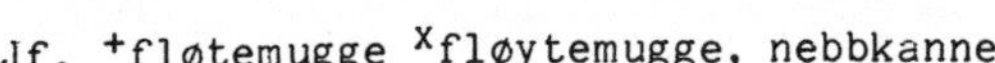

Jf. [+]fløtemugge [x]fløytemugge, nebbkanne

Synonymer: cocktailmugge, melkemugge, mjølkemugge, nebba, nebbe, punsjemugge, saftmugge, sjokolademugge, vannmugge, vassmugge, ølmugge

References to actual literature.

Index for all standard terms and synonyms.

The reference in bold-faced print refer to the use of standard terms, the others to pages where the term is found in the synonym lists.

Conclusion

To do nomenclature work is very time-consuming. This pilot project lasted for three years. On one occasion, I raised the question before my advisory group whether it was acceptable to produce roughly one list per year, which seemed to be the norm if a certain standard was to be held. Then an old professor of lexicography replied, 'If the Swedish Academy had not started their work on the large Swedish dictionary in the 1890s, they would not have got as far as to the letter ('S') today'.

61 ICOM INTERNATIONAL COMMITTEE FOR MUSEUMS AND COLLECTIONS OF COSTUME: VOCABULARY OF BASIC TERMS FOR CATALOGUING COSTUME

Naomi Tarrant

Secretary, ICOM Costume Committee 1983–89
National Museums of Scotland
Edinburgh

Introduction

The International Committee for Museums and Collections of Costume is one of ICOM's subject committees. With the more widespread use of information retrieval systems, Committee members felt it was important that the information recorded was what they considered to be most relevant, so in 1971 the Committee set up a working party to look at the cataloguing of costume.

Some members were already committed to schemes which had been developed for their entire museum, and it became clear that it was not therefore desirable to devise a particular system. What was needed was a fundamental scheme for identifying garments and recording the basic information which was relevant to them. The approach chosen was to take the garments themselves and ask what we, as students of costume, wanted to know from them.

This was to be the basic information, and included the usual details incorporated in museum records. Figure 61.1 shows an outline of the fields (Buck, 1976).

This list of criteria was fairly clear and did not cause any great problem. However, the name of objects created the biggest difficulty and this had to be overcome. Contemporary fashion terms are useless and historic terms are not always easy to assign to a particular garment. There is also confusion with a common language, for example, the English word *Pants* does not mean the same in American English. It was therefore necessary for the Committee to look at this problem in a different way and it was decided to make a list of basic terms which could be used by anyone (International Committee for Museums and Collections of Costume, 1982). Because there are distinct differences between men's and women's clothes, these were treated separately, as were babies' clothes, as there are some garments which are unique to them.

The principle followed is that the basic term should be the first catalogue name, followed by a second term to identify it more precisely within the main category, with other variables following if necessary, such as 'Trousers' (general term), 'jeans' (second term). The use of general terms makes it easier for a non-specialist cataloguer to achieve a reasonable degree of accuracy for grouping garments.

The garments were considered in relationship to the human body and grouped according to the layers of clothing as listed under the classification in Figure 61.1. The terms were then worked out according to the area of the body covered, with a long-established term of general use selected as the basic term. For example (Figure 61.2):

Figure 61.1 Recommended fields for cataloguing costume

Registration number plus number of pieces of a garment
Classification divided by age and sex, with each category subdivided into
- Main dress
- Outerwear
- Protective wear
- Underwear
- Nightwear
- Accessories worn on the body
- Accessories for adornment
- Accessories carried
- Accessories for care of the person
- Accessories for care of clothing
- Accessories for making clothes

Name of object
Function
Date of object
Materials of which it is made
Cut and construction
Basic measurement
Condition
Maker
Wearer
Related specimens and documents
Acquisition
Pedigree
Authority for identification
Photographs and sketches
Conservation
Published and exhibition references
Cataloguer
Position in store

Figure 1.2 Extract from costume classification

1.2 Covering the body above the waist.

1.21 BODICE

BODICE Blouse

1.22 BODICE Jacket Cardigan

1.23 BODICE Jacket Waistcoat

1.24 BODICE Pullover

BODICE Pullover (Tee-shirt)

A numerical classification was added to the lists, for use as a reference code. It is not offered as a full system and has not been elaborated.

The basic terms used do not specify function, only the parts of the body covered. Thus, both a wedding dress and a bathing costume come under the same basic term 'Dress'. This has caused confusion to some curators who are not used to looking at the problem in the same logical way that the working party did. They still feel that the term should describe its function. This has led several American colleagues to try to devise a system which uses contemporary fashion terms, but this has not answered the underlying problem.

For other reasons, the system does not work so well for non-European dress, but the Committee does not really cover these areas, so they were not considered. An attempt was made by some members to look at the problem for Middle Eastern clothing, but this did not report any success.

Use of the ICOM system does depend on how it can be adapted to fit into any broad classification which is already being used by the main institution, as it is rare for there to be a completely separate costume museum. It is possible with a manual index to use this system for storing the cards quite easily, and it works well. However, unless each department adopts a system for itself, it is possible that the ICOM system is too dissimilar to others to make it compatible. Some computerised systems being installed would not allow enough space for the idea to be fully used. But for the costume curator it does work as a logical and simple system for cataloguing costume, without the problems that other, more elaborate, ones possess.

62 CLASSIFYING DECORATIVE ARTS COLLECTIONS

Karol A. Schmiegel
Registrar
Winterthur Museum
Winterthur, Del.

The decorative arts — often called minor arts, applied arts or material culture — are objects which may have had a utilitarian purpose but which are collected and exhibited more for their artistic and aesthetic merit than for their role in everyday life. These domestic, public and ecclesiastical objects are of diverse types and materials: for example, furniture, ceramics, glass, precious and base metals, textiles and carpets. The objects tend to be high style or representative of special cultural groups, such as the Shakers. Collections primarily of decorative arts usually also include graphics, paintings and sculpture, and museums whose major collections are fine arts often include decorative art objects.

The interpretive emphasis in a decorative arts collection is usually on transmission of style, the artist/maker and his *œuvre,* iconography, and regional characteristics. Exhibitions and installations tend to be based on these factors and aesthetic considerations. These practices contrast to those in the historic house museum, which aims to show how people lived in that house, or in history museums such as the Museum of London or the Strong Museum, which use objects to illustate different facets of history.

With such a variety of types of objects, the museums must draw upon many sources for documentation. The art historian and subject specialist may be from the museum, academic or commercial areas. These people usually provide and seek data directly related to the object or its maker. However, cultural, social and even political historians view these objects as supplementary to written documents rather than as primary sources or documents in themselves. They and picture researchers seek illustrations for lectures and for publications ranging from history textbooks, to books, articles and films on collecting antiques, decorating, tourism, life in a particular period or place, techniques such as quilting, materials such as ivory, types of objects such as beakers, or themes such as childhood.

Collectors, genealogists, staff interpreters, students, amateur subject specialists and craftsmen who want to make reproductions ask an amazing variety of questions which the documentation officer, registrar, or curator endeavour to answer. The easy question is, what objects were made by a particular person. The more difficult ones relate to such queries as craft practices (what chairs do you have with the seat rails tenoned through?), activity, content or subject (e.g. musical trophies, people tea drinking, or dogs).

Such queries also bring out the variety of names used for the same or similar objects. A Pembroke table may also be called a breakfast table. Names change over time, and a piece of furniture called a couch in the early eighteenth century may be referred to as a daybed, a chaise lounge, or a Récaumier in later times. Different languages are often represented in the same collection for similar types of objects. The object identified by the Dutch word *Kas* looks similar to the *schrank* of the Pennsylvania Germans, which is closely related to a wardrobe in English or the French *armoire.* The wide range of enquiries and of data make classifying objects and controlling terminology especially useful techniques to facilitate the recording and provision of information about decorative arts. However, there is no tradition of a generally accepted system or vocabulary.

Winterthur Museum offers a case study in the development of classification and documentation systems. Since the mid-1950s, shortly after the museum opened in 1951, the registrar's office has been the central repository for collections information. The master (ordered by identification or registration number), location, and source files were established first. The confidential, security, curatorial, slide library, and dispersed files were created in the mid-1960s. The manual card file system was expanded to provide faster access and more access points to the data on approximately 89 000 objects which range in date from 1640 to 1860. Added were origin and association (proper name) files, plus the object research file, which was inconsistently organised by type of object generally based on material. It includes photographs with the catalogue cards but does not follow a classification system. These 11 manual card files have been a great help, but they still do not enable the staff to answer all types of questions easily and quickly, and they require much time to maintain.

Our search for a classification system led us in the mid-1970s to look at the *Human Relations Area Files* (edited by Murdock *et al.*, revised 1987). We experimented with expanding the three-digit index numbers and found the system could work. It was, however, implemented only for approximately 1 000 prints in our graphics collection and for some slides in our slide collection. Later we looked at the first edition of *Nomenclature* (Chapter 58) (Chenhall, 1978). We attempted to use the object name list from *Nomenclature* (Chenhall, 1978). However, the book uses the object's function as the basis for classification, and this is not the primary way in which we view our collection. We attempted to use the object name list from *Nomenclature,* but it did not include many of the objects in our collection. Because *Nomenclature* uses different names for objects which look very similar and differentiates by function, it was not appropriate for our collection. In that system, a jug is an object with a spout and handle used in food preparation,but an object which appears similar but is used for food service is called a pitcher. Some objects could have been used for either, and we did not want to infer more than we could document.

In the late 1970s and early 1980s, we looked to automation for assistance. The primary goal, however, was inventory control for the collection, and providing other types of information was viewed as secondary. We began by using a word-processing system. The list-process feature enabled us to sort objects by registration number, permanent location and location on various tours or exhibitions. Later we added the category code, (e.g. F for furniture, C for ceramics) and abbreviation for the primary material used for the object. We inverted the object name, for example, chair-side, rather than side chair, so that we could retrieve all of the chairs in a simple sort.

In 1986, some students from the University of Delaware used the data from the word-processing system and some utility features on our Hewlett-Packard computer system to create a simple inventory control system called Collect. It enabled us to track loans and temporary object moves, for example, to a conservation laboratory, photography studio, or for a workshop conducted by a staff member.

In planning for a true collections information management system, we prepared comprehensive specifications that included all types of data, reports, and collection management activities which were used or needed. However, the cost of customised software development made us reduce the scope of the project. The module which would divide the object's description and comments into discrete fields is not being implemented initially. However, the use of an optical character reader for the major portion of the data entry allowed this information to be entered as text, and it can be searched.

The system as implemented includes basic data (registration number, object name, date, maker, title, origin, measurements, physical relationships to other objects, category, former owner and special collection); the inventory controls needed; acquisition, loan, insurance and appraisal data. We also have a thesaurus capability, which allows three alternate names or synonyms, and five fields for a classification system.

When I presented this talk at the terminology conference in Cambridge, I suggested retitling it 'Collections in Search of a System'. The National Endowment for the Humanities (an agency of the United States government) had just given Winterthur funding to hire a project assistant to implement classification systems. In the grant application, we had stressed that we wanted to use existing systems and not create new ones.

We have decided to use the Art and Architecture Thesaurus (AAT) to control object names and parts of objects, and to allow retrieval by style name, design elements, process and technique, events, and associated concepts. The major problem is that AAT is not complete, and our grant calls for us to implement the systems by October 1989. We are using the completed portions of the AAT and adding as we need, knowing that we will have to make some global corrections for codes as the AAT staff complete additional sections. The five areas for classification were chosen because they fill the major gaps in our existing data and systems and will be of the greatest benefit to the diverse groups of people who use our collections information.

Heretofore, there has been no method for us to retrieve objects related to an 'event', such as the American Revolution. Using AAT, all depictions of incidents which occurred during that war and objects used in the conflict can be located. The 'associated concept' field is used for abstract ideas such as childhood, patriotism, and dissident art — again topics for which we had no system of retrieval. The style and period names in American decorative arts are currently being reviewed. One idea was to rename the Queen Anne period (1730–55 in the United States) the Early Georgian period which would be more nearly accurate in terms of dates. However, following AAT's use of style names, these objects are now classified as Early Baroque — a term which is more visual and less associated with British history.

Where AAT has not assigned codes, we have added our own to the system and informed the AAT staff so that our work will help advance the project. AAT has not yet worked with glass, but Lynn Brocklebank (Winterthur's Project Assistant) has developed codes for processes and techniques which allow us to retrieve free-blown, blown-moulded, three-mould, or pressed glass. The design elements,such as diamond and eagle from AAT are used, and codes for the pattern numbers developed by George and Helen McKearin for moulded glass have been assigned. Until the implementation of the AAT as our classification system, the only way one could locate objects in these groups was to look at the catalogue cards for the entire glass collection which were organised by form (bottle, bowl, dish, flask, plate, etc.) in the object research file.

We also plan to use ICONCLASS to develop a detailed classification system for iconography and subject. Each type of object has types of data which its specialists believe are extremely important, and we hope in the future to be able to accommodate most of these needs. We will add an additional screen to our computer system to accommodate more than five areas of classification and the long codes which ICONCLASS requires.

Our goal is to provide easy access to all aspects of our collection for a wide variety of users. We hope by the end of 1989 to have taken a major step toward achieving that goal.

---

63 SUBJECT INDEXING OF OBJECTS IN THE NATIONAL MUSEUM OF SCIENCE AND INDUSTRY

Dr Leonard D. Will

Acting Head of Research and Information Services Division
Science Museum
London

Introduction

The National Museum of Science and Industry is a blanket title which we have adopted to cover our several sites throughout the country, of which the major ones are the Science Museum, in London, the National Railway Museum, in York, and the National Museum of Photography, Film and Television, in Bradford. These are all part of a single management structure and we are developing an integrated documentation system to record objects at all sites in a uniform manner, on a central computer, accessible online from all locations. We use Databasix Computer Services' Adlib software package, running on a Prime 4150 minicomputer. Our database now contains entries for almost all the 200 000 objects at the Science Museum, although there is a lot of work still to do in improving the quality of the records and extending the coverage to include the other sites.

Indexes are already provided to give direct access by personal and corporate names, inventory numbers, photographic negative numbers, materials, dates, places, and so on. All these need rules and standards for form and content, but indexing by subject is the most difficult, because judgement is required both in deciding first what concepts are worth indexing and then how these concepts can be expressed in a form which will match that used by someone using the index, perhaps years later.

No single subject indexing method meets all our needs, and our present approach is to use three complementary techniques; these can be combined with each other and with the use of the other indexes mentioned above, or with manual or computer scanning of records to narrow down the items retrieved to the required degree of precision.

Free text indexing of inventory descriptions

We give each object a brief 'inventory description' of one to three lines, describing in natural language what the object is, any particularly significant features, and by whom, where and when it was made. These descriptions were a central feature of our previous manual documentation system, and they have been input to the computer, with a minimum of editing, to form the basis of the automated system. They are used in producing all sorts of brief lists of items, both for housekeeping purposes and as responses to enquiries, and fulfil the same role as the titles of journal articles do in a bibliographic system. Some typical examples of inventory descriptions are shown in Figure 63.1, together with some other parts of the records which relate to subject retrieval.

We have generated a 'free text index' which allows us to retrieve quickly any inventory description containing any word or combination of words, without the computer having to read through all entries.

Figure 63.1 Examples of extracts from database records, showing inventory descriptions, collection-specific classification numbers and ROOT thesaurus terms

```
1988- 290: Slide rule for triangle-mesh-reinforced concrete slabs, celluloid,
copyright 1909 by the American Steel and Wire Company
  ROOT TERMS : slide rules; reinforced concrete

1986-1502: Experimental bed for continuous weight measurement during psychic
experiments, used by Prof. J.B. Hasted in his research, English, c.1980
  ROOT TERMS : beds; weighing machines; electronically-operated devices;
               recording instruments (measurement); psychology

1982- 228: Hallade track recorder (Manufacturers No.80)
  CLASS 12.03  : Permanent Way
  ROOT TERMS : railway track; recording instruments (measurement);
               accelerometers

1986-1009: Diorama (1:32 scale) depicting a V2 missile being prepared for launch
from a site outside the Hague Municipal Museum, late 1944
  CLASS 1.3    : Scale model rockets and missiles
  CLASS 1.5    : Test and launch equipment
  ROOT TERMS : guided missiles; space centres (ground); scale models
  [The non-ROOT term "dioramas" will be added to our thesaurus]
```

Advantages:

implementation is quick, as the index can be generated and maintained automatically by the computer. No specific effort is required from curators, apart from writing informative and consistent inventory descriptions;

searching on the actual words used in the inventory descriptions is helpful in identifying half-remembered items, and will retrieve by specific terms peculiar to individual objects, trade names and jargon, such as 'triangle-mesh' or 'Hallade', to take two examples from Figure 63.1.

Disadvantages:

many existing inventory descriptions are inadequate, and editing them will take a lot of work, generally requiring examination of the objects;

inconsistencies in description require the searcher to think of all terms which might have been used, including synonyms, grammatical and typographic variants. An item described as a 'V-1' would be missed by a search for the term 'V1', and someone looking for 'missiles' would miss something described as a 'flying bomb';

there is no guarantee that items retrieved represent all items of that type in the museum, because other items may have been differently described, using broader or more specific terms than the ones sought. The description 'Hallade track recorder' does not show its connection with the broader subject of railways, and someone looking for material on 'levitation' may miss Hasted's bed because that term does not occur in its description, only the broader terms 'weight' and 'psychic'.

Classification numbers and subject headings

Our objects are grouped into about 130 separate 'collections', each curator being responsible for one or more collections. Many curators subdivide their collections into

Figure 63.2 Example of part of a collection-specific classification scheme: Photography

```
0.00 : Photography, classification uncertain

1.00 : Camera obscuras

2.00 : First photographic cameras (to c1850)

3.00 : [Early cameras (c1850-1875)]
3.10 :    Early box cameras (c1850-1875)
3.20 :    Early bag or bellows cameras, c1850-1875

4.00 : Box plate cameras

5.00 : [Bellows plate cameras]
5.10 :    Bellows plate cameras: drop front
5.20 :    Bellows plate cameras: tailboard
5.30 :    Bellows plate cameras: others

6.00 : Magazine cameras

7.00 : Detective cameras

8.00 : Early roll film cameras (up to 1900)

9.00 : [Box and rigid bodied roll film cameras]
9.10 :    Box & rigid bodied cameras: roll film
9.20 :    Box & rigid bodied cameras: 126 cartridge
9.30 :    Box & rigid bodied cameras: 110 cartridge
9.40 :    Box & rigid bodied cameras: sub-miniature
9.50 :    Disc cameras
```

subject groupings, such as those which they have used in the past as headings on guide cards in a card file. These groupings may have purely verbal headings, or they may also have a numerical notation to allow sorting in a classified order rather than alphabetically. An example of part of one of these schemes of classification is shown in Figure 63.2.

It is not possible to construct a consistent scheme of this type covering the whole museum, because of the different principles on which the collections themselves are defined and subdivided. Classification numbers are specific to individual collections, and when using them to search the database it is also necessary to specify the collection number.

Advantages:

subject lists can be produced under complex subject headings, which may relate to the context of the collection, such as 'Babbage items' or 'Methods of working: coal mining';

the subject order can sometimes be used for the physical arrangement of a collection of objects in store, like books in a library;

the headings define pre-determined subsets of a collection, which can be printed out or used to define the domain for more detailed searches.

Disadvantages:

a searcher needs to have a copy of the classification scheme for the collection being searched, to identify the classification headings used;

classification schemes become complex if they try to specify too much detail. Items may fall into several categories, and one has to be given priority if a list is required in which each item appears only once;

there is no consistency between collections, because objects are grouped in accordance with their role in each specific collection. For example, in Medical Sciences a Wimshurst machine might be grouped with 'Electrotherapy equipment' while in Physical Sciences it would be grouped with 'Electrostatic generators'.

Thesaurus of subject terms

The intention of this is to have a single set of subject indexing terms which will be applied consistently to all collections, so that searches across the whole database will be possible. I consider that these indexing terms should replace the use of 'simple name' and 'full name' fields which we have used in the past but which have never been properly distinguished or defined. If it is desired to give one term precedence over the others, as when sorting a list in which each item is to appear once only, then that term can be listed first.

The construction of a comprehensive thesaurus for a broad subject field is a major task, and we intend to use an existing thesaurus as far as possible, building on it as necessary to reflect those aspects of our collections which it does not cover adequately. We looked at many possible thesauri, and concluded that our needs were best matched by the ROOT thesaurus published by the British Standards Institution. Examples of ROOT, in the form in which we have loaded it into our system, are shown in Figures 63.3 and 63.4.

This thesaurus was originally compiled for indexing material related to standards and standardisation, and it therefore covers technology in detail, with a more object-oriented approach than other thesauri intended primarily for bibliographic material. It also covers physical science and medicine quite well, these being the other two subject areas of interest to us. It includes terms for geographical areas and materials, so we can use it for these parts of the records as well as for the subject index. ROOT has been adopted by

Figure 63.3 Hierarchical display of thesaurus terms

```
Machine tools
..Finishing machines
....Calenders
....Textile finishing machinery
......Stenters
..Gear-cutting machines
..Machines working by stock removal
....Boring machines
....Broaching machines
....Drilling machines
......Percussion drills
....Grinding machines
....Honing machines
....Lathes
......Centre lathes
......Copying lathes
......Turret lathes
......Vertical boring and turning lathes
......Woodworking lathes

Machine tools (cont.)
..Machines working by stock removal (cont.)
....Milling machines
....Mortising machines
....Planing machines
....Routing machines
....Sanders
....Sawing machines
......Band saws
......Chain saws
......Circular saws (machines)
......Jig saws
....Slotting machines
..Machines working without stock removal
....Bending rolls
....Extruding machines
....Hammers (machines)
....Presses
```

standardisation organisations in several other countries, and we are thus confident that it will be supported and developed for the foreseeable future.

There are two main areas in which we have to add to ROOT. It has only skeleton coverage of the social sciences and humanities, and we shall probably use another source of terms for this area, although fitting them as far as possible into the ROOT structure. It also does not include historical names for objects, but this is not a major problem, because it is usually clear where any particular item should be placed in the hierarchies of function and application. Its structure is one of its main strengths, because it conforms closely to the recommendations of the British and International Standards on thesaurus construction (BS 5723 and ISO 2788-1986) (British Standards Institution, 1987 and International Organization for Standardization, 1986). So long as we keep to these recommendations too we should be able to add terms without invalidating the overall structure.

We hope that our work on developing this thesaurus will also be of value to other museums, and we are collaborating with the Science and Industry Curators Group on the STOT (Scientific and Technical Objects Thesaurus) project and with the Scientific Instruments Commission on their plans to develop terminology for scientific instruments of historic interest.

Advantages:

any object will be given the same indexing terms irrespective of the collection in which it is located. A higher proportion of relevant objects will therefore be recalled;

Figure 63.4 Alphabetical display of thesaurus terms

```
Machineability [CYI.WP]
BT  Workability
RT  Free-machining alloys

Machinery housing facilities
USE Equipment housing facilities

Machines working by stock removal [PQF]
BT  Machine tools
NT  Boring machines
    Broaching machines
    Drilling machines
    Grinding machines
    Honing machines
    Lathes
    Milling machines
    Mortising machines
    Planing machines
    Routing machines
    Sanders
    Sawing machines
    Slotting machines

Machines working without stock removal
    [PQH]
BT  Machine tools
NT  Bending rolls
    Extruding machines
    Hammers (machines)
    Presses

Machining tolerances [BBP.GGX]
BT  Dimensional tolerances

Machmeters [BFU.FO]
BT  Speedometers

Macrogenerating programs [MXE]
UF  Macros
BT  Computer programs

Macrographic examination [BND.C]
BT  Non-destructive testing
NT  Baumann test

Macros
USE Macrogenerating programs

Macroscopic examination [BND.BN]
BT  Visual inspection (testing)

Maculation tests
USE Stain tests

Madagascar [AYM.MX]
UF  Malagasy Republic
BT  Southern Africa
```

terms will be linked in a hierarchy which depends on the inherent nature of the objects, so the software allows us to do 'generic' searches, i.e. to search for a term and all levels of its narrower terms as a single search statement. Each object need therefore be given only the most specific term from each applicable section of the hierarchy. An item indexed as 'lathes' can be retrieved by a search for all types of 'machine tools', and 'cabbages', 'carrots' and 'cauliflowers' will all be retrieved in a search for 'vegetables and all its narrower terms';

proper use of such indexing assumes online computer searching, so that terms are combined when a search is being done rather than when records are input. It is thus not appropriate to invent compound terms such as 'slide rules for reinforced concrete'; by using separate terms it is easy to find either 'all types of slide rule' or 'anything to do with reinforced concrete' without having to enumerate applications under 'slide rules' or calculating devices under 'reinforced concrete';

the Adlib software provides for automatic replacement of non-preferred terms by preferred terms on input and on searching, so that searches can be done successfully even though the preferred indexing term is not known;

a thesaurus display function allows searchers to examine the thesaurus structure on screen and select terms for indexing or searching.

Disadvantages:

indexers have to refer to the thesaurus to allocate terms when cataloguing objects, and some training will be required to ensure that consistency is maintained;

the thesaurus will not necessarily group objects in the way they are grouped in any particular collection;

some professional and curatorial time will be needed for thesaurus maintenance, for considering candidate terms and building those selected into the proper places in the structure.

Conclusions

We hope that by adopting this threefold approach to subject indexing we shall have a structure which is capable of meeting the many different demands which are made of it. With any such system there is a trade-off between powerful features and ease of use. We hope to make it simple enough to be used with a minimum of training, and we are looking forwards towards the eventual use of public access terminals. On the other hand we have to ensure that curators indexing objects have sufficient grasp of the underlying principles not to take too simplistic a view of the problem; it is easy to wander into a quagmire of confused and inconsistent terminology, and that is what we must at all costs avoid.

64 THE CLASSIFICATION OF LIGHTING DEVICES — A CASE STUDY

Anne Serio

Museum Specialist, Division of Domestic Life
National Museum of American History, Smithsonian Institution
Washington, DC

Lighting devices are basic tools of civilisation. As such, they have been in use in one form or another for centuries. Individual devices have acquired multiple names over those centuries: names which have caused problems for those who need to identify and classify lighting artefacts.

Figure 64.1 Wick support oil lamp of type referred to as betty lamp

The National Museum of American History

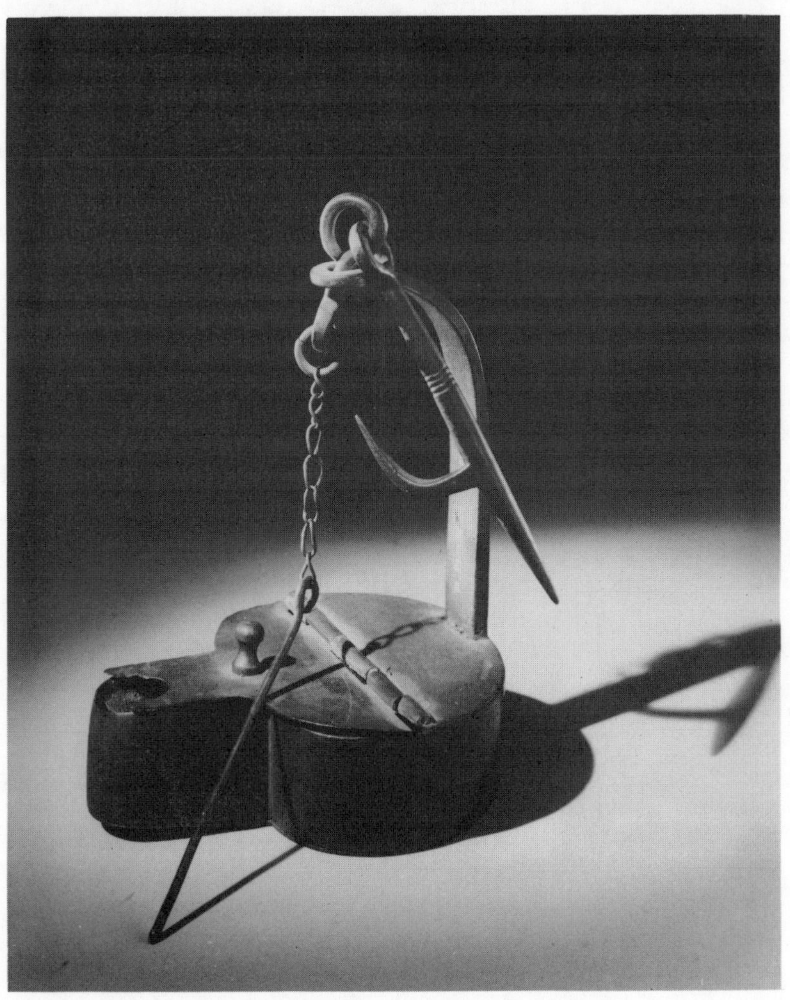

Figure 64.2 Central draft oil lamp commonly called an Argand lamp

The National Museum of American History

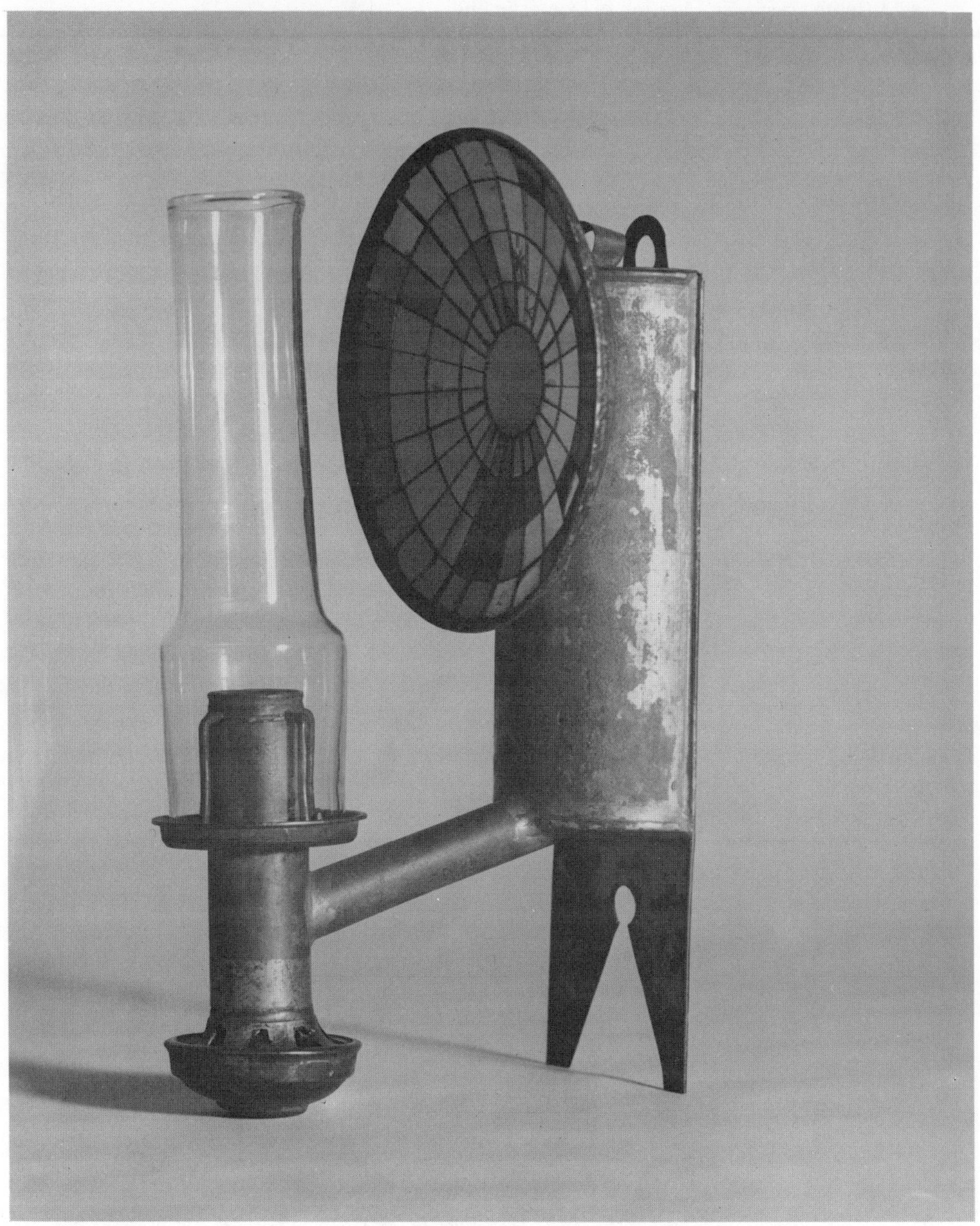

The Rushlight Club, an organisation dedicated to the study of early lighting, recognised the problem by establishing a committee on the classification of lamps shortly after its formation in 1932. The editor of *The Rushlight*, in describing a meeeting of the committee, reported that one of the committee members had written an article on the subject and 'naturally he thought that his classification could not be improved on' and also naturally one of the other committee members did not agree with him. The 'customary brilliant verbal fireworks followed' as the committee debated the names to be applied to particular lamps (Rushlight Club, 1935). But they never did resolve the issue: the matter was tabled. In the years since that meeting, various classification schemes have been proposed and glossaries produced to define the many names used for lamps and other lighting devices. Despite this, people have continued to use a multitude of names for the same device.

Identifying and classifying lighting devices in a truly meaningful way involves coming to terms with these various names: sorting them out and reconciling them. This became

Figure 64.3 Wick support oil lamp

The National Museum of American History

apparent in managing the National Museum of American History's extensive collection of American and European lighting devices dating from the sixteenth to the twentieth centuries — researching the devices in it, adding to it, providing for its physical care, answering enquiries about it and assisting others in its use. The enquiries in particular made it obvious that people were using different names for the same object and the same name for different objects. Something had to be done to ensure that people understood what was meant when an object was described using chosen terminology, if the collection and information on it were to be readily available to the public. Simply selecting a single object name for each device and organising the collection and information on that basis does not solve the problem of the multiple names. As more than one name applies to the same object, a lighting device might be given one of those names by one person, while a second person might give the same device a different one.

The issues of which of the various names should be chosen as the object name for a particular device and what should be done with the other names remained unresolved. For example, should the lamp illustrated in Figure 64.1 be called a wick support lamp, an oil lamp, or a betty lamp, when in fact all three names apply? The lamp in Figure 64.2 is also an oil lamp but it is not a wick support lamp nor a betty lamp. The third lamp is a wick support lamp and an oil lamp but not a betty lamp (Figure 64.3). They are, however, all lamps. By calling them all lamps and subdividing them on the basis of the characteristics that result in the other names, one can accommodate the commonly used terms and group the objects in a meaningful way.

The classification categories

The Museum Information Retrieval and Documentation System, known by the acronym MIRDS, is a generalised cataloguing system developed at the National Museum of American History. It provides classification categories (Figure 64.4) that can be used to solve the multiple name problem. MIRDS is not a classification system itself, it is a set of structured categories into which a classification scheme can be fitted. The MIRDS

Figure 64.4 MIRDS classification categories

SUPERCLASS IV–II
SUPERCLASS I
CLASS NAME
ALTERNATE CLASS NAME
FOREIGN CLASS NAME
PROPER NAME
SUBCLASS I (Fuel)
II
ALTERNATE SUBCLASS I (Form)
II
ADDITIONAL SUBCLASS (Placement)
ADDITIONAL SUBCLASS
MISNOMERS
OBJECT TYPE

categories can be used manually or they can be adapted for use in a computerised system. In addition to a category for the common generic name of the object (Class Name), MIRDS provides a series of categories for the names of larger groupings to which the object might belong (Superclasses) and various categories for groupings narrower than the object name (Subclasses). Specific categories are identified for recording titles and trade names (Proper Names); other generic object names commonly applied to the object being classified, but not selected as the object name for this particular classification (Alternate Class Names); discarded class names and incorrectly applied proper names (Misnomers); the object name in languages other then English (Foreign Class Names); and the identification of certain special types of objects such as patent models, facsimiles and miniatures (Object Type). Since MIRDS provides separate categories for recording material, style, production method, date, maker and related details, such information need not be included in the classification.

Existing classification systems for museum objects are usually subject orientated, they begin with broad concepts and narrow down to the object which, in most cases, is where they stop. The lighting classification is object orientated, it begins at the object level subdividing objects into smaller groupings based on shared attributes. The superclasses mentioned above can be used for the broad concepts of systems such as the *Social History and Industrial Classification* (SHIC Working Party, 1983) or *Nomenclature* (Chenhall, 1978) or for a classification system developed within the museum. The subclasses are used to further define and classify the object class. This is what has been done for lighting devices.

Selection of object names

Object names (entered in the MIRDS category called Class Name) have been identified for the devices and those names or classes have been subdivided to further define specific devices. The only grouping broader than the object or class name that has been assigned at this point is lighting devices. Lighting devices are all apparatus used to produce artificial light. The lighting classification was developed specifically for this one large grouping of objects and only the superclass needed to identify that grouping has been included. Superclasses above the level of lighting devices would need to be determined in the context of other man-made objects and broad cultural concepts. This was outside

Figure 64.5 Selected list of Class (Object) Names for lighting devices

CLASS (OBJECT) NAMES
Candleholder
Chandelier
Cresset
Fixture
Lamp
Lantern
Rushlight holder
Splint holder
Torch

the scope of this project, the intent of which is to provide specific identification of individual items. Any of the existing classification systems for museum objects could be used for the broader concepts if one wished to include them.

In deciding which names to use as object names and how to subdivide them, terminology and classifications used over the years by students and collectors of early lighting have been used. No new terms have been invented. The existing terms have been structured so that they can be recorded in a consistent manner.

The names selected as object names are the most commonly used generic names consistently applied to a particular device (Figure 64.5). For lighting devices these names are frequently based on the general nature of the fuel or power source used. Devices that employ a fuel that is sufficiently rigid to support itself in a holder are called candleholders, rushlight holders, etc.; one in which the fuel, because of its liquid or semi-liquid state, is contained in a vessel are called lamps; and devices permanently fixed in place to which gas or electricity is delivered are called fixtures. Gas and electric devices that are not permanently fixed in place are also called lamps. In addition there are lanterns — devices, fixed or portable, designed to enclose and protect a light source (lamp, candle, etc.), usually with sides of glass, horn, or pierced metal, allowing light to emerge — and chandeliers — ornamental branched supports or frames to hold a number of lamps, candles or burners, usually hung from the roof or ceiling. These are the principal object names used for lighting devices. There are others but it is not necessary to list them all to demonstrate the classification system.

Consistency and common usage are the guidelines in determining object names. Where there is more than one name frequently used for an object, the one most consistently used has been selected. For example, the term fixture is sometimes used interchangeably with chandelier, usually when it is a gas or electric device. Chandelier is the preferred term because it is more commonly and consistently used for such devices and because it applies to similar devices for which the term fixture is rarely, if ever, used. Another example is the term candlestick. Candlestick is often used for the device called candleholder, usually when the holder is for a single candle. However, not every device holding a single candle is called a candlestick. The name is applied to some but not to others with often no clear understanding as to when it does or does not apply. Candleholder applies consistently to any device that holds a candle and is therefore preferred as the object name in this classification. Candlestick can be recorded as an alternate class name in those cases where it applies, making it possible to retrieve the device under either term.

Subclasses and proper names

The groupings below class or object name are poly-hierarchical. They are alternate or parallel ways of subdividing the class. The poly-hierarchical structure avoids the problem sited by Dr Loris Russell in the introduction to his lighting classification, 'A scheme that attempts to classify all devices for providing artificial lighting is more uniform if based on the source of the light rather (than) the physical design of the device. The latter can be the basis of the more detailed subdivisions. Such a system of classification is not perfect, because some lamps work with more than one kind of fuel, and an arbitrary choice has to be made' (Russell, 1968). In a poly-hierarchical structure this arbitrary choice does not have to be made.

Lamps are classified according to the specific fuel or power source they employ, according to form, and according to placement while in use. The partial listing in

Figure 64.6 Examples of subclasses for lamps

LAMP

- (By fuel)
- Grease
- Oil
- Lard
- Burning Fluid
- Kerosene
- Gas
- Gasoline
- Electric

- (By form)
- Pan
- Saucer
- Wick Channel
  - Crusie (Alternate Class Name)
  - Chill (Alternate Class Name)
  - Crasset (Alternate Class Name)
  - Phoebe (Alternate Class Name)
- Wick Support
  - Betty (Proper Name)
- Spout
- Float
- Wick Tube
- Central Draft
  - Argand (Proper Name)
- Flat Wick

- (By placement)
- Ceiling
  - Pendant (Alternate Class Name)
- Wall
  - Sconce (Alternate Class Name)
  - Bracket (Alternate Class Name)
- Floor
  - Piano lamp (Proper Name)
- Table
  - Banquet lamp (Proper Name)
- Hand

Figure 64.7 Classification of two wick support lamps in Figures 64.1 and 64.3

SUPERCLASS IV–II		
SUPERCLASS I	Lighting Devices	Lighting Devices
CLASS NAME	Lamp	Lamp
ALTERNATE CLASS NAME		
FOREIGN CLASS NAME		
PROPER NAME	Betty	
SUBCLASS I (Fuel)	Oil	Oil
II		
ALTERNATE SUBCLASS I (Form)	Wick Support	Wick Support
II		
ADDITIONAL SUBCLASS (Placement)		
ADDITIONAL SUBCLASS		
OBJECT TYPE		

Figure 64.6 shows some of the names that would be recorded in these categories. The subclasses can be divided further if necessary. Candleholders, lanterns and fixtures can be subdivided in much the same manner, although fuel is redundant for candleholders. Other devices may not need to be subdivided so extensively.

As there is a set of categories in MIRDS specifically reserved for classifying objects on the basis of their use, a subdivision for use is not needed in this classification scheme. A name given to a lighting device based on its use, such as binacle lamp or railroad lantern, would be recorded in the use category. This provides another alternative subdivision.

Some names applied to the devices can best be categorised as proper names: special names given to specific devices at a particular period, trade names, model names and the like. Names such as Betty lamp, Argand lamp and Astral lamp are examples of proper names. These names frequently relate to a certain form or use, but they do not apply to all devices of that form or use and are usually not applied consistently.

Figures 64.7 and 64.8 illustrate how the classification works. The two wick support lamps in Figures 64.1 and 64.3 would be classified as shown in Figure 64.7. These lamps are grease lamps as well as oil lamps as any heavy oil or grease would burn in them. To record this fact a second entry, the term grease, would be made in the fuel subclass. The oil lamp that is not a wick support lamp is classified in Figure 64.8.

While it is not reasonable, nor indeed necessary, to record every name applied to a particular object, this structured approach makes it possible to record those names most frequently used for lighting devices. It avoids the necessity of having to make arbitrary choices to exclude commonly used terminology. The terms can all be recorded. The classification gives one an object name for indexing and as many other terms, consistently recorded, as needed to meaningfully identify and group the artefacts and/or information about them. It provides the flexibility to record the distinguishing characteristics of specific devices on a case-by-case basis, including as much information as is known or desired for each piece. Information can be retrieved using any

Figure 64.8 Classification of oil lamp in Figure 64.2

SUPERCLASS IV–II	
SUPERCLASS I	Lighting Devices
CLASS NAME	Lamp
ALTERNATE CLASS NAME	
FOREIGN CLASS NAME	
PROPER NAME	Argand
SUBCLASS I (Fuel)	Oil
II	
ALTERNATE SUBCLASS I (Form)	Central Draft
II	
ADDITIONAL SUBCLASS (Placement)	Wall
ADDITIONAL SUBCLASS	
OBJECT TYPE	

combination of the categories: all lamps, only wick support lamps, all kerosene lighting devices and so forth.

To date the lighting classification has been used in physically organising the National Museum of American History's collection, in inventorying the collection, and in preparing a checklist of the devices in a large addition to the collection. It has made it possible to organise the collection and the information about it in a consistent, readily retrievable form, identifying each object using all of the terminology commonly applied to it. The same structured approach can be applied to subdividing other object groups.

65 WHAT'S IN A NAME? A CLASSIFICATION, AND A DEFINITION

Shelly Foote

Museum Specialist, Division of Costume
National Museum of American History, Smithsonian Institution
Washington, DC

For the last ten years, the Division of Costume at the Smithsonian Institution has successfully used a modified version of the ICOM costume classification system (a hierarchical structure) and our own standardised system of terminology (generic object names). Viewed as a tool, these systems have helped us to reorganise our collections and to gain a better understanding of our collection holdings. Although adopting standardised terminology was time-consuming, especially in the implementation phases (and the process is far from complete), the end benefits to the Division have made it a worthwhile investment in time and personnel.

Background

To understand the enormity of this undertaking, one must first understand our collections. The costume collection houses about 30 000 civilian costume artefacts, including men's, women's and children's garments and accessories as well as objects used for making and selling clothing. The emphasis of the collection is on American made or used materials; therefore, the collection spans in date from the seventeenth century to the present. Since collecting began in the late nineteenth century, record-keeping, as in most older museums, is uneven in its quality.

In the 1960s the Division recognised the need for a classification system to facilitate record-keeping and accessible storage. A system was implemented that came to the museum via the Valentine Museum in Richmond, Virginia. It was basically a word list without accompanying definitions. As a finding aid, the Division developed a series of cross-referenced cards. The catalogue card, filed by catalogue number, contained most of the available information on an object. There were also donor, manufacturer, area of use, and most importantly, subject cards. These latter were filed by classification, then further by object name, then divided by the sex/age of the wearer (i.e. man, woman, boy, girl, child), and then by the date of use. This system worked well manually, as the staff knew they might find related objects.

Then in 1978 the United States Congress mandated that the Smithsonian Institution physically inventory its collections. Our museum, The National Museum of American History, decided to computerise this inventory. The minimal record was to include museum number, object name and location of the object. The administration scheduled the Division of Costume as one of the first divisions to be inventoried. We knew that our then-current system of classification was going to create problems for us when we tried to computerise it. It did have an hierarchical structure, but items were not compared equally. For example, underwear was on the same level hierarchically as trousers. We also knew that we had not always called like items by the same name and that there were many objects in our collections for which there were no provisions in the listing.

To change our classification and terminology systems was a major decision, as it meant physically rearranging the collection, since, like most costume collections, it is stored by subject. In part, the storage requirements of different kinds of objects (hats versus gloves, for example) necessitates this arrangement. Additionally, the collection is most often used in this manner. Staff and visiting researchers usually want to view or compare similar kinds of objects. Therefore, changing our classification and terminology systems meant more than just changing existing manual records or creating new computerised records. It meant looking at each object and deciding what it should be called and where it should be stored based on the new classification. Since our previous records had inconsistently named objects, we could not use the cards alone to change the names. It was necessary to consult the objects themselves. Since object storage is (and will probably always be) a manual operation, the scale of the undertaking forced us to examine carefully, the available classification and terminology systems. We knew that no system would be perfect, but we wanted something that would require minor changes in storage and would also allow for some flexibility for new kinds of objects in the future.

Costume classification schemes

We started by comparing existing classification systems. We evaluated their worth by testing their structure against the contents of our collection to determine if our wide range of objects was accommodated in a logical manner. The first system we investigated was the widely known *Nomenclature for Museum Cataloguing* (Chapter 58). From a costume historian's point of view the objects were not grouped logically. For example, 'Clothing, Headwear' was the name of one large grouping of what are commonly called 'accessories' but other accessories such as gloves, mitts and mittens were listed in 'Clothing–Accessory' and additional accessories, such as purses and fans were part of 'Personal Gear'. We then looked at a system developed by Marilyn Horn, then a professor at the University of Nevada. Her system reflected the traditional groupings used by costume historians, but it did not accommodate the wide range of objects present in our collections. Propitiously, the English costume historian, Anne Buck, told us about a system being developed by the ICOM Costume Committee (Chapter 65). Miss Buck had published an in-progress report in the December 1976 issue of *The Museums Journal* (Buck, 1976). The adoption of the ICOM system had an additional advantage (if it worked) in that we would be using a system accepted internationally. We, as Americans, would not be creating something totally different; it would also ease communication in the international community. The ICOM system had not been finalised at this point, but we found that in principle it worked. Objects were organised by layers on the body (underwear, main garments and outerwear for example) and then by parts of the body, since the human body is the common element in all costume.

We modified the ICOM system, sometimes intentionally, sometimes not. We deliberately added a new category or 'superclass', called 'Accessories for the Selling of Clothing' to accommodate objects in our collections such as department store mannequins (Figure 65.1) and display cases for which there was no provision in ICOM. Additionally, we did not separate 'Underwear' and 'Supporting or Shaping Structure' but considered all of these items to be 'Underwear'. We eliminated 'Accessories Added to Body or Clothing for Ornament' by adding these items to 'Accessories Worn on the Body' as we felt there was some question as to the functionality or ornamentality of many garments and accessories. Lastly, the titles we used for these superclasses are superficially different. ICOM names had not been finalised at this time. For example, we used 'Accessories for the Care of the Person' where ICOM finally selected 'Accessories

Figure 65.1 The Smithsonian's Division of Costume collects a wide range of artefacts, including department store mannequins, such as these from 1988. To accommodate these objects, a new classification, 'Accessories for the Selling of Clothing', was added to the existing ICOM classification

Dane A. Penland, Smithsonian Institution

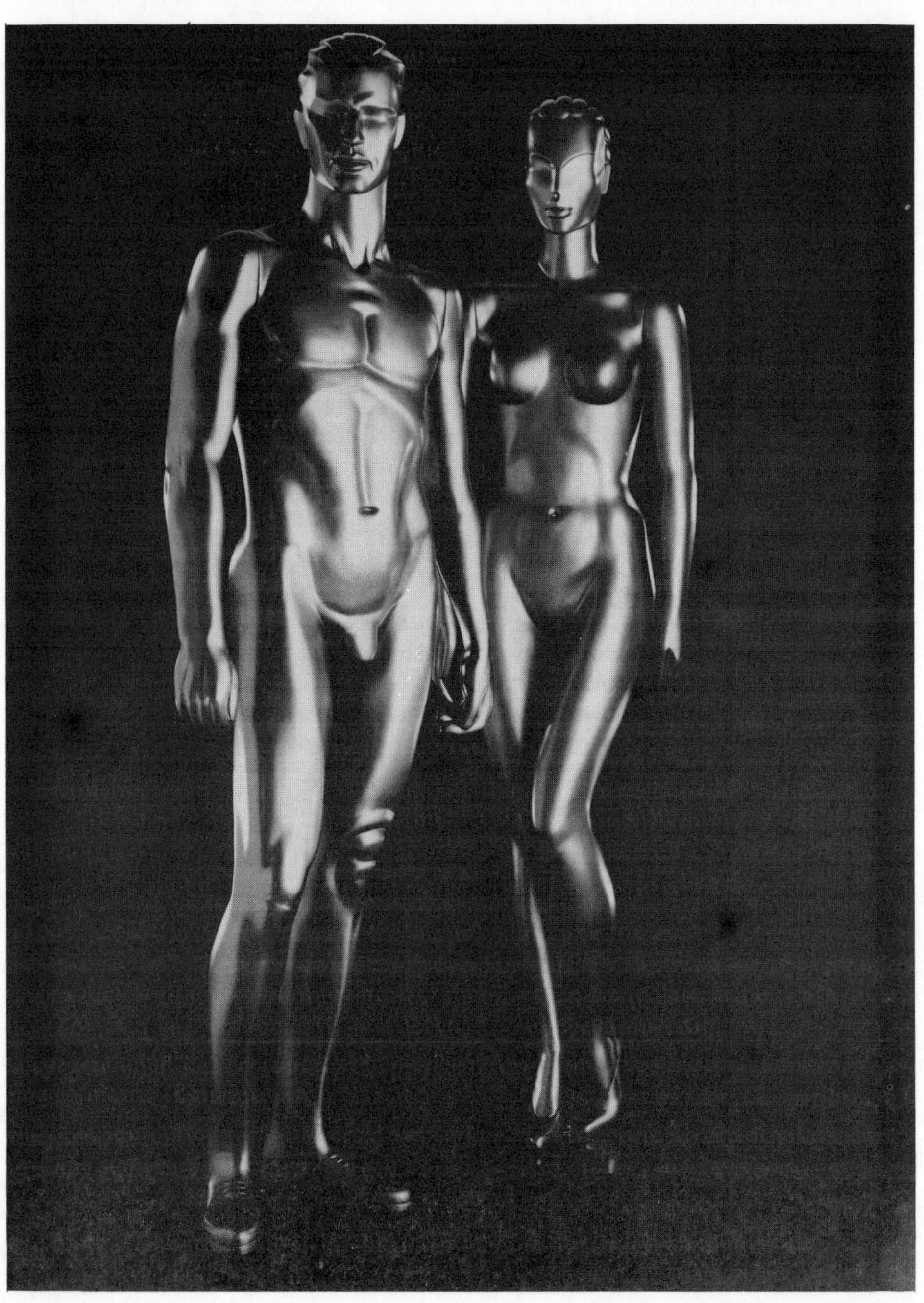

Figure 65.2 The ICOM and Division of Costume classification systems differ most from each other in the intermediate 'superclass' listing. This sampling shows some of the differences

INTERMEDIATE SUPERCLASSES

ICOM	DIVISION OF COSTUME
Main Garments	Main Dress
Covering body above and below waist	Entire Body
Covering body above waist	Upper body
Covering body below waist	Lower Body
Underwear	Underwear
Worn next to the body above and below waist	Entire body
Above and below waist with shaping for legs	Entire Body
Above waist	Upper Body
Below waist with shaping for legs	Lower Body
Above and below waist immediately beneath main garment	Entire Body
Below waist immediately beneath main garment	Lower Body

Used in the Care of the Person'. These differences are so minor as to be practically non-existent.

We also used an 'intermediate' grouping or 'superclass' between the object name and these larger classifications. Given the size of our collection, it was necessary to group some items together for storage and record-keeping purposes. We decided to use parts of the body (as did ICOM for most groupings). For example, gloves are part of Accessories Worn on the Body (using our classification terminology). Other related objects are mitts and mittens because they are all worn on the hand. In this instance, the term chosen for the intermediate 'superclass' was 'handwear'. Whenever possible we used the shortest term possible for these intermediate groupings, both for clarity and for minimal use of computer space. In the future we need to compare closely our intermediate superclasses with ICOM, for this is, as can be seen from the accompanying chart (Figure 65.2), where we differ the most. We may modify some of our terms to fit ICOM, but we may, in some instances, continue with our own.

By adopting a standardised classification system, we were allowed to add all these 'superclasses' to the computerised inventory records (where the emphasis was on skeletal records for accountability purposes). This addition made the computer records much more valuable to us. We have been able to use the classification for collections management, but we also foresee using it for research and exhibition needs in the future.

Object name definitions

Most of our efforts concentrated on selecting generic object names. At this time, we had little information on what ICOM was doing in this area. Published costume dictionaries were of little assistance, since they were often based on the vagaries of fashion terminology or, if they were historical, they only covered a specific period of time. No one dictionary would serve our purpose. Whatever we adopted had to be meaningful to

Figure 65.3 Is this object a bag or a purse? By the Division of Costume's definition it would be a bag, since it has no fixed closure

Laurie Minor, Smithsonian Institution

ourselves, other costume historians, and to a certain extent, the general public, who often uses our collections. Being realistic, we knew that the selection of terms would be somewhat artificial, but we wanted the terms to be commonly understood as much as was possible. We also decided to use preferred American terminology since the majority of our users are American. Lastly, given the size of our collections it was essential that the definitions could not be so broadly written that many objects be assigned the same name.

Probably the most important decision we made was to document the object names selected. We felt that too often word lists have been published without definitions or illustrations. The user has always had to determine what was meant by these terms. Several people using a listing meant that several interpretations could be made. For example, one individual might call an object a bag and another person might call it a purse when both terms are listed as preferred terms in a word list (Figure 65.3). What distinguishes a bag from a purse? Without documentation in written or visual form it would be difficult to know. As a consequence of this decision, we ended up creating our own costume dictionary. We hoped that by having definitions we would be consistent in our naming of objects, both then and in the future. With the inevitable changes in personnel, having clear definitions might make consistency possible. Also, if we later decided we were wrong in the choice of the term, we would be consistently wrong. It would then be much easier to change the records and change the information on the object itself.

Once we decided to write a dictionary, we were faced with the issue of how to differentiate objects. Was it to be on the basis of form or function? And, more importantly, what did we mean by form and function? The answer is far from being clear. We felt objects should be distinguished from one another on the basis of form (cut or construction), not on how they were used. But you cannot ignore function entirely since costume is meant to be worn and is used in many situations (in public and in private). For example, a dress is a dress, no matter for what occasion or by whom it was worn. That seemed clear. But how do you define a dress without indicating how it was used? You cannot. Our definition of dress (which is classified as Main Dress, Entire Body) is that it is a 'skirted garment, cut in one or more pieces, worn in public . . .'. As one critic has pointed out, this definition combined construction (a skirted garment) with function (in public and where and in what layer on the body it was worn). There is simply no way to get around using some functional aspects as part of the distinctions. If we did not we would find that other garments, such as nightgowns, chemises, etc., would be defined as dresses as they are also skirted garments. This would be too artificial a distinction. No one would come asking to see dresses when they were interested in nightgowns. Additionally, we would be mixing up these various kinds of garments in storage. So, we had to take the long-standing usage of clothing into account when we wrote the definitions.

We eventually defined function as a special usage, such as occasions for which a particular kind of clothing is often worn (weddings or for mourning) or by a group of people who are readily distinguishable by their clothing (the Amish or Quakers). This usage was not to be used as the part of the object names (not wedding dress, but dress). But we knew that this kind of information was of great interest to ourselves as well as to users of the collections.

We are fortunate that the Museum Information Retrieval and Documentation System (MIRDS), used by The National Museum of American History, provides for all kinds of information required by the large scope of the museum. Therefore, we included this special function information in two ways. One category was defined for a function that was obvious to someone looking at the object. For example, many white dresses are immediately recognisable to many people as wedding dresses, usually by their fabrics and trimmings. Therefore, wedding would be indicated in this category. However, suits and other dresses have been worn by women for weddings, but only the background information that came with the object would tell us that. A second functional category was defined for these objects. For example, a 1945 woman's suit worn for a wedding would have the object name 'suit' but would also have 'wedding' listed in this second category. The information, when computerised, could be retrieved in many ways. We could compare similar objects, such as head-dresses. Or we could retrieve by one of both of the functional fields, depending on our needs.

We also decided that the name of the object should be dependent on its construction, not upon which sex or age group wore it (men, women, girls, boys and children). We hoped this would eliminate sexual bias in our definitions. In our manual files, subject cards are filed by object name within their proper classification and then by the sex/age of the wearer. In our computer records the sex/age of the wearer is a separate field and we can, therefore, retrieve either by all objects of the same name or by the sex/age of the wearer or any permutations of these fields. ICOM, on the other hand, first divided items by the sex/age of the wearer. We hoped that by starting with the cut of the garment we might reduce the amount of sexual biases in the definitions. But some bias cannot be avoided given the long history of usage of some terms. For example, a skirted entire body garment worn for nightwear has traditionally been a nightgown or nightdress for women and a nightshirt for men. Common usage over time had to influence our decision.

Members of the staff developed definitions and possible generic object names for sections of the collections by collecting various published definitions and comparing them with the objects themselves. New definitions were written based on both of these sources. As the definitions were completed for a large grouping of objects, such as underwear, all the divisional staff were given copies of the definitions and were encouraged to ask questions and make suggestions. The end result was a written costume dictionary verified by the objects themselves.

Even though we standardised our terminology as a tool for record-keeping and collections management purposes, we did not want to forget the historical or fashion terminology previously used to describe objects. To do so would be to lose the richness of our heritage. Again, luckily MIRDS has categories where this kind of information can be recorded. However, so far we have had the time to record this information in only one instance. In this instance, a curator emeritus has researched the original terms used for the items in the Copp collection of everyday clothing from the late eighteenth and early nineteenth centuries and this information has been added to our computer records. For the rest of the collection, the information exists in our manual files and needs to be recorded in our central computerised catalogue to make it more accessible.

Future direction

We know that the classification and terminology we use is not perfect. It needs refinement. Even though we tried to be as careful as possible in developing these systems, we were under time constraints and decisions had to be made quickly. We need to make a final reconciliation with the ICOM classification system. Whatever the outcome, our revised ICOM classification system is so close to the official version that there will not be a problem of international communication. More needs to be done with our dictionary. We need to rewrite many of our definitions for clarity. Some need to be changed. In our zeal to define terms, we may have made some of the definitions too narrow. Terms that should be subgroupings or subclasses are listed as object names. We need to add synonyms to the ends of the definitions and these terms should also be cross-indexed in the dictionary. The definitions will probably always have some sexual bias given the material with which we are dealing and our own unconscious prejudices. The dictionary is in the process of being revised. The Division has a major exhibition opening in the spring of 1989 and most of our time is devoted to that project. However, we shall have a re-written version of the dictionary and a thesaurus available for public distribution as soon as is possible after the exhibition opening.

For the foreseeable future, we will be forced to work with both manual and computerised records, neither of them being complete. Our computer records are skeletal and much background information and cross-referencing (such as for sets) needs to be added. Additionally, our computer records are not available online, creating a time lag between entering data and having the information available to us. Until this data is readily accessible, the records will continue to be most useful for collections management and less helpful for research enquiries.

Establishing standardised classification and terminology has been a time-consuming project that will never be totally complete. As new information on objects comes to light or we are presented with new kinds of objects we will need to refine the dictionary and possibly the classification. It will be a living, growing system, not a static one. We would never have attempted such an enormous task if it had not been for our inventory. But the divisional staff feels that it was a worthwhile endeavour. We have never examined our collections so widely and so intensely. The results have helped us evaluate the strengths and weaknesses of our collection. We have also organised our slide and photograph files to correspond to the classification and terminology systems. As a result, we believe that our records and collections are in better order than they have ever been in before.

---

66 NOMENCLATURE FOR MUSEUM CATALOGUING AT THE MARGARET WOODBURY STRONG MUSEUM

Jan Guldbeck

Registrar
The Strong Museum
Rochester, NY

Introduction

The Strong Museum in Rochester, New York, which opened to the public in October 1982, developed largely out of the collections amassed by one woman with diverse and eclectic tastes and out of a mission statement that endeavoured to bring some conceptual coherence to those collections. *Nomenclature for Museum Cataloging*, now the standard reference in the history museum field, was itself an outgrowth of the effort to bring physical and intellectual order to a wide array of historical artefacts. The traditional classification system used most often in art museums was not adequate for a history museum that is often more interested in an object's function than it is in style or materials.

Margaret Woodbury Strong (1897–1969) was a wealthy widow whose fortune was based on an early and enduring family investment in Rochester's Eastman Kodak Company. An insatiable collector, Mrs Strong's most consuming interest was dolls — she collected 30 000 before she died — but she also collected many thousands of other artefacts, including inkwells, silver, household objects, prints, regional art, doll houses, trade cards and canes. Mrs Strong did not collect the finest and most expensive artefacts. Instead, her interests seemed to focus on the common machine-made object. For example, she did not collect many one-of-a-kind oil paintings; however, we estimate that the ephemera collection numbers 80 000 pieces. It consists of paper objects which are not easily saved because they either deteriorate rapidly or are thrown out. Yet, as ephemeral as they were meant to be in their own time, they have become valuable historical evidence today.

When Mrs Stong died, she left behind much more than a very large collection; she left the trustees of her estate with the charge of determining whether the artefacts she had accumulated could form the basis of a museum. Holman J. Swinney, then the director of the Adirondack Museum and later the Strong's first director, was hired to study these collections and to recommend an answer to this question. Because of Mrs Strong's inarticulate but apparent interest in mass-produced goods, Swinney advised that the collections would form an effective material basis upon which to interpret the domestic life of 'ordinary Americans' in the north-eastern United States in the age of industrialisation, roughly taken to embrace the years between 1820 and 1940.

Nomenclature

Swinney hired a professional staff to bring the collection — about 500 000 objects — under control and make it into a museum, an enormous task that took about ten years to complete. In the 1970s, few museums in the United States used computers. But to Swinney, who realised that in order to organise such a vast collection and make the accumulated knowledge about it easy to retrieve, computers had obvious potential. He hired Dr Robert Chenhall to consult with Strong Museum staff and museum professionals around the country to devise a classification system for man-made objects based on function. In 1978, Chenhall's classification system was published as *Nomenclature for Museum Cataloging* (Chenhall, 1978) and hundreds of history museums have since used the system to manage their collections and records (Chapter 58). *Nomenclature* can be used to manage records in a manual as well as in a computerised record keeping system. Its relevance to the field was effectively demonstrated when the published volume sold out in 1984. By that time it had become apparent that *Nomenclature* needed more than reprinting. Since its publication, many users had suggested changes to make the system more useful for cataloguers of man-made artefacts. The *Revised Nomenclature* was published in 1988 (Blackaby, 1988).

Since 1978, the Strong Museum has used *Nomenclature* to catalogue and organise the collections. To date, about 85 000 objects are in the computerised catalogue. But, after the system was developed, the staff realised that a controlled vocabulary was necesary in addition to the classification system and the set of object names that *Nomenclature* provided. Between 1979 and 1983, Mary Case, then registrar at the Strong Museum, wrote a cataloguing manual which serves as an instruction book for whoever is cataloguing the collection, whether it is a full-time curator, the curatorial cataloguer, or a volunteer.

Before the advent of computers, vocabulary control was not as important as it is today. Not only is it important to use a single object term consistently when cataloguing, but it became evident that imposing vocabulary control on other data fields would make the information more useful and more easily retrieved. Case worked with staff curators to write 'authority lists' for Material/Technique, Style/Type, Subject, and Theme. Having the authority lists in conjunction with *Nomenclature* has enabled the museum staff to take full advantage of computers.

The *Revised Nomenclature* and the cataloguing manual are very effective tools for managing the collections and the catalogue information. However, the curatorial staff has embarked on another project that makes the collections and collections data even more useful. Though we have an estimated half million objects in the collection, there were holes that were easily identified at the outset. For example, while Mrs Strong collected many artefacts of daily life between 1820 and 1940, she did not seem to be drawn to furniture; consequently, collections have been continually supplemented to fill out the material record. About 4 000 objects were added to the collection in 1987, both by donation and purchase.

We do not have infinite storage space (who does?), so we cannot accept or purchase every object that comes along. We have a very precise statement of purpose which guides members of the collections staff in acquisition decisions. In addition, the museum's five curators, as well as the librarian, registrar, and an historian, sit on an Acquisitions Committee. The committee is chaired by the Vice President for Collections and meets twice a month to consider additions to the collection.

Even though we are guided by the statement of purpose, that policy is not specific enough to help curators and historians identify gaps and plan for the future of specific museum collections.

Scope statements

In 1985, Vice President for Collections Lynne Poirier visited the Smithsonian Institution to talk with staff involved in archival projects and learn about how their scope statements have helped manage collections growth. In the archives field, collections development statements are written that describe specific collections. It seemed to Ms Poirier that such statements might be applicable and useful for museum collections.

The purpose of writing the 'scopes' is to gain a solid handle on what the museum now has and what future growth or reduction would entail. The process of preparing them has helped the staff define our major collections and sub-collections. So far, since 1985, 66 scopes have been written. This is a project without end because there are so many sub-collections that need to be studied and written up in this way, and it is possible conceptually to divide the collections in any number of ways. As the collections continue to evolve and as gaps are identified and filled, scope statements become outdated. However, there is no better way to get to know a collection than to work on a scope statement.

In 1985, each of the five curators started working on their collections and deciding how best to divide them into manageable sizes that would suit the scope method of analysis. First of all, they looked at the collection from the *Nomenclature* vantage point. The curators listed the collections under their care according to the major *Nomenclature* groupings, such as written communication equipment and sub-groupings such as inkwells, paperweights and stationery. Their lists were arranged hierarchically, in classification and object term order, just as *Nomenclature* is. Having *Nomenclature* already in place made such a project possible.

Structure of scope statements

Each scope is divided into three sections. The first discusses the collection using the following descriptors Collection Size, Date Range, Style/Type, Material, Special Manufacturers, Artist/Artisans, Geographical Identification, Image/Subject, Theme and Handwork or Manufactured. Other descriptors may be added as appropriate. The second is a discussion of storage or conservation needs. The third section is a subjective statement on future use, growth or reduction of the collection. Each scope statement should be no longer than two pages, single-spaced.

The project has been underway now for nearly three years. As more scopes were written, a format was developed to provide uniformity and consistency. Experience showed that a scope statement should treat a sub-collection that includes no less than aproximately 100 objects. An exception to this at-least-100 rule is made if there is an important smaller collection used in interpretation and exhibition. There is enough data in common among 100 objects to make the scope statement useful and to make the data manageable.

Of course, many sub-collections are far bigger than 100 objects. In such a case, collections are divided up by other appropriate descriptors. For example, the museum has thousands of coins. A useful way to sub-divide the object term Coin was to do a scope statement on just those coins that depict American heroes, a useful category in view of the museum's plans for a 1989 exhibition on the subject.

Since early 1987, one person, the curatorial cataloguer, has been responsible for writing scopes. The full-time job of the curatorial cataloguer is to work with the curators, one at a time, to develop these statements. Each curator is given ten weeks a year of the cataloguer's services. Together, the curator and cataloguer choose a sub-collection to work on. In many instances, the objects in the sub-collection are not completely catalogued. Doing the scopes has meant that many objects are getting catalogued and accounted for the first time in years.

Rather than go to the computer and find out what is catalogued in a particular sub-collection, the cataloguer and curator first work with the objects. In some cases this means moving objects in order to have them all stored in the same storage space. This project has done much to improve storage conditions and the accessibility of the collections. The curator and cataloguer meet several times to decide on the best sources of information about that particular sub-collection, and they agree on how the sub-collection fits into the *Nomenclature* hierarchy. Each scope statement starts by naming the category, classification and object name. In most cases, cataloguing must be completed before the scope can be developed. The cataloguer and curator agree on what features to look for and describe about each object. They also discuss which themes and subjects are most likely to be searched later in the computerised catalogue. This can be a very subjective decision: the same image on a Staffordshire plate, on a trade card, and on a portrait print might evoke a different theme for each curator looking at it, as well as when regarded in the light of different exhibition topics. For example, the image of Tom Thumb's wedding scene might 'say' romanticism to one curator, celebrity to another and courtship to yet another. The cataloguer/scope writer must be sure to look at each object from as many different points of view as possible.

After all the objects are catalogued in a targeted sub-collection, the catalogue cards are assembled and studied. It might take ten weeks to catalogue a sub-collection, but the familiarity with the collection that cataloguing develops, coupled with the precise guidelines for writing a scope, make it possible to prepare a scope in a day.

For the third section of the scope statement, the subjective part, dealing with future additions or deletions from the collection, the curatorial cataloguer again consults with the curator, whose point of view is sufficiently broad to make judgements about if and how the collection should grow.

Many benefits have come out of the Strong Museum scope project. For one, it has enforced and reinforced cataloguing. Dealing with a large number of similar objects one after the other has proven to be a very efficient way of cataloguing. We have found that volunteers, who are not subject experts, can be easily taught how to catalogue. If we were to acquire a collection of objects for which there already was a scope statement — commemorative medals, for example — the volunteer could study the scope statement to learn what is deemed important to note in the catalogue. The advantage of cataloguing along with developing the scope is that there is a beginning, a middle and an end to such a project. No matter what the project, people always appreciate having an end in sight.

At the Strong Museum, scopes are used by the curators each time the Acquisition Committee meets. A curator is able to say how many objects just like the one offered there are in or are *not* in the collection. While that information is in the computer, the notebook of scope statements has proven to be a more 'user-friendly' tool in some respects; because not every curator has a computer, it is quicker to refer to the scope notebook.

As more scope statements are completed, we come closer to having a comprehensive overview of the collections. As I described, scope statements are written on objects in the collection. No attempt has yet been made yet to write a scope statement on a whole class of objects. An example of what we want to do might be Written Communication T & E, a classification in Category 6 of *Nomenclature*. The objects in this class include pens, pencils, writing paper, sealing wax and typewriters. Although our collections are divided among the curators roughly along the lines of classes in *Nomenclature*, there are exceptions. In the case of written communication, the curator of household accessories is in charge of pens and pencils; the curator of paper is in charge of writing paper; and the curator of furnishings takes care of typewriters. Having scope statements on all the objects in the class will enable us to write a scope statement on the entire class. Once scopes have been written on many classifications, taking into account the scope statements about hundreds of objects, we will be closer to having a collection survey and collections goal statement.

Conclusions

We find that it has been beneficial to have taken on such a project, particularly in view of our goal of managing our collections to their best advantage. The scope exercise has made it possible to learn more about the collection every day. The original intent of this project was to provide a history of the collection and a way of projecting future collection goals. As far as we know, no other museums are doing such scope statements. The curators appreciate the new understanding they have of the collections for which the scopes have been developed and curators in other institutions have begun to show interest in how the project is proceeding and what we have learned from it.

---

67 INVENTORYING AND DOCUMENTING OBJECTS IN REGIONAL MUSEUMS

Dr W. Eckehart Spengler

Rheinisches Museumsamt
Bonn

Introduction

The *Kleine Museen* project to computerise the records of regional museums has been set up by the museum administrations in Rheinland and Westfalen-Lippe, together with the *Institute für Museumskunde* (Stiftung Preußisher Kulturbesitz) and the *Konrad-Zuse-Zentrum für Informationstechnik Berlin*, both situated in Berlin-West (Saro and Wolters, 1988).

The regional museums in Rheinland have wanted a central inventory of their objects since 1925. However, it was nearly 40 years before the aim could be pursued, on the formation of a central administration for the welfare of the regional museums, the *Rheinisches Museumsamt* (RMA), near Colgne. In 1964, RMA appointed the first documentation expert to help these small museums, which were not able to make their own documentation because they had no curatorial staff.

RMA had to develop a system for describing the different objects found in such mixed collections. It developed a reference manual, including guidance on describing objects, producing accession- and catalogue-numbers, and how to record materials, technique, artist, manufacture motif, style or type, publications and photograph numbers (Rheinisches Museumsamt, 1985). This information is noted on a record card, together with a photograph and sketches, showing one or more pictures or copies of the object or its marks, decoration and so on. Our central documentation now contains details of 75 000 objects and object groups from 25 museums in Rheinland (about 20 per cent of all museums in this region).

The record cards of these museums have been copied for the RMA and our central archive. They are arranged by accession number, sometimes connected with an alphabetical system of object types, periods or materials. This leads to problems when looking for a specific object, such as 'Frechener Henkelkrug — Bartmannskrug, 1. H. 18.Jh.' when it is needed for publication or an exhibition.

Classification systems

We had to look for a way to introduce a computer-based object classification system, such as *Système descriptif des objects domestiques francais* (Chapter 13) or Trachsler's *Systematik kulturhistorisches* for the Schweizer Landesmuseum in Zürich (1981).

By 1987 we had a general view of our objects, with indexes and cross-references, a first systematic classification of our registered objects and the permutation of the main and leading elements of the words and object names. We also began to write thesauri for special collections, for we saw the general problem and necessity of a controlled vocabulary (Spengler, 1988). We have produced systematic and alphabetic indexes of these collections (Figures 67.1 and 67.2). We then had a means of putting in order our central archive and the possibility of helping other regional museums to register their objects in the right way.

Figure 67.1 Systematic index

```
Archivgut (Fortsetzung)

.  Archivgut außer Büchern usw.
.  .  Zeugnisse
.  .  .  Gesinde-Dienstbuch
                          M 438        Gesinde-Dienstbuch 1873
.  Archivgut: Bücher usw.
.  .  Kalender: Sachgruppe
.  .  .  Bauern-Wandkalender
                          K 61         Bauern-Wandkalender 13.Jh.
                                       Material: Holz
.  .  Religiöse Bücher, Schriften
.  .  .  Andachts-Gebetbuch
                          M 437        Andachts-Gebetbuch
                                       ("Himml.Wegweiser") Köln 1785
                                       Foto: LBR 28/15306/3
.  .  .  Antiphonarblatt  M 432        Antiphonarblatt? ca.15./16.Jh.
                          M 433        Antiphonarblatt 15./16.Jh.
                                       Foto: LBR 28/15310/3
.  .  .  Meßbuch          M 434        Meßbuch ca.1640/50  Foto: LBR
                                       28/15310/4
.  .  Zeitungen - Flugblätter
.  .  .  Zeitung          M 442        Zeitung: Gülich- und Bergische
                                       wöchentliche Nachrichten 1789
                          M 443        Zeitung: Bensberg-Gladbacher
                                       Anzeiger 1867
.  .  .  Zeitungsbildnis  M 441        Zeitungsbildnis Maurer ? c.1840/50


Aufzüge - Hebegeräte

.  Wäng                   HH 93        5-t-Winde/Wäng 1.H.20.Jh.
                                       Material: Eisen  Material:
                                       Eichenholz  Foto: LBR 28/15178


Bekleidung

.  Accessoires
.  .  Bänder - Spitzen
.  .  .  Band             HH 73        Band 1.H.20.Jh.  Material: Eisen
                                       Foto: LBR 28/15166
.  Schmuck
.  .  .  Anhänger: Sachgruppe
.  .  .  .  Holz-Perlmutt-Anhänger
                          K 373        Holz-Perlmutt-Anhänger 19.Jh.
.  .  .  .  Kupfer-Anhänger
                          H 274        Kupfer-Anhänger
                                       Antoniterkreuz/Umschrift 18.Jh.
                                       Foto: LBR 28/15074
.  .  .  .  Zinn-Anhänger
                          H 275/1-2    Zinn-Anhänger Kevelaer Mutter
                                       Gottes 19.Jh.  Foto: LBR 28/15050
.  .  .  Brosche          K 82         Brosche 1901  Material: Kupfer
                                       Material: Silber
.  .  .  Fibeln
.  .  .  .  Fibel         F 7          Fibelreste Refrath Frkzt.
                                       Material: Bronze  Foto: LBR
                                       28/15128
.  .  .  Nadeln (Schmuck)
.  .  .  .  Nadel-Kopf    K 81         Nadel-Kopf 2.H.19.Jh.  Material:
                                       Silber
Systematisches Register                          Seite 106
```

We now needed to input more categories and to get a catalogue of all important information concerned with the objects. We also needed a good and typical description of museum objects: the so called 'Bestimmungsfibeln'.

The documentation of objects is impossible without a controlled vocabulary for the precise object names and systematic terminologies and indexes, combined with an alphabetical index for a common standard dictionary.

Developing thesauri

My thesaurus of agricultural tools and instruments and those for timber and woodwork, means of transport and so on, is an effort to develop dictionaries for such groups of objects. I aim to find out a systematic structure of such tools from their historical beginnings until the machine-age, and their regional and dialect forms, their constructions, functions, uses and significant names and terms.

Many technical or professional terms contain words of the common popular language of slang, which became parts of a special terminology by defining them. This is the connection between real and nominal definitions.

I tried to order the historical tools of agricultural implement farming instruments, harvesters and tools of trade in a terminological nomenclature. Here are the basic words in the vocabulary. The museums can provide the simple names of the objects and also their regional connections and dialect-forms. Beneath these terms there are the objects themselves and their terminology in the scientific and folklore literature and the special nomenclature of technology. Bringing these together is one way to get a systematic index of cultural objects.

But we also need other original reseach, as we find in the Atlas of German Folklore (ADV) and the special dictionaries of regional slang and dialects, such as our *Rheinisches Worterbuch* or the materials and notes of the dialect atlas of Rheinland or of the other German regions. In an international context, we also need a European Atlas of Folklore, one of which was begun some years ago, with all the manifestations of folklore in the different territories of our continent.

But this is not enough, because we also need our own explorations in the region to find our special vocabulary and cultural background for our objects.

This type of research demonstrates that you also need a short definition of many words, if you want to understand the object name or the function of a tool. Only in this way does the word become clear and unequivocal. The functional and constructive definitions of my thesaurus will follow in a separate part, where we also have to take a look at the origins of the objects, for example the tools from prehistoric time until now, and especially their historical, regional, functional and technical development, forms and formations, and the development you find also in the object names themselves.

Literature referred to in Figures 67.2–71.4

H = Hansen, Wilhelm, *Hauswesen und Tagewerk im alten Lippe. Ländliches Leben in vorindustrieller Zeit* (Münster, Aschendorff, 1982).

S = Siuts, Hinrich, *Bäuerliche und handwerkliche Arbeitsgeräte in Westfalen. Die alten Geräte der Landwirtschaft und des Landhandwerks 1890–1930* (Münster, Aschendorff, 1982).

DG = Droysen – Gisevius, *Ackerbau einschließlich Bodenkunde, Düngerlehre, Maschinenlehre und Meliorationslehre etc.* (Berlin, 1906) u.ö.

The numbers following the abbreviations refer to pages (S) and plates (T).

Figure 67.2 Alphabetical index

Ackerbaugerät - Feldbestellung
. Bodenbearbeitungsgerät
. . Pflug
. . . Karrenpflugteile

• • • • **Pflugkarre (Karrenpflug)**
Syn: „Pleogkorrn"(Karrenpflug)

• • • • **Pflugschar (Karrenpflug)**
• • • • **Pflugsohle (Karrenpflug)**
Syn: „Grotsohle"(Karrenpflug)
„Grotsole"(Karrenpflug)

• • • • „Reuster"(Karrenpflug)
• • • • **Sech (Karrenpflug)**
• • • • **Sterz (Karrenpflug)**
Syn: „Stert"(Karrenpflug)

• • • • Streichbrett (Karrenpflug)
• • • • Vorschneidemesser (Karrenpflug)
Syn: „Lenguisen"(Karrenpflug)
„Vorschnier"(Karrenpflug)

• • • Kartoffelpflüge (Lit.: H 164, T 67/1-3)
• • • • Kartoffelpflug (Normalform) (Lit.: S 32, T 12/10)
• • • • Kartoffelpflug mit Pflugkarren
• • • • Kartoffelpflug mit Rad
• • • • Kartoffelpflug mit Radstelze
• • • Kippdampfpflug (Lit.: DG 104)
• • • Kipppflug
• • • Krümelpflug (Lit.: H 166, T 68/10)
• • • Krümelsohlenpflug (Lit.: S 32, T 12/11)
• • • Krümmer mit Gänsefuß (Lit.: H 166, T 68/11)
• • • Löffelschar (Lit.: H 166, T 68/11)
• • • Mehrscharepflug (Lit.: DG 74/79 f)
• • • Rajolpflug (Lit.: S 27, T 8/5)
• • • Saatpflug
• • • Saatpflug mit Sterz (Lit.: S 26, T 15)
• • • Saatpflugteile
• • • • Achse (Saatpflug) (Lit.: S 26/37, T 15)
• • • • Grindel (Saatpflug) (Lit.: S 26/37, T 15)
• • • • Grindelhalter (Saatpflug) (Lit.: S 26/37, T 15)
• • • • Lichte (Saatpflug) (Lit.: S 26/37, T 15)
• • • • Pflugbaum (Saatpflug) (Lit.: S 26/37, T 15)
• • • • Pflugbrücke (Saatpflug) (Lit.: S 26/37, T 15)
• • • • Pflugkette (Saatpflug) (Lit.: S 26/37, T 15)
• • • • Pflugmaul (Saatpflug) (Lit.: S 26/37, T 15)
• • • • Pflugstock (Saatpflug) (Lit.: S 26/37, T 15)
• • • • Rad (Saatpflug) (Lit.: S 26/37, T 15)
• • • • Schar (Saatpflug) (Lit.: S 26/37, T 15)
• • • • Sech (Saatpflug) (Lit.: S 26/37, T 15)
• • • • Sterz (Saatpflug)
Syn: „Stert"(Saatpflug)

Figure 67.3 Agricultural thesaurus hierarchy

Ackerbaugerät - Feldbestellung
. Bodenbearbeitungsgerät
. . Pflanzgerät

• • • **Erdbohrer** (Lit.: S 20/21, T 5)
• • • **Kartoffelpflanzbrett** (Lit.: S 22/23, T 6)
• • • **Pflanzenlochstoßer** (Lit.: S 20/21, T 5)
• • • **Pflanzholz** (Lit.: H 174, T 72/2)
Syn: **„Plänter"** (Lit.: H 174, T 72/8)

• • • **Pflanzstock**
• • • **Reihenzieher** (Lit.: S 22/23, T 6)
• • • **Rillenzieher** (Lit.: H 174, T 72/6-7)
• • • **Rübenpflanzer** (Lit.: H 174, T 72/5)
• • • **Setzstock** (Lit.: S 29/21, T 5)
• • **Pflug**
Syn: **„Pleog"**

• • • Baupflug (Lit.: S 27, T 8/6)
• • • Beetpflug (Lit.: S 27, T 8/5)
• • • Bockpflug (Lit.: S 26, T 8/4)
• • • Dampfpflug (Lit.: DG 104)
• • • Dampfpfluglokomobil (Lit.: DG 104)
• • • Doppelpflug (Lit.: DG 74/79 f)
• • • Doppelsterzpflug (Lit.: DG 74/79 f ; H 158, T 63/1-3)
• • • Eisenpflug mit Grubber (Lit.: S 38/39, T 15a)
• • • Gänsefuß (Lit.: H 166 ; S 44/45, T 68/11 ; S 38/39/15a)
Syn: „Gausefoot" (Lit.: H 166 ; S 44/45, T 68/11 ; S 38/39/15a)
„Porter" (Lit.: H 166 ; S 44/45, T 68/11 ; S 38/39/15a)

• • • Grubber (Lit.: H 166 ; S 44/45, T 68/11 ; S 38/39/15a)
Syn: Kultivator

• • • Hackpflug, keilförmig (Lit.: H 166, T 68/10)
• • • Häufelpflug (Lit.: H 164, T 67/1-3)
• • • Häufelpflug mit Pflugkarren (Lit.: H 164, T 67/4)
• • • Hakenpflug
• • • Haubergspflug (Lit.: S 24, T 7/1)
• • • Hunspflug (Lit.: S 24, T 7/2)
• • • • Pflugschar (Hunspflug) (Lit.: S 24, T 7/2)
• • • • Streichbrett (Hunspflug) (Lit.: S 24, T 7/2)
• • • • Vorwagen (Hunspflug)
• • • Igel (Krümelpflug) (Lit.: H 166, T 68/10)
• • • Karrenpflug (Lit.: H 156, T 62/1-2)
• • • Karrenpflugteile (Lit.: H 152, T 61/1-3 ; DG 74/79 f)
• • • • Grindel mit Pflugsohle
• • • • Pflugbaum (Karrenpflug)
• • • • Pflugeisen (Karrenpflug)
Syn: „Ploeguisen"(Karrenpflug)

• • • • Pfluggestell (Karrenpflug)
Syn: „Pleoggstell"(Karrenpflug)

Figure 67.4 Organisation of object names

Ackerbaugerät - Feldbestellung
. Erntegerät
. . Schneidende Erntegeräte
. . . Sicheln - Sichten

• • • • **Kurzsense mit Mahdhaken** (Lit.: H 178, T 74/9 ; S 58 f., T 26/8)
Syn: **Sichte mit Mahdhaken** (Lit.: H 178, T 74/9 ; S 58 f. T 26/8)

• • • • • **Kurzsense**
Syn: **Hausense** (Lit.: H 178, T 74/9 ; S 58 f. T 26/8)
Kniesense (Lit.: H 178, T 74/9 ; S 58 f. T 26/8)
„Sait" (Lit.: H 178, T 74/9 ; S 58 f. T 26/8)
„Sichte" (Lit.: H 178, T 74/9 ; S 58 f. T 26/8)
Sichte ohne Mahdhaken (Lit.: H 178, T 74/9 ; S 58 f. T 26/8)

• • • • • **Mahdhaken**
Syn: **„Bick"** (Lit.: S 58, T 26/9)
„Bickhook" (Lit.: S 58, T 26/9)
„Mathaken"
„Matthaken"
„Pick, zweizinkig" (Lit.: S 58, T 26/9)
„Pickhook, zweizinkig" (Lit.: S 58, T 26/9)

• • • • Plaggensichel (Lit.: S 58 f. T 26)
• • • • Sichel (Lit.: H 178 T 74/1-5 ; S 58, T 26/1)
Syn: „Sech"(Sichel) (Lit.: H 178 T 74/1-5 ; S 58, T 26/1)
„Seckel" (Lit.: H 178 T 74/1-5 ; S 58, T 26/1)

• • • • Sichel, gezähnt (Lit.: S 58, T 26/3)
• • • • Sichelteile
• • • • • Griff (Sichel)
• • • • • Klinge, gebogen (Sichel)
• • • • Unkrautsichel (Lit.: S 58 f. T 26/4-5)
• • • • Weidensichel (Lit.: S 58 f. T 26/4-5)
• • • • Wellerhaken (Lit.: S 60; T 27/6)
Syn: „Striekhook" (Lit.: S 58, T 26/1-5)

• • • • Wiesenbeil (Lit.: H 178)
Syn: „Wiesebüil" (Lit.: H 178)

• • • • Wiesenhaue (Lit.: H 178)
Syn: „Wiesehogge" (Lit.: H 178)

• • • Wetzgerät - Schleifgerät - Dengelgerät
• • • • Dengelgerät
Syn: „Dengeltuig" (Lit.: H 180, T 75/1-3 ; H 346, T 158/5-7)
Dengelzeug (Lit.: H 180, T 75/1-3 ; H 346, T 158/5-7)
„Haartüg"
Haartüg zu Mittelhochdeutsch hare (=scharf), haren=schärfen
(Lit.: S 54/55, T 24)
„Kloppetuig" (Lit.: H 180, T 75/1-3 ; H 346, T 158/5-7)

• • • • • Amboß mit Hammer (Dengelgerät) (Lit.: S 54/55, T 24)
• • • • • Dengelamboß (Lit.: S 54/55, T 24 ; H 180, T 75/2; 4)

Figure 57.5 Illustration of different types of sickles

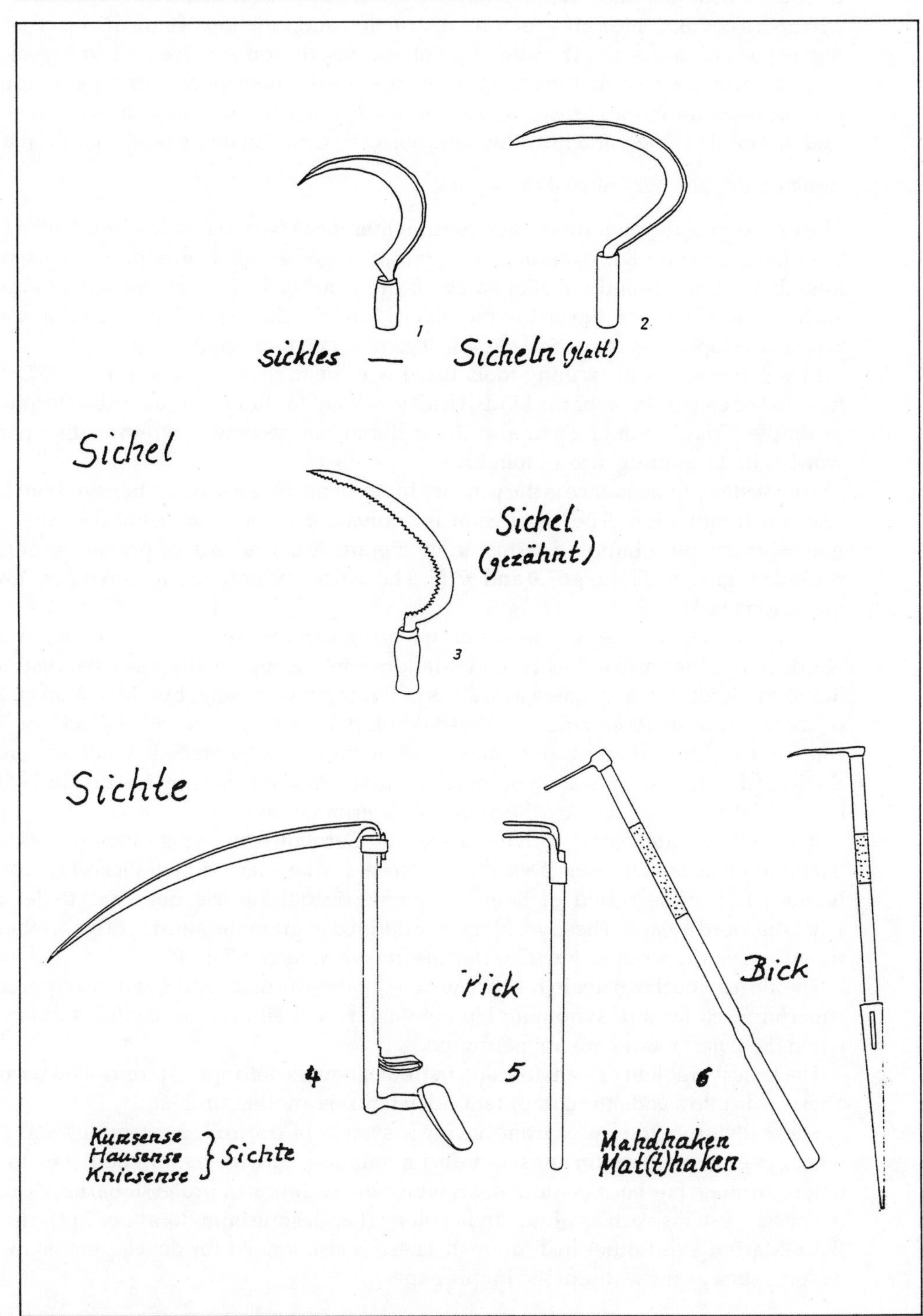

Besides the vocabulary in our thesaurus, we have recorded the most important literature on the object and acquired a picture or a photograph of it. We can print our thesaurus with this information and get by this way a short definition of the object. We also give a compact indication of the construction and function of similar objects in other regions or museums. On the other end of our description we give a short bibliography and a drawing or photo of the object; drawings mostly show more of its typical properties than photography does. Also, we can produce a distribution map showing where we find this kind of object and how the same object is named in the several regional dialects.

Constructing the agricultural thesaurus

The first step in developing the agricultural thesaurus was to find the broad structure of the object groups. For example, we brought together all words or names with the ingredient 'messer' and we eliminated all the words which were not knives and tools such as 'Fiebermesser' (fever-thermometer), 'Luftdruckmesser' (barometer) and so on. So we developed a systematical survey of groups and subgroups.

In my thesaurus of farming-tools there is a hierarchical system (Figure 67.3). The function or construction or the kind of fruit you want to show becomes the determination of simple 'Pflug' (plough); but also the material can become a determinative part in a word as in 'Eisenpflug' (iron-plough).

This systematic sequence is the primary index of the thesaurus, for here you can find all relevant information. The succession is equivalent to the composition of the simple names under superimposed terms, in its hierarchical structure of primary groups and secondary groups (Figures 67.4 and 67.5). The dialect forms of the synonyms are given in quotation marks.

Here one can see the way in which we bring together the different regional dialect words in our thesaurus. 'Sichte' and 'Mahdhaken' belong together as a harvesting-tool found in Nordrhein-Westfalen as well as in Southern Germany, but 'Mat(t)haken' is the regional name in Rheinland. In Westfalen-Lippe, this tool is called 'Pick' or 'Bick', sometimes with a different construction, while the name 'Sichte/Sait' you find here as in Rheinland. The first consonant or initial-sound in Pick or Bick shows what kind of tool it is (slized shaft or not) and are the marks of determination.

It would be interesting to have a look at German synonyms, such as 'Axt–Beil', 'Hammer–Feustel–Dechsel/"Dexel"', 'Hacke–Harke–Haue–Karst–Picke(1)', or the homonyms such as 'Schild' of 'Band', where we need the article 'der', 'das' to determine what the word means. These problems are defined in grammars and in our normbook for thesaurus work, produced by *Deutches Institut für Normung* (DIN).

The alphabetical register in the thesaurus contains the names and, where required, any superimposed term or synonym. Homonyms have their own declarations in brackets, when the object names are not permuted.

The lexical problem of transforming natural language into special controlled terms and afterwards into a code the computer understands is another problem.

We really are a long way from having a system of controlled categories and terms, which everybody uses for museum documentation, but we had a good start in some fields. Progress has been made in fields which use technical or professional terminologies or special systems such as photo-archaeology (Landesmuseum Bonn), or in the fine arts (Foto-Marburg and other institutions). There is also a need for developments in social history, such as those discussed in this paper.

68

ARCHITECTURAL TERMINOLOGY

Eiji Mizushima

Curator
Science Museum, Japan Science Foundation
Tokyo

Introduction

The Tokyo Science Museum has developed an image information retrieval system as part of the refurbishing of the exhibition galleries.

When visitors select keywords for 'houses' of the world on the screen, the system provides corresponding images of dwellings. The output information shows differences in living conditions related to climate, history, culture and the like. This paper introduces architectural terminology and this system.

Construction classification

Buildings, especially dwellings, are classified into three categories:

by geographical location, to show the variety of structures used in each part of the world;

by construction material to show the kinds used;

by purpose to show the different types of buildings.

These are subdivided as given in the list below:

Geographical location

1. Japan
2. China
3. South-east Asia, India, Oceania
4. North America
5. South America
6. Near and Middle East
7. North Europe
8. West and South Europe
9. Africa
10. South Pole

Construction material

1. stone, brick
2. soil, mud
3. wood
4. grass
5. ferroconcrete
6. steel-frame
7. tent

Purpose

1. independent dwellings
2. ensemble, group dwellings
3. church, religious architecture
4. palace, castle
5. village

Construction information for data input

The following categories show the construction information to be input into the system. Architectural data are input into the computer using data cards as shown in Figure 68.1.

Figure 68.1 Architectural data input card

name of the dwelling			
area and location		period	
classification		construction method	
keyword			
explanation			
input operator		photographer/source	

This data includes the name of the dwelling, area and location, period, classification (purpose), construction method, keyword for the visitor, a brief explanation, the curator or input operator, and the photographer and source of the image.

Requirements for system development

If additional information rapidly increases, the data cannot be neatly arranged by using ordinary data cards. The following are the minimal requirements for system development.

An easy procedure for updating data. The value of scientific technological information rapidly deteriorates year by year. It is necessary, therefore, to organise a system that will always provide up-to-date information. For this reason, the updating procedure must be simple.

Technical terms with illustrations included. Architectural information focuses on the buildings themselves, and therefore needs to include illustrations as well as text.

Operational simplicity. For visitors, the picture must appear on the screen instantly and easily after touching the key words. For curators, the operation to add information must be simple.

Future objectives

The Science Museum, as a place for popular scientific eduction, has two objectives in the development of this architectural system and its terminology. One goal is to increase young people's interest in houses and show them buildings of the world. The second objective is to use a computer for storing architectural data — mainly photographs — because this museum has a great resemblance to photographic archives. Future objectives include the improvement of the retrieval system (for example, by adding a thesaurus) and studies on how to use the computer system to make available informative objects or illustrations.

Conclusion

The development of this system is the first step. The second step is to create the data management of the architectural terminology. The third is to combine an image information database with a terminological database. The final step is to create an artificial intelligence database dealing with buildings.

---

69 DOCUMENTATION OF CONTEXTUAL INFORMATION ON MUSEUM OBJECTS: THE EXAMPLE OF THE ATLANTIC CANADA NEWSPAPER SURVEY

Dr Peter E. Rider

Atlantic Provinces Historian
Canadian Museum of Civilization
Ottawa

Debra A. McNabb

Registrar
Museum of Industry and Transportation
Stellerton, Nova Scotia

Museological setting

For many years museums in Canada focused their attention on natural history and aboriginal cultures. A redefinition of museological concerns in the past 20 years, however, has shifted the emphasis to the heritage of contemporary society. This process has been accompanied by a rapid increase in the number of human history museums and their attendance figures. The subject-matter of exhibitions and the composition of collections in these institutions reflect the populism of the process. Commonplace objects of ordinary folk rather than works of art or of exquisite craftsmanship are the principal targets for acquisition and display. Unfortunately museums have not always demonstrated informed selection and careful planning in adding to their holdings. Haste and lack of foresight have resulted in some ill-considered acquisitions and deficient documentation. Items added in order not to offend their owners or to satisfy the eccentric interests of someone in authority form part of many artefact collections. History collections, moreover, tend to reflect the view, stated or otherwise, that artefacts are not distinct documents embodying unique evidence of material culture but samples of things which are best comprehended principally through other historical evidence. Canadian museums, thus, have few icons or historical type specimens and many examples of ordinary objects. Ironically the methodology for documenting historical artefacts reflects an approach best suited to items of particular significance.

Although institutional guidelines for documenting holdings were shaped to meet specific needs and operational capacities, the advent of the National Inventory Programme in 1972 provoked efforts to reach a broadly-based consensus of what would constitute the common points of artefact documentation. The outcome, after years of debate, reveals an overwhelming emphasis upon physical description. The principal field in Canada's Humanities National Database for recording cultural background information on historical artefacts is 'Culture Context', and it is not one that is heavily used. Physical description is absolutely necessary for inventory control and is an important first step in the interpretation of material history, but it neglects many of the concerns which museums face in serving the public. The number of visitors interested in a bottle, for instance, is far exceeded by those interested in drinking. Thus the shortfall in data which characterised the rapid blooming of museum history collections is

Figure 9.1 Original property advertisement and ACNS computer printout

PARIS NUMBER	12729
DATE OF BIRTH	850918
DATE OF CHANGE	880829
PROVINCE OF ORIGIN	NS
CONTRIBUTOR	ATLANTIC CANADA NEWSPAPER SURVEY
CATALOGUER	ROWLAND
TRANSCRIPTION DATE	19830624
RECORD NUMBER	83-1869
NEWSPAPER NAME	WEEKLY CHRONICLE - HALIFAX
NEW. VOLUME NO.	5
NEW. ISSUE NO.	257
NEW. PAGE NO.	3
NEW. COLUMN	2
DATE FIRST APPEAR.	17910611
DATE CONTIN. APPEAR.	17910625; 17910709; 17910723; 17910806; 17910827; 17910903
ILLUSTRATION	YES
SUBJECT, GEN. CONTEXT	PROPERTY, EXCHANGE TRANSACTIONS OF; PROPERTY, REAL; MARKETING, RETAIL
GROUP, ANNOUNCE. TYPE	LAND
LAND TRANSACTION	FOR SALE
LAND TYPE	TOWNLOTS; LOTS
LAND FEATURES	BUILDINGS; HOUSES; BUILDING, COMMERCIAL; FENCES; HOUSE INTERIORS; GARDENS; OUTBUILDINGS; WHARVES
PLACE-COUNTRY/PROV/ST	NOVA SCOTIA
PLACE-MUNICIPALITY	HALIFAX; LUNENBURG
PLACE-COUNTY	HALIFAX COUNTY?; LUNENBURG COUNTY
PERSON / BUSINESS	SHOALS, JOHN-LAND AGENT?-ADVERTISER;
DESCF	T, WITH ON FIRST , WITH OR 2 OR 3 BY 15 N WHARF. Y BOARD WITH SPUTABLE ULARS OR H(SIC)

TO BE SOLD,

A HOUSE, STORE, WHARF, GARDEN and LOTS, in the town of *Lunenburg*, the property of the Subſcriber.

The Houſe is new, and in complete order, 42 by 36 feet, encircled with a pale fence. It contains three rooms with fire places, three bed-rooms, and an excellent kitchen on the firſtfloor, a ſpacious garret, that will admit a number of additional rooms, and a cellar under the whole, which has proved impenetrable to the ſevereſt froſt.

A pleaſant garden adjoins the houſe, with a ſtable ſufficient for two or three cows or horſes. The ſtore is 42 by 15 feet, conveniently placed in the rear of the garden on the wharf, where boats conſtantly load and unload, and renders the above a moſt advantageous ſituation for a merchant, or a private gentleman.

Ten TOWN-LOTS, incloſed in a board fence, within a quarter of a mile of the houſe, are laid down in graſs, and may be converted into a productive garden.

An indiſputable title will be given, and the payment made eaſy to the purchaſer.

For particulars enquire of Major CORTLAND at Halifax, or the ſubſcriber, on the premiſes, at Lunenburgh.

John Shoals.

Figure 69.2 Original service announcement with ACNS Computer printout

PARIS NUMBER	12752
DATE OF BIRTH	850918
DATE OF CHANGE	880818
PROVINCE OF ORIGIN	NS
CONTRIBUTOR	ATLANTIC CANADA NEWSPAPER SURVEY
CATALOGUER	LANDRY
TRANSCRIPTION DATE	19830816
RECORD NUMBER	83-2197
NEWSPAPER NAME	NOVA SCOTIA GAZETTE, THE
NEW. VOLUME NO.	13
NEW. ISSUE NO.	890
NEW. PAGE NO.	4
NEW. COLUMN	2
DATE FIRST APPEAR.	17830527
SUBJECT, GEN. CONTEXT	COMMUNITY; SOCIAL CONTROL; PROPERTY, SLAVERY; OCCUPATIONS: SLAVE MASTER?
GROUP, ANNOUNCE. TYPE	RUNAWAYS
PLACE-COUNTRY/PROV/ST	NOVA SCOTIA
PLACE-MUNICIPALITY	HALIFAX
PLACE-COUNTY	HALIFAX COUNTY?
PERSON / BUSINESS	KIRKHAM, HUGH-SLAVE MASTER?-ADVERTISER; PETER-SLAVE?
DESCRIPTION	RAN AWAY, A SMART WELL-LOOKING NEGRO BOY, NAMED PETER, ABOUT 17 YEARS OLD. WAS WEARING A BLUE JACKET, ROUND HAT, NEW TROUSERS OF WHITE DUCK, NEW SHOES WITH LARGE PLATED BUCKLES. HE IS ROUND FACED, … HE HAS A REMARKABLE … , HE MAY ATTEMPT TO … SKILLED IN … EIGHT DOLLAR REWARD … M. IF HE IS … NTY MARKS ON HIS … QUARE. ANY PERSON … G HIM WILL BE … ON HIS OWN HE WILL … D HALIFAX, MAY

HALIFAX, 8th May, 1783.

RAN Away a ſmart Well-looking Negro BOY, named Peter, about Seventeen Years of Age; had On when he went away a blue Jacket; round Hat, New Trouſers of white Duck; new Shoes and large plated Buckles; he is round faced, ſpeakes broken Engliſh, and when ſpoke to has a remarkable Smile on his Countenance, ſhort and ſtout maid; has been uſed to the Carpenters buſineſs, and may attempt to paſs for a free Man; this is to warn all Maſters of Veſſels and Others not to harbour or Carry of ſaid Negro, as he is the property of the Subſcriber; any one that will apprehend the ſaid Negro ſo that his Maſter may receive him, Shall receive Eight Dollars Reward from.

HUGH KIRKHAM.

N. B. If he is ſtript he has his Country marks on his back in the form of a Square, thus.

Any Perſon harbouring or Concealing ſaid Boy will be proſecuted to the utmoſt rugoir of the Law.——if he returns of his Own Accord there will be nothing done to him.

compounded by the focus that curators have in the documentation which they provide. The objectives of the Atlantic Canada Newspaper Survey (ACNS) are to compensate for the weaknesses found in the provenance of museum collections and to increase the contextual information on the region's material heritage.

Project development

The initial impetus for the development of ACNS lay in the experience of re-opening the Newfoundland Museum a decade ago. To plug the gaps in artefact documentation, museum staff were obliged to refer frequently to primary documents, principally newspapers. Often the same sources were canvassed several times for different reasons. The prospect of a single reading of the richest source of information, newspaper advertisements, for information on objects had great allure.

The National Inventory Programme (NIP) of the National Museums of Canada was approached in 1979 by the Newfoundland Museum to participate in such an endeavour using the technology which was being developed for the documentation of major museum collections. Three years later the Canadian Museum of Civilization sponsored a similar project in conjunction with the New Brunswick Museum and the Canadian Heritage Information Network (CHIN) successor to NIP, to develop a body of data for that province. Data from the Newfoundland project, which had become dormant, was incorporated with the research from New Brunswick and made available online. In subsequent years projects were undertaken as well in Nova Scotia and Prince Edward Island. In all cases the national agencies worked in collaboration with the provincial museums. More recently three universities, St Mary's in Halifax, Nova Scotia, University of New Brunswick in Saint John, New Brunswick and Memorial University in St John's, Newfoundland, have joined the consortium. The database at present includes approximately 45 000 records with an additional number researched and awaiting entry (examples of two records and the original advertisements are shown in Figures 69.1 and 69.2). When complete, material will cover the major newspaper sources from the principal city of each province for the eighteenth and nineteenth centuries. Some parts of the material will be covered using a cluster sample technique in which three consecutive years in nine are selected for indexing. This will be mainly for the period after 1860 and is being employed to bring the undertaking to an end within a reasonable time.

Database structure

The initial focus of the project on the availability of trade goods in a specific colonial market-place (nineteenth-century Newfoundland) led to a database structure that focused on the commodities offered for sale in newspaper advertisements (Figure 69.3). Products were organised into nine types or groupings based on Statistics Canada's *Trade of Canada Commodity Classification* (Canada. Department of Industry, 1975) with some modifications to reflect nineteenth-century conditions. Each of these broad categories of commodities was given a field in the database and a field for services was also added. Other fields identified the newspaper source, provided details concerning the advertiser, and noted the place of origin of the commodity and the name of the vessel by which it arrived. The content of each of these fields retained significant words and phrases as they appeared in the original documents. With a few additional fields for remarks and record keeping purposes, the whole database comprised 25 fields.

Over a period of several years, refinements were made to the methodology to increase the precision of indexing, facilitate access to data and widen the scope of the information

Figure 69.3 Field Table: Atlantic Canada newspaper survey

MNEMONIC	NUMBER	TYPE	LABEL
PAR	1	I KEY	PARIS NUMBER
DOB	4	S NP	DATE OF BIRTH
DOC	5	S NP	DATE OF CHANGE
RL	10	S	RECORD LANGUAGE
ORPR	11	S	PROVINCE OF ORIGIN
CON	20	S	CONTRIBUTOR
CAT	21	S	CATALOGUER
CDTR	22	I	TRANSCRIPTION DATE
CRN	23	S	RECORD NUMBER
NPNAM	30	S	NEWSPAPER NAME
NPVOL	31	S	NEW. VOLUME NO.
NPISS	32	S	NEW. ISSUE NO.
NPPAG	33	S	NEW. PAGE NO.
NPCOL	34	S	NEW. COLUMN
NPDFA	35	I	DATE FIRST APPEAR.
NPDCA	36	I	DATE CONTIN. APPEAR.
NPILL	37	S	ILLUSTRATION
SUB	45	S	SUBJECT, GEN. CONTEXT
SGRP	47	S	GROUP, ANNOUNCE. TYPE
SCAT	48	S	PRODUCT CATEGORY
SSCAT	49	S	PRODUCT SUB-CATEGORY
SPROD	52	S	PRODUCT TRANSACTION
SLTR	54	S	LAND TRANSACTION
SLTY	55	S	LAND TYPE
SLSZ	56	S	LAND SIZE
SLFE	57	S	LAND FEATURES
SPCRY	59	S	PLACE-COUNTRY/PROV/ST
SPMUN	60	S	PLACE-MUNICIPALITY
SPCTY	61	S	PLACE-COUNTY
SPADL	62	S	PL-STR/ADDR/LANDMARK
SPER	65	S	PERSON / BUSINESS
SBUSTY	67	S	TYPE OF BUSINESS
SOCC	69	S	OCCUPATION
SBUSNM	70	S	BUSINESS NAME
SVNAM	71	S	VESSEL NAME
SVTY	72	S	VESSEL TYPE
SVPROV	73	S	VESSEL PROVENANCE
SRAL	74	S	SUBJECT, RAILWAY
DE	80	S	DESCRIPTION
DELA	81	S	LIVE ANIMALS
DEFFBT	82	S	FOOD/FEED/BEV/TOBACCO
DECM	83	S	CRUDE MATERIALS
DEFM	84	S	FABRICATED MATERIALS
DEMACH	85	S	MACHINERY
DETCE	86	S	TRANSPORTATION EQUIP.
DEOET	87	S	OTHER EQUIP. / TOOLS
DEPHG	88	S	PERS. HOUSEHOLD GOODS
DEMEP	89	S	MISC./END PROD./OTHER
DESERV	95	S	SERVICES
CREM	99	S	CATALOGUER REMARKS

contained in the database. Each of the broad categories was subdivided into 52 specific sub-categories to define category content. Additional fields were created to capture information which was not incorporated in the original 25 fields. There are now 50 fields that can be arranged into four classes according to function: the administrative fields used primarily for internal record management; those providing bibliographical details of the newspaper source; the descriptive fields for commodities and services; and fields in which authority lists are used to index subject matter or content from a number of levels and a variety of perspectives. The key to understanding the interconnected nature of the field structure is an appreciation of the latter subject fields. Taken collectively, these fields index subject matter according to a hierarchical structure. Levels range from general context and broad classifications of advertisement type to more specific references to person and place. As noted, the language of the subject fields is controlled by authority lists of standardised index terms. These generic terms are representative of the descriptive phrases of advertisements that express content in various ways. Overall, fields have been designed to be integrated and overlapping to ensure that all relevant information is captured and organised in a cross-referenced structure.

An analysis of the source data completed several years ago revealed that only 42 per cent of the content of early newspaper advertisements was being categorised by the commodity classification system. An additional 8 per cent was contained in the field for services. Land transactions accounted for 20 per cent of the advertisements, and the rest relating to financial matters, public events, transportation and communication, and other subjects came to 30 per cent of the whole. The new fields accordingly were designed to incorporate information dealing with land transactions, and a general subject cross-reference field was created to provide major groupings of data which did not refer to commodities, land or people. The three general kinds of information found in this field are occupation, business and event.

Reference aids

A key piece of documentation for ACNS is a directory of all commodities appearing in the database. Called the *Any Files* for want of a better title, the directory contains the names of approximately 8 000 commodities together with the sub-categories and the categories in which the objects may be found. It is an exhaustive list which reflects the complete terminology found in the sources.

ACNS is being developed as a public reference database. As such it is intended for widespread use by persons possessing a considerable range of computer skills. Access to it can be made via the hundreds of institutions connected to CHIN in Canada and abroad. A *Users' Guide* has been prepared to assist those not familiar with the BASIS software of the CHIN computers. It contains an overview of the project, field definitions, copies of the authority lists, various commands for the retrieval of data and the *Any Files*. Examples of various search procedures are provided to demonstrate the practical application of the commands. With it researchers can locate the items that interest them and be informed of the field in which such items can be found. While the methodology of ACNS has been adopted with specific objectives in mind, the comprehensiveness and flexibility of its integrated structure makes it adaptable to any project that systematically extracts information from newspaper sources.

To simplify access to ACNS and to alert users to all of the relevant content of the database, CHIN and the Canadian Museum of Civilization have begun the development of a thesaurus of commodity names. For cross-referenced retrieval, 'preferred' terms link similar terms within the ACNS database and, in addition, group objects according to broad concepts and classifications. Examples of the latter include measurement and architectural features and tools and kitchenware. Dictionary definitions and contextual references are supplied to assist retrieval further by clarifying the identification of objects. Online access to the thesaurus would also enable a user to switch easily from the database to the thesaurus before formulating search requests. A completed thesaurus would moreover provide and authoritative guide to the material culture of Atlantic Canada from 1750 to 1900.

Artefact and context

The thesaurus is also the key with which the contextual information of ACNS can be brought into contact with the physical description of artefacts in the museum collections. A thesaurus for ACNS could serve as well for the PARIS database which contains the artefact records. By referring first to one database and then to the other, researchers could juxtapose information concerning the objects and their context. In this way the carefully documented background data of ACNS could be made to redress in part the inadequacies of collections documentation which is part of the inheritance of our recent boom in historical museums. Similarly researchers in material history would be able, with greater ease, to anchor their studies to concrete examples of the actual objects.

---

70 THE RATIONALE FOR CATEGORISATION AND NAMING: FUNCTION AND CONTEXT

Stephen H. Delroy
Curator, House of Commons
Ottawa

One of the largest decisions that a museum can make is to choose a system of documentation. Every documentation system has one or more rationales underlying the categorisation of items. Since the publication of *Nomenclature* (Chenhall, 1978) (Chapter 58), museum staff have been told they must decide whether function or context was the best organising principle. But should the organising principle be the determining factor?

'Function', as an organising principle of categorisation and naming, has a precise meaning. It is the presumed original function or reason for the creation of the object. At the most abstract level, each function is used as a major category. More concrete reasons are used as lower level categories. In practice, the *Nomenclature* group has chosen precision over function for the naming of objects where more than one name is possible.

'Contextual' categorisation and naming from the *Nomenclature* perspective, involves the use of another principle instead of or besides function.

The essence of the *Nomenclature* argument for function is that it is a single rationale and, of all the single rationales, the only one which is common to all man-made objects.

Most museums do not follow *Nomenclature* or any other published system, nor have they entered the debate between *Nomenclature* and the other published systems. Evidently, they are not convinced that it is necessary to adopt any published system. Hence, this paper adopts their point of view by examining what museums require rather than what the opposing principles offer.

From the museums' perspective, the following issues are relevant: first, the nature of the collections being documented; second, the purpose and audience for the categories and names; and third, museum resources. Since goals are partly determined beforehand by the nature of collections and only limited afterwards by resources, it is best to begin with museum collections.

With a large museum and an online museum network background, the following collections topics were relevant: the disciplines involved; and the types of items and activities being documented.

Although a museum may focus on social history, it cannot shut out the other disciplines. Almost all history museums have art and archaeology objects in their collections. In this case, the organising principle has a subtle effect. The *Nomenclature* method categorises a ballet slipper under clothing whereas the *Social History and Industrial Classification* (SHIC Working Party, 1983) (Chapter 59) might place it under Theatres or Recreational Services. Both would classify a drawing as art, *Nomenclature* as original art, *SHIC* as picture. Again the functional view is that of the maker, the artist who would say he is creating original art, whereas the contextual approach considers the user, who bought it to hang on his wall. Murdock's *Outline of Cultural Materials* (Murdock *et al.*, 1987) falls in between by distinguishing decorative art from representative art.

From a disciplinary perspective, the functional view has most often been criticised by military and art historians and by archaeologists. Galleries and war museums complain that virtually all their collections would fall under one or two major categories. Archaeologists complain that vast amounts of their prehistoric materials can have any of a number of functions and some rely more on shape and process, in the same way that galleries rely on medium and support.

Given that neither the functional nor the contextual approach solves these problems, the question of organising principle might be broadened. Strategies to consider include organising information by function, context, shape or process.

Even more relevant to the choice of organising principle than discipline is the type of item being categorised and named. *Nomenclature* only deals with objects. The contextualists deal with any items collected, including documentary items from other museum activities such as research and exhibition. At first sight, it appears that context is more useful than function. However, function is more likely to include the mutually exclusive and reliably assigned categories required for reporting purposes than to broaden the functional categories to document non-object items such as bibliographies and biographies.

A museum network finds that the number of museums is also relevant, The more institutions that are involved, the less likely they are to want idiosyncratic categories or systems that are complex. To the extent that the functional categories are simpler to manage, they have an advantage. At the same time, with more museums, it is more likely that there will be numbers of specialised museums desiring non-functional, non-contextual criteria to make their own categories. A railway museum and a postal museum are two examples.

Given its collections, a museum must consider its goals. In particular, it must decide who is the audience for the documentation system? What types of users will there be? Why would anyone retrieve by category and item name? There are several groupings of users such as curators and researchers; administrative staff; exhibition and outreach staff; the public; and the staff of other museums.

Curators and researchers prefer categories that are relevant to their particular discipline. But how much agreement is there between historians about the categories of material history? In an internal study by Philippa Syme of 28 CHIN databases, it was found that only one category was used in more than a third of the databases, and that was 'miscellaneous'. Over 2 600 unique terms were in use. To be fair, many of the categories would disappear if variants were collapsed and terms describing less than 100 objects were ignored.

Administrative staff worry less about the content of the categories than the degree to which they can be reliably assigned with the minimum of effort. Anyone who has been grilled by an auditor will understand what is meant.

Exhibition and outreach staff share the curators' preference for categories organised by discipline. However, they may also want the categories to make sense to the tour guides they train.

Up to now, the public has had little contact with museum categories. Natural historians proudly label their displayed specimens with both taxonomic and common names. Why do social historians hide their categories? Has anyone ever seen either a functional or a contextual category on a label?

Lastly, we come to the group that is least served by our home-grown categories, the staff of other museums. When a breakdown of collections by an internally-assigned category is given, it usually requires a definition of most of the terms.

CHIN did not include a 'category' field on the Humanities National Database for this reason: that the terms used meant something different in each museum. There was far more consistency in the naming of objects than in their categorisation.

In conclusion, it should be argued that the rationale for categorisation is not the most important aspect of a documentation system of categorising and naming items. Given limited resources, a museum should not waste time inventing yet another system. Instead it should choose one of the existing systems. This choice should be influenced by the relative simplicity, comprehensiveness, presentation and mutual exclusion of the categories. The function versus context issue is primarily important when items other than historical objects are being documented.

X
DISCIPLINE DEVELOPMENTS: NATURAL HISTORY AND GEOLOGY

71 DISCIPLINE DEVELOPMENTS IN NATURAL HISTORY AND GEOLOGY

Mike Budd

Advice and Training Officer
Museum Documentation Association
Cambridge

It is a common misconception that terminology control in the natural sciences is well developed, and compared to other disciplines, well coordinated. In part this may be due to the perception of biology and geology as 'hard' systematic sciences. More probably it stems from the long history and obvious structure of Linnaean taxonomy.

Cooper (Chapter 72) in a review of the history of terminology control in the geological and biological sciences establishes that terminology control is neither well developed nor well coordinated, and that recent progress has been rather disappointing. In geology, for instance, he states that there is 'no agreed stratigraphic framework, and no agreed keyword lists for a whole range of descriptors'. In biology, he hints that concentration on environmental data and nomenclature may have lead to the neglect of equally important collections management information. In taxonomy, name changes and the multiplication of names are causing sufficient problems for Harding (Chapter 76) to suggest that the work of the Bern Convention and the World Conservation Monitoring Centre are being hampered by 'bewildering nomenclature'.

The papers in this section identify a variety of factors inhibiting the development of terminology control standards in natural history, and a series of interesting approaches to their solution. Both the problems and the solutions range from the political to the technical.

The essential need for central coordination, adequate funding and defined responsibility is touched on by a number of authors. Harding (Chapter 76) for instance, notes that it is unlikely that financial support for a European nomenclatural database of plants or animals would be found 'because no international or national organisation would consider the database to be its responsibility'. Cooper (Chapter 72) wonders whether, in retrospect, the MDA regrets its decision to absolve itself of responsibility for the development of specialist terminologies. Cooper also makes the perceptive point of the importance of clearly establishing the rationale for terminology inititatives. In the political climate of the early nineties, little will be achieved in the development of terminology unless we can unambiguously establish that very tangible benefits will follow.

Technical solutions to similar problems of nomenclature are discussed by Pettitt (Chapter 78) and Heppell (Chapter 79). Heppell notes that Linnaean taxonomic names have become progressively more inscrutable because of naming instability, and the multiplication of species and genera. Both naming instability and confusion arising from the multiplication of names can be avoided by the use of abstract hierarchical biocodes, which have the further property of correct systematic sorting. While biocode systems for some areas of nomenclature already exist, an overall system has yet to be developed. Pettitt reports on the development of an abstract coding system for Manchester Museum. In this case the system extends beyond the limits of biological nomenclature into other disciplines.

Harding (Chapter 76) and Walley (Chapter 75) report on an alternative approach to the problems of biological nomenclature — the development of standard checklists. Walley assesses the value of checklists and summarises UK sources. Along with other authors in this section, he lays great stress on the value of automated aids. Harding approaches the question from the European perspective and, despite his pessimism, makes a strong case for the development of a European nomenclature database.

Perhaps the brightest note is sounded by the papers by Clark (Chapter 74) and Wentz and Shearer (Chapter 73) which deal with substantial ongoing projects. Clark reports on a project to update the Chemical (or Hays) Index for mineralogical coding/nomenclature, which is scheduled for completion in 1991. Wentz and Shearer review Geosaurus, a thesaurus developed for the indexing and retrieval of items in the GeoArchive database. The thesaurus is wide in scope covering geophysics, geochemistry, geology, palaeontology, mathematical geology, and geo-resources. The paper includes an interesting discussion of the special characteristics of geoscience data.

---

72 TERMINOLOGY CONTROLS FOR THE NATURAL SCIENCES IN UK MUSEUMS

John A. Cooper

Booth Museum of Natural History
Brighton

Introduction

As a museum geologist and a working curator, I am disappointed that there are no nationwide agreements about the terms that I need to use in my museum documentation system to describe specimens in my care. Although I have produced my own classifications and word lists these are not necessarily ones which would find approval within the profession. I know that in other museums, curators have done much the same and I hope that, by and large, there is some measure of similarity. Moreover, there are many other museums where curators are not using any form of standardised terminology, nor indeed, curating geological collections at all.

Within all subject areas in museums, I am confident that the number and kinds of information fields which are used to describe objects and specimens have been well worked out, particularly through the good services of the Museum Documentation Association (MDA). But certainly within geology we do not seem to have got any further. For example, there is no agreed taxonomic classification at superfamily or order level, no agreed stratigraphic framework and no agreed keyword lists for a whole range of descriptors. Even if internal conventions are in force, when curators produce records relating to many thousands of specimens, errors in the ways in which the specimens are classified and described soon produce data which is either inaccurate, incomplete or simply useless. This results in poor data retrieval for the users of museum collections, and severely inhibits their proper management by curators. On a national scale, our resultant lack of ability to demonstrate a full and detailed strategy for specimen documentation undermines all the good work geological curators have done and are doing.

The geologists do not appear to be alone, however. While there have been great strides forward in terminological control in some other museum disciplines (social history, ethnography), when I looked for guidance from my near neighbours the biologists, it struck me that they too lacked any cohesive documentation strategies for museum specimens. This view did not come from my research alone: it was also that of museum biologists with whom I have had long discussions. As a result, I became interested in discovering how it could be that two highly active and dedicated groups of museum workers could have got to this position. This paper summarises my findings and makes some suggestions for action.

In common with many other museum disciplines in Britain, natural history (and here I use the term to include geology) has its own specialist groups to provide forums for curatorial development. This movement away from the generalist approach of the Museums Association was perhaps spearheaded by the Geological Curators' Group (GCG), founded in 1974, and the Biological Curators Group (BCG) in 1975. One of the constitutional aims of the GCG related directly to the improvement of standards of geological curation. While the constitution of the BCG was rather more tacit on the subject, it certainly embraced the same issues.

Since both Groups produce journals and hold meetings, it is useful to begin a review of the development of terminology control for the natural sciences in UK museums by examining the published accounts of the Groups' deliberations in this area. In time-honoured stratigraphic fashion I will first turn the pages of the earliest formation, the GCG.

The Geologists

Perhaps the earliest reference to a standard terminology in GCG literature appears in Peter Embrey's 1975 critique on machine cataloguing, where he refers to a French (BRGM) scheme started in 1965/6 'to commit all the mineral collections in France to a central machine catalogue' (Embrey, 1975). This culminated in an alphabetical index of mineral names reducing all varieties and synonyms to single species and allotting a six-digit totally unintelligible numerical code. This reference at least alerts us here that some of our European colleagues were some way ahead of us in ideas.

In the same year that Chenhall published his perceptive *Museum Cataloguing in the Computer Age*, the GCG held a meeting with IRGMA (The Information Retrieval Group of the Museums Association) in March 1975 and published an account of the meeting in April (Jones, 1975). This meeting (and many later ones) was rather too concerned with the layout and format of a Geology Specimen Record Card than with the strategies of documentation which should surely precede anything else. Little of this point appears to have been made at the time. Incidentally, 1975 also saw the GCG initiative on Geological Site Documentation reported in its Newsletter (Anon., 1975 and Jones and Cooper, 1975). A meeting held in September with IRGMA had as one of its objectives 'to define . . . a suitable record format to allow for both manual and computer handling of this information'. Again, no consideration of terminology control is apparent.

An interesting non-IRGMA development was reported in the *Newsletter* of 1976 by its progenitor David Gittins (1976a). He described a system using a package called INFOL 2 which had been experimentally applied to molluscs in the British Museum (Natural History). One of the selling points of this system was its relative user-friendliness and input was 'free-format' which, with hindsight, makes it all the more surprising that the implications for terminology control were apparently ignored. Gittins continued his crusading with INFOL 2 at Leicestershire Museums, where it was applied to the then burgeoning collection of geological site data (Gittins, 1976b). This pilot project was successful not only in achieving the ready recording and retrieval of site information itself, but also in demonstrating the ease with which this could be done. Many of the lessons learnt were incorporated into the proposals for a National Scheme for Geological Site Documentation aired in a GCG Special Publication (Cooper and Jones, 1976) and provided some opposition to the IRGMA methodology (Roberts, 1976b). Clearly Gittins had learnt some lessons about terminology control since he now placed emphasis on the definition of recording categories and on the formulation of '. . . the necessary detailed instructions for recorders outlining the contents of each category' (Gittins, 1976c). Furthermore, at least in this regard, he saw a distinct insufficiency in the instructions for recorders provided by IRGMA and which provided the material for a rather provocative letter to the Museums Bulletin in 1977 (Gittins and Scotter, 1977). The new Museum Documentation Advisory Unit (MDAU) replied in the same issue that 'we wholeheartedly support the aim of standardization itself but . . . this is a task for curators and others in the discipline concerned and not the MDAU' (Porter and Roberts, 1977).

The GCG, together with the Palaeontological Association, held a major colloquium on the curation of Palaeontological collections in March 1978 which included three presentations on computer cataloguing (Light, 1979; Brunton, 1979 and 1980; Jones, 1979). Richard Light described the use of GOS and the standards derived by IRGMA (now the Museum Documentation Association — MDA) for cataloguing geological specimens. Perhaps for the first time in a geological context he refers to word lists and thesaurus construction and says that 'most museums have adopted some internal conventions to improve the consistency of their records . . .', In the discussion to his paper, Light replies to the concerns about museums each acting individually in developing computer-based systems by saying that, '[The MDA] certainly cannot begin to collate different systems until individual museums send us copies of their own conventions'. Both the other two contributions to the proceedings neglected to mention terminological control in describing their systems.

The papers presented at the Cardiff Colloquium were published with a summary (Bassett *et al.*, 1979). Six recommendations further summarised the themes of the meeting and these were presented in the hope that they could be used as a basis for future action. Last of these was the following: 'In addition to computer technologies and data-formats, terminology and hierarchies require standardisation if computerised cataloguing techniques are to become widely used and effective for indexing and data-exchange in palaeontology'. On 29 October 1980, all the recommendations were presented to a meeting of the International Committee of Natural History Museums in Mexico City and as resolution No. 3 were adopted in their entirety (Anon., 1981).

Two publications in 1978 provided welcome relief to curators desperate to build terminologies. Catriona McInnes (McInnes, 1978) published her contribution to 'IRGMA card geology vocabulary and grammar' as used in the Hunterian Museum (Glasgow University) in *MDA Information*. She included word lists for 'Form', 'Collection Method', 'Acquisition Method', etc., and included a long list of terms for *Aspect: Description*. Unfortunately, I am not aware that her work was widely discussed and it might better have appeared in the *GCG Newsletter* where it would more readily have been available. In September 1978, Pettigrew and Holden (1978) published the internal conventions used by the Tyne and Wear Museum Service with the IRGMA Geology and Mineral Specimen cards. The authors aimed to 'provide a basis for comparison, criticism and improvement by other museum workers . . .'. Curiously, as with the Hunterian conventions, there is no published response to these conventions, though from memory, reaction among curators was somewhat negative.

Susan Turner and Peter Robson of the Hancock Museum, University of Newcastle, extended the north-east's progression into computer cataloguing by publishing in 1979 an account of their use of the SPIRES system (Turner and Robson, 1979). In this case, however, despite the lead of Pettigrew and Holden, no mention of terminologies is made, only 'improved' file definitions.

Perhaps the most significant publication of 1980 in this field was the MDA's instructions for the Geology Specimen card (Museum Documentation Association, 1980). The card itself was issued in 1976 together with companion instructions but this new version included many revisions derived from advice and discussions from and with GCG members. On this account one might be forgiven for looking for detailed advice on terminologies but no, once again only a bland generalisation is given: 'We also suggest that you adopt INTERNAL CONVENTIONS. These may be an extension of the MDS [Museum Documentation System] proposals such as a list of approved terms or a decision to record names by one method selected from several possibilities. Opportunities for devising such conventions are mentioned in the following pages'. To be fair, some examples of word lists are given, but little guidance is offered as to how conventions should be developed.

About this time it was becoming clear to curators and the MDA alike that there was a lack of coordination among those who were using computer and computer-compatible systems and this realisation led to a series of meetings and publications. The first of these was a joint meeting between the GCG and the Institute of Geological Sciences at Leeds in June 1980 (Roberts, 1980) entitled *Towards a Common Standard*. The problems of terminology were acknowledged and some descriptions of current systems were presented but further discussion was reserved for a future meeting with the MDA. The meeting's title had obviously been carefully chosen.

The second meeting was much more fruitful, with the GCG and MDA tackling mineralogical terminologies to the extent that several word lists and agreements on further actions resulted (Roberts, 1981b). It is a pity that these conclusions have not been more soundly implemented. The meeting mooted at Leeds between the GCG and the MDA was held in June 1981 as a *Workshop on Geology Documentation* (Roberts, 1981b) where Andrew Roberts suggested that the progress made with the MDA Mineral card might well be emulated by consideration of the Geology card. He referred to the 'sad lack of co-ordination' and the 'key importance of strict internal conventions'. The sterility of the descriptions of individual procedures and the astounding conclusion that 'recording conventions should be improved' is only tempered by the apparent agreement to convene a 'Standing Committee for Natural Sciences Documentation' which among other tasks would 'provide a forum . . . to standardise recording procedures'. Sadly, this committee is yet to materialise.

An attempt to make some headway was the Brighton meeting held in June 1985 optimistically titled *Specimen Documentation and Data Standards*, which was intended to be a springboard for further action on the part of the GCG towards a common terminology. Though the moment was right — the GCG *Guidelines for the Curation of Geological Material* had just been published — no action followed. No report of the meeting appeared but two of the most thoughtful papers presented were eventually published in the *Geological Curator*. David Price of the Sedgwick Museum emphasised two important points in his 'honest' verbatim account (Price, 1986). First, he drew attention to the need for quality in specimen documentation and pointed out that we have clearly failed to achieve this quality by traditional means. Second, he claimed that salvation may well lie in the advantages offered by the rapidity and effectiveness of computer-based data handling methods but that as long as individual museums produce internally standardised catalogues and indexes, 'does it matter if we all do it in rather different ways'.

These ideas are at variance with some of the views put forward by Andrew Roberts in his paper 'Towards a common strategy for geological documentation: the MDA view' published in the same GCG issue (Roberts, 1986). Furthermore Roberts was able to show that despite differences in the recording style and strategy of catalogue records from six separate museum projects, cumulative indexes could be produced successfully. Roberts clearly recognised the position that had been reached with geological specimen documentation and on behalf of the MDA proposed a research project to continue the development of a common documentation strategy. The GCG and MDA jointly submitted this proposal to the Museum and Galleries Commission but it was unfortunately rejected due to lack of funds.

The Biologists

The Biology Curators Group was established in 1975 following four conferences on the subject: Cardiff (1971), Leicester (1973), Dundee (1975) and Oxford (1975). From the very first issue of its *Newsletter*, the flavour of concern over documentation has been linked to 'biological' i.e. environmental recording. This emphasis is not surprising when one recognises the national role of the Biological Records Centre (BRC) of the Institute of Terrestrial Ecology as the authoritative agency for the recording of Britain's flora and fauna. Its existence provided a compelling rationale for the creation of local record centres in museums. Collections, however, were not forgotten, and in the second issue of the *Newsletter*, notes of a committee meeting record that 'as a matter of policy the Group should give its support to national documentation schemes for biological specimens . . .'.

It was not until 1977 that the question of terminology arose in print. In April of that year, the first meeting of the Museum Association's Working Party on Environmental Record Centres in Museums was held and in the report of that meeting two agreements are noted (Anon., 1977):

> that responsibility for adopting and reviewing recording terms should rest with the disciplines.
>
> that agreement should be reached on environmental descriptors

Mention is also made of the need for 'inter-disciplinary consultation'. This theme of agreeing that agreements should be reached should by now be familiar. Considering that some 37 recording schemes for biological records were by this time already in operation it is surprising that no comprehensive guidelines for information recording had been laid down.

What was to become a core activity of natural scientists was conceived at a joint meeting of BCG, GCG and the Systematics Association in 1977. A proposal was made to organise a body to collect data on the location of natural history collections in north-west England. This Collection Research Unit was to be the forerunner of many other regional projects, grouped finally under the title of FENSCORE — the Federation for Natural Sciences Collections Research (Hancock, 1977 and 1978).' Data has been collected centrally in Manchester using a package called FAMULUS and several articles and notes have appeared in the *BCG Newsletter* and elsewhere describing its operation (e.g. Pettitt, 1979; 1986). Data on collections are entered on coding sheets which are accompanied by a set of instructions for their completion. These instructions include minimal guidance for terminological control, relying only on a few examples. A more recent description (Pettitt, 1986) explains more:

> Curators are allowed to use free text when completing almost all of the sections . . . : . . . supervising the use of a controlled vocabulary . . . would have been very difficult . . . Curators are more prepared to assist if data capture is uncomplicated. However an unordered mass of free text is not very useful . . . Therefore all the records are scanned . . . and a series of sort/search codes is added to each.

This approach doubtless has its advantages, though it necessarily produces useful generalisations than might otherwise have been achieved. Although it remains very useful, the 1979 publication *Collections and collectors in NW England* reveals the consequent flaws (Hancock and Pettitt, 1979). The indices in Volume 2, especially the subject index show many examples of poor term control. That the instructions for completing the data entry forms were never improved seems a pity. The MDA has now taken on the task of processing the data returned by recorders and as a result FENSCORE is undergoing a welcome resurgence.

If one considers that the field of biological recording is another desert of non-controlled terminologies, then there is at least an oasis comparable to the efforts of Pettigrew and Holden in geology. Geoff Halfpenny published his *Natural History Classification Scheme* in 1983 (Halfpenny, 1983) as part of a feature on the Natural History Section of Stoke on Trent Museum. The scheme consists of a list of taxa from Kingdom to orders spanning some 14 pages and which to my knowledge it is the only list of its type to have been published. In 1984 the question of the need for 'standardised' recording again arises, but still largely in the context of biological records centres. Among a number of papers in the *BCG Newsletter* issued prior to a conference on *Biological Recording and Museums*, Charles Copp considered the future of environmental recording and local records centres and identified a number of problems (Copp, 1984). Although he did not highlight terminology control specifically, he did suggest that a new national federation could 'foster the interchange of information on techniques e.g. cards, computers, recording formats and data standards'. Subsequent to the conference in Leicester, Graham Walley published some thoughts on the proceedings and gave some consideration to the priorities for the development of biological information recording techniques (Walley, 1984). He refers only in passing to the need for 'agreed standards', for 'dictionary files to facilitate input' and for 'checklists'. He concludes with a plea for a forum for the development of biological recording, which earlier he had described as being 'parallel to museum documentation', and ends by saying 'Whether we need the equivalent of the MDA remains to be seen'.

The proceedings of the conference were published as a complete issue of the *BCG Newsletter* (Garland, 1985) and although several of the contributors address issues of data recording and retrieval, there is no mention of problems of terminology control. Clearly by this time the many individual institutions and curators involved in site-based data recording had solved the problems of data entry for themselves and in their own way.

In April 1986 the concerns over biological recording culminated in the launching of the National Federation for Biological Recording. 'The Federation seeks to bring together the many agencies that are involved in biological recording and, in so doing, improve their effectiveness in gathering, managing and disseminating biological records'.

This development has great potential, in particular concerning computer methods of data recording. A package called *Recorder* has been produced by Stuart Ball which, despite the fact that it is still unreleased in a finalised format, is quickly gaining acceptance among a wide range of biologists. Terminological controls are in hand and it is hoped that check-lists will be available on disc. Habitat classification and description has been recently developed by the NCC and should be made generally available soon (Jan. 1990). European initiatives will follow.

Conclusions

The preceding review is not comprehensive; I have attempted to discover all the essential published sources, expecially those indicated by reference to the two specialist curatorial groups where I would expect to find the most useful guidelines for curatorial practice. I am less familiar with coverage of the biological arguments for specimen documentation than the geological and hope that I have not been unjust. However, certain conclusions seem inescapable.

First, despite a large number of references to various museum documentation systems (and I have not included them all), terminological control is rarely mentioned by either curatorial group. Secondly, the Museum Documentation Association and its predecessor IRGMA, whilst always championing the need for specialist terminologies, absolved themselves at an early stage from actively carrying out the necessary work. Though there is clearly a willingness to provide guidance for the construction of terminologies, the onus was placed most definitely with curators. I cannot help but think that this was short-sighted and now regretted. For museum geology, I would conclude thirdly that although the requirement for standard terminologies was recognised relatively early (certainly by some individuals), little work was done towards producing concensus decisions, based perhaps on the leads offered by McInnes (1978) and Pettigrew and Holden (1978). One might ask why we have not seen the published lists of the more active computer users such as Leicester and Ulster and indeed my own institution, Brighton, as well, presumably, as many others. Publication alone of course is no answer. Decisions with at least a glimmer of consensus views are required and need to be published as at least a first attempt at uniting each curatorial discipline. The geologists have started this process with the GCG's 1985 *Guidelines for the Curation of Geological Materials* (Brunton, Besterman and Cooper, 1985). The guidelines, however, stop short of comprehensive terminologies, the bulk of the book being more concerned with specimen handling and care. For documentation, the guidelines are nevertheless a good foundation but the GCG must build on it. The GCG/MDA proposal for a research project was the right approach despite its rejection and must be resubmitted.

For the biologists, my fourth conclusion must be that the documentation of museum objects has been almost totally ignored in preference to that of site-based data. This may be a reflection of the great diversity of interests among biological curators, together with the great diversity of specimens they curate. It is therefore far more difficult for a single grand plan of terminology control to be conceived, though I confess a difficulty in understanding why, with the single exception of Halfpenny's 1983 *Natural History Classification* no terminologies at all have appeared or are referred to in the *BCG Newsletter*. (There are now various American manuals available giving guidance on different kinds of collections management (such as Genoways, Jones and Rossolimo, 1987), but I have not been able to consult these.)

Presumably biologists, like palaeontologists, have placed their trust in the natural order of things, Linnean nomenclature, sex, age and anatomy, leaving, it has been hoped, little room for subjectivity. Despite this optimism, there is still enormous variety in recording terminologies, if not in sex, then certainly in nomenclature and classification and I see no reason for the present indifference to proper terminological control. While it is certainly true that proper habitat description is essential to the proper description of museum specimens, this is not enough by itself. The bias towards environmental and habitat data must be a reflection on the important role of museum biologists and their collections within the framework of the National Federation for Biological Recording which is greatly more advanced than the equivalent in the geological sector. The NFBR package *Recorder* does not, however, concern itself with any of the data required for collections management.

Clearly any resolutions of the problems I have identified are the responsibility of the curatorial professions. But natural history curators cannot afford to be myopic. They are either generalists or specialist; in both cases there is a need to consult a wide cross-section of users of the information museums are purveying and not just other curators.

Crucially, we should be talking with the research institutions to find out exactly what is wanted from us. Not just the universities and polytechnics but also the botanic gardens, the zoos, the Geological Survey, etc. Furthermore, the scope for international collaboration, especially European is enormous, though whether we should get our own national house in order first or enter the international circuit through CIDOC (the Documentation Committee of ICOM) is a moot point. We must even agree on non-specialist terminologies, an area which still does not seem to have been settled. Too many meetings have been held where the individual efforts of a few have been presented to the many with no resolve to reach consensus views and there has been little if any joint work between the two curatorial groups.

If we are to make progress we must begin by reviewing the rationale of terminologies. Most importantly, it seems to me, they present us with a formula for consistent and appropriate specimen documentation to a high professional level. But we must avoid the building of a discipline of terminology in its own right. Information is there for the user and his or her purposes must continually be verified. Should we for instance be concerned with standards which address information of little value. Is the reason of not being able to predict future use of collections strong enough to justify some of the highly complex and detailed records proposed? Is the goal of national and international union catalogues a realistic one, and if so what terminologies should we be working on to produce them? I am greatly encouraged by the early success of the Museum Databases project pilot scheme in this respect. But at the most basic level of proper inventory and stock control, natural history curators, perhaps above all others, must remember the context in which they work — millions of specimens in the country's provincial museums lie neglected and unrepresented by curators and millions more are in the national museums, Internationally the situation must be at least as bad.

I would wish that natural history curators in British museums find ways to agree terminologies between them, but I am not optimistic. It seems to me that by and large curators have actually preferred their own methodologies and terminologies which are thus private property and not the common stock of the profession. I am, however, grateful to see the advances made by the MDA Terminology Working Party, and natural history curators should perhaps concern themselves closely with the deliberations of this group and by a determined and collaborative effort of the specialist groups achieve a breakthrough even at this late stage.

---

73 GEOSAURUS: A SYSTEMATIC THESAURUS OF GEOSCIENCE

Pnina Wentz and James R. Shearer

Department of Information Studies and Technology
Ealing College of Higher Education
London

Introduction

This paper considers the principles involved in the design and use of Geosaurus, a structured thesaurus covering the geosciences, developed for indexing and retrieval of items in the GeoArchive database. GeoArchive is a computerised bibliographic database aiming at world-wide coverage of geoscience literature in all its forms (Geosystems, 1981). Its scope includes geophysics, geochemistry, geology, palaeontology, mathematical geology, mineral and petroleum production and resources, as well as new taxa, new minerals and new stratigraphic names. GeoArchive is available online through Dialog Information Services.

The database started in 1969 and it now contains about 590 000 records. Geosaurus was issued in its fourth edition in 1981 (Charles, 1981) and a fifth edition is scheduled for publication in 1989. The thesaurus is shortly to become available online as part of the GeoArchive database on Dialog.

The paper begins with an outline of the characteristics of geoscience information. This is followed by a detailed discussion of the structure of Geosaurus and its distinctive features as a thesauro-classification: a thesaurus in which the main presentation is in a systematic form, exhibiting the relationships between the terms used and providing full synonym and homograph control, with access through an alphabetical index. The use of Geosaurus in indexing and retrieval is discussed, with specific reference to the indexing policies of the GeoArchive database and the need for structured representation of knowledge for effective retrieval in the geosciences. Consideration is also given to the review/updating procedures and to the development of software for thesaurus construction. The paper concludes with a discussion on the suitability of the structured approach and software used in Geosaurus for the construction of thesauri in other disciplines.

Characteristics of geoscience information

Interdisciplinarity

Geology began as an inductive science where observation of the structures and stratigraphy of the rocks led to the development of ideas about their history. As the science matured geologists began applying physical and chemical laws to geological studies, and increasingly deduction rather than induction characterised the subject. Today the geosciences are inter- and multi-disciplinary, developing and adapting the theories, hypotheses and practices of other scientific disciplines and applying them to geological phenomena.

The relationship between the sciences, and their application to the geosciences, may be illustrated in an abstraction-complexity series (Lea, 1978):

PURE SCIENCE SERIES	ABSTRACTION	INTERDISCIPLINARY GEOSCIENCE SERIES
Mathematics	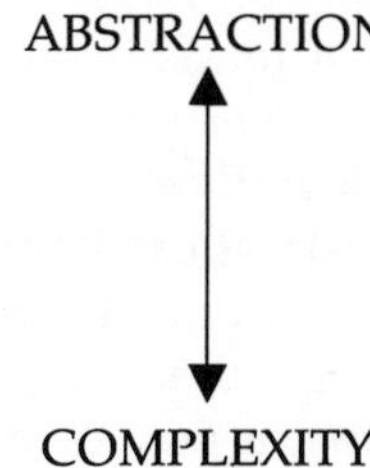	Mathematical geology
Physics		Geophysics
Chemistry		Geochemistry
Geology (sensu lato)		Geology (sensu stricto)
Biology		Palaeontology
	COMPLEXITY	

Classificatory/taxonomic nature

The geosciences include a number of disciplines which are classificatory/taxonomic/descriptive in nature, at least in part. The literature of palaeontology contains descriptions of new taxa (species, genera, families and orders); the literature of mineralogy includes details of new minerals; the stratigraphic literature details of new stratigraphic units. In each case the description is highly formalised and the new nomenclature is approved by the appropriate international body. The references are of permanent importance, since they are not subsumed by more recent writing.

Long half-life

A considerable proportion of the geological literature has a long half-life (i.e. it does not become obsolete rapidly). In particular this applies to descriptive/taxonomic writing and to the many early reports and surveys which have not, or in some cases cannot, be repeated. Thus, early palaeontological descriptions of new species are constantly referred to, and old regional surveys of obscure areas may be the only guide as to whether further exploration is worthwhile.

Regionality

Much primary geological research is carried out by studying a single location or a small group of locations covering a relatively small area; only later can broader interpretive studies be made.

Publication practices in the geosciences

The periodical is the most frequent medium for publishing geoscience literature, but there is a substantial amount of semi-serial and monographic material. In addition there is an ever-increasing quantity of material published in special forms, such as standards and patents, and in specialised formats, such as maps, audiovisual materials, machine-readable files, etc.

One of the results of the regional characteristic of geoscience information mentioned above is that local studies are often published in local journals, which may have limited circulation and be little-known.

The scientific and economic significance of the geosciences is reflected in the types of organisations active in publishing the literature. National and regional government surveys and departments of mines and mining are the most important publishers in this field, followed by commercial publishers, learned and professional societies, universities, museums and individuals.

Implications for thesaurus construction and maintenance

The characteristics of geoscience information discussed above have considerable implications for thesaurus construction and maintenance.

The inter-disciplinary nature of the geosciences may result in difficulties defining the scope and the perspective of terms in the thesaurus. It is not sufficient to combine existing terminologies of various relevant subject fields; terms derived from other disciplines may lack the geological perspective. Thus, the same term may appear several times in different contexts and this can lead to cross-classification.

Since taxonomies feature in a number of geoscience disciplines, users are familiar with classificatory structures. It is, therefore, advantageous to incorporate a classified arrangement in the thesaurus. It may be possible to use existing taxonomies for some parts of the thesaurus, but these classifications are subject to review and thus necessitate a corresponding review of the thesaurus.

The long half-life results in a need to relate older literature to current materials. There is a need to maintain records of changes in terminology over a period of time. On the other hand the long half-life may lead to fossilisation and a reluctance to update terminology.

The regional aspect of geoscience literature requires fully detailed geographical classes with adequate provision to specify geographical adjacency.

In view of the various media of publication, provision should be made for indicating form and format of publication.

Terms selected for the thesaurus should reflect the interests of the varied bodies involved in geoscience information transfer without value judgements.

Geosaurus: Scope and coverage

Materials indexed

GeoArchive aims at world-wide coverage of the geoscience literature and inclusion of all publicly available relevant material, regardless of form.

Over 5 000 current periodicals are scanned (Shearer, 1979) as well as relevant new monographs and maps. In addition, older material is gradually added to the database, as there is a need for considerable retrospective coverage in view of the long half-life of the literature. In particular, this involves indexing the older publications of the major national geological surveys and the major core journals.

Scope

The subject scope of Geosaurus closely reflects the inter-disciplinary nature of the geosciences. Terms in the thesaurus are grouped into subject and auxiliary series. The subject series covers the geosciences and related fields. The auxiliary series includes language, geographical, stratigraphical and palaeogeographical terms.

Subject series

The major divisions of the subject series are:

Regional Geology
Applied Geology
Mineral Geology
General Geology
Physical Geology
Methodology
Geoscience Information

The *Regional Geology* section includes all types of maps and data resulting from regional surveys, but excludes reference to the theoretical and technical aspects of mapping and surveying. These feature in the Appied Geology section.

The *Applied Geology* section includes economic geology (petroleum and minerals exploration, production, processing and management), geodesy, cartography and remote sensing, and the applied fields of engineering geology, environmental geology and oceanography.

The *Mineral Deposits* section includes fossil fuel and mineral resources, ore genesis, and hydrology. Many of the mineral rock names which appear here also appear in the Mineralogy and Petrology sections which cover the theoretical study of mineral and rocks.

The *General Geology* section contains the pure and theoretical disciplines of the geosciences: mineralogy, petrology, sedimentology, palaeontology, geochemistry, geophysics and geomathematics.

Physical Geology includes tectonics, structural geology, geomorphology, historical geology and planetology.

Methodology contains field methods, laboratory methods, computer methods, graphical methods and equipment and instrumentation.

The *Geoscience Information* section incorporates all aspects of geoscience information, documentation, organisation and policy.

Auxiliary series

Major divisions of the geographic series are locational, physiographical and political, and palaeogeographical sections.

The locational descriptors include concepts such as offshore areas, urban areas, swamps, etc. They may be used to qualify other geographical descriptors, or on their own as subjects. There are descriptor groups for the universe and planets and for international organisations and alliances.

The political and physiographical descriptors are merged to provide a unified classification. Areas which are physically contiguous are adjacent, or as nearly as adjacent as possible, in the classification. Where possible, physiographical features situated geographically between two political areas are inserted between them. When it is not convenient to integrate political with physiographical terms, the physiographical terms are given first.

Geosaurus — Structure and arrangement

Overview

Most indexing and retrieval tools employ implicitly or explicitly some elements of classification (see for example discussion in Vickery (1975)). Creating a classificatory structure provides a systematic, analytical tool for developing the thesaurus: 'The more effort that is taken creating [the classificatory] underlying structure, the higher the quality of the relationships and consequently the performance of the thesaurus' (Aitchison, 1986).

Combining and displaying hierarchical and other semantic relationships in a unified conceptual framework is particularly suitable for the geosciences. As discussed above, a number of disciplines within the geosciences are classificatory/taxonomic in nature, thus structuring the indexing language to correspond to the structure of the discipline, follows

Figure 73.1 Systematic display in Geosaurus

557000 Sedimentation

See also: 540900 Petrogenesis; 729900 Tectonic controls of sedimentation; 740500 Transportation (geomorphology); 743800 Fluvial deposition features; 746400 Glacial & fluvioglacial deposition features;- 747600 Coastal deposition features

557100 Sediment provenance

Includes: Heavy mineral zones; Mineral stability (sediments); Mineralogical maturity of sediments; - Sediment source rocks

See also: 418800 Heavy mineral deposits

557200 Sediment dispersal

Includes: Sedimentary facies; Sedimentary petrologic provinces

See also: 230300 Facies maps; 550500 Sedimentary environments; 771000 Paleogeography; 771300 Paleocurrents

557300 Sedimentary basins

Includes: Ancient shorelines; Basin configuration

557400 Physical parameters of sedimentation

Includes: Current direction; Current stability; Current velocity; Depth of water (sedimentation)

557500 Rate of sedimentation

557600 Deposition of clastics

Includes: Deposition of turbidites; Turbidity currents

See also: 383200 Submarine canyons; 552300 Clastic textures; 553000 Clastic sediments

557700 Deposition of non-clastics

See also: 552900 Non-clastic textures; 554000 Non-clastic sediments

557800 Carbonate sedimentation

See also: 555000 Carbonate sediments; 772100 Calcretes

557900 Cyclic sedimentation

See also: 556300 Internal bedding structures

558000 Diagenesis

Used for: Catagenesis

See also: 740400 Chemical weathering

558100 Lithification

558200 Authigenesis

Used for: Neogenesis

558300 Cementation & decementation

Figure 73.2 Geosaurus alphabetical index

the principles of 'literary warrant' and 'user warrant' and offers considerable advantages in retrieval.

Geosaurus is a thesauroclassification: a thesaurus in which the main presentation is in a systematic form with a fully displayed hierarchical structure, and including details of definitions and semantic relations between concepts (Figure 73.1). An alphabetical section is necessary to act as an index to the location of terms in the systematic part (Figure 73.2); in addition, it also provides a useful grouping of terms spelled in similar ways. A notation is required as a link between the systematic and the alphabetic sections. The notation is a six-digit code assigned sequentially, to reflect the order of descriptors in the systematic display.

It is important to note, however, a number of disadvantages of the structured thesaurus. There is a potential conflict between the formal structure of knowledge representation in a systematic thesaurus and the dynamic nature of knowledge. Any form of knowledge representation has to include provisions for revision and updating. These may involve the addition of new concepts, often to increase specificity, but also of new fields of specialisations or new inter-disciplinary approaches. Sometimes a 'scientific revolution' requires a reworking of an entire section because thought patterns within the area have undergone a sea change (e.g. plate tectonics).

While the addition of specific concepts into existing hierarchies is a relatively straightforward matter, the addition of new specialities or inter-disciplinary perspectives may require more fundamental structural changes and regrouping of the main sections/classes of the thesaurus. Such modifications are possible; however, there is an inevitable '. . . time-lag in the recognition of the developments in the relationships of interacting components in the subject' (Gopinath and Seetharama, 1979). However, frequent structural modifications may conflict with a fundamental function of the thesaurus: to enable consistency in indexing and retrieval, for which a degree of stability is required.

As mentioned above, structured thesauri require an alphabetical index and a notation to link the two parts. The notation reflects the order of concepts in the systematic part and represents a fixed linear sequence. Using notational symbols tends to reinforce a static impression and a quality of permanence. Alphabetical thesauri, on the other hand, do not embody a linear sequence of concepts and do not require a symbolic representation. They are, therefore, considered more flexible and dynamic, amenable to immediate modifications. Lacking an explicit ordering device, however, they are forced to use the arbitrary alphabetical sequence for tasks for which it is ill-suited.

In Geosaurus, it was considered appropriate not only to use classificatory techniques as an analytical tool for the development of the thesaurus, but to maintain the resulting systematic structure as the main part of the thesaurus, thus making available its considerable advantages as a retrieval tool. In this context, it is important to note the additional indexing features which provide a mechanism for enhancing the thesaurus, and the provisions for modification and updating of the thesaurus (see later).

The systematic section

Descriptors

The first section of the thesaurus is a systematic presentation of descriptors and the relationships between them. All subject and locational descriptors are nouns or noun phrases and are given in the plural, except for discrete concepts (e.g. Geochemistry) and systematic mineral names (e.g. Kyanite). Geographical descriptors are proper nouns, stratigraphical and language descriptors are adjectival phrases.

A significant number of Geosaurus descriptors are phrases or multi-word descriptors. These are used either because it is not possible to express some concepts with a single word, or because it is considered preferable to use compound terms in certain circumstances.

In the first instance there may be no one-to-one relationship between concepts and their verbal representations. This situation becomes particularly apparent using multilingual dictionaries or thesauri, in which a concept may be represented by a single word in one language and by a phrase in another (Railway/Chemin de fer; Railway station/Bahnhof). Alternatively, a single word may represent a compound concept (Mother — a female parent).

In inter-disciplinary subject fields, it is often necessary to express newly formed concepts by a phrase, as a single suitable word may not exist. Using a number of words to form a new concept may result in the new concept having a distinct meaning, different from the meaning of its constituent words. When such multi-word concepts are accepted as descriptors in the thesaurus, the semantic relationships of the descriptor as a whole may be different from the semantic scope of the individual words. (For a full discussion of compound terms in indexing and retrieval see, for example, Austin (1984), Aitchison and Gilchrist (1987) and British Standards Institution BS 5723 (1987).)

The second situation, deliberately using multi-word phrases as descriptors, is intended as a device to increase precision in retrieval. For example, using Asbestos Deposits as a single descriptor may reduce 'false drops' in retrieval (i.e. retrieving irrelevant documents which were indexed under Asbestos and Mineral Deposits as independent descriptors which do not necessarily relate to each other).

An interesting phenomenon in concept formation in multidisciplinary subject fields, is the frequent amalgamation of two distinct discipline names into a single word representing the new field (Geochemistry, Biogeochemistry and Geothermometry). This phenomenon is of considerable significance because of the widespread acceptance of American usage and the growing suppression of hyphens (e.g. in-house/inhouse, on-line/online, data-base/database).

Relationships between descriptors

Hierarchical relationships are indicated implicitly by typeface and indentation such as:

390000 ENERGY SOURCES
395000 Hydropower
    395200 Tidal energy

Although the codes are assigned sequentially, they have in general no special hierarchical significance, though major terms tend to end with more zeros.

Narrower terms are distinguished by typeface and are listed under their relevant descriptors in alphabetical order. Where a narrower term itself has one or more synonyms, all are listed as narrower terms. For example, allanite and orthite are both given as narrower terms under Epidote group (Figure 73.3).

A number of descriptors occur more than once in the thesaurus. Some are homographs (e.g. Eucrites (igneous) and Eucrites (meteoritic)) and others are terms which may be used in several different contexts (e.g. Asphalt (economic), Asphalt (mineralogy) and Asphalts (sedimentology)). In such cases, the descriptors have qualifiers in parentheses and are disinguished by the different descriptor codes, indicating the different contexts.

Figure 73.3 Narrower terms

521800 Epldote group
Includes: Allanite; Angaralite; Canasite; Carpholite; Cebollite; Chevkinite; Clinozoisite; Deerite; Delhayelite; Fenaksite; Ferrocarpholite; Hancockite; Howieite; Hsianghualite; Ilvaite; Latiumite; Llevrite; Lombaardite; Mukhinite; Muromonfite; Orthite; Perrlerite; Pledmontite; Piemontite;Pistacite; Tanzanite; Tawmawite; Thulite; Tranquillityite; Treanorite; Tscheffkinite; Tuhualite;Zoisite; Zussmanite

'Used for' relators indicate synonyms or near-synonyms for descriptors, such as:

410600 Lignite
Used for: Brown coal

The non-preferred terms feature as entry vocabulary in the alphabetical index.

Related terms are shown by 'See also', providing cross-references to other relevant descriptors, such as:

540900 Petrogenesis
See also: 547000 Metamorphism; 557000 Sedimentation

'See also' references are always made reciprocally.

The index

Overview

As discussed above, it is necessary to provide an alphabetical index as a key to the location of terms in the systematic section. The notation is the link between the systematic and the alphabetical sections. The alphabetical index lists all preferred and non-preferred terms included in the thesaurus.

Synonyms or near synonyms (Used for) are indexed directly: a direct reference is made to the code both from the preferred and non-preferred term, such as:

519200 Bitumen
. . . . . .
519200 Macerals (the non-preferred term)

In this way users are guided directly to the relevant section in the systematic file, even though they may have searched the index under the non-preferred term.

Homographs are distinguished by the different context as indicated by the codes and are qualified in brackets, such as:

734000 Cleavage
510400 Cleavage (mineralogy)

Other semantic relationships provided in the main systematic section (i.e. hierarchical and associative relationships) are not repeated in the alphabetical index, as it is always preferable, even essential,. to consult the systematic section for full display of semantic relationships.

Structure

In order to provide access to all constituent parts of multi-word descriptors, the alphabetical index to Geosaurus is a rotated (permuted) index, generated automatically from the main systematic file after ignoring stop words (Figure 73.4).

Such provision is particularly important for the English language in which the typical word order in compound phrases is of modifiers (e.g. abverbs, adjectives) preceding the substantive part (the noun) of the phrase. Rotation enables useful collocation in the alphabetical index under the noun.

'igure '3.4 Rotation feature of alphabetical index

(192500)	Lihou
536500	Likasite
(097000)	Likhvinian
572400	Liljevalliinae
(087300)	Lillburnian
534800	Lillianite
(866100)	Lima
(363850)	Limassol
735100	Limbs
(203310)	Limburg
546500	Limburgites
532100	Lime
547600	Lime metasomatism, alkali &
(186600)	Limerick
451400	Limestone
(207000)	Limestone Alps, French
(208000)	Limestone Alps, Northern & Southern
(782184)	Limestone County (TX)
(780567)	Limestone County(al)
478000	Limestone deposits
478100	Limestone deposits, lacustrine
744600	Limestone pavements
555400	Limestones, algal
555900	Limestones, allochthonous
555100	Limestones, autochthonous
555300	Limestones, biohermal
555400	Limestones, biostromal
555400	Limestones, crinoidal
555900	Limestones, detrital
555950	Limestones, dolomites & magnesian
555700	Limestones, evaporitic
555900	Limestones, exogenetic
555400	Limestones, foraminiferal
555800	Limestones, oolitic & pisolitic
555200	Limestones, organic
555600	Limestones, orthochemical
772100	Limestones, pedogenic
555200	Limestones, pelagic
555300	Limestones, reef
555400	Limestones, shelly
772200	Limestones, vermicular
772100	Limestones, vlei
554000	Limestones), non-clastic sediments (excluding
576500	Limidae
575500	Limnadiidae
575500	Limnadopsidae
573200	Limnocnididae

Rotation also provides access to parts of descriptors which are not indexing terms themselves 'and therefore do not occur anywhere else in the thesaurus' (Aitchison and Gilchrist, 1987, page 72).

However, a rotated index cannot provide access to parts of descriptors embedded in another word. For example, there is no access to the term Biology embedded in the term Paleobiology. The problem could be solved by providing a 'See also' reference in the index, as:

Biology
See also Paleobiology

though this approach is not currently adopted in Geosaurus.

Additional indexing features

Identifiers

As discussed earlier, the literature of the geosciences contains descriptions of new taxa, new minerals and new stratigraphic units. These descriptions are of considerable importance, but they present a number of problems. Inevitably, they introduce new terminology, which cannot be ignored. At the same time, it would not be desirable to include all these new terms in the thesaurus, for two reasons: the thesaurus would grow beyond reasonable bounds very rapidly, and thus lose utility; and in general, the new terms will be too specific for the thesaurus, and have the effect of dividing the literature too finely, when one purpose of the thesaurus is to enable like material to be grouped together.

The solution that has been adopted in GeoArchive is to introduce fixed format identifiers. These use a prefix code or tag before the new term to identify its nature. The user can retrieve on the highly specific term when it was first used and defined. The identifiers do not replace thesaurus terms; they supplement the appropriate descriptors with specific identifier information. Thus descriptors such as:

572000	Brachiopoda
763000	Lithostratigraphy
923000	Nomenclature and terminology

will be used as appropriate in conjunction with the following new terminology identifiers:

*NSPE	New species
*NGEN	New genus
*NFAM	New family
*NORD	New order
*NTAX	New taxon other than those above
*NMIN	New mineral
*NSTR	New stratigraphic name

For example:

New taxon
Trigoniids from the Berriasian of the Crimea [*NSPE Myophorella mordvilkore]

New mineral
Helmutwinklerite, a new arsenate mineral from Tsumeb, SW Africa [*NMIN helmutwinklerite PbZn2(AS04) 2H20]

A further set of identifier codes are used to identify personal data relating to an individual. Using these codes, it is possible to retrieve specific information about named individuals, a facility which is difficult to provide for through the thesaurus itself, because of the unlimited number of names and the generally poor control of personal name use. The codes available and their meanings are:

*OBIT	Obituary
*BIOG	Biography
*FEST	Festschrift
*PORT	Portrait
*BIBL	Bibliography
*TRAN	Translator
*REVI	Book review by

For example:

Mario Taschini [*OBIT *PORT *BIBL TASCHINI, M 1932–1975]

The Anthropogene of the USSR [*TRAN OWEN, CR from Russian]

The Earth [Academic Press, New York, 1978, 502 pages] [*REVI Bambach, RK]

Fixed format identifiers of this kind are also used to link together the publications relating to a particular conference. A typical conference generates a great deal of material, ranging from the initial call for papers to the final published proceedings, including preprints and abstracts, and possible changes in the title of the conference itself, or of individual papers. The approach used in GeoArchive is to assign a unique annual number to each conference, and link the records together through this number and appropriate identifiers. The identifier codes used are as follows:

*CONF Conference announcement
Entry includes conference details, including title, venue, dates, organiser's name and address
*CABS Conference abstract
*CPRE Conference preprint
*PROC Conference proceedings
Entries are made for the proceedings as a whole and for the individual papers
*CREP Conference report

For example:

The entry:
Geology of the Sierra de Falcon [Falcon State, NW Venezuela]
[*CABS (48–2/21:2/23) 80]
indicates that this is the abstract of a paper given at conference no. 48 of 1980, held from 21–23 February.
Retrieval of the entry tagged with
[*CONF (48–2/21:2/23) 80] would reveal the full details of the conference.

This approach to identifiers for terms that do not warrant inclusion in the thesaurus proper has obvious potential for thesauri in other areas. It provides a mechanism for identifying specific neologisms which are important for retrieval purposes but do not merit inclusion in the thesaurus proper. It must be noted, however, that this method is not a substitute for the regular review and update of the thesaurus with new concepts as they emerge.

Data

Certain categories of factual data can be extracted from documents and arranged in sets. Each element of information in such a data set can then be retrieved independently as required. This technique is applied to map indexing, with special data fields such as scale, form, edition, latitude and longitude.

Geosaurus in indexing and retrieval

Indexing policy

Geosaurus is used as the controlled vocabulary for indexing the GeoArchive database. The indexing philosophy is based on the premise that a systematic, structured approach to thesaurus construction is required to ensure consistency in indexing and accessibility in retrieval. Indexing policy is based on a number of broad principles.

Documents are indexed at the most specific level, using the most specific descriptors and supplementing them with identifiers, data elements and natural language, to increase specificity as appropriate.

Indexing is carried out by subject specialists, who have substantial knowledge of the subject domain, in addition to their expertise in indexing.

Indexers scan the full text of documents. The interdisciplinary scope of the geosciences requires wide coverage of core and fringe publications. Titles and abstracts, in particular of fringe publications, may have been written from a non-geological viewpoint and may not provide adequate information on the geological content of the document. Full text scanning is also necessary to determine appropriate identifiers, data elements and natural language phrases which may be added to the record to increase specificity.

Geosaurus in retrieval

Geosaurus is used as a tool for translating search topics into the indexing and retrieval language of the database: the codes and descriptors used for indexing GeoArchive.

The structured approach adopted for the construction of Geosaurus provides the facility for searching by classification codes representing concepts, or by natural language, or by a combination of both. Using the classification structure as a tool in online retrieval provides a number of important search features.

The structured presentation acts as a guide on how to expand or narrow searches, and provides cross-references to other relevant parts of the thesaurus.

The policy of indexing at the most specific level is common to many databases. While this has considerable advantages in providing access to specific topics, it may cause problems in searching for broader subjects. There is no autoposting to broader terms (i.e. a document on the Isle of Wight is not also indexed under Hampshire) and retrieval under the broader terms identifies the more general material only.

Using classification codes to formulate search strategies overcomes this problem. A broader concept can be specified either by truncating a class code (e.g. 553?) or by searching on a range of codes (e.g. 553000:553999). Both examples cover all codes between 553000 and 553999. Range searching is the more versatile of the two methods, since it is possible to search on a range of codes which do not share significant common digits (e.g. 553000:554999 when truncating by 55? is considered too broad).

Range searching is a useful method to ensure that relevant unpublished new terms are incorporated into the search strategy as appropriate. This is achieved by using a range of codes which begins with the desired descriptor code and ends with the number immediately preceding the next descriptor code. For example, the code for Sedimentary geochemisty is 668000 and the next descriptor code is 669000; using the range 668000:668999 will ensure inclusion of any new descriptors added to the end of Sedimentary geochemistry section.

Using class codes instead of verbal representations of concepts reduces possible ambiguities. A class code provides a context for homographs, control of synonyms and of changes in terminology (e.g. geographical names: Rhodesia/Zimbabwe or Falklands/ Malvinas). Control of geographical names can cause considerable problems, in particular in retrospective searches. Class codes offer an easy method to handle place-names.

A classified structure facilitiates online browsing, similar to subject browsing through a classified bibliography. It is possible to sort search results on class codes and then prepare classified lists of references.

However, it is important to recognise situations in which natural language searching offers advantages over searching with class codes. It is particularly useful for refining results already achieved using code searching, for searching fringe subjects or highly specific subjects, or when the specific concept of interest is consistently and unambiguously named.

Revision and updating

The problem of fossilisation

A major problem with any thesaurus is that its structure and content can rapidly become fossilised with time. This is because:

new terms are invented for both new and old concepts;

old terms acquire additional or changed meanings;

old terms become obsolete as a concept 'dies';

new ways of thinking, using new terminologies, develop, both in major areas (e.g. plate tectonics) or at a very specific level (e.g. reassignment of species to genera and families).

It is essential that any current thesaurus be regarded as a dynamic product requiring constant updating. Ideally, this should be done regularly and systematically.

Continuous review of new terms

For Geosaurus, the basic principle for inclusion of terms is literary warrant (though some terms are included to show steps in division which are never used in classification). Editors and indexers work with and respond to the terminology in use, and note new terms as they appear. Regular editorial team meetings debate their inclusion in the thesaurus, and their appropriate notation. All new terms are entered with the date when they were first introduced. It is worth noting that even before the term has been formally included in the thesaurus, it is possible to retrieve items including it by using natural language. However, such a retrieval will only identify items with the chosen term present in the title, rather than the larger set of items dealing with the selected concept.

Systematic review

In addition, there is systematic periodic review of the various sections of the thesaurus. In part, the basis of review is the frequency count of usage of thesaurus terms. Consideration is given to subdividing heavily posted terms earlier than lightly posted ones, but equally, attention is paid to maintaining an even degree of subdivision so that adjacent classes are not divided to widely different degrees. Particular attention is given to topical areas; thus Environmental Geology, Geoarcheology and China are all under current review.

Hierarchy checking and term lapsing

During systematic reviews, the hierarchical structure of the section and the ordering is carefully checked. Occasionally such checks reveal a structural error in the thesaurus, in that an existing term is misplaced. The term involved is then lapsed: the code is marked and never re-used, and the term is reassigned to its proper position. The machine readable file records the term in each position and links them together. In a few cases a term may lapse because the concept is not needed (e.g. Federation of Rhodesia and Nyasaland). The term is then retained in the thesaurus, but not used except when indexing older materials when its use may be appropriate.

Review of geographical areas

Geographical thesaurus development has generally followed the systematic work of Geosystems in indexing the geological maps of the world. Geosaurus has generally been revised and enhanced according to the need for subdivision identified when examining the maps of an area prior to indexing them. Index maps are commonly used to define the boundaries of the divisions identified, but for reasons of cost these have not been published. In a number of cases overlays to distinguish political and physiographic divisions are employed. The oceans present a particular problem in this respect, since the boundaries of most oceanic features are poorly and ambiguously defined and used in the literature.

Scope variations

Changes in the scope of GeoArchive also result in new additions to the thesaurus. Thus, Mineral processing has recently been developed, and Ore deposits revised and expanded.

Software for thesaurus construction

It is important to distinguish between using computers to generate thesauri automatically and using the computer as a tool in the process of conventional thesaurus construction.

Techniques for automatic thesaurus construction evolved from research of automatic indexing. These techniques employ statistical methods to group terms into clusters, compute term similarities and frequencies of occurrences, to identify terms which are good 'discriminators' for purposes of indexing and retrieval. (For a full discussion, see Salton and McGill, 1983, Chapters 3 and 4 and Lancaster, 1986, Chapter 21.) However, these methods remain largely experimental, as they do not provide a satisfactory solution to the problem of identifying conceptual relationships between terms, which may not be revealed by statistical analysis.

At present, most operational thesauri are constructed by human intellectual effort, involving subject analysis and identification of semantic relationships. The computer may have a significant role as a tool for recording, storing and updating the terms included in the thesaurus. The resulting machine-readable file may be processed by appropriate software that:

automatically indicates reciprocal relationships (BT/NT,RT,U/UF);

creates an alphabetical display and generates hierarchies;

creates an alphabetical display from a systematic file;

generates rotated displays;

derives specialised lists of terms from larger thesauri;

merges several thesauri;

enables the creation of an online thesaurus, to provide an up-to-date interactive tool for indexing and searching.

Most commercially available software packages for thesaurus construction are designed to handle primarily the alphabetical section of thesauri. In addition, a number of packages (such as CAIRS) provide facilities for displaying machine generated hierarchies derived from the main alphabetical section.

Geosaurus software adopts a different approach, closely reflecting the principles employed in the construction of the thesaurus and highlighting the advantages of a systematic subject analysis and a classificatory structure as the underlying basis of the thesaurus.

As discussed above, the main presentation of Geosaurus is in a systematic form, displaying a hierarchy of up to 11 levels. The hierarchical relationships between descriptors are indicated typographically and by indentation and incorporating other semantic relationships (synonyms, homonyms and associative relationships) in the main display (Figure 77.1). The software is designed to generate automatically the full systematic structure from the initial input records and to create the rotated alphabetical index (Figure 77.2).

Following the subject analysis, a machine-readable input file is created. Each descriptor is represented in the input file by a record which consists of four parts:

[CODE] [LEVEL] [DESCRIPTOR] [A NUMBER]

The CODE is a six-digit notation allocated to each descriptor, reflecting its position in the systematic structure.

The LEVEL is a number indicating the level of subordination of each term, representing the hierarchical relationships (BT/NT). In addition there are special numbers reserved to indicate the other semantic relationships incorporated in the main display (associative relationships shown as See also, equivalence relationships shown as Used for and scope notes).

The NUMBER indicates a cross-reference, or dates for new terms, or links between new and lapsed terms.

The main part of the thesaurus, the systematic presentation, is generated automatically from the input file. The rotated index is derived from the main file after removal of stop words.

When the thesaurus is updated, each new term is analysed, and assigned a code appropriate to its location in the systematic structure, and a number reflecting its level of subordination.

Discussion and conclusions

Geosaurus is designed to reflect the characteristics of earth sciences information and documentation and to meet user needs for an efficient retrieval tool for the GeoArchive database. However, the principles and methodology employed in the development and maintenance of Geosaurus have wider applicability.

Whenever a classificatory approach, reflecting a common understanding of the relationships between concepts in a subject, is appropriate, the Geosaurus methodology may be suitable. There are considerable advantages in using a classificatory approach as an analytical tool and including the resulting classification as part of the thesaurus. In addition, the classificatory structure can serve as a powerful retrieval tool.

A rotated index provides a simple and efficient mechanism to enable access to all parts of multi-word descriptors.

The geographical part of Geosaurus is of particular interest. The entire world is covered in reasonable depth and the general sequence, determined by physical contiguity rather than political affiliation is suitable for applications where a regional classification is required. A significant number of current databases have no regional vocabulary control or regional access, although such facilities would greatly enhance retrieval.

The use of identifiers for terms which do not warrant inclusion in the thesaurus proper, is potentially suitable for other taxonomic/descriptive disciplines, in which it is necessary to identify the first definition and use of a term.

The approach adopted for designing the software is equally suited to other thesauri which employ classificatory techniques for subject analysis and incorporate a hierarchical display with distinct levels and codes and a rotated index. Both parts of the thesaurus are generated fully automatically from the initial input file.

With appropriate develoment of relevant sections, Geosaurus could be extended to form a terminological tool for specimen databases, with the ultimate objective of linking specimens with pertinent documentation through shared terminology.

---

74 SOME STEPS TOWARDS UNIFORM TERMINOLOGY IN MINERALOGY

A. M. Clark

Department of Mineralogy
British Museum (Natural History)
London

Introduction

The standardisation of terminology in mineralogy is one of the major aims of the International Mineralogical Association (IMA), an association of the principal mineralogical societies of the world. Their recommendations, as far as mineral names and symbols are concerned, are expressed through its Commission on New Minerals and Mineral Names. These recommendations are widely applied in museum mineralogy departments, where mineral nomenclature documentation is recognised to be one of their core activities. The publication and access to appropriate databases now forms the cornerstone of this activity.

A major part of the British contribution to the standardisation of mineral nomenclature arose in 1942 from an enquiry to the Natural History Museum, London, concerning the silicates of magnesium that were known in nature. The enquiry was dealt with by Dr Max H. Hey and, since there was no single up-to-date reference to which he could turn, he had to make a complete listing. After that immediate question had been answered, the resulting card catalogue continued to grow as a departmental work of reference. It proved so useful that it was published in 1950 as *An Index of Mineral species and Varieties arranged chemically, with an Alphabetical Index of accepted Mineral Names and Synonyms* or in its shortened form: *The Chemical Index of Minerals* (Hey, 1950).

Its purpose, as stated in the introduction, was 'to provide a ready answer to anyone inquiring what minerals of a given qualitative chemical composition are known, to assist in eliminating superfluous mineral names, and to serve as a collective index . . . bearing on the individuality and chemical composition of minerals'.

The work was an immediate success and a second edition followed (Hey, 1955) which was reprinted with corrections in 1962 and reprinted again in 1975. Two appendixes followed, in 1963 and 1974 (Hey, 1963 and Hey and Embrey, 1974), and the three volumes remain in print. This paper outlines the role played by the *Chemical Index* in the establishment of uniform terminology in mineralogy and the steps now being taken to bring the publication up-to-date in order to make it increasingly accessible to those requiring information in documenting mineral collections.

Application and development of the system

Experience with the *Chemical Index* over the last 28 years has revealed several interesting facts.

Firstly, although the index was intended primarily as a mineral analyst's determinative aid, placing all minerals of similar composition near together, many of its readers were found to consult the alphabetical index first, as a comprehensive and authoritative guide to mineralogical nomenclature.

Secondly, and probably the main reason for this paper, each mineral or important chemical variety was allocated a number in the chemical section. These numbers have since been widely used in museums and private mineral collections for documenting mineral species and for labelling collections.

It will probably be useful at this point to look at the structure of the classifiction devised by Max Hey:

> Based on its chemical composition, a mineral is placed in its appropriate anionic group: oxide, sulphide, silicate, phosphate, etc. Each group is numbered, the numbers ranging from 1 (native elements and alloys) to 33 (hydrocarbons to which mineral-type names have been applied). Sections 34 and 35 are reserved for partially or inadequately characterised materials.
>
> Within each anionic group, the minerals are arranged by metals following the order of the periodic classification. Where more than one metal is present, appropriate cross-references are included and the main entry is made under "the noblest or rarest metal present"; the latter discrimination has been difficult to apply consistently across the whole range of chemical components found in minerals.

The intention was to group minerals in sets of about 30 species, with the final group obtained by ordering the minerals according to increasing oxidation state, degree of hydration, etc. As an example, a fragment of the index lists some of the manganese oxides as:

7.18.1	Manganosite	MnO
7.18.2	Pyrochroite	$Mn(OH)_2$ [trigonal]
7.18.3	Bäckströmite	$Mn(OH)_2$ [orthorhombic]
7.18.4	Hausmannite	Mn_3O_4
7.18.5	Partridgeite	Mn_2O_3 [cubic]
7.18.6	Pyrolusite	MnO_2

The number 7 refers to the oxide-hydroxide section, 18 to the manganese group, and the final numbers to the position in the sequence, starting with manganosite, the manganese oxide in the lowest oxidation state.

Since the publication of the second edition of the index in 1955, individual species numbers have not been changed unless gross errors in a mineral's chemical formulation have been discovered. Newly described species have been inserted into the classification by appending a letter to the number sequences. As an example, an addition made in the first appendix to the above sequence is:

7.18.5a α–Kurnakite Mn_2O_3 [tetragonal]

Probably the only modern classification system with which Hey's system can be compared is that developed through succeeding editions of Dana's System of Mineralogy (Dana, J. D., 1837, 1844, 1850, 1855 and 1868; Dana, E. S., 1892; Palache, Berman and Frondel, 1944 and 1951; and Frondel, 1962). The latter system does lend itself to the systematic display and storage of minerals, as it combines both the chemical and structural aspects of a mineral compound. But it does not have a satisfactory numerical system, as the numbers were changed in succeeding editions. Additionally, the final edition, the seventh, has remained incomplete, lacking the numerically largest mineral group, the silicates.

So Hey's system has found application amongst those who prefer a numerical system for documenting their collections. But it does have some shortcomings as shown below, some of which are being rectified in the third edition now in preparation:

members of an isomorphous series often appear widely separated in the classification (e.g. the two clinopyroxenes diopside, $MgCaSi_2O_6$, and hedenbergite, $CaFeSi_2O_6$, are numbered 14.6.9 and 14.22.2, respectively);

multiple chemical substitutions in minerals often require extensive cross-referencing;

changes in numbering are not generally made unless gross errors in the chemical determination are detected. For example, the gem mineral painite (Claringbull, *et al.*, 1956 and 1957) was originally described as $Al_{40}Ca_8B_2Si_2O_{75}$, number 17.5.9a. Later work showed that zirconium had been overlooked in the original analysis and the new formulation, $CaZrBa_9O_{18}$ (Moore and Araki, 1976), no longer accords with its place in the classification;

new minerals are being described at a rate approaching 100 species per year. Placing new entries in the system can pose difficulties in retaining a rational numerical system;

many workers have found the chemical classification difficult to follow and apply.

In view of the growth of mineralogical data since the publication of the second appendix in 1974, Hey had planned and spent many years working on a completely revised third edition of the *Chemical Index*. From experience gained with the earlier editions he had intended to place most of the information under the names in the alphabetical section, referring to it at times as the 'Index Mineralium'.

Furthermore, the availability of computer search facilities covering mineralogical data, such as a computer identification program and database called MINIDENT (Smith and Leibovitz, 1986) and a mineral database created by Aleph Enterprises and CSIRO, have to some extent reduced the potential demand for a publication searching for mineral species from the qualitative chemical composition. Nevertheless, following consultations with mineralogists in this country and overseas, it became evident that demand remains for a complete index to mineral species, varietal names and synonyms.

In his lifetime, Hey had completed work on just over half the species, working not alphabetically, but systematically through the species, starting with the native elements. At the time of his death in 1984, he was in the middle of the alumino-silicates, having dealt with the important varieties and synonyms as well as the accepted species up to that point. He had not documented the minor synonyms and varieties, mixtures, trade names, erroneous spellings, etc., which abound in the literature.

Concurrently with this work, Peter Embrey, also at the Natural History Museum, had arranged for the transfer to floppy disks of the whole text of the second edition and the two appendixes via an optical character reader. These disks have been edited to eliminate reading errors and can be accessed on a microcomputer.

Following our survey, work on the revision of the index is being carried out using the following guidelines:

the compilation is to contain the main body of information in an alphabetical listing by mineral name;

cross-reference chains are to be eliminated;

a much simpler species-finding index, arranged chemically, is to be included;

primary sources of reference data are to be cited, not secondary sources such as Dana's System or Mineralogical Abstracts;

basic unit cell data and the Powder Diffraction File Numbers are to be included. This recognises that minerals are not defined solely on the basis of their chemical compositions, but that some crystal structure data are essential. Their inclusion means that the title 'Chemical Index' no longer strictly applies and the publication is provisionally titled 'The Mineral Index',

type localities, where known, are to be included;

the origin of the species names is to be documented, where known;

the nature of the mineral synonymy or varietal status is to be qualified. Some synonyms are local names or language variants. Others were applied when a mineral was thought to be a species in its own right: only subsequent work relegated the name to that of a synonym. Similarly, species varieties may be of a chemical nature or they may be crystal habit or colour variants;

accepted IMA nomenclature directives are to be followed.

A specimen entry is given here as an example:

Apuanite, $Fe^{2+}Fe^{3+}{}_4Sb^{3+}{}_4O_{12}S$.

M. Mellini, S. Merlino, and P. Orlandi (1979)

Amer.Min. 64, 1230 and 1235. Tetragonal, *a* 8.367, *b* 17.959 Å, Z = 4 [PDF 33–642]. (TL) Bella della Vena mine, Stazzema, Tuscany, Italy. Named for Apuan Alps.

Compilation of the index started at the beginning of 1988 and is expected to take three years with publication soon thereafter. The final extent of the file is thought to be some 17 000 entries, of which around 3 000 will be accepted species names. The index is being compiled using the British Museum (Natural History) database system, with software written inhouse. The expected size of the complete index is 20Mb and should be accessible to an IBM AT compatible microcomputer. Although the prime objective is to produce a printed reference index, the file can also be used to generate indexes based on fields such as the chemical components of mineral species and chemical varieties, mineral type localities, authors, publications, etc., and the index will be available on a floppy disk.

---

75 UNITED KINGDOM BIOLOGY CHECKLISTS

Graham Walley

Senior Keeper (Natural Sciences)
Nottingham City Museums

Introduction

Checklists of names in biology, zoology and geology are such readily available tools that they are easily taken for granted. My interest here is to concentrate on the actual and potential use of electronic checklists — checklists in machine-readable form. As background, I would like to summarise the origins and uses of checklists, with specific reference to the UK.

Crowson (1970) describes the creation of classifications as a basic aid to survival. Certainly the ability to discriminate, analyse, group like with like and extrapolate from patterns is very well developed in humans. In our writing-based cultures, listing the names of the rich variety of life found in the natural world has been basic to natural historians from Aristotle to Francis Willoughby to Darwin and his successors in the present day.

A list represents what is out there, or is being studied in field observations or inside an experiment; as such it is basic to the study of all aspects of natural history.

Checklist uses

Natural historians have many uses for checklists. They form the common currency by which biologists formulate the transfer of information and improve the understanding of their work. Bringing all names used in a work into line with a published checklist removes an area of potential confusion and allows ready access to its contents. Environmental inventories make use of checklists of species according to the area and range of groups concerned. Over and above any pure reference work, 'to get the name right', they can be appended with many kinds of experimental, habitat and geographical data.

Checklists are a convenient way to update the names and the classification of a group. With a complete synonymy they provide a reference for the history of name changes. They can be physically cut up or copied for collections management and cataloguing uses and provide a means of access to literature and databases, which increasingly are indexed by taxonomic keywords. This last aspect shows the main use of checklists as a system of common currency.

Increasingly, biological information-gathering, especially that with an ecological or geological base, is geared towards the tailoring of data for transmission and use either nationally (and internationally) or locally. To this end, the gatherers make use of the lists being produced by specialist recording groups or older composite lists as appropriate.

Using checklists to update names does not alter the validity of an identification. That will remain as correct or dubious as before — checklists with synonymy can only link *names*.

Checklist production

A checklist can be compiled by anyone at any level of expertise, using any language, within the taxonomy of their choice. Most workers, at least as a starting point, enjoy the opportunity of being able to buy a checklist produced by professionals. This often gives them access to the combined work of many taxonomists in a convenient, clearly set out printed form, and increasingly in an electronic, machine-readable form.

Dedicated checklists are produced as name lists only. The lists produced by J. E. Dandy (Dandy, 1958) and those of the Royal Entomological Society (RES) are well known to UK naturalists. Other works form *effective checklists*, but are in fact synopses of species, that have the checklist function because of their comprehensiveness and authority. The *Flora Europaea* (Tutin, Heywood, Burges, Valentine, Walters and Webb, 1964–80) now provides the base for UK vascular plant nomenclature. It is the reference for most of the 3rd edition of *Excursion flora of the British Isles* (Clapham, Tutin and Warburg, 1981) which is the more available (and portable work) for the UK flora. Both these are systematic works with keys and detailed descriptions and distribution information as well as the latest thoughts of many experts botanists on nomenclature.

Checklists by their nature are always out of date. The UK has an increasing number of alien species establishing themselves and a declining natural and semi-natural landscape. Some of these species' gains and losses escape any published checklist, especially a paper one. The cost of publication of major revisions and the work they entail means that they are very infrequent. Workers in the 1990s will still be using lists published in the 1970s, if not earlier.

Authoritative checklists are compiled by one or more authors after a review of the published and unpublished work of perhaps hundreds of individuals. Their reliability and hence usefulness as a standard depends on this bedrock of informed opinion from these group experts. In addition, authors often allow their own consideration to override other expert opinion in some cases. So for example the 2nd edition of *English Names of Wild Flowers* (Dony, Jury and Perring, 1986) largely reflects the nomenclature used in *Flora Europaea*, but not completely. The traditional use of a name can still be seen as being a valid reason for inclusion, often with sound systematic reasons, sometimes not.

Revisions published in journals, synopses and monographs can keep a published checklist more up to date. They are a basic part of the checklist process and can be comprehensively included to form a next edition.

The long time lag between the original work of the revisor and the paper publication is a disincentive to continue their work and a loss to the natural history world of their expertise for considerable lengths of time.

Checklist structure

The checklist itself can be a basic name list, or increase in complexity (and usefulness) by citing the authorities and dates of publication of species names, together with any synonyms they replace and possibly a hierarchical numbering system. They can be set out systematically, for example to include family/sub-family divisions, or be listed alphabetically. Indexes may or may not be included as may sub-species/variety details.

Most published checklists can be seen to have the following overall structure:

title, author/editor details;

introduction, explanation of revisions and sources, acknowledgements;

checklist proper;

index.

Within the checklist proper:

higher classification taxa;

genus, species, infraspecies names, authority name, date;

species number (with or without encoded classification);

synonyms, authority and note on validity or explanation;

vernacular/regional names;

ancillary data — distribution, ecology, descriptions.

(Sometimes species lists are alphabetically arranged rather than taxonomically arranged.)

Generally speaking a greater degree of detail given in a checklist makes it available for more uses, but increases the cost of production considerably. Layout is very important for ease of use.

UK checklist sources

The production of checklists in the UK has changed over the years. Once the territory of individual enthusiasts, many publishing privately, in recent years their production has come increasingly under the remit of the national specialist societies and organisations. Individual authors are commissioned to coordinate and review the work of many separate experts, but the societies formed for the study of specific groups have taken their responsibilities very seriously. As well as the Botanical Society of the British Isles (BSBI) and RES, the work of the Linnean Society in this sphere is also well known.

In recent years, the Lichen, Bryological and Pteridological societies have been at the forefront of their group revisions. The Freshwater Biological Association (FBA) has produced work across many groups in that environment. In addition, individual authors have published without the benefit of an umbrella organisation (for example, Bradley and Fletcher, 1979).

The checklists from these sources provide the basis for most of the lists used day to day in the UK. In addition, their production of synopses of species provides a means, for many workers the only practical means, of updating group systematics and names whilst providing the source to identify individual species.

What might be termed secondary sources of checklists are organised by the Environmental Information Centre (Biological Records Centre) (BRC) which has been collecting and working with lists of species names across all animal and plant groups in the UK for nearly 20 years. Based at the centre of a wide array of National Recording Schemes with a remit to publish national summaries of the known status of species, it is a key user and potential disseminator of checklists. A small number of local museums have attempted to do similar work and these lists are also available.

Rearranging checklists for local use

Checklists summarise the species of a geographic area — British Isles, Fennoscandia, Australasia, etc. Unless you are very lucky, these areas never coincide with your own area of concern. The creation of checklists for use at the local level is often necessary at sometime. Species relevant to an area often have to be abstracted from published longer lists for larger areas. To these need to be added species discovered or introduced since the compilation date of the published checklist, plus any alteration to taxonomy suggested by a more recent published note or monograph. 'Inside' knowledge from an authoritative colleague may also be incorporated where the compiler believes it important enough. The local list therefore has a mixture of sources for names which are in themselves important to document for future use by other workers. When creating a local checklist to cover several groups the complication increases. A full invertebrate list for one county in the UK could involve abstracting names from publications of the RES, FBA, Linnean Society and many published notes, some of which are out of print. In total some 30 000 species would need to be considered. This would be increased considerably if synonyms were included. There is great scope for confusion and errors if this were to be carried out manually across the UK.

Major systematic works might not be used locally where a readily available popular field guide seems to serve the purpose: this is more frequently met with where the success of local natural history recording depends on local amateur workers, a tradition still strong in the UK.

Case for computerisation of checklists

Handling lists of such a specialised form that also requires acurate reproduction and use by many workers would seem to be a prime candidate for computerisation. In addition to the obvious convenience towards production of checklists, computerisation is being encouraged by other user needs.

Firstly, there is a greater need to handle a broad spectrum of species data across many groups at the local level. In the UK, local biological record centres, conservation and planning organisation, the Nature Conservancy Council and various research projects want to use, adapt and expand existing checklists.

Secondly, there is an increased need to compare and amalgamate biological information at the local, regional and national levels. National statuses are based on contributions from the local level; local interests ask for feedback from centrally run national schemes. Pressures on the natural/semi-natural environments mean that reassessments of status needs to be carried out at shorter periods and the exchange of data needs to speed up. This would be greatly facilitated by a common format that could be derived from a common checklist format in machine readable form or *vice versa*. Checklists are always expensive to produce in whatever format. But the compilation, distribution and maintenance of checklists by computerised means would seem to have clear advantages.

Benefits of electronic checklists (ECs)

The main benefits of publishing *computerised* standard checklists are in the efficient use of inputting time and the accuracy of replication between sites. Speed of distribution would encourage a reduction in the intervals between major revision. Revision could be more cheaply undertaken and encourage individuals to submit their work to the compiler because there would be both early use of it and credit for it. In addition, the end-users might have the opportunity to receive updates regularly and checklists would be immediately available for editing for local use.

Published ECs would be a great encouragement towards standardising a data transfer format with great benefits for exchanging data horizontally as well as vertically.

At the local level, ECs would provide the base material for producing a large range of locally developed lists for local use in data processing, record keeping and publications. There would also be security benefits.

Progress with ECs in the UK

On behalf of the National Federation for Biological Recording (NFBR) the author elicited the views of the national societies and other research and recording organisation about their existing or planned use of ECs. All the national societies in the UK have clearly recognised the usefulness of computerisation and accept that future lists should be ECs. Equally clearly the costs of transferring existing lists and distributing future ones are recognised. Some of the respondents were creating databases containing a wide range of data from which ECs could be derived; this work is also being undertaken by some water authorities. The Marine Conservation Society at present stands alone in having recently published its multi-group EC.

In botany, the work of the European Documentation System under V. H. Heywood at Reading University has produced a computerised version of the *Flora Europaea* which has great potential as source material for the whole of Europe.

The British Museum (Natural History) with responsibility for coordinating future RES publications is looking at cooperating with users to ensure future checklists are ECs. The Environmental Information Centre has established itself as a key organiser of ECs and is about to make copies of its lists available in microcomputer format to outside users.

The future of ECs in the UK

There is enough activity at present to suggest that production of ECs across many groups is likely to happen. The author suggests that their production needs to be formerly supported so that they are produced to a standard with the widest possible use.

Indeed their production is too important for them to be a by-product of other activities and should not be seen to be the sole property of any one institution. Agreement to commercial production by an institution would need to be seen to be on behalf of the community and an archive safety net would need to be assured if the venture failed. Financial support is necessary and some commercial rights will need to be established as for any printed checklist production.

In addition the users of ECs would need some input into their design, maintenance and distribution method.

The importance of ECs and their maintenance needs to be formally recognised. The UK has a tradition of producing its checklists principally for the benefit of the naturalist and scientist and not as a commercial operation. In recent years the commercialisation of services that were once freely given in the UK natural history world has increased. The goodwill so necessary in the production of checklists and their EC successors might also end, in which case a commercially based replacement will be required.

EC coordinating responsibilities

Whoever might coordinate EC production and EC standards will need to address the following issues.

The content, data structure and transfer format would be key considerations. Any data structure would also need to accommodate or be linked to habitat and distribution information.

The way working ECs are formulated at the local level indicates that the end-users need to know the source of the component names. The coordinator needs to ensure that procedures for authenticating the inclusion of particular names from particular groups are clear and documented and that links with group specialists are recorded.

Links with the full range of end-user biologists and geologists would be important. A formally set up body would be needed to ensure that the widest range of interests are heard and incorporated into EC standards.

ECs would be a large investment and they need careful archiving. This task would need to be a requirement of at least one body.

Distribution of original lists and updates would need to be carried out competently. There needs to be means of automatically updating locally used lists on a regular basis, and support for this would need to be a key task for any distributor, whether commercially based or otherwise.

Compatibility with other international ECs needs to be maintained and areas of disagreement identified. Some coordinating body will need to have this liaison responsibility.

Copyright of the information and its subsequent use by end-users at all levels would need to be investigated and procedures agreed. Many users will wish to create published works based, at least in part, on ECs. This needs to be recognised from the start and acknowledgement procedures and royalty agreements would be required.

76 BIOLOGICAL CHECKLISTS, A EUROPEAN PERSPECTIVE

Paul T.Harding

Head, Biological Records Centre
NERC Institute of Terrestrial Ecology
Monks Wood Experimental Station
Abbots Ripton, Huntingdon, Cambridgeshire

Introduction

The need for standardised biological check-lists, at a national level, has already been described by Walley (Chapter 75) and at the international level many of the needs are the same.

Taxonomists have reached broad agreement on how biological nomenclature should proceed, through the international codes for botanical and zoological nomenclature (Greuter, 1988 and International Commission on Zoological Nomenclature, 1964). However, the work of the International Commissions is inadequately funded and is directed towards the establishment of a set of rules and making decisions on particular problems in nomenclature. The establishment of nomenclatural base-lines and standard lists is a haphazard process dependent on the interests and activity of individual taxonomists.

Taxonomic reasearch is a continuing process and scientific names are constantly changing: new genera are described, species are split or amalgamated and species new to science are described. Added to these factors are natural and man-assisted changes in the geographical range of species. It can be seen that keeping up-to-date with the names of the flora and fauna, of even such a small and well-researched area as Europe, is a formidable task. There is no organisation in Europe which analyses each of these changes and recommends whether changes should be followed. Even if there were such an organisation, it is probable that not all biologists would agree with its proposals and decisions.

Problems for the user

Keeping up-to-date with nomenclatural changes and additions is difficult enough for taxonomic specialists. Few are lucky enough to have an international 'clearing house' for information, such as exists for Myriapoda in Paris at the *Centre International de Myriapodologie.*

Collaborative international scientific projects, such as those listed in Figure 76.1, have to establish an agreed nomenclature (or a way of temporarily bypassing it) *before* beginning their collaboration. However, most such projects approach the problem with good sense and caution because taxonomic experts are involved from the beginning.

Pity the poor international wildlife conservationist or legislator who is rarely a taxonomic expert! The projects listed in Figure 76.2 have all come up against the problem of bewildering nomenclature when information is collated internationally. International organisations in Europe need to find ways of avoiding nomenclatural complexities to be able to do their work.

Figure 76.1 International collaborative projects on the flora and fauna of Europe

Flora Europaea
Atlas Florae Europapeae
Atlas des reptiles et amphibiens de l'Europe
Atlas des mammifers de l'Europe
European Ornithological Atlas
European Invertebrate Survey
Faunistica Lepidopterorum Europaeorum

Figure 76.2 Examples of European projects using check-lists

COUNCIL OF EUROPE
Bern Convention

EUROPEAN COMMISSION
CORINE Biotopes Project

IUCN (International Union for the Conservation of Nature)
World Conservation Monitoring Centre
Bonn Environmental Law Centre

The increasing use of computers to exchange information, both between taxonomists and between other potential users of biological check-lists, has increased the need for stability in nomenclature because opportunities to exchange data are increased. Computers also have the potential to provide more flexible and easily interpreted systems for compiling, storing and using check-lists.

Solutions to the problem

Most organisations or projects have adopted similar approaches to the problems of nomenclatural instability. Whether stated or not, in most cases, a recent authoritative, pan-European, western Palaearctic, or global publication which reviews a taxonomic group, has been used as a principal source of scientific names.

In 1986, a Council of Europe working party recommended that the choice of reference works was fundamental to the adoption of standard nomenclatural lists for use by data banks in member states (Council of Europe, 1986). In 1987, the Ministerial Committee of the Council of Europe approved a recommendation that *Flora Europaea* (Tutin, Heywood, Burges, Moore, Valentine, Walters and Webb, 1964–80) should be the source of 'standard names' of flowering plants to be used by data banks dealing with the flora of Europe.

Unfortunately, when the Council of Europe initiated the compilation of a list of 'standard names' for the vertebrates of Euope, mainly for legislative purposes, it did not follow this earlier advice. As a consequence, the consultants used by the Council of Europe produced an incomplete list containing confused nomenclature. Also, their work ignored the check-lists compiled by, and available in computerised form from, the Nordic Code Centre and the lists of amphibians, reptiles, birds and mammals compiled for the European Commission (Nowak 1977, 1979,1981). It has taken two, two-day meetings of an international select committee of experts and the production of four draft versions of the list to achieve a publishable list which follows the Council of Europe's own recommendations (Council of Europe, 1988)!

Vernacular names

The preceding sections of this paper have dealt with scientific (Latin) names. Vernacular names also merit consideration because they are widely used in national legislation (for example, in Great Britain, the Wildlife and Countryside Act, 1981) and have to be interpreted when information is collated or exchanged between countries.

The Council of Europe's select committee of experts working on the list of standard names for the vertebrates of Europe recommended that vernacular names, in at least French and English, should be included in the computerised version of the list (Council of Europe, 1988). Again, there is need for a principal source reference for each group because vernacular names are subject to variation and imprecision. For example, the British Ornithologists' Union Records Committee (1988) published suggested changes to the English names of 190 species of birds, to standardise with Englsh language usage elsewhere, especially in North America. Learning to call common garden and hedgerow birds (see Figure 76.3) by longer, more complicated names, may meet with resistance from several generations of British birdwatchers and the general public, but the suppression of the old names in field guides and in publications would probably lead to the adoption of the new names within a few decades.

European biological nomenclature database

The need for a nomenclatural database of the plants and animals of Europe was discussed by a select committee of the Council of Europe in 1987 (Council of Europe, 1987).

Figure 76.3 English names of Western Palaearctic birds — examples of proposed changes

Present name	Proposed name
Swallow	Barn swallow
Wren	Northern wren
Robin	European robin
Blackbird	Common blackbird
Jay	Acorn jay
Magpie	Black-billed magpie
Jackdaw	Western jackdaw
Linnet	Brown linnet

Proposals for the content of such a database were formulated by the committee and a slightly modified version is included as an Appendix. It is improbable that financial suport for a database would be found, because no international or national organisation would consider the database to be its responsibility. However, the proposed content of this database serves as a benchmark for future consideration of the topic.

Where do we go from here?

Any individual or organisation requiring a list of standard names of European plants or animals has several choices, for example:

find out what others have done (but where does the non-specialist start?);

develop a list from first principles (a lengthy process requiring taxonomic expertise);

employ a consultant (and hope that they do what is required).

Figure 76.4 Examples of computerised European biological check-lists

NORDIC CODE CENTRE (Stockholm)

European vertebrates
Nordic vascular plants, bryophytes, phytoplankton
Nordic molluscs, some insects
Baltic invetebrates and benthic algae

SECRETARIAT DE LA FAUNE ET DE LA FLORE (Paris)

European vertebrates
French fauna and flora

MEDIFAUNE (Nice)

Mediterranean marine fauna

INSTITUTE FOR NATURE CONSERVATION AND ANIMAL ECOLOGY (Bonn)

European vertebrates excluding fishes (Nowak, 1977, 1979, 1981)

MARINE CONSERVATION SOCIETY (Ross-on-Wye)

British Isles marine flora and fauna (Howson, 1987)

BIOLOGICAL RECORDS CENTRE (Huntingdon)

British Isles fauna and flora (terrestrial and freshwater)

NATURE CONSERVANCY COUNCIL (Peterborough)

British insects and macro-invertebrates

EUROPEAN INVERTEBRATE SURVEY — NEDERLAND (Leiden)

Invertebrates of inland waters in the Netherlands (Mol, 1984)

FACULTÉ DES SCIENCES AGRONOMIQUES (Gembloux)

Belgian invertebrates

Many European biological check-lists already exist, but their existence is often unknown outside a small group of specialists. Many national data centres, museums or individuals have national lists, often in computerised form. A few examples of national and international lists (some of which have also been published) are included in Figure 76.4. International lists are few, but the Nordic Code Centre is expanding the coverage of its lists using the RUBIN code system of numbers and nmemonics (Österdahl and Zetterberg, 1981).

There is potential for collaboration between organisations: for example, the lists of the Nordic Code Centre, Medifaune and the Marine Conservation Society could be used to compile a basic list of European coastal fauna. However, collaboration requires a sense of common purpose and financial support. At the same time as central governments are withdrawing support for taxonomy and systematics, the products of taxonomy and systematics are beginning to become of importance to legislators. The need for the compilation of international biological check-lists comes as much from legislators as from taxonomists or biogeographers.

Some duplication of effort could be avoided if an inventory of major biological check-lists in Europe was compiled and publicised. A 'list of check-lists' could easily be kept up-to-date using a computer. For someone to take this initiative, it is essential that a potential user, such as the Council of Europe, the Euopean Commission or the International Union for the Conservation of Nature (IUCN) should provide the financial incentive.

Computers provide the ideal medium for storing and keeping up-to-date biological check-lists. Computer-readable media (disks, tapes, etc.) provide a simple means of transferring information from one user to another. Europe is, for most groups of flora and fauna, the best documented continent. Data centres now exist in many countries. If the production of European biological checklists is a worthwhile objective, then we have the knowledge and the facilities. All we need now is the money!

Appendix. European biological nomenclature database: proposed content

The Council of Europe hosted a select committee of experts on data banks in conservation in September 1987. The committee, chaired by P. T. Harding, identified the need for a nomenclatural database of European vertebrates as the first step towards a series of such databases (Council of Europe paper PE-R-BD (87) 3 rev). The following is a slightly modified version of the proposal in the report of the select committee.

The database for a given taxonomic group has, as its basis, the Central Reference Publication(s) which would provide a working list of the species of Europe. In the absence of pan-European publications, individual national publications would be used to compile a composite list.

The database should contain scientific nomenclatural information and indexing fields. Coding systems for the database have not been considered, but codes should allow access to all levels of scientific names and indexing fields.

Scientific nomenclatural information

1 current accepted scientific binomials derived from the central reference publication(s) for each group and from subsequent revisionary publications;

2 supra-specific taxa (Order, family, etc.);

3 infra-specific taxa (sub-species, variety, race, etc.);

4 valid synonyms;

5 authors (authorities) and dates of publication;

6 bibliographic references to original descriptions or re-descriptions.

Note: Items need not necessarily be held in the database if they are included in the central reference publication(s).

Indexing fields

Information to be used to sort the database and to enhance its use, particularly at an international level.

1 standard names to be used for legislation purposes: in some cases these will differ from the current accepted scientific binomials for example, valid synonyms. Standard names are intended to have greater stability than current accepted binomials;

2 vernacular names: where thought relevant these could be compiled for each country. It should not be necessary to 'invent' vernacular names;

3 geographical information: a summary of the known range of each species (either as resident or visitor), or least to the level of countries and to distinct biogeographical units within countries (e.g. Crete, Madeira, Azores, Faroes) where relevant;

4 protection status: whether the taxon has been covered by international or national legislation (e.g. Bern Convention, CITES or national wildlife legislation (including permitted hunted species)); whether the taxon is listed in international, national or local Red Data lists/books;

5 nomenclatural updates: bibliography of publications used for interim minor revisions of the nomenclatural lists; to be included only where the 'current binomial' is changed from that in the central reference publication.

---

77 AUTOMATION POLICY AND STANDARDISED INVENTORY FORMS FOR FRENCH NATURAL HISTORY COLLECTIONS

Philippe Guillet
Office de Coopération et d'Information Muséographiques, Dijon

The French Ministry of Education (which is responsible for Natural History Museums) has recently undertaken the development of an automation policy for their collections. This is intended to allow the exchange of data between museums and, especially, to make it possible to produce national collections inventories.

In order to achieve this, it was appropriate to standardise the form of information recorded and to choose software that could be used by all the museums concerned.

After consultation with curators and with the aid of the MDA cards, five inventory forms have been developed and published. These cover the principal areas of Natural History: Zoology, Botany, Petrology, Mineralogy and Palaeontology.

The software adopted was the MDA's MODES package, which is well suited to small institutions like the Natural History museums of France. The French version of MODES has been available since July 1988.

At present, the use of the inventory forms and the automation of collections are both increasing, allowing us to foresee the imminent production of national inventories for a heritage which is very valuable and almost totally unknown.

78 SORT/SEARCH CODES: A PRAGMATIC APPROACH TO RATIONALISING MUSEUM INFORMATION ON COMPUTER

Charles Pettitt

Keeper of Invertebrates
Manchester Museum
The University
Manchester

Background

Ten years ago I was faced with the task of computer cataloguing the Manchester Museum collections, using a large untrained team of people funded by a government job creation scheme. The collections in question covered archaeology, botany, egyptology, entomology ethnology, geology, toxophily and zoology (Pettitt and Hancock, 1981). At the same time hundreds of input sheets with information about UK natural science collections were flowing in from fellow curators, and I had also somehow to create a usable database from that information (Pettitt, 1981). This paper explains some of the methods I used to achieve the above objectives with the resources at my disposal, while also striving to maintain the integrity of the original information.

It is only worth computerising information if by so doing you can make more efficient and effective use of it. This implies being able to sort information into various meaningful orders and form helpful correlations, and to be able to selectively retrieve information according to logical combinations of search terms. The raw information attached to the objects in the collections we had to deal with, however, had to be captured from the labels and registers, and was inconsistent both within and between different collections because:

the information was presented in differing formats;

the information was often incomplete or, especially on old labels, partially illegible;

the terminology used tended to vary depending upon the date the object was originally accessioned.

The Register of Natural Science Collections Project (FENSCORE) also had variable terminology because over 200 curators across the UK were involved in completing the input sheets, and a non-restrictive free-text approach had deliberately been adopted by the Project committee (Pettitt, 1986). The current accepted practice in museums for dealing with such heterogenous information is, of course, to attempt to fully concord every part of the information using an agreed data standard and conventions. This would have meant re-formatting practically all the information, standardising every term with the aid of vocabulary lists and supplying missing terms wherever possible. This total concordance approach was rejected because:

the concordance approach can possibly be misleading to the end user, who could be uncertain what is *objective* information actually present in the written documentation, and what is *subjective* information that has been added or altered by the database compiler, who may not be a subject expert;

total concordance may not necessarily help to produce meaningful indexes, as an alpha-numeric listing is not always what a curator requires; neither does concorded information always lend itself to efficient searching, as will become apparent later;

to be fully effective, it needed staff with at least some relevant training, whereas I had to use inexperienced and frequently changing staff;

and finally, it would have slowed down the rate of work very significantly, whereas my remit was to cover as much as possible of the Museum's holdings as quickly as possible, before the government stopped funding the staff.

At Manchester, therefore although we adopted a formal, museum-wide data specification and standard, we were selective in the degree of concordance applied to the information. People's names and measurements of objects, for example, were entered in a consistent format, and some small controlled vocabularies were constructed where the gain in the utility of the information in the database outweighed the cost in data capture and checking time, and where the integrity of the information was not affected. However, concordance was soon seen to be inefficient for three important facets of the information we had to deal with:

supra-generic taxa in the natural sciences;

chronological information (e.g. archaeological and geological eras);

source localities.

My pragmatic approach, born of necessity, was to have the cataloguers input the information appertaining to these aspects exactly as it was attached to the object, and then to arrange for people with some subject knowledge to add simple sort/search codes to the computer entries, to permit post-coordinate indexing and retrieval.

Taxonomic names

For taxonomic names we used a Biocode system; the use of Biocodes has been covered by Heppell (Chapter 83) and therefore is not further elaborated here.

Chronological information

Geological eras

For geological eras, at first sight a simple controlled vocabulary including all the main terms from Caenozoic to Pre-Cambrian might be thought all that was necessary. Unfortunately this would not allow the database entries to be sorted into the chronological sequence required by a geologist. Initially this problem was overcome by adding the 'FENSCORE' Sort/Search codes shown in Figure 78.1. While sorting entries on these codes will provide the required chronological sequence, on closer inspection the haste with which this system was set up is apparent, for the major divisions of Mesozoic and Palaeozoic have had to be inelegantly inter-coded and the important subdivisions of the Tertiary are not differentiated. In addition the coding is not hierarchical, so that, for example, a search for Mesozoic material means requesting the four terms from 'A12A' to 'A15', which is clumsy, time-consuming and error-prone; the same retrieval problem would have applied if we had merely strictly concorded the names of the eras.

To correct these faults I later developed the 'Mk 2' codes. Since C, M and P happen to sort in the desired order it was easy to make the codes at least partially mnemonic; they are also arranged to be hierarchical. Thus just specifically Pleistocene entries can be

Figure 78.1 Sort/Search codes for the geological eras

	'FENSCORE'	'Mk.2'
Caenozoic	A10	C
Quaternary	A11	C1
Tertiary	A12	C2
Eocene	"	C21
Pleistocene	"	C22
Pliocene	"	C23
Miocene	"	C24
Mesozoic	A12A	M
Cretaceous	A13	M1
Jurassic	A14	M2
Triassic	A15	M3
Palaeozoic	A15A	P
Permian	A16	P1
Carboniferous	A17	P2
Devonian	A18	P3
Silurian	A19	P4
Ordovician	A20	P5
Cambrian	A21	P6
Pre-Cambrian	A22	P7

extracted by searching for 'C22', while Tertiary entries are retrieved by asking for all codes starting 'C2' and Caenozoic entries found by selecting entries whose code starts 'C'; all good modern database management packages permit this type of search-term truncation. These new codes are presently being applied retrospectively to existing Manchester databases. Similar code sequences were devised for the Egyptian dynasties and for the European Archaeological periods.

Source localities

Existing coding systems

Many systems for coding localities have been proposed over the years. Some have been extremely arcane and idiosyncratic, such as that of Rhumbler (1910) which involved the

Figure 78.2 Sketch map showing the major subdivisions of the globe on which the locational reference codes at Manchester Museum are based (*after* Wijk, *et al.*, 1959)

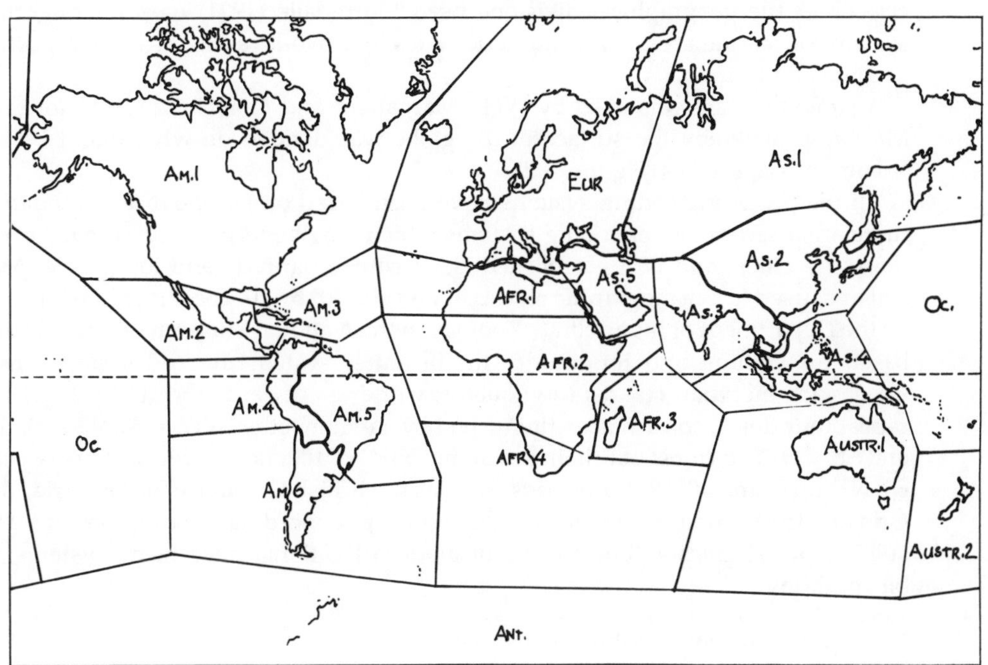

intricate use of accents to convey meaning. In his system, for example, u = Australian while ü = Cosmopolitan ('überall'), and an acute accent indicated 'eastern' while a grave one meant 'western', and so on. Such a complex system would have been difficult enough to use manually, but its use on a computer which often has difficulty *representing* accents let alone sorting and retrieving them would have been a nightmare. Heikertinger (1918) modified Rhumbler's system; the continents were assigned single letters, scattered through the alphabet, and then biogeographical regions such as Holarctic and 'Neoboreal' were assigned the remaining letters, apparently quite at random. To indicate sub-regions Heikertinger substituted digits for Rhumbler's accents, so that 1 = Northern, 5 = Northwestern and 9 = 'middle', for example. Although a marginal improvement on Rhumbler's, Heikertinger's system was still illogical, and useless for computer use (for which it was not intended, of course).

A much more detailed system of four-letter group alphabetic locality codes has been proposed by Gould (1968 and 1972), and he has supported these by publishing detailed outline maps of every country, etc., showing his intended boundary of each code. Gould's codes are a good example of data compression, but although much more systematic than the earlier codes, and despite having a degree of hierarchy built-in, the codes are not ideal for computer use, and they are not mnemonic. Also the marine divisions are not natural or logical, which would cause problems when cataloguing natural history collections.

The Food and Agriculture Organisation (FAO) codes (1960), based on those of the United Nations (1949), understandably treat the sea areas more rationally. The codes are numeric for land areas and alphabetic for marine areas; they are not to any extent mnemonic. The numeric codes incorporate a degree of hierarchy, but are somewhat eclectic in the geographical divisions used. Borradaile (1921) uses a straightforward system for marine areas, with numeric codes in a two-level hierarchy, supported by a gazetteer and a map.

A simple system was used by Wijk, Margadant and Florschutz (1959) for the *Index Muscorum*, whereby the surface of the globe was divided on what might be called a 'common-usage' basis (Figure 78.2).

All the preceding coding systems have been based on geo-political boundaries, but there are a second set of coding systems which may be termed 'coordinate' codes. Of these the oldest and best established is, of course, latitude and longtitude. Marsden squares, used in oceanographic research, and the 10° by 10° coordinate system adopted by the Department of Invertebrate Zoology in the National Museum of Canada, are both based on latitude and longtitude. In the latter system the codes start where the Greenwich meridian crosses the Equator; working outwards the 10° by 10° rectangles repeat four times, so each is distinguished by a region letter, NW = A, NE = B, SW = C and SE = D. Thus most of Britain lies in the 'box' A 50 00, i.e. the rectangle between 50° & 60° N. and 0° and 10° W. Local grids, such as the British Ordnance Survey Grid, the Irish Grid and the European Grid, form another group of coordinate coding systems. Chorley (1987; App. 7) gives a good review of modern locational referencing systems, with a bibliography.

Manchester Museum locality coding system

In deciding upon a coding system for a particular application there are two primary considerations:

the system should suit the nature of the information actually being dealt with; there is no point in having a complex system that lets you pin-point a 100m square on an individual oceanic island if most of the labels in the collection being catalogued say only 'Indo-Pacific';

the system should suit the indexing and retrieval required by the users of the database. In our case this meant the ability to search hierarchically so that, for example, all European entries could be retrieved without having to search for every European country name.

Although coordinate systems are ideally suited to manipulation by computer, have a built-in multi-level hierarchy and are independent of any political name or boundary changes, they were rejected for use at Manchester because in practice they proved difficult to apply to our information and were less than ideal for the type of retrieval queries were envisaged. Thus the task of relating the place-name information attached to an object with the correct coordinate was found to be difficult. Although gazetteers exist which give the latitude and longtitude for places, it still meant that every entry involved a 'look-up' to code, and the assignment of the correct coordinate code for a 'square' to a given latitude/longtitude fix proved non-trivial and error-prone for inexperienced cataloguers. On the retrieval side users tend to define their requirements in geo-political terms, and because of the non-correspondence of coordinate codes and geo-political boundaries the search could never be precise; there would usually be a proportion of unwanted entries retrieved as most counties, countries, states, etc., are not rectangular.

Devotees of the coordinate approach have suggested this imprecision could be compensated for by adopting conventions such as coding a country by the square in which most of its area fell, or within which its capital city lay. However, such distortions destroy one of the great strengths of coordinate codes, their independence from political changes. Such a system is an unsatisfactory hybrid. The tale of Blossom Village is salutary. In 1932 some snails were collected in 'Blossom Village, Little Cayman', a quite precise location. On a collecting trip in 1975 a colleague, Dr M. V. Hounsome, discovered that since 1932 Blossom Village had been translocated by its inhabitants to an entirely different site; of the old village no trace remained. Thus anyone using a modern map to assign coordinates to the 1932 specimens would get it wrong, but an area based location reference code is less likely to be invalidated by such changes.

In my opinion, for museum-related work, coordinate locality codes are mainly suitable on land for detailed local research projects and surveys, where the coordinate intervals are 10 km or less, and where a local standard grid is available. Recently collected material, of course, often now has grid references or latitude and longtitude recorded in the field, and coordinate coding can with advantage be used for assemblages of such material, but the reality of the information in most existing collections makes coordinate coding a non-starter. Coordinate based codes are much more useful when dealing with an oceanographic collection, especially as oceanographic specimens routinely have their latitude and longtitude attached; but even here there is a problem in that some early oceanographic expeditions used latitude and longtitude based on the Paris rather than the Greenwich meridian.

Therefore we chose to adopt a geo-political approach for our coding system. Of the existing systems already mentioned the *Index Muscorum* system (Wijk, Margadant and Florschutz, 1959) appeared the most suitable as a basis; it had been adopted by the Museum for a previous project (Franks, 1973). The objective was to provide a set of pigeonholes each of which would contain roughly the same number of entries when the cataloguing was complete. Most of our natural sciences collections appeared to contain roughly equal amounts of British, European and 'foreign' material, so a totally pragmatic approach was taken, whereby objects would be coded to county level within the British Isles, to country level within Europe and elsewhere to continent or sub-continent level (Figure 78.2). The humanities collections required a different approach as, for example, all the Ethnographical Inuit material fell in area code AM1, so 30 subdivisions were erected relating to the tribal culture and used only for this collection. Some collections did not receive any locality coding; for the Egyptian collection, for example, the finding-site name was deemed sufficient by the responsible curator.

The *Index Muscorum* alpha-numeric codes proved easy to remember and simple to apply. The Manchester extensions under EUR were primarily devised to be as mnemonic as possible to reduce 'look-ups' to a minimum. Thus many British specimens had the county recorded on the label so by adopting the first three letters of the county name as the usual code the need to 'look-up' was then eliminated; the Manchester codes for some of the English counties are given in Figure 78.3. The mnemonic approach leads to a few ambiguities, as where three English counties start with the letters 'HER'; this was accommodated by coding none of them 'HER', so that any entry absent-mindedly so coded would at once be picked up by the computer code-checking routines. The treatment of county amalgamations and name changes can be seen by examining the

Figure 78.3 Examples of Sort/Search codes for the English counties, illustrating use of mnemonics and the hierarchical treatment of new, amalgamated, counties

XB$	British Isles, General
XN	England, General
XNAVO	Avon (incl. Bristol)
XNBED	Bedfordshire
XNBER	Berkshire
XNBUC	Buckinghamshire
.....	
XNCUR	Cumbria (includes Cumberland and Westmorland)
XNCURC	Cumberland (the old county)
XNCURW	Westmorland (" ")
.....	
XNHET	Hertfordshire
XNHEW	Herefordshire and Worcestershire (new county)
XNHEWH	Herefordshire (the old county)
XNHEWW	Worcestershire (" " ")
.....	
XNNRA	Northamptonshire
XNNRF	Norfolk
XNNRU	Northumberland
.....	
XNSUF	Suffolk
XNSUR	Surrey
XNSUS	Sussex (general)
XNSUSE	East Sussex
XNSUSW	West Sussex
.....	
XNYOR	Yorkshire, general
XNYORE	East Yorkshire
XNYORN	North Yorkshire
XNYORW	West Yorkshire

codes for Westmorland, Cumberland and Cumbria, where the first two are 'old' counties now included in the 'new' county Cumbria. The hierarchical arrangement means that entries can be indexed and retrieved logically, but that the greater locational precision of the 'old names, when present, is not obscured in the coding. The various anomalies were quickly learnt by the cataloguers, most of whom had no difficulty in remembering the non-standard codes.

The country was introduced as an additional level of hierarchy for Great Britain; XN signifies England, XS Scotland, etc. This again reflected the type of enquiries the curators indicated they wished to make of the final database. The leading 'X' is a 'singularity character' added to make the combinations of letters used unambiguous and unlikely to occur elsewhere within the database, primarily to prevent errors when doing string searching on more than one field. Locality codes can cope with ambiguous information, as when an object in a British collection is just labelled 'Cheadle', say. There are two

Cheadles in different counties and, if there is no other information available, the cataloguing problem can be resolved simply by adding the codes for Cheshire and for Staffordshire to the entry, so that the entry will be listed and retrieved under either county. This transfers the onus of decision onto the database user, who is likely to be a subject expert, to decide the relevance or otherwise of that entry to their needs. Since it is patently obvious that the Sort/Search codes have been added to the database and do not occur on the original documentation there is little chance of a user being mislead by the delphic effect of 'it must be right because the computer said so'. It is accepted good curatorial practice that the authority for any information added to labels or registers is clearly indicated. Sometimes, unfortunately, the substansive information in computerised databases is 'improved' (for example, by concordance) without the changes being rigorously indicated as such. This may be acceptable if the database is purely for local use next to the collection and its original labels, but one of the great advantages of computerised information is the ease with which it can be reproduced and disseminated, and any user distant from the collection is then liable to be misled by the altered information.

Summary

Well-designed Sort/Search codes added to entries in a computerised database will allow sensible indexing and retrieval of information despite the use of variable terminology. Assigning and adding the codes is much simpler and quicker than full concordance using controlled vocabularies. The information attached to an item by the person who first made it a museum object should be sacrosanct, and using Sort/Search codes has the added advantage that the integrity of the original information relating to the object is maintained for the benefit of later workers.

79 BIOCODES AND REGISTRATION OF NAMES

David Heppell
Department of Natural History
National Museums of Scotland
Edinburgh

Biocodes defined

The term 'biocode' is used here to denote any system of letters or numbers used with or in place of the name of a taxon. A biocode may indicate the position of that taxon in the taxonomic hierarchy or merely serve as a unique and unchanging reference to it.

There is a vast and rapidly increasing body of published biological information, most of it in scientific journals. Unlike much other scientific literature, its usage is relatively long-lived. For taxonomic papers, the effective life may exceed 200 years. Biology has a built-in, internationally used, basic retrieval code in the scientific (or 'Latin') names applied to living things — the taxa — especially at the genus and species levels. The type-concept provides an objective basis for the application of these names which are the principal keywords of zoology and botany.

The binominal system of Linnaeus was devised as a coded system. The binomen combined the uninominal specific name (which often indicated a characteristic of the species and was consequently of mnemonic value) with the name of the genus. The resulting combination was unique, and therefore usable for unambiguous exchange of information about the species and as a key to its published literature. Moreover an indication of its position within the systematic hierarchy was contained within itself. As genera were of broad concept, the zoologist or botanist of the late eighteenth century could reasonably be expected to be familiar with most of those described.

We have now to ask why, with biology having a self-contained and universal system of nomenclature, do we need any additional or alternative system of coding for information retrieval? The problem is that not only has the number of keywords grown apace with the fragmentation and increase in the number of genera, but the passwords themselves to this store of biological information keep changing. The main causes of this instability are briefly mentioned below.

Instability of names

Names change for taxonomic or for nomenclatural reasons. As the generic name indicates its systematic position, and may change with progress of knowledge, there can be no stability until all the facts are in. An absolutely stable nomenclature would represent intellectual stagnation. Certain changes of name are as real and important to the taxonomist as any other advance in science.

Changes due to nomenclatural causes are those resulting from the provisions of the internationally accepted codes of zoological and botanical nomenclature. Two cardinal provisions are that each taxon may have only one name and each name may apply to only one taxon (otherwise the name of one synonym or one homonym must be changed). Such changes are unavoidable and acceptable. It is changes due to the retrospective Principle of Priority which have caused most disagreement between those taxonomists who consider established usage as of paramount importance and those who accept priority (with few exceptions) as a democracy in which there is no respecting of persons.

With the refining of the Linnaean classification, and the recognition of more and more smaller genera, especially among the invertebrates, it became impossible for any zoologist to remain familiar with all the genera of animals described, even within a limited field. A defect of the Linnaean nomenclature is that with the addition of hundreds of additional genera, the generic name no longer effectively indicates the systematic position of the known species. Needham (1910) recognised the problem of the enormous growth of systematic knowledge and that the Linnaean system could provide for the recording of its progress only by a proportionate growth in terminology. It could remain simple only while the known organisms were comparatively few, so inevitably the new generic and family names proposed should grow ever more complex and cumbersome. Consequently some zoologists addressed the problem of whether the taxonomy could in some way be linked with classification so that the name itself would be an indication of the place of the taxon within the animal kingdom. Two kinds of solution were proposed and are still being proposed to overcome this problem: the first modify or replace names of taxa with some system of coding, or alternative system of nomenclature (see, for example, Michener, 1964; Rivas, 1965; Hull, 1966), while the second seek some means of stabilising the names derived from the orthodox system of nomenclature, usually by limiting the effects of the Principle of Priority (see, for example, Brummitt, 1987, and Cornelius, 1987). Compromise solutions use a code in association with the orthodox names.

The pressure on taxonomists from the users of names of organisms to produce more stable systems of names is increasing. The International Commission on Zoological Nomenclature (ICZN) has periodically been criticised for failing in its aim to promote stability of nomenclature. Recent correspondence in the columns of *Nature* indicates that the topic is still very much alive (Tubbs, 1986; and see references cited in Hawksworth, 1988). Some biologists have called for the regular issue of definitive lists of names for each group of organisms. Others have suggested conservation of names used in certain 'protected' works, normally group revisions on a world-wide basis. Such names would be exempt from the application of the principle of priority. Yet others reject the introduction of nomina conservanda, with an official register of protected names, as 'a recipe for taxonomic chaos'.

Taxonomic data sorting and retrieval

The vexing problems of the species migrating from genus to genus, and the rules of nomenclature reflecting those of Latin grammar, requiring the agreement of adjectival species names with the gender of their current genus, became an issue again when mechanical sorting methods became widespread. The more recent spread of computer systems has made some solution to this problem an even more pressing requirement (Jahn, 1961).

Information retrieval problems arising directly from the orthodox system of taxonomy include not only the difficulty of associating closely related (or dissociating distantly related) genera whose names alphabetically are in an inverse relationship (e.g. *Anodonta* is more closely related to *Unio* than *Mya* is to *Mytilus*), but also because most established retrieval systems do not allow searching at higher more inclusive levels (e.g. entries for *Arianta*, *Cepaea*, *Cochlicella*, *Eobania*, *Theba* or *Trichia* would not be found by a search for

'Helicidae', although data associated with these particular names might be very relevant to the information being sought). Thus any taxonomic code would need to indicate a degree of relationship and allow for coding at a more inclusive level. In this way it would resemble, for instance, a library classification such as the Universal Decimal Classification (UDC) where related subjects are sorted close together (598 = birds, 599 = mammals) and there is a built-in hierarchy in the decimal system from the general to the particular (5 = natural sciences, 59 = zoology, 599 = mammals).

Coding systems and alternative systems of nomenclature

Many novel and ingenious coding systems have been proposed with the object of restoring to the generic name its original function of being a positional indicator. In some cases higher taxa were also coded or renamed in some logically hierarchical manner. Our accepted convention of the -idae termination for zoological names of family rank is an example of coding of this sort.

The earliest attempt at introducing a coded taxonomy (Harting, 1871) used a cumulative hierarchical system of vowels and consonants to indicate the systematic position of a taxon, either standing alone (as substitute names for the higher taxa) or as suffixes to part of the generic name. Herrera (1899) used a system of more or less mnemonic prefixes and suffixes attached to the generic name. Rhumbler (1910) increased the amount of information that such coding could carry by extending his system to the specific names, and devising a complicated system of prefixes (letters combined with diacritical marks) which indicated zoogeographical distribution. It should be noted that these coded forms are considered to be formulae, and not names, and have no separate status in nomenclature (Opinion 72, 1972; see also Smith and Smith, 1980).

The universal adoption of symbols in mathematics and chemistry inspired other systems which used more abstract codes, based on fairly arbitrary sequences of letters and numbers. Tornier (1898) for example developed his ideas from a comparison of the traditional names of chemicals with their structural names and formulae: e.g. saltpetre – potassium nitrate – KNO_3, corrosive sublimate – mercuric chloride – $HgC1_2$. By analogy: the snake genus *Zamenis* (Ophidia: Colubridae) would have the formula $VROCZ_1$ [Vertebrata; Reptilia; Ophidia; Colubridae; and genus *Zamenis* Z_1 (genus *Zaocys* was Z_2)]. Species would be similarly numbered alphabetically within the genus, thus species of *Zamenis* would be numbered from $VROCZ_1$,1 (*Z. algirus*) to $VROCZ_1$,32 (*Z. ventrimaculatus*). Thus unlike mere names, the formulae would automatically indicate the systematic position of the taxon.

Early considerations of introducing coding to link scientific names to their place in classification overlooked what came to be regarded later by many workers as an inherent weakness of the binominal system itself — the instability of the name of the species arising from its linkage not permanently with its original generic placement but temporarily with whichever generic name is subjectively considered to be its proper position at any time. Prefixes for higher taxa also become archaic unless there is an unchanging classification, but even the number of phyla is far from generally agreed.

Rather than link the generic name to a prefix which in its indication of systematic position could soon become outmoded, suggestions have been made to link the specific name to a code which represented approximately the family level as we know it, so that the position of a large percentage of names would be recognised on sight. I refer to these group names, which are true keywords or verbal biocodes, as 'tribal' names. Needham

(1910) believed the purely clerical work of biology might be accomplished with less waste of time and energy if in addition to the 'taxonomic' name, a terminology, expressing the same system with fewer, shorter and simpler names and symbols, were agreed for general use. Species had to be represented by names or symbols; either would have to be used an equal number of times, but symbols would be preferable as they simplified not the knowledge but effort, time and space. An analogy might be the use of grid references and coordinates as an adjunct to geographical names.

The ideal would be to have a combined designation (biocode + specific name) which is both unique and indicative of systematic position. The biocode + specific name could freely move from genus to genus or family to family, but an unchanging code would thereby lose much of its second, systematic, function. Some authors have suggested that the code could be the generic name used in the last catalogue or revision so that the current binomen is preserved (i.e nomenclaturally stabilised). Berio (1953) proposed a system using the original genus as part of a 'suffix' (e.g. *Vespula maculata* (*Vespa* Linnaeus)), which could be expanded to a dual authorship system such as used in botany.

Amadon (1966) suggested an alternative approach to stability, designed to overcome the problems of binomina changing for taxonomic reasons, often with resultant homonymy of the specific name within the revised generic placement. Although the generic name has lost its original function of providing a clue to the relationship of the species, it cannot be omitted without the creation of thousands of homonyms among the existing specific names. Reminding us that Linnaeus used very large genera, Amadon suggested the return on a more formal basis to a system which postulates one 'tribal' name for each family (or subfamily or tribe when the family is divided). For example 'Corvus' would serve as a 'tribal' name in forming the species names for the entire family Corvidae, and only in strictly taxonomic work would a further division be required. A new term 'suneg' was coined (= 'genus' reversed) to indicate the type genus of families (and their subdivisions) when used in the special way recommended by Amadon. The generic name could then continue to be used as at present, but would no longer, as such, be a part of the name of a species. The suneg would be printed in Roman type not italics and used, except in strictly taxonomic publications, in lieu of generic names for all species in any given family, subfamily, or tribe. This could result in homonymy between identical specific names within the same family division, but solutions avoiding renaming the junior homonym have been proposed. A species moved from one family to another would acquire a new suneg.

Requirements of biocodes

All these various attempts at introducing a coded taxonomy had the object of providing a more logical or symbolic reference to biological information than the more or less random system of coining taxonomic names which is in general use. All sought to bring order to the perceived chaos and provide more reliable maps to the endless jungles of taxonomic names which had grown from the original seeds planted by Linnaeus.

Although many biologists have lost faith in the ability of the existing Codes of Nomenclature to produce the desired stability, none of the coding systems proposed has won any lasting acceptance. This is partly due to the size and complexity of the living world, and we have to accept that there are no easy solutions. But many of the systems of biocodes proposed in the past either aimed impossibly high or viewed the problem with such blinkered naïvety that their failure was foredoomed. Can anything be salvaged from the array of coding systems proposed not only in biology but in other fields which will ease our path to the twin goals of stable nomenclature and efficient storage and retrieval of biological data? The requirement is a code which may be used for computer sorting, but combined with implied information (Hull, 1986). The *notation* should express the *classification*.

Although names for species are convenient and useful, an alternative proposal is that all species should be numbered and that only the common, conspicuous, or important ones need be named (Michener, 1963). The numbering system would then be the important, all-inclusive device for keeping track of the kinds of organisms and the system of names could become informal. For example, the phylum, class, order, family, and genus could be represented by numbers separated by hyphens, so that the following might represent the classification and reference numbers for *Musca domestica*: 10-7-26-081-052-0325761. All numbers in front of the last hyphen represent the classification and can be omitted or changed without influencing the specific designation. If a species were described whose generic placement was uncertain, the genus could be represented by zeros (the empty set) (e.g. 10-7-26-081-000-0751201). The parataxa (and collective groups) are the equivalent of zeros at the generic or sometimes higher levels (e.g. graptolites). All this assumes the setting up of some international numbering agency. It is also relevant to question what is the advantage of the reference number over a name, so long as the whole term is unique. Perhaps in the interim there could be a combination biocode + specific name (e.g. 25-168.03-cellarius = *Zonites cellarius*, where 25 = Mollusca, 168 = Gastropoda: Zonitacea, and subdivision .03 = *Zonites*).

It is evident that two types of biocode must be considered (or a single biocode with two functionally separate elements): one to indicate taxonomic position, and one to provide a unique reference number (or name). No biocode could be permanent if it were accurately to represent the systematic position of the coded taxon. This lack of stability would be a serious, if not fatal, objection to the introduction of a new system planned to correct precisely the same defect in the old. Conversely any code independent of changing views of position and relationships would after a certain time become ossified. If this is accepted, however, it does not mean that there is not a place for biocodes if provision is made for their periodic updating as, say, with library classification schedules.

The most important requirement of a comprehensive system of nomenclature for biology is a uniform method whereby data on all organisms, both fossil and recent, with all associated data, may be coded, identified within, or retrieved. A uninominal designation (biocode + specific name) must be both unique and indicative of systematic position. Generic changes must not cause changes in names, and homonymy must not arise. The requirements of such a system are that it should be simple enough to be easily adopted, and flexible enough not to break down or require basic revision because of growth and future nomenclatural changes. If numbers are substituted for names, provision should be made for reducing the chances of undetected errors.

In designing this numbering system it is important to avoid Linnaeus's error of incorporating into the designation information which is subject to change with improved knowledge or changing ideas. The registration number could be a unique and in itself meaningless reference number for each taxon, to be looked up in a catalogue or in a database when the name is needed. In front of this reference number, however, could be meaningful numbers containing classificatory information. Such numbers collectively could be called the biocode and could be cited in a taxonomic paper in place of the author and date information which of itself can frequently be ambiguous.

It has been claimed that a central numbering bureau would be required for each group and for that to go back and number all the forgotten species in the literature, but I believe it is quite unnecessary to provide numbers for names which have fallen into disuse. To avoid accusations of limiting taxonomic freedom of choice, it will be best to make the registration of all new names voluntary (although it can be agreed that after a date to be determined such names will not receive any protection from the Codes of Nomenclature). The retrospective numbering of taxa should be achieved by a parallel system, but applied only to names accepted on whatever registers of approved names may be required.

Recently published systems of biocodes

There seem to be few papers commenting on biocodes of limited scope. Bullis and Roe (1967) reported on the use of the United Nations Food and Agriculture Organization (FAO) biocodes for handling large quantities of commercial fisheries data in Mississippi. The basic code consists of nine digits divided into phylum-class, class-order, family, genus and species categories (in the form (0)0-(0)00-(0)00-(0)00-(0)00 where the (0) allows for each taxon to be magnified by a factor of ten (this dates from the punched card/tape days when such expansion would have reduced capacity for other data). They concluded that a universally agreed code was an urgent need to eliminate the hundreds of man-years that would go into each user making up his own. That code should be a simple compromise between an ultimate in classification and a working tool for automatic data processing.

In Scandinavia the National Swedish Environment Protection Board has funded the BIODATA project, started in 1967 as a computerised system for environmental data with biological, ecological, faunistic and floristic connections. This project uses a routine known as RUBIN (RUtin för Biologiska INventeringar) which enables data entered by the field workers as species codes and coded ecological keywords to be linked to species numbers used by the computer to organise the data systematically (Österdahl, *et al.*, 1977; Österdahl and Zetterberg, 1981). The systematic input files, derived from the systematic literature, are assigned the species numbers at the Nordic Code Centre (Kodcentralen) housed at the Naturhistoriska Riksmuseet in Stockholm. The database facilitates the production of checklists and distribution lists, as well as the correlation of the cumulated ecological data. Other more local biocoding systems have been proposed, e.g. for British freshwater animals (Maitland, 1977), and for the British marine fauna and flora (Howson, 1987), but these are too inflexible for more general application.

The International Species Inventory System (ISIS) maintains a database of births, deaths, pedigrees and inter-institutional movements of living specimens held by zoological gardens. It uses codes for both taxon and institution, both hierarchical. ISIS taxonomic codes are a name, and also contain the complete classification of the organism from kingdom to subspecies (e.g. 5 30 14 10 002 030 024 001 *Sciurus vulgaris*). Thus the name and the classification are linked much more extensively than in the Linnaean binominal, and taxonomic revision changes the taxonomic code. ISIS may eventually decouple the numeric code from the taxonomic classification, use the numeric code for database purposes only, and construct input/output software so that incoming data and outgoing reports used the Latin name only. A hierarchical auxiliary file would then be built to indicate the current classification and relationship of each taxon (Flesness, *et al.*, 1984).

Biocodes in universal uses: problems and solutions

Many institutions have of necessity introduced some kind of coded system for retrieval of biological data, but these efforts are uncoordinated and done in ways which are not in line with present and future needs of biologists. There is, in effect, a lack of a universal standardised 'conversion factor'. The term 'numericlature' was coined for a proposed system of biological numerical nomenclature, which the proposer (Little, 1964) believed 'should be agreed upon, or at least developed, immediately if time and money are not to be needlessly wasted on unnecessary duplication of effort with various short-term, localized, or narrowly specialized systems and their subsequent costly conversion, adaption, or even discard, in order to achieve compatibility with the finally accepted system'. Little's system extended to 36 digits, in the format 00(0)-00(0)-000(0)-000(0)-000(00)-0000(00)-0-000-0000000, which allowed not only for coding at phylum, class, order, family, genus and species levels, each with possible subgroups within the parentheses, but also at the individual specimen level the type status, institution and institutional reference number (e.g. museum register number). In fact it is not necessary to code all levels of the hierarchy, and a three-level code (of the form 000: 000.000) should be adequate. The categories encoded could vary according to the stability and pattern of subdivision within different systematic groups, e.g. phylum : class + family : genus for molluscs, or class : order : family for insects. The lowest level of coding would represent a subdivision within which specific name homonymy would be undesirable.

BIOSIS, producers of the *Zoological Record*, have over the last ten years been developing the concept of a Taxonomic Reference File (TRF) — a computerised collection of organism names and associated data (Dadd and Kelly, 1984; Walat, 1986). Its objective is to provide scientists with an online, interactive tool for sharing taxonomic information. So far a more or less complete database is available for bacteria, although this does not appear to relate to the taxonomic limits imposed since 1980 by the obligatory registration of bacteria for nomenclatural purposes. A pilot study has also been undertaken using 40 000 records from the *Zoological Record*, mostly I believe for vertebrates. Although the TRF has not been developed for that purpose, it would seem to be adaptable for use as a centralised and multidisciplinary database for a general taxonomic register, although no biocoding on the ISIS model has so far been introduced.

Registers of names

One thing that taxonomists are not required to do under the Codes is to register their nomenclatural innovations. It is left to others to find the published announcements, and that may take decades. Many names are thus duplicated, and unnecessary confusion results. This has led to criticisms of taxonomy as essentially unscientific. Brown (1961), concerned about the unmangeable growth of information in systematic entomology, put forward preliminary proposals for an international taxonomic register. Since 1980 new taxa in bacteriology have had to be registered (Hawksworth, 1988). A number of initiatives are in progress to consider some means of compiling taxonomic registers which could make access to information about the taxa more efficient.

A resolution of the III International Congress of Systematic and Evolutionary Biology (ICSEB) meeting in Brighton, 1985, urged the General Committee for Botanical Nomenclature and the International Commission on Zoological Nomenclature (ICZN) to take steps to establish formal registration procedures for new scientific names. As a result, the Committee for Registration of Plant Names was set up, which considered the problem and made a number of proposals for further consideration (Greuter, 1986). These were discussed at the XIV International Botanical Congress in Berlin, 1987, and a committee established to report to the next Congress in Tokyo, 1993. The feasibility of producing lists of names in current use in botany was discussed at a joint IUBS (International Union of Biological Sciences) / IAPT (International Association for Plant Taxonomy) meeting at Kew in April 1988, and yet another committee was proposed to report to the Tokyo Congress. In October 1988 the XXIII General Assembly of IUBS requested the ICZN to study, in conjunction with appropriate agencies (such as the publisher of *Zoological Record*) the feasibility of indexing, on an international basis, scientific names in zoology. A system of biocoded references, such as an International Standard Taxonomic Code, could be effected in parallel with all such registers of names.

Summary of the problem and some possible solutions

The coding value of the Linnaean system of naming taxa (in which the binomen provides a unique, concise name code — specific name — within a memorable, concise name code — generic name — indicating its place in the classification) is reduced with the increase in the number of known species (and the correspondingly greater increase in the number of names). Names of taxa become inscrutable as a result of instability, rate of change, lack of classification (position) information, and change of classification with progress of systematic zoology.

All the following possibilities should be considered in seeking the best solution for the biological nomenclature of the future:

ossification of the nomenclature at least partially: by nomina conservanda; supplanting of the Linnaean generic function by 'tribal' names, allowing genera to 'float' taxonomically; according artificial stability to names used in current checklists or monographs; registration of names or works; adoption of cut-off dates, after which new regulations will apply; accepting statutes of limitation;

limitation of the present free-for-all for descriptions of new taxa;

simplified retrieval of taxonomic information by use of a biocode (either alphanumerical or mnemonic) in place of or added to the generic element of a name; stabilisation of endings of higher taxa;

terminology control on higher taxa names (but these are often non-synonymic) or enough 'slack' in biocoding to allow for reinterpretation of phylogenies (or periodic issue of new 'editions' of higher codes). This in fact seems to be the most difficult problem, but may be both small-scale and long-term; higher taxa biocodes may need to be recognised as artificial and 'convenient'.

XI
DISCIPLINE DEVELOPMENTS: CONSERVATION

80 DISCIPLINE DEVELOPMENTS IN CONSERVATION

Michael Corfield

Head of Conservation
National Museum of Wales

The papers presented in the conservation sessions demonstrate clearly the fundamental shift in the emphasis and role of conservation recording. Historically, conservation recording has developed in isolation, and stands as a major body of information isolated from the main curatorial object records; this is unfortunate, because it is during conservation that much of our knowlege about the techniques used in the creation of the objects is gained. Similarly, it is the conservation record that provides the information about the changing condition of the object. In part, this dichotomy has been due to the difference in the nature of the records: the curatorial record has been perceived as basically static, non-variable data which may occasionally change; while the conservation record is dynamic and documents the changes in condition of the object, its various treatments, and any restrictions which may be placed on its use.

The advent of the philosophy of collections management has resulted in a change in the role of the conservator and a change in the perceptions of the conservation record. The passive service role of the past has given way to a more pragmatic involvement in all aspects of collections management; the conservation record is more and more being integrated into a museum wide documentation and collection management structure (Miles, 1988). These changes are described in the ensuing papers.

Not only must there be a sensible policy for management of the collections, there must equally be an effective management of conservation resources; in most major museums, single departments of conservation are the norm. Departmental managers, whether in a major museum conservation department or in a curatorial department, are required to organise programmes of work and to allocate resources according to the needs of the collection in a manner that utilises the resources to the maximum effect. To do so requires access to a body of information about the collections and their impending use which will allow work to be prioritised, according primary treatment to the items most in need of attention. Condition reporting provides the necessary data, and three examples of condition reporting are described by Carlyle, Miles and Perry (Chapters 83, 85 and 86).

Museum collections are increasingly being seen as an international resource; prestigious exhibitions are assembled drawing on the collections of many institutions. In these circumstances, the condition report becomes an essential tool for the protection of the object and for the peace of mind of lender and borrower alike. It is important that both lender and borrower should understand the terminology of the report and to this end any moves towards standardisation of terminology is welcome. Although the importance of the conservation record is constantly emphasised, it must be borne in mind that the actual processes of conservation are the primary objective of the conservator; Perry (Chapter 86) observes that technical records are tools, and indeed any documentation system must serve conservators and their colleagues, not be the slave. Documentation must equally be in proportion to the work in hand: recording a major work of conservation could take many days; such details would be inappropriate to a simple process applied to a less significant object.

Conservation documentation will generally be a dossier of information on different media — photographs, drawings, radiographs, written notes and so on. The full record may include the curatorial request for treatment, condition reports, specifications of treatment, technical records as well as the treatment record (as described by Jones in Chapter 87). Not all this information can be easily confined within a strict structure and terminology control, although as Jones reports, free text recording may actually cloud the issue rather than support it. In practice, it is often found that given a free choice, conservators will use a fairly restricted vocabulary to describe their work.

The record of object conservation is not the only documentation required. It is essential that full data is maintained of any materials used on objects; this is especially true of propriety materials where formulations may change frequently, without any consequent change of trade name. Analysis of contents and observations of performance in conservation practice are an important component of the material databases which are currently being developed. With the development of health and safety legislation, particularly in the United Kingdom with the *Control of Substances Hazardous to Health Regulations*, it has become a legal obligation to keep records of materials used by individuals.

Conservation documentation cannot stand alone; it must interrelate with curatorial documentation systems. Conservators themselves must work with others in the museum, such as scientists, designers, architects and services engineers. The essential purpose of the museum is preservation of objects, and all other functions should be subsidiary to that: the priorities of the museum must be planned to ensure that nothing is done to the detriment of the objects, to which end the fullest flow of information must be directed.

In all this, the need for terminology control is gaining wider recognition. The importance of avoiding ambiguity when describing an object's condition, or the conditions under which it may be used, is paramount in the current climate, where maximum utilisation of collections is urged upon us, particularly where this may involve inter-museum loans on a national or even international scale. None the less, we should be aware that much work has already been done by industry and by the various national standards institutes; Horie has given a valuable resume of areas of their work which may be of relevance to conservators (Chapter 82).

It is a matter of concern that few conservators are systematising their recording; there is a great gulf between those who have come to accept the need for control, even in a manual system, and those who maintain that recording is an art form, not to be encumbered by any discipline of teminology control. It is surprising that in a sample of professionals who claim science as the basis of their work, only 1 per cent should be using computers within the practical area of their work and only 7 per cent some form of computer management. This surevey reported by Miles (Chapter 85) also found no fully integrated system in use; it is hoped that the implementation of the system described by Jones (Chapter 87) and similar developments will redress the deficiency.

There are several international initiatives. Carlyle has described the systems in use in Canada and Dearing and Uginet the information retrieval system in the ICCROM Library in Rome (Chapters 83 and 84). At the conference, a paper was presented by Perkins who described the latest situation of the Conservation Information Network of the Getty Conservation Institute. The databases of the Network are becoming an increasingly powerful tool for conservators: the bibliographic database has well over 100 000 citations and is constantly updated — this represents almost the entire world conservation literature; the materials database is a growing database or information on many of the materials used in conservation; and the suppliers' database gives information about where to obtain materials and equipment. Of themselves these databases stimulate standardisation, particularly of materials descriptions. The Conservation Information Network also provides subscribers with an electonic mailing facility which enables them to keep in day-to-day contact; through such contacts the work of an ever widening spectrum of conservator is served and further establishes the profession on a truly international footing.

---

81 CONSERVATION TERMINOLOGY

Gwyn Miles

Victoria & Albert Museum
London

Introduction

The process of conservation results in an altered object. It is essential to be able to reconstruct what the object was like before conservation took place and what intervention took place. The information about treatment carried out is important to future generations of conservators. The documentation of conservation requires careful thought on the part of the conservator. There is a need to decide what purpose the information will serve, rather than record copious details in the hope that it may prove useful at a later date.

The conservator is placed in the ideal position to carry out technical examination. It is the conservator, using magnification and further analytical techniques, who will examine the object in detail. This results in the elucidation of the fabrication of the object: providing the details of the composition of an object, the techniques used in its manufacture and the method of construction. The conservator needs to record carefully the state of an object (i.e. its condition at a given point in time). It should be quite clear from the condition report what the state of preservation of the object was when it first came to the attention of the conservator. Any practical treatment given to an object by a conservator involves some type of interference. This must be clearly described so that the treatment procedure, conservation-materials and equipment used can be easily retrieved for future reference. Finally, the success or failure of a given treatment should be assessed.

Thus, the purpose of practical record-keeping, in the first instance, should be to provide a snapshot of an object at a given time. Details of the composition and construction of the object are noted and its condition clearly stated. The process of treatment, including the quantities and concentration of conservation-materials employed, must then be described. Ideally an evaluation of the treatment should also be given.

The conservation record is required for more than simply the conservators within the institution that houses the objects. Conservators in other institutions, for example one that borrows an object for temporary exhibition, may need access to the conservation record. Even within a particular museum, conservators may work within different project groups, each group contributing to the conservation record of a single object. Conservation scientists use the conservation record to provide data to back up or disprove hypotheses about methods of treatment. They may also need to use the conservation record of an object to ascertain whether the prevailing environment has caused a particular alteration to its state. Curators need to use the conservation record both to manage their collections efficiently and also to guide their research. Lastly the manager of any organisation requires information from the conservation record to balance the use of resources against the needs of the collection.

Thus, conservation should not be seen in isolation, but as an integral part of the successful management of any collection (Miles, 1988). It is concerned with information about what the object is, what has happened to it throughout its history and how it should be best cared for. Collections management is concerned with the procedures of acquisition and disposal of objects, their placement both on display or in store, their security and movement (i.e. entry and exit and also movement around the building) and, most importantly, the documentation of the collections. All activities carried out within the institution, whether conservation, mounting or photography, must be properly recorded. Any information gained by conservators should be easily accessible to other people concerned with that object. Interchange of information between all staff concerned with the well-being of an object is vital.

Conservation recording in United Kingdom museums

A recent survey of Conservation Departments in the United Kingdom was carried out in 1987 (Miles and Umney, forthcoming) in order to provide some idea of the methods of information handling in the field of conservation.

A questionnaire was sent to each Conservation Department; it was divided into two parts. The first part asked specific questions: on the organisation; number of conservation staff; which conservation specialisms were covered by the laboratory; what administrative support was available; the nature and extent of computer facilities and technical support available.

The second part asked for a description of current documentation procedures. Respondents were asked to cover the following points: the scope of documentation kept (i.e. condition, treatment reports, contracts, etc.); the physical form of the documentation system (whether card index or computer database); how the information is retrieved; what it is used for; who uses it; whether automated systems are in use and, if so, what software and hardware.

It was clear from the preliminary results of the survey that three areas of conservation recording are apparent. These are administrative, dealing with the number of objects being conserved, the location of those objects, the resources used and the actions carried out. The second, practical area comprises the results of technical examination, the condition report and the treatment report. Lastly, the supporting area includes information on conservation materials, bibliographic references and some form of index of equipment and suppliers' addresses.

Within these areas it was found that the use of computers by conservators was still fairly limited. Of the replies to the survey, 83 per cent recorded no usage of computers, 50 per cent having no access to computers, but 33 per cent having access, but making no use of automation. Ten per cent were actively planning to use computers, but not doing so as yet; seven per cent were using some form of computerised management system, but only one per cent were using automated methods to record within the practical area. No fully integrated system was in use within the UK in 1987.

Looking at each area, the use of computers depends on a number of factors. The administrative area is primarily concerned with the ability to trace an object. If the numbers of objects treated within one year exceeds 1 000, or there is more than one location for the work to be carried out, a database management system will be a more efficient means of tracking an object than the daybook, with a sequential list objects in date order. This has the advantage of simplicity, but it can be extremely time-consuming to compile, say, a list of objects still in the studio after two years. If there is also the need to record time spent on conservation, particularly for more than one client, a more sophisticated system is necessary. It is hardly surprising that conservators are starting to look towards microcomputers to provide a relatively cheap solution to the management of this information.

Very little work on automation has been carried out in the practical area. The most typical method of information retrieval is the use of cards or data sheets. A large percentage of laboratories used the MDA card format, but more (particularly large-scale units) were using museum originated forms. Either way the format is unimportant, as long as the data capture is adequate for the purpose.

The supporting area has been traditionally served by Art and Archaeology Technical Abstracts (AATA) and supplemented by individual lists and card indices of conservation-materials and their suppliers. This area has been revolutionised by the advent of the Conservation Information Network (Perkins, Jelich and Lafontaine, 1987). As yet there are only a small number of users in the UK. But as the use of the network grows, particularly if conservation students gain access and familiarity with it during their studies, acceptance of computers and the benefits of this system will spill out into other areas. As the new technology gains more ground in other disciplines and many museum staff are presented with a computer on their desks, so the conservation profession will become more used to the idea of automation and the benefits that it can bring. However, as yet the conservator remains wedded to the paper record.

The conservation profession is still at a formative period in the development of its documentation. This point was made at a conference in Halifax in 1985 (Perkins, 1986) and we have moved little since then. Conservators need to seize the opportunity to specify their requirements and not be constrained by the perceived limitations in computerised systems. Analysis of the requirements for conservation to provide working systems should be carried out.

Preparation for automation has brought an appreciation of the need for analysis of requirements. This, in turn, is bringing a degree of discipline to recording systems, whether automated or not. Work being done in Canada and here in UK (Victoria & Albert Museum and National Museums of Scotland) on condition reporting is part of this movement to tighten up the approach to information gathering and its effective retrieval.

The ICOM Conservation Committee Documentation Working Group held a meeting in Cambridge in September 1987, before the Terminology Conference. One of the stated aims of this group is to improve communication between people working in the field of conservation documentation and that conservators are made aware of world-wide developments such as the Art and Architecture Thesaurus (AAT) (Chapter 56). It is important that duplication is avoided — we do not need the re-invention of the controlled vocabulary. The Materials Hierarchy of AAT along with the work of Canadian Conservation Institute (CCI) to develop a glossary of terms (Jewett, 1983) should be built upon, rather than each institution setting out along the hard and difficult road of providing its own glossary of terms.

It is hoped that the working group will in the future be in a position to put forward a framework for conservation recording which will be flexible enough to suit the needs of all specialisms within conservation. This should take the form of a data standard similar to that being developed by the ICOM Documentation Committee (CIDOC) for museum recording generally. Another area for discussion by the group is the need for exchange of information on reference materials used in conservation. In the first instance it is proposed that all laboratories holding standard reference materials should be listed within some form of directory. The first stage will be to identify all laboratories holding information of interest and then a system for making the information available will have to be found.

Adoption of a standard for the interchange of spectral data relevant to the reference materials will be of assistance in allowing exchange of information between different laboratories. Using a standard method of representing spectral data as alphanumeric characters will allow the data to be stored and accessed remotely on a variety of computer-based systems. It is hoped to investigate the possibilities of adopting such a standard.

In an age of rapid, world-wide communication, the conservation profession should be prepared to exploit the new technology to gain access to the information it needs to carry out its work satisfactorily. Conservation techniques change rapidly and the ability to disseminate new information quickly and easily must be recognised and used. Conservators are in the fortunate position of having the tools they need to do this, but it requires a leap of the imagination to use these tools effectively. The first few faltering steps are being taken, but we still have a long way to go.

---

82 INDUSTRIAL STANDARDS OF TERMINOLOGY FOR CONSERVATION

C. V. Horie

Keeper of Conservation
The Manchester Museum, The University
Manchester

Introduction

I take a 'terminology' to be a system of terms which express concepts for a discipline. Dealing with these components in turn:

'system' implies that the number of terms are limited, usually to provide structured coverage of only a single (or part of a) discipline;

'terms' are usually verbal descriptors, though numbers and even symbols may be employed to summarise the concept;

'concepts' implies that the meaning and limits of usage of each term is outlined, using verbal, numerical and/or pictorial representations, though frequently no exact meaning (or definition) could be possible or desirable;

'discipline' implies that those knowledgeable and active in and around the field of activity have reached agreement, usually after considerable discussion, concerning both the terms and their usage.

Traditional industrial activities are similar to museum conservation in that both work with objects rather than, say, concepts. Descriptions are formed in similar hierarchies:

Class of objects
- object
  - part
    - material
      - property
        - process
          - authority

Each stage of the hierarchy is described in terms, using concepts, derived from the lower stages.

Agreed terminologies develop out of the need for workers in the same field, but in different times and places, to communicate with minimal errors of understanding. The common usage of words is apt to change their meanings to suit the context. Desirable in literature, dangerous in technology. As a subject grows, concepts are refined so that nuances of differences in meaning require more terms than there are available words. Various solutions have been employed, such as:

inventing new words (e.g. biological taxonomy);

using a dead language, usually Latin (e.g. anatomy);

concatenating 'words' like building blocks (e.g. chemical nomenclature);

using numerical designations (e.g. colour descriptors);

employing ordinary words in a special technical sense.

Figure 82.1. The term 'engineers wrench, single head' (and its equivalents in other languages) is defined by this illustration which alone is used to identify the concept; from *BS 6416: 1983, Nomenclature for assembly tools for screws and nuts.* In this and the following illustrations of definitions, it can be seen that each term is further identified with a unique number

Reproduced by permission of the British Standards Institution

2.1 **Spanners and wrenches**
Clés
Ключи гаечные

No. №	Application Применение	Tool Outil Инструмент	Designation Dénomination Наименование
1			Engineers wrench, single head
			Clé à fourche simple
			Ключ гаечный с открытым зевом, односторонний

Figure 82.2 This simple stitch, 'number 204', is defined by the illustration and text working together, no term is given; from *BS 3870: Part 1: 1982, Stitches and seams. Part 1. Classification and terminology of stitch types*

Reproduced by permission of the British Standards Institution

204

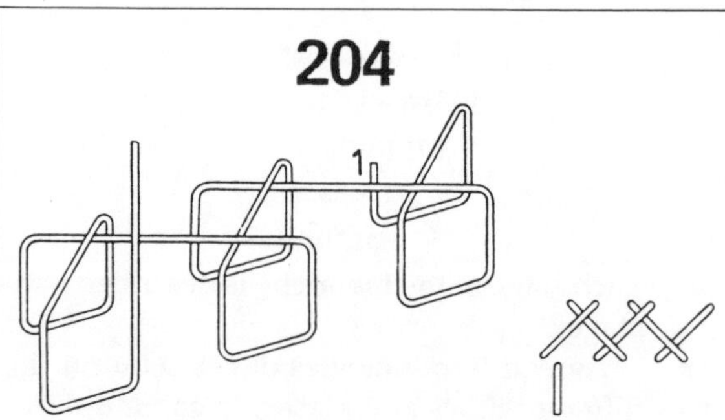

This stitch type is formed with one needle thread (**1**), which is passed through the material, moved diagonally across the material the width of the stitch, passed back through the material and brought back a suitable length before passing again through the material. It is then returned diagonally across the material the width of the stitch, passed through the material and back through the material a similar length behind. This process is repeated to form parallel rows of separated and offset stitches on the needle side and a criss-cross pattern on the other side. (When done by hand, this stitch type is normally worked from left to right.)

A minimum of two stitches describes this stitch type.

Figure 82.3 This definition of leather was the result of some years of discussion and compromise between manufacturers, converters and end-users of 'leather'; from *BS 2780: 1983, Glossary of leather terms*. The notes provide a commentary on the definition but do not form part of it

Reproduced by permission of the British Standards Institution

No.	Term	Definition
159	leather	Hide or skin with its original fibrous structure more or less intact, tanned to be imputrescible. The hair or wool may or may not have been removed. It is also made from a hide or skin that has been split into layers or segmented either before or after tanning. NOTE 1. If the leather has a surface coating, the mean thickness of this surface layer, however applied, has to be 0.15 mm or less. See 56, 156, 189, 190 and 191. NOTE 2. If the tanned hide or skin is disintegrated mechanically and/or chemically into fibrous particles, small pieces or powders and then, with or without the combination of a binding agent, is made into sheets or forms, such sheets or forms are not leather.

The effort needed to invent and develop a totally synthetic vocabulary (and structure to regulate it), as in the first three solutions, presupposes the cooperation of a large body of workers who have considered the use of language important over many decades, or centuries. Most industrial activities have been too short-lived to develop this level of terminological sophistication. Industrial terminologies therefore make most use of the two latter solutions to extend the language, which can be developed and understood with less investment of time and energy. This paper primarily addresses the resources of such industrially derived terminologies.

The units of a terminology, terms, must be defined or described. Although there are strong proponents for a purely verbal definition of a concept, there are various established methods for summarising the meaning of a concept:

a unique object as definition: a primary standard, such as the old metre standard of length, or the biological type specimen;

a visual image as definition: various standards (e.g. BS 6416 (Figure 82.1) or the *Munsell Book of Color*) rely solely on a picture to convey the meaning;

annotated diagrams: frequently used when the relationship of parts must be described (e.g. BS 3870 (Figure 82.2));

purely verbal: the usual method in formal 'terminologies' (e.g. BS 2780 (Figure 82.3));

numerical: many materials and properties are described (at least in part) by numbers, usually derived from measurements.

Where do the terminologies come from?

Industrial standards were initially — and are still mainly — primarily concerned about ensuring that the materials of production have a minimum and established variation in properties. These standards have frequently grown from internal procedures within one company to become practices that are accepted world-wide. The process by which this happens can vary.

The legally enforceable trade name (e.g. Perspex, a poly(methyl methacrylate) sheet manufactured by ICI) is the lowest level of public industrial standard. A commercial product may become so useful that it achieves world-wide use as a terminology (e.g. *Munsell Book of Color*). Many specialist technical societies, both national and international, have established agreed vocabularies which have been published for widespread use (e.g. *Federation of Societies for Coatings Technology*, 1978). One of the largest sources of standards is a society, the American Society for Testing and Materials (ASTM). Similarly, scientific bodies have established systems of nomenclatures for international communication, such as the International Union of Pure and Applied Chemistry (1979), the International Trust for Zoological Nomenclature (1985) and the Commission Internationale de l'Eclairage (1987).

These terminologies have no method of enforcement except that implied by widespread acceptance. However, most countries have national standards organisations which prepare terminologies that can be made to have the force of law. For instance, some British Standard terms, if not applied correctly in a description leave the user open to charges of misrepresentation. Frequently, national standards incorporate the terminologies from elsewhere, though unfortunately they may be modified from those agreed through international organisations (e.g. BS 2474). Increasingly, national standards are following those agreed through the International Organisation for Standarization (ISO) which enable translations between equivalent terms in different languages.

All these various terminologies are developed by committees, published after consultation and consensus within (and sometimes outside) the discipline intended to be covered, and (hopefully) revised regularly to reflect changes in technology and to improve the descriptions used. They may reflect a narrow view of the prospective users of the terminology or represent a compromise between best and existing practice. Even the best prepared terminology may prove misleading when used in a context for which it was not envisaged (Heymann, 1983). Though compilations (American Society for Testing and Materials, 1986) can provide a short cut to a succinct definition, the primary source must be checked in order to establish that the defined concept is the one which is wanted. Obsolete standards might provide useful terminologies for objects and processes which are related to historic collections.

Some large libraries maintain sets of their national standards, and perhaps collections of the ASTM and ISO documents. There are perhaps 450 000 industrial standards in the world. This paper reflects the material readily available to me, some vocabularies published by technical societies, the standards of the British Standards Institution (BSI, the oldest national standards organisation in the world (Woodward, 1972)), the ASTM and, to a small degree, the ISO. It is to some extent idiosyncratic, but should provide a guide to the type of standards that are available in other countries.

Terminologies of what?

Material specification and designation

The properties of a material are found by subjecting it to a series of tests identified within the standard. Depending usually on scientific measurements producing numerical results, the material will be given an appropriate designation from the available terminology. For example, a lac material can be designated as 'orange shellac grade B to ASTM D237–57' if it has the following properties:

insoluble in hot solvent	1.25	max %
iodine no.	15	max
moisture	2.0	max %

wax	5.5	max %
orpiment	0.03	max %
soluble in water	0.5	max %
ash	1.0	max %
rosin	none	

As can be seen, the designation has three aspects (Dretske, 1981). First, the designation 'orange shellac grade B to ASTM D237–57' is a shorthand which conveys a large amount of implicit information, known to all those who consult the standard. Secondly, a portion of the information is lost (the results of the analysis), deemed by those who drew up and use the standard as insignificant in terms of the standard. Thirdly, the designation implies nothing about properties of the material not specified in the standard. Surprisingly, these designations are frequently omitted from standard terminologies.

Some materials such as wood are not described by their properties, performance or components, but by their source. Standardised nomenclature has been found necessary to fix the frequently shifting relationships between botanical species, the colloquial names of the tree and the resulting timber. The industrial names of the same botanical species are different in the USA, UK and Australia.

Industrial standards for specifiction and designation have been developed for most materials of industrial importance. Except for major compilations of specifications, this mass of standards will not be discussed further because they employ analytical techniques not available to conservators. These analytical techniques are further specified with their own methodologies and management procedures, and indeed can form the major part of the corpus of standards. The designations and specifications can be used reliably only for materials that have been tested under the standard. Objects recently produced, a few conservation materials and materials specifically tested fall into this category. When a material (or procedure) is described using a standard specification, it can be helpful to have this stated.

Commonly applied terms for materials, such as 'shellac' or 'lime' (BS 6100) can become meaningless (i.e. undefined), within the structure of these industrial terminologies. Their very vagueness may be desirable for conservators in demonstrating the lack of detailed knowledge about the material. More misleading would be a description like 'orange shellac', which happens to be an approved designation for a grade of shellac but not used in this manner. The terms used by conservators must be chosen with regard to the practice of related technologies.

Names of things

The names of objects (e.g. BS 6416) or their parts (e.g. ASTM D547 (Figure 82.4)) are not commonly the subject of industrial terminologies. For objects being treated by a conservator, the names and part-names should usually be obtained from (or agreed with) the appropriate collection specialists using, where possible, widely accepted terms.

Glossaries, terminologies and vocabularies

It is now well recognised that workers in a field must use terms in the same way to describe the same concepts. These may cover all or some of the activities of a discipline: from the materials, their properties, methods of test and use. Initially, many of the definitions were part of materials or process specifications, leading to duplication and conflicting definitions for one term. As a result, many disciplines have established

Figure 82.4 These illustrations of the types of nail points provide guidance only in the choice of the correct name which is defined in words in the standard; from *ASTM F547–77, Standard definitions of terms relating to nails for use with wood and wood-base materials*

Reproduced by permission of the American Society for Testing and Materials

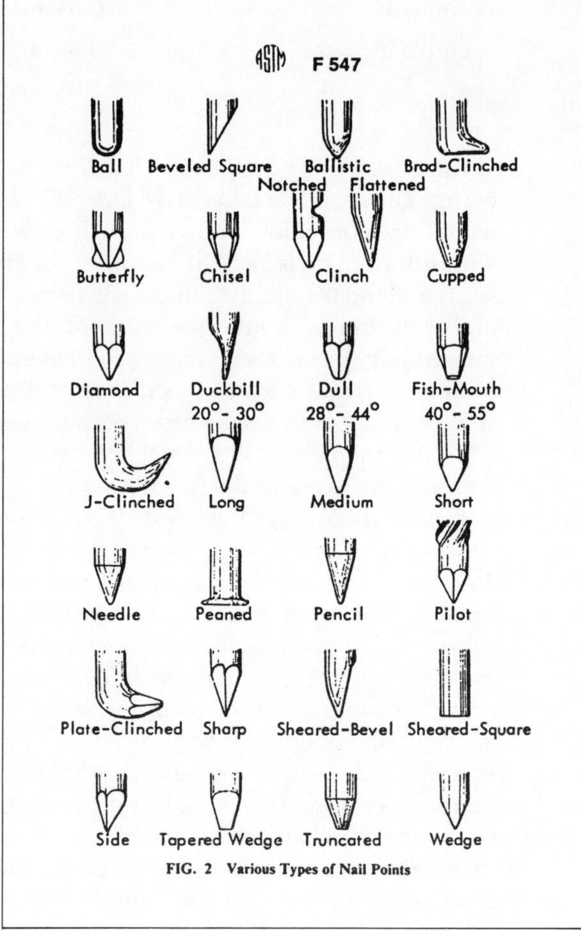

FIG. 2 Various Types of Nail Points

specialist committees to draw up agreed usages and definitions (Felber, Krommer-Benz and Manu, 1979). These are increasingly available as separate standards or publications and form the bulk of the sources listed in the appendix. Care should be taken in employing those sources that do not present a formal definition but only a statement of agreed usage(s). The term one uses should be able to be applied to only one concept as referenced. Well tested techniques are available and increasingly applied to the development of terminologies, both the structure and content (American Society for Testing and Materials, 1990, BS 3669, ISO 704, Strehlow, 1988).

Descriptions of properties

A number of standards are used to describe the state of a material, using largely visual inspection techniques. These have been included here because of their ease of use by conservators. These methods result in a numerical designation corresponding usually to a pictorial representation. Colour samples are commonly used but potentially of great use are pictorial illustrations of defects in paints or other objects which can be used to describe both type and degree of occurrence (Figure 82.5).

Figure 32.5 The imperfections on a surface are compared visually against standard photographs (originals are in colour) and dot diagrams to obtain an estimate of the extent of damage; from *ASTM B537–70, Standard practice for rating electroplated panels subjected to atmospheric exposure*

Reproduced by permission of the American Society for Testing and Materials

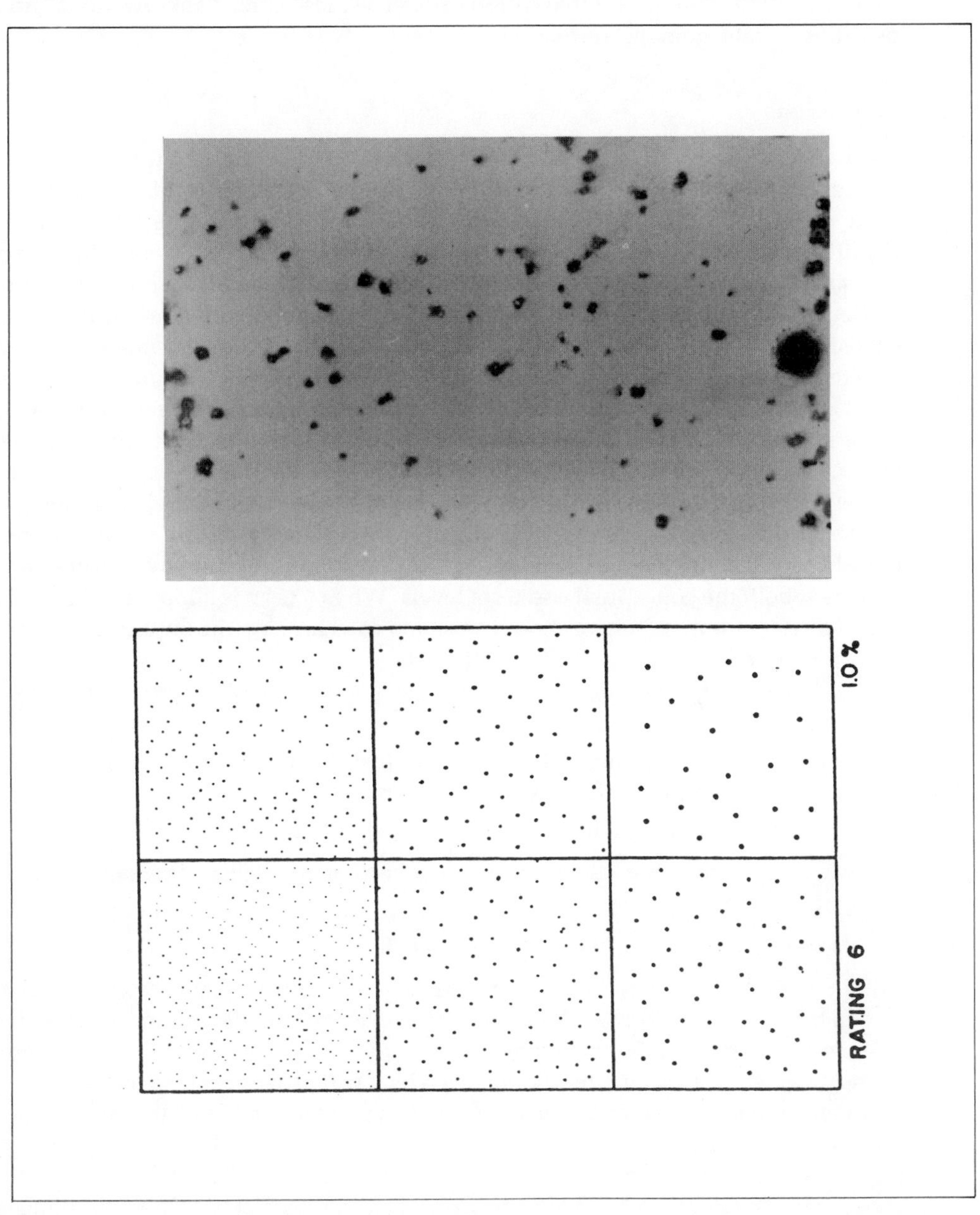

Abbreviations and symbols

Many industrial and scientific terminologies make use of inconveniently long terms which can impede rather than aid communication. Abbreviations of terms is widespread and, for universal understanding, need to be standardised. Examples are PVAC for poly(vinyl acetate) and cm for centimetre (International Organization for Standardization, 1982). It is important that conservators use these agreed abbreviations and do not use idiosyncratic nomenclature.

Conclusions

As has been shown here and made clear elsewhere in this volume, a terminology is a tool. Conservation has adopted tools (e.g. epoxy resins, RH meters and chemical analysis), from many sources with little modification. Some tools became useful only when modified, such as honeycomb core picture supports, lighting evaluation. Where a need is pressing, purpose-built tools may be proposed, developed and put into operation, such as Beva 371, vacuum hot table and condition reports. At the start of the process of choosing/developing a tool, a wide range of possibilities must be inspected and most rejected. The extent of applicability will be discovered during evaluation of the proposed tool. Experience in conservation has shown that a material or method that is well understood is frequently of greater usefulness than one, which although theoretically better, is novel.

The appendix includes a wide range of (mostly English language) terminologies that have been subjected to refinement over many years. They therefore represent a resource that should be considered in developing tools for communication by conservators. This applies at both the conceptual and term levels. When a term is adopted (or modified) for use in conservation, its source should be stated as a check on the implicit assumptions in its formulation.

The choice of a terminology depends on the likely recipients of the term. These might be:

the individual conservator, both in refining distinctions between concepts and ensuring consistency in the use of terms over time;

successor conservators who make use of conservation records;

professional colleagues: conservators, collection specialists, managers, scientists, architects, etc.;

the public, from schoolchildren to politicians.

Within institutions or narrow fields of conservation, the meanings of some terms may be understood without formal definition. However, when communicating with those outside this expert circle, meanings must be made explicit. In many cases, terms are already available in existing terminologies which will prove cost effective to use.

An effort of unknown but enormous size has gone into the construction of industrial terminologies. These, and the analysis on which they are based, can reveal concepts and implications that would otherwise remain unsuspected. Frequently, the recognition of a concept is a function of knowing the word used to describe it. One's thinking can be clarified once the words are available to describe reality. There are dangers in adopting a new language. The concepts must be adequately understood before the terms can be applied accurately.

Conservators should where possible apply this body of expertise in both carrying out and reporting their work on objects. This can be achieved only by gaining familiarity with these intellectual tools early in training and during work. The accompanying listing of terminologies (augmented where necessary) can act as a source both for training institutions and for those preparing controlled vocabularies for conservation use.

Appendix. Compilation of standard terminologies useful to conservators.

Index

American Society for Testing and Materials (ASTM) standards are indicated by an initial capital e.g. C1717; British Standards Institution (BSI) standards are indicated by an initial BS e.g. BS 6138; other standards are preceded by the relevant acronym.

Adhesives: BS 6138, C717, C797, D907
Aluminium: BS 3600, B209M, B275, G34, ANSI H35.1
Building(s): BS 3827, BS 4049, BS 5578, BS 6100, C11, C43, C119, C125, C219, C717, C797, D1554, E631, F547
Chemistry: BS 1755, BS 2474, BS 5775, IUPAC (1979 a & b)
Cinematograph: BS 5550
Colour: BS 1006, BS 4727, D1535, D1729, E308, E805, CIE, Munsell, SF
Copper: E310, CDA
Detergents: D459
Environment: BS 1339, BS 4727, BS 5643, D1356, D4023, E41, E344, F856
Furniture: BS 2005, BS 3827, BS 5557, BS 5578, D1554, D2825, D4523, F547
Glass: BS 952, BS 3130, BS 3447, BS 6100, C162, Int.Comm.Glass
Lead: B275
Leather: BS 2780, D1517
Magnesium: B275
Metal:
Materials: BS 3130, BS 3660, B209M, B275, E527
Objects: BS 3827, BS 6040, A644, A802, B374, B537, C286, D610, D2200, E186, E272, E280, E310, E446, F547, F592, F788, F812, G15, G46
Natural Products: BS 881, BS 2005, BS 3724, D9, D123, D1165, D4523
Objects: BS 185, BS 6040, BS 3827, BS 6456, BS 6528
Packaging: BS 3130, D996
Paint: BS 2015, BS 3900, D16, D610, D659, D660, D661, D662, D714, D772, D1848, FSCT
Paper: BS 2961, BS 3130, BS 3203, BS 6456, F592
Pesticides: BS 1831
Plaster & Cement: BS 2787, BS 4049, BS 6100, C11, C57, C125, C219
Polish: D2825
Polymers: BS 1755, BS 3130, BS 3502, BS 3558, BS 4589, BS 6138, D1418, D1566, D1600, ISO 1043, ISO Handbk21, IUPAC (1974 & 1976)
Pottery: C43, C71, C242, C286, F109
Properties: BS 1006, BS 3900, BS 6741, A802, B537, D448, D523, D610, D659, D660, D661, D662, D714, D772, D1442, D1535, D1729, D1848, D2200, E186, E253, E272, E280, E284, E308, E310, E447, F109, F788, F812, G15, G34, G46
Rope: BS 3724
Science: BS 3763, BS 5775, E12, E170, E175, E344, E456, ISO Handbk2
Stone & Earth: BS 610, C119, D125, C294, D448, D653, D2488, D2607, D4083
Terminology & Documentation: BS 3669, BS 4760, BS 5374, BS 5408, ISO 704, ISO/R 919, ISO/R 1087, ISO Handbk1
Textiles: BS 946, BS 1903, BS 3870, BS 4440, BS 4817, BS 6172, BS 5523, BS 6189, D123, D3990
Tools: BS 498, BS 876, BS 1296, BS 3066, BS 6416, ISO Handbk6
Water: D1129
Wear: G40
Wood: BS 881, BS 3130, BS 4261, BS 6100, BS 6566, D9, D1083, D1165, D1554

Standard Terminologies

American National Standards Institute (ANSI)

H35.1–1982: Alloy and temper designation systems for aluminum
[in ASTM vol. 02.01]

American Society for Testing and Materials (ASTM)

1916, Race Street, Philadelphia, PA 19103–1187, USA

Compilation of ASTM Standard Definitions 6th edn, ASTM (1986)

A644–86a: Standard Terminology relating to iron castings
[industrial practice, metallography]

A802–86: Steel castings, textures and discontinuities, evaluating and specifying, by visual inspection

[reference photographs, drawings and a tactile surface indicator]

B209M–86: Specification for aluminum and aluminum-alloy sheet and plate (Metric)
[reference photographs of corrosion effects]

B275–80: Codification of certain nonferrous metals and alloys, cast and wrought
[listings for aluminum, magnesium with some lead and zinc]

B375–80: Standard definitions of terms relating to electroplating

B537–70: Standard practice for rating electroplated panels subjected to atmospheric exposure
[rating assessed by protection or appearance, with many useful dot diagrams for evaluating percentage area affected]

C11–87: Standard definitions of terms relating to gypsum and related building materials and systems

C43–85a: Standard definitions of terms relating to structural clay products

C51–71: Standard definitions of terms relating to lime and limestone (as used by industry)
[relating to plasters and cements]

C71–85: Standard definitions of terms relating to refractories
[for architectural and industrial]

C119–86: Standard definitions of terms relating to natural building stones
[useful summary of composition and properties]

C125–86: Standard definitions of terms relating to concrete and concrete aggregates

C162–85a: Standard definitions of terms relating to glass and glass products
[useful]

C219–84: Standard terminology for hydraulic cement

C242–86: Standard definitions of terms relating to ceramic whitewares and related products
[useful]

C286–83a: Standard definitions of terms relating to porcelain, enamel and ceramic metal systems
[only a few terms for describing the finished product]

C294–86: Standard descriptive nomenclature for constituents of natural mineral aggregates
[lists and describes the rocks used]

C717–87a: Standard definitions of terms relating to building seals and sealants

C797–87: Standard practices and terminology for use of oil- and resin-based putty and glazing compounds

D9–87: Standard definitions of terms relating to wood
[timber and its defects]

D16–84: Standard definitions of terms relating to paint, varnish, lacquer and related products

D123–87: Standard terminology relating to textiles
[definitions referred to the relevant standards and other sources, names of fibres (commercial and systematic) with their uses]

D448–86: Standard classification for sizes of aggregate for road and bridge construction
[numerical designations for gravels, coarse sands, etc.]

D459–87: Standard definitions of terms relating to soaps and detergents

D610–85: Standard method of evaluating degree of rusting on painted steel surfaces
[photographic standards]

D653–86: Standard terms and symbols relating to soil and rock
[largely civil engineering]

D659–86: Standard method evaluating degree of chalking of exterior paints
[photographic standards]

D661–86: Standard test method for evaluating degree of cracking of exterior paints
[photographic standards]

D662–86: Standard test method for evaluating degree of erosion of exterior paints
[photographic standards]

D714–56: Standard method of evaluating degree of blistering of paints
[photographic standards]

D772–86: Standard test method for evaluating degree of flaking (scaling) of exterior paints
[photographic standards]

D907–82: Standard terminology of adhesives
[useful]

D996–85a: Standard terminology of packaging and distribution environments

D1083–83: Standard definitions of terms relating to veneer and plywood

D1129–82b: Standard definitions of terms relating to water

D1165–80: Standard nomenclature of domestic hardwoods and softoods
[Commercial (USA & Canada) and botanical names are cross-tabulated]

D1356–73a: Standard definitions of terms relating to atmospheric sampling and analysis

D1418–85: Standard practice for rubber and rubber latices nomenclature
[classification and abbreviations]

D4449–85: Standard method for visual evaluation of gloss differences between surfaces of similar appearance
[defines different types of gloss]

D1517–80: Standard definitions of terms relating to leather
[useful with 1 illustration]

D1535–80: Standard method for specifying color by the Munsell system
[uses real colour samples for comparisons]

D1554–86: Standard definitions of terms relating to wood-base fiber and particle panel materials

D1566–87a: Standard terminology relating to rubber
[simple definitions]

D1600–86a: Standard abbreviations of terms relating to plastics
[includes both polymers and additives]

D1848–63: Standard classification for reporting paint film failures characteristic of exterior latex paints
[definitions of defects]

D2200–85: Standard pictorial preparation standards for painting steel surfaces
[photographic standards]

D2488–84: Standard practice for description and identification of soils (visual-manual procedure)
[for civil engineering]

D2607–64: Standard classification of peats, mosses, humus and related products

D2825–84: Standard definitions of terms relating to polishes and related materials
[surface finishes with a few defects]

D3990–87: Standard terminology relating to fabric defects
[useful with photographic illustrations]

D4023–82a: Standard definitions of terms relating to humidity measurements

D4083–83: Standard practice for description of frozen soils (visual-manual procedure)
[civil engineering]

D4523–85: Standard terminology relating to feather-filled and down-filled products

E12–70: Standard definitions of terms relating to density and specific gravity of solids, liquids and gases

E41–86: Standard definitions of terms relating to conditioning
[temperature and relative humidity]

E170–84b: Standard terminology relating to radiation measurements and dosimetry
[nuclear radiation]

E175–82: Standard definitions of terms relating to microscopy

E186–84: Reference radiographs for heavy walled (2 to 4 in. (51 to 114 mm)) steel castings

E253–85: Standard definitions of terms relating to sensory evaluation of materials
[a guide to the practice of evaluation]

E272–75: Reference radiographs for high-strength copper-base and nickel-copper alloy castings

E280–84: Reference radiographs for heavy walled (4 to 12 in.) steel castings

E284–81a: Standard definitions of terms relating to appearance of materials
[useful]

E308–85: Standard method for computing the colors of objects by using the CIE system
[adopts an internationally agreed methodology]

E310–75: Reference radiographs for tin bronze castings

E344–84: Terminology relating to thermometry and hydrometry

E375–75: Standard definitions of terms relating to resinography

E446–84: Reference radiographs for steel castings up to 2 in. (51 mm) in thickness

E456–83a: Standard terminology for statistical methods
[useful for describing the conclusions as well as the methods]

E527–83: Practice for numbering metals and alloys (UNS)
[numerical codes for each group of alloys, detailed listings are derived from elsewhere]

E631–87: Standard terminology of building constructions
[types, methods and components, includes definitions of conservation, restoration, etc.]

F109–73: Standard definitions of terms relating to surface imperfections on ceramics
[defects illustrated by drawings]

F547–77: Standard definitions of terms relating to nails for use with wood and wood-base materials
[useful with names of parts]

F592–84: Standard definitions of terms relating to collated and cohered fastenings and their application tools
[illustrations]

F577–82: Standard specification for surface discontinuities of bolts, screws, and studs, inch and metric series
[defects defined and illustrated]

F812–83: Standard specification for discontinuities of nuts, inch and metric series
[defects defined and illustrated]

F856–83: Standard practice of symbols — heating, ventilation and air conditioning (HVAC)
[for design and drawings]

G15–86: Standard definitions of terms relating to corrosion and corrosion testing
[some relevant to appearance]

G34–86: Standard test method for exfoliation corrosion susceptibility in 2xxx and 7xxx series aluminum alloys (Exco test)
[classified series of photographs, pitting and exfoliation]

G46–76: Standard practice for examination and evaluation of pitting corrosion
[fairly useful]

British Standards Institution (BSI)
Linford Wood, Milton Keynes, Bucks MK14 6LE, UK

BS 185: Glossary of aeronautical and astronomical terms
[aircraft, engines, parachutes, spaceships]

BS 498: Part 1: 1960 (ISO 234) Specification for files and rasps
[types and parts defined by diagram]

BS 876: 1981 Specification for hand hammers
[types defined by diagrams]

BS 881 & 589: 1974 Nomenclature of commercial timbers, including sources of supply
[names are different from those used in USA and Australia]

BS 946: 1970 Methods for designation of yarns

BS 952: Glass for glazing
[classification and terminology of work]

BS 1006: 1985 Colour fastness of textiles and leather
[grey scales for assessing differences]

BS 1296: Part 2: 1972 Single point cutting tools: Nomenclature

BS 1339: 1965 Definitions, formulae and constants relating to the humidity of the air

BS 1755: (ISO 472–1979) Terms used in the plastics industry
[uses verbal and IUPAC definitions]

BS 1831: Recommended common names for pesticides
[three additional supplements]

BS 1903: Glossary of terms used by the clothing industry

BS 2005: 1966 Glossary of terms for fillings for bedding, upholstery and other domestic articles
[verbal definitions, some historically based]

BS 2015: 1965 Paint terms
[verbal with photographic aids for defects]

BS 2474: 1983 Recommendations for names for chemicals used in industry
[follows IUPAC — with exceptions]

BS 2780: 1983 Glossary of leather terms
[aided by a few diagrams]

BS 2787: 1956 Glossary of terms for concrete and reinforced concrete

BS 2961: 1967 Typeface nomenclature and classification

BS 3066: 1981 Specification for engineers' cold chisels and allied tools
[defined by diagram]

BS 3130: Packaging terms
[multi-component standard (verbal with descriptions), dealing with metal, glass, paper, plastics, wood]

BS 3203: 1979 (ISO 4046–1978) Paper, board, pulp and related terms
[verbal definitions]

BS 3447: 1962 Glossary of terms used in the glass industry
[inadequate]

BS 3502: 1978 Common names and abbreviations for plastics and rubbers

BS 3558: 1980 (ISO 1382) Rubber terms
[verbal with some diagrams on uses]

BS 3660: 1976 Terms used in the wrought aluminium industry
[little applicability]

BS 3669: 1963 Recommendations for the selection, formation and definition of technical terms
[useful guide]

BS 3724: 1964 (ISO 1968) Glossary of terms relating to fibre ropes and cordage
[short but useful]

BS 3763: 1976 The International System of units (SI)

BS 3827: Glossary of terms relating to builders' hardware
[purely verbal descriptions, locks, catches, door furniture, etc.]

BS 3870: ISO 4916–1982, Stitches and seams
[Classification and terminology]
[numerical designations defined using a combined verbal/pictorial description]

BS 3900: Group H: 1983, ISO 4628–1982, Methods of test for paints, part Hl. Designation of intensity, quantity and size of common types of defect: general principles and rating schemes
[terms defined by diagrams and photographs]

BS 4261: 1985 Terms relating to timber preservation
[classification including defects]

BS 4049: 1966 Glossary of terms applicable to internal plastering, external rendering and floor screeding
[verbal, obsolescent]

BS 4440: Glossary of basic terms for fishing nets

BS 4589: 1970 Abbreviations for rubber and plastics compounding materials

BS 4727: Part 4: 1972 Electrotechnical, power, telecommunications, electronics, lighting and colour terms; Part 4, Terms particular to

lighting and colour
[verbal]

BS 4760: 1971 Numbering of weeks

BS 4815: 1975, ISO/R 2076, Generic names for man-made fibres
[short]

BS 5172: 1975 Fishing nets; description and designation of knotted netting

BS 5374: 1981 (ISO 3166) Codes for the representation of names of countries

BS 5408: 1976 (ISO 5127) Documentation terms
[verbal definitions with a useful classification]

BS 5523: 1977, ISO 3572–1976, Textiles- weaves- definitions of general terms and basic weaves
[verbal definitions with added diagrams]

BS 5550: Section 8.1: 1980 Cinematography, Part 8, Glossaries
[verbal descriptions, film, equipment and exhibition]

BS 5557: 1978, ISO 2424, Textile floor coverings: classification and terminology
[verbal definitions with diagrams]

BS 5578: Part 1: 1978, ISO 3880/1–1977, Building construction stairs, Part 1, Vocabulary
[verbal descriptions with diagrams]

BS 5643: 1984 Refrigeration, heating, ventilating and air conditioning terms
[verbal, no classification or cross-referencing]

BS 5775: Specification for quantities, units and symbols
[space, time, light, chemistry, etc.]

BS 6040: 1981, ISO 1891–1979, Nomenclature for bolts, screws, nuts and accessories
[useful, graphical definitions with numerical/verbal designations]

BS 6100: Glossary of building and civil engineering terms
[multi-component standard, well structured and classified, building, glass, operations, civil engineering, services, wood based products, masonry, concrete and plaster]

BS 6138: 1981 Glossary of terms used in the adhesives industry
[useful, verbal, well organised]

BS 6189: 1981 Terms relating to fabrics and associated fibres, yarns and processes
[verbal, classified]

BS 6416: 1983, ISO 1703–1983, Nomenclature for assembly tools for screws and nuts
[pictorial definitions of tools]

BS 6456: 1983, ISO 6924–1983, Glossary of terms for correspondance envelopes
[verbal/pictorial definitions]

BS 6528: 1984, ISO 5408–1983, Terms for cylindrical screw threads
[verbal/pictorial definitions]

BS 6566: Part 2: 1985 Plywood, Part 2, Glossary of terms
[verbal, see BS 6100 section 4.3]

Copper Development Association (*CDA*)

Standard designations for copper and copper alloys
[in ASTM vol. 02.01]

Commission International de l'Eclairage (*CIE*)

International Lighting Vocabulary 4th edn (1987), ISBN 3 900734 0070

International Commission on Glass

Terminology of Defects in Glass (1969)

Dictionary of Glass Making (1983), ISBN 0444 42048 7

International Organization for Standardization (*ISO*)

Case postale 56, CH–1211 Genève 20, Switzerland

For many industrial, commercial and organisational activities, ISO has produced relevant standard vocabularies in two or three languages (English, French, Russian). Only a few compilations (*Handbooks*) and sample terminology standards are given here.

Catalogue 1988, ISBN 92 67 01049 2

Handbook 1, Information Transfer 2nd edn (1982), ISBN 92 67 10058 0

Handbook 2, Units of Measurement 2nd edn (1982), ISBN 92 67 10051 3

Handbook 6, Tools (2 vols) (1987), ISBN 92 67 10136 6

Handbook 21, Plastics, vol. 2, Terminology, sampling and policy (1984), ISBN 92 67 10093 9

ISO 704: 1968, Principles and methods of terminology

ISO/R 860: 1968, International unification of concepts and terms

ISO/R 919: 1969, Guide for the preparation of classified vocabularies (example of method)

ISO 1043–1: 1987, Plastics-Symbols-Part 1: Basic polymers and their special characterestrics

ISO/R 1087: 1969, Vocabulary of terminology

ISO 6354: 1982, Adhesives-Vocabulary, Bilingual edition

International Union of Pure and Applied Chemistry (*IUPAC*)

IUPAC (1974) List of standard abbreviations (symbols) for synthetic polymers and polymer materials, *Pure and Applied Chemistry* 30, 475–76

IUPAC (1976) Nomenclature of regular single strand organic polymers, *Pure and Applied Chemistry* 48, 373–85

IUPAC (1979a) Manual of symbols and terminology for physicochemical quantities and units, *Pure and Applied Chemistry* 51,1–51

IUPAC (1979b) *Nomenclature of Organic Chemistry* Pergamon Press, London, ISBN 0 08 022369 9

Federation of Societies for Coatings Technology Philadelphia (FSCT)
Paint/Coatings Dictionary (1978)

Munsell Color Co.
Munsell Book of Color

Scandinaviska Farbinstitutet (SF)
Riddargatan 38, PO Box 140 38, S-10440 Stockholm, Sweden
Natural Colour System, Atlas, ISBN 91 7162 076 1

83 COMPUTERISED SUMMARIES OF CONDITION AND TREATMENT REPORTS FOR PAINTINGS

Leslie Carlyle

Canadian Conservation Institute
Ottawa, Ont.

Introduction

The Canadian Conservation Institute (CCI) has a mandate to carry out conservation treatments and research for publicly owned museums and art galleries across Canada. The Conservation Services Division provides treatments, consultations, surveys and training in collections care. The Conservation Research Services Division provides analyses of materials used in the construction of objects, as well as research on conservation treatments and on deterioration caused by environmental agents.

Between 1983 and 1985, CCI and the Canadian Heritage Information Network (CHIN) as sister organisations then within the National Museums of Canada Corporation, collaborated to provide CCI with an overall computerised application for information management in all its facets.

Called ICARUS (Index of Conservation and Analytical Records: Unified System), the application incorporated facilities for the registration of objects entering and leaving the Institute, and retrieval of data on their condition and treatment. It also contained research information, such as analytical records and an adhesive database (Wainwright, 1986). The latter has been incorporated in the Materials Database of the Conservation Information Network.

During the initial stages of the development project, one conservator from each of the conservation laboratories was assigned to a task force to participate in the design of the database for conservation records. The task force worked directly with a computer systems analyst. The aim, was to develop a system that would simultaneously serve the needs of each of the separate laboratories: Works of Art on Paper, Ethnology, Archaeology, Furniture and Wooden Objects, Textiles and Fine Arts.

Application design

Initially the database was looked upon as an indexing system: it was not meant to replace the typewritten condition and treatment reports altogether but was to exist in addition to these dossiers.

As a result of the collaboration with the task force and the systems analyst, a format was designed which involved reporting on an object according to discrete components of its structure. Using an oil painting as an example, the support, ground, paint, surface coating and frame were listed as separate components. In the database, each of the 'components' forms a separate record which is linked to a main record. Each laboratory then determined the vocabulary and the amount of detail that they wished to have entered for each component.

The issue of standard terminology was left to be developed after a substantial number of records had been entered from each laboratory. By using the indexing software

Figure 83.1 A sample from the terminology print out

Records	Term	Laboratory
75	Abraded	(E/F) (TEX) (FAP)*
46	Abrasion	(WOP) (FAP)
37	Abrasions	(FAP)
3	Surface Abrasion	(WOP)
8	Scratched	(WOP)

The term chosen was 'Abraded'.

*(E/F) is Ethnology and Furniture
(TEX) is Textiles
(FAP) is Fine Arts (paintings)
(WOP) is Works of Art

available in CHIN's PARIS system, an alphabetical list of the keywords, the number of times they were used and by which laboratory, was printed out (Figure 83.1). From that list, standard terminology was established. This approach effectively avoided the conflicts and loss of time which can be associated with the process of deciding on a fixed vocabulary in conjunction with designing a system.

Condition and treatment reporting

In order to determine the type of information to enter into the computer, a study was made of the existing condition and treatment records. The review of past records in the paintings laboratory (Fine Arts) revealed that there was a general lack of consistency; not only with what was reported upon, but also in the amount of detail given. As well, where materials were identified, there was often no information on how that identification was made. For example, if a ground material was described as 'chalk', there was no indication of whether this was positively identified as calcium carbonate. Given the similar appearance of calcium carbonate and calcium sulphate the question of a positive identification is significant.

As a result of this study in the paintings laboratory, it became apparent that a clarification of the objectives and techniques in condition and treatment recording was necessary. If even the traditional condition and treatment records are going to be valuable to future research on painting materials and techniques, and on conservation treatments, it is vital that the amount and depth of detail of the the information recorded is consistent and that the level of accuracy in any given identification procedure for materials is reported upon.

Ideally in a full condition report on a painting, the presence or absence of a ground layer should be recorded. If present, its colour, texture, and layer thickness in proportion to the paint layer is then described. If an analysis of the materials present in the ground layer is deemed necessary, then the method of analysis and the results would be included as well.

Each method used in reporting on the identity of a material, from a visual examination up to the use of instrumental analysis, reflects a certain level of confidence in the accuracy

Figure 3.2 Table of contents of recording manual

TABLE OF CONTENTS

Page #

of the information. Therefore, it is important that the method which has been used is identified. For example, if the description of a material rests purely on a visual examination by the conservator, or if the materials have been examined microscopically and compared with control specimens (i.e. fibre or pigments), this should be recorded.

The basic question which arose regarding the computerised summaries from the conservation records was how much of this information should be included in the summary, should the computer be able to provide a search only of all paintings where a ground layer was or was not present with no further details, or would it conceivably be more valuable to be able to search for all paintings according to the colour or proportion of ground layer present.

One possible reason for valuing a computer search on the colour of grounds is related to the opinion held by some painting conservators that red coloured grounds from certain early Italian paintings have a tendency to react violently to high moisture levels. If enough records are entered to make a search statistically viable, it may be possible to identify such a trend by searching for paintings with such red grounds, and noting whether their condition or the conservation treatments performed on them indicated a tendency for problems associated with moisture damage. Comparing this information with a search of cream or white coloured grounds could indicate whether there is a significant difference in condition associated with deep red and light coloured grounds.

Many other as yet unanticipated relationships between the materials and techniques of paintings and their subsequent condition and treatment may become evident once a significant number of records are available in computerised databases.

The manual for condition and treatment reporting

In view of this, and the lack of restrictions in storage posed by the computer system available, it was decided that as comprehensive a summary as possible would be made for the computer records in the paintings laboratory. Thus, a system that was initially planned as simply a way of pointing to specific hard copy files from a variety of subject headings, for example, the name of the painting, the artist, the conservator, the owner institution, etc., came to be viewed as potentially of significant value as a research tool.

A condition and treatment reporting manual was developed for the paintings laboratory. There were two objectives: to help systematise traditional reporting techniques by providing a check-list and to provide a prompt for translating the text already written for the dossiers into summarised computer entries.

The manual was designed so that users could choose the section that related most closely to the object they were reporting on. This can be seen in the table of contents (Figure 83.2). Thus, if the painting was executed on a canvas support, the user would turn to the section relating to fabric supports and be offered a set of prompts relevant to this material; if it was on ridged support, the appropriate section would then be chosen.

Each separate component was reported on according to its name, its materials, details of the materials, their condition, and the treatment received. An example from the section on fabric supports is given in Figure 83.3. The headings on the left side of the page were presented as possible items to report upon, with suggested modifiers given in brackets on the right. A sample summary is provided in Figure 83.4 using the fabric section as an example. Where information was not present for the object, it was decided that the heading should be left out: since the manual listed this item, its absence in the summary was considered a negative report.

Figure 83.3 Extracts from recording manual

SUPPORT : FABRIC

COMPONENT NAME

SUPPORT : FABRIC

COMPONENT MATERIALS

Fabric:	(canvas: linen; canvas: linen ?; canvas: cotton ?; canvas: jute; etc; synthetic; polyester; polyester ?; etc;);

COMPONENT DETAILS

Fibre Identified:	(linen; cotton; bast fibre; jute; ramie; polyester; etc;);
Weave:	(not recorded; plain; tabby; basket; twill; herringbone; etc;);
Thread Count:	(not recorded; number horizontal/cm x number vertical/cm; number warp/cm x number weft/cm;);
Selvedge Edge:	(top: bottom: back: left side: back: right side;);
Tension Garland:	(top: bottom: back left side: back: right side: all sides;);
Attachment To Auxiliary Support:	(tacks: staples: patent fasteners: etc;): (distance: even; distance: uneven; etc;);
Stamp(s):	(record all information);
Label(s):	(number): (owner related; artist related; see dossier;);
Inscription(s):	(number): (owner related; artist related; see dossier;);

CONDITION

Surface:	(dusty: dirty: grimey: mould:): (slight; substantial;);
Colour:	(yellowed; darkened; discoloured; fresh;);
Strength:	(weak; strong; embrittled;);
Tension:	(slack; taught; uneven;);
Distortion(s):	(bulge; cockled; rippled; dent; corner draw; etc;);
Damage(s):	(tear: hole: puncture: rip: slash:): (large; small;);
Patch(s):	(number): (h x w); adhesive: (animal glue; starch paste; synthetic adhesive; PVA emulsion; pressure sensitive tape; etc;);
Stain(s):	(water ?: dye: ink: etc:): (run: spot: splatter: stream:): (overall; local;);
Accretion(s):	(unidentified: liquid residue: foodstuff: fly specs: etc:): (run: spot: splatter: stream:): (overall; local;);
Tacking Margins:	(clean: dusty: dirty: grimey:): (fresh; discoloured: yellowed; etc:): (strong; weak; embrittled;); (attachment: secure; attachment: insecure: uneven: attachment: insecure: rusty;); (torn: turn over edge; torn: at attachment; etc;);

Figure 83.4 Sample of summary record for computer entry

Component Name:	Support: Fabric
Component Materials:	Fabric:canvas:linen
Component Details:	Fibre Identified:bast fibre; Weave: plain; Thread Count: 10/cm × 8/cm; Tension Garland: top: left side; Attachment to Auxiliary Support: tacks; distance: even; Label: one: owner related;
Condition:	Surface: dusty:substantial; mould: slight; Colour: yellowed: darkened; Strength: weak; Tension: slack; Distortion: bulges; Damage: puncture:small; Accretion: unidentified:spot: local; Tacking Margins: dusty: weak: attachment: insecure;

Although the information listed in the manual does represent the amount of detail which is expected to be present in the written reports, again, it was difficult to decide which of these details should be entered in the computer summary. Which pieces of information will prove relevant or irrelevant in a computer search?

Future

The manual as presented is currently in draft form. For the computer summaries, the amount of detail to enter and the lack of headings where the item was not present are still unresolved issues. A complete review of the information in the computer summary is planned and an evaluation of it is to be made once a significant number of reports have been entered.

Ideally, any computerised system for condition and treatment records should include free-text as well as keyword summaries to eliminate the necessity of searching hard copies of the dossiers for an elaboration on the information present in the computer. Such freetext entries would also eliminate the need to anticipate once and for all what keywords are relevant, since keyword summaries could be relatively easily extracted from the text sections as the need arose.

As the use of computers becomes more and more familiar to conservators, their potential for surveying aspects of conservation treatments, and the materials and technique of manufacture associated with the objects will be further exploited. Already the very exercise of preparing information for data entry has been of significant value as it has promoted a re-evaluation of existing methods of documentation.

84 INFORMATION RETRIEVAL IN ICCROM LIBRARY

Julie A. M. Dearing and Marie Christine Uginet
ICCROM
Rome

Introduction

ICCROM, the International Centre for the Study of the Preservation and the Restoration of Cultural Property, was created as an intergovernmental organisation in 1959, following an agreement between UNESCO and the Italian Government. Soon after that, a small library was organised with the help of a grant from the Gulbenkian Foundation. The library aims to cover every aspect of the conservation of moveable and immovable cultural property, primarily archaeology, architecture, archives, libraries, museums, art objects and materials. It now has approximately 15 000 volumes and offprints and more than 650 periodicals.

This paper discusses the organisation of the library from the point of view of access to its collections. User access is primarily on a subject basis, so the collection has been organised with this in mind. The development of ICCROM's list of descriptors is outlined.

Organisation of the library

A topographical classification was decided on for the shelf arrangement of the library's collections. A very simple scheme from I to XXXIII (I bibliography, II History and Theory of Restoration, III Museology, etc.) is used for books. Within each subject division there is a further alphabetical subdivision of the subject. For example:

XIII Furniture/Music

A Furniture

B Frames/stretchers

C Marquetry

D Music (instruments of)

E Gilding

Alphabetic order of the countries is used for serials, and an alphabetical list of simple subject headings for the collection of offprints.

Apart from the main subject arrangement on the shelf, a subject analysis of each item entering in the library was necessary for bibliographic research through a manual card catalogue. A French subject index was created with the following structure:

Batiment, conservation consolidation
(Building, conservation consolidation)

Batiment, conservation nettoyage
(Building, conservation cleaning)

For each item analysed, one or more subject catalogue cards were typed for the manual catalogue. Such analysis was limited for practical reasons to main subject headings, those of more relevance justifying the typing of a card. This system seemed to work well, giving good access to the information available in the library. Unfortunately such access was only possible for researchers in Rome. One of the functions of ICCROM as stated in its Statutes (1963) is to 'collect, study and circulate documentation concerned with scientific and technical problems of the preservation and restoration of cultural property'. Thus the system's limitation convinced ICCROM to switch in 1977 to a computerised system for the input and retrieval of library records.

Computerisation of the library records

For the computerisation of library records, the UNISIST Reference Manual for Machine-Readable Bibliographic Descriptions (Martin, 1974) was chosen as a guideline for bibliographic description and system design. The bibliographic description of the library documents had to include an analysis of the documents in terms of their subject content so that the users of the library records (either in the form of the card catalogue, the printed subject index or the computerised database) would be able to retrieve relevant references and assess the likely value of the documents to them. Thus it was decided to write a short abstract for each document. The 1974 edition of the UNISIST reference manual did not mention controlled or uncontrolled indexing terms, but it was decided to append some additional fields for subject analysis after the abstract: one field for controlled index terms, one for uncontrolled index terms and other fields for technical information such as dating, place, typology, artist and object names, names of products.

Controlled index terms

The list of French descriptors used for the manual card index was reworked in order to create a new codified semi-hierarchical list in English and French. A machine generated alphanumeric code of four digits with a control character was assigned to each descriptor. The code is used only for data input and is automatically translated by the machine in both languages, thus avoiding typing errors. The following is an example of some of the descriptors for paper:

1006X	Manuscript, paper
1110R	Miniature, paper
1400D	Painting, paper
1242W	Paper, acidity
1243S	Paper, adhesive
3875O	Paper, adhesive removal
1285H	Paper, ageing
1286N	Paper, ageing accelerated
1246R	Paper, analysis
0175E	Paper, bactericide
1248V	Paper, biodeterioration
29496	Paper, biodeterioration bacteria
2595B	Paper, biodeterioration fungus

It was agreed that references to dating, location and typology of objects were not to be included in the subject list. These were input into other fields which are described below. During the work, all adverbs and prepositions were removed from the subject headings.

Figure 84.1 Syntax order of subject terms

General concept or collection of objects	Cultural property, Museum
Object	Sculpture
Material of the object	Stone
Test, study, analysis of the object	Test, dating, documentation
Deterioration of the object	Corrosion, biodeterioration
Conservation of the object	Consolidation, cleaning
Material used in the conservation	Synthetic-resin
Test, study of analysis of material used in the process of conservation	Penetration, removal, study
Deterioration of the material used in conservation	Yellowing

This has sometimes given descriptors unclear meanings: 'painting on metal' has become 'painting, metal'.

The reworking of the structure of the descriptors was rather rudimentary. The syntax itself required clearer definition and rationalisation, but the first years of computerisation were almost all dedicated to the processing of pre-1977 acquisitions into the new system. Recently work has begun again on the syntax. It was decided to adopt the word order for the descriptors illustrated in Figure 84.1.

Many descriptors do not have this correct syntactic structure. A slow process of restructuring some descriptors has started and is still in progress. An updated descriptor list should be issued in 1989. There are and there will still be a certain number of inconsistencies, but fortunately this does not affect online bibliographic research or the use of the printed subject index. All the words are available for online research and in the printed annual subject index all the descriptors are permuted so that the syntax order of the words is not too disturbing. It is, however, essential to rationalise the whole descriptor list to allow the future passage to a more hierarchical structure and a thesaurus.

Uncontrolled index-terms (stand-by keywords)

This field is used for the proposal of new descriptors by the abstractor. It is also useful as a check the understanding of the descriptors by the abstractor. Sometimes a proposed new descriptor exists already, but formulated in a different way. That means either that the existing descriptor is not clear or that the abstractor has missed it in searching the list. Thus doubtful meanings due to the syntax may be corrected. New descriptors are first discussed between the library staff and the abstractor, then if accepted assigned a code.

Other subject fields

Additional information such as dating, location and typology are put in fields separate from the subject index terms fields. Fields for dating and geographic location are semi-controlled.

The dating field is used to indicate the date or range of dates of an object or topic discussed in the document. After the date (dates *post quem* and *ante quem* with the mention of AD or BC) a space is available to indicate the historical period. A tentative list of periods with the corresponding dates has been elaborated for this purpose.

For geographic location, a list of the world's regions and of nations (divided sometimes to a lower level of state, region or department), with the corresponding codes, has been prepared by ICCROM. It is bilingual in English and French. The code is entered and is automatically decodified in the two languages without the possibility of error or misspelling. A space is available to indicate the name of the specific town or site on the vernacular language.

The material of the object discussed in the publication is entered if it is not adequately described in the general categories of the list of descriptors; for example a local type of stone, such as 'parian marble'. The name of the object (e.g. 'vase' or 'Il Cenacolo'), the name of the artist (e.g. Leonardo da Vinci) and the trade name of the products used or tested during the restoration (e.g. Paraloid B72) may also be recorded.

Detailed instructions have been prepared for the abstractor, in order to have as much uniformity as possible for the data entered into these fields but it is evident that without authority lists there will be some inconsistencies. Therefore, it is highly desirable to standardise as much as possible the information found in these fields.

The future

ICCROM is now part of the Conservation Information Network (CIN) and the question of harmonising the indexing systems and taking advantage of the experience of other institutions is *à l'ordre du jour*. The list of descriptors will be rediscussed, taking note of the other database in CIN, for example the Material Database. Reference will also be made to the experience of the Getty Art History Information Program, which has worked for some years on terminology.

Our system, with all its imperfections, is operating and may be a starting point for any improvement in the frame of CIN.

---

85 CONDITION REPORTING AT THE VICTORIA & ALBERT MUSEUM

Gwyn Miles

Victoria & Albert Museum

Introduction

The purpose of a condition report is to provide an acurate assessment of the state of a given object at a particular point in time. The reason for providing a form is to capture all the information that is required, leaving as little as possible to chance.

In the case of the Victoria & Albert Museum, a report is always completed before any treatment is carried out on an object. This provides a clear record of the state of an object before any intervention by the conservator. A report is completed before an object is acquired; this allows the resources required to make the object fit for display or study to be assessed. Also, a condition report is required to act as a record both before and after an object leaves the museum on loans. The purpose of the record is to show whether or not an object is fit to travel and also to determine what resources will be required to make it fit to travel.

The use of a written condition report when making a choice of conservation treatment in consultation with curatorial staff has been found to be useful and may help to determine the priorities for conservation treatment.

Essential features of a condition report

Essential information on any condition report is the identification of the object in question. This includes: the museum number; the department in the museum to which it is assigned; a simple name; title (if it has one); and a brief identifying description. This description should include: the date of manufacture; place of origin; artist, designer or maker associated with it; materials and techniques used in its manufacture. It is also desirable to record: whether or not the object is complete; whether or not it is intact; its dimensions (height, width, length, weight, etc.).

Normally the condition report is completed by a member of the Conservation Department. However, the volume of potential acquisition and loans may necessitate preliminary examination by curatorial staff. In such cases the purpose will be to determine whether the object is in sound condition. Sound here is taken to mean in good repair and suitable for display or study. If the object is not considered to be sound, it should be throughly examined by a conservator and a full condition report completed.

It is essential that the condition report is written in an objective fashion and it must include all the relevant information. This can be achieved best by analysing the factors involved in determining the condition of an object, and then trying to quantify those factors. Merely to say that an object is in 'good' or 'poor' condition conveys little information. It is better to use a structured form than to write a three-page essay. All relevant information must be noted; it has been found that a structured record form will help the conservator to do this, it will also produce data suitable for automated storage and retrieval.

Figure 85.1 Pages 1–4 of ceramics conditions report

V&A CONSERVATION DEPARTMENT — CONDITION REPORT

CERAMICS SECTION

MUSEUM NO.	2433 ta – 1876	DEPARTMENT	CERAMICS
OBJECT TYPE	JAR (+ METAL COVER)	CONSERVATION NO.	10678
DATE	19TH C ?	MAKER	—
MATERIALS	EARTHENWARE + TURQUOISE GLAZE	ORIGIN	PERSIA

DIAGRAM: include dimensions; major damage/degradation

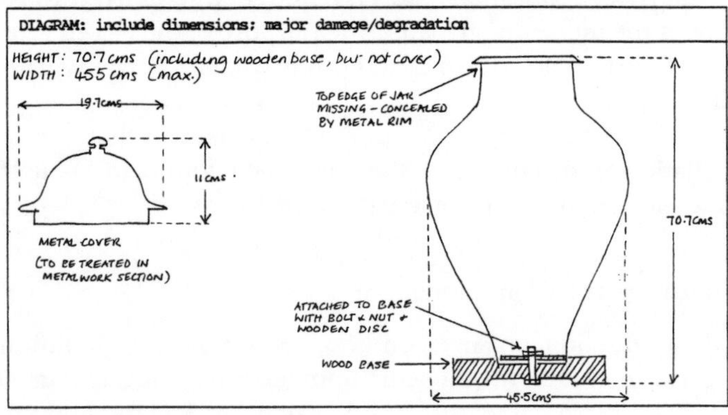

GENERAL CONDITION REPORT/COMMENT

Has sustained damage to rim area, which is concealed by metal addition and cover. Base drilled with central hole for attachment with bolt to wooden support. Extensive chipping of turquoise glaze. Extensive crazing (stained) over entire surface. Much superficial dust and dirt.
(Metal cover and rim to be reported on by metal work Conservation Section)

1 SOUND		2 DISFIGURED		3 DAMAGED	✓	4 UNSTABLE		5 HIGHLY UNSTABLE	

SUITABLE FOR LOAN	YES	✓	NO		Subject to conditions on back page.	
CONSERVATION	YES	✓	NO		TIME	COST
EXAMINER	V.L. Oakley				DATE	16·2·90

CONDITION

[ ] SOUND (no damage)
[ ] MANUFACTURING DEFECTS
[✓] DIRT/STAINING Thick layer of superficial dust and dirt – especially on interior and trapped in relief decoration. Also where glaze is abraded dirt has been retained in scratches, and also in areas of glaze loss where body is exposed.
[ ] ENCRUSTATIONS/SALTS
[✓] ABRASIONS/SCRATCHES Very extensive abrasion of all vulnerable 'raised' relief areas.
[✓] CRAZING Network of crazing over all surfaces. Closer, more pronounced (stained) crazing on interior than exterior. Dirt trapped in fissures of crazing
[ ] FLAKING
[✓] CHIPS Numerous large chips over entire surface
[ ] BREAKS/CRACKS
[✓] LOSS Upper neck area missing, now concealed by metal rim.
[ ] OTHER

Figure 85.1 *continued*

MOUNTS/SUPPORTS - describe and indicate position

Square wooden base (painted black) secured to pierced base of jar with nut and bolt system - to give stability.

LABELS - indicate position and condition

NONE

PREVIOUS TREATMENT - indicate extent and condition

[] NO PREVIOUS TREATMENT

[] CONSOLIDANT

[✓] ADHESIVE Shellac - attaching metal rim to neck

[] DOWELS/RIVETS

[✓] FILLER Packing between metal rim and damaged break-edge of jar's neck - shellac with fibrous material (straw?)

[] RETOUCHING

FURTHER COMMENTS/ DIAGRAMS

Metal cover will require a separate condition report.

PROPOSED TREATMENT

(to be agreed with Ceramics Dept.)
MINIMUM – cleaning interior and exterior surfaces.
MAXIMUM – as above, but in addition filling and retouching all damaged areas.
Metal rim removed, traces of old adhesive and filler removed. Rim reattached (after cleaning)

DISPLAY REQUIREMENTS

Environment: Temperature C; Relative Humidity % +/-
Light Ultra Violet

As for general loan conditions

Mounting:

STORAGE REQUIREMENTS

NOTES FOR PACKING AND TRANSIT

Extremely heavy. Should be packed upright in strong container, padded with tissue wads.

Use of terms

Condition reports should be brief but accurate. To ensure proper understanding and to facilitate information retrieval, the consistent use of terms is essential, as are certain conventions in the recording of data such as dates and names. It is vital that this information should be consistent within the museum; standards for the description of museum object data are at present under active discussion. The conventions currently used by the Conservation Department will be reconciled with the museum standard once it has been set up.

The term condition refers to the state of preservation of an object. The state is determined by three basic factors: instability, damage and disfigurement (Buck, 1979).

Instability is the sign of active physical, chemical or biological deterioration; it is understood that the object will continue to deteriorate unless some steps are taken to stop or at least slow down the process of deterioration.

Damage is loss or distortion due to physical, chemical or biological agents, now inactive; an object may be damaged because deterioration has become so advanced that there are actual losses or ruptures, or it may be damaged by mechanical or physical violence or chemical change.

Disfigurement refers to the aesthetic impact of losses, additions or alterations; an object may be disfigured by dirt, stains, discoloured coating, poor restoration or by damage. Use of this term implies that disfigurement is superficial and may be reversed.

In determining the condition of an object these three aspects should be considered. When the condition of an object is described, it is compared in its present state to some ideal 'original' state or a previous record. Any losses, additions or alterations that have occurred since manufacture, excavation or at some other previous date should be recorded.

Categories of condition

Once the overall description of the condition of an object has been assessed it is categorised according to a five-point scale:

1 Sound
2 Disfigured
3 Damaged
4 Unstable
5 Highly unstable

The use of this five-point scale allows some quantification of the state of the collections and the type of objects undergoing treatment. The same scale is used when condition surveys are carried out.

A detailed breakdown of defects follows. The description of any defect must include its nature, its location and its extent.

Nature: there are standard terms used to describe defects. (Buck, 1979; Jewett, 1983). These vary according to the type of object under examination. Each specialism of Conservation tends to use specific terms to describe condition. Because of this fact it has been our experience within the Museum that it is much simpler to provide condition reports which are specific to a type of object.

Location: it is useful to know if a specific defect is general and to be found across the object in question, or whether it is to be found in a restricted area. Some defects, such as superficial dirt, are likely to be spread evenly across the object, other defects, such as a tear or dent, are more likely to be in a specific location.

In practice the location can be described most easily by means of a sketch or marked up photographs. For this reason each condition report includes either a photograph or a sketch of the object. This is then labelled with the nature and extent of any defect.

Extent: this is dependent to some extent on the nature of the defect — a tear, hole or stain may be measured fairly exactly in terms of length or area. However, abrasion, dirt, embrittlement, corrosion, etc., are not so easily measured and adjectives are needed. There are five standard adjectives which are normally used across the conservation department: negligible, slight, moderate, marked and extreme. This could as easily be a five point numerical scale, but the use of an understandable word makes it less confusing.

Further instructions for care of objects

The condition report is frequently used as a channel of communication, particularly where objects are about to be loaned to special exhibitions. It is useful to record the requirements for display or storage and any instructions for handling and packing. Proposed treatment may also be given in order to provide a clear picture of the scope of work which needs to be carried out, the finish to be expected and the dimensions to expect. It will also include the details of any mount which will be necessary.

Examples of condition reports in use at the Victoria & Albert Museum

The format of condition reports in the Conservation Department of the Victoria & Albert Museum is similar for each of the nine separate sections dealing with discrete specialisms, such as Paintings, Paper, Textiles and Ceramics. However, the exact details vary considerably. Generally each form is a minimum of four sides of A4, the front and back of which provide a summary of the state of the object and recommendations for display and storage, packing and handling and proposed treatment. The centre two pages provide space for detailed descriptions of defects and diagrams or marked photographs (Figure 85.1).

The design of these reports has involved the conservators working in each specialism. The enthusiasm for examination and reporting on the condition of an object has affected progress in the design of the report. There has been a definite tendency to look on the report as a personal statement, rather than a tool for informatioin retrieval. As the requirements of the report becomes clearer, with pressure for condition reports to be completed for every loan and acquisition, the need for clarity has become paramount. The exact design of the forms still needs to be refined to provide information quickly and easily to both conservators and curators as they care for the collections. Nevertheless, the principle items of information and categorisation of the state of a given object is unlikely to change.

86 CONSERVATION RECORDS FOR PAINTINGS AT THE TATE GALLERY

Roy A. Perry

Deputy Keeper, Conservation Department
The Tate Gallery
London

Introduction

The existing Conservation record systems at the Tate Gallery are the accumulation of many decades' efforts to meet changing demands and occasional sorties to rationalise and improve the formats. Current influences are the increasing requirement to supply more comprehensive, detailed information for technical art history and conservation and the introduction of computerised, information handling systems for the management of the collections. Whereas the demand for ever more detailed technical information applies pressure to expand and complicate the records, computerisation imposes uniformity and conciseness.

The purposes and formats of Conservation Department records

Technical records and reports are prepared for many documentary and managerial reasons.

Pre-Acquisition Reports are prepared in confidence:

to advise staff, trustees and donors as to the existing and potential condition of proposed acquisitions;

to estimate the conservation commitment involved;

to provide technical evidence of authenticity where doubt arises.

Conservation Records are established on all acquisitions entering the main collections and previously unrecorded items undergoing examination and treatment. Technical records are made to:

describe the original structure of an object (materials and techniques used to make it);

describe any alterations and additions to the original structure affecting the present condition;

record treatments applied to it (materials and techniques);

record special handling, display, storage and transport requirements assessing restrictions on environmental conditions and suitability for loan;

assess inevitable future changes in condition and conservation requirements, where appropriate.

This provides a chronological history of the object's structure, changing condition and the conservation procedures and restoration treatments applied to it.

At this time, basic technical information (e.g. medium, support, dimensions), is provided for cataloguing and collections management use. Generally, formated record sheets and photography are used for paintings.

Figure 86.1 Treatment sheet

TATE GALLERY CONSERVATION DEPARTMENT: TREATMENT		NO:	REF:
		ARTIST:	
CONSERVATOR:		TITLE:	
DATE:	URGENCY:	LOCATION:	
REQUEST:			

✓	WORK DONE	MATERIAL USED	
	ANALYSIS	SUBJECT	
	X – RADIOGRAPHY		
	CONSOLIDATION	ADHESIVE:	
	DE-ACIDIFICATION	AGENT:	
	CANVAS REPAIR (TEARS/LOSSES)	MATERIAL:	ADHESIVE:
	PANEL REPAIR (SPLITS/LOSSES)	MATERIAL:	ADHESIVE:
	LINING/RELINING	MATERIAL:	ADHESIVE:
	STRIP LINING	MATERIAL:	ADHESIVE:
	MAROUFLAGE	MATERIAL:	ADHESIVE:
	ATTACHMENT		
	NEW STRETCHER/ACCESSORY SUPPORT	MATERIAL:	
	LOOSE LINING	MATERIAL:	
	PANEL TRAY/ACCESSORY SUPPORT	MATERIAL:	
	OTHER SUPPORT TREATMENT	MATERIAL: ADHESIVE:	
	SURFACE CLEANING	AGENT:	
	VARNISH REMOVAL	AGENT:	
	VARNISH REFORMING	AGENT:	
	RESTORATION REMOVAL	AGENT:	
	FILLING	MEDIUM:	
	RETOUCHING/INPAINTING	MEDIUM:	
	INITIAL VARNISH	RESIN:	
	FINAL VARNISH	RESIN:	
	OTHER SURFACE TREATMENT		
	FRAME REPAIRED/RESTORED		
	NEW FRAME	MATERIAL:	FINISH:
	BUILD UP		
	BACKBOARD	MATERIAL:	
	GLAZING	MATERIAL:	
	STORAGE/TRANSIT FRAME/BOX		
	RECORD MADE		TREATMENT COMPLETED
	PHOTOGRAPHY COMPLETED		DISPLAY/STORAGE/TRANSPORT REQUIREMENTS MADE
	ACQUISITION FORM COMPLETED		RETURNED TO DISPLAY/STORE/LOAN OUT
	CONSERVATOR:	DATE COMPLETED:	

Dd 8819600 10 Pads 6.86 H.D.B. Ltd. 3657

The technical record is used as a source of information for:

conservation and restoration of the object;

assessing changes in its structure and appearance;

technical art history including identification and authentification, and the history of conservation;

assessing the success and failure of treatments;

assessing the conservation requirements, identification and authentification of related objects.

For Major Treatment and Examination, when structure and condition are explored in greater depth, an open-plan format is normally adopted, following the order and main headings of the formated sheets, for ease of reference. The basic black and white photographic recording of the front, the front in raking light, and back, is also extended as necessary (e.g. using details, IR, UV, colour, X-radiography, etc.), and all stages of treatment involving changes in appearance are photographed.

Treatment is always recorded using an open plan format, each operation being given in the order in which it was carried out, giving details of the materials and techniques employed.

Treatment Sheets (Figure 86.1) are the job sheets for work on paintings and do not contain technical information not recorded in the main record. Used initially to allocate work, they include a check-list of work done, which is completed by the conservator. They are kept for reference and departmental management purposes.

Treatment Priority Lists are compiled to assist conservation and curatorial staff set programmes for conservation and treatment. They are particularly important in the case of stored items with no other priority for attention, such as new acquisitions or items required for display or loan out. They are in the process of being computerised.

Loan Reports are prepared to advise the Loans Committee and Trustees as to the physical suitability of a work to undergo a proposed loan. As well as briefly reporting on the condition of an object in relation to the proposed display venue and transport arrangements, the conservation commitment involved in preparing the work, type of packing and desirability of courier are also considered. For major loans, technical documentation is prepared to accompany them.

Exhibition Condition Reports are different in that they concern items loaned to the Gallery, are often prepared with limited access, within tight time restrictions and are intended for the consumption of owners as well as gallery staff. Usually designed for each exhibition, taking into account the nature of the objects involved, their main functions are to:

enable staff to provide the best conditions of packing, transport, handling and display;

identify any defects requiring remedial action for the loan to proceed;

inform the owner of the general condition of the work and where necessary advise on treatment;

protect the borrower from unwarranted claims for damage or deterioration.

They concentrate on recording hazardous defects, only briefly describing structure and general condition. Some form of photograph is essential for marking purposes and any serious adverse condition found is immediately photographed.

Record format for paintings

The record format for paintings is an expansion of the core features first collated by a committee of the American Association of Museums (Stout, 1935). This has been the basis of all technical records for paintings at the Tate, since their full establishment in the 1950s.

Similar formated short record sheets are used for works on paper, but not as yet for sculpture. The diversity of materials, techniques and degrees of complexity of sculpture make formated records impractical except in the most basic format. As the section develops we hope to produce them for basic categories of object, such as carved, modelled, cast, constructed and kinetic.

Notes on Compiling Technical Records is an in-house guide to compiling records giving full instructions, explanations of the terms employed in the forms and bibliographies of relevant sources of terminology. Written as an instruction manual for new staff and students, it also performs as an *aide memoire*. It is updated as records are modified. The Tate Gallery also produces a manual on 'Catalogue Style', written by Leslie Parris.

All records are filed by accession number in gusseted wallets. The record sheets are kept in a folder which carries full catalogue information and lists contents. The first enclosed sheet is *Record of Examination* which lists all examinations and the reason for them, whether or not any addition has been made to the main record.

The record sheets are then inserted chronologically, page numbered, signed and dated. There are four styles for paintings (Figures 86.2–86.5):

woven fabric support/priming;

panel support/priming;

paint film/image/surface films;

framing/inscriptions.

Labels, photographs and flat samples are kept in appropriately labelled 'Melinex' envelopes.

In most instances of works by living artists, a questionnaire will be prepared and sent to the artist, hopefully to acquire first-hand information concerning the materials and techniques employed, the artist's opinions on the work's display and conservation.

As well as contributing information and entries to Gallery collections' catalogues and reports, we regularly contribute articles to technical publications, exhibition catalogues and occasionally books. The format and language are determined by the audience for the publication.

Vocabulary principles

Although the record always includes information expressed in word and number, the use of photographs and explanatory diagrams has become increasingly important.

For example, although many eloquent vocabularies have been devised for describing cracks in paintings, none are as comprehensive, accurate and easily understood as good photographs in normal, raking or transmitted light. Photographs are more consistent and objective in their representation of surface appearance than verbal descriptions and can be confidently used in identifying many kinds of surface change.

Objective description is highly valued, and in written aspects of the record every attempt is made to distinguish between observed 'fact', which would be acceptably

Figure 86.2

TATE GALLERY CONSERVATION DEPARTMENT

WOVEN FABRIC SUPPORT PRIMING

PAGE

CAT NO. ARTIST

WOVEN FABRIC SUPPORT — REF PHOTO

PRIMARY SUPPORT FABRIC
WEAVE PATTERN
THREAD TYPE
THREAD COUNT warp ends per cm weft picks per cm
WARP DIRECTION SELVEDGES
No. OF PIECES JOINS

OTHER MATERIAL
CONDITION: GOOD FAIR POOR
DEGRADATION/EMBRITTLEMENT
DEFECTS IN PLANE/DIMENSIONAL STABILITY

TEARS, DAMAGE & LOSS

DIRT: MINIMAL VISIBLE HEAVY SOILING
LINING/REINFORCEMENT: ORIGINAL
MATERIAL
ADHESIVE/ATTACHMENT
CONDITION: ADEQUATE INADEQUATE HARMFUL

ATTACHMENT TO ACCESSORY SUPPORT: ORIGINAL
METHOD

CONDITION: ADEQUATE INADEQUATE FAILED
ORIGINAL TACKING EDGES: INTACT DAMAGED MISSING

STRETCHER ACCESSORY SUPPORT

TYPE: ORIGINAL
No OF MEMBERS MATERIAL
OUTER MEMBERS: W mm T mm FOREWARD FACES FLAT/BEVELLED INNER EDGES SHARP/ROUNDED
CROSS MEMBERS: W mm T mm MAX CANVAS CLEARANCE mm INNER EDGES SHARP/ROUNDED
JOINTS: EXPANSION FIXED

EXPANSION KEYS: COMPLETE MISSING
CONDITION: ADEQUATE INADEQUATE HARMFUL
DEFECTS IN PLANE
FAILURE OF JOINTS
DAMAGE & LOSS

PREVIOUS TREATMENT

PRIMING GROUND — REF PHOTO

UNPIGMENTED PRIMING/SIZING
MATERIAL

DISTRIBUTION & APPLICATION

PIGMENTED PRIMING/GROUND
MEDIA

PIGMENTS/INERTS

COLOUR
CONSISTENCY: GRANULAR VEHICULAR LEAN/PASTE/RICH

DISTRIBUTION

LAYERS
THICKNESS
HANDLING/CONFORMATION

CONDITION: GOOD FAIR POOR
SOLUBILITY: NOT TESTED
HEAT RESISTANCE: NOT TESTED
DISCOLOURATION

CRACKS

CLEAVAGE/FLAKING

OTHER DAMAGE & LOSS

PREVIOUS TREATMENT: CONSOLIDATION COMPENSATION

COMMENTS DIAGRAMS

SUPPORT PREPARED BY

EXAMINER

Figure 86.3

TATE GALLERY CONSERVATION DEPARTMENT

FRAMING INSCRIPTIONS

PAGE

CAT NO. ARTIST

DISPLAY FRAME — REF PHOTO

TYPE: ORIGINAL
MATERIAL: SOFTWOOD HARDWOOD
CONSTRUCTION/JOINTS

SHAPING: CARVED MOULDED APPLIED MOULDINGS

FINISH: NATURAL SEALED/VARNISHED STAINED PAINTED GILDED

FLAT
SLIPS
DOOR
GLAZING: NONE ADEQUATE INADEQUATE

BACKBOARD: NONE ADEQUATE INADEQUATE

FITTING OF PAINTING: ADEQUATE INADEQUATE HARMFUL
SECURED BY
SPACERS/CUSHIONS
REBATE CAPACITY: ADEQUATE TIGHT SHALLOW
REBATE FACE: SMOOTH ROUGH BARE FACED

CONDITION: GOOD FAIR POOR HARMFUL
APPEARANCE: ACCEPTABLE UNACCEPTABLE

PROTECTION GIVEN TO PAINTING: ADEQUATE INADEQUATE

DEFECTS IN PLANE

FAILURE IN JOINTS

OTHER DAMAGE & LOSS

DIAGRAMS

LOCATION EXAMINER DATE

FRAME TREATMENT/REPLACEMENT — REF PHOTO

STORAGE FRAME

GLAZING
BUILD-UP
BACKBOARD
REBATE
FITTING
CONSERVATOR TECHNICIAN DATE

INSCRIPTIONS LABELS

ITEM	LOCATION

Figure 86.4

TATE GALLERY CONSERVATION DEPARTMENT — PAINT FILM/IMAGE SURFACE FILMS

PAGE

CAT NO. ARTIST

PAINT FILM/IMAGE — REF PHOTO

MEDIA

PIGMENTS/INERTS

OTHER MATERIAL

CONSISTENCY: GRANULAR VEHICULAR LEAN/PASTE/RICH PELLICULAR

DISTRIBUTION

INITIAL DRAWING
LAYERS
THICKNESS
HANDLING/TOOLMARKING

TRANSPARENCY/GLOSS

CONDITION: GOOD FAIR POOR
SOLUBILITY: NOT TESTED
HEAT RESISTANCE: NOT TESTED
DISCOLOURATION

DRYING DEFECTS/CONTRACTION CRACKS: GENERAL LOCAL MINOR SEVERE

AGE CRACKS:	GENERAL	LOCAL	MINOR	SEVERE
FRACTURES:	BRITTLE	DUCTILE	SMOOTH	RAGGED
APERTURES:	OPEN	CLOSED	COMPRESSED	
EDGES:	FLAT	ELEVATED	CUPPED	
PATTERNS:	LINEAR	BRANCHED	NETWORK	IMPACT

CLEAVAGE/FLAKING: GENERAL LOCAL MINOR SEVERE

MECHANICAL WEAR/DEGRADATION: GENERAL LOCAL MINOR SEVERE

CHEMICAL/BIOLOGICAL DEGRADATION: GENERAL LOCAL MINOR SEVERE

OTHER DAMAGE & LOSS

PAINT FILM/IMAGE cont'd — REF PHOTO

PREVIOUS TREATMENT: CONSOLIDATION CLEANING COMPENSATION

SURFACE FILMS

APPLIED SURFACE FILMS

LAYERS
DISTRIBUTION
APPLICATION

COLOUR/TRANSPARENCY/GLOSS

SOLUBILITY: NOT TESTED

CONDITION: GOOD VISUALLY DISTURBING HARMFUL

CHANGES IN COLOUR/GLOSS/TRANSPARENCY

CRACKS/CRAZING: GENERAL LOCAL MINOR SEVERE

OTHER DEGRADATION, DAMAGE & LOSS

PREVIOUS TREATMENT: CLEANING REVIVAL COMPENSATION

SURFACE DIRT: MINIMAL VISIBLE HEAVY SOILING
TYPE
DISTRIBUTION

REMOVABILITY

COMMENT

GENERAL CONDITION/RECOMMENDED TREATMENT

DISPLAY/STORAGE RESTRICTIONS

LOAN RESTRICTIONS: UNSUITABLE FOR UK FOREIGN TOURING LOAN

LOCATION EXAMINER DATE

Figure 86.5

TATE GALLERY CONSERVATION DEPARTMENT — PANEL SUPPORT PRIMING

PAGE

CAT NO. ARTIST

PANEL SUPPORT — REF PHOTO

PRIMARY SUPPORT PANEL
SPECIES

MEMBERS No
CUT
GRAIN DIRECTION
JOINTS

CONFORMATION: FRONT
BACK
EDGES
OTHER MATERIAL

CONDITION: GOOD FAIR POOR
DEGRADATION: MECHANICAL BIOLOGICAL

DEFECTS IN PLANE/DIMENSIONAL STABILITY

DEFECTS IN JOINTS

SPLITS/CHECKS

OTHER DAMAGE & LOSS

DIRT: MINIMAL VISIBLE HEAVY SOILING

CRADLE/ACCESSORY SUPPORT: ORIGINAL
STRUCTURE

CONDITION: ADEQUATE INADEQUATE HARMFUL TO PRIMARY SUPPORT

DIAGRAMS

PREVIOUS TREATMENT

PRIMING GROUND — REF PHOTO

UNPIGMENTED PRIMING/SIZING
MATERIAL

DISTRIBUTION & APPLICATION

PIGMENTED PRIMING/GROUND
MEDIA

PIGMENTS/INERTS

COLOUR
CONSISTENCY: GRANULAR VEHICULAR LEAN/PASTE/RICH

DISTRIBUTION

LAYERS
THICKNESS
HANDLING/CONFORMATION

CONDITION: GOOD FAIR POOR
SOLUBILITY: NOT TESTED
HEAT RESISTANCE: NOT TESTED
DISCOLOURATION

CRACKS

CLEAVAGE/FLAKING

OTHER DAMAGE & LOSS

PREVIOUS TREATMENT: CONSOLIDATION COMPENSATION

COMMENTS DIAGRAMS
SUPPORT PREPARED BY

EXAMINER

consistent between most observers, and opinion derived from that observation. For example, there may be technically unresolvable disagreements about why a painting exhibits certain physical features — are they 'original' or not? — even though their physical form is not disputed (e.g. abraded paint, soiled collage or yellow varnish).

The vocabulary of records evolves like any other, as words fall into disuse, change and diversify in meaning and new terms are incorporated from other relevant disciplines. The 'Notes on Compiling Technical Records' includes bibliographies of standard sources in use.

However determinedly controlled, all disciplines contain differing practices and undergo change. For example, the nomenclature of chemicals has continually changed (wood spirit: wood alcohol: methyl alcohol: methanol); that in common use today often containing names from different disciplines (propan-2-ol, xylene, white spirit).

Terminology when writing about works of art is even more erratic. 'Medium' can refer to any form of communication or mean precisely the fluid vehicle/binder of a paint system. Occasionally the word 'pigment' will be used where the writer was obviously refering to 'paint'. Their context, however, normally makes their meaning clear. For example, whereas the word 'pencil' in a nineteenth-century manual could refer to a brush, if written today we would take it to mean a graphite drawing instrument. Serious problems of meaning, however, can arise for art historians and conservators, such as what is meant by W. Blake's 'tempera' or 'fresco'. Another example is the abbreviation PVA which has been used to denote both polyvinyl alcohol and polyvinyl acetate.

Conservators must leave, for future reference, full explanations of the terms they use. This is of particular importance with regard to treatments where full technical data and samples of materials should be kept.

Computers

The current use of computers in the Conservation Department is severely restricted by their technical limitations, lack of resources and staff skills.

Most preparation of written documents and some information storage is carried out on an IBM PC using Multimate and dBase III programs.

Within the department, the major research program into J. M. W. Turner's materials and techniques is being documented on dBase III, the Treatment sheet information is to be computerised, as is a program for working out and recording the packing foam requirements of paintings for transport. The Treatment sheet program known as CONTRE (Conservation treatment record extract) will hopefully enable us to quickly search and cross-reference treatments as well as provide managerial information.

In the current circumstances, it is not envisaged that we will use computerisation for the main records although serious consideration is being given to producing more consistency in terminology and layout, with computerisation as the long term aim. Unfortunately, the most consistent 'vocabulary' we have for recording visual appearance, photography, is not well served by affordable computer technology, either in terms of handling or visual presentation. Until this is available at the easel or in the store, the question of the applicability of computers to the main conservation record will remain in doubt. We will still need the photographic prints, and of course, the painting itself as our main source of information.

Conclusion

Technical records are a tool in conservation and aid to the appreciation of works of art, not a self sufficient activity. As such, they are continually revised and honed to meet current use while maintaining a continuity with past forms. In addition to an orderly preservation of the records themselves, it is important to maintain adequate glossaries and archives of materials for future reference.

---

87 CONSERVATION TERMINOLOGY CONTROL IN THE BRITISH MUSEUM

Dr Lea D. Jones

Collections Data Management Section
The British Museum
London

Introduction

The Conservation database in the British Museum is in a stage of transition from a manual system to an automated one. In some respects this paper represents an interim statement about proposed intentions and current realities of the Conservation information system as a whole. However, the role of terminology within this system and its potential control will be given specific emphasis. A general introduction to terminology control in the British Museum can be found in Chapter 18.

The Conservation Department comprises six sections: Western Pictorial Art, Eastern Pictorial Art, Organics, Ceramics, Stone (including wall-paintings and mosaics) and Metals. The Conservation database is not merely a specialist system serving the needs of the Conservation Department, but also exists as a sub-system of the Museum's object database, constituting as it does a collections management resource.

Preparations for automation began ten years ago, with the intention of using the Research Laboratory computer, a Hewlett-Packard 1000 mini-computer running the Museum Documentation Association's GOS processing package. However, shortage of funds and man-power delayed a serious review and implementation of the proposed system. Recently, the Museum has purchased a new online system (a Prime 9955 Mark 2, running MAGUS). A fuller account of this system and the reason for its choice can be found in Jones and Allden (1988). This investment has stimulated a reassessment of the situation and preparations for automation have begun anew.

The present manual system, a legacy of the original preparations, represents an important phase in the institution of a uniform method of recording with, in theory, each section using the same type of document to record the same sort of information.

The conservation documentation system

The main documentation elements are divisable into *primary documentation* (Requisition form, Envelope and Treatment Card), providing very direct information about object treatment, and *secondary documentation* (Collection Surveys and Technical Reports) providing supportive information arising from object treatment or relating to the general management of systematic collections conservation. Briefly, the specific functions of the documents are as follows:

Requisition Form: notifies basic details about the object as issued from the Antiquities departments and acts as a receipt and invoice for the object as well as an authorisation from the curatorial staff for treatment to be undertaken;

Envelope: a filable container for documents associated with object treatment (e.g. Treatment Card, also photographs, samples, etc.);

Treatment Card: used to record details of object condition, composition, technique and materials used in treatment;

Collection Surveys: the result of systematic investigation and recording of the state and urgency of treatment required for the object collections. Intended to allow the curatorial staff to prioritise their demands on Conservation resources;

Technical Reports: information of interest noted during the treatment of the object. Offered to the curatorial staff for interest only.

Record structure

The mainstay of the Conservation database concerns the primary documentation. Although fields are provided for certain specific types of information, they most consistently relate to details of object identification (e.g. registration number) and description as received from the antiquities departments involved (e.g. object name, cultural/historical affiliation, etc.). However, as far as the recording of object treatment is concerned, there is a heavy emphasis on free-text within which keywords for tools, techniques and treatment materials are distinguished by underlining (once for materials and tools, twice for techniques). There is no standard, agreed list of terms to govern the choice of keywords.

Despite an apparent uniformity in the format for data recording, there is still a degree of variation in the ways in which individual Conservation Officers perceive the role of the fields involved and the type of data necessary for the work of their individual section. It is also apparent that some new fields are required, especially those dealing with time management and resource deployment.

In addition, other data requires a greater degree of definition and structure than is currently possible in the manual system. This is especially noticeable with the text field dedicated to object treatment, in which other categories of data have also been recorded, resulting in an unpredictable mix of subject matter within the free-text entry.

This illustrates that there is currently a problem in satisfying the needs, both during recording and recall, of six sections each occasionally generating very different types of data. In part, these idiosyncracies may be accommodated within one system by creating new, more appropriate fields within a global data structure, from which subsets may be selected to suit the needs of each section. Redundant fields can be removed from input screens at the same time that a core of common fields is retained, and the relationships of all fields within the technical structure can be preserved.

Terminology control

The role of free-text recording, particularly on the treatment card is one aspect which will have to be critically re-examined in the light of the automated system. The versatility of free-text, and accessibility to information described in natural language, is not matched by the specificity of data association and speed of retrieval. In addition, the ability of the individual Conservation Officer to discriminate between essential data, incidental observations of interest, and superfluous padding may become a handicap during recording. Indeed, during a recent systems analysis exercise a common complaint was that the quantity of text recorded often constituted an obtrusive and unwelcome corollary of object treatment. It is also, of course, a bulky method of information storage. In contrast, structured fields provide the dual advantages of speed of retrieval with the ability to control more tightly the type of information involved by the use of authority lists, and the potential breadth and flexibility of retrieval offered by thesauri. However, making coherent sense of the data is not so easily achieved from single words lacking necessary conjunctions of defined relationships with other data elements.

One remedy would be to accommodate both free-text and structured information within the record, but with the proviso that the free-text be used only to record the information not conveyable by single key-words (i.e. that which is incidental, supporting information not critical for specific retrieval). In this way the full integrity of the information may be preserved, without a significant loss of either data or user-friendliness.

Thesauri are being developed to control fields in the object collections database. Those governing composition and technique of manufacture already exist. The potential exists for these thesauri to be extended to accommodate the terminology of conservation materials and treatments. In other areas of the Conservation record, such as those specifically relating to object details, information may be available directly from the object collection database. Some object records are already in existence as a result of the Collections Data Management Section's (CDMS) activity in various departments around the Museum. Where and when these records exist, the object ID(s), the object name and other essentially object-oriented data will already be present within the System and in some cases, controlled by authority lists and thesauri.

The cross-section of object records available is dependent on CDMS progress within individual departments as well as throughout the Museum as a whole. It is planned that the necessary sections of these records will be referred to during the creation of Conservation records. In this way, terminology can be controlled without the necessity for entering the data afresh, and without duplicating data that already exists.

As far as the specific contents of the Conservation automated authority lists and thesauri are concerned, some foundations already exist. Standard lists are currently used governing brand names and their equivalent chemical formulae, a list of codes for techniques and specific material types, and a more complex series of relationships between materials and techniques for the Organics section. However, the provision of equivalent terms for brand names and chemical formulae raises the issue of synonyms and how this will be resolved within the general handling of a thesaurus.

The technical aspects of terminology control present few problems; its the actual substance of thesauri and authority lists that will provoke the greatest debate, especially between six sections which have had the opportunity to develop terminology in virtual independence during the past ten years. Terminology can only be rendered controllable if there is a consensus on definitions and applications in the first place. The six sections, dealing with different object compositions and treatment materials, will need a high degree of communication in order to remove some inevitable divergence of use and supposed content. Some flexibility exists to accommodate differences in opinion or usage through the facility to retrieve on non-preferred terms, although necessarily the dependent relationships will only be available via the preferred terms.

The mechanics of creating the relevant controls may be tackled in various ways. One method would be to enter the existing records, discriminating relevant keywords as they are defined within the manual system, and generating lists for amendment and discussion as a subsequent process. In this way, specific elements may be targeted as being either acceptable or otherwise, and the focus for discussion consequently more precise. Alternatively, where comprehensive manual lists exist they could form the basis of an independently constructed thesaurus or list. This has the advantage of providing online vetting facilities during initial data entry of the estimated 36 000 existing manual records. In this way, unvetted elements can be signalled for immediate attention. However, this may constitute a possible disadvantage, as immediate attention may not be available in order for the records to be satisfactorily completed on an *ad hoc* basis.

The next phase in automating the Conservation Department's records will be a pilot scheme, whereby a new record structure will be tested for its suitability. It is hoped that this will stimulate a greater awareness of the value and importance of terminology controls, not merely as a convenient adjunct to automated data entry, but as a means of communication that will define and describe the Conservation sections' varied specialisms.

XII
INTERNAL AND EXTERNAL USERS: WORKING WITH MUSEUM TERMINOLOGY

88 WORKING WITH MUSEUM TERMINOLOGY

D. Andrew Roberts

Museum Documentation Association
Cambridge

The following papers concentrate on the experience of a number of users of museum documentation systems and terminology facilities. These include an external system developer, two external users and two museum professionals.

Toni Petersen describes her impressions of the receptivity of museums to terminology control, based on her experience in developing the Art and Architecture Thesaurus. She is clearly concerned that museums have been slow to respond to the potential of AAT, showing less interest than colleagues in libraries, archives and pictorial collections.

Despite this, she argues very strongly that museums can and indeed must benefit from such cooperative schemes. Whether for use when developing databases or when sharing information she is convinced that the best standardised products will come from a community effort.

Michael Greenhalgh and Elizabeth Orna are both equally forceful in their conviction that museums must take more account of the needs of different types of users.

Taking the viewpoint of a user of art historical databases, Michael Greenhalgh is concerned with the need for flexible help facilities, including thesauri, and the value of image databases. Like later contributors (Chapters 95 and 97), he is concerned about the need to provide appropriate support for different types and level of user.

Similarly, Elizabeth Orna is concerned that users should be given direct access to documentation so that they can explore it themselves and thereby decide how to use the museum. Based on her experience in designing information systems, she argues that good terminology control facilities can be an important tool in helping users gain this type of entry into museum resources. She notes the importance of making a thesaurus seem invisible to the user and also the value of image-based facilities.

Based at the National Museum of American Art, Rachel Allen and Christine Hennessey both have experience in using the evolving collection and library documentation systems of the Smithsonian Institution.

Rachel Allen concentrates on the experience of moving records from one computer system to another, a process which has entailed a complete reappraisal of data and terminology standards. She illustrates the inter-relationship between a data dictionary and its component fields and data content, showing how field names can be transformed into data content as the new system model provides greater flexibility. She also stresses the importance of working towards long-term goals, such as providing shared access to information about collections across the whole Institution.

The aims of the Inventory of American Sculpture are described by Christine Hennessey. In assessing the needs of the project, its staff and potential users, it was recognised that access by medium or material was of crucial importance. In the absence of an existing media term list, the project has developed a new thesaurus to support effective retrieval. She stresses that the Inventory will only be successful if it serves the needs of its researchers and that a resource like the media thesaurus should help in this process.

89 CAN A STANDARDISED VOCABULARY MEET THE NEEDS OF MUSEUM STAFF AND OTHER INDEPENDENT TYPES? PRELIMINARY EXPERIENCES OF A VOCABULARY BUILDER

Toni Petersen
Director
Art and Architecture Thesaurus
Williamstown, Mass.

Introduction

Museums of all sizes and types of collections all over Europe and America are faced not only with automating elements of their cataloguing procedures, but at the same time must deal with the necessity of finding controlled vocabularies to use in their automated systems. Many are building their own vocabulary lists; others seek standardised vocabularies that are shared by a community of users.

The developing standardised vocabulary that I direct, the Art and Architecture Thesaurus (AAT), has a growing user group of well over 100 organisations, so we have acquired some experience in knowing where in the art community there has been the most use of controlled vocabularies. Interestingly enough, in our experience thus far it is the museum community that has been lagging behind in the use of standardised vocabularies. This paper will attempt to speculate why and to project where museums might be headed in this regard.

The application of a standardised vocabulary in a museum catalogue or database assures consistency of the data both for cataloguing and retrieval purposes, and allows for the sharing of information among institutions. An example may be in order here. The 5 000 000 records in the Canadian Heritage Information Network (CHIN) are a testimony to the success of a program that allows separate Canadian museums to input their collection records into a single network. The records as input reflect the cataloguing practices of each museum, with little coordination of vocabulary across museums.

Sharing space with one another on this network allows for real opportunity for other kinds of sharing as well, such as the sharing of information about each other's collections, without the bother of switching from one database program to another. But since there has been no use of standardised vocabularies across the museums, the retrieval of information is hampered. CHIN is now looking into using existing vocabularies like Nomenclature (Chapter 58) and the AAT (Chapter 56) as sort of frontend thesauri into their vast database of somewhat 'uncontrolled' records.

The Canadian Centre for Architecture, engaged in building an integrated database of records pertaining to bibliographic and archival materials, and photographs, prints, drawings and slides of architectural subjects, has taken an opposite tack to that of CHIN. It has spent several years investigating computer and cataloguing systems and has also expended a good deal of effort into identifying vocabulary sources before actually inputting full records into their database.

One could say that these two organisations provide a paradigm for the state of museum information today. We are all engaged in common tasks, with relatively common goals, yet most of us are going about it in different ways. Why then should I try to persuade you to consider the use of standardised vocabularies? I find myself thinking about the care that is given to the objects in museums, and what comes to mind is that information is like preservation. We all know of at least one museum, hardly worthy of the name, that has little idea how to preserve its collection; where wooden objects expand all through the hot and humid summer and contract and crack through the dry, artificially heated winter; where dust collects and workers leave coffee cup rings on pieces they have commandeered as temporary work stations. Can we jump to the assumption that the care they give their objects is similar to the way they manage information about those objects; that their registrarial and collections management records are cluttered, messy and inconsistent? And holding this analogy just a bit further, may I suggest that the care that goes into the production of a sound cataloguing record is as important, in the light of history and the needs of scholars, as the care with which the object is preserved. In other words, it is *good* for your object!

Museums and vocabulary control: the current state

My observation of what museum professionals are doing about automation and vocabulary control is that they are either diverting their own staff with the task of developing thesauri on their own, or that they are often leaving it up to the vendors of the many software packages being developed in this field. This is based on two factors in the experience of the AAT. The first is that although we receive many enquiries from individuals who are slide and photograph curators (some of whom are in museums), librarians and archivists, we have received relatively few from museum curators and registrars. The second is that every software vendor who exhibited at the 1988 annual conference of the American Association of Museums called our office to enquire whether they might display the AAT as part of their software packages. A couple of museum consultants working with specific vendors have also called to say that they are preparing a particular program for a museum and wonder whether the AAT might be mounted in the resulting cataloguing system. I am beginning to draw the conclusion that many museum professionals, for whatever reasons, are imposing a layer of computer system experts between themselves and their systems of vocabulary control and cataloguing.

There is nothing wrong with seeking expert advice and assistance in areas in which you have little or no experience, and for most of us, developing a computer system is one of them. Database programs are becoming more sophisticated, with artificial intelligence-like elements being applied to them, and vendors have a very important role to play in providing the necessary expertise to translate your institution's needs into a computer system that makes sense to you. But I wish to throw out the warning that it is a rare software vendor who has expertise in the areas of vocabulary control and thesaurus construction. Some may give the impression that storing and retrieving information can be made as simple as childs' play. Nothing could be further from the truth.

There are four functions of an automated cataloguing system: information preparation; description analysis and storage; indexing and cataloguing; and information retrieval. At every stage in this process, expert and intelligent human intervention is still acutely necessary. Even those working in the domains of natural language processing and knowledge representation systems, stress the importance of human indexing and cataloguing. To be sure they may be aided by expert systems doing the 'dumb' parts of the task, but the necessity for a lexicon or well-structured thesaurus to undergird the database, allowing for the application of rule-based expert systems to aid in indexing and retrieval becomes even more important in these sophisticated systems than in their simple predecessors. There is still no easy way for the computer to make sense of partial and inconsistent data. Compounding the problem is the fact that no matter how good a 'user-friendly' interface is, it cannot deal well with a heterogeneous user population. (Studies are showing that there is no homogeneous user population, by the way.) We are still in the infancy stage concerning research into how to provide for the lack of consistency in behaviour both by indexer/cataloguers and end users.

Software developers and vendors, valuable as they have been in museum automation projects, have provided the bare rudiments of vocabulary control. In most cases they simply generate lists of terms from the museum's own cataloguing or registrarial records. What are these records like? Unlike librarians, who have a long history of accepting vocabulary standards from outside sources, museum staff have maintained a certain independence in their use of terminology to describe objects in their collections. Perhaps it is because a history of adherence to vocabulary standards has simply not been there. Indeed, there has been no necessity even for a single curator to use consistent terminology when filling out the typical object card. A curator once told me that what he named an object depended on his mood on a particular day. Imagine this compounded by the number of curators within one institution; with curators who change over time; with curatorial records differing from registrarial records on the same object. With no history of vocabulary control within a single institution, there has been no incentive to provide community-wide standards. The exception that comes to mind is the support *Nomenclature* has been gathering in the United States, especially among history museums that are automating their collection records.

The lack of consistency in museum cataloguing applies to much of the data on museum records, not only to the names of objects. There has been a lack of consciousness about the need to make distinct the various parts of object descriptions that are retrievable items of information. If on one card a piece is called 'footed bowl' and on another a similar piece is described as 'bowl with bird feet', there is a problem. Imagine a computer-generated list of such terms, multiplied by the number of objects held in any one museum, and try to think about how you would make order out of it. How successful would natural language free-text searching be? There are other examples of problem areas. Do you want to keep terms like 'footed' rather than the noun form 'feet'? Do you want to be specific enough to maintain records of what kind of feet? Should the fact that the piece is footed remain an integral part of the object name, or should the footness be expressed in a separate item in the cataloguing record? What other parts of description should be singled out for retrieval: how about materials, process or technique, style, condition, subject matter, manufacturer, artist? The list can go on and on.

There is nothing magic about the word lists generated by vendors selling museum automation programs, nor are they immediately helpful in solving consistency and retrieval problems. They are, however, useful as a tool in the first stage of bringing some order to the use of vocabulary by the museum staff, but on the other hand, there are few museums that can afford the time in staff resources to build a genuinely useful thesaurus out of such lists. Having seen some of them, I know it would be daunting on the part of an individual institution to take on the task of ordering their vocabulary. It requires more than normalising spelling and choosing a single term for identical concepts.

I hope I have not implied in my previous statements that curators take no care in their cataloguing records. I am aware of the amount of scholarly labour that goes on, but I think that the emphasis is on describing the piece in hand, noting its condition, researching its provenance and how it matches up to similar pieces in other collections. The emphasis is not on the words used to name and describe it. And of course, here is the rub. The computer does not care about the depth of scholarly research or the particular scholarly judgement about a piece. It does care very much about the words chosen to be used about that piece and how they are identified in the computer record. In other words, it is here that the fields of thesaurus construction and cataloguing directly intersect with museum curatorship.

Building controlled vocabularies for museums

Where *should* the vocabularies needed for museum cataloguing come from? Despite what has been said above, those lists generated from museums should indeed provide the initial gathering for a controlled vocabulary to be used in museum object cataloguing. The operative word here, though, is 'initial', for I believe very strongly in the standardisation of vocabulary. And in order to build a standardised vocabulary, one has to engage in a community effort.

Both *Nomenclature* and the AAT are products of such community efforts. Community enters into the standardisation effort in a number of ways. Firstly, the original terminology should be gathered from existing sources: from the community of users. The sources will be museum catalogue records as well as published sources. Secondly, the terms should be analysed and put through a rigorous authority control process that chooses the likeliest preferred term, identifies synonyms and variant spellings, and sets the term within a context of broader and narrower terms. Thirdly, the resulting thesaurus should be reviewed by advisory groups of users and scholars to make sure it represents the needs of the entire community of users. Fourthly, a stable organisation should be put together that will undertake to maintain the vocabulary in the long term, to disseminate changes and updates, and to ensure its stability over time. Without this last feature, a vocabulary becomes stagnant and irrelevant, and eventually its usefulness will wither and die.

If the vocabulary is strongly built and structured well, the community of users stands to gain a great deal, especially if their own vocabulary is assimilated into the larger product and if they may continue to suggest new terminology to be added as needed. There will be a significant comfort factor, when filling out a computer cataloguing workform, to having a well-structured list of terms from which to choose, instead of having to search one's mind for relevant descriptive terms. The thesaurus will also provide lead-in terms, or synonyms, already laid out, and in those systems that integrate thesauri with cataloguing records, the synonyms will be automatically generated.

Hierarchically structured thesauri like the AAT will lay out in a conceptual array terms that are broader and narrower than the original term chosen, allowing the cataloguer to browse the list up and down and to find a term that is perhaps even more pertinent to the piece at hand. And of course, one might assume that if a community of users is all applying terms from a single source, terminology within and among museums would be consistent. Retrieval of information would be enhanced and sharable.

What do museums lose, if anything, to join this community effort? There is the time it takes to find one's way around a large and complex thesaurus, and one has to learn how it is structured and how to apply its rules for term combination. There may be terms in it that are not relevant for one's own collection. There may also be some delay when the thesaurus being used does not have the particular term that is needed. There can be a lack of effective two-way communication in place for the receipt of new vocabulary, and for the dissemination of changes to users. Responsiveness on the part of a standardised vocabulary is a crucial element to maintaining satisfaction among its users.

Another disadvantage might be having to adhere to the accepted way of referring to a concept or object. However, computerisation holds out the promise that an institution using a standardised vocabulary may still have freedom of choice in the form of a particular term, if its computer system can provide an adequate switching mechanism between the term preferred in the thesaurus, and the term chosen by the institution, and as long as the chosen term appears as a synonym in the thesaurus.

This last point might be especially important in the context of an international community where a standardised vocabulary, especially one in American English like the AAT, may not at all meet the needs of its European, or even its French-Canadian neighbours. In order for the sharing of information to occur on an international level, there will be an urgent need for the linking of standardised thesauri across languages. Creating bilingual or multilingual thesauri is an especially difficult task, requiring the expertise of linguists as well as scholars in particular subject areas who are fluent in the language being translated as well as the language being translated into. It becomes critical to agree on definitions of terms, and to work out a methodology for dealing with instances where there are terms in one language which have no equivalent in the other.

In spite of these difficulties, are there advantages to be gained by the use of standardised vocabularies in the museum community? Perhaps I may be forgiven for backing into the answer to this question by referring to the interest shown by museum systems vendors in supplying controlled vocabularies to their museum clients. It is clear that at the most elementary level, museum professionals are faced with the problem of the need for consistency and control over many of the data elements they must provide in their automated catalogues. Some museum professionals have also expressed the desirability of individuals from different departments within a museum coming together over issues like standardising vocabulary within their institution, with a new spirit of collegiality emerging as a positive result. Beyond this first goal of building a database from which information can be easily and successfully retrieved within a single institution, there is the benefit to be gained from being able to share information with other institutions, even across national and linguistic barriers.

The terminology conference clearly showed the eagerness with which museum professionals are approaching the difficult task of controlling terminology. It also showed that at present we are preparing a seething cauldron of individually chosen or produced ingredients. I do not think any of us is willing to predict whether the end product will be a delicious stew, or a pot of stone soup.

---

90 A USER VIEW OF ART DATABASES

Michael Greenhalgh

Australian National University
Canberra

Introduction

Art history has long been a leading area for humanities computerisation: by 1984, for example, there were no less than 162 projects connected with the subject (Corti, 1984). What is more, the subject is amenable to the use of various kinds of graphics, and hence to a deep involvement with the various technologies involved (Kirsch, 1984). But many difficulties have been encountered with computerisation, and are perhaps endemic when the technology moves fast, and when there are large collections — whether of bibliographical or pictorial data — to be entered.

This paper assesses the prospects for databases in the discipline from the point of view of the *user*, who may well not understand the system, and who is to be distinguished from the information professionals to whose needs many current systems are unfortunately geared. It examines the inadequacies of many of the help systems currently available by looking at database hosts and the bibliographical databases they support. Mindful of the dilemma of the bewildered user who will surely need to consult *several* databases, it suggests alternatives and improvements (including better access to terminology controls) based around the standardisation of elements of the user interface, rather than at the data level.

Those databases which generally have to pay their way by selling their data, may provide an overview of difficulties which art historical databases, many of them still at the project stage, also face. Deiss (1988) has identified the following universal problems with online systems:

> As compared to card catalogs, the content and extent of the online database is not apparent: parts of it become visible only in response to appropriate search strategies. When searches are conducted by librarians on behalf of researchers, the researcher is dependent on the librarian's expertise *and* on his or her interpretation of the researcher's requirements. Remote from the data, and at a remove from the search process, the researcher cannot be certain that the results (if any) are the product of an adequate search. Only first class performance, enabled by subject knowledge as well as technical proficiency, involving imagination and serendipity, and facilitated and sustained by sympathetic management, will inspire confidence in online reference services.

To add to the confusion, the same data are sometimes available under *different* software control.

It should go without saying that the database of the future will *not* be the preserve of the library professional or information scientist; as machines get cheaper and software smarter, everyone will want to do their own searching, reporting and cloning into sub-sets. It is a matter for dismay that, in so many existing online systems, albeit experimental ones, modern technology in the form of the CD-ROM is coupled with outdated and restrictive searching facilities, and poor help facilities (Helgerson, 1986).

Boyles (1987 and 1988) has added more difficulties that are specific to art history, namely limited subject coverage, poor retrospective indexing of the literature, inadequate currency in the indexing, lack of coordination among the services, and vocabulary difficulties. These are of course but a microcosm of the bigger world of information systems, which some see as facing critical problems.

The limited subject coverage is improving (with online versions of RILA, RAA, etc.), while the poor retrospective indexing and inadequate currency are probably a reflection of the speed with which computerisation has come upon us. Boyles identifies lack of coordination (and its off-shoot, vocabulary difficulties) as the major problem with existing working systems. RILA and ARTbibliographies Modern, being on DIALOG, require a different search strategy from the Art Index. And RILA (some parts) and ARTbibliographies Modern require different terminology and formats. He concludes (Boyles, 1988, page 30):

> A gateway system which is developed to help search an entire databank like DIALOG cannot possibly handle the individual quirks of each database and must, therefore, allow only broad searches that homogenize the databases by ignoring the details. Gateway systems that attempt to span databanks can only be more simplistic. CD-ROM systems that give access to a few databases [. . .] increase the problem of multiplicity of access methods.

As for vocabulary, he suggests that:

> Computer systems demand a precise usage of language, a precision that art, based upon nonverbal communication, does not readily provide. Unfortunately, users are notorious for employing terminology that is either too broad (producing too much) or too narrow (producing too little, if anything).

In other words, large-scale working implementations such as the hosts sometimes seem to lack those very facilities which anyone with a personal computer would demand and indeed find in micro packages, whether shareware or bought.

The importance of flexible help facilities

There is no more a 'typical' art historian than there is a 'typical' museum collection, and the purposes to which computerised databases of art works may be put are equally various — although they *all* share problems unlikely to be speedily resolved (Greenhalgh, 1987). This is because art history is itself a very diverse subject: Jacques Thuillier describes it as 'a discipline which has neither unity, nor homogeneous multiplicity [. . .] brings together a series of domains of different natures' — and he instances objects, narrative accounts, original sources, analyses, judgements, techniques, etc. (Thuillier, 1987). But there are further difficulties with the myth of the 'typical user'. If, in the past, computerisation has been 'focused', this seems to have been done with museum personnel or computer experts in mind — which is no help to the art historian in the street (which is where such arrangements tend to leave him). What is more, different people believe they have different needs, such as indexing on free-text; an irregular (and changeable) record length; repeating groups; different treatment for the great variety of art matters — patrons, painters, prints, etc. — and the documents they involve. Such diversity in set-up and audience (which is no less than one might expect of *any* group of users, perhaps) has decided implications for the way in which the data are presented to the user (the *user interface*) and the way in which they are stored and manipulated (the database and its associated language).

One lesson for the art historical database world is that the user interface — whatever form it may take — can smooth out at least some of the inconsistencies in the search strategies of some of the programs that might lie underneath it. Although there is a wide variety of online help systems available, and research in the field is lively, many of them are antiquated and based on the needs of programmers rather than ordinary users. The main difficulty is that the database designer cannot easily anticipate the problems the user — whoever he is — is likely to encounter.

There are two basic reasons for this, the one to do with the nature of searching itself, the other with both the nature and extent of desirable help facilities. For not only is it difficult to avoid intellectual ambiguities (Schwartz, 1986–87), but 'users feel unable to specify what they want because they don't know what is possible' (Oliver and Langford, 1987, page 114). This may be related to observed cases of beginners doing badly even with online help aids. With some online systems, indeed, one sometimes gets the feeling not only that the help facilities are something of an afterthought, but also that the person specifying them is none too familiar with *how* a database works, let alone how a beginner perceives it *might* work — which is why some knowledge of programming (even of the easy database language kind, that the database program constructs for you) can surely help to oil the wheels (Greenhalgh, 1986). Another avenue is the development of interfaces that benefit from research in expert systems, and can actually offer advice.

A related problem is that it is often difficult to judge just how successful search strategies are. This is a highly technical matter, but it does seem to be the case that, for example, natural-language *automatic* indexing of documents in text-retrieval systems performs significantly better than controlled language *manual* indexing — given the swings and roundabouts results as between recall and precision. From a test conducted by NASA in the mid-70s with 100 queries on 44 000 documents, 'it is certainly not possible to conclude that searches of natural-language abstracts are inferior, in general, to controlled language indexing. [There are] recall advantages of over 20 per cent compared to the manual system' (Salton, 1986).

In most cases, it is probable that one particular help strategy will be insufficient to cater for the majority of users. In the future, command line querying must surely co-exist with the menu approach, probably implemented as windows — which is essential to some, and tedious to others. Menus can, after all, be enlivened with graphics. I can see no reason why *both* methods should not co-exist with others (such as Query By Example), given that *all* querying methods have advantages and disadvantages. Again, the promised 'fifth generation' database management system is predicted not only to use the relational model, but also to offer interfaces such as expert systems using natural language, access through forms, and navigation through images, all conceivably rule-based. In France, for example, work is afoot on EXPRIM, an EXPert system to retrieve IMages (Crehange, *et al.*, 1984), which will include a work station, a pictorial base, a descriptive base, a database management system, and an expert system and knowledge base to drive the system. And for two of its databases, the Library of Congress is using INTELLECT, which employs a keyword-parser and a user-customised lexicon with software to convert from natural language to the formal database query language (Warner, 1988).

Help facilities: the thesaurus

One aspect of help facilities is the thesaurus, which sometimes seems to be thought of exclusively as a tool for data entry. The construction of thesauri can today be largely automated, although as with user interfaces, anybody who needs to use thesauri is often hampered by the technology: 'we are using models developed a generation ago — in the 50s and 60s — to meet the challenge of new and rapidly developing information retrieval technologies' (Petersen, 1984, page 55). What is more, I have looked in vain for evaluations of different types or sizes of thesauri, for the matter seems to interest neither librarians nor statisticians, for 'little has been written recently on the general process of constructing and evaluating thesauri' (Schwartz and Esienman, 1986). This is perhaps a matter for surprise, because 'little is known about the consistency among indexers of visual materials' (Markey, 1983, page 361; Markey, 1984). But the problem is a complicated one — much more so than the 'blockbuster' methods of concordancing or dictionary construction — which explains why automatic thesaurus construction continues to be a live topic at conferences. Solutions need to be found, especially for full-text systems.

Indeed, some recent research suggests that the very concept of *le mot juste* in thesaurus construction *might* be misdirected: thus Gomez and Lochbaum (1985) experimenting with computer-naive people, found that:

> information systems with many different and not necessarily unique names for each system object will dramatically increase the likelihood of finding a target object over more standard retrieval systems in which each target has only one or a few names [. . .] those people using systems with richly-indexed vocabularies needed slightly fewer, rather than more, key-word entries to find a given target object'.

What is more:

> contrary to some naive expectations, we have shown that providing users with a word-aid list did not improve target identification.

Hence automatic thesaurisation could probably be a decided help in the recommended path of what is called 'unlimited aliasing' by some, and 'the side-of-a-barn principle' by others. In Markey's opinion, 'Online computerized information retrieval is the only practical way to provide satisfactory keyword indexing of visual resources' subject matter' (Markey, 1986, pages 148–49). A profusion of terms is *not* the same as a structured thesaurus; and it remains to be seen whether the online version of the Art and Architecture Thesaurus, or the new classification and indexing system being designed for the *Repertoire d'Art et D'Archeologie* and RILA: Lucker (1988) notes that 'it is far from clear that using just one source or the other will suffice: rather, it is likely that the best option will be to use both thesauri'.

Furthermore, the question must be asked: when is a thesaurus 'ready'? This is an aspect of computerisation that worries me, and I present it as a variation on the 'chicken and egg' conundrum: how can one test a thesaurus without a large working database to practice upon, and how can one test a database without a large working thesaurus?

A new type of user interface: Hypertext

In our search for ways of improving the user interface of databases, we can look for hints to recent micro-based productions. This is entirely logical, for micros were developed for *users*, and not for *programmers*. Commonly available facilities on today's micros include help with authority lists at data entry time, switchable on-screen help, including a 'tutor' mode, and, not far in the future, the non-linear text-and-graphical resources of Hypertext.

Hypertext makes use of both natural language test and the computer's capacity for interactive branching. It is also user-definable. Not surprisingly, therefore, it has been suggested that Hypertext is the direction to go in order to provide better user interfaces: the help screens can be moved around, and the system provides not only different levels of detail, but also navigation aids and pop-up explanations. And because Hypertext can express both relations and hierarchies, perhaps the concept might be employed to display graphically the intricacies of thesauri, which *also* have these features. Using Hypertext, lower levels of each hierarchy are easily suppressed (for clarity's sake) if the need arises; and the user can choose the terms required because Hypertext screens can be *interactive*. Two additional advantages (besides the support of standard windowing operations) are that the user can create new windows ('nodes'), and also that these can if necessary be graphical. One thinks of the Italian 'blue books' for data entry of the national treasures, with drawings of the range of items (e.g. the various elements of medieval armour) so that each can be correctly identified and the correct terminology employed. Hypertext illustrations could short-cut this procedure. But the supreme advantage of Hypertext is its *generality* for, in essence, Hypertext is *itself* a database, which need not be linked to the art-works database on top of which it would sit. It therefore offers a facility similar to that of the Structured Query Language (SQL) — namely that of a consistent and simple user interface. It is certainly arguable that the success of the Apple Macintosh is due as much to its consistent user interface (across *all* programs from system files to applications) as it is to its bit-mapped graphics.

Of course, more or less elaborate extensions to the above types of user interface aids are possible. Thus Bates (1986) proposes a FSM (for *Front-end System Mind*) to help the computer-naïve with browsing. She distinguishes between an *indexer* thesaurus and a *user* thesaurus, specifying that the latter must include 'a vast entry vocabulary, including very colloquial terms, to help the searcher get started' — this being necessary because of the mismatch between the restricted indexer 'set' and the broader user 'set' of terms. As she admits (Bates, 1986, page 97), 'end user thesauri could actually have been developed a hundred years ago for library catalogs. We have helped ourselves locate terms for cataloguing by providing indexer thesauri for ourselves, but we have not done as much for the poor users, who must think up the right search terms all by themselves'.

Such difficulties underneath the surface, so to speak, can be smoothed out by using the relational model of database, which makes a canonical separation between physical and *logical* views of the data and, unlike the hierarchical model, does not impose a user view upon the data. This separation between the data itself and the programs which manipulate them means that *one* HELP system keyed to *one* Data Manipulation Language (which must be some variety of SQL because it is well established and popular) can be valid across a range of packages. More and more this is a version of SQL, originally a mainframe language, but for which there are now no less than six versions available under MS-DOS; and work is constantly afoot to make this interface more user-friendly for beginners — a language that, like SQL itself, would be as universal as the database packages that used it.

A similar approach to the same problem is to use semantics techniques; these could either build a good help facility on top of SQL which would produce good error messages and trap erroneous queries, or act as a 'pre-processor' for query optimisation. A slightly different one is to build, specifically for casual users and straightforward queries, a pseudo-intelligent front-end retrieval system that would be *separate* from any specific database, although oriented to the relational model.

Help from videodisks

It has long been considered desirable — and not just in the art works or museum areas — to link pictures with databases (Blaser, 1980). For although videodisks present great organisational, copyright and hence financial problems of enregistration, they offer the prospect of easy access to large quantities of images or text, and are therefore of the greatest interest to all of us (Greenhalgh, 1982), firstly with museums and libraries, for obvious reasons, and then University and college art and art history departments (Cash, 1985; Nyerges, 1983; Hausman, 1986; Montevecchi and Papaldo, 1987; Sorkow, 1983; and Sustik, 1981). Many experiments, over the last few years, have demonstrated the advantages of this technology (Laurent, 1983; Okun, 1984) so that there are now sufficient videodisks and CD-ROMs (in many fields) to fill directories — although the searching problems endemic to online systems still exist. Because of the expense, however (Hastings, 1986), only well-funded (and usually large) projects can afford to experiment with videodisk enregistration, the very organisation of which can itself require a database, as with the Warburg/Hertziana project.

A decided difficulty for projects just beginning is that this is a technology which is still developing (McQueen and Boss, 1986). Competing with present-day analog videodisks and CD-ROMs are optical digital data disks (OD3s for short), which are analogous to the CD-ROM but store much more, and can be written by the user, either in 'digital' or in 'captured image' form. In the near future, the erasable compact disk will provide still greater flexibility, helped perhaps by better compression algorithms. At present, the CD-ROM would seem to be the natural solution for the storage of digitised image data (such as works of art), except that capacities — at about 5 000 video image frames — are too low in comparison with analog encoding, which manages 108 000 images. Fortunately, help is at hand, for development work is proceeding on a compact videodisk that would allow an *analog* channel and a separate *digital* channel on the same disk.

With such high-storage and user-writable technologies, we may envisage the databases of the future with text linked to visual data, and the latter available in OD3-packs, ten or 20 platters to a pack: speed of access to any image in the pack would be very fast, but network transmission could be very slow. One answer already suggested is that, properly exploited, networking software together with relational databases, and all using variants of SQL, can abolish the need for any large, central and monolithic database: sets of files can easily be created, stored and maintained in *different* locations (with relevant specialisms), to be accessed, manipulated and even downloaded by users onto their own machine for further processing (Roberts, H. E., 1985). Indeed, the very availability of such technologies *should* enable database designers to short-cut some of the labour-intensive (and storage-intensive) data entry and data description procedures current today (including the construction of thesauri), because the ability to access relevant images quickly should mean that a less detailed description of the data object will suffice (Shatford, 1984). In this respect as in others, a picture *should* be worth a thousand words.

Conclusion

I have taken it for granted in this paper that *all* users need gradated help, and I believe that this is the direction to which help systems should look. Although museums may well develop computerised and even videodisk systems for in-house use, user needs *must* be addressed if such expensive technologies are to 'pay' for themselves by being widely distributed. Hence system designers should first consider who the system is *for* and, if for everyone, design the required flexibility into the user interface. I would even venture to suggest that designers should *begin* with the user (rather than with the data), and continue to ask: who will use the database(s), and in what way(s)?

I suspect that some current institutional schemes are propelled by delusions of grandeur, often linked to notions of national prestige: the motto is not 'Keep it simple', but rather 'Make it complicated' – presumably on the assumption that a computer can deal with anything thrown at it. Their conception, though admirable, can therefore take either a far too inflexible 'user view', or a far too complicated one — which goes against the evidence of what users want and expect.

Fortunately, several institutions have already learned their lesson from the burdens (of time, effort and money) they have incurred in the attempt to computerise everything in great detail, and we can hope that future launches will be informed by a more realistic appreciation of the possible fruits to be derived from the time-scales available. Other mistakes have been made as well, the most serious of which is to cement one's data into hierarchical and specially written software. It is, of course, very easy to come along and criticise, pointing out solutions which were not available when projects were begun: if we waited for ever, everything would certainly be perfect. The important things in any database, text and/or visual, is the *data*: if it can be gathered and preserved with as few structuring decisions as possible, then succeeding generations can do what they will with it. But if we impose *our* view and hence *our* structure on it, we will tend to tie the data to specific systems of computer software and hardware so closely that disentangling it will prove difficult.

It is for these reasons that I propose the relational model as the only one to preserve our data for the future in 'neutral' format; digitised images as the best way to preserve visual information; and a panoply of help facilities as the best way of doing what databases *should* be there for, namely making the data available to the users — whoever they may be, and at whatever level of expertise.

All the above might easily be encapsulated in a set of principles, maxims and related comments. I suggest the main principles in any database project (whatever the subject area) are as follows:

planning and administration are of the essence;
understand computers as well as the subject area, or you may be misled;
conduct trials with data and potential users, and ascertain what the database is *for;*
use a relational package which supports SQL.

The maxims are:

users want one viable authority list (thesaurus, or whatever) for each area — not ten;
terminology is not a theology, but a severely practical matter which *should* be minimalist, and not an end in itself;
nobody wants an unfinished database; and
dismiss megalomania, for the computer is a tool, and should not become a bucket.

Suitably cynical comments, all heard at the conference were:

for every simple problem there is a complicated solution;
you can sit around all day talking about terminology controls, but sooner or later reality catches up with you; and
Linnaeus created a taxonomy, but he did not have to live with it.

91 HELPING USERS TO COME TO TERMS WITH THE DOCUMENTATION

Elizabeth Orna

Orna/Stevens Consultancy
Norwich, Norfolk

Asked what he would undertake first,
Were he called upon to rule a nation,
Confucius replied: 'To correct language . . .
If language is not correct,
Then what is said is not what is meant,
Then what ought to be done remains undone;
If this remains undone, morals and art will deteriorate;
If morals and art deteriorate, justice will go astray;
If justice goes astray,
The people will stand about in helpless confusion.'

from Heathcote Williams, 'Mokusatsu'
(reproduced in *Sanity*, August 1988)

Introduction

Unlike most of the authors represented in this volume, I write from a position outside the museum world, as a visitor to museums, who sees them both 'front of house' and 'back-stage'. In respect of museums, I am therefore an amateur, in all senses of the word. On the other hand, I am a professional in the use of words, especially the use of words to help people to find the information they need.

I have been interested in the application of this aspect of information management to museums, since the days when few people within the museum profession had considered the importance of terminology. It is gratifying that the situation has so far changed as to attract a wide audience to a conference on terminology, and to make a volume of the proceedings worth publishing.

The thesis of this paper

The argument I advance in this paper is twofold: I argue, first, that users should be helped to use documentation for themselves, so that they can make their own decisions about how to use museums; and, second, that terminology control, if properly used, can be a useful tool in helping them to do this.

Definitions

It is necessary first to clarify the terms used in these arguments.

Users: There are two main groups. First, those who *come* with a question in mind, which they have formulated in specific or general terms. They may be learned researchers, or the most general of general public, or anything in between. Second, those who do not arrive with a question, but who become interested to the point where what they encounter in a museum may lead them to want to know more, and to formulate questions.

Documentation: This term covers everything that represents the museum's resources, gives information about them, and points users to the actual objects. The medium can be print on paper, electronic on-screen display, or audio-visual.

First questions

It is now necessary to ask and answer some questions about users and documentation.

What does museum documentation represent for the users I have defined?

It represents, in potential, a store, which may have just the goods they are looking for: something that will answer a question, promote an interest, prompt and answer questions.

What do they want to experience when they use the store?

Continuing the metaphor of using a store, it is probably fair to say that users want to be able to:

come in through their own particular concerns;

move freely through the store;

see what it offers that meets their requirements;

pick up the goods they want;

come out again with them quickly, ready to get on with their own interest, or move on easily to find new things.

What will displease them?

Finding no entrance that matches their own interest;

Being offered information that is irrelevant to their question, mixed up with that which is relevant and of use to them, and having to undertake tedious sifting in order to find what they want.

Emerging empty-handed from the store.

What features of documentation operate to create these negative experiences?

The commonest cause is probably still documentation that does not provide enough 'ways in' to the would-be user: from collections which offer only an accessions list, and perhaps a donor index, to those which have a classification but lack the index to it which is indispensable for productive use.

If there is no more than a single list arranged in accession order, users are under the painful necessity of scanning from start to finish to see if there is anything that matches their needs. If there is a classification, and a single set of records arranged according to it, that is good news for those whose interest runs with the grain of the classification, but it is not much help to those whose frame of reference cuts across that of the classification. Imagine, for instance, trying to find photographs of housing conditions in a particular area at a given period of time, in a museum of photography where the main classification is by techniques, and the only supplement to it is an index of photographers.

This is the problem identified more than a century ago by Antonio Crestadoro (1856) at the British Museum library:

'How can an alphabetical Catalogue on the existing plan of joint inventory and index, or one entry and one heading, satisfy inquirers that seek the same book from different data, and for different purposes? . . . Freedom is, in all things, an essential condition of growth and power. The purposes of readers in search of a book are as manifold as the names and subjects, or headings under which the book may be traced. Entering the book only once is giving but one of its many references and suppressing the remainder; — it is serving the purpose of one reader and defeating that of others. So far the book is withdrawn from the public, its light is extinguished and destroyed.'

His words are as valid today as when they were written, and as relevant to museums as to libraries.

If that particular obstacle is removed, by using technology that allows multiple ways in to the documentation — as it can be, for example, by means of information retrieval software that permits free-text searching on multiple criteria — another is liable to take its place. The new difficulty arises from the sheer richness and variety of language.

There are so many possible ways of describing things and of expressing concepts, that, even when we have a tireless electronic slave that will find any word or phrase we ask for, what it brings us may be only a fraction of what is relevant. This disappointing performance will happen if some records which we would find useful do not contain the *exact* words we have asked for. Alternatively, what the electronic slave presents us with may be quite irrelevant; that will be the case when the people who created the records have used our words in quite a different sense from that in which we intended them; consider, for example, the meanings which differing specialisms attach to such words as 'wardrobe' or 'terrier'.

This is a kind of difficulty that has, in the past, often not been appreciated by the designers of the technology. The situation is getting better with modern text-based systems, most of which allow some facilities for controlling the terminology. The more recent image-based systems, however, still offer little help in finding all the relevant images.

What can we do with words to help the users?

Having reached this point, let me now ask, and try to answer, the main question: What can we do to make words help rather than hinder the users of museum documentation?

The nature of the help is fairly easy to define. We need to help users:

to get from the words they use to *all* the things they need, whether or not the words they use are the same as the ones used in the records;

to find exactly what they want at the *most precise level* of detail they need, without having to sift through a lot of things that are irrelevant to their needs;

to find everything relevant to a *generally formulated interest*, without having to guess at the detailed elements that make it up;

to remind them of *related* things that may also be useful.

Cost-effective ways of giving the help users need

These are the standard kinds of help that thesauri seek to give; they do it by providing a strongly structured terminology, with well thought out links between terms, and guidance on using them. The interesting and difficult question is: What is the cheapest and most effective way of helping:

the people who create the documentation to use tools of terminology control to help the users?

the users to put their questions and take control in their interactions with the documentation?

You will note that I say the *users* have to take control: it is the *terminology* that has to be controlled, not the users, and the mechanism of terminology control should be invisible to them. It should help them unobtrusively and never on any account should it give them negative or incomprehensible messages.

Helping the people who create the documentation

Many forms of help with terminology control are already available in existing commercially available software for the people who create this documentation. But they are not all brought together in an easily usable form, particularly one which could be applied in medium to small museums without documentation specialists.

My own list of desirable features for software is on these lines:

it should allow you to integrate the building and use of a thesaurus with the creation of records;

it should let you link as many entry (non-preferred) terms as you wish to relevant index (preferred) terms, so that they can be used interchangeably. This means that when you are creating records, the software will let you use any of the entry terms, and will index the record with *both* that term and the relevant index term; and when any one of a group of terms linked in this way is input as a search term, the software will retrieve records containing any of the terms, starting from the ones where the term actually input has been used in indexing;

the software should allow you to set up authority lists for different fields, and to call up in a window the lists for different fields (for example, periods of time, or materials) as you are creating records. Then you should be able to scan through them, and key Enter for the ones relevant to the record you are working on, so that the software automatically assigns them as index terms for it.

Apart from making the software kinder to the people who have to use it in creating records, there is another urgent need. That is for more off-the-peg smallish thesauri for specific subject areas. They should be available in machine-readable as well as hard-copy form, and museums could buy them and extend them to meet their own needs, rather than facing the problem of starting to compile a thesaurus from scratch, which usually means never starting at all.

Helping the end users to take control

So much for developments that would help the creators of documentation to help the end users. What are the possibilities for direct help to the end users, so that they can take control of their own searches for information?

Large museums with resources to match their size should be able to offer an online public access catalogue, based on a really well-designed and powerful information retrieval system, with carefully planned links to a videodisc system, all held together by a well-concealed thesaurus that will unobtrusively help users to get to the right place, without alarming them. Some steps have already been taken in this direction. A solution on these lines has been pioneered at the Prins Hendrik Maritime Museum in Rotterdam (Vries, 1987 and personal communication). The Musée D'Orsay in Paris has in operation a database of images, text and sound; these are linked by a thesaurus, with what are

Figure 91.1 A public index, based on an 'invisible' thesaurus

```
Lets you go direct from a non-preferred term to all the
information about the subject:

PRESTEL                        1992410a          0p
Occ - Oce                      Subject Index

10 Occupational guidance
   (CAREERS GUIDANCE)
11 Occupational health
   (SAFETY AT WORK)
12 Occupational information
   (CAREERS GUIDANCE)


Shows you detailed terms under their 'parent' terms
as well as individually in their own place in the
alphabetical list

PRESTEL                        1991830a          0p
Bui - Bul                      Subject Index

10 BUILDING
11    BUILDING SERVICES
12       AIR CONDITIONING
13       HEATING
14       PLUMBING
```

described as 'consultation programs accessible to the public', making use of the powerful facilities of BASIS software (Anon., 1987).

The systems being developed in some museums in the UK should ultimately make it possible to apply this approach, especially where there is already an emphasis on careful structure of information, technology under users' control, and users determining for themselves the direction they want to take in seeking information.

Using a thesaurus without frightening the users

I emphasise again how important it is to make terminology control unobtrusive; a thesaurus in all its glory is an alarming creation, even for some information professionals, let alone the general public. We therefore have to find ways of making its benefits available without revealing the works.

My own experience with designing indexes for a public videotex system suggests that people untrained in the techniques of information search find it reasonably easy to cope with an index based on a thesaurus, with very simple displays of related terms and more precise terms. The Prestel subject index is of this kind (Figure 91.1), and it also allows users to select any term — including non-preferred ones — and to go direct to the relevant records (Orna, 1986). The practical solution adopted by the Prins Hendrik Museum in Rotterdam is on the same lines (Vries, personal communication).

The visual thesaurus

There is one other desirable development, which could help museum users greatly: a thesaurus that combines text and images, so that it is possible to move from words to related images, from images to related images, and from images to related words, as well as from words to related words. Not only is it desirable, it is also feasible; the technology, in the form of software and hardware which permit this kind of linkage of words and images is now available, and, more important, a number of people are working on the problems. The solution will not be an easy one, because of the intellectual difficulty of structuring the information so that the possibilities of navigation allow users to move constructively, without becoming lost.

Respect for the customers' interests

This has been a rather speedy tour of some developments that I think could help users to make good use of museum documentation for their own purposes and on their own terms. If it has seemed too oriented towards the technology, let me now correct that.

The real essential is that museum professionals should try to put themselves in the place of the widest range of potential users when they look at their collections. Then they should think how they can manage the information and use the terminology so as to allow users to find their own ways in, even if their ways of looking at the material are very different from the museum's own conception of what it is there for. Curators saying 'We're not there to serve people who are looking for X, *we're* a museum of Y' can be doing a disservice to their institution by taking a wilfully narrow view, and the people who are looking for X may have the key to new and exciting ways of looking at the collections it contains.

That kind of failure to respect the interests of the customers is not confined to the 'old-fashioned' curators who think the museum exists for them and their scholarly pursuits, and regard the public as a tiresome distraction. It is implicit, in an even more dangerous form, at the other extreme, in those museums which are dedicated to 'outreach' and 'integration with the community', which are public relations-conscious, and keen on high-tech information retrieval, but still regard the public as, in Eilean Hooper-Greenhill's words (1987), 'passive recipients of the museum's work'. That prevents them from seeing that their use of technology should include resources for exercising skills in managing information and using terminology, so as to give their public the means of controlling for themselves what they get out of the museum's riches.

It is only when museum professionals start trying to put themselves in the place of the people who come in through the front door that terminology and the means of using it creatively and helpfully takes on its true significance.

---

92 COMING TO TERMS WITH A NEW DATA STRUCTURE

Rachel M. Allen

Acting Chief, Research Support
National Museum of American Art
Smithsonian Institution
Washington, DC

Introduction

Since 1971 and the establishment of the Inventory of American Paintings Executed before 1914, the National Museum of American Art (NMAA), Smithsonian Institution, has taken a leading role in developing database projects to serve the needs of art researchers. The projects are:

Inventory of American Paintings Executed before 1914, a nationwide census of paintings in public as well as private collections;

Inventory of American Sculpture, a new programme to locate and reference sculptures in public and private collections, indoor and outdoor locations, around the country;

Permanent Collection Data Base, utilised for management of the 33 000 objects in the NMAA collections;

Slide and Photograph Archives enabling multiple access to images in the museum's visual collections;

Peter A. Juley and Son Collection of 127 000 negatives of works of art and artists produced between 1896 and 1975 by this New York City firm;

Smithsonian Art Index, providing information on artworks located in scientific and technical bureaus at the Smithsonian;

Art Exhibition Catalogue Index, an item-level listing from art exhibition catalogues dated before 1877. The Index was published in 1986 by G. K. Hall.

In 1987, in preparation for migration to a new computer system, the National Museum of American Art with the six other art bureaus of the Smithsonian Institution began a structured process to analyse the data and supporting functions required to describe and manage collection objects and related information. Other participating bureaus include the Cooper-Hewitt Museum of Decorative Arts and Design in New Nork City, the Freer Gallery of Art, the Hirshhorn Museum and Sculpture Garden, the National Museum of African Art, the National Portrait Gallery and the Arthur M. Sackler Gallery.

One of the primary results of this work is a logical data model (also referred to as an entity-relationship model) for the art community, which is being enlarged by other Smithsonian museums to provide a map for ongoing development of the Institution's Collection Information System (CIS) (Chapter 21). The challenge in defining a data model for the Smithsonian art bureaus rests in adopting a structure broad enough to support diverse information about African tribal masks, contemporary photographs or eighteenth-century American portraits; yet specific enough to support the complex information management requirements of individual bureaus, departments, offices, and programmes. The Smithsonian art collections cross the disciplines of art, anthropology, archaeology and history, to name just a few. Achieving a common understanding of our data has not been easy. At times our differences seem to outweigh our similarities. Yet, the complexity of interests, differences in collections, and the discipline-specific ways of describing objects underscore the need and value of using a structured methodology to design an information system. (For an overview of the methodology used at the Smithsonian, see Reed and Sledge, 1988.)

Participation by the user community — or teamwork — was essential to a successful result. The process of developing the data model provided a forum for exchanging ideas, methods for analysing information, structures for documenting results, and a graphic representation which allows ideas and concepts to be expressed, reviewed, revised and refined. Involvement by users also heightened expectations for what the system would deliver. The first half of this paper summarises some of the user expectations which have become long-range goal objectives for the system. Unfortunately, for various reasons, existing data cannot be moved directly to the new structure defined by the model. Our existing data records — structured according to standard museum practice of 15 years ago — by today's standards are often ambiguous, imprecise, and inconsistent. The second half of this paper describes the practical realities — as well as opportunities — of defining a transition (or interim) file to bridge the distance between our existing database structure into the model proposed by the Smithsonian art community.

User expectations: working towards long-range objectives

The model embodies many of the expectations of the Smithsonian art community, which can be summarised as follows:

shared, cross-bureau access to Smithsonian holdings;

data integrity, or elimination of duplicate information;

more information, through automation/utilisation of research results;

better information, by taking advantage of specialised expertise within each bureau.

The Smithsonian is not a single building, but a complex of museums and facilities in Washington and beyond. Research by scholars and the general public is often serendipitous, requiring tenacity and persistence by phone and foot to succeed. There is no office in the Smithsonian that can answer a seemingly simple question, such as:

'Where can I view artworks by Winslow Homer at the Smithsonian?'

Participation by the Smithsonian art bureaus in the data modelling effort represents a commitment to the concept of a shared information system. Recognising a common data structure is one of the first steps towards providing cross-bureau access to information.

In the future, we should be able to tell the researcher that works by Winslow Homer may be found in the collections of the Hirshhorn Museum and Sculpture Garden, Freer Gallery, National Museum of American Art, National Museum of American History's Division of Graphic Arts, Cooper-Hewitt, and furthermore that references to other works are found in the National Portrait Gallery's Catalog of American Portraits and the National Museum of American Art's Inventory of American Paintings.

By extending this access to more complicated enquiries that cross discipline boundaries, the resources of the Smithsonian will be accessible for discovery of new relationships. A researcher may enquire about the inventor Samuel F. B. Morse (1791–1872) to discover that the telegraph he invented is owned by the National Museum of American History; his cameras and photographic equipment are in its Division of

Figure 92.1 A page from NMAA's Comprehensive Artist Listing. Shows the extent of data duplication in the existing computer databases. The entry for the artist, George Catlin, reflects a combined total of 4 398 records each containing biographical information for this artist.

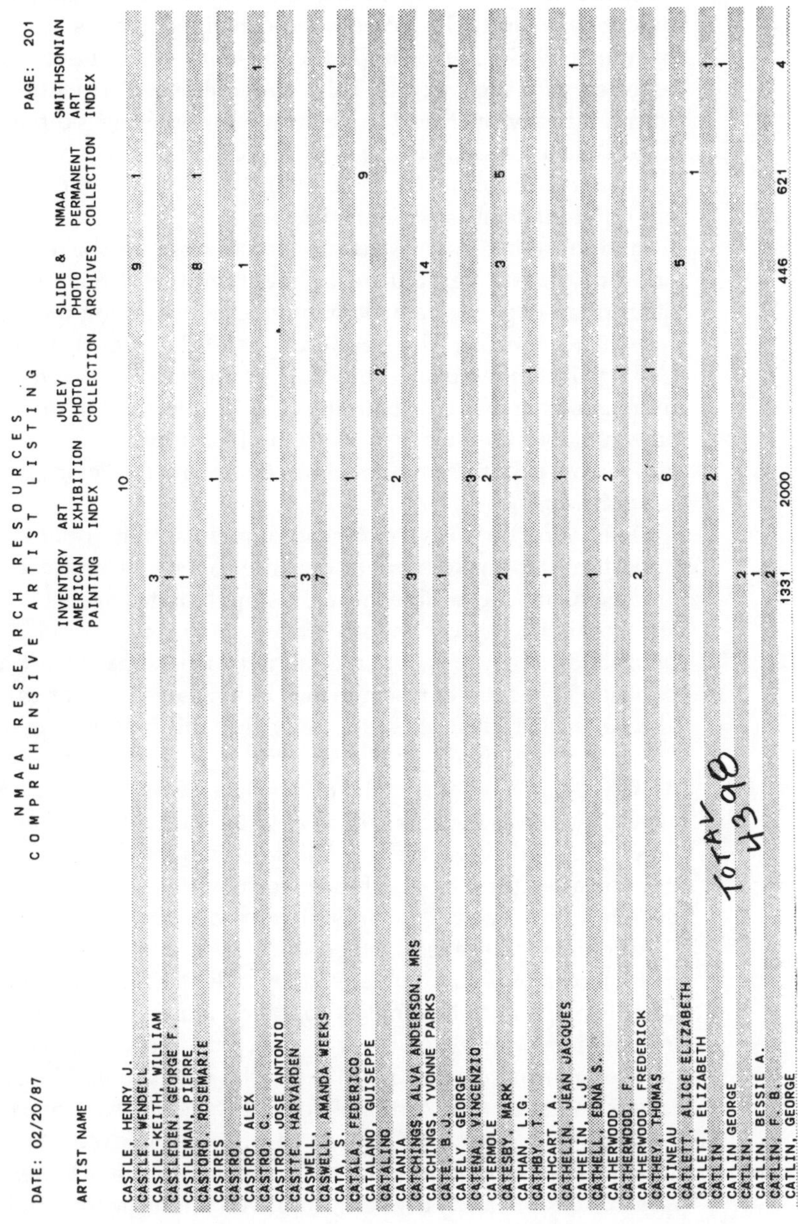

NMAA RESEARCH RESOURCES
COMPREHENSIVE ARTIST LISTING

DATE: 02/20/87 PAGE: 201

ARTIST NAME	INVENTORY AMERICAN PAINTING	ART EXHIBITION INDEX	JULEY PHOTO COLLECTION	SLIDE & PHOTO ARCHIVES	NMAA PERMANENT COLLECTION	SMITHSONIAN ART INDEX
CASTLE, HENRY J.		10				
CASTLE, WENDELL				9	1	
CASTLE-KEITH, WILLIAM	3					
CASTLEDEN, GEORGE F.	1					
CASTLEMAN, PIERRE	1					
CASTORO, ROSEMARIE				8	1	
CASTRES		1				
CASTRO,	1					
CASTRO, ALEX				1		
CASTRO, C.						1
CASTRO, JOSE ANTONIO		1				
CASTTE, HARVARDEN	1					
CASWELL,	3					
CASWELL, AMANDA WEEKS	7					
CATA, S.						1
CATALA, FEDERICO		1				
CATALANO, GUISEPPE					9	
CATALINO			2			
CATANIA		2				
CATCHINGS, ALVA ANDERSON, MRS	3					
CATCHINGS, YVONNE PARKS				14		
CATE, B.J.	1					
CATELY, GEORGE						1
CATENA, VINCENZIO		3				
CATERMOLE		2				
CATESBY, MARK	2			3	5	
CATHAN, L.G.		1				
CATHBY, T.			1			
CATHCART, A.	1					
CATHELIN, JEAN JACQUES		1				
CATHELIN, L.J.						1
CATHELL, EDNA S.	1					
CATHERWOOD		2				
CATHERWOOD, F.			1			
CATHERWOOD, FREDERICK	2					
CATHEY, THOMAS			1			
CATINEAU		6				
CATLETT, ALICE ELIZABETH				5		
CATLETT, ELIZABETH					1	
CATLIN		2				1
CATLIN GEORGE						1
CATLIN,	2					
CATLIN, BESSIE A.	1					
CATLIN, F. B.	2					
CATLIN, GEORGE	1331	2000		446	621	4

TOTAL 4398

Photographic History; two medals awarded to Morse are in its Division of Political History; he is depicted in a portrait at the National Portrait Gallery; and his paintings are owned by the National Museum of American Art. By this single example, the career of this artist/inventor comes full circle, for the receiving end of the Morse telegraph is constructed from a painting stretcher.

The concept of data integrity, or information in one place only, is implicit in the structure of the model. In concept this is radically different from our existing file structure. In the existing automated file, each record contains all of the data required to describe an object. The record is self-contained. It can stand alone. But, for each of the 500 paintings by George Catlin in the museum's collection, information about the artist is repeated with each record. This commonly used structure, sometimes called a flat file, carries a heavy overhead in staff time for entering, editing and maintaining duplicate data. To take it a step further — since we maintain, not one, but seven different databases — in our case information about the artist, George Catlin, is duplicated over 4 000 times in our different databases (Figure 92.1).

In contrast, in the new structure, information will be recorded *one time only*. The record of an object will be built up by identifying and relating different components of its description (e.g. the data element groups describing the creator, the materials used to construct the object, the classifications of the object). Biographical data about George Catlin will be entered once, but this information will be referred to many times to describe his relationship with the paintings in our collection. In the same way, information about an exhibition, the owner or location of a sculpture, or a bibliographic reference can be entered once, but used many times by linking (or keying) data groups to form multiple relationships.

Eliminating the heavy overhead of maintaining duplicate information affords us the opportunity to make more of our information — products of ongoing research at the Smithsonian — accessible through our automated systems. Every year collection objects are researched for exhibitions, catalogues or other projects. Some of this research is published; much of it remains buried in personal or office research files. While the published products of research may be available in libraries (albeit, sometimes only very specialised libraries), it is rare to include this new information in our automated files. Providing additional data element groups and efficient formats for recording the results of staff research unlocks many of our closed files to enhance research for staff and visitor alike. Since we no longer will have to duplicate data about George Catlin thousands of times, instead of recording a minimal amount of information, now we can afford to develop a complete biographical record for this artist, eventually building a biographical file referring to each of the artists in our collection.

Automating these research products raises the possibility of sharing the results. In the Smithsonian of today, bureaus independently research and catalogue their collections. The development of a single application allows us to consider referencing each others information to supplement our own records. Individual bureaus can concentrate on their particular areas of expertise in research. The National Museum of American Art could take advantage of the National Portrait Gallery's extensive biographical files on historic persons. The Portrait Gallery, in turn, could link records to American Art's extensive artist files: each bureau taking advantage of the other's strength, eliminating redundant research efforts, and providing improved reference for scholars and the general public.

Transition: coming to terms with a new data structure

The data model embodies future expectations and ideals of the Smithsonian art community. Like a whack on the side of the head, the transition file brings us back to reality. But, why transition? Fifteen years and thousands of data records create both problems and opportunities in preparing to move information to a new system. Opportunities to analyse and understand our information and how it is used. Problems because of text fields that combine data elements and standards that have been inconsistently applied or that have evolved over time. We have learned from the experience of the Division of Fishes in the Smithsonian's National Museum of Natural History which became the prototype project for the migration. For Fishes, a period of 12 months for an intensive editorial project to clean-up and revise data was required prior to moving to a new system. Our transition database provides an editorial work space to resolve data ambiguities and inconsistencies and to split categories of information into more discrete elements.

It offers other opportunities as well. The process of defining the transition file forced a critical analysis of existing information, causing revision in some areas of the model, testing the logical structures of the model. When we can break apart the numerous combined fields of data from our old file, we can study the existing terminology, and develop the new word lists and terms that will be required to move into the model. Even though the transition file falls far short of the user expectations enumerated earlier, it is a first, and important, step towards attaining the fully relational 'ideal' structure embodied in the model. By structuring the transition file as closely as possible to the model, the next step towards the goal objective should be much easier.

It should be emphasised that both the data modelling process and transition file definition have focused on structure over vocabulary or syntax. While this emphasis on structure may represent the general trend in museum computerisation projects, as noted in a recent *Museum News* article (Anon., 1988), it is not a new concept. The MARC (or Machine Readable Cataloguing) format, implemented by the Library of Congress in the 1960s for the exchange of bibliographic information, was developed similarly. The MARC format can be likened to a series of storage containers each labelled with the kind of information (e.g., title, date) that it holds. The repositories using the format have accepted and promoted standards, such as the Anglo-American Cataloging Rules or Library of Congress Subject Headings, to provide syntactic and vocabulary consistency to facilitate the exchange of information. A similar recognition and acceptance of common standards to control syntax and vocabulary is expected as the Smithsonian information system is implemented and used.

In the meantime, the transition file provides a practical laboratory for proving the structure of the data model, rethinking vocabulary, and testing new access to collection information. One specific area — Marks and Inscriptions — serves to illustrate the kinds of opportunities and possibilities identified in the transition file.

Marks and inscriptions (objects marks)

Our existing structure for marks is quite simple: a text field for signatures and an identical field for inscriptions. By default, anything not a signature is an inscription. Multiple occurrences of signature or inscription are separated by punctuation in the appropriate field.

This data group provides an interesting example of how understanding the way we describe object signatures, inscriptions and marks prompted revision in the structure of the data model. Originally, in developing the data model we divided marks into a deceptively logical structure, as follows:

Objects marks: a working concept

MARK TYPE: e.g. signature, inscription, date, or other

MARK LOCATION: e.g. lower right

MARK METHOD: e.g. incised, cast, applied

Figure 92.2 Paul Manship's *Flying Figure, Doodle* (National Museum of American Art, Gift of the Estate of Paul Manship).
Illustrates a typical object mark that combines signature, date and inscription

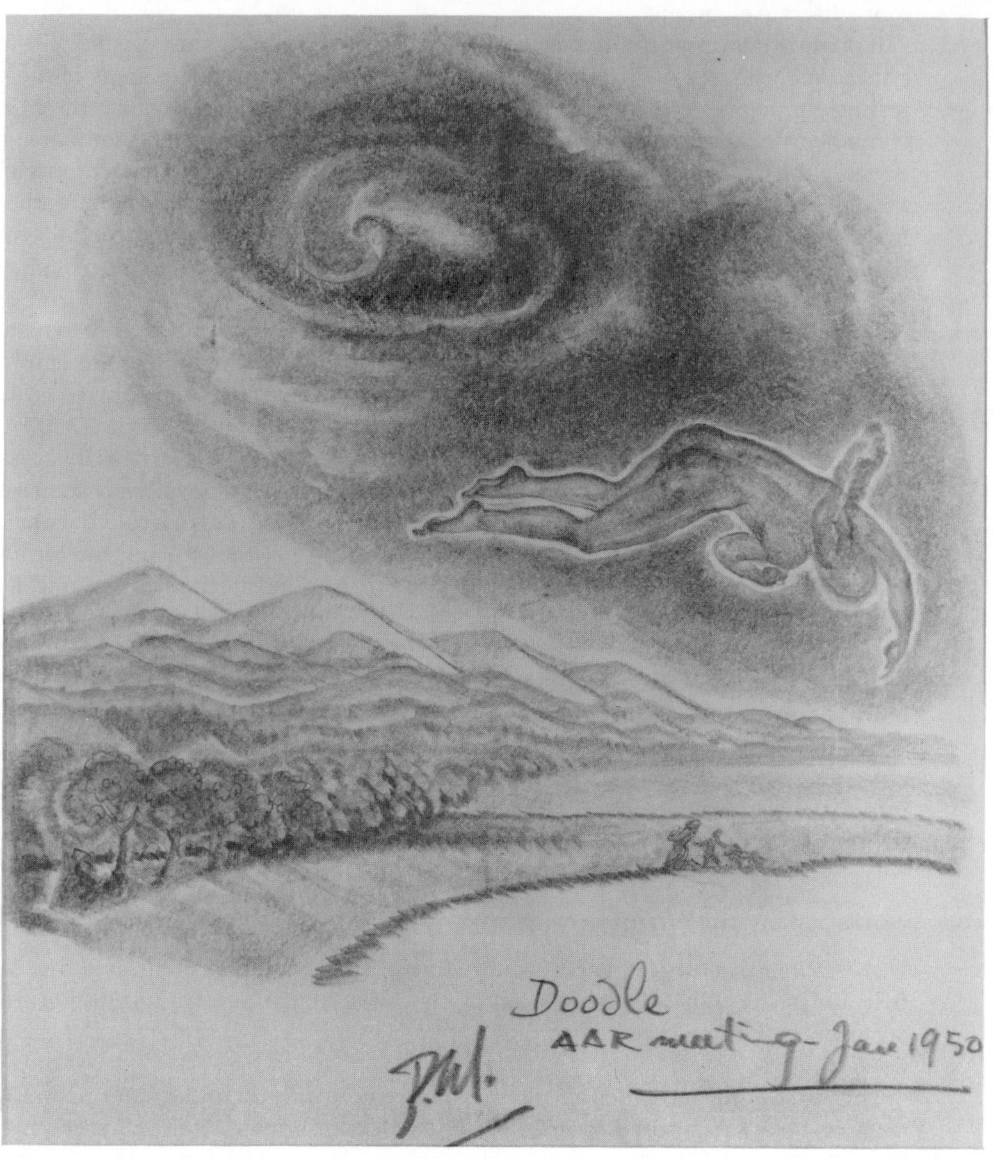

MARK MEDIUM: e.g. pencil, paint, gold-leaf

MARK TEXT: e.g. 'To my good friend and confidante, Jane Sledge'

What comes to mind is a painting or drawing inscribed in the lower right, in pencil, with the artist's signature, a date, or an inscription.

While this seems logical, defining a transition file forced more rigorous analysis of the existing data. This revealed that information in the field is typically made up of several types of marks which are expressed together because they appear in the same location. While an artwork might have a single signature or a date, it also might be signed and dated in the lower right corner, or inscribed, signed and dated, lower right, in pencil (Figure 92.2). Instead of 'Mark Type' controlling the incidence of this group, it is actually 'Mark Location' that signals a new repetition.

Because we may want to query the database for all paintings that are dated, or signed, the transition file provides a structure that allows these common 'Mark Types' to be flagged. It also permits the literal recording of the text as it appears on the object. The inscription from Paul Manship's *Flying Figure, Doodle* would be configured in the new file as follows:

Object marks: a new structure

	Yes	No	Undet
SIGNED:	[X]	[ ]	[ ]
DATED:	[X]	[ ]	[ ]
INSCRIBED:	[X]	[ ]	[ ]

OTHER MARK TYPE:

MARK LOCATION/TECHNIQUE: Signed, dated, and inscribed, lower right, in pencil

MARK TEXT: Doodle/AAR meeting — Jan 1950/P.M.

FORM OF SIGNATURE: P.M.

In this structure it will not be necessary to describe a mark as either an inscription or a signature. Monogram, edition number, founder's mark, watermark, and even title are examples of terms that more precisely define a particular mark which can be accommodated in the field called 'Other Mark Type'. In contrast to the limited structure of the old file, this use of generic fields (such as Other Mark Type) in combination with precise, but an unlimited number of, data values offers more flexibility. Repeatedly we find what were field names in the old structure, such as signature or inscription, become data values in the new.

Experience with research enquiries to the museum's art research databases prompted the addition of a new field for 'Form of Signature'. Being able to search on a particular name or pattern of initials may assist with attributions when little else is known *except* a signature or initials.

Conclusion

It should be clear that much work remains to migrate our existing data into a transition file and, eventually, into the proposed relational data model structure. It should also be clear that a great amount of planning, analysis and conceptual thinking has already taken place. Having a commonly understood goal and framework provided through the data model, has helped to focus the efforts of the Smithsonian art bureaus. In introducing a new journal, *Smithsonian Studies in American Art*, Charles Eldredge, former Director of the National Museum of American Art, summarises the opportunities and frustrations of the scholar. He says:

> In the rush to discover ourselves through our art we have taken many divergent paths, adding to traditional Wolfflinean formalism a new fascination with social context, patronage, technique, and relationships that cut across national, cultural, and disciplinary boundaries. Some historians of American art look for private meaning and insight in specific objects, while others seek the broad sweep of general cultural trends. Clearly, no one tendency or methodology suffices today to cope with our complex twentieth century interests: Never before have we been faced with so many perplexing questions and so few incontrovertible answers. But this situation, which can seem confusing and contradictory, contains an invigorating energy, as we realize that we have only begun to excavate the riches that lie within our art (Eldredge, 1987).

Before us at the Smithsonian is the challenge and the opportunity of defining a System that can begin to cope with our complex twentieth-century interests. If we can make our information available to new lines of enquiry — both broad and specific that cross disciplinary boundaries — perhaps we can begin to understand and answer those 'perplexing questions' that the scholar would like to pose.

---

93 DEVELOPING A MEDIA THESAURUS FOR THE INVENTORY OF AMERICAN SCULPTURE: MEETING PROJECT, USER AND STAFF NEEDS

Christine Hennessey

Office of Research Support
National Museum of American Art
Smithsonian Institution
Washington, DC

Introduction

The Inventory of American Sculpture is the newest art database to be implemented by the Smithsonian's National Museum of American Art. Intended to serve as a national census, the Inventory records descriptions of works in public and private collections created by artists who were born in America or whose works are identified with this country. From the outset of the project, careful consideration was given to choosing, developing and controlling vocabulary for access. This paper will focus on the difficulties encountered in developing and implementing a thesaurus to control media terms. Project, user and staff needs will be addressed. Before discussing those needs and the thesaurus in more detail, however, a brief overview of the Sculpture inventory is warranted.

Inventory of American Sculpture

The primary goal of the Inventory is to compile and maintain a central base of information on American sculpture from the earliest colonial days to the present. Whereas considerable critical and scholarly attention has been devoted in recent years to American painting, architecture and the decorative arts, sculpture remains largely undocumented (Craven, 1984). In part, its inherent properties — its size, weight and often fragile nature — have acted as deterrents to its inclusion in exhibitions. Moreover, many significant pieces are located in outdoor sites, inaccessible to the scholar who does not know their local whereabouts. A national survey has never been taken of the thousands of statues and memorials scattered in parks and town squares throughout the country, or of the sculptures in museums, historical societies, corporate and private collections.

To allow these works to remain undocumented, anonymous and unnoticed is to lose a fundamental part of the cultural heritage of the United States. Even more crucial, our neglect of outdoor sculpture — vulnerable to weather, environmental pollution and vandalism — promises its untimely deterioration through lack of conservation. Thus, the National Museum of American Art has begun a comprehensive Inventory of American Sculpture. To be included in the Inventory, a work:

may be sculpted using traditional methods of modelling, carving or casting;

may be sculpted using contemporary materials or techniques, such as plastics or neon, assemblage or site construction;

must have been created by an artist who was born in or whose works are identified with the United States.

Figure 93.1 Sample record from the Inventory of American Sculpture

```
  ARTIST:  Manship, Paul Howard, 1885-1966, sculptor.
   TITLE:  Lyric Muse, (sculpture).
   DATES:  1912.
  MEDIUM:  Bronze.
   DIMEN:  11 3/4 x 6 15/16 x 5 9/16 in.
 FOUNDER:  Roman Bronze Works, founder. 275 Greene Street, Brooklyn, New York
   MARKS:  (Inscribed top of base:) PAUL MANSHIP ROMA C 1912. (Right side of
           base:) ROMAN BRONZE WORKS N-Y-. signed founder's mark appears
   OWNER:  Cincinnati Art Museum, Eden Park, Cincinnati, Ohio
 SUBJECT:  Mythology Classical Muse
           Performing Arts Music
  SOURCE:  Index of American Sculpture, University of Delaware, 1985
           Cincinnati Art Museum, 1970.
  REC ID:  ias 75006670
```

The Inventory references works in public and private collections; records works in indoor or outdoor sites. In fact, a significant component of the inventory is a planned comprehensive survey and conservation/conditions assessment of all outdoor sculpture in America. Co-sponsored with the National Institute for the Conservation of Cultural Property, this collaborative 'Save Outdoor Sculpture' effort will be done in cooperation with the American Association for State and Local History, the National Conference of State Historic Preservation Officers, the United States National Park Service and the Smithsonian's Conservation Analytical Laboratory.

As a national census, the Inventory of American Sculpture is necessarily comprised of information culled from a variety of published and unpublished sources. A substantial core of records from the University of Delaware's sculpture index files have been entered already. Additionally, in response to a recent nationwide appeal, museums, historical societies, public libraries and private collectors are contributing collection and exhibition catalogues, computerised checklists, photocopied registration cards or hand-written reports.

Since data entry began in December 1985, over 25 000 records have been entered (Figure 93.1). Essential information recorded for each sculpture includes: artist, title, creation dates, medium, foundry, cast numbers and other markings, owner/location, provenance, subject, historical and exhibition notes. For outdoor sculptures, basic condition and conservation treatment reports will supplement this information. Data is being entered using an adaptation of the USMARC Visual Materials format on the Smithsonian Institution Bibliographic Information System (SIBIS).

As a research database on SIBIS, the Inventory of American Sculpture is designed to answer questions, such as:

what themes were depicted by American sculptors working in the 20 year span following the Civil War?

where can one find the early bronze works done by Louise Nevelson?

are there any statues of Winston Churchill in the United States?

User needs defined

In developing the Inventory of American Sculpture, consideration was given to project, user and staff needs. In contrast to the museum's other, well-established art databases, the sculpture inventory is a relatively new initiative, so we could build upon experiences learned. User registration forms (in place for many of our projects) provided statistics and insights into who and how those resources are utilised.

Museum professionals, scholars, students and private collectors use the resources as a starting point in researching and planning exhibitions and publications, to locate related works for comparative analysis or for interdisciplinary research and thematic studies. Historians, publishers and picture researchers from all disciplines also routinely consult the databases to locate images pertinent to the particular themes they are researching.

Of the nearly 2 000 research requests received last year, 70 per cent were for artist access, 20 per cent for subject access and 10 per cent for other types of queries, including owner/location, medium or exhibition information. However, these statistics seen by themselves might be misleading. One can easily argue that the structure of existing data pre-determines the kinds of questions likely to be asked. Thus, in designing the Inventory of American Sculpture, we sought a more flexible structure with multiple access points.

Medium (or the material of which a sculpture is composed) was identified early on as a crucial access point, especially given the conservation/conditions assessment component of the project. Although the Inventory of American Sculpture is not yet open for research use (as initial efforts must necessarily be concentrated on gathering and entering information), potential queries can be projected.

The United States National Park Service, for example, working on an acid rain study, has already expressed an interest in retrieving sculptures by specific material in combination with particular geographic locations. Curators and conservators, studying an artist's style and technique, are likely to ask for a listing of all known reproductions or models of a particular work, whether in plaster or bronze. Historians, researching foundries, might request entries for all bronze works cast in a specific year, so that markings can be studied for possible foundry identification. And the media index could be used to help curators track the history and use of a particular medium, be it painted wood or Minnesota red granite.

Form and structure of media terms

Recognising the need for access in the medium field, however, was only the first step. The problem was how to structure and control terms to permit efficient and reliable access. Several difficulties became apparent. American sculptors have employed a wide range of media, from the traditional marble and bronze, to the more *avant garde*, such as plexiglas and neon with transistors. It is not possible nor would it be practical for the three staff members working on the inventory project to examine each and every sculpture to identify its physical characteristics. Rather, the inventory is dependent on a variety of published and unpublished source materials compiled by a variety of

Figure 93.2 Catalogue entry from Museum of Fine Arts collection catalogue (1987)

Cat. No.	Artist	Title	Date	Foundry	Casting Technique	Copper	Tin	Zinc	Lead
53	John Quincy Adams Ward	*The Indian Hunter*	about 1860		Sand	87.7	3.5	7.0	1.8

Figure 93.3 Inventory of American Sculpture primary media terms

Medium:	
ceramic:	
concrete:	
fiber:	
glass:	
light:	Includes electric and neon works.
metal:	
mixed:	Use this term when the work is composed of several media and no single media predominates; do not use for outdoor monuments when material of base differs from the sculpture's.
paper:	
plaster:	
plastic:	
readymade:	Use this term when you are dealing with, for the most part, unadapted found objects.
rubber:	
site:	Use for outdoor, site-specific earthworks, such as Robert Smithson's Spiral Jetty.
sound:	
stone:	
wax:	
wood:	
undetermined:	Use this term when sources does not state media and it is impossible to determine from available photograph or source record.
other:	Use this term when media does not fit into any of the above categories or the material cannot be identified from existing source reference. Always assign secondary term to identify other medium. (Example: other:bensite).

individuals and institutions of varying expertises. Few reports from museum curators, registrars and conservators provide the very detailed, well-researched media information illustrated by Figure 93.2 from the Boston Museum of Fine Arts (Greenthal, Kozol and Ramirez, 1986). In contrast and much more typical are the numerous reports received from small museums and non-traditional art repositories (zoos, courthouses and historical societies among them), where fine arts may be only a minor part of their holdings. Often, these institutions can distinguish only that a work is metal or stone or wood.

To accommodate varying source reports and to serve the needs of researchers, a hierarchical thesauri structure for recording media terms was implemented by the Inventory of American Sculpture. Initially, we had hoped to utilise an existing media thesaurus, naively assuming that such a thesaurus would already exist. However, a search for an applicable thesaurus proved frustrating. Since the Art and Architecture project (AAT) had not yet fully developed or released their materials hierarchy (in 1985), questionnaires were sent to selected museums, who had either published sculpture collection catalogues or who had automated collection systems. Responses to those questionnaires and a search of museum and library literature (under the headings for 'information storage and retrieval systems', 'vocabulary control' and 'cataloguing and indexing') turned up little. In fact, only one article mentioning a media thesaurus was subsequently found (Small, 1988)

It became evident that despite the prevalence of medium as a data element in museum registration records, there are as yet no agreed upon standards for recording this information, either for the structure of the data or for the terminology used. Instead, it

Figure 93.4 Sample page from the Inventory media thesaurus

MEDIA TERMS

PRIMARY TERM	SECONDARY TERM	Use for:
stone:	greenstone	
	jade	
	jasper	
	lapis lazuli	
	lepidolite	
	limestone.................	Burgundian limestone
		Chauvigny limestone
		Dakota limestone
		Dunville stone
		French limestone
		Indiana limestone
		Mankato stone
		limestone
		Oolitic limestone
		Texas limestone

remains common practice for terms to be entered in whatever spelling or degree of specificity provided by the curator or registrar cataloguing the object.

Yet, control of museum terminology seemed essential to the success of the sculpture inventory so a media thesaurus was undertaken. Frequency lists from the museum's other art databases and a search of specialised art reference sources (such as Mayer, 1969), provided a basic alphabetical listing of media terms upon which to build.

A hierarchical structure was then imposed on these terms. Nineteen 'primary terms' were defined to categorise the broadest types of media (Figure 93.3). Included is a category for 'Undetermined', assigned when the medium is unknown or cannot be determined and a category for 'other', which can be used to reference terms for which no immediate definitions can be found, or for those terms that do not fit into any of the other primary categories. Each primary term can be further qualified by a 'secondary term' to distinguish, for example, that a work in stone is alabaster or granite; or a wooden sculpture is mahogany or pine (Figure 93.4).

These structured primary and secondary terms do not appear on the online public catalogue display. Assigned solely for indexing purposes, they provide a means of collocating or bringing together like terms. For example, if a researcher were to ask for all acrylic works, entries for the generic acrylic as well as brand names, Plexiglas, Lucite, Persplex, and Shinkolite, would be retrieved.

To supplement these highly structured primary and secondary terms, a free-text medium field is used for the public catalogue display. This 'user-friendly' field might include generic medium, trade names, support, processes, techniques, implements or colours (Figure 93.5). Keyword and Boolean searching of this field provides enhanced access for the researcher.

Currently, over 500 terms are referenced in the Inventory's media thesaurus. Approximately ten new media terms are added per month. Admittedly, building the thesaurus has not been without its problems. Chief among them, no one in our office is a materials expert. Even with the basic primary and secondary categories defined, it is often difficult to classify terms. For example:

should artificial stone be listed under stone or other?

if we make a distinction between synthetic and natural latex, classifying one as a plastic, the other as rubber, how do we avoid mis-classifying a work when the source does not specify which type of latex has been used?

Moreover, incoming reports sometimes list 'mystery' media for which no immediate definition can be found (i.e. siryne, bensite and bellplast were just a few that have come

Figure 93.5 Expanded media display

```
EXAMPLE OF MEDIUM STRUCTURE

PRIMARY:     stone

SECONDARY:   marble

DISPLAY:     Carved Vermont White marble.
```

in). Often, these terms turn out to be regionally-named materials or commercial trade names. In these cases, calls to non-art reference centres (such as the Department of Volcanology at the Smithsonian) have often proved helpful.

For the future, there is still much work to be done. AAT has recently released their materials hierarchy which will provide great assistance. However, since many of our terms are uniquely American, regionally-named sculpture materials, they are not yet referenced by AAT. Thus while we await approval of the candidate terms from AAT, we will continue to research and maintain our inhouse thesaurus. As the size of our thesaurus increases, the need for clear definitions of terms as well as defined standards for choosing between variants of terms becomes more crucial. Decisions in classifying terms need to be better documented so future staff will assign terms consistently. And, we are in the process of developing a cross-referenced alphabetical index to supplement the hierarchical list.

Conclusion

While specialists might debate classifications of various materials, use of a thesaurus structure provides some assurance that there will be consistency in the spelling and classification of media terms. The Inventory of American Sculpture, clearly ambitious in scope and intent, is successful only to the extent that it can serve the needs of its researchers. Certainly, creating a media thesaurus has been a learning experience for our office and we hope will be of benefit to our researchers. We welcome the efforts of others, such as AAT, in developing more comprehensive thesauri; and, as we begin to enter condition and conservation treatment information, we seek help from conservators in defining and structuring terms. Control of museum terminology should ultimately asssure efficient retrieval for the researcher.

XIII FUTURE EXPECTATIONS

94

FUTURE EXPECTATIONS

D. Andrew Roberts

Museum Documentation Association
Cambridge

The final section briefly explores some of the technological and policy developments that will be needed to support museums in the future.

Lene Rold describes the plans of the National Museum of Denmark to design a data structure which makes full use of the features of a relational system. This research has lead to a deeper understanding of the data itself. She develops the concept of multiple classification systems being used in parallel within a museum and the increasing use of new combinations of information to generate research ideas.

Those of us with an Anglophone background need to be made more aware of the greater complexity of some other languages. Christof Wolters does this in a masterly way with his description of the museum terminology problems faced in Germany. Future terminology systems will need to cope with demanding characteristics of the German language, such as allowing you to create complex compound words which cannot easily (or automatically) be broken down into their original elements. He notes the importance of computer systems coping with national variations of this type.

Finally, Peter Welsh concentrates on a series of principles about museums and museum information. These include a realisation of the cultural significance of objects and the importance of preservation and access. Like Lene Rold, he stresses the new opportunities that will be opened up by improved terminology strategies.

95 APPLICATIONS OF COMPUTER SCIENCE IN MUSEUMS AND HUMANISTIC RESEARCH

Lene Rold

Nationalmuseet
Copenhagen

Introduction

At the National Museum of Denmark, we have over the past year been registering information about our collections in a database. Substantial funds have been granted to the project from both private and public sources, enough to transfer the entire collections from the museum's central departments in about five years. This means that about 1 000 000 objects will be registered before the end of 1993.

There is a quite varied assortment of information to be entered, since the objects — for both practical and traditional reasons — have been treated from diverse viewpoints, using diverse registration systems and diverse classification methods.

None the less we have succeeded in transferring information about the objects to a common database, without doing violence either to the material or to the involved departments' accustomed registration practices.

This paper is divided into two parts. The first section is an example of a data structure in the database mentioned above. This is followed by some thoughts concerning classification of objects and future techniques of machine-aided classification.

The reason for touching on two seemingly very different subjects in one paper is that in fact both topics are dependent on one another, even though it may not seem so at first notice. Our work with data structures has necessitated insight into the nature of the data involved in a research process. Gaining a deeper understanding of this nature has lead to the rearrangement of our data into new structures.

Data structures in a relational database

The database GENREG for registering objects in the collections encompasses the same data that were previously entered manually on cards and in special registers.

We must admit that even for brief texts, natural language can be far superior to a structured database when the task is to describe precisely the involved relations and complex inter-relationships. We could have chosen to enter such documentation as free-text; but that would have been a quite expensive project, and the associated advantages too small to have been worth the price. Furthermore, we plan eventually to be able to photograph or scan the old texts, so they can be recalled together with the database's structured information.

Information which would normally not be regarded as transferable to database fields can in fact be entered by using the data structures we have devised.

The real subtlety in the work of designing the database consists in structuring the data so as to preserve a high level of precision, simplicity and comprehensibility, and simultaneously to achieve a reasonable ability to record fine nuances.

The case history of an object

One characteristic of a well-designed relational database is that identical information is entered in only one place in the base. For example, the creator and user of an object can have been one and the same person, consequently with the same name, life time, position, address and so on. This collection of information should thus be placed in one table and be given a unique code.

In all places where this person figures in the database, one can use the code alone, and if changes in the information occur, for example a change of address, then this need be changed only in one place; the code stays invariant.

I will describe one of GENREG's central data structures which makes full use of this technique. Figure 95.1 shows one way to present an object's 'case history'. The problems solved by this table are how to relate in chronological order the various information concerning the object's production, use, collection and acquisition. If one separates this information by entering it in two or more tables, then one risks that information about two users of the same object with their respective places of usage may be impossible to bring together again. One could no longer be able to tell whether user 1 was associated with user site 1 or 2, and one is also unable to find out which of the two users was the first.

The first field in 'case history' contains a key composed of no, sit and seq. The record displayed thus contains information about an object's number (no = '103') and the first occurrence in a possible sequence (eg. seq = '1') of production situations (eg. sit = 'A'). Note: an object may have more than one production situation.

Figure 95.1 A simplified presentation of the principles used in constructing the case history table

CASE HISTORY

no	sit	seq	place	time	person	role
103	A	1	85	1986	714	artist
103	B	2				

CASE HISTORY CODES

code	text
A	provenance
B	use
C	collection
D	accession

PERSON-CODES

code	lname	fname	add	tel
714	Scott	David	22	03458

ADDRESS-CODES

code	st	town	cip	count
85	haven	oslo	6000	norge
22				

A production place (code = '85') is bound to this occurrence, a time of production (time = '1986'), a person (person = '714'), and this person's role in the production situation (role = 'artist').

Most of the fields in this table are code fields whose codes refer to auxiliary tables. In these auxiliary tables, the code is a unique key and consequently Scott, represented by code 714, may occur many times in the main tables but only once in the 'Person-Codes' table. Note that the address codes are placed in three quite different relations. One code represents a production place (code = '85'), the second appears in an auxiliary table representing a person's address (code = '22') and both of these codes appear as keys in 'Address-Codes'. Thus all addresses are entered into 'Address-Codes', and this also concerns addresses that may occur in other places in tables not shown here.

The example given here is an example of the internal schema for the database. Externally, that is to the user, most of this structure may not be apparent at all, and a user may never enter codes or even be aware that they exist.

Classification systems

Another more philosophical aspect is the importance of distinguishing between on the one hand raw empirical data (if such things exist), and on the other hand data which are the result of some research process. The latter type of data would, for instance, be any classification assigned to an object, and often even the name of an object.

By a classification system I mean a system like the *Outline of Cultural Materials* or *SHIC*, not nomenclatures, word lists, and not even most thesauri.

The best known of the early classification systems used in archaeology is surely the old *material-based* division into stone, bronze and iron. It served scholars well for decades in putting some order into the various rarity cabinets of the early nineteenth century.

Registration in museums has throughout time followed the development of research in their respective fields. From the end of the last century and for several years after, typological studies were the backbone of archaeological research. Practically all statements were based in *typology*, whether they concerned age, use or distribution of artefacts. Exact description of objects therefore became an important discipline.

Descriptive systems gradually developed by means of which, ideally, any object could be placed, determined and registered.

Later — from the 1930s onwards — objects' *functions* became the primary research interest, especially in ethnology, and this manifested itself in the development of registers based on objects' usage, such as SHIC.

Recent research projects have tended to aim towards revealing symbolic values and non-visible connections. If these projects produce lasting results, we will see before long that it is both possible and desirable to classify objects according to their symbolic content or other forms of value judgement. An example of an object which can only be fully understood if the symbolic aspects are explained is The Shrine of St Columba.

From this short survey, it is apparent that the 'perfect' classification system is — if more than a passing fantasy — still only a utopian dream.

One can foresee over a longer perspective that the classification systems themselves will be removed from the database, since this type of information can better be handled through a knowledge based superstructure or 'shell', built on top of the raw data.

A classification will thus not be a piece of stored data which is bound to the object and is recorded in the database, but a data value that can be *created* according to need by running an AI (artificial intelligence) program. In such a situation one could classify objects by as many systems as one might desire, provided the classification programs are installed in a knowledge based superstructure, and provided there is enough information in the database for the classification program to be able to work.

Conclusion

It probably takes more than just raw data like an object's size, age, material, colour, etc., to do a successful classification job. We also need information about the original and secondary contexts and comparison to similar or related objects and their 'case histories'.

We might therefore dedicate more thought to problems such as *which information* about objects makes it possible to classify them; and *which raw data* is necessary in such a research process.

If we can make a machine carry out classification tasks we are indeed, as just mentioned, getting very close to simulating a research process; but if we want 'to teach' a machine how to do our research jobs for us we may have to structure our ways of thinking and cannot any longer get by with the 'Eureka-method'.

This does not mean, however, that we should allow computer science concepts to become a strait-jacket. On the contrary, we must insist that the data structures used respect humanistic research traditions.

Associations and gradually increasing understanding are still the basis for the birth and development of research ideas. This process is unlikely to become easier even though we can structure the source material and test the research theories at an earlier time. Further, data structures can aid the research process by making the process itself easier to comprehend and thereby more accessible by others than the researcher himself.

In the National Museum's object registration database we have used several other data structures in addition to those described above. Among others we use hierarchical structures incorporated inside relations to record information about different objects' mutual interrelationships. In forthcoming systems we intend to apply knowledge-based systems as a superstructure over the database. Furthermore, we plan to involve other forms of data, for example pictorial material, in the scientific and expository treatment of the collected data. The intention is to obtain a better integration between research and registration.

---

96 ON THE NEED TO SUPPORT LANGUAGE SPECIFIC PROBLEMS IN TERMINOLOGY SYSTEMS

Christof Wolters

Institut für Museumskunde
Berlin

Introduction

There seems to exist a widespread conviction among museum people that the documentation of museum objects is (or should be) more or less the same anywhere in the world. People using the computer take part in international working groups and conferences on subjects like *Data Standards* and *Terminology Control*. The idea of a national or even international exchange of data is very much alive.

In our daily work we seem to act quite differently. Quite often we tend to develop our own systems. I am sure that there are many good reasons for that and some bad reasons too. Are some of the reasons language specific? What role do natural languages, their vocabulary, their grammar and, last but not least, their underlying concepts, play in this context? How about 'dialects' or 'jargons' like the discipline-oriented professional languages of the archaeologist or the art historian?

There is no simple answer to this question. Museum people may talk several languages, but usually they are not linguists, they may even be quite naïve concerning language problems. The problem has been adequately described in 'My Fair Lady'. Some of us may identify with Professor Higgins, but in fact most of us resemble more or less Eliza before the play starts. I myself have only discovered these problems in the last years.

Projects concerned with terminology are necessarily based on detailed and sometimes endless discussions about the meaning of words in the one context or the other. A lot of effort is being put into the translation of all this into more or less general regulations. Working in this context there is no way to avoid the question of language specific problems and I will try to report on some of those we have met in our work.

In doing this, I will concentrate on problems for which computer support seems possible and useful in day-to-day activities. I will talk about computer programs which do something with the words we are using in the documentation of museum objects. I will leave aside the more sociological and philosophical questions, even though they can be quite fascinating.

Problem areas

My field of experience in vocabulary control is based on a project which had the task of 'getting some order into the central archives of two regional museum organisations in Western Germany' (Saro and Wolters, 1988). The computer work to which I will refer has been undertaken by the Department of Symbolics of the Konrad-Zuse-Zentrum für Informationstechnik, Berlin. In the first 20 museums we worked on, we found for instance more than 10 000 different Object Names and the work of getting some degree of order into them was done by using thesaurus methods. The result of course was not a 10 000-word thesaurus, but at least a considerable progress in order. This preliminary order (we called it 'Broad Classification') was the starting point to some real thesaurus projects (see Chapter 67).

During our work, we encountered a lot of problems with words and the usual difficulties in translating possible solutions into generally useful regulations. Among them I want to pick three problem areas as examples, one where a general solution is possible using regulations of German grammar ('Orthography'), one where a general procedure seems to be acceptable at least inside the German language ('Syntax') and one where we will have to try to get away from general rules to local rules ('Synonyms'). These three problem areas have been chosen because they are relevant to a practical application in day-to-day work.

In these three examples, I shall concentrate on only one characteristic of the German language: instead of using a short sentence you may create a new term by putting two or more words directly together, usually without any hyphen (German 'Haustüre', English 'front-door', French 'porte de la maison').

In German these compound terms are almost excessively used in giving names to museum objects. Sometimes they even seem to be created *in lieu* of a short description, indicating that the person did not remember the correct term. A real beauty we discovered in our files was 'Blutsenkungsgeschwindigkeitsmesser' (indicating an apparatus to measure the speed of segmentation of blood). In German you can easily transform a long sentence into one word.

Many of these compound terms will not be in any general dictionary: to understand them you must be able to break them up into their original elements. A computer program cannot do that in a simple and straightforward way. Compound terms will not be broken up correctly by word processors having an automatic hyphenation feature.

As an illustration, I will show you what kind of nonsense you may get when you carry out retrieval based on character-strings. The words you are looking for will appear in many cases as a part of a compound term and so there may be other letters before of after the string you are looking for (Figure 96.1).

Figure 96.1 Examples for problems with compound terms in text retrieval

If you want to include compound terms in your search you not only get a lot of normal 'noise' (use of the same 'word' for different purposes), you get a lot of complete nonsense too. The terms you might want to be included in your retrieval might be, for example:

'Damen*schuh*', 'Haus*schuhe*', 'Holz*schuh*', 'Schlitt*schuh*stiefel', 'Schnür*schuhe*', '*Schuh*schnalle', 'Stöckel*schuh*absatz' but

If you look for	you also get nonsense like
Schuh (shoe)	Ti*schuh*r (table clock)
Tisch (table)	Quittungsbuch der stä*tisch*en Sparkasse (receipt-book of the municipal savings-bank)
Scherbe (potsherd)	Flei*scherbe*il (butcher's hatchet)

Looking for compound terms containing '*Schuh*' ('shoe') you will also get 'Ti*schuhr*' ('table clock'); looking for '*Tisch*' ('table') you will find out that 'isch' is a very common suffix for adjectives and quite often preceded by a '*t*' (in English, adverbs like 'accep*table*' would have the same effect). Looking for '*Scherbe*' ('potsherd') you will be quite astonished to get 'Flei*scherbe*il' ('butcher's hatchet').

The following three examples treat problems we had with the wide spread use of compound terms. The computer programs written to help with these problems may have a wider application one day.

Orthography

My first example is concerned with orthography. There are many cases where the same character or the same word can be written in slightly different ways. This will inevitably be the case when the documentation is based on older sources, while regional differences can also play a considerable role.

If you put several words together in a compound term the rules of orthography become (at least in German) much more complicated (Figure 96.2). The first element, for instance, may finish with a double character and the second may start with the same. In the case of 'ss' ('ß'), all of these characters will be preserved, for example 'Reissschiene' ('drawing-rule'). In the case of other consonants, this will depend on whether the following character is also a consonant ('Betttruhe', a chest to store bed-linen) or not ('Bettisch', a small table one can put on a bed). A small but further complication arises when you put a

Figure 96.2 Orthography problems

Automatic Treatment of characters (without or within the context of other characters) for comparing, sorting and retrieval purposes

Single Characters	treated as if
ä, Ä	AE
ö, Ö	OE
ü, Ü	UE
ß	SS
-	(deleted)
Characters in the Context of Compound Terms	
Rei*ßs*chiene	REIS*SS*CHIENE
Rei*ß*-*S*chiene	,,
Rei*ss*schiene	,,
Rei*ss*-*S*chiene	,,
Be*tt*truhe	BE*TTT*RUHE
Be*tt*-*T*ruhe	,,
Be*tt*isch	BE*TT*ISCH
Be*tt*-*T*isch	,,

hyphen between the two words, which one should not do too often, but which is allowed for reasons of readability. In that case the double characters will be conserved ('Bett-Truhe', 'Bett-Tisch').

Such rules lead not only to a lot of mistakes but also to considerable variations in correct spelling. I suppose that there will be more or less similar rules of orthography in many languages. It is a big help when a computer program is able to identify a word even if it is spelled differently. If you can introduce 'Duerer' (spelled without Umlaut) into your artist's file when 'Dürer' (with Umlaut) is already there, something is wrong with your programs.

A terminology system should be able to support specific rules of orthography. It will need for that a kind of slot where we can lay down such regulations.

Syntax

My second example is concerned with syntax in a very wide sense. It is in fact quite difficult to make general rules about how to formulate for example an Object Name for a given object. Before we can furnish complete lists of such ames (and this is very far in the future), we must allow for a wide variation of terms. Meanwhile we will have to have access to the already existing vocabulary. We need to know whether a similar term is

Figure 96.3 Syntax problems

Some Examples for the permutation of compound terms or short sentences

Special characters may be used to cut up a word (*), to suppress an automatic permutation (_) or to suppress an additional letter from a compound term in a permutation (<.>). Lower case letters at the beginning of a permuted term are changed to capital letters.

Original Term (Input)	Permutation by Program
Türschlüssel	—
Tür-Schlüssel	Schlüssel (Tür-)
Tür*schlüssel	Schlüssel (Tür-)
Haus*tür*schlüssel	Türschlüssel (Haus-) Schlüssel (Haustür-)
Schwarzwälder Holzräderuhr	Holzräderuhr (Schwarzwälder)
Schwarzwälder Holz*räder*uhr	Holzräderuhr (Schwarzwälder) Räderuhr (Schwarzwälder Holz-) Uhr (Schwarzwälder Holzräder-)
Egge_mit Rutschbalken	Rutschbalken (Egge mit)
Holz-,_Stahl-,_Eisen*spaten	Spaten (Holz-, Stahl-, Eisen-)
Schiffs*anker	Anker (Schiffs-)
Schiff<s>anker	Anker (Schiff)

Useful word elements will appear before opening brackets and can be easily identified and retrieved already in the computer or not. In German this may become quite difficult. The reason (again) is the widespread use of compound terms.

The problem of finding an already existing similar term can best be illustrated by some difficulties in the creation of alphabetical indexes. The widespread use of compound terms and the great number of new words introduced by their use make it advisable to give such an index the form of a permuted index.

A computer program to make 'front door' also appear under 'door' is easily written and may even be part of a standard program package. But in German there is no simple way in analysing a term like 'Haustüre', to decide whether it should be broken up for a permuted index and where this should be done.

So we need some computer support in doing this, if possible without making it appear in the way we write the original term. Syntax regulations should not violate the language. I will not go into the details of our regulations and computer-programs. They have to cover a wide field not only of compound terms but also of short sentences. They have to take care of the fact that a word may be slightly changed by the combination with another word (Figure 96.3).

The result is that a term like 'Haustürschlüssel' ('front door key') can be made to appear in an alphabetical index also under 'Türschlüssel (Haus-)' and under 'Schlüssel (Haustür-)'. This kind of decision is of course taken in the thesaurus file. Using these methods we gain access to relevant word elements and quite often to similar terms already filed in the thesaurus.

This handling of compound terms is facilitated by computer programs which are activated during input or update sessions of the thesaurus. It has taken considerable time and effort to define rules which lead to a result which is both easy to understand and aesthetically pleasing.

Again: terminology systems should incorporate this kind of program.

Synonyms

My third example is concerned with synonyms in a thesaurus environment. The usual thesaurus rules for synonyms did not seem to be really helpful in our work on object

Figure 96.4 Synonym problems

Synonymity established by several fields at the same time

The most appropriate term (underlined) in this and many other cases is not in accordance to general rules for syntax (in this case: diminutive). 'Redundant' information in the Simple Name is indicated by inverted commas in brackets.

SIMPLE NAME	MATERIAL	FUNCTION
Kanne	Messing	Taufgerät
Kännchen	Messing	Taufgerät
<u>Taufkännchen</u>	Messing	('')
Messingkännchen	('')	Taufgerät
Messingtaufkännchen	('')	('')

names. Again it is the compound terms which add considerably to these difficulties. I can perhaps describe this with two statements:

if you look only at the field Object Name there are virtually no 'full synonyms'. Even terms which originally were simple translations tend to develop a life of their own. The same goes for terms in dialect which are so dear to people doing research on folklore;

if you look at some additional fields at the same time, you will find a great number of 'full synonyms' or rather a lot of information identical to the information contained in the compound terms mentioned above.

The fields concerned the most often are Material, Function and fields describing context (like Part of) or giving descriptive details like Dimension. In many cases their contents will already be part of the Object Name.

I will give just one example. The object is one of those rather small jugs used during ceremonies of baptism (French: 'burette de baptême'). Some of the variations in writing down exactly the same information are shown in Figure 96.4.

The first term ('Kanne') would follow the often used regulation to put each kind of information into it's proper field and to avoid 'unnecessary' variations in language (the ending '. . . chen' in the following lines signals that it is a small object). The correct term ('Taufkännchen') in this and in many other cases would be a compound term in which at least the content of one other field would already be implied. The other lines give often used variations.

What can we do about this kind of 'synonym'? There are quite obviously no general rules about when and how terms should be combined or not. The immediate result is an enormous and quite undesirable inflation in the number of terms used.

Our first attempt at a practical solution was to experiment with an extension of the regulations we find in thesaurus norms. Before making a decision about preferred terms, descriptors and non-descriptors we tried to describe the equivalence relation by using fields of our data standard.

We could then state that for instance the Object Name 'Porzellantasse' ('china cup') is an equivalent to the combination of the Object Name 'Tasse' ('cup') and the Material 'Porzellan' ('porcelain'). We could also state that 'Tonpfeife' (a clay pipe used for smoking) implies the Material 'Ton' although the simple combination of 'clay' and 'pipe' in German might also be used for a musical instrument or a toy.

In using such equivalences the user then had three options:

automatic replacing of one expression in the object file by the other (including the possibility to add information implied by the term into other fields). This is quite useful in treating variations in orthography. It also helps in getting rid once and for all of undesirable but unkillable compound monstrosities, without being obliged to repeat this cleaning up process from time to time and without loosing implied information from other fields;

declaring them as synonyms for retrieval purposes only, without changing the data in the object files and without making all the variations appear in an alphabetical index. This mode seems to be quite useful during the first stages of thesaurus work when it is still too early for definitive decisions. It also helps to conserve a lot of historically interesting or even valuable variations of words in the object files without inflating the number of 'officially accepted' terms;

- treating them as full synonyms but declaring one of them as 'preferred term' (the only but important function of this explicit preference would be to enforce the sequence of these terms in printing the thesaurus, rather then chance to alphabetical order or an arbitrary decision while making the input).

The advantage in describing equivalence relations in terms of the data standard used for the object files obviously lies in the possibility to formulate easily accessible 'local rules' in the thesaurus file without being obliged to extend them as a general rule of syntax in the data standard (there would be too many exceptions for a general rule).

The importance of context

This small extension of the thesaurus rules for synonyms also made us think about a more general approach to computer support of 'local rules' in the future. There is of course a very wide field of possible applications. The often numerous exceptions to general regulations might be treated differently. In the context of computer support of language specific problems I want to refer to just two:

- the necessity of unambiguous standardised terms in a field like Object Name is a nuisance, especially in treating older sources or working in fields like folklore. It will be quite interesting to treat this problem not so much by inventing new words or by adding to them something in brackets, but by putting them in their context;
- a word-by-word translation of thesaurus terms into another language is a very difficult business, often leading to the creation of artificial and linguistically undesirable terms. Including context information may be a considerable help.

We will try to go in this direction in a project starting in 1989. The introduction of local rules will need a lot of experimentation before we can evaluate positive and negative repercussions on (for example) the consistency of the regulations applied to the data and last not least the data standard.

This project should coincide with a more systematic approach to vocabulary control in the Federal Republic and West Berlin which is in the planning stage.

---

97 IMAGINING THE FUTURE

Dr Peter H. Welsh

Director of Research/Chief Curator
The Heard Museum
Phoenix, Arizona

Introduction

There are different ways to imagine the future. We can concentrate on applications that we wish were available today, and then try to imagine ways that these areas can be addressed. We might also dream of completely unexplored realms and consider how they might be entered. For each of us the future charts a different course. Some of us are still seeking ways to get our collections out of boxes, while others seek ways to put the words that describe our collections into conceptual boxes called data fields.

In discussing the future, one could mention relational databases, expert systems, digital imaging or any of a number of technology intensive techniques. While they might be future techniques from my point of view, for some museums they are part of the past and the present. To speak of specific techniques that hover (some would say 'loom') over the horizon, is of limited utility — and doomed to immediate revision. Thus, I will do no more than suggest several future techniques that seem to hold some promise. I will then discuss those fundamental concepts that must be served by any future techniques.

Techniques

First of all, any discussion of the future presupposes the presence of computers. The ability to search simultaneously (for practical purposes) among a variety of variables is a prerequisite for any other future techniques that might be discussed.

We can enhance our capabilities for learning more about our collections by developing 'expert systems'. So-called expert systems have a clear appeal for applying terminological knowledge to questions commonly asked in museums. An example of the ways that expert systems could be helpful would be in object identification, in which the user is prompted to make observations of the object, and the computer compiles the responses to suggest an attribution.

More advanced applications of expert systems will depend on more advanced utilisation of terminology. Yet, exploring new domains may take us in many directions. We might go beyond terminology into other types of communication to 'languages' of form, colour and pattern. With advances in digitising images, it may become practical to develop libraries of forms, for instance. A query might take the form of a scanned drawing and a request to find things that 'look like this'.

Many who imagine the future envision a time when information from many different institutions will be coordinated through a centralised database. Of course, the Canadian Heritage Information Network (CHIN) is the landmark institution for this approach. Less centralised but also effective has been the growing network among institutions using similar database software. Such a network can develop simply through the use of modems, and an agreement to make data available to another institution in the same way that we would permit a researcher in our own institution query the database. The most active proponents of this approach in the United States are the users of the ARGUS database system.

The future holds great excitement: many challenging problems are being addressed. Certainly, the challenges of the present must be addressed with an eye to the future, but without a clear vision of those principles from the past that serve as our landmarks, our course into the future will be perilous.

Therefore, instead of just looking to the future, I am going to suggest that we reflect on the past and keep in mind some general principles. In the end, I will suggest some general techniques that we might apply to bridge between yesterday and tomorrow.

First principles

It is essential that we do not lose sight of those principles that must serve as the primary landmarks for our work. Unlike much technology and many techniques, first principles do not become obsolete. We will want future techniques to enable us to better meet the ideal states suggested by first principles.

First is the realisation that the people who make and use objects imbue them with significance (Appadurai, 1986 and especially Kopytoff, 1986). Although this observation seems so obvious as to be trivial, in fact it is in our efforts to ascertain the significance of objects that we make advances in our disciplines. This principle appears trivial only when we ask trivial questions of the objects. When we recognise the special place that objects have in human life, and that the functionality of objects includes their ability to condense symbols, meaning, and potency in entities which have physical presence, then we begin to appreciate the possibilities of using objects for expanding our understanding of human possibility.

As we move into the realms of greater sophistication in asking what objects can tell us about the past and the present, the terminology that we use must also become more sophisticated. Future techniques need to combine observations of the physical qualities of objects with their conceptual qualities. Objects without the knowledge that animates them are nothing more than empty husks.

A second principle is that objects alone are mute. They do not speak for themselves. Anthropologists who work with the objects made and used by people from other cultures are particularly aware of this fact. We struggle to find ways to make meaningful in one context — such as a museum — those things produced in another context — such as a native society. However, in this task anthropologists are not much unlike historians, art historians, or, for that matter, zoologists. Practitioners of each discipline attempt to translate across contextual boundaries to make meaningful distinctions. In this effort, of course, terminology becomes a primary tool. Objects somehow speak to us, and we need to find the words that let us speak to others about what we have learned.

Preservation and access

Then there are institutional first principles of preservation and access that together constitute an irresolvable dilemma. While I addressed this topic previously (Welsh and LeBlanc, 1987), the role of terminology in this matter may bear repetition. Documentation is the intellectual investment that professional museum people make toward mitigating the impact of access on the objects we are charged to preserve. The more closely the documentation of an object represents the object itself, the less frequently the object itself will have to be consulted to answer research questions.

While documentation means many things, the terminology that we use to document the objects is a central and critical element of the documentation programme. Terminology, language, is our primary tool for organising our ideas about objects. Even with the most sophisticated electronic imaging systems, the terminological system must be capable of enabling us to select appropriate objects that we have not physically examined, or our intellectual investment in the documentation system will have been wasted.

Preservation from the ravages of entropy and disorder is a responsibility that we who work in museums take seriously. Yet, one of the key topics that was repeated frequently at the Terminology conference is that we are responsible to preserve not only the objects in our trust, but also the richness of understanding that has been passed on to us from our predecessors.

This is particularly a concern when we consider terminology revisions. We need to resist the tendency to dismiss earlier terminologies simply because modern consensus has made a different choice. Our movement into the future depends on the understandings of the past, and we have a reponsibility to preserve knowledge from the ravages of consistency and organisation.

Access represents the other side of our dilemma. Preservation would be much less of a problem if we did not feel obligated to make the objects in our collections accessible to a wide range of users. We could simply store collections in environmentally controlled vaults kept free of light and oxygen. To do so would, however, rob us of much of the reason for following this particular occupation. We keep collections in the public trust so that they can be appreciated by audiences in the present as well as in the future.

Access defies prediction. We cannot know the questions that we need to be prepared to answer. The kinds of questions that could be predicted — historical, functional or hermeneutic — can only suggest the kinds of information that should be included in our documentation. Good documentation encourages access as well as preservation. The more often we are able to depend on documentation to successfully respond to a researcher's or visitor's request without having to jeopardise the objects themselves, the happier we will be to facilitate such requests. Our participation in increased access is directly proportional to our confidence that we can fulfil the questioner's request through our documentation.

Access is not only unpredictable, it is heterogeneous. We cannot predict what questions will be asked, and we cannot predict who will ask them. For purposes of simplicity, I can mention two extreme kinds of users: popular and specialised.

Popular access means many things. It means accommodating the movement to treat museums as a form of popular entertainment. In this sense we need to be responsive to wider, more varied, and more vocal audiences. The more actively we participate in this movement, the more likely we are to be putting our collections at risk. Galleries that must be changed frequently to 'keep it interesting' are reflecting an attitude towards objects that is completely compatible with an age of sound-bites and spin-control in which history is measurable in milliseconds.

Furthermore, among the populace who are interested in popular access are groups we might describe as constitutents rather than simply as audiences. They are constituents in that they want more than entertainment — they want to have some say about the ways that we manage and interpret objects in our collections. In some cases, constituents want to have access to the objects in our collections. For example, The Heard Museum is focused primarily on the cultures of American Indians. We attempt to represent

American Indian peoples of the American Southwest to visitors who come from all over the world. We see American Indian people as more than simply an audience; we see them as constituents. Thus, depending on the circumstance, American Indian people are consulted in matters of collections management, interpretation and, in fact, terminology development. In all cases, our audiences want — and we probably want to give them — greater knowledge about the objects we hold. Surely, our terminology needs to reflect this response to popular access.

Popular access offers tremendous educational potential. We can use the information about the objects in our collections to offer glimpses into the resources of the museum's collections. Access by constituents can also offer tangible benefits to the museum. Constituents who feel that they have an investment in the care and preservation of the collections can often assist in increasing our knowledge about those collections.

Specialised access, meaning access by specialists, has its own challenges. On the one hand, our terminologies need to be able to respond to the queries of specialists. We need to speak the specialist's language — just as for popular access, we need to be able to use terminology that is not daunting to the non-specialist. On the other hand, our terminologies must be able to accommodate the added insights and discriminations that specialists can offer, for it is these additions that continue to refine the quality of our database.

We can further expand the accessibility of collections by developing parallel terminological systems. Such parallel terminologies would reflect the needs of popular users as well as specialised users of a database. Although each group would soon be frustrated by having to employ the terminology of the other, we could construct our systems in such a way that a user would enter and move through the system using terms that are most comfortable for them. At any point, however, they could switch to the terminology developed for an academic specialist, say, or even a native speaker.

Conclusion

The language we use to talk about objects has occupied a prominent place in the thinking of linguists and semanticists. Less well developed is the way that we use objects to communicate ideas. Though the growing interest in semiotics has offered an opportunity for us to consider new ways to look at objects as carriers of significant messages, there remains a great deal to be done in this regard. Museums are the most obvious and appropriate places for this work to be centred. However, for museums to undertake this project while remaining true to their responsibility to preserve cultural and artistic heritage poses great problems. It is through further refinement of terminologies that we will be able to offer increased access to those audiences who can help us increase our knowledge of the objects in our collections and, by further extension, of the lives and times of the creators of those objects.

The first principles concerning our assumptions about the value of objects for learning, for expanding our understanding of the lives of others and of the need to make those objects available to as many people as possible, while preserving them for as long as possible, are principles which will remain valid for some time. They are also principles which provide us with clear goals that we can strive to achieve.

PRIMARY SOURCES AND BIBLIOGRAPHY

PRIMARY SOURCES

This checklist refers to some of the main sources of information about museum terminology. Details of the references are given in the following bibliography.

The compilation of the list has been assisted by a bibliography prepared by the CIDOC Terminology Control Working Group in 1989 and an artist name union list produced by the Getty Art History Information Program Vocabulary Coordination Group in 1988 (with acknowledgement to Eleanor Fink and Jim Bower). Chapter authors and a few other advisors have also made an input. Despite this help, we make no apology for the end result being idiosyncratic. It demonstrates the need for the development and maintenance of a full and annotated directory of terminology sources. In particular, the sections on discipline-based systems are highly selective, based in part on the scope of this volume. They are intended to indicate the types of resources that are available.

Andrew Roberts

General guidelines about documentation and cataloguing practice

Museum registration methods	Dudley and Wilkinson (1979)
Practical museum documentation	Museum Documentation Association (1981 and others in press)
Planning	Roberts (1985)
Collections management	Roberts (1988)

General guidelines about terminology control principles

Guidelines	Aitchison and Gilchrist (1987) Austin and Dale (1981) Foskett (1982) Lancaster (1986) Orna (1983) Wersig (1985)

Terminology standards

See Chapters 3, 5 and 6

Monolingual thesauri	
ISO 2788	International Organization for Standardization (1986)
ANSI/N1SO Z39.19	American National Standards Institute (1980) (new edition in preparation)
BS 5723	British Standards Institution (1987)
NF Z 47–100	Association français de normalisation (1981)
DIN 1463 Teil 1	Deutsches Institut für Normung (1987)
GOST 7.25–80	GOSSANDART (1981)
Multilingual thesauri	
ISO 5964	International Organization for Standardization (1985)

BS 6723	British Standards Institution (1985a)
NF Z 47–101	Association français de normalisation (1977)

Museum standards: national schemes

Canada

See Chapters 15 and 70

Humanities data dictionary	Canadian Heritage Information Network (1985a)
Natural sciences data dictionary	Canadian Heritage Information Network (1985b)
Recording practices research publications	Canadian Heritage Information Network (1985c and others in preparation)

France

See Chapter 13

Système descriptif of the *Ministère de la Culture*

Architecture	Chatenet and de Montclos (1989)
Classical antiquities	Villard (1984)
Iconography	Garnier (1984)
Movable artefacts	Arminjon, Blondel and de Reyniès (1987)

Vocabulaires méthodique

Objects	Arminjon and Blondel (1984)
Movable artefacts	Reyniès (1987)
Sculpture	Baudry (1978)
Tapestries	Viallet (1971)
Architecture	Montclos (1972)

Italy

See Chapters 14, 35, 44 and 45

Archaeology material	Badoni (1980)
Armour	Boccia (1982)
Arms	de Vita (1983)
Church furnishings	Montevecchi and Vasco Rocca (1985, 1987 and 1989)

United Kingdom

MDA's *Museum Documentation System*

New versions of primary standards publications in preparation.

Individual subjects supported by a range of instruction manuals such as Museum Documentation Association (1980a and b)

Application by one museum service described in	Norgate (1986)

Museological terminology

Dictionary of museology	Éri and Vegh (1986)
Glossary of museology	Blanchet and Bernard (1989)

Library and archive standards

Anglo-American Cataloguing Rules	Anglo-American Cataloguing Rules (1988)
MARC Manual	British Library (1989) and Library of Congress (1988)
MARC archive format	Evans and Will (1988) Hensen (1989)
LC subject headings	Library of Congress (1988)

Personal and corporate body name standards and checklists

See Chapters 22–28

Anglo-American Cataloguing Rules	Anglo-American Cataloguing Rules (1988)
Name authorities list	Library of Congress (1977–) British Library (1981–)
Outline of World Cultures	Murdock (1983)
Herbaria: international	Stafleu (1974)
UK	Kent and Allen (1984)
Museums: international	Hudson and Nicholls (1981)
UK	Museums Association (1989)
USA	American Association of Museums (1985) American Art Directory (1984)
Artist names	Allgemeines Künstler-lexikon (1983–) Bénézit (1976) Chilvers and Osborne (1988) Cummings (1982) Delli (1987) Encyclopedia of World Art (1959–1983) Havlice (1973) Logan and Sullivan (1987) Piper (1988) Read and Stangos (1985) Thieme and Becker (1907–1950) Witt Library (1978)

Place name guides and checklists

See Chapters 29–33

General guides

Mapping	Parry and Perkins (1987)
Conventions	Anglo-American Cataloguing Rules (1988)

Systems

Geo-Code	Gould (1968 and 1972)
Outline of World Cultures	Murdock (1983)
USMARC code lists	Library of Congress (1988b and 1988c)
Atlases	New International Atlas (1986) Times Atlas of the World (1985) Websters New Geographical Dictionary (1964)

General descriptive and administrative concepts

See Chapters 17–21 and 80–87 and 93 and museum standards referred to above.

Specific systems

Conservation	Conservation Information Network (1987)
Condition	Jewett (1983)

Selective checklist of sources for archaeology, anthropology and ethnography

See Chapters 34–40

General systems

Archaeological thesaurus	Royal Commission on the Historical Monuments of England (1986) (Chapter 36)	
British Archaeological Thesaurus	Lavell (1989)	(1989)
Outline of World Culture	Murdock (1983)	

Specific systems

Bronze Age/Iron Age material	Badoni (1980) (Chapter 35)
Classical archaeology	Villard (1984)
Glass glossary	Jones and Sullivan (1985)
Pitt Rivers system	Blackwood (1970) (Chapter 39)
Canadian archaeology	Loy and Powell (1977)

Selective checklist of sources for art

See Chapters 22–28, 41–62 and 89–93

For *artist names*, see Personal name entry above.

Dictionaries of terms	Chilvers and Osborne (1988) Lucie-Smith (1984) Mayer (1969) Piper (1988) Read and Stangos (1985)

General systems

Art and Architecture Thesaurus	AAT (1988a, 1988b, 1989 and 1990) (Chapters 53, 56 and 89)

Iconography and visual representation

Iconclass	Van de Waal (1968 and 1973–85) (Chapter 43)
Thesaurus iconographique	Garnier (1984)
Library of Congress system	Parker (1987) and Zinkham and Parker (1986) (Chapters 46 and 51)
Subject index for visual arts	Glass (1969)
Abbreviations for image descriptions	Schuller (1987)
Lexicon iconographicuum mytholgiae classical	Lexicon iconographicuum (1981–)

Selective checklist of sources for decorative art, social and industrial history

See Chapters 54–70

General systems

Art and Architecture Thesaurus	AAT (1988a, 1988b, 1989 and 1990) (Chapters 53, 56 and 89)
Nomenclature	Blackaby *et al.* (1988) (Chapters 58 and 66)
Social History and Industrial Classification (SHIC)	SHIC Working Party (1983) (Chapter 59)
Pitt Rivers classification	Blackwood (1970) (Chapter 39)
Outline of Cultural Materials	Murdock (1983) and Murdock *et al.* (1987)
Systematik kulturhistorischer Sachgüter	Trachsler (1981)
ROOT thesaurus	British Standards Institution (1988)

Specific systems

Armour	Boccia (1982)
Arms	de Vita (1983)
Church furnishings	Montevecchi and Vasco Rocca (1985, 1987 and 1989) (Chapters 44 and 45)
	Dirsztay (1988)
Costume	International Committee for the Museums and Collections of Costume (1982) (Chapter 61)
Domestic artefacts	Østby (1982, 1983, 1984 and 1985) (Chapter 60)
Domestic and movable artefacts	Arminjon, Blondel and de Reyniès (1987)
	Arminjon and Blondel (1984)
	Reyniès (1987)
Shoes	Thornton and Swann (1986)
Sculpture	Baudry (1978)
Tapestries	Viallet (1971)

Selective checklist of sources for natural history and geology

See Chapters 71–79

General guides

Biological nomenclature	Jeffrey (1977)
Key works to European fauna and flora	Sims, Freeman and Hawksworth (1988)
Guide to floras	Frodin (1984)
Guidelines for geology curation	Brunton, *et al.* (1985)
Guide to geology cataloguing	Knell and Taylor (1989)

Codes for taxonomic nomenclature

Botany	Greuter (1988)
Zoology	International Trust for Zoological Nomenclature (1985)

Systems and Treatise

Geosaurus	Charles (1981) (Chapter 73)
Chemical index of minerals	Hey (1955) (Chapter 74)
Glossary of mineral species	Fleischer (1987)
Dana's mineralogy	Frondel (1962)
Rocks	Murray (1981)
Stratigraphy	Holland (1978)
American ornithology	Committee on Classification and Nomenclature of the American Ornithologists' Union (1983)

American mammals	Jones, Carter and Genoways (1986)
Vertebrate palaeontology	Carroll (1988)
Invertebrate palaeontology	Geological Society of America (1970–)
British marine fauna and flora	Howson (1987)
British freshwater animals	Maitland (1977)

BIBLIOGRAPHY

References marked with a * are available from the MDA Book Service.

Adams, M. (1988). *The study of sub-Saharan art history in the United States in the nineteen seventies and eighties*. Paper commissioned by the Joint Committee on African Studies of the American Council of Learned Societies and the Social Science Research Council for presentation at the 31st annual meeting of the African Studies Association, 28 October, 1988. Chicago.

Aitchison, J. (1977). *Unesco thesaurus: a structured list of descriptors for indexing and retrieving literature in the fields of education, science, social science, culture and communication*. 2 vols. Paris: Unesco. ISBN 92 3 101469 2.

Aitchison, J. (1986). A classification as a source for a thesaurus: the bibliographic classification of H. E. Bliss as a source of thesaurus terms and structure. *Journal of Documentation, 42*, 160–181.

Aitchison, J. and Gilchrist, A. (1987). *Thesaurus construction: a practical manual*. 2nd ed. London: Aslib. ISBN 0 85142 197 0. *

Allen, R. F. and Kraft, C. (1984). Transformations that last: a cultural approach. In: Adams, J. D. *Transforming work*. Alexandria, Virginia: Miles River Press.

Allgemeines Künstler-lexikon (1983–). *Allgemaines Künstler-Lexikon die bildenden Künstler aller Zeiten und Völker*. Leipzig: E. A. Seeman. (Updates Thieme-Becker (1907–50).) (See also Volmer (1953–62).)

Allwood, J. (1977). *The great exhibitions*. London: Studio Vista.

Amadon, D. (1966). Another suggestion for stabilizing nomenclature. *Syst. Zool., 15*, 54–58.

American Art Directory (1984). 50th ed. Edited and compiled by Jaques Cattell Press. New York: R. R. Bowker.

American Association of Museums (1985). *Official museum directory for the United States of America.*: National Register Publishing Co.

American National Standards Institute (1980). *ANSI Z 39.19–1980. Guidelines for thesaurus structure, construction and use*. New York: ANSI.

American Society for Testing and Materials (1986). *Compilation of ASTM standard definitions*. 6th ed. Philadelphia: ASTM.

American Society for Testing and Materials (1990). Part E — Terminology in ASTM standards. In: *Form and style for ASTM standards*. Philadelphia: ASTM.

Anglo-American Cataloguing Rules (1988). Prepared under the direction of the Joint Steering Committee for Revision of AACR . Edited by M. Gorman and P. W. Winkler. 2nd ed. 1988 revision. London: Library Association. xxv, 677p. *

Anon. (1975). Report of meeting on geological site documentation. *GCG Newsletter, 1* (5), 206.

Anon. (1977). The Museums Association Working Party on Record Centres in Museums. *BCG Newsletter, 6*, 13–15.

Anon. (1981). ICOM adopts Cardiff Colloquium recommendations. *Geological Curator, 3* (1), 39.

Anon. (1985). *ICOMOS-ICOM Cultural Heritage Thesaurus: historic monuments and sites; museums and museology* (draft). Paris: Unesco-ICOM and Unesco-ICOMOS Documentation Centres.

Anon. (1986). *Guida alla Catalogazione per Autori delle Stampe*. Rome: Istituto Centrale per il Catalogo Unico delle Biblioteche Italiane e per le Infomazioni Bibliografiche; Istituto Centrale per il Catalogo e la Documentazione.

Anon. (1987a). *Format INTERMARC: notice bibliographique des images fixes*. Paris: Bibliothèque Nationale.

Anon. (1987b). Most modern museum. *Computer Systems*, October.

Anon. (1988a). The Common Agenda Museum Information Survey. AASLH Special Report 2. *History News, 43* (4), insert.

Anon. (1988b). *Catalogacion de Materiales Graficos.* Madrid: Biblioteca Nacional.

Anon. (1988c). Museum automation: defining the need. *Museum News, 66* (6), 42–48.

Appadurai, A. (ed.) (1986). *The social life of things: commodities in cultural perspective.* Cambridge: Cambridge University Press.

Arminjon, C. and Blondel, N. (1984). *Vocabulaire des objets civils domestiques, vocabulaire typologique.* Paris: Imprimerie Nationale. 672p.

Arminjon, C., Blondel, N. and de Reyniès, N. (1987). *Système descriptifs des objets mobiliers.* Paris: Ministère de la Culture. Inventaire Général.

Art and Architecture Thesaurus (1988a). *Art and Architecture Thesaurus introductory brochure.* Williamstown, Ma.: AAT.

Art and Architecture Thesaurus (1988b). *Art and Architecture Thesaurus: synopsis.* Williamstown, Ma: AAT.

Art and Architecture Thesaurus (1989). *AAT Bulletin, 18.* Williamstown, Ma.: AAT.

Art and Architecture Thesaurus (1990). *Art and Architecture Thesaurus.* 3 vols. Oxford: Oxford University Press. ISBN 0 19 506403 8. *

Association Francais de Normalisation (1977). *NF Z 47-101:1977. Principes directeurs pour l'éstablissement des thésaurus multilingues.* Paris: AFNOR.

Association Francais de Normalisation (1981). *NF Z 47-100. Documentation. Règles d'éstablissement des thésaurus monolingues.* Paris: AFNOR.

Austin, D. W. (1984). *PRECIS: a manual of concept analysis and subject indexing.* 2nd ed. London: British Library.

Austin, D. and Dale, P. (1981). *Guidelines for the establishment and development of monolingual thesauri.* 2nd rev. ed. (PGI–81/WS/15.) Paris: Unesco.

Badoni, F. Parise (1980). *Materiali dell'etá del Bronzo finale e della prima etá del Ferro.* (Dizionari Terminologici, 1.) Firenze: Centro Di. ISBN 88 7038 005 X. *

Barasch, M. (1987). *Giotto and the language of gesture.* Cambridge: Cambridge University Press.

Bartoli, R., Grita, G., Papaldo, S. and Signore, O. (in press). *Indici CNUCE.*: CNUCE.

Bascom, W. (1969). Creativity and style in African art. In: Biebuyck, D. (ed.) *Tradition and creativity in tribal art.* Berkeley: University of California Press. Pages 98–119.

Bassett, M. G., Ball, H. W., Bassett, D. A., Rickards, R. B., Rolfe, W. D. I., Torrens, H. S. and Waterston, C. D. (1979). Concluding discussion and summary. *Special Papers in Palaeontology, 22,* 269–275.

Bates, M. (1986a). Subject access online catalogues: a design model. *Journal of the American Society for Information Science, 37,* 357–376.

Bates, M. J. (1986b). An exploratory paradigm for online information retrieval. In: Brookes, B. C. *Intelligent information systems for the information society. Proceedings Sixth International Research Forum in Information Science, Frascati, 1985.* Amsterdam: North Holland. Pages 91–99.

Bateson, G. (1979). *Mind and nature: a necessary unity.* New York: Bantam Books.

Baudry, M.-T. (1978). *Vocabulaire de la sculpture, méthode et vocabulaire.* Paris: Imprimerie Nationale. 768p.

Bearman, D. (ed.) (1982). *Data elements used in archives, manuscript and records repository information systems: a dictionary of standard terminology.* National Information Systems Task Force report October 1982. (Reprinted in Sahli, N. ed. (1985). Marc for archives and manuscripts: the AMC format. Chicago: Society of American Archivists*).

Bearman, D. (1987). *Towards national information systems for archives and manuscript repositories: the National Information Systems Task Force (NISTF) papers — 1981–84.* Chicago: Society of American Archivists.

Bearman, D. (in press). Strategies for developing national description standards for archives. In: *Proceedings of the International Council on Archives, Meeting of Experts on Description Standards*, October 1988.

Beazley, J. D. (1956). *Attic black-figure vase painters.* Oxford: Clarendon Press.

Beer, S. (1972). *Brain of the firm*. London: Penguin Press. ISBN 0 7139 02191.

Bénézit, E. (1976). *Dictionnaire critique et documentaire des peintres, sculpteurs, dessinateurs et graveurs de tous les temps et de tous les pays.* Paris: Gründ. 10v.

Bergengren, G. (1978). Towards a total information system. *Museum, 30* (3/4), 213–217.

Berio, E. (1953). The rule of priority in zoological nomenclature. *Bull. zool. Nomencl., 8*, 30–40.

Betz, E. W. (compil.) (1982). *Graphic materials: rules for describing original items and historical collections.* Washington, DC: Library of Congress.

Biblioteca Nacional (1988). *Catalogacion de materiales graficos.* [Chapter 13 in draft cataloguing rules.] Madrid: Biblioteca Nacional.

Bibliothèque Nationale (1987). *Format INTERMARC:* Notice Bibliographique des Images Fixes. Paris: Bibliotheque Nationale.

Bird, J. (1988). On newness, art and history: reviewing *Block* 1979–1985. In: Rees, A. L. and Borzello, F. (eds.). *The new art history.* Atlantic Highlands, N.J.: Humanities Press International Inc.

Blackaby, J. R., Greeno, P. and the Nomenclature Committee (1988). *The revised Nomenclature for museum cataloging.* Nashville, Tenn.: AASLH. *

Blackwood, B. (1970). *The classification of artefacts in the Pitt Rivers Museum Oxford.* (Occasional Papers on Technology, II). Oxford: Pitt Rivers Museum.

Blanchet, J. and Bernard, Y. (1989). *Glossary of museology/lexique de museologie.* (Terminology Bulletin, 188.) Ottawa: Canadian Government Publishing Centre. ix, 263p ISBN 0 660 54662 0.

Blaser, A. (ed.) (1980). *Data base techniques for pictorial applications. Proceedings of Conference, Florence, 1979.* (Lecture Notes in Computer Science, 81.) Berlin: Springer.

Block, C. (1987). *RLG Geo-Referenced Information Network functional requirements.* Stanford, CA: Research Libraries Group. (Unpublished).

Block, C. (1988a). *Data design.* Stanford, CA: Research Libraries Group. (Unpublished).

Block, C. (1988b). *Command design.* Stanford, CA: Research Libraries Group. (Unpublished).

Boccia, L. G. (1982). *Armi difensive dal medioevo all'etá moderna.* (Dizionari Terminologici, 2.) Firenze: Centro Di. ISBN 88 7038 050 5. *

Booth, B. (1988). The SAM Record — past, present and future. In: Rahtz, S.P.Q. (ed.). *Proceedings of the 1988 Computer Applications in Archaeology Conference.* B.A.R. International Series. (S446). Pages 379–388.

Borradaile, L. A. (ed.) (1921). *Bibliography of the marine fauna. Synopsis of the card catalogue.* 3rd ed. London: The Challenger Society.

Boyles, J. C. (1987). Bibliographic databases for the art researcher: developments, problems and proposals. *Art Documentation, 6* (1), 9–12.

Boyles, J. C. (1988). The end-user and the art librarian. *Art Libraries Journal, 13* (2), 27–31.

Bradley, J. D. and Fletcher, D. S. (1979). *A recorder's log book or label list of British butterflies and moths.* London: Curwen Books.

Brilliant, R. (1984). *Visual narratives: story telling in Etruscan and Roman art.* Ithaca: Cornell University Press.

British Library, Bibliographic Services Division (1980). *UK MARC manual.* Second edition. London: British Library. ISBN 0 900220 84 8.

British Library. National Bibliographic Service (1981–). *Name authority list.* London: British Library. (Monthly.)

British Library. National Bibliographic Service (1989). *UK MARC manual.* 3rd ed. Part 1.

London: British Library. ISBN 0 7123 1060 6. (Part 2 in press, 1990.)

British Ornithologists' Union. Records Committee (1988). Suggested changes to the English names of some Western Palaearctic birds. *Ibis, 130,* Supplement; *British Birds, 81,* 355–377.

British Standards Institution (1985a). *BS 6723: 1985. Guidelines for the establishment and development of multilingual thesauri.* London: BSI.

British Standards Institution (1985b). *Root thesaurus.* 2nd ed. Milton Keynes: BSI. 2v. 580 and 620p. ISBN 0 580 14677 4.

British Standards Institution (1987). *BS 5723: 1987. British Standard guide to the establishment and development of monolingual thesauri.* 2nd ed. London: BSI. ISBN 0 580 16101 3. (See also ISO 2788–1986.)

British Standards Institution (1988). *Root thesaurus.* 3rd ed. London. BSI. 2v.

Brown, W. L. (1961). An international taxomonic register: preliminary proposals. *Syst. Zool.* 10: 80–85.

Brummitt, R. K. (1987). Will we ever achieve stability of nomenclature? *Taxon, 36,* 78–81.

Brunton, C. H. C. (1979). The development of a computer-based curatorial system for palaeontology at the British Museum (Natural History). *Special Papers in Palaeontology, 22,* 159–173.

Brunton, C. H. C. (1980). The use of a computer based curatorial system in the Department of Palaeontology B.M.(N.H.). *Geological Curator, 2* (9–10), 624–628.

Brunton, C. H. C., Besterman, T. and Cooper, J. A. (eds) (1985). *Guidelines to the Curation of Geological Materials.* Geological Society Miscellaneous Publication, 17. London: Geological Society. *

Bryson, N. (1983). *Vision and painting: the logic of the gaze.* New Haven: Yale University Press.

Buck, A. (1976). Cataloguing costume. *Museums Journal, 76* (3), 109–110.

Buck, R. D. (1979). Inspecting and describing the condition of art objects. In: Dudley, D. H. and Wilkinson, I. B. (eds). *Museum registration methods.* Washington, DC: American Association of Museums. Pages 237–244. *

Budin, G., Galinski, C., Nedobity, W. and Thaller, R. (1988). Terminology and knowledge processing. In: Czap, H. and Galinski, C. (eds). *Terminology and knowledge engineering.* Supplement. Proceedings of the International Congress on Terminology and Knowledge Engineering, Trier, 29 September–1 October 1987. Frankfurt: INDEKS.

Bulaong, G. (1982). Authorities and standards in the changing world. *International Cataloguing, 11,* 35–36 and 41–44.

Bullis, H. R. Jr and Roe, R. B. (1967). A bionumeric code application in handling complex and massive faunal data. *Syst. Zool., 16,* 52–55.

Canada. Department of Industry, Trade and Commerce (1975). *Trade of Canada commodity classification.* Ottawa: Statistics Canada.

Canadian Heritage Information Network (1985a). *Humanities Data Dictionary.* (Documentation Research Publication, 1.) Ottawa: CHIN. *

Canadian Heritage Information Network (1985b). *Natural Sciences Data Dictionary.* (Documentation Research Publication, 2.) Ottawa: CHIN. *

Canadian Heritage Information Network (1985c). *Standards and terminology for the recording of culture in the humanities data dictionary.* (Documentation Research Publication, 3.). Ottawa: CHIN. *

Carroll, R. L. (1988). *Vertebrate palaeontology.* Chicago: University of Chicago Press.

Cash, J. (1985). Spinning toward the future: the museum on laser videodisc. *Museum News, 63* (6), 19–35.

Chadburn, A. (1988). A review of approaches to controlling archaeological vocabulary for data retrieval. In: Rahtz, S. P. Q. (ed.). *Proceedings of the 1988 Computer Applications in Archaeology Conference.* B.A.R. International Series. (S446). Pages 315–322.

Charles, R. (1981). *Geosaurus: Geosystems' thesaurus of geoscience.* 4th ed. London: Geosystems.

Chatenet, M. and de Montclos, J. M. P. (1989). *Système descriptif de l'architecture.* Paris: Ministère de la Culture. Inventaire Général.

Chenhall, R. G. (1978). *Nomenclature for museum cataloging.* Nashville: American Association for State and Local History. ISBN 0 910050 30 9. (See Blackaby *et al.*, 1988, for later edition.)

Chilvers, I. and Osborne, H. (eds) (1988). *The Oxford dictionary of art.* Oxford: OUP. ISBN 0 19 886133 9. *

Chorley, R. R. E. (1987). Spatial units and locational referencing. In: *Handling geographic information: report to the Secretary of State for the Environment of the Committee of Enquiry into the Handling of Geographic Information.* London: HMSO. ISBN 0 11 752015 2. Pages 162–171.

Clapham, A. R., Tutin, T. G. and Warburg, E. F. (1981). *The excursion flora of the British Isles.* 3rd ed. Cambridge: Cambridge University Press. ISBN 0 521 23290 2.

Claringbull, G. F., Hey, M. H. and Payne, C. J. (1956). *Mineralogical Society Notice,* 95.

Claringbull, G. F., Hey, M. H. and Payne, C. J. (1957). *Mineralogical Magazine, 31,* 420.

Clark, T. J. (1974). On the conditions of artistic creation. *Times Literary Supplement,* 24 May 1974, 561–562.

Clark, T. J. (1985). *The painting of modern life: Paris in the art of Manet and his followers.* New York: Knopf.

Clubb, N. (1988). Computer mapping and the Scheduled Ancient Monuments Record. In: Rahtz, S. P. Q. (ed.). *Proceedings of the 1988 Computer Applications in Archaeology Conference.* B.A.R. International Series. (S446.)

Commission Internationale de l'Eclairage (1987). *International lighting vocabulary.* 4th ed. Vienna: CIE. ISBN 3 900734 070.

Committee on Classification and Nomenclature of the American Ornithologists' Union (1983). *Checklist of North American birds.* 6th ed. Lawrence, KS: American Ornithologists' Union.

Conservation Information Network (1987). *The Conservation Information Network data dictionary.* Vols 1–3. Los Angeles: The Getty Conservation Institute.

Cooper, J. A. and Jones, M. D. (1976). Proposals for a National Scheme for Geological Site Documentation. *GCG Special Publication, 1,* 6–17.

Copp, C. J. T. (1984). Local record centres and environmental recording — where do we go from here? *BCG Newsletter, 3* (9), 489–497.

Cornelius, P. F. S. (1987). Use versus priority in zoological nomenclature: a solution for an old problem. *Bull. zool. Nomencl., 44,* 79–86.

Corti, L. (ed.) (1984). *Census: computerization in the history of art.* Pisa: Scuola Normale Superiore. *

Council of Europe (1986). *Computer applications in the field of nature conservation.* Working group on taxonomic problems and coding systems. Secretariat Memorandum CDSN-Inf(86)2 revised. Strasbourg: Council of Europe.

Council of Europe (1987). *Select Committee of Experts on Data Banks in the Field of Nature Conservation.* (PE-R-BD.) Secretariat Memorandum PE-R-BD(87)3 revised. Strasbourg: Council of Europe.

Council of Europe (1988). *Select Committee of Experts on Data Banks in the Field of Nature Conservation.* (PE-R-BD.) Secretariat Memorandum PE-R-BD(88)2 revised. Strasbourg: Council of Europe.

Craven, W. (1984). *Sculpture in America.* Newark, Delaware: University of Delaware Press. ISBN 0 87413 225 8.

Crawford, W. (1984). *MARC for library use: understanding the USMARC formats.* White Plains, NY: Knowledge Industry.

Crawford, W. (1986). *Technical standards: an introduction for librarians.* White Plains, NY: Knowledge Industry. 299p. ISBN 0 86729 191 5.

Crehange, M., Ait Haddou, A., Boukakiou, M., David, J. M., Foucaut, O. and Maroldt, J.

(1984). EXPRIM: an expert system to aid in progressive retrieval from a pictorial and descriptive database. In: Gardarin, G. and Gelenbe, E (eds). *New applications of databases.* Orlando, Florida: Academic Press. Pages 43–61. ISBN 0122755562.

Crestadoro, A. (1856). *The art of making catalogues of libraries or, a method to obtain in a short time a most perfect, complete, and satisfactory printed catalogue of the British Museum Library.* [London]: The Literary Scientific and Artistic Reference Office.

Crowson, R. A. (1970). *Classification and biology.* London: Heinemann Educational Books. ISBN 0 435 629840.

Cummings, P. (1982). *Dictionary of contemporary American artists.* New York: St Martin's Press.

Dadd, M. N. and Kelly, M. C. (1984). A concept for a machine-readable taxonomic reference file. In: Allkin, R. and Bisby, F. A. (eds). *Databases in Systematics. Systematics Association Special Volume, 26,* London: Academic Press. Pages 69–78. *

Dana, E. S. (1892). *A system of mineralogy.* 6th ed.: John Wiley.

Dana, J. D. (1837). *A system of mineralogy.* 1st ed.: Durrie & Peck and Herrick & Noyes.

Dana, J. D. (1844). *A system of mineralogy.* 2nd ed.: Wiley and Putnam.

Dana, J. D. (1850). *A system of mineralogy.* 3rd ed.: G. P. Putnam.

Dana, J. D. (1855). *A system of mineralogy.* 4th ed. Two volumes.: Trũber and Co.

Dana, J. D. (1868). *A system of mineralogy.* 5th ed.: John Wiley.

Dandy, J. E. (1958). *List of British vascular plants.* London.

Darvill, T., Saunders, A and Startin, B. (1987). A question of national importance: approaches to the evaluation of ancient monuments for the Monuments Protection Programme in England. *Antiquity, 61,* 393–408.

De Vita, C. (1983). *Armi bianche dal Medioevo all'etá moderna.* (Dizionari Terminologici, 3.) Firenze: Centro Di. ISBN 88 7038 084 X. *

Deiss, K. (1988). Databases: artful reference tools or convenient alibis? *Art Libraries Journal, 13* (2), 24–26.

Delli, B. (1987). *Art index.* New York: H. W. Wilson.

Deutsches Institut für Normung (1987). *DIN 1463 Teil 1. Estellung und weiterentwicklung von thesauri. Einsprachige thesauri.* Berlin: Beuth.

Dirsztay, P. (1988). *Church furnishings: a NADFAS guide.*: Routledge.

Dony, J. E., Jury, S. L. and Perring, F. H. (1986). *English names of wild flowers.* 2nd ed. Botanical Society of the British Isles. ISBN 0 901158 15 1.

Dretske, F. I. (1981). *Knowledge and the flow of information.* Oxford: Blackwell. ISBN 0 631 12765 8.

Drewal, H. J. and Drewal, M. T. (1984). *Gelede: art and female power among the Yoruba.* Bloomington: Indiana University Press. ISBN 0253325692.

Dubois, C. P. R. (1984). The use of thesauri in online retrieval. *Journal of Information Science, 8* (2), 63–66.

Dudley, D. H. and Wilkinson, I. B. (1979). *Museum registration methods.* Washington, D.C.: American Association of Museums. lx, 437p.

Dutton, P. (1986). Geschäft über alles: notes on some medallions inspired by the sinking of the Lusitania. *Imperial War Museum Review, 1,* 30–42.

Eco, U. (1979). *A theory of semiotics.* Bloomington: Indiana University Press.

Edwards, E. (1989). The innocent in computing: the Pitt Rivers Museum Photographic Archive documentation system. *Journal of Museum Ethnography,* 1, 85–91.

Eliot, T. S. (1934). *Choruses from 'The Rock'.* London: Faber.

Eldredge, C. C. (1987). Preface. *Smithsonian Studies in American Art, 1.*

Embrey, P. G. (1975). Some thoughts on machine cataloguing. *GCG Newsletter, 1* (3), 148–150.

Encyclopedia of World Art (1959–83). New York: McGraw-Hill.

Eri, I. and Vegh, B. (1986). *Dictionarium museologicum*. CIDOC Working Group on Terminology. Budapest: Hungarian Esperanto Association. 1v, 774p. ISBN 963 571 174 3. *

Evans, L. J. and Will, M. O. (1988). *MARC for archival visual materials*: a compendium of practice. Chicago, Ill.: Chicago Historical Society.

Fédération Internationale des Archives du Film. Cataloguing Commission (1979). *Film cataloging*. New York: Burt Franklin. ISBN 0 89102 076 4.

Federation of Societies for Coatings Technology (1978). *Paint/coatings dictionary*. Philadelphia: FSCT.

Felber, H. (1984). *Terminology Manual*. (Unesco PGI 84/WS/21.) Paris: Unesco. 426p.

Felber, H., Krommer-Benz, M. and Manu, A. (eds) (1979). *International bibliography of standardized vocabularies*. (Infoterm series, 2.) Munich: K. G. Saur. ISBN 0 89664 075 2.

Fischer, E. (1978). Dan forest spirits. *African Arts, 11* (2), 16–23.

Fischer, E. (1984). The masquerade of the Dan: a classification. In: Fischer, E. and Himmelheber, H. *The arts of the Dan in West Africa*. Zurich: Museum Rietberg. ISBN 3907070046.

Fleischer, M. (1987). *Glossary of mineral species*. 5th ed. Tucson, AZ: Mineralogical Record.

Flesness, N. R. Garnatz, P. G. and Seal, U. S. (1984). ISIS — an international specimen information system. In: Allkin, R. and Bisby, F. A. (eds), *Databases in Systematics. Systematics Association Special Volume, 26*. London: Academic Press.' Pages 103–112. *

Foskett, A. C. (1982). *The subject approach to information*. 4th ed. London: Clive Bingley. ISBN 0 85157 339 8. *

Foskett, D. J. (1959). *The construction of a faceted classification for a special subject*. London: Butterworths.

Foucault, M. (1970). *The order of things: an archaeology of the human sciences*. New York: Vintage Books.

Franks, J. W. (1973). Herb. Manch. A guide to the contents of the Herbarium of Manchester Museum. *Manchester Museum Publications, N.S.*, 1.73.

Frodin, D. G. (1984). *Guide to the standard floras of the world*. Cambridge: Cambridge University Press.

Frondel, C. (1962). *Dana's system of mineralogy*. Vol. 3.: John Wiley.

Fuchs, R. H. (1972–73). Henri van de Waal 1910–1972. *Simiolus, 6* (1), 5–7.

Galinski, C. and Nedobity, W. ([1986]). A terminological data bank as a management tool. In: Albrecht, J., Drescher, H. W., Göhring, H. and Salnikow, N. (eds). *Translation und interkulturelle kommunikation*. 40 Jahre Fachbereich Angewandte Sprachwissenschaft der Johannes Gutenberg-Universität Mainz in Germersheim. Frankfurt: Peter Lang. Also in *Unesco/ALSED-LSP Newsletter, 9* (2), 2–10.

Garland, S. (ed.) (1985). Biological recording and the use of site-based biological information. *BCG Newsletter, 4* (2), 1–72. *

Garnier, F. (1984). *Thésaurus iconographique. Système descriptif des représentations*. Paris: Le Léopard D'Or. *

Garrard, T. (1980). *Akan weights and the gold trade*. (Legon History Series.) London: Longman. ISBN 0582646316.

Genoways, H. H., Jones, C. and Rossolimo, O. L. (eds) (1987). *Mammal collection management*. Lubbock, Texas: Texas Tech University Press. IV, 219p. *

Geological Society of America (1970–). *Treatise on invertebrate palaeontology*.: University of Kansas Press.

Geosystems (1981). *GeoArchive users guide*. London: Geosystems. ISBN 0 901806 05 6.

Gittins, D. (1976a). Computer-based collection documentation using INFOL/2. *GCG Newsletter, 1* (6), 302–309.

Gittins, D. (1976b). Computer-based museum information systems. *Museums Journal, 76* (3), 115–118.

Gittins, D. (1976c). Computer-based museum information systems. *Museums Journal, 76*, (3), 115–118.

Gittins, D. and Scotter, C. N. G. (1977). Letters to the Editor. *Museums Bulletin, 17* (1), 9–10.

Glass, E. (1969). *A subject index for visual arts.* London: HMSO.

Gomez, L. M. and Lochbaum, C. C. (1985). People can retrieve more objects with enriched key-word vocabularies. But is there a human performance cost? In: Shackel, B. (ed.). *Human-computer interaction — Interact '84. Proceedings of the IFIP Conference, London, 1984.* Amsterdam: North-Holland.

Goodenough, W. H. (1956). Componential analysis and the study of meaning. *Language, 32*, 195–216.

Goodenough, W. H. (1965). Rethinking 'status' and 'role': toward a general model of the cultural organization of social relationships. In: Banton, M. (ed.). *The relevance of models for social anthropology.* London: Tavistock Publications. Pages 1–24.

Gopinath, M. A. and Seetharama, S. (1979). Interdisciplinary subjects and their classification. In: Neelameghan, A. (ed.) *Ordering systems for global information networks. Proceedings of the Third International Study Conference on Classification Research.* Bombay: FID/CR. Pages 121–135.

Gordon, C. (1988). Report of ICONCLASS workshop, 2–4 November 1987. *Visual Resources, 5* (3), 197–258.

Gorman, M. and Winkler, P. W. (eds) (1978). *Anglo-American cataloguing rules.* 2nd ed. Chicago: American Library Association and London: Library Association.

Gorman, M. and Winkler, P. W. (eds) (1988). *Anglo-American cataloguing rules.* 2nd ed. 1988 revision. London: Library Association. 667 p. ISBN 0 85365 598 7. (Also cited under Anglo-American Cataloging Rules, 1988.)*

GOSSTANDART (1981). *GOST 7.25–80. [Monolingual thesaurus for information retrieval.]* Moscow: GOSSTANDART.

Gould, S. W. (1968). *Geo-Code.* Vol. 1 [West edn.] New Haven, Conn: The Gould Fund.

Gould, S. W. (1972). *Geo-Code.* Vol. 2 [East edn.] New Haven, Conn: The Gould Fund.

Great Britain. Central Statistical Office (1981). *Standard industrial classification.* London: HMSO.

Great Britain. Science and Art Department (1877). *Catalogue of the Special Loan Collection of Scientific Apparatus at the South Kensington Museum MDCCCLXXVI.* 3rd ed. London: HMSO.

Greenhalgh, M. (1982). New technologies for data and image storage and their application to the history of art. *Art Libraries Journal, 7* (2), 67–81.

Greenhalgh, M. (1986). Why should art historians learn programming? *Computers and the History of Art, 2*, 7–13.

Greenhalgh, M. (1987). Databases for art historians: problems and possibilities. In: Denley, and Hopkin, (eds). *History and computing.* Manchester: Manchester University Press. Pages 157–167.

Greenthal, K., Kozel, P. M. and Ramirez, J. S. (1986). *American figurative sculpture in the Museum of Fine Arts, Boston.* Boston: Museum of Fine Arts. ISBN 0 87846 272 4. Page 479.

Greuter, W. (1986). Proposals on registration of plant names: a new concept for the nomenclature of the future. *Taxon, 35*, 816–819.

Greuter, W. (1988). *International code of botanical nomenclature.* Köningstein: Koeltz Scientific Books. ISBN 3 87429 278 9.

Hagen, M. A. (1986). *Varieties of realism, geometries of representational art.* London: Cambridge University Press.

Halfpenny, G. (1983). Natural History Classification Scheme in use at the City Museum and Art Gallery, Stoke-on-Trent. *BCG Newsletter, 3* (6), 305–320.

Hancock, E. G. (1977). Zoological Collections in North West England. In: The function of local natural History collections. *Museums Journal, 77* (4), 130.

Hancock, E. G. (1987). The North West Collections Research Unit. *Museums Journal, 77* (4), 188–189.

Hancock, E. G. and Pettitt, C. (eds) (1979). Collections and Collectors in North West England (Botany, Geology and Zoology). Manchester: Manchester Museum.

Hancock, M. (1987). Subject searching behaviour at the library catalogue and at the shelves: implications for online interactive catalogues. *Journal of Documentation, 43*, 303–321.

Harrison, H. W. (1988). *FIAF cataloguing rules, review draft*. Brussels: Fédération Internationale des Archives du Film.

Harting, P. (1871). Schets van een nieuw stelsel van zoologische nomenclatuur. *Versl. Meded. K. Akad. wet. Amst.* (Natuurk.), (2) *5*, 311–324. [A German translation, "Skizze eines rationellen System der zoologischen Nomenclatur", was published in *Arch. Naturgesch. 37*, 25–41, the same year.]

Hastings, A. (1986). Interactive videodisc project at University College, Dublin. *Art Libraries Journal, 11* (4), 19–23.

Hausman, J. (1986). Art history core videodisc retrieval project at the School of Art and Art History and Weeg Computing Centre, University of Iowa. *International Bulletin for Documentation of the Visual Arts, 13* (1), 13–16.

Havlice, P. (1973). *Index to artistic biography*. Metuchen, NI: Scarecrow Press. (Supplement in 1981.)

Hawksworth, D. L. (1988). Improved stability for biological nomenclature. *Nature, Lond., 334*, 301. [A revised version of this paper, 'Increased nomenclatural stability through Lists of Names in Current Use', was published in *Bull. zool. Nomencl., 45*, 183–185, the same year.]

Heikertinger, von F. (1918). Das Patriazeichen beim Artnamen. *Zoologische Anzeiger, 50*, 41–54.

Helgerson, L. W. (1986). CD-ROM search and retrieval software: the requirements and the realities. *Library Hi-Tech, 14*, 69–77.

Hensen, S. L. (1989). *Archives, personal papers and manuscripts*: a cataloguing manual for archival repositories, historical societies and manuscript libraries. 2nd ed. Chicago: Society of American Archivists. 196p.

Herrera, A. L. (1899). *Sinonomía vulgar y científica de los principales vertebrados mexicanos*. Méjico: Oficina Tipográfica de Secretaría de Fomento. 31p.

Hertfordshire Curators' Group (1984). *Hertfordshire simple name list*: Standing Committee for Museums in Hertfordshire. ISBN 0 901354 30 9. *

Hey, M. H. (1950). *An index of mineral species and varieties arranged chemically*. 1st ed. London: British Museum (Natural History).

Hey, M. H. (1955). *An index of mineral species and varieties arranged chemically*. 2nd ed. London: British Museum (Natural History).

Hey, M. H. (1963). *Appendix to the second edition of an index of mineral species and varieties arranged chemically*. London: British Museum (Natural History).

Hey, M. H. and Embrey, P. G. (1974). *A second appendix to the second edition of an index of mineral species and varieties arranged chemically*. London: British Museum (Natural History).

Heymann, F. J. (1983). Summary and conclusions. In: Interrante, C. G. and Heymann, F. J. (eds). *Standardization of technical terminology: principles and practices*. (ASTM STP 806.). Philadelphia: American Society for Testing and Materials.

Holland, C. H., *et al.* (eds.) (1978). *A guide to stratigraphic procedure*. (Geological Society of London Special Report, 11.) London: Geological Society.

Holt, B. P., McCallum, S. H. and Long, A. B. (eds) (1987). *UNIMARC manual*. London: IFLA UBCIM Programme.

Hooper-Greenhill, E. (1987). Knowledge in an open prison. *New Statesman*, 13 February 1987, 21–22.

Horsfall, A. (1987). *The awareness and use of terminology control in museum documentation.* A study submitted in partial fulfilment of the requirements for the degree of Master of Science in Information Studies. Sheffield: The University.

Houghton, B. (1969). *Standardization for documentation.* London: Bingley. 93p. SBN 85157 078 X.

Howson, C. M. (ed.) (1987). *Directory of the British marine fauna and flora. A coded checklist of the marine fauna and flora of the British Isles and its surrounding seas.* Ross-on-Wye: Marine Conservation Society. ISBN 0 948150 04 1.

Hudson, K. and Nicholls, A. (1981). *The directory of world museums.* 2nd ed. London: MacMillan.

Hull, D. L. (1966). Phylogenetic numericlature. *Syst. Zool.* 15: 14–17.

Hull, D. L. (1968). The syntax of numericlature. *Syst. Zool.* 17: 472–474.

Hughes, D. O. (1988). Representing the family. In: Rotberg, R. I. and Rabb, T. (eds). *Art and history.* New York: Cambridge University Press.

International Commission on Zoological Nomenclature (1964). *International code of zoological nomenclature.* London: The International Trust for Zoological Nomenclature. (See also International Trust for Zoological Nomenclature, 1985).

International Committee for the Museums and Collections of Costume (1982). Vocabulary of basic terms for cataloguing costume. *Waffen- und Kostümkunde, 24,* 119–152. *

International Organization for Standardization (1974). *ISO 2788–1974. Guidelines for the establishment and development of monolingual thesauri.* Geneva: ISO. (Superseded by ISO 2788–1986.)

International Organization for Standardization (1982a). *Information transfer.* 2nd ed. (ISO Standards Handbook, 1.) Geneva: ISO.

International Organization for Standardization (1982b). *Units of measurement.* 2nd ed. (ISO Standards Handbook.) Geneva: ISO.

International Organization for Standardization (1983). *Standardization and documentation: an introduction for documentalists and librarians.* Geneva: ISO. 93p. ISBN 92 67 10071 8.

International Organization for Standardization (1984). *ISO 7498–1984. Basic reference model.* Geneva: ISO.

International Organization for Standardization (1985a). *ISO 5964–1985. Guidelines for the establishment and development of multilingual thesauri.* Geneva: ISO.

International Organization for Standardization (1985b). *Photography.* (ISO Standards Handbook, 26.) Geneva: ISO. 434p. ISBN 92 67 10111 0.

International Organization for Standardization (1986). *ISO 2788–1986. Guidelines for the establishment and development of monolingual thesauri.* Geneva: ISO.

International Organization for Standardization (1988). *Information Transfer.* 3rd edition. (ISO Standards Handbook, 1.) Geneva: ISO. 1021p. ISBN 92 67 10144 7.

International Trust for Zoological Nomenclature (1985). *International code of zoological nomenclature.* 3rd ed. London: ITZN with the British Museum (Natural History). ISBN 0 85301 003 X.

International Union of Pure and Applied Chemistry (1979). *Nomenclature of organic chemistry.* London: Pergamon. ISBN 0 08 022369 9.

Istituto Centrale per il Catalogo Unico delle Biblioteche Italiane e per le Informazioni Bibliografiche and Istituto Centrale per il Catalogo e la Documentazione (1986). *Guida alla Catalogazione per Autori delle Stampe.* Rome: The Institutes.

Jahn, T. L. (1961). Man versus machine: a future problem in protozoan taxonomy. *Syst. Zool.* 10: 179–192.

Jeffrey, C. (1977). *Biological nomenclature.* London: Edward Arnold. ISBN 0 7131 2615 9. *

Jewett, D. F. (1983). *A glossary for recording the condition of an artefact.* Ottawa: Canadian Heritage Information Network. *

Jones, B. (1979). Data storage and retrieval for the palaeontological collections, University of Alberta. *Special Papers in Palaeontology*, 22, 175–187.

Jones, J. K., Carter, D. and Genoways, H. (1986). *Revised checklist of North American mammals north of Mexico*. El Paso: Texas Tech University.

Jones, L. D. and Allden, A. J. (1988). How the British Museum computerised its collections. *Government Computing*, 2 (2), 17–20.

Jones, M. D. (1975). Workshop on geological cataloguing. *GCG Newsletter*, *1* (3), 138–140.

Jones, M. D. and Cooper, J. A. (1975). A national scheme for the documentation of geological sites. *GCG Newsletter*, *1* (5), 225–230.

Jones, O. R. and Sullivan, C. (1985). *Glass glossary*. Ottawa: Parks Canada. 184 p. ISBN 0 660 11775 4. *

Kasfir, S. (1984). One tribe, one style? Paradigms in the historiography of African Art. *History in Africa*, *11*, 163–193.

Keesing, R. M. (1970). Towards a model of role analysis. In: Naroll, R. and Cohen, R. (eds). *A handbook of method in cultural anthropology*. Garden City, NY: Natural History Press. Pages 432–453.

Kent, D. H. and Allen, D. E. (1984). *British and Irish herbaria*. London: Botanical Society of the British Isles. iv, 333p. ISBN 0 901158 05 4.

Kindleberger, C. F. (1983). Standards as public, collective and private goods. *In* Kyklos, *Internationale Zeitschrift für Socialwissenschaften*, *36* (3), 377–396.

Kirsch, J. L. and Kirsch, R. A. (1988). The anatomy of painting style: description with computer rules. *Leonardo*, *5*, 437–444.

Kirsch, R. A. (1984). Making art historical sources visible to computers: pictures as primary sources for computer-based art history data. In: Corti, L. (ed.) *Second International Conference on Automatic Processing of Art History Data and Documents, 1984. Papers*. Pisa: Scuola Normale Superiore. Vol. 2, Pages 275–290. *

Knell, S. J. and Taylor, M. A. (1989). *Geology and the local museum*. London: HMSO. xii, 150p. ISBN 0 11 290459 9. *

Knight, G. N. (1979). *Indexing, the art of* London: Allen and Unwin.

Kopytoff, I. (1986). The cultural biography of things: commoditization as process. In Appadurai, A. (ed.). *The social life of things: commodities in cultural perspective*. Cambridge: Cambridge University Press. Pages 64–91.

Lancaster, F. W. (1986). *Vocabulary control for information retrieval*. 2nd ed. Arlington, Virginia: Information Resources Press. ISBN 0 87815 053 6. *

Lane Fox, A. (1874). On the principles of classification. *Anthropological Journal*, *4*, 293–308.

Laurent, B. (1983). L'utilisation des vidéodisques dans la documentation iconographique: un exemple. Le vidéodisque URBAMET. *Documentaliste*, *20*, 98–100.

Lavell, C. (1989). *British Archaeological Thesaurus*. (CBA Practical Handbooks in Archaeology, 4.) London: Council for British Archaeology. ISBN 0 9067 8077 2.

Lea, G. (1978). GeoArchive: Geosystems' indexing policy. *Proceedings of the Geoscience Information Society*, *8*, 42–56.

Leites, N. C. (1986). *Art and life: aspects of Michelangelo*. New York: New York University Press.

Lexicon iconographicuum mythologiae classical (1981). (LIMC.) Zurich: Artemis.

Library of Congress (1977–). *Name authorities cumulative microform*. Washington, DC: Library of Congress.(Also available on CD-ROM as *CDMARC names, 1989–* .)

Library of Congress. Network Development and MARC Standards Office (1988a). *USMARC format for bibliographic data*. Washington, DC: Library of Congress.

Library of Congress (1988b). *USMARC code list for countries*. Washington, D.C.: Library of Congress.

Library of Congress (1988c). *USMARC code list for geographic areas.* Washington, D.C.: Library of Congress.

Light, R. B. (1979). Computer-based cataloguing in British museums. *Special Papers in Palaeontology, 22,* 149–157.

Little, E. J. Jr. (1964). The need for a uniform system of biological numericlature. *Syst. Zool., 13,* 191–194.

Logan, A.-M. and Sullivan, K. (1987). *British artists authority list* developed by the Yale Center for British Art Photograph Archive. Eugene, Or: Visual Resources Association. *

Loy, T. and Powell, G. R. (1977). *Archaeological data recording guide.* (Heritage Record, 3.) Victoria: British Columbia Provincial Museum.

Lucie-Smith, E. (1984). *The Thames and Hudson dictionary of art terms.* London: Thames and Hudson. ISBN 0 500 20222 2. *

Lucker, A. (1988). The right words: controlled vocabulary and standards. (An editorial.). *Art Documentation, 7* (1), 19–20.

Lyons, J. (1977). *Semantics.* Cambridge: Cambridge University Press.

McCracken, G. (1988). *Culture and consumption. New approaches to the symbolic character of consumer goods and activities.* Bloomington, Indiana: Indiana University Press.

MacDonald, R. S. and Wilks, P. A., Jr (1988). JCAMP-DX: a standard form for exchange of infrared spectra in computer readable form. *Applied Spectroscopy, 42* (1), 151–162.

McInnes, C. (1978). The Hunterian IRGMA geology vocabulary and grammar. *MDA Information,* 2 (2), 11–17.

McKie, E. W. (1980). Using the MDA cards in the Hunterian Museum. *Museums Journal, 80,* 86–89.

McLeod, M. (1984). Akan terracottas. In: Picton, J. (ed.) *Earthenware in Asia and Africa.* London: Percival David Foundation of Chinese Art. ISBN 0728601206. Pages 365–380.

McQueen, J. and Boss, R. W. (1986). *Videodisc and optical digital disk technologies and their applications in libraries, 1986 update.* Chicago: American Library Association. ISBN 8389 7041 9.

Maitland, P. S. (1977). *A coded checklist of animals occurring in fresh water in the British isles.* Edinburgh: Institute of Terrestrial Ecology. 76p.

Markey, K. (1983). Catalog use studies — since the introduction of online interactive catalogs: impact on design for subject access. *Library and Information Science Research, 5,* 337–363.

Markey, K. (1984). Interindexer consistency tests: a literature review and report of a test of consistency in indexing visual materials. *Library and Information Science Research, 6,* 155–177.

Markey, K. (1986). *Subject access to visual resources collections. A model for computer construction of thematic catalogs.* Westport, Conn.: Greenwood Press. ISBN 0 313 24031 0. *

Martin, M. D. (compil.) (1974). *Reference manual for machine-readable bibliographic descriptions.* Paris: Unesco.

Mayer, R. (1969). *A dictionary of art terms and techniques.* New York: Crowell.

Michener, C. D. (1963). Some future developments in taxonomy. *Syst. Zool.* 12: 151–172.

Michener, C. D. (1964). The possible use of uninominal nomenclature to increase the stability of names in biology. *Syst. Zool.* 13: 182–190.

Miles, G. (1988). Conservation and collection management: integration or isolation. *International Journal of Museum Management and Curatorship, 7,* 159–163.

Miles, G. and Umney, N. (forthcoming). *Information handling in conservation.*

Miles, M. R. (1985). *Image as insight: visual understanding in western Christianity and secular culture.* Boston: Beacon Press.

Mills, J. and Broughton, V. (1984). *Bliss bibliographical classification.* 2nd ed. Class K. Society. London: Butterworths. ISBN 0 408 70820 4.

Mol, A. W. M. (1984). Limnofauna Neerlandica. *Nieuwsbrief European Invertebrate Survey — Nederland, 15*, 1–124.

Montclos, J. M. (1972). *Vocabulaire de l'architecture*. Paris: Imprimerie Nationale. 720p.

Montevecchi, B. and Papaldo, S. (1987). *Modello di banca-dati per un museo: i dipinti della Galleria Spada in Roma*. Rome: Multigrafica Editrice.

Montevecchi, B. and Vasco Rocca, S. (1985). *Le suppellettili ecclesiastiche — thesaurus dei termini*. Rome: Multigrafica Editrice.

Montevecchi, B. and Vasco Rocca, S. (1987). *Suppellettile ecclesiastica*. (Dizionari Terminologici, 4.). Florence: Centro Di. ISBN 88 7038 142 0. *

Montevecchi, B. and Vasco Rocca, S. (1989). *La Suppellettile Ecclesiastica. Metodologia di Catalogazione*. Florence: Centro Di. *

Moore, P. B. and Araki, T. (1976). *American Mineralogy, 61*, 88.

Murdock, G. P. (1983). *Outline of world cultures*. Sixth revised edition. New Haven, Conn.: Human Relations Area Files. ISBN 0 87536 664 3. *

Murdock, G. P., Ford, C. S., Hudson, A. E., Kennedy, R., Simmons, L. W. and Whiting, J. W. M. (1987). *Outline of cultural materials*. 5th ed. New Haven, Conn.: Human Relations Area Files Inc. ISBN 0 87536 645 6. *

Murray, J. W. (1981). *A guide to classification in geology*: Ellis Horwood division of John Wiley & Sons.

Musée Picasso (1988). *Demoiselles d'Avignon*. Paris: Editions de la Réunion des musées nationaux.

Museum Documentation Association (1980a). *Museum object instructions*. (Museum Documentation System.) [Cambridge]: MDA. *

Museum Documentation Association (1980b). *Geology specimen card instructions*. (Museum Documentation System.) [Cambridge]: MDA. *

Museum Documentation Association (1981). *Practical museum documentation*. 2nd ed. Cambridge: MDA. VIII, 188p. ISBN 0 905963 41 5. *

Museums Association (1989). *Museums Yearbook*. London: Museums Association.

National Library of Medicine (1988). *Medical subject headings*. Bethesda, Maryland: National Library of Medicine.

Nedobity, W. (1983). Terminology and its application to classification, indexing and abstracting. *Unesco Journal of Information Science, Librarianship and Archives Administration, 5* (4), 227–234.

Nedobity, W. (1987). *International bibliography of standards and non-standardized guidelines for terminology*. (BT 6.). Vienna: Infoterm.

Needham, J. G. (1910). Practical nomenclature. *Science, N.Y., 32*, 295–300.

New International Atlas (1986). Chicago: Rand McNally.

Nicoll, D. (1984). Grace beyond the rules: a new paradigm for lives on a human scale. In: Adams, J. D. *Transforming work*. Alexandria, Virginia: Miles River Press.

Norgate, M. (1986). *WILTM Group Conventions*. Steeple Ashton, Wilts: The Author. *

Nowak, E. (1977). *Die Lurche und Kriechtier der Länder der Europäischen Gemeinschaft*. Greven: Kilda-Verlag. ISBN 3 921427 19 3.

Nowak, E. (1979). *Die Vögel der Länder der Europäischen Gemeinschaft*. Greven: Kilda–Verlag. ISBN 3 921427 03 7.

Nowak, E. (1981). *Die Säugetiere der Länder der Europäischen Gemeinschaft*. Greven: Kilda–Verlag. ISBN 3 921427 24 X.

Nyerges, A. L. (1983). Museums and the videodisc revolution: cautious involvement. *Videodisc/Videotext, 2* (4), 267–274.

Odak, O. (1988). *Material culture and ethnic identity*. Paper presented at an international Workshop on Resources and Documentation of African Material Culture, Bellagio, Italy, May 1988. [Unpublished].

Okun, H. (1984). Picassofile, or using the computer to look at Picasso. *Picturescope, 31* (4), 114–118.

Oliver, I. and Langford, H. (1987). Myths of demons and users: evidence and analysis of negative perceptions of users. In: Galliers, R. (ed.). *Information analysis: selected readings.* Sydney: Addison-Wesley. Pages 113–123.

Onyeneke, A. (1985). The masquerade: a social symbol in Igboland. *Ikoro, 6* (1), 19–34.

Opinion 72 (1922). Herrera's zoological formulae. *Smithson. misc. Collns, 73* (1), 19–22. [Reprinted 1958 in *Opin. Decl. int. Commn. zool. Nomencl., 1B,* 503–504.]

Orna, E. (1983). *Build yourself a thesaurus. A step by step guide.* Norwich: Running Angel. ISBN 0 946600 00 7. *

Orna, E. (1986). Information management by design: improving information retrieval on Prestel. *Information Design Journal, 5* (1), 61–68.

Orna, E. and Pettitt, C. W. (1980). *Information handling in museums.* New York: K. G. Saur and London: Library Association. 190 p. ISBN 0 85157 300 2. *

Østby, J. B. (1982). *Nomenklatur for drikkestell.* [Illustrated dictionary of drinking vessels and containers.] Oslo: Norske Kunst-og Kulturhistoriske Museer. *

Østby, J. B. (1983). *Nomenklatur for spise-og serveringsbestikk.* [Illustrated dictionary of flatware.] Oslo: Norske Kunst-og Kulturhistoriske Museer. *

Østby, J. B. (1984). *Nomenklatur for melkestell.* [Illustrated dictionary of appliances for milk and butter.] Oslo: Norske Kunst-og Kulturhistoriske Museer. *

Østby, J. B. (1985). *Forelopig nomenklatur for esker, tiner og skrin.* [Illustrated draft dictionary of boxes, chests and trunks.] Oslo: Norske Kunst-og Kulturhistoriske Museer. *

Österdahl, L. and Zetterberg, G. (1981). RUBIN species codes and species numbers. *Statens naturvårdsverk Forskningssekretariat Rapport.* SNV PM 1427. ISBN 91 7590 065 3

Österdahl, L., Zetterberg, G. and Andersson, I. (1977). Introduktion till RUBIN. *Statens naturvårdsverk Forskningssekretariat Rapport.* SNV PM 909.

Palache, C., Berman, H. and Frondel, C. (1944). *Dana's system of mineralogy.* Vol. 1: John Wiley.

Palache, C., Berman, H. and Frondel, C. (1951). *Dana's system of mineralogy.* Vol. 2: John Wiley.

Papaldo, S. and Signore O. (1989). *Un approccio metodologico per la realizzazione di una banca dati storico-geografica.* (A methodological approach to producing a historical/geographical databank.) Roma: Multigrafica Editrice. 573p. ISBN 88 7597 105 6.

Parker, E. B. (compil.) (1987). *LC thesaurus for graphic material: topical terms for subject access.* Washington, DC: Library of Congress. *

Parry, R. B. and Perkins, C. R. (1987). *World mapping today.* London: Butterworths. ISBN 0 408 02850 5. *

Perkins, J. (ed.) (1986). *Computer technology for conservators.* Proceedings of the 11th annual IIC-CG conference workshop. Atlantic Group of IIC-CG. ISBN 0 9691347 1 1. *

Perkins, J., Jelich, H. and Lafontaine, R. (1987). The Conservation Information Network. In: *Reprints of the 8th Triennial Meeting.* Paris and Los Angeles: ICOM Conservation Committee. Pages 255–260.

Petersen, T. (1984). [Thesauri.] In: Corti, L. and Schmitt, M. (eds). *Second International Conference on Automatic Processing of Art History Data and Documents, 1984. Proceedings.* Pages 55–59. *

Pettigrew, T. and Holden, J. (1978). Internal Conventions used with the IRGMA Geology and Mineral Specimen cards in the documentation of the Geology collections of Tyne and Wear County Council Museums. *GCG Newsletter Supplement,* 2 (3), 1–26.

Pettitt, C. W. (1979). A Comparison of the Famulus and GOS packages for handling museum data. *BCG Newsletter,* 2 (3), 105–108.

Pettitt, C. W. (1981). The Manchester Museum Computer Cataloguing Unit: a STEP in the right direction? *Museums Journal, 80* (4), 187–191.

Pettitt, C. W. (1986). Collections research in the United Kingdom. In: Light, R. B., Roberts, D. A. and Stewart, J. D. (eds). *Museum*

Documentation Systems. London: Butterworths. ISBN 0 408 01081 5 0. Pages 221–228. *

Pettitt, C. W. and Hancock, E. G. (1981). Natural Sciences Collections Research Units, their origin, aims and current status. *Museums Journal, 81* (2), 73–74.

Picht, H. and Draskau, J. (1985). *Terminology: an introduction*. (Department of Linguistics and International Studies Monographs, 2.) Guildford: University of Surrey. 265p. ISBN 0 9510943 1 9.

Piggott, M. (1988). *A topography of cataloguing*. London: Library Association.

Piggot, S. (1976). *Ruins in a landscape: essays in antiquarianism*. Edinburgh: Edinburgh University Press.

Piper, D. (1988). *Dictionary of art and artists*. London: Collins. ISBN 0 00 434358 1. *

Porter, M. F. and Roberts, D. A. (1977). Letters to the Editor. *Museums Bulletin, 17* (1), 10.

Price, D. (1986). Documentation after 'The Guidelines'. *Geological Curator, 4* (8), 481–483.

Quine, W. V. (1969). *Ontological relativity and other essays*. New York: Columbia University Press.

Read, H. and Stangos, N. (1985). The Thames and Hudson dictionary of art and artists. London: Thames and Hudson. ISBN 0 500 20223 0. *

Reed, P. A. and Sledge, J. (1988). Thinking about museum information. *Library Trends, 37* (2), 220–231.

Rees, A. L. and Borzello, F. (eds) (1988). *The new art history*. Atlantic Highlands, NJ: Humanities Press International Inc.

Rey, A. (1979). *La terminologie: noms et notions*. Paris: Presses Universitaires de France. 127p.

Reyniès, N. de (1987). *Vocabulaire du mobilier domestique*. Paris: Imprimerie Nationale. 2 vol. 1300p.

Rheinisches Museumsamt (1985). *Inventarisierung*.: Rheinland-Verlag. ISBN 3 7927 0900 7.

Rhumbler, von L. (1910). Über eine zweckmässige Weiterbildung der Linnéischen binären Nomenklatur. *Zoologische Anzeiger, 36*, 453–471.

Rivas, L. R. (1965). A proposed code system for storage and retrieval of information in systematic zoology. *Syst. Zool.* 14: 131–132.

Roberts, D. A. (1976a). *Introduction to the IRGMA documentation system*. (Part 1.) London: Museums Association. 29p.

Roberts, D. A. (1976b). IRGMA Proposals for locality records. *GCG Special Publication, 1*, 18–55.

Roberts, D. A. (1980). Documentation of geological material — towards a common standard. *MDA Information, 4* (5), 28–31 and *Geological Curator, 3* (1), 14–17.

Roberts, D. A. (1981a). MDA/GCG Mineralogical Terminology Documentation. *Geological Curator, 3* (1), 10–13.

Roberts, D. A. (1981b). GCG/MDA Workshop on Geology Documentation. *GCG Newsletter, 3* (2/3), 74–76 and *MDA Information, 5* (3), 15–18.

Roberts, D. A. (1985). *Planning the documentation of museum collections*. Cambridge: MDA. v, 568p. ISBN 0 905963 53 9. *

Roberts, D. A. (1986). Towards a common strategy for Geological Documentation: the MDA view. *Geological Curator 4* (8), 477–480.

Roberts, D. A. (ed.) (1988). *Collections management for museums. Proceedings of an international conference . . . September 1987*, Cambridge. MDA. xx, 237p. ISBN 0 905963 61 X. *

Roberts, D. A. and Light, R. B. (1980). Progress in documentation. Museum documentation. *Journal of Documentation, 36* (1), 42–84.

Roberts, H. E. (1985). Visual resources: proposals for an ideal network. *Art Libraries Journal, 10* (3), 32–41.

Roberts, N. (1984). The pre-history of the information retrieval thesaurus. *Journal of Documentation, 40*, 271–285.

Robins, R. H. (1979). *A short history of linguistics*. 2nd ed. London: Longman. ISBN 0 582 55288 5.

Romer, A. S. (1966). *Vertebrate paleontology*. 3rd ed. Chicago: University of Chicago Press.

Royal Commission on the Historical Monuments of England (1986). *Thesaurus of archaeological terms*. London: RCHME. 122 p.

Royal Commission on the Historical Monuments of England (1987). *Draft thesaurus of architectural terms*. London: RCHME.

Rushlight Club (1935). Committee on the Classification of Lamps. *The Rushlight*, *1*, 8.

Russell, L. S. (1968). *A heritage of light*. Toronto: University of Toronto Press.

Sahli, N. (1985). *MARC for archives and manuscripts. The AMC format*. Chicago, Ill.; Society of American Archivists. ISBN 0 931828 65 1. *

Salton, G. (1986). Another look at automatic text-retrieval systems. *Communications of the ACM*, *29* (7), 648–656.

Salton, G. and McGill, M. J. (1983). *Introduction to modern information retrieval*. New York: McGraw Hill.

Sanders, T. R. B. (ed.) (1972). *The aims and principles of standardization*. Geneva: ISO. 121p.

Sarasan, L. (1981). Why museum computer projects fail. *Museum News*, *59* (4), 40–49.

Sarasan, L. (1988). Standards: how do we get there from here? *Museum News*, *66* (6), 36.

Sarasan, L. and Neuner, A. M. (1983). *Museum collections and computers*. Lawrence, Kansas: Association of Systematics Collections. ISBN 0 942924 03 7.

Saro, C. and Wolters, C. (1988). EDV-gestützte Bestandserschließung in kleinen und mittleren Museen, Bericht zum Projekt "Kleine Museen" für den Zeitraum 1984–1987. *Materialien aus dem Institut für Museumskunde* (Berlin), *24*.

Schama, S. (1988). *Embarrassment of riches: an interpretation of Dutch culture in the Golden Age*. Berkeley: University of California Press.

Schmitt, M. (ed.) (1988). *Object — image — inquiry: the art historian at work*. Report on a collaborative study by the Getty Art History Information program (AHIP) and the Institute for Research in Information and Scholarship (IRIS), Brown University. Santa Monica: The Getty Art History Information Program. *

Schuller, N. S. (1987). VRA Special Bulletin for photographic documentation of the visual arts: standard abbreviations for image descriptions for use in fine arts visual resource collections. *Visual Resources Association Special Bulletin*, *2*. *

Schupbach, W. (1985). Some cabinets of curiosities in European academic institutions. In: Impey, O. and MacGregor, A. *The origin of museums*. Oxford: Clarendon Press. Pages 169–178.

Schwartz, C. and Esienman, L. M. (1986). Thesaurus development. *Annual Review of Information Science and Technology*, *21*, 38–39.

Schwartz. G. (1986–87). Le Musée Documentaire: reflections on a database of works mentioned in art treatises and town descriptions before 1800. *Bulletin of the Archives and Documentation Centres for Modern and Contemporary Art*, *2* (1986) and *1* (1987), 56–59.

Shatford, S. (1984). Describing a picture: a thousand words are seldom cost-effective. *Cataloging and Classification Quarterly*, *4* (4), 13–30.

Shatford, S. (1986). Analyzing the subject of a picture. *Cataloging and Classification Quarterly*, *6*, 39–62.

Shearer, J. (1979). *Geosources: Geosystems' list of geoscience serial titles and non-serial publishers*. London: Geosystems.

Sheridan, W. (ed) (1986). *Anglo-American cataloguing rules (second edition) for the pictorial collection, Science Museum, London*. London: Science Museum.

SHIC Working Party (1983). *Social History and Industrial Classification*. Sheffield: University of Sheffield, Centre for English Cultural Tradition and Language. *

Signore, O. and Bartoli, R. (1989). *Managing art history fuzzy dates: an application in historico-geographical authority*. Paper presented at the Cologne Computer Conference, 7–10 September, 1988. *Historical Social Research*, *14* (3), 98–104.

Signore, O., Campari, I., Magnarapa, C., Ferrari, O., Grita, G. and Papaldo, S. (1988). *Schema di realizzazione di elaborazione cartografica di un thesaurus Storico-geografico.* [Internal report C88–14.] Pisa: CNUCE.

Sims, R. W., Freeman, P. and Hawksworth, D. L. (1988). *Key works to the fauna and flora of the British Isles and north-western Europe.* (Systematics Association Special Volume, 33.) 5th ed. Oxford: Clarendon Press. xii, 312p. ISBN 0 19 857706 0. *

Skinkel-Taupin, C. (1984). A propos d'un vase italiote: problèmes de terminologie. *Bulletin des Musées royaux d'Art et d'Histoire* (Brussels), *55* (2), 39–51.

Sledge, J. E. (1988). Survey of North American collections management systems and practice. In: Roberts, D. A. (ed.). *Collections management for museums.* Cambridge: Museum Documentation Association. ISBN 0 905963 61 X. Pages 9–17. *

Small, J. P. (1988). A database for classical iconography. *Art Documentation, 7* (1), 3–5.

Smith, D. G. W. and Leibovitz, D. P. (1986). MINDENT: a database for minerals and a computer program for their identification. *Canadian Mineralogist, 24*, 695–708.

Smith, H. M. and Smith, R. B. (1980). Herrera's formulae are not names. Proposed Direction supplementary to Direction 32. *Bull. zool. Nomencl., 36*, 246–248.

Smither, R. B. N. (1987). Formats and standards: a film archive perspective on exchanging computerized data. *American Archivist, 50* (3), 324–337.

Smithsonian Institution. Office of Information Resource Management (1984). *A plan for the acquisition of an integrated, generalized, collections management information system.* Washington, DC: Smithsonian Institution.

Smithsonian Institution. Office of Information Resource Management (1986). *Data administration standards manual.* Washington, DC: Smithsonian Institution.

Solkin, D. H. (1982). *Richard Wilson: the landscape of reaction.* London: Tate Gallery.

Sorkow, J. (1983). Videodiscs and art documentation. *Art Libraries Journal, 8* (3), 27–41.

Spengler, W. E. (1988). *Projekt 'Kleine Museen'. Thesaurus zu Ackerbaugerät, Feldbestellung Landwirtschaftliche Transport- und Nutzfahrzeuge Werkzeuge.*: Rheinsches Museumsamt and Institut für Museumskunde.

Stafleu, F. A. (1974) *Index Herbariorum*: a guide to the location and contents of the world's public herbaria. Compiled by P. K. Holmgren and W. Keuken. Utrecht: Oosthoek, Scheltema and Holkema for the International Bureau for Plant Taxonomy and Nomenclature.

Stanley, J. L. (1986). African art and the Art and Architecture Thesaurus. *Museum Studies Journal, 2* (2), 42–53.

Steiner, W. (1988). *Pictures of romance: form against content in painting and literature.* Chicago: University of Chicago Press.

Stevenson, R. B. K. (1954). The National Museum of Antiquities of Scotland. *Museums journal, 54*, 56–59.

Stout, G. L. (1935). A museum record of the condition of paintings. *Technical Studies in the Field of Fine Arts, 3* (4), 203–212.

Strehlow, R. A. (ed) (1988). *Standardization of technical terminology.* Vol. 2. (ASTM STP 991.). Philadelphia: American Society for Testing and Materials.

Sustik, J. M. (1981). Art history interactive videodisc project at the University of Iowa. *Videodisc/Teletext, 1* (2), 78–85.

Teichert, C. (1970–). *Treatise on invertebrate paleontology.* 2nd ed. Boulder, Co.: Geological Society of America.

Thieme, U. and Becker, F. (1907–1950). *Allgemeines Lexikon der bildenden Künstler von der Antike bis zur Gegenwart.* Leipzig: E. A. Seemann. 37v. (See also Volmer (1953–62) and Allgemeines Künstlerlexicon (1983–).)

Thornton, J. H. and Swann, J. M. (1986). *A glossary of shoe terms.* Northampton: Central Museum. *

Thuillier, J. (1987). An opinion: relationships among databases serving the history of art. *Art Documentation, 6* (3), 108–109.

Tickner, L. (1988). *The spectacle of women: imagery of the suffrage campaign, 1907–1914.* Chicago: University of Chicago Press.

Times Atlas of the World (1985). London: Times Books Ltd.

Toney, S. (1988). Planning techniques for collections information systems. In: Roberts, D. A. (ed.). *Collections management for museums.* Cambridge: Museum Documentation Association. ISBN 0 905963 61 X. Pages 82–87. *

Tornier, G. (1898). Grundlagen einer wissenschaftlichen Thier- und Pflanzennomenclatur. *Zool. Anz., 21,* 575–580.

Trachsler, W. (1981). *Systematik kulturhistorisches Sachgüter. Eine klassifikation nach funktionsgruppen zum gebrauch in museen und sammlunger.* Bern: Paul Haupt Bern. ISBN 3 258 02942 3.

Trendall, A. D. (1967). *The red-figured vases of Lucania, Campania and Sicily.* Oxford: Clarendon Press.

Treuherz, J. (1987). *Hard times: social realism in Victorian art.* London: Lund Humphries; Mt Kisco, NY: Moyer Bell, in association with Manchester City Art Galleries.

Tubbs, P. K. (1986). The stability of zoological nomenclature. *Nature, Lond., 321,* 476.

Turner, S. and Robson, P. (1979). Computer controlled databank system at the Hancock Museum. *GCG Newsletter,* 2 (7), 443–445.

Tutin, T. G., Heywood, V. R., Burges, N. A., Valentine, D. H., Walters, S. M. and Webb, D. A. (eds) (1964–80). *Flora Europaea.* 5 vols. Cambridge: Cambridge University Press.

United Nations (1949). Nomenclature of Geographic Areas for Statistical Purposes. *U.N. Statistical papers Series,* M(1).

United Nations. Food and Agricultural Organization (1960). Geographic classification and codes. In: *Current bibliography for aquatic sciences and fisheries.* Volume 3, Pages 3 (1) ex 24–25. London: Taylor & Francis.

Ure, P. N. (1927). *Boeotian pottery of the geometric and archaic styles.* (Classification des céramiques antiques, XII.) Mâcon: Protat (Union académique internationale), 18.

Vajda, E. (compiler) (1980). *Unisist guide to standards for information handling.* Paris: Unesco. 304p. ISBN 92 3 101833 7.

Van de Waal, H. (1955). Some principles of a general iconographical classification. *Actes du 17 ème Congrès international d'Histoire de l'Art,* Amsterdam 23–31 Juillet 1952. Pages 601–606. (Reprinted in Aler, J. (ed.) (1968). *Actes de 5 ème Congrès international d'Esthétique,* Amsterdam 1964. The Hague: Mouton. Pages 727–783.

Van de Waal, H. (1968). *Decimal Index of the Art of the Low Countries (DIAL).* Abridges edition of the ICONCLASS system. The Hague: Riksbureau voor Kunsthistsorische Documentatie.

Van de Waal, H. (1973–85). *ICONCLASS — an iconographic classification system.* 17 volumes. (System, Bibliography and Index.) Amsterdam: North-Holland Publishing Co. for Koninklijke Nederlandse Academie van Wetenschappen.

Vansina, J. (1984). *Art history in Africa: an introduction to method.* London: Longman. ISBN 0582643678.

Vasco Rocca, S. and Montevecchi, B. (1985). Le suppellettili ecclesiastiche — thesaurus dei termini. In: *Automazione dei dati del Catalogo dei Beni Culturali, atti del convegno* Rome: Multigrafica Editrice. Pages 131–136.

Viallet, N. (1971). *La tapisserie, méthode et vocabulaire.* Paris: Imprimerie Nationale. 148p.

Vickery, B. C. (1975). *Classification and indexing in science.* 3rd ed. London: Butterworths.

Viet, J. (1980). *International thesaurus of cultural development.* Paris: Unesco.

Villard, L. (1984). *Système descriptif des antiquités classiques.* Paris: Ministère de la Culture. *

Virginia Museum of Fine Arts (1987). *Information systems framework.* Richmond, VA: Virginia Museum of Fine Art.

Virshup, A. (1988). The great art explosion. *Art News,* April 1988, 103–109, and Renaissance or deluge. *Art News,* April 1988, 119–122.

Vollmer, H. (1953–62). *Allgemeines Lexikon der bildenden Künstler des X.X. Jahrunderts*. Leipzig. E. A. Seeman. 6v. (Updates Thieme-Becker (1907–50).) (See also Allgemeines Künstlerlexicon (1983–).)

Vries, E. A. de (1987). *Museum information by means of computer and videodisc for public use*. Paper presented at the International Conference of Maritime Museums, September 1987.

Wainwright, I. N. M. (1986). A conservation information retrieval system of the Canadian Conservation Institute. In: Perkins, J. (ed.). *Computer technology for conservators*. [S.L.]: Atlantic Regional Group of the International Institute for Conservation of Historic and Artistic Works: Canadian Group. ISBN 0 9691347 1 1. Pages 249–264. *

Walat, J. (1986). The BIOSIS taxonomic reference file: a microcomputer-based pilot project for an organism data network. *Science Software Quarterly, 2* (4), 10–14.

Walley, G. (1984). Thoughts on the Leicester biological recording meeting. Where to next? *BCG Newsletter, 3* (10), 541–547.

Warner, A. J. (1988). Natural language processing in information retrieval. *Bulletin of the American Society for Information Science, 14* (6), 18–19.

Websters New Geographical Dictionary (1964). Springfield, MA.: G & C. Merriam.

Weller, M. and Fink, E. (1987). *Geographic name authority survey*. Los Angeles, CA: Getty Art History Information Program. (Unpublished).

Welsh, P. A. and LeBlanc, S. A. (1987). Computer literacy and collections management. *Museum News, 65* (5), 42–51.

Wersig, G. (1985). *Thesaurus-leitfaden*. Eine einführung in das thesaurus-prinzip in theorie und praxis. (DGD-Schriftenreihe, Band 8.) München: K. G. Saur. ISBN 3 598 21252 6.

Wijk, R.,Margadant, W. D. and Florschutz, P. A. (1959). *Index Muscorum*. Vol. 1. (Vol. 17 of *Regnum Vegetabile*). Utrect: International Bureau for Plant Taxonomy and Nomenclature.

Wilkinson, G. G. and Winterflood, E. R. (eds) (1987). *Fundamentals of information technology*. London: John Wiley.

Witt Library (1978). *A checklist of painters c. 1200–1976 represented in the Witt Library, Courtauld Institute of Art*. London: Mansell.

Wood, S. (1987). Military museums: the national perspective. *Museums Journal, 87* (2), 65–66.

Woodward, C. D. (1972). *BSI — the story of standards*. London: British Standards Institute. ISBN 0 580 07591 5.

Zinkham, H. and Parker, E. B. (eds) (1986). *Descriptive terms for graphic materials: genre and physical characteristic headings*. Washington DC: Library of Congress. *

CONTRIBUTORS

ALAN ABERG
Royal Commission on the Historic Monuments of England

Currently Principal Investigator of the RCHM England, and head of the Archaeology Record Section of the National Monuments Record. Previously Lecturer in Archaeology at the University of Leeds, and has also held appointments in museums at Ipswich and Southampton. Has published papers on medieval archaeology in several journals and reports on excavations apart from papers on the work of the Archaeology Record Section.

ALISON ALLDEN
The British Museum

Alison Allden joined the Collections Data Management Section of the British Museum in 1985. This section is currently computerising the collections' documentation, and management of this project includes the supervision of specialist teams compiling the database and liaison with the curatorial staff in the antiquities departments — to define the user requirement and plan the work programme. The recent acquisition of a new computer has involved her in detailed systems analysis and design work, incorporating a review of data standards and terminology controls, in order to develop a consistent museum-wide information system. During the last year the development of thesauri and authority lists has been a high priority.

Before moving to the British Museum she was responsible, as County Archaeological Officer, for setting up a computerised County Sites and Monuments Record for Gloucestershire; this followed a period spent developing a computerised national Scheduled Monuments Record for the Department of the Environment Inspectorate of Ancient Monuments (now English Heritage). She has a degree in archaeology and several years experience in the field, is a Member of the Institute of Field Archaeologists and the Institute of Information Scientists. From 1988–89, she spent a year at the London School of Economics undertaking an MSc course in Analysis, Design and Management of Information Systems.

RACHEL M. ALLEN
National Museum of American Art, Smithsonian Institution

Rachel M. Allen is Acting Chief in the Office of Research Support at the National Museum of American Art. The Office of Research Support encompasses a variety of specialised art resources which include the Inventory of American Paintings Executed before 1914, the Inventory of American Sculpture, the Peter A. Juley and Son Collection, the Smithsonian Art Index, the Slide and Photographic Archives, and the museum's database for the permanent collection. Mrs Allen has served on the staff of the National Museum of American Art for 15 years, with experience in the areas of office administration, information management, archival management, rights and reproductions and photographic services. For the past two years, she has been actively involved with the development of the Smithsonian's Collection Information System. She holds a BA from Duke University.

CATHERINE ARMINJON
Ministère de la Culture et de la Communication

Diplômée d'Etudes Supérieures d'Histoire de l'Art de la Faculté des Lettres de Paris. Conservateur de l'Inventaire général, à la Direction du Patrimoine au Ministère de la Culture. Responsable des Objets Mobiliers (spécialistes des Arts décoratifs de l'Orfèvrerie et des arts du métal ainsi que des Objets d'Art religieux et des instruments de musique.) Auteur du Dictionnarie des *Objets Civils domestiques* publié à l'Imprimerie Nationale en 1984. Co-auteur du *Système descriptif des Objets Mobiliers* de l'Inventaire général. Responsable du programme de recherche sur l'orfèvrerie française dans le cadre du Laboratoire de Recherches du CNRS (Central National de la recherche scientifique) (publication sur les *Orfèvres de Nantes* 1989). A participé aux travaux de coordination des différentes bases de données informatiques du Ministère de la Culture ainsi qu'aux travaux de l'AFNOR sur l'analyse de l'Image. Participe aux travaux de méthodologie de l'Inventaire général.

FRANCA PARISE BADONI
Istituto Centrale per il Catalogo e la Documentazione, Roma

Laureata in Lettere classiche nel 1961 all'Università di Milano, ha studiato presso le Università di Mainz e di Bonn (1963–64) ed ha frequentato la Scuola Nazionale di Archeologia di Roma e la Scuola Archeologica Italiana di Atene. 1969: ispettore archeologo presso la Soprintendenza archeologica di Chieti. 1976: soprintendente aggiunto. Dal 1978 dirige il Servizio Beni Archeologici dell'Istituto Centrale per il Catalogo e la Documentazione. 1974–79: direzione della scavo della necropoli di Alfedena. 1977–80: direzione e coordinamento della campagna speciale di rilevamento fotografico e di documentazione dell'area archeologica di Pompei. 1981: mostra documentaria *Pompei 1748–1980* (Roma). Edizione degli indici topografici *Pitture e pavimenti di Pompei*, I, II, III, Roma 1981, 1983, 1986.

DAVID BEARMAN
Archives and Museum Informatics

David Bearman is a consultant on archives and museum information systems and the editor of *Archival Informatics Newsletter and Archival Informatics Technical Report*, journals that focus on museum and archives issues. Prior to establishing Archives & Museum Informatics in Pittsburgh, David was Deputy Director of the Office of Information Resource Management at the Smithsonian, an office he helped establish in 1982. David serves on the board of the Museum Computer Network and was President of MCN in 1988/89. He directed the National Information Systems Task Force of the Society of American Archivists in the development of communications standards for archives and has written extensively on the politics and technical issues surrounding the development and maintenance of standards. David served as chairman of the Arts and Humanities Special Interest Group of the American Society for Information Science in 1989, is a fellow of the Society of American Archivists, and has been an active member of other archival and museum associations. He is author of over 60 papers and reports, including a number in his academic speciality, the history of science.

JAMES R. BLACKABY
Mercer Museum

Originally from Palo Alto, California, James R. Blackaby was educated at the University of Oregon. He was a lecturer in English Literature at that institution, and he later taught at Temple University in Philadelphia, Pennsylvania.

Mr Blackaby became involved with museums as a member of the Research Department of Old Sturbridge Village in Massachusetts and in collection management as project director to create storage and records systems for the collection of the Mercer Museum, an encyclopaedic collection of pre-Industrial American material culture. For eight years he has served as Curator of the Mercer Museum and of Fonthill, Mercer's castle-like home.

Mr Blackaby has lectured extensively on aspects of material culture, collection management, and computerisation. He has served as officer and committee member of regional and national museum organisations and as board member of national museum support programs. He was an editor of the *Revised Nomenclature for Museum Cataloging*, he is Chairman of the Common Agenda for History Museums Data Base Task Force, and he serves on the Steering Committe of the American Association of Museums 'Decade Survey'.

Besides having designed several computerised collection management systems, Mr Blackaby has particular interest in the possibilities of museums sharing information. Most recently he has been involved in projects to consider computerised applications for *Nomenclature* and the possibilities of using electronic imaging systems as an adjunct to museum cataloging.

JAMES M. BOWER
Getty Art History Information Program

James M. Bower has been Technical Information Specialist with the Getty AHIP Vocabulary Coordination Group since 1987, developing systems and resources supporting application of controlled vocabularies. Prior to 1987 he was Assistant Archivist/Head of Technical Services with the Getty Center Photo Archive, where he designed cataloging and authority databases for the research photograph collections. He has been active in the Art Libraries Society of North America and the Research Libraries Group in promoting descriptive standards for visual materials.

MICHAEL BUDD
Museum Documentation Association

Mike Budd joined the MDA in 1988 as an Advice and Training Officer, having previously worked at Perth Museum & Art Gallery, Berwick Borough Museum, and the Scottish Fisheries Museum. He completed the Graduate Certificate Course in Museum Studies at the University of Leicester in 1985 and is currently working on an MSc project relating to computerised cataloguing systems.

JOHN BURNETT
National Museums of Scotland

John Burnett was born and educated in Glasgow, and later read Natural Sciences at the University of Cambridge. He holds a Master's Degree in Information Studies from the University of Sheffield. From 1978 to 1986 he worked at the Science Museum, London, and he is now Head of Documentation at the National Museums of Scotland, Edinburgh.

LESLIE CARLYLE
Canadian Conservation Institute/Courtauld Institute of Art

Leslie Carlyle is a paintings conservator, currently on education leave from her position at the Canadian Conservation Institute in Ottawa, Canada. Now enrolled at the Courtauld Institute of Art in London as a PhD candidate, she is conducting research in the history of nineteenth-century oil paintings, materials and techniques. Part of the research involves the development of a computer database containing information on the materials and techniques of nineteenth-century painters in oil.

LARRY CARVER
Map and Imagery Laboratory, University of California

Larry Carver is the Director of the Map and Imagery Laboratory at the University of California, Santa Barbara. He is a member of the RLG Taskforce for the creation of the GRIN system, a member of the American Society of Photogrammetric Engineering and Remote Sensing Preservation and Information Access Committee, and is on the Board of Directors of the United States Geological Survey's Earth Sciences Information Centers state affiliated offices.

AMANDA CHADBURN
English Heritage

Amanda Chadburn was educated at the University of Durham, where she read Archaeology and Anthropology, and at the University of Oxford where she took the 'in-service' course in practical archaeology. From there, she went on to work on the Sites and Monuments Records of Surrey and East Sussex, and became the Assistant Records Officer at English Heritage's Records Office in 1987, working on the Scheduled Ancient Monuments Record. Ms Chadburn began excavating whilst at school, and has continued to dig and fieldwalk on sites in the UK, Hungary, France and Italy. Recently she co-directed and published a Neolithic site at Hengistbury Head, Dorset, with Julie Gardiner. Main interests in archaeology include British prehistory, especially the Iron Age, and records management.

ANDREW CLARK
The Natural History Museum, London

After obtaining a physics degree at the University of Wales in 1966, Andrew Clark spent three years as a research assistant in the Geology Department at University College, London, where he helped introduce the technique of electron-probe microanalysis for the analysis of geological materials. This work was continued as a PhD student in the Department of Mineralogy and Petrology at Cambridge University.

In 1969 he joined the staff in the Mineralogy Department at the British Museum (Natural History), where he has worked mainly on minerals of the niobium-tantalum and platinum groups. Since 1988 he has been engaged on the production of a revised computer-based index of mineral species, one of its uses being in the classification and indexing of mineral collections. The compilation of this index forms the subject matter of his contribution to this volume.

JOHN A. COOPER
Booth Museum of Natural History, Brighton

John Cooper joined the Booth Museum of Natural History in Brighton as the Keeper of Geology in 1981. Previously, he worked in the Earth Sciences Section of Leicestershire Museums.

Born in Hull and educated at the Marist College and Leicester University where he read Geology, John Cooper saw a year's service for VSO in Nigeria after completing the Museum Studies Course in 1973 and before joining Leicestershire Museums for seven years. He has been highly active in the Geological Curators' Group for which, apart from being treasurer for some five years and now Chairman, he developed the National Scheme for Geological Site Documentation and latterly co-edited and substantially authored the innovative *Guidelines for the Curation of Geological Materials* (Geol. Soc. Miscell. Pub.17, 1985). He has had a long term interest in the advancement of professional standards of specimen documentation and has wide experience of both European and

American museum methods. In Brighton, he is responsible for the computerised system of the Royal Pavilion, Musems and Art Galleries Department and founded the highly regarded Brighton and Hove Geological Society. Current research centres on Brighton's typed and figured collections and biographic studies.

He is married with one daughter and one son.

MICHAEL CORFIELD
National Museum of Wales

Michael Corfield started in conservation in 1969 with the Ministry of Public Buildings & Works Ancient Monuments Laboratory (later Department of the Environment, now English Heritage). During his four years with the Laboratory he studied for the Diploma in Conservation of the Institute of Archaeology.

In 1973 he moved to Wiltshire to set up a county-wide conservation service and soon became involved with the establishment of conservation record systems and eventually became one of the conservation laboratories to use the MDA record cards and the GOS package for indexing data. Subsequently, the inadequacies of this system for conservation recording became apparent and he worked with the MDA developing a microcomputer-based database.

In 1986 he was appointed Head of Conservation in the Department of Archaeology and Numismatics, National Museum of Wales.

From 1984 to 1988 he was Chairman of the United Kingdom Institute for Conservation and he has published a number of papers on information storage and retrieval in conservation.

STEPHEN H. DELROY
Canadian House of Commons

Steve Delroy was born in Montreal, Canada but grew up in Ottawa. He took his BA Honours degree from Carleton University in 1972 and completed a M.Phil. from the University of Edinburgh in 1980. From 1974 to 1977, he was an Archive Technician at the Canadian Centre for Folk Culture Studies of the Museum of Man. During this period, he did various experimental projects to computerise folkloric information using a Varian minicomputer and worked extensively with a cataloguing system based on Murdock. From 1977 to 1982, he was Senior Cataloguer at the centre. During this time he founded the computer users group at the National Museum of Man and acted as the User Representative to the Canadian Heritage Information Network. In 1982, he was seconded by the Canadian Heritage Information Network as a Museum Consultant. In 1983, he became Chief of Research at CHIN and then, in 1986, Chief of Research and Consulting. During this time the Humanities and Natural Sciences Data Dictionaries of CHIN were published and made available online. In 1989, he left CHIN to become the first Curator of the collections at the Canadian House of Commons.

ROBIN DOWDEN
National Gallery of Art, Washington

Robin Dowden received a BA in art history from Arizona State University and did her graduate work in eighteenth-century British art at the University of California, Davis. She worked for the Office of the Registrar at the Crocker Art Museum in Sacramento and served as Assistant to the Director at the Richard L. Nelson Art Gallery. In 1980, she attended the Attingham Summer School as the Sir George Trevelyan Scholar. In 1981, after completing an internship in the Department of Prints and Drawings at the National Gallery of Art, Washington, she was hired to manage the transfer of the Gallery's data on works of graphic art to a computer-based cataloguing system. Since 1985, she has worked in the National Gallery's Department of Data Processing, where she is in charge of the development of the Art Information System.

ELIZABETH EDWARDS
Pitt Rivers Museum, University of Oxford

Elizabeth Edwards is Archivist at the Pitt Rivers Museum, University of Oxford and has a special interest in photography curatorship.

AXEL ERMERT
DIN Deutsches Institut für Normung e.V., Berlin

Secretary, ISO/TC 46/SC 3. Born 1952 in Berlin (Federal Republic of Germany). Studied sociology and information science. It was there where it came to training in the spirit of information science as an overall subject/discipline, as such encompassing libraries, documentation work, museums, archives, publishing. After studies, joined West Germany's standardisation body DIN (in 1978) at the committee for library science and documentation which holds the secretariat of the international standardisation committee ISO/TC 46 in the same technical field. Here, to a considerable degree also a coordinative work, the overall approach as established by information science is substantiated which also materialises in the scope of

ISO/TC 46: its subjects ranging from bibliographic description, technical terminology, editing, classification, printing, geography, script/character set and transliteration practices, linguistics, translation sciences, and computer applications.

Runs as a Secretary several national and international standardisation groups. First contact during this work with museums as information institutions through work at the 'Vocabulary of information and documentation' at Leiden and Paris (ICOM). Member of West Germany's professional association of documentalists (DGD). Presented results of documentation standardisation work there and at congresses.

PROFESSOR ORESTE FERRARI

Istituto Centrale per il Catalogo e la Documentazione, Roma

Oreste Ferrari, nato a Roma il 5 Aprile 1927, si è laureato in Filosofia nell'Università di Roma. Ha studiato Storia dell'Arte come allievo di Lionello Venturi e di Giulio Carlo Argan. Dal 1949 è nella pubblica amministrazione dei Beni Culturali, prima nelle Soprintendenze di Venezia e di Napoli, poi a Roma. Nel 1969 ha fondato lo speciale ufficio per la catalogazione del patrimonio culturale italiano, che nel 1975 diverrà l'Istituto Centrale per il Catalogo e la Documentazione, del quale egli è tuttora il Direttore. E' libero docente di Storia dell'Arte nell'Università di Roma. Si è specializzato nello studio della pittura e della scultura napoletana del Seicento e del Settecento ed ha publicato una monografia su Luca Giordano (in collaborazione con G Scavizzi) e numerosi saggi. E' redattore della rivista *Storia dell'Arte*.

ELEANOR E. FINK

J. Paul Getty Art History Information Program

Eleanor E. Fink has a graduate degree in Medieval Art and fifteen years of art research, database management, and visual resource experience gained at the Smithsonian Institution's National Museum of American Art and most recently at the J. Paul Getty Art History Information Program where she is manager of the Vocabulary Coordination Group. As Chief of the Office of Research Support at the Smithsonian's National Museum of American Art, she directed several computerised art research projects including the museum's nationwide inventories of American painting and sculpture. As part of the Smithsonian's institution-wide planning process for the establishment of information networks, she and her staff designed a data model for art which is to be implemented among all Smithsonian art bureaux. The Vocabulary Coordination department she is establishing at the Getty Art History Information Program (AHIP), facilitates the development and use of standard lists of names and terms for proper name vocabulary among AHIP's art-historical databases. Projects currently underway include an international union list of artists' names and a geographic place-name authority file.

Eleanor serves on the board of several national and international organisations and currently holds positions of President of the Visual Resources Association, Chairperson of the Terminology Control Working Group of the International Committee for Documentation (CIDOC), and member of the Board of Directors of the Museum Computer Network.

SHELLY FOOTE

Smithsonian Institution

Shelly Foote obtained a BA from Scripps College in California and an MA in American Studies from the George Washington University in Washington, DC. She has been employed by the Smithsonian Institution since the early 1970s and is currently a senior museum specialist in the field of historic costume. Ms Foote's duties include answering public enquiries, dealing with potential donors and ensuring the proper use of the classification and terminology systems used in the division's computerised records. She is also the author of several articles on the history of costume.

FRANÇOIS GARNIER

Institut de Recherche et d'Histoire des Textes (CNRS) Orléans, France

Né en 1923, études de philosophie et enseignement des lettres pendent 25 ans. Travaux sur Max Jacob, publication de deux volumes de sa *Correspondance* (1953 et 1955).

Etude sur la bataille de Lépante et les galères, publication du *Journal de la bataille de Lépante*, 1956.

Constitution d'une photothèque personnelle, environ 70 000 documents à ce jour. Publication de *La Légende dorée des saints de France*, 1965. Iconographie et édition d'une *Bible* illustrée en 22 volumes, Lausanne 1970–1973, environ 4 000 documents reproduits.

Enseignement de l'iconographie médiévale à l'université du Mans, depuis 1970. Chercheur à l'Institut de Recherche et d'Histoire des Textes (CNRS) en 1973. Publication de nombreux articles et chapitres de livres collectifs, catalogues d'expositions.

Principaux livres publiés sur l'iconographie: *Le vitrail de Charlemagne*, 1969; *Le langage de l'Image au Moyen Age*, 1982; *Thesaurus iconographique*, 1984; *L'Ane à la lyre, sottisier d'iconographie médiévale*, 1988; *Le Langage de l'Image au Moyen Age*, 1988.

DR CATHERINE GORDON
Courtauld Institute of Art

Dr Catherine Gordon is Project Director of the Witt Computer Index, part of the Getty Art History Information Programme, which aims to increase access to the photo collections of the Witt Library by building a detailed database covering categories such as subject matter, ownership, location and previous history. Born in New Zealand, graduated English, Victoria University of Wellington, and Art History, Courtauld Institute of Art, London. Publications include *British Painting of Subjects from the English Novel, 1740–1870*, Garland Press, New York, 1988; 'The Witt Computer Index', *Visual Resources*, IV, 1987, pp. 141–51, (with John Sunderland); and various articles and exhibition catalogues on literary painting. In preparation are a report on the ICONCLASS International Workshop, held Santa Barbara, November 1987 and *A Checklist of British Paintings in British Public Collections*, (Sotheby Publications) with Christopher Wright.

MICHAEL GREENHALGH
Australian National University

Born Stafford 1943; Lecturer and then Senior Lecturer in the History of Art, University of Leicester, 1968–1987; 1987ff: Foundation Professor of Art History, Australian National University, Canberra.

Books include *The Classical Tradition in Art*, (London 1978); *Donatello and his Sources* (London 1982); *Computing for Non-Scientific Applications* (Leicester 1987: joint author with D. Andrews); a book on *Database for Historians* is in preparation, and another on *The Making of Art* (jointly with Dr A. Yarrington).

I was involved with the computerisation of the Warburg/Hertziana *Census of Antique Works of Art known to the Renaissance* at the beginning of that process; I had a short Fellowship at the British Art Center, Yale, to study their computerised database; I have advised the Ministère de la Culture, Paris, on the computerisation of the Patrimoine Nationale; I am a regular contributor to CHArt, the British Journal dealing with Computers and the History of Art.

PHILIPPE GUILLET
Office de Coopération et d'Information Muséographiques, Dijon

Studied geology (tectonophysics) at University of Nantes. Since 1986, at Office de Coopération et d'Information Muséographiques, department of the Ministère de l'Education Nationale.

JAN GULDBECK
The Strong Museum

Jan Guldbeck has worked with Robert Chenhall's *Nomenclature for Museum Cataloging* in two institutions since 1980. As Registrar of the Rochester Museum and Science Center and of the Margaret Woodbury Strong Museum, both in upstate New York, she appreciates how a classification system can help to bring an enormous body of information under control.

Ms Guldbeck earned her Master of Arts Degree in History Museum Studies from the Cooperstown Graduate Program, adminstered by the State University of New York and the New York State Historical Association. Prior to 1980, she worked as a curator, a conservator of works of art on paper and a museum instructor in museums in the US and Canada. At the Rochester Museum, she managed the records of approximately two million objects in the natural science, anthropology and local history collections. The first edition of Chenhall's *Nomenclature* (1978) was used to classify the historical objects and to organise the manual files.

As Registrar of the Strong Museum since 1984, Ms Guldbeck shepherded the transition of the records management system from a time-shared mainframe computer system to an in-house minicomputer. As a member of the *Nomenclature* Revision Committee, she worked with the two authors to assure that the revision delivered what was promised — a classification and naming system which is 'user-friendly'.

PAUL T. HARDING
Biological Records Centre, NERC Institute of Terrestrial Ecology

Paul Harding has been head of the national Biological Records Centre for the UK since 1982. Previously he carried out research on various topics within the NERC Institute of Terrestrial Ecology including invertebrate ecology and woodland management and conservation. He is the author of over 130 papers, reports and books on invertebrates, woodland conservation and biological recording. As a delegate to various meetings of the Council of Europe on databases, and as a Council member of the European Invertebrate Survey, he has wide experience of biological recording in Europe.

CHRISTINE HENNESSEY
National Museum of American Art, Smithsonian Institution
Christine Hennessey is Coordinator of the Inventory of American Paintings Executed before 1914 and the newly implemented Inventory of American Sculpture, administered through the Office of Research Support, National Museum of American Art, Smithsonian Institution. She has dual masters degrees in Art History and Library and Information Science from the University of Maryland (1982 and 1986 respectively) and has written articles on name authority control, on the use of the MARC format for cataloguing art objects, and on Joseph Cornell. She has also actively worked with the Library of Congress Network Development and MARC Standards Office in redefining the Visual Materials MARC format to accommodate three-dimensional materials.

DAVID HEPPELL
National Museums of Scotland, Edinburgh
David Heppell is Curator of Mollusca in the National Museums of Scotland, Edinburgh, and has been that museum's representative on the committee of FENSCORE, the Federation for Natural Sciences Collection Research. He is a Council Member of the International Commission on Zoological Nomenclature and a member of the scrutinising committee set up to consider wider implications of proposals for amendments to the zoological Code. Among his particular interests are the history of natural history and its bibliography and documentation. He is currently involved in a study of the importance of errors in the history of malacology, in tracing the pedigree of the horned hare and, jointly with Charles Pettitt of the Manchester Museum, is compiling a database of illustrations of molluscs in malacological periodicals.

JENNIFER HIRSH
Museum Documentation Association
Jennifer Hirsh joined the MDA in 1981. After several years of working on museum cataloguing applications in GOS, she is currently an advisory officer with primary responsibility for the training and support of over 300 MODES users world-wide. Her job includes giving basic instruction and guidance in the use of terminology control to new computer users in museums. She has a degree in Mathematics and worked for many years as a freelance computer programmer. Prior to joining the MDA, she worked at Saffron Walden Museum for 5 years. She is a keen botanist and gardener and gives guided tours of the Cambridge University Botanic Gardens. Her other activities include being Chairman of the Parish Council and woodturning.

STUART HOLM
Museum Documentation Association
Stuart Holm began his career, after voluntary work on an archaeological excavation at Hertford, when he was appointed as Museum Assistant with the Pembrokeshire County Museum Service. Having gained experience in general museum work, Stuart moved to Scunthorpe as Assistant Curator (Local History) where the need for better subject retrieval led him to experiment with classification schemes. Moving to the Black Country Museum he spent nearly ten years as Keeper of Social and Industrial History. Achievements during this period were the development of techniques for recording and dismantling brick buildings and subsequently recreating them authentically on the museum site, and a major contribution to the SHIC classification system, now widely used by UK museums. He was the first chairman of the West Midlands Social and Industrial History Collections Research Unit and was responsible for introducing a computerised documentation system at the Black Country Museum. This increasing commitment to documentation led to his appointment as MDA Advisory Officer in February 1985. Currently he is Assistant Director, heading a small team responsible for providing documentation advice and training throughout the UK and Channel Islands.

C. V. HORIE
The Manchester Museum
During my degree course in Chemistry at Bristol University, I became the curator of a small archaeological museum — good preparation for subsequent activities. Vocation training came from the Diploma in the Conservation of Archaeological Material, Institute of Archaeology (London). Varied practical experience was gained in three years as Archaeological

Conservatory for the North of England Museum Service. Since 1978, at the Manchester Museum, I have been involved with many storage and display improvements as well as the excavation and publicity of Lindow Man. Experience and research has demonstrated the urgent need for the development of adequate conservation techniques used on organic materials, particularly natural history and archaeological specimens, and I am currently coordinator of the ICOM Conservation Committee Working Group on Natural History Collections. I am the author of two books and about 40 articles.

Dr COLUM HOURIHANE
Courtauld Institute of Art

Colum Hourihane is senior assistant on the Witt Computer Project at the Courtauld Institute of Art. Born in Ireland he graduated from the National University of Ireland with an MA in Archaeology in 1979 and subsequently received his doctorate in Art History at the Courtauld Institute in 1983. His interests and publications range from medieval art to systems of subject classification.

WILFRIED JANSSENS
Royal Institute for the Cultural Heritage, Brussels

1969, Graduate of Modern History from the Catholic University of Louvain; 1972, Scientific assistant at the Royal Institute; since 1984, co-responsible for the Photo-Archives department at the above institute.

Dr LEA D. JONES
The British Museum

Lea Jones joined the British Museum in 1985 and is responsible for the supervision of schemes (Oriental and Japanese, and Egyptian Antiquities) within the Collections Data Management Section (CDMS). Latterly, responsibility for analysis and design of a Conservation records database has been assumed. Other tasks have recently involved the detailed systems analysis and design of object records with other colleagues in CDMS preliminary to the acquisition of a new online computer system. Supervision of working parties has also been necessary as terminology comes under close scrutiny in preparation for thesaurus and authority list compilation.

Previous work with data management comprises several years with the Scheduled Monuments Section of the Department of Environment's Historic Buildings and Monuments Commission. More recently she was responsible for the Devon and Cornwall section of the Natural Monuments Records Project (Royal Commission on Historic Monuments) compiling a country-wide excavation index database.

She is an archaeologist by training, specialising at Doctoral level in the petrographic analysis of Mesoamerican ceramics, an interest maintained privately in the role of analyst for two current projects.

GRETCHEN N. KUHN
National Geographic Society

As a member of the National Geographic Society's Cartographic Division, I have been associated with the Geographic Names Data Base for five years and presently direct research for the project.

GILLIAN H. LEWIS
RILA — Getty Art History Information Program

Gillian H. Lewis, Associate Editor for Authorities at RILA (*International Repertory of the Literature of Art*), was formerly Head of Technical Services at Skidmore College Library. Earlier positions at Skidmore and other institutions include those of Fine Arts Librarian, Cataloguer and Reference Librarian. Since joining RILA she has been concerned primarily with the automation of the authority files and with plans for the merger of RILA and the RAA (*Répertoire d'Art et d'Archéologie*) for which RILA will do all the authority work. She holds degrees from the University of New Brunswick (Canada) and McGill University and has also taken courses toward the doctorate at Columbia University.

RICHARD B. LIGHT
Museum Documentation Association

Born and educated in Yorkshire, Richard Light attended Cambridge University to read Mathematics and Theoretical Physics. In 1974 he moved to the Sedgwick Museum, Cambridge, as a Research Assistant on a British Library-funded research project. His primary role was to manage the transfer of data on 440 000 fossils to a computer-based system, but he was also involved in helping the IRGMA committee to develop and test its multidisciplinary recording system. In 1977, Richard joined the newly-formed Museum Documentation Association as a Research Officer. He is currently Deputy Director of the MDA, and has particular responsibility for standards, system development and computer-related aspects of the Association's work.

ROSANNE McCAFFREY MACKIE
The Historic New Orleans Collection

Rosanne Mackie is the Director of Systems at the Historic New Orleans Collection, responsible for that Institution's computer applications, including the FACETS system she developed. Her former positions have included curator and assistant archivist, working on everything from cataloguing to exhibitions; in 1987 she edited the *Encyclopaedia of New Orleans Artists, 1718–1918*.

A Phi Beta Kappa graduate of Newcomb College of Tulane University, she completed a fellowship in museum practices at the Whitney Museum of American Art in New York, and has been investigating automation in museums since 1979.

Active in the museum community, Ms Mackie hosted the Museum Computer Network meeting in New Orleans in 1986, has spoken at numerous professional conferences, and serves as president of the Louisiana Association of Museums, an organisation which recently developed MUSEBASE, a database management system for museum service associations.

DEBRA A. McNABB
Museum of Industry and Transportation, Stellerton, Nova Scotia

Debra McNabb is an historical geographer formerly affiliated with the Gorsebrook Research Institute, Saint Mary's University, Halifax, Nova Scotia. She has been involved with the Atlantic Canada Newspaper Survey database since 1983. She has developed documentation standards for the database and facilitated coordination among its four provincial contributors. In association with the Canadian Museum of Civilization and the Canadian Heritage Information network, she began work on a thesaurus search tool. Ms McNabb's other research interests lie in the historical geography of Nova Scotia, and particularly in the colonisation of parts of that province by New Englanders in the late eighteenth century.

GWYN MILES
Victoria & Albert Museum

Gwyn Miles received a BSc in Physiology from Bristol University in 1969. She joined the Department of Antiques in the Ashmolean Museum, Oxford, in 1972, and in 1982 became Head of Conservation. She has held the post of Deputy Keeper of Conservation at the Victoria and Albert Museum since 1985. She chairs the Documentation Committee for the Museum and is the Coordinator of the ICOM Conservation Committee Documentation Working Group.

Gwyn lives in Oxford with her husband (an archaeologist), daughter and son; she has written books and articles on knitting and gardening as well as conservation topics.

EIJI MIZUSHIMA
Science Museum, Japan Science Foundation

Curator, Science Museum, Japan Science Foundation, Department of Planning & Development, Exhibition and Science Research Office. Chief of the Meeting for the Study of Display Engineering Project. Born in 1956, Yokohama, Japan. Graduated from Tokyo University of Science, Faculty of Science & Technology in 1981, BSc. Postgraduate course in the following year specialised in System Engineering. Since 1981 at the Science Museum. Up to now as a system designer; planned and developed many interactive, new-media, computer-exhibitions at Science Museum. At the present post since 1985. In the last few years, studying the computerisation of museum information and planning for the study of the application of Artificial Intelligence to develop a museum expert system. From last September, studied in France, Museologie Scientifique, at Cite des Sciences et de l'Industrie, CNRS (Centre National de la Recherche Scientifique) and University of Paris VII. Translated *Dictionarium Museologicum* into Japanese.

BORIS MOLLO

Boris Mollo recently retired as Deputy Director and Keeper of Records at the National Army Museum. He joined the museum in 1966 as keeper of books and archives, becoming deputy director in 1974. He has always been interested in documentation and was an early member of the Information Retrieval Group of the Museums Association. He has worked closely with the Museum Documentation Association since its formation and helped with the development of the military artefact card. At the National Army Museum he has been responsible for the introduction of computer cataloguing, first through the use of GOS and latterly with the adoption of the &MAGUS system following the lead of the British Museum. At the time of his retirement, this system held over 30 000 records online.

Mr Mollo has always worked closely with smaller museums in his field, particularly with regimental museums, where he carried out a survey of holdings of photographic and manuscript records and where he encouraged improvement in documentation methods. He has also been involved in the deliberations of the International Association of Museums of Arms and Military History.

BENEDETTA MONTEVECCHI
Istituto Centrale per il Catalogo e la Documentazione, Roma

Benedetta Montevecchi è nata a Roma, il 21/IX/1948. Si è laureata in Lettere presso l'Università degli studi di Roma con una tesi in Archeologia Cristiana sull'iconografia dei primi martiri. Ha frequentato il corso di Perfezionamento in Storia dell'Arte presso l'Università di Roma. Dal 1973 al 1980 ha compiuto lavori di catalogazione di opere d'arte per le Soprintendenze di Roma, Arezzo e Urbino. Nel 1980 è stata nominata Ispettore storico dell'arte presso la Soprintendenza delle Marche (Urbino). Dal 1982 lavora presso l'Istituto Centrale per il Catalogo e la Documentazione dove si occupa di metodologia della catalogazione anche sotto il profilo terminologico-lessicale.

YOLANDE MOREL-DECKERS
Royal Museum of Fine Arts, Antwerp

Studied in history of art at the University of Gent.

Assistant at the Royal Museum of Fine Arts in Antwerp since 1975. Since 1985 responsible for the development and implementation of an automated collections information system.

LINDA MOWAT
Pitt Rivers Museum, Oxford

Linda Mowat has been research and Documentation Assistant at the Pitt Rivers Museum for the last four years.

WOLFGANG NEDOBITY
International Information Centre for Terminology (Infoterm)

Wolfgang Nedobity was educated in philology and librarianship in both Austria and the United Kingdom. He joined the International Information Centre for Terminology (Infoterm) in 1980, where is he responsible for research and training activities in the General Theory of Terminology and in particular for the application of terminology as a management instrument. He is in charge of the Infoterm documentation and the Wüster Research Library. In addition, he is a lecturer in foreign language documentation at the University of Vienna.

MARTIN NORGATE
Hampshire County Museum Service

Martin Norgate joined Hampshire County Museum Service as Keeper of Documentation in May 1989. He has a degree in Physics and Mathematics and was a mathematics teacher for five years in England and Zambia. He was curator of the local museum in Dunfermline, Fife; director of the Scottish area museum council; and county museums officer for Wiltshire. In this last role he co-ordinated the documentation of two dozen museums, carrying out the recording, storage and data processing of eighteen of them. A major element in the work was to control terminology for the group of museums, which lead to the publication of WILTM Group Conventions – comprehensive terminology rules for the MDA object data structure — in 1986.

ELIZABETH ORNA
Orna/Stevens Consultancy

Elizabeth Orna has been visiting museums since being introduced to the Hancock and Sunderland museums at the age of four, and still isn't tired of it. In the early 1970s she became interested in the application of information science to them. This led to meeting the MDA and so to books on *Information handling in museums* (1980), thesaurus construction for museums (*Build yourself a thesaurus* 1983) and *Information policies for museums* (1987). Since 1979 she has worked in partnership with the typographer Graham Stevens, with whom she has written a book on *The presentation of Information* (to be published by Aslib). Her work as an information consultant has given her a strong interest in interdisciplinary co-operation in designing systems where information technology works with rather than against human ways of information processing. She has lectured to museum curators and students in Australia and to curators in the UK.

JON BIRGER ØSTBY
Norwegian Folk Museum, Oslo

Jon Birger Østby, 42, is curator and currently Head of the scientific department at the Norwegian Folk Museum, Oslo, Norway.

1981–84 he was the leader of a pilot project of developing nomenclature for ethnological material. In cooperation with a working group, nomenclature for four selected groups has been published: Flatware, Drinking vessels, Appliances for milk and butter, Boxes — Chests — Trunks. These publications are meant to be models for the continuing work on nomenclature in Norway.

1984–86 he worked on a two-year computing project for museums of art and cultural history in Norway. The project was carried out in collaboration with the Norwegian Computing Centre for the Humanities and was aimed at creating a joint system for the entry and storage of source data in museums.

ELISABETH BETZ PARKER

Prints and Photographs Division, Library of Congress

Since 1971, Elisabeth Parker has been a cataloguer and is now Head of the Processing Section in the Library of Congress Prints and Photographs Division, probably the largest single pictorial collection in the United States. In 1982, the Library published her *Graphic Materials: Rules for Describing Original Items and Historical Collections*, a manual based on and supplementing the *Anglo-American Cataloguing Rules* (2nd edn). She subsequently participated in the development of the MARC (Machine-Readable Cataloguing) Format for Visual Materials. In 1987, the *LC Thesaurus for Graphic Materials: Topical Terms for Subject Access* was published for use — particularly, but not necessarily — in large general collections of historical images which are found in many libraries, historical societies, archives and museums. 1986 saw the publication of *Descriptive Terms for Graphic Materials: Genre and Physical Characteristic Headings*, which she co-authored with Helena Zinkham, cataloguer in the Prints and Photographs Division.

CHRISTOPHER SPALDING PEEBLES

Indiana University, The Glenn A. Black Laboratory of Archaeology

Christopher Spalding Peebles is Director of the Glenn A. Black Laboratory of Archaeology at Indiana University. He also is a member of the Department of Anthropology and the Research Center for Language and Semiotic Studies at that institution. He is a 'corresponding member' of the Albert Egges van Giffen Institute for Pre- and Proto-history at the University of Amsterdam and an adjunct member of the faculty at the University of Alabama. Professor Peebles received the AB in anthropology and philosophy from the University of Chicago and the PhD from the University of California, Santa Barbara. He has taught at the University of Windsor, Canada and the University of Michigan. He was curator of the Division of the Great Lakes at the University of Michigan Museum of Anthropology. He has been a visiting associate professor at Northwestern Northern Illinois, Indiana, and the Pennsylvania State University. He was visiting Professor of Cultural Prehistory at the University of Amsterdam. His scholarly interests include the later prehistory of the Southeastern United States and the Iron Age of northern Europe. His first work with computers was in 1959, on an IBM 709 owned by his employer, the US Air Force. He has maintained an interest in database and management information systems over the last three decades. His current research in this area includes the construction of intelligent knowledge based management systems and the application of expert systems and other techniques from artificial intelligence to archaeological research. His work has been supported by the National Science Foundation, the US Department of the Interior, and the US Army Corps of Engineers. He has served as a consultant to several state and federal agencies and to the J. Paul Getty Trust.

PAUL PELOWSKI

Formerly National Maritime Museum

Born and brought up in London. Married in 1985 to Mary Murray, music librarian. Now living in Colchester, Essex.

Paul graduated from the University of Hull in 1978 with a degree in English Language and Literature and in the following year from the University of Reading with a Master of Arts degree in Modern English Literature.

He worked for the Corporation of London in various library posts before joining the National Maritime Museum in September 1980. There for the next four years he worked in the Readers' Services Section of the Printed Books and Manuscripts Department, having particular responsibility for reprographic services and becoming a qualified librarian by studying part-time at University College London.

In 1984 he became one of the orginal members of the Information Project Group set up primarily to attack the Museum's large backlog of documentation. Since then he has been particularly responsible for data standardisation, including terminology control. He has been awarded a Master of Arts degree in library and information studies for work including a dissertation on data standardisation in museum documentation. He has served on the MDA Working Party on Terminology Control.

About to move on to technologies new, Paul is taking up a new post as coordinator of a film and video company in Colchester.

JOHN PERKINS
Getty Conservation Institute

For the past two years John Perkins has been the Projects Coordinator for the Documentation Program of the Getty Conservation Institute (GCI). In this capacity he manages the GCI's participation in the Conservation Information Network in the areas of user services, data management, the development of microcomputer applications and the creation of a thesaurus in collaboration with the AAT. He also represents the GCI on the Conservation Information Network project coordination team.

Prior to this he was a conservator for the Canadian National Parks Service, Atlantic Region working on automation projects in the areas of environmental monitoring and control and conservation laboratory management.

ROY A. PERRY
Tate Gallery

Camberwell School of Arts and Crafts Dip AD (Fine Art) 1967. Joined the Conservation Department of the Tate Gallery in 1968. Deputy Keeper since 1981.

SUSANNE PETERS
International Council of Museums

Susanne Peters trained as a school teacher before gaining a law degree at the University of Graz, Austria. Migrated to Australia in 1969 where she studied librarianship at the Royal Melbourne Institute of Technology and Monash University (Melbourne). Appointments at several academic libraries with specialisation in automated information retrieval, and audiovisual material. Founding audiovisual librarian at Melbourne University. Administered the Technical Assistance Programme at ICCROM, Rome, from 1982 to 1986. Since July 1986, head of the Unesco-ICOM Documentation Centre, Paris.

TONI PETERSEN
Art and Architecture Thesaurus of the Getty Art History Information Program

Director of the Art and Architecture Thesaurus and one of the original founders of this project to build a comprehensive hierarchical structured thesaurus for the fields of art and architecture. Previously Director of the Bennington College Library (1980–86), and Executive Editor of RILA (International Repertory of the Literature of Art) (1972–80). Background is as a library cataloguer, having worked at Harvard University and Boston University prior to going to RILA. Lectures widely on authority control and on the AAT. Most recent publications: *Multiple Authorities in Library Systems*, published in *Authority Control Symposium: Papers presented during the 14th Annual ARLIS Conference, New York, NY* (Art Libraries Society of North America, 1987); and 'The AAT: A Model for the Restructuring of LCSH', *Journal of Academic Librarianship*, vol. 9, no. 4 (September 1983). Has recently been appointed to the Subject Access Committee of the American Library Association. Is a past-president of the Art Libraries Society of North America (1985–86). Serves on the Advisory Board of the Clearinghouse Project of Art Documentation and Computerisation, on the RLG/AAPC Taskforce on AAT Application Protocol, and on the Advisory Committee for a list of subject headings in specialised collections in Numismatics.

CHARLES PETTITT
Manchester Museum

After graduating, Charles Pettitt spent a year as a Research Associate in the Mollusca Section, BM(NH), moving to the Institute of Oceanographic Sciences as Curator, *Discovery* Collections, in 1963. In 1964 he started computer processing of data from Atlantic plankton samples. Charles moved to Manchester University Museum in 1968, where he is now Keeper of Invertebrate Zoology and Controller, Computer cataloguing Unit. Here he has overseen the computer cataloguing of about two million objects from the Museum's collections; this has involved developing in-house data standards and terminology control. Most of the data preparation has been done using large Manpower Service Commission assisted teams, for which he has been managerially responsible. This work has also meant writing and supporting a comprehensive Museum Application Package on the successive University mainframes. This package allows curators to access their databases easily via a series of menus and help screens, using the terminals sited within their departments. Recently the Museum has been re-equipped with microcomputers, onto which he has transferred some of the database work for his colleagues.

Charles is database manager for the Federation for Natural Sciences Collections Research (FENSCORE), and was Chairman of the Museums Computer group from 1984–87. From 1965 to 1975 he was a member of the National Committee on Biological Information, and from 1972 to 1977 a member of the British Library Review panel for Information Research in Biology. In addition to the methodology of computerised collection cataloguing and management, Charles' research interests include various aspects of Malacology and Ethnoconchology.

VICKI PORTER
Foundation for Documents of Architecture, Washington

Vicki Porter received a PhD in the History of Art from The John Hopkins University in 1977. She has held the following posts: Assistant Professor of Art History at the State University of New York, Binghamton; Assistant Curator of Manuscripts and Rare Books at the Walters Art Gallery; Assistant Professor, College of Continuing Studies, The Johns Hopkins University; Curator for the City of Baltimore, Maryland.

In 1983, she began working on a wide range of art historical automation projects undertaken by the J. Paul Getty Trust. One of these was the Architectural Drawings Advisory Group, where she gradually focused her energies as Acting Senior Research Associate, Center for Advanced Study in the Visual Arts, National Gallery of Art, Washington, DC. In 1987, when this group evolved into a separate organisation, the Foundation for Documents of Architecture, Porter became its Project Manager.

MARYSE RAHARD
Centre National de la Recherche Scientifique

In charge of the online dissemination of FRANCIS, a French human and social bibliographic database containing 1 130 000 citations produced by INIST (Institut de l'Information Scientifique et Technique) of CNRS. Mrs Rahard is involved in the database vocabulary work and concerned with the organisation of training sessions in France and abroad.

Dr PETER E. RIDER
Canadian Museum of Civilization, Ottawa, Canada

Dr Peter Rider is a graduate of Carleton University, Ottawa and the University of Toronto. He has held appointments at several universities and heritage institutions and has been Atlantic Provinces Historian at the Canadian Museum of Civilization in Ottawa since 1978. A specialist in the history of Canada in the post-Confederation era, Dr Rider has published in the fields of intellectural, urban and material history and has filled editorial positions connected with *Material History Bulletin* and *Urban History Review*. Since 1982 he has coordinated the development of the Atlantic Canada Newspaper Survey as part of the museum's programme of research into the history of the Maritime provinces and Newfoundland.

D. ANDREW ROBERTS
Museum Documentation Association

Andrew Roberts joined the MDA in 1977. After an initial appointment as Research Officer he became Secretary in 1979. He read a BSc in Geology/Archaeology at Leicester University and an MSc in Information Science at The City University, London. He became a Research Assistant on a project at the Sedgwick Museum, Cambridge, with initial responsibility for establishing the parameters for a national survey of cataloguing practice, then acting as secretary of the IRGMA committee chaired by Geoffrey Lewis and Philip Doughty. Currently concerned with the further development of the MDA, with particular responsibilities including conferences and publications. On the Boards of the Museum Computer Network and CIDOC.

HELENE E. ROBERTS
Fogg Art Museum, Harvard University

Helene E. Roberts is the Curator of Visual Collections, Fine Arts Library, Fogg Art Museum, Harvard University, Cambridge, MA, USA. She has written on Victorian art and art periodicals, as well as dress and the image of women in art. Over thirty years of experience with art book and visual libraries at Dartmouth College and Harvard University have led her to the belief that subject access is essential. She has written supporting this view, including an *Iconographic Index to Old Testament Subjects Represented in Photographs and Slides of Paintings in the Visual Collections, Fine Arts Library, Harvard University* (NY, Garland Press, 1987). She is the Editor of *Visual Resources: an International Journal of Documentation*, a periodical devoted to the history of visual documentation, the organisation of visual collections and the impact of new technology on visual resources.

SANDRA VASCO ROCCA
Istituto Centrale per il Catalogo e la Documentazione, Roma

Sandra Vasco Rocca è nata a Roma il 1947. Si è laureata presso l'Università degli Studi di Roma con una tesi in Storia dell'Arte sul manierismo bolognese. Ha conseguito il diploma di perfezionamento con tesi sulla pittura umbra del Quattrocento presso l'Università di Roma, dove è rimasta in qualità di vincitrice di una Borsa di studio triennale del Ministero della Pubblica Istruzione. Ha compiuto lavori di catalogazione per le Soprintendenze di Roma e Campobasso. Nel 1976 è entrata in servizio presso l'Istituto Centrale per il Catalogo e la Documentazione, dove tuttora lavora, occupandosi di metodologia della catalogazione anche sotto il profilo terminologico-lessicale.

LENE ROLD
The National Museum of Denmark

Earned the degree of cand.mag in Archaeology in 1981 at the University of Aarhus, Denmark, with major subject and thesis in medieval archaeology and with prehistory as minor subject. She took the first two years of coursework in Computer Science at the University of Copenhagen, finishing in 1987. Lene Rold worked at the Prehistoric Museum, Aarhus from 1976 to 1983, mainly in public relations (information, teacher training, planning exhibitions etc.), where she became department leader. She has been curator at the National Museum of Denmark since 1987, employed in the Documentation Unit. Her responsibility is the development of computer-based registration, retrieval and research systems, covering all the museum's collections.

LENORE SARASAN
Willoughby Associates

Lenore Sarasan heads Willoughby Associates, an Illinois based museum consultancy.

KAROL A. SCHMIEGEL
Winterthur Museum, Delaware

Karol Schmiegel is the Registrar at Winterthur Museum, where she has implemented a computerised Collections Information Management System for 89 000 decorative and fine art objects. She is the author of six articles on American painting and five on museology. She received an AB degree from Smith College and an MA degree from the University of Delaware, both in art history. She is also an alumna of the Museum Management Institute. Ms Schmiegel is the Vice-President of the Mid-Atlantic Association of Museums and the past Chairman of the Registrars Committee of the American Association of Museums.

MARILYN SCHMITT
Getty Art History Information Program

Marilyn Schmitt, Program Manager for Scholarly Coordination in the Getty Art History Information Program, was educated at Lawrence University, BA, the University of California, Berkeley, MA, and Yale University, PhD. A specialist in Romanesque art, she has published articles on that subject as well as on ancient and modern art. She pursued a teaching career at the University of Miami, Florida, Southern Connecticut State University, Yale University, and Dickinson College, Pennsylvania, before joining the Getty Trust in 1983. She has been the recipient of research fellowships from the National Endowment for the Humanities, the American Association of University Women, the Woodrow Wilson Foundation, the Belgian American Educational Foundation and Earthwatch. During her time with the Getty Art History Information Program, she has co-authored (with Elizabeth Bakewell, William Beeman, and Carol McMichael Reese) the study *Object, Image, Inquiry: The Art Historian at Work*, and co-edited (with Laura Corti) the *Proceedings of the Second International Conference on Automatic Processing of Art History Data and Documents*.

ANNE MARIE SERIO
National Museum of American History, Smithsonian Institution, Washington

Anne Marie Serio is a Senior Museum Specialist in the Division of Domestic Life at the National Museum of American History. She is responsible for answering enquiries about the division's collections and the subject areas covered by them, as well as assisting researchers in using the collections. In addition, she cares for an extensive collection of lighting devices and The Harry T. Peters 'America On Stone' Lithography Collection, over 1 600 nineteenth-century lithographs documenting American life. Ms Serio has been a member of the ad hoc group of curatorial and registrarial staff members who developed the Museum Information Retrieval and Documentation System (MIRDS) since 1972 and is currently involved in the Museum's efforts to convert MIRDS to a new computer system that is part of the Smithsonian Institution's Collection Information System (CIS). Born in Buffalo, New York, Ms Serio holds a BA (D'Youville College) and an MA (University of Rochester) in American History. Her publications include articles on the history of lighting and the use of lithographs as social documents.

JAMES R SHEARER
Ealing College of Higher Education

Principal Lecturer in Information Retrieval Systems and Head of Department of Information Studies and Technology at Ealing College of

Higher Education. Employed for ten years as Database Development Manager with Geosystems, engaged in producing and enhancing GeoArchive and other databases, and in consultancy work in providing database systems for a range of clients. Currently lectures on the design, specification and implementation of relational databases. Current research investigates ways of making the wider community aware of the possibilities of online information systems for meeting their information needs.

ORESTE SIGNORE
CNUCE - Institute of CNR, Pisa, Italy

Born in 1946, took the degree in Physics at University of Pisa in 1970. Initially he had been working on high energy physics and nuclear fusion.

From 1973, as staff member of CNUCE (Institute of CNR, Pisa) he started work in the area of computer science, covering different areas of interest (operating systems, information retrieval systems, database management systems, database design).

Since 1984, he is managing the cooperation between CNUCE and ICCD in order to build an automated catalogue of Italian cultural heritage.

In the meantime, he worked at several other applications of database technology to the management of history of art data (Roma Project, historic-geographic authority).

CLAIRE SKINKEL-TAUPIN
Musées royaux d'Art et d'Histoire, Brussels

Licence in Art History and Archaeology, section of Classical Antiquities, Université Libre de Bruxelles.

Mémoire de licence (equivalent to MA Thesis): Towards a Unified Typology for Roman Terracotta Lamps, 1969.

Attachée aux Musées royaux d'Art et d'Histoire, Department of Classical Antiquities (assistant curator).

Publications: *Lampes romaines de tradition hellénistique* in *Bulletin des MRAH*, 43–44 (1971–72), pp. 53–62. *Notes sur la restauration des lampes antiques aux XIXes* in *Bull., cit.*, 49 (1977), pp. 89–102. *Une nouvelle coupe du peintre d'Euaion* in *Bull., cit.*, 50 (1978). *Lampes de la Méditerrannée greque et romaine* (Guidê du Visiteur), Bruxelles, 1980. *A propos d'un vase italiote: problèmes de terminologie* in *Bull., cit.*, 55 (1984).

Forthcoming publications: *Guide to the Classical Department: Attic Black-Figure, Attic Black-Glaze, Southern Italian and Hellenistic Vases; Terracotta's from the Daedalic to the Hellenistic period. Catalogue of the Terracotta Lamps in the Classical Department of the MRAH.*

JANE SLEDGE
Office of Information Resource Management, Smithsonian Institution

With undergraduate degrees in history and fine arts from Concordia University in Montreal, and a Master of Museum Studies from the University of Toronto with a thesis on 19th-century Ontario gardens, Jane Sledge began a career in the automation of museum collections information. She worked with the Canadian Heritage Information Network from 1977 to 1985, developing the Museum Services area to support museum projects, training and documentation research. She now works with the Office of Information Resource Management at the Smithsonian Institution as Collections Information System Administrator.

ROGER SMITHER
Imperial War Museum

Roger Smither joined the staff of the Imperial War Museum as a film cataloguer in 1970 after completing a history degree at Cambridge University. Since 1977 he has been Keeper of the Museum's Department of Information Retrieval. The Department has a staff of five and responsibilities extending over documentation work in all the Museum's seven collecting departments. He has worked with various national and international organisations involved in the cataloguing and documentation of museum and audio-visual archival collections, and is the author of several papers on cataloguing practice and procedures and the application of computers to them.

Dr W. ECKEHART SPENGLER
Rheinisches Museumsamt, Pulheim

From 1971 to 1977 Wiss. Assistent of the University of Freiburg/Breisgau (Germanistik/Deutsche Volkskunde). Since 1978: Landschaftsverband Rheinland/Rheinisches Museumsamt for history of civilization; invertorying and documentation in the regional museums in Rheinland.

JANET L. STANLEY
National Museum of African Art Library, Smithsonian Institution

Janet L. Stanley is chief librarian of the National Museum of African Art at the Smithsonian Institution. She holds a masters degree in library science from Catholic University of America, Washington, DC and did African Studies as an undergraduate. Prior to her position with the Smithsonian, she worked in Nigeria as head reference librarian at the University of Ife (now Obafemi Awolowo University) in Ile-Ife, and in Washington, DC at the Library of Congress. Her publications include a bibliographic guide to African art, articles on African art and culture, and numerous book reviews for *African book publishing record*, *Art documentation*, *Africana Journal*, and *Library journal*. She is currently preparing the first in a new biennial bibliographic series on African art. She serves on a Working Group on the African Humanities of the Joint Committee of African Studies of the American Council of Learned Societies and the Social Science Research Council. In May 1988 she presented a paper on the African material culture information network at the International Conference on African Material Culture, Bellagio, Italy.

JENNIFER STEWART
City of Bristol Museum and Art Gallery

Jennifer Stewart is Curator of Archaeology, City of Bristol Museum and Art Gallery where she is currently developing an integrated manual and computerised inventory and cataloguing system for the Department's estimated five million groups of artefacts (ranging from British Archaeology, Egyptology, Ethnography, Numismatics, mediterranean archaeology, medals and, for some reason, also of firearms). After receiving a degree in Archaeology (Edinburgh University) she spent several years excavating and researching in Cyprus, Turkey, Syria and Iran. Ill-health and lack of funds forced her back to the UK where she worked in museums and studied for the Leicester University Certificate in Museums Studies. A happy five years followed at the MDA, then at Duxford Airfield, as their advisory officer where she travelled the country, spreading the MDA gospel. Later she moved back into the 'real' world of museums as Curator of Collections, Museum of East Anglian Life where she learned invaluable skills in how to groom shire horses and how to steer steam traction engines. She has published on archaeological documentation and the use of microcomputers in archaeology.

NAOMI TARRANT
National Museums of Scotland

Curator of Costume and Textiles in the National Museums of Scotland and Secretary of the ICOM Committee for Museums and Collections of Costume, 1983–1989.

MARIE CHRISTINE UGINET
ICCROM, Rome

Degree in history at the University of Grenoble, France. Diploma from the Vatican School of Librarianship. Head of Library at ICCROM since 1974.

MICHAEL A. VANNS
Ironbridge Gorge Museum Trust

Michael Vanns graduated from Leicester University in 1977 after having studied history of art. A short stay at Tamworth Castle Museum introduced him to IRGMA/MDA and in 1978 he was taken onto the curatorial staff of the Ironbridge Gorge Museum to catalogue the Elton Collection of prints, drawings and paintings of the industrial and transport revolutions. Since then his hands have been soiled with social and industrial history cataloguing problems at Ironbridge, leading him on to be intimately involved with the creation of the Social History & Industrial Classification in the early 1980s. As the 1990s approach, he grimly remains as the reactionary 'rump' of this Working Party.

GRAHAM WALLEY
Nottingham Museums

Born Manchester 1951, graduate of University of Glasgow 1973 (Zoology specialising in Systematics). Associate Member of the Museums Association 1977. Since 1975 a keeper at the Nottingham Natural History Museum, Wollaton Hall, Nottingham. Senior Keeper (Natural Sciences) since 1984. Council member of the Nottinghamshire Wildlife Trust 1976–1980, 1983–1988, secretary of its Scientific Policy Committee 1980–1985.

Main tasks at Nottingham have been establishing environmental records centre, including one of the most comprehensive botanical inventories in the UK, and cataloguing and re-storing the Museum's collection of 500 000 specimens. Working with computerisation of field and collection documentation since 1978. Member of the National Federation for Biological Recording Council since 1986. Member of the All Midland Collections Research Unit and chairman since 1985. Standards Coordinator of the Federation of Natural Science Collection Research Units 1990–1992.

Dr PETER H. WELSH
The Heard Museum, Phoenix, Arizona

Peter H. Welsh holds a PhD in anthropology from the University of Pennsylvania. He has been involved in museum computerisation projects since 1982, supervising the conversion to computerised systems at both the Southwest Museum in Los Angeles and The Heard Museum in Phoenix. He has authored several articles on museum computerisation, given a variety of professional papers and workshops on the subject and has taught a graduate level course on the use of computers in museums.

PNINA WENTZ
Ealing College of Higher Education

Senior Lecturer in Information Retrieval Systems at Ealing College of Higher Education.

Dr LEONARD WILL
National Museum of Science and Industry, Science Museum

Born and brought up in the northern highlands of Scotland, Leonard Will learned to handle invoices and statements, screwdrivers and soldering irons while helping in his father's radio and electrical retailing business. His interest in combining the theoretical and the practical led him to take a degree in physics from the University of Edinburgh, going on to a PhD which required precision measurement of electrical and mechanical properties of metal crystals at cryogenic temperatures. Having married a librarian, he became increasingly interested in the problems of information storage and retrieval, so that after teaching appointments in physics at the University of Edinburgh and The City University, London, he became Head of Information and Research Services in The City University Library and qualified as a Chartered Librarian. Having developed the use of commercial online information systems at City, he moved to the Science Museum in 1978 as Systems Manager with the hope of applying these techniques to the emerging field of museum object documentation. He managed the installation of the Science Museum's online computer documentation system in 1982 and has been nurturing its development since then into a comprehensive networked service which supports all aspects of the Museum's work, including library, finance and personnel. He is responsible for the Science Museum Library's service to users, which is playing an increasingly active role in improving the general public's knowledge of, and attitude to, science and technology. He served for three years as a member of the MDA Executive Committee, and is currently Chairman of the CIDOC Working Party on Documentation Centres.

PETER WILSON
Tate Gallery

Peter Wilson heads the Technical Services section at the Tate Gallery and is a member of the MDA's Board.

CHRISTOF WOLTERS
Institut für Museumskunde, Berlin

Christof Wolters has been working in the field of museum documentation since 1972 and is currently head of the small department for museum documentation in the Institute for Museum Studies in Berlin.

INDEX